MIDWAY:
DAUNTLESS VICTORY

By the same author:

NAVAL
Action Imminent
Arctic Victory
Battle of Midway
Battles of the Malta Striking Forces
Battleship *Royal Sovereign*
British Battle Cruisers
Cruisers in Action
Destroyer Action
Destroyer Leader
Eagle's War
Fighting Flotilla
Hard Lying
Heritage of the Sea
Hit First, Hit Hard
H.M.S. *Wild Swan*
Hold the Narrow Sea
Into the Minefields
Pedestal; the convoy that saved Malta
Royal Navy Ships' Badges
Task Force 57
The Great Ships Pass
War in the Aegean

AVIATION
Close Air Support
Fairchild-Republic A10A Thunderbolt
North American T-6, SNJ, Harvard & Wirraway
Lockheed C-130 Hercules
Ship Strike
RAF Squadron Badges
T-6; the Harvard, Texan and Wirraway
The Sea Eagles
The Story of the Torpedo Bomber

MILITARY
Massacre at Tobruk
The Royal Marines: A Pictorial History
Per Mare, Per Terram
Victoria's Victories

DIVE BOMBERS
Aichi D3A1/2 *Val*
Curtiss SB2C *Helldiver*
Dive Bomber!
Dive Bombers in Action
Douglas SBD *Dauntless*
Douglas AD *Skyraider*
Fist from the Sky
Impact; the dive-bomber pilots speak.
Into the Assault
Jungle Dive Bombers at War
Junkers Ju.87 *Stuka*
Luftwaffe Colours – Stukas – 1
Luftwaffe Colours – Stukas – 2
Petlyakov Pe-2 *Peshka*
Straight Down!
Skua; The Royal Navy's Dive Bomber
Stuka at War
Stukas over the Mediterranean
Stukas over the Steppe
Stuka Spearhead
Stuka Squadron
Vengeance!

MIDWAY: DAUNTLESS VICTORY

*Fresh perspectives on America's seminal naval victory
of World War II*

by

Peter C. Smith

Pen & Sword
MARITIME

First published in Great Britain in 2007 by
Pen & Sword Maritime
an imprint of
Pen & Sword Books Ltd
47 Church Street
Barnsley
South Yorkshire
S70 2AS

ISBN 978 1 84415 583 5

Typeset in Bulmer by
Phoenix Typesetting, Auldgirth, Dumfriesshire

Printed and bound inEngland by
CPI UK

See all Peter C. Smith's books at www.dive-bombers.co.uk

Pen & Sword Books Ltd incorporates the Imprints of Pen & Sword Aviation, Pen &
Sword Maritime, Pen & Sword Military, Wharncliffe Local History, Pen & Sword
Select, Pen & Sword Military Classics and Leo Cooper.

For a complete list of Pen & Sword titles please contact
PEN & SWORD BOOKS LIMITED
47 Church Street, Barnsley, South Yorkshire, S70 2AS, England
E-mail: enquiries@pen-and-sword.co.uk
Website: www.pen-and-sword.co.uk

Depend on it, he who pretends to give a general account of a great battle
from his own observation deceives you – believe him not.
He can see no farther (that is, if he be personally engaged in it)
than the length of his nose.

Captain Alexander Cavalie Mercer, Royal Horse Artillery. (1783–1868)
(*Journal of the Waterloo Campaign*, 1870)

To Pat –

for fifty joyful years –
for two wonderful children –
for patience and tolerance –
for following my restless footsteps around the globe –

this book is for you.

Contents

List of Illustrations   viii
List of Maps   xv
List of Diagrams   xvi
List of Tables   xvii
Author's Note   xviii
Acknowledgements   xix

Part One – BUILD-UP

Chapter 1 – Intelligence 1 – Seeking   3
Chapter 2 – Intelligence 2 – Knowing   31
Chapter 3 – Preparing the Ambushes   51

Part Two – THE BATTLE COMMENCES

Chapter 4 – The 1st *Kidō Butai* Under Siege   81
Chapter 5 – The Wide Blue Yonder   104
Chapter 6 – The 'Barge' Saves the Day   124
Chapter 7 – Inquest   152

Part Three – DUEL TO THE DEATH

Chapter 8 – One against Three   173
Chapter 9 – The Fog of War   200
Chapter 10 – The Final Blows   232

Part Four – THE MIDWAY LEGACY

Chapter 11 – Conclusions and Consequences   257
Chapter 12 – Post-War Conclusions   269
Chapter 13 – The Chimera of 'Orient'   299

Appendix 1 – The Japanese Charting of Enemy Action and Damage Suffered
              by their carriers at Midway. (ONI translation). Table A–*Akagi*;
              Table B – *Kaga*; Table C – *Soryū*; Table D – *Hiryū*.   330
Appendix 2 – Midway and the Media   334

Select Bibliography   337
Glossary   346
Index   351

Illustrations

(1) The Commander-in-Chief of the Combined Fleet, Admiral Isoroku Yamamoto. (Courtesy Library of War History Department, National Institute for Defense Studies, Tokyo)

(2) The Commander of the First Air Fleet, Vice Admiral Chuichi Nagumo. (Courtesy Library of War History Department, National Institute for Defense Studies, Tokyo)

(3) The Chief of Naval General Staff, Admiral Osami Nagano. (Courtesy Library of War History Department, National Institute for Defense Studies, Tokyo)

(4) The Chief of Staff, Combined Fleet, Rear Admiral Matome Ugaki. (Courtesy Library of War History Department, National Institute for Defense Studies, Tokyo)

(5) The Commander and staff of the Combined Fleet. (Courtesy Library of War History Department, National Institute for Defense Studies, Tokyo)

(6) The Commander and staff of the First Air Fleet. (Courtesy Library of War History Department, National Institute for Defense Studies, Tokyo)

(7) The young officer cadets of the Imperial Japanese Navy trained hard to fight hard. Here a kendo class is underway at the Etajima Training College across the bay from Kure. They were highly disciplined and taught that a superior spirit and better weapons would obviate the numerical advantage held by the United States and Great Britain. (This photograph was part of a series taken in the 1930s by famous photographer Matsugu. Reproduced by courtesy of his daughter Miss Mitsa Matsugu.)

(8) Here the young officer cadets of the Imperial Japanese Navy move from one classroom to another with their books and notes, in strict file and always at the double. Fiercely proud and ruthless in combat, many declared even then that to die in combat was their avowed aim. With such an inbuilt attitude, the Western Allies found them more than a handful when talk changed to action in the Pacific. (This photograph was part of a series taken in the 1930s by famous photographer Matsugu. Reproduced by courtesy of his daughter Miss Mitsa Matsugu.)

(9) Captain Joseph John Rochefort, an unorthodox maverick, whose work at Station *Hypo* gave the Americans unrivalled insight into the war plans and intentions of their enemy and gave them a 'priceless advantage' in the ensuing naval battle. He outthought his opposite numbers in Washington DC, but they quickly got their revenge and Rochefort was recalled, and kicked out of Intelligence ('They don't think like we do,' said one of his detractors – too right he didn't, for he got it right and they got it mainly wrong!). He turned down a destroyer command and ended up in charge of a floating dock on the west coast. (Naval Historical Center, Washington DC)

(10) Captain John Redman, pictured at Tarawa in November 1943. The younger of the two brothers. Rochefort was consigned to years in the wilderness after his brilliant deduction on Japanese intentions before Midway negated their own interpretation of the evidence. 'Not the most glorious episode in the history of the US Navy,' was one historian's verdict on what took place. (Naval Historical Center, Washington DC)

(11) Rear Admiral Joseph R. Redman, seen here in 1957 with Fleet Admiral Nimitz. The elder of the two brothers who extended their control over Navy Intelligence after Midway. (Naval Historical Center, Washington DC)

(12) Aerial view of the Japanese aircraft carrier *Akagi,* sunk at Midway. (Courtesy Library of War History Department, National Institute for Defense Studies, Tokyo)

(13) Overhead view of the Japanese aircraft carrier *Kaga,* sunk at Midway. (Courtesy Library of War History Department, National Institute for Defense Studies, Tokyo)

(14) Starboard-side view of the Japanese aircraft carrier *Soryū,* sunk at Midway. (Courtesy Library of War History Department, National Institute for Defense Studies, Tokyo)

(15) Portside view of the Japanese aircraft carrier *Hiryū*, sunk at Midway. (Courtesy Library of War History Department, National Institute for Defense Studies, Tokyo)

(16) Nakajima B5N (Type 97) *Kate* torpedo-bomber. (Courtesy of War History Department, National Institute for Defense Studies, Tokyo)

(17) Lieutenant-Commander Zenji Abe, with his Aichi D3A/1 Val dive-bomber, aboard the aircraft carrier *Akagi* in 1941. Abe took part in the Pearl Harbor attack that December and served right through the war in dive-bombers, his final action being at the Battle of the Philippine Sea in June 1944, when, piloting a Yokasuka D4Y *Comet* (code-named 'Judy'), he scored a very near miss on the aircraft carrier *Bunker Hill* (CV-17) and escaped to Rota Island. (Zenji Abe)

(18) Aichi D3A (Type 99) Val carrier-(dive-)bomber. (Courtesy Library of War History Department, National Institute for Defense Studies, Tokyo)

(19) The A6M3 Type O Reisen (codenamed 'Zeke' by the Allies but more commonly known as Zero, after the Japanese year of manufacture, 2600) was the best combat fighter in the Pacific Theatre in 1942. Here a Zero is cheered on as she takes off from the deck of a carrier to attack. (Courtesy Library of War History Department, National Institute for Defense Studies, Tokyo)

(20) Some of the top American officers involved in the Midway encounter from left to right, Admiral Raymond A. Spruance, Admiral Ernest J. King and Admiral Chester W. Nimitz. They are seen here later in the war at Saipan with Brigadier-General Sanderford Jarman (far right). (National Archives via Naval Historical Foundation, Washington DC)

(21) Captain Arthur C. Davis, Aviation Officer at Hawaii, one of a small group of experienced naval aviators who gave advice to former submariner Nimitz before and during the course of the battle. (Naval Historical Center, Washington, DC)

(22) Frank Jack Fletcher, as a Vice-Admiral later in the war. The senior naval officer on the spot and the tactical commander of the US forces at the Battle of Midway. (Courtesy of Mr George Fletcher, donated 1976, via Naval Historical Foundation, Washington DC)

(23) Japanese ace Zero pilot Iyozo Fujita during the war. He stacked up a heavy count of 'kills' and even lost track of just how many in the end, assigning his later victims to his squadron rather than himself. (Iyozo Fujita)

(24) The *Hikōchō's* domain. The small size and fragility of the bridge structure of Japanese aircraft carriers, when compared with American or British ships of the same vintage, is made clear in this view of the *Soryū*. She is undertaking her sea trials in the Bungo Suido Channel. The much smaller profile was due to the fact that, instead of incorporating a single upright funnel into the structure, with trunked uptakes leading to a single vent, Japanese carriers often had their uptakes curved over outboard to take the fumes and smoke away from the flight decks. The actual air defence station can be seen atop the compass bridge, and a direction finding loop antenna, a 60 cm signal lamp, signal flag hoists, ratio aerials and a 1/5 m rangefinder can all be seen. (Author's collection via *Ships of the World*)

(25) Lieutenant-Commander John C. Waldron. Commander of torpedo-bomber squadron VT-8 from the carrier *Hornet* (CV-8). Waldron disagreed with the Air Group plan on the morning of 4 June 1942, and led his unit to their destruction in a gallant but hopeless attack, alone and unaided. This rather fuzzy photo was taken before the war. (Courtesy of South Dakota Hall of Fame)

(26) The ill-fated Douglas TBD-1 Devastator torpedo-bomber. Here seen before the war, a TBD-1 ended up in the catwalk abaft the bridge of the USS *Yorktown* on 3 September 1940 following a landing accident. This particular aircraft was subsequently repaired and assigned to Torpedo Eight, and was one of the many such aircraft lost during the Battle of Midway on 4th June 1942. (Naval Historical Foundation)

(27) & (28) (Double Photo). **Déjà vu**.

(27) Top: Date: 13 June 1940. Location: deck of the British aircraft carrier *Ark Royal* off the coast of Norway. Aircraft: fifteen Blackburn Skua dive-bombers. Mission: attack on German battle-cruiser *Scharnhorst* at Trondheim. Result: fighter escort failed to show up, defending German fighters in the air waiting for them, eight Skuas lost. (Author's collection via Dickie Rolph)

(28) Bottom: Date: 4 June 1942. Location: deck of the American aircraft carrier *Enterprise* off Midway Island. Aircraft: fourteen Devastator torpedo-bombers. Mission: attack on Japanese aircraft carriers off Midway. Result: fighter escort failed to intervene, defending Japanese fighters in the air waiting for them, ten Devastators lost. (US Navy Official)

(29) The ill-fated Torpedo Eight, led by Waldron, forms up prior to departure from the USS *Hornet* on the morning of 4 June 1942. The last known photograph of the unit in battle formation, taken by the official

Hornet photographer, William B. Gibson (Copyright William B. Gibson)

(30) The US Army Air Force employed four of their new twin-engined Martin B-26 Marauder medium bombers as makeshift torpedo-bombers at Midway. Fast and brand new, they were no sitting ducks like the Devastators, but for the loss of half their number they were equally unsuccessful, despite the usual claims to the contrary. Here the crew of Lieutenant James Muri pose for the cameras on their return to Midway, with more than 500 bullet holes in their aircraft. (US Air Force via Naval Historical Foundation, Washington DC)

(31) A famous still from the John Ford film of the battle showing US Marine Corps SB2U-3 Vindicator dive-bombers of Scout-Bombing 241 taking off from Midway Island airstrip to strike the Japanese fleet on the morning of 4 June 1942. Known derisively as the 'wind indicator' (because one could judge wind direction by the way the sealing tapes used to patch up the old machines were blowing), the Vindicator saw her first and last major action at Midway. (NARA, Washington DC)

(32) Not even close! Bomb patterns well clear of the circling carrier *Hiryū* during the opening engagements of the battle. The US Army Air Corps B-17s never justified the boastful propaganda of the air force top brass and the baying headlines of the *New York Times*. Not once, in the entire Pacific War, did an altitude bombing attack score a hit on any carrier or battleship of the Imperial Japanese Navy. The photograph is significant in other ways also, for it shows the carrier's flight deck almost bare of aircraft: only two Zero's can be seen, and there is no sign of a massed 'spotting' of any counter-attack force at this time. (Naval Archives via Naval Historical Foundation, Washington DC)

(33) The author seated in the cockpit of the preserved Mitsubishi Zero fighter at the Mitsubishi Heavy Industries factory in Nagoya, Japan. This particular aircraft is a salvaged and rebuilt Model 52, serial number 4708, of a later type of Zeke than those used at Midway. (Copyright Peter C. Smith)

(34) The starboard-side view of the cockpit of a captured Mitsubishi A6M Zero fighter (AI-154) that was recovered after the Pearl Harbor attack and examined at Hickham Field. The Type 96-Ku-1 radio control box can be seen in the centre with the transmitter on the shelf below and astern of it. (Hickham Base Photograph Laboratory via LRA)

(35) The black box on the right-hand side of the cockpit of the preserved Mitsubishi Zero fighter at the Mitsubishi Heavy Industries factory in Nagoya is a replica of the Type 3-Mark 1 radio set used at Midway. (Copyright Peter C. Smith)

(36) The USS *Enterprise* (CV-6) steaming at high speed during the Battle of Midway. Two SBDs can be seen 'spotted' aft, and on the right. In the distance, is the heavy cruiser USS *Pensacola* (CA-24), one of her screening escorts. (Naval Archives via Naval Historical Foundation, Washington, DC)

(37) The bridge structure of the carrier *Hornet* (CV-8) (the *Yorktown* and *Enterprise* were near-sister ships and just about identical with similar camouflage-pattern paintwork). The Union Flag can be seen at the gaff, with radar atop her foremast in front of the large funnel and the HA director atop the three-tier bridge. The large bridge island makes a stark contrast to the scanty upperworks of the Japanese carrier *Soryū* of the roughly the same vintage (see Illustration 24)

(38) The SBDs of VS-6 in immaculate formation. This is an obviously posed shot as the bomb crutches are empty and they rarely used this type of stacked-up *en echelon* formation in combat conditions. The old-type Gunsight can clearly be seen and the pre-war markings are plain. (Norman J. 'Dusty' Kleiss)

(39) The radiomen/gunners of Scouting Squadron Six aboard USS *Enterprise* (CV-6) on 12 May 1942. Radioman Third Class John W. Snowden is in the centre of the front row. Many of the other radio-gunners have signed their names. (Norman J. 'Dusty' Kleiss)

(40) The officers of Scouting Squadron Six aboard USS *Enterprise* (CV-6) on 12 May 1942. (Norman J 'Dusty' Kleiss)

(41) Scouting Squadron Six aboard USS *Enterprise,* 24 January 1942. (Norman J. 'Dusty' Kleiss)

(42) Rear Admiral Tamon Yamaguchi, Commander Carrier Division 2, who fought back with the *Hiryu* against three US carriers. *(Courtesy of his son Mr Soukei Yamaguchi)*

(43) Lieutenant (junior grade) Norman J. 'Dusty' Kleiss of Scouting Squadron Six aboard USS *Enterprise* 24 January 1942. (Norman J. 'Dusty' Kleiss)

(44) Dauntless *en masse*. Deck part of SBDs aboard the USS *Enterprise* (CV-6) on 4 March 1942, *en route* to raid Marcus Island. Note the individual aircraft numbers on both wings and old-style 'red meatball' in the centre of the white star national markings on the wings, still carried at this date. (National Archives, College Park, Maryland)

(45) The pilots 'Ready Room' aboard an American aircraft carrier. This photograph was taken aboard the *Essex* Class carrier *Lexington* (CV-16) later in the war, but all were generally similar. Here the squadron aircrew assemble prior to a combat sortie to be briefed fully on the nature of the target, its bearing, course and speed and prevailing and predicted weather conditions, and on aircraft allocation prior to take-off. Note that they have their individual chart boards to plot the information relayed by teletype and verbally. (US Navy Official)

(46) A US carrier pilot's chart-plotting board. Used to compute outward and homeward courses from the information provided at the pre-flight, on-board briefing and subsequent updates. This is a photograph from an exhibition and features a TBD navigator's set. (Author's Collection)

(47) Lieutenant-Commander Joe Taylor (left) and Lieutenant-Commander Wallace O. Burch Jr, of VT-5, pictured with a TBD-1 on Ford Island , Pearl Harbor, on 6 June 1942. They had been transferred ashore just prior to the battle, a fact which saved their lives. Note their flight gear, with 'Mae West' life jackets and the chart plotting boards. (NARA, Washington, DC)

(48) Douglas SBD-*3* Dauntless dive-bombers 'warming up' aboard the carrier *Yorktown* (CV-5) prior to take-off for a strike on the morning of 4 June, 1942. (Naval Institute Photo Collection via Naval Historical Foundation, Washington DC)

(49) Commander Stanhope C. Ring, 'Sea-Hag' of *Hornet*'s Air Group on the 'flight to nowhere' on 4 June 1942. One of the most controversial factors of the battle was the failure of *Hornet*'s entire Air Group (other than Waldron's doomed VT-8), to make any contact with the enemy. This abject performance is attributed by some to Ring's choice of course to the target. Ring himself never filed the required mission report giving the course he chose, nor was it mentioned in the selected extracts from a letter he wrote after the war, other than as a 'predetermined interception course'. This vagueness has left a wide field of speculation open for historians. (US Navy Official, via Clayton Fisher)

(50) Manhandling the SBD. Aircraft 11 of Bombing-8 aboard the *Hornet* is hand-manoeuvred across the carrier's flight-deck. Note the mixture of old-style and new-style helmets at this stage of the war, and the freshly painted white stars on the Dauntless, now with no trace at all of any hint of the 'red meatball', illustrating the dominance of the rising sun marking in the spring of 1942. (Clayton Fisher)

(51) 'Bombing up' an SBD on the deck of an American carrier during the Battle of Midway. The bomb is resting on its loading trolley and the three-man ordnance team are preparing to affix if to the swinging crutch beneath the aircraft. (US Navy Official)

(52) After the Ready Room information and briefing and the agreed flight details to the target had been decided upon, the SBD pilots were fed last-minute updates and information on the flight-deck right up to the moment of departure via the flight-deck information boards. This is *Hornet*'s despatch team with one such piece of interesting data. (Clayton Fisher)

(53) Ready to go! This is the first launch of *Hornet*'s Air Group 8 on the morning of 4 June 1942. Immediately astern of the ten F4F Grumman Wildcat fighters of VF-8, are the SBD-3s of VS-8, with aircraft 9 (centre), the mount of Ensign Clayton Fisher, who had been assigned, much to his dismay, as one of two wingmen for 'Sea-Hag' (CHAG or Commander, *Hornet* Air Group), Commander Stanhope Ring. (Clayton Fisher)

(54) Early in the war SBD pilots used the Mk III Mod IV type gunsight to align their targets on the way down in the dive attack. The main problem with this instrument was that differing layers of density tended to make the sight 'mist over' during the descent. This rather old-fashioned method and sight was later replaced by the M VIII adjustable sight from the SBD-5 onward, but Royal Navy Skua dive-bomber pilots had been using such an electronic 'ring-and-bead' sight since 1939. (US Navy Official via Clayton Fisher)

(55) Target nicely centred! Pilot's-eye view of a turning warship through the gunsight. Allowance for wind speed and drift, speed and course of the target vessel, correct altitude for release of type of bomb carried, and so on, all had to be calculated by the SBD pilot on the way. During the dive the sight had a tendency to mist up and the layers rapidly changed. This was quite apart from distractions like incoming anti-aircraft fire and Zeros on their tail! (US Navy Official via Clayton Fisher)

(56) 'There was only one hero at Midway' (Admiral Raymond Spruance, commander Task Force 16). Commander Clarence Wade McClusky Jr, 1943, a former fighter pilot who led the SBDs to fame and glory. (Courtesy of Mrs C. Wade McClusky Jr, via Naval Historical Foundation, Washington, DC)

(57) The incomparable *Sugar Baker Dog*. Despite the plethora of books and conflicting theories that continue to surround the Battle of Midway, the cardinal fact is that it was by dive-bombing, as conducted so efficiently by the SBD Dauntless aircraft, and dive-bombing alone, that the battle was won. (Ray Wagner courtesy of N. Paul Whittier Historical Aviation Library at the San Diego Aerospace Museum)

(58) The Bel-Geddes diorama depicting the attack by the VB-6 and VS-6 from USS *Enterprise* upon the Japanese aircraft carriers *Kaga* and *Akagi* on the morning of 4 June 1942. (National Archives, College Park, Maryland)

(59) Admiral William I. Martin, seen here when he was commander of the US Sixth Fleet in the Mediterranean, 1967–9, one of the many former SBD pilots who fought at Midway and went on to achieve flag rank in the navy, having established the power of the dive-bomber and the navy's Air Arm during the darkest days of 1942. As a young Dauntless pilot, Bill Martin had been blooded at the Battle of Midway. Serving with VS-10 aboard the famous USS *Enterprise* (CV-6), he later fought in the Guadalcanal campaign and at Santa Cruz and the Eastern Solomons carrier duels, before taking over as commander of that unit from Commander James R. Lee in February 1943. (Admiral William I. Martin)

(60) 'Dusty' Kleiss and John Snowden making their exit aboard S-7 after hitting the *Kaga* with one 500 lb and two 100 lb incendiary bombs. Snowden added to that tally by managing to shoot down a Zero fighter which tried to attack them. (Original painting reproduced by permission of Dave Gray)

(61) Sturdy defence. It is an amazing and still little-acknowledged, fact that hardly any of the 'slow but deadly'. Dauntless dive-bombers were shot down by the outstanding Mitsubishi Zero-Sen fighters on the first day of the Midway encounter. By contrast, several of the hitherto 'invincible' Zekes fell to the .303 guns of the allegedly obsolescent 'barge'. (US Navy via Clayton Fisher)

(62) The SBD's sting in the tail. The twin .303 mounting in a Dauntless, which proved quite effective in defending the dive-bomber from marauding Zekes at Midway. Not a single SBD was shot down by the Japanese Combat Air Patrol during the first attack on the morning of 4 June. (Author's collection)

(63) A Douglas SBD-3 Dauntless dive bomber (Bu No 4542), coded B-15, of Bombing Squadron Six (VB-6), is manhandled across the flight-deck after landing back aboard the carrier *Enterprise* (CV-6) with damage taken during her attack on a Japanese target during the morning of 4 June 1942. The dive-bomber's crew were Ensign George H. Goldsmith,

A-V (N), USNR, pilot: and RM1c J. W. Patterson, USN, radioman and rear-gunner. (Naval Institute Photo Collection via Naval Historical Foundation, Washington DC)

(64) Welcome back! A hive of activity as SBDs crowd the deck part forward aboard the USS *Hornet* following the return of a strike. Watched by Admiral Mitscher (forward in peaked cap) and other observers from the bridge, the deck crew wheel away a 500 lb bomb that has been brought back undelivered; aircraft 10 bears the scars of the Japanese reception committee on her starboard aileron; an armourer removes the ammunition belt from the starboard wing of 15; while a pair of jeeps manoeuvre as aircraft movers across the flight-deck. A photo taken later in the war. (Clayton Fisher)

(65) A fire-fighting station aboard the USS *Yorktown* (CV-5). Although rather primitive and limited these facilities, especially the Foamite foam generator with the funnel-shaped delivery, enabled the damage-control parties to contain the damage caused by the three dive-bomber hits on 4 June. (Naval Historical Foundation, Washington DC)

(66) The scene inside the hangar deck of a US carrier earlier in the war. Artisans are shown working on a Grumman F4-F Wildcat (3-F-14) fighter under the watchful eye of a petty officer. Across the hangar roof run the mass of pipes, including the all-important sprinkler system. To create maximum space for working and arming aircraft, the planes could be hung from the hangar roof itself, and both TBD Devastator torpedo bombers (3-T-3) (left) and SBD Dauntless dive-bombers (2-S-3) can be seen so stacked. The calm, measured, pristine world of the pre-war US Navy hangar deck bears little resemblance to the chaos, hell and frenzy of the Japanese carriers' combat rearming and rearming again on the morning of 4 June 1942, but it conveys the claustrophobic working conditions. (NARA, Washington)

(67) A Japanese Val dive-bomber attacking the *Yorktown*. A dramatic still from a movie film shot by Photographer's Mate Second Class William G. Roy, with a 35 mm Bell & Howell motion picture camera, which was later recovered by Otis Kight (VF-42). (Copyright William G. Roy, Naples, FL.)

(68) On the receiving end. The flight deck of the USS *Yorktown* (CV-5) after the Japanese dive-bomber assault. Corpsmen can be seen treating casualties around one of the quadruple 1.1 in anti-aircraft mountings near the carrier's bridge structure. (National Archives via Naval Historical Foundation, Washington DC)

(69) A Japanese Kate torpedo bomber from *Hiryū's* second attack wave. Having dropped her torpedo at the *Yorktown* she receives flak hits and trails smoke as she makes a low-level turn to try and escape across the screen. Another still from a movie film by William G. Roy, with a 35 mm Bell & Howell motion picture camera, which was later recovered by Otis Kight (VF-42). (William G. Roy, Naples, FL)

(70) William G. Roy, with the hand-held camera with which he shot some of the most memorable photographs of the battle from on board the carrier *Yorktown*. (Copyright William G. Roy, Naples, FL)

(71) Japanese Kate torpedo-bombers brave the barrage at low level to deliver a pincer attack against the carrier *Yorktown*. (William G. Roy, via NARA, Washington, DC)

(72) The *Yorktown* listing after heavy damage. She was hit by three bombs and four torpedoes and abandoned twice before she finally gave up the fight. (William G. Roy, via NARA, Washington (DC)

(73) The *Yorktown* settling after heavy damage. She was hit by three bombs and four torpedoes and abandoned twice before she finally gave up the fight. (William G. Roy, via NARA, DC)

(74) The final plunge of the USS *Yorktown*, as recorded by naval photographer William G. Roy. A massive hole caused by torpedo hits can be seen in her hull (left) and her LSO platform can be discerned on the right. On arrival back at Pearl Harbor, Roy was forbidden to look at the very photographs that he had taken! (Naval Historical Foundation)

(75) How 'Flags' Karetka remembers the *Yorktown's* last moments. Drawing from memory by Kelly Lewis (Copyright Peter E. Karetka, Chicopee, MA)

(76) The destroyer USS *Hughes* (DD-410) was sent to stand by the abandoned *Yorktown* overnight on the 4/5 June. (Naval Historical Foundation, Washington DC)

(77) The forward twin 5 in gun mount of a *Fubuki* class destroyer. This photograph show the guns at low depression for surface action, but this mounting was designed specifically for a dual-purpose capability and, as can be seen by the gun-barrel slots in the forward mounts face and roof, the guns could elevate to 75° to engage aircraft. The *Tanikaze* proved their value during the battle. (Courtesy *Ships of the World*)

(78) A division of the Imperial Japanese Navy's *Kagero* class destroyers. When these ships joined the fleet they were regarded as the finest destroyers in any navy in the world. They carried six 5 in guns in twin mount-ings capable of elevating 75 degrees to engage aircraft as well as two sets of torpedo tubes carrying the most powerful underwater punch then known. One of the ships of this class, the *Tanikaze*, showed just what they were capable of by surviving attacks by both B-17s and several dozen SBDs and managed to shoot down at least two of her attackers in return. (Courtesy Jim Culberson, *Sea Bird Publishing*, Inc, Melbourne, FL)

(79) The one that got away! On 5 June 1942, the solitary Japanese destroyer *Tanikaze* (Wind from the mountain to the valley) of the *Kagero* Class, commanded by Captain Katsumi Motoi, was subjected to almost non-stop attack by eight Boeing B-17 heavy bombers and no fewer than thirty-eight SBDs from both *Enterprise* and *Hornet*, and survived them all. This was largely due to Signalman Masashi Shibata, who lay on his back half in and half out of the ship's bridge window, watching each aircraft as it attacked and calling down to the helmsman just as the bomb was released. Many years later, in 1991, Shibata, now a successful businessman, met some of his former tormentors at a reunion at the Hotel del Coronado, San Diego. Left to right: Don Adams, Mr Masashi Shibata, Clayton Fisher and Roy Gee. (Copyright Clayton Fisher)

(80) Colonel Ernest Roderic Manierre. As a captain pilot in the USAAC with Patrol Wing Two, based at Oahu, Hawaii in June 1942, Manierre led one of the many small formations of Boeing B-17 Flying Fortress four-engined bombers against Japanese naval targets during the battle. Despite their dedication and bravery, the army precision altitude attacks, utilizing the much-vaunted Norden bomb sight, failed to score a single hit throughout the entire battle. The B-17 later proved herself more successful as a long-range bomber against static city-sized targets, where precision was not such an issue. (USAAF Official)

(81) Another one that got away! The submarine USS *Grayling* (SS 202*)*, running at 12.9 knots on the surface. It was in just such configuration that she was attacked by B-17s during the battle and forced to crash dive. The USAAF claimed that they had 'sunk a Japanese heavy cruiser in record time' and refused to believe Layton when he explained that, actually, they had not! (Naval Historical Foundation, Washington, DC)

(82) And one that *didn't* get away! The Japanese heavy cruiser *Mikuma* after heavy attacks by *Enterprise* and *Hornet* SBDs on 6 June. This photograph was taken from the *Hornet's* combat file (serial 0018) and shows smoke from three different bomb hits pouring away from her. This photograph has never been published before and is also the only one that shows the two destroyers, *Arashio* and *Asashio,* in position upwind of the crippled ship in her last hours. (NARA, Washington DC)

(83) Another view of the Japanese heavy cruiser *Mikuma* on fire after attacks by SBDs from *Enterprise* and *Hornet* on 6 June 1942. (Naval Historical Foundation, Washington DC)

(84) Flying log book of an SBD at Midway. This is the battle record of Clayton Fisher of the *Hornet*'s Scouting squadron. Note the first mission on 4 June, with a four-and-a-half hour flight duration marked up. (Clayton Fisher)

(85) Japanese prisoners of war on board the USS *Ballard (*AVD-10), after being found in a lifeboat after the Battle of Midway. They are engine-room survivors from the aircraft carrier *Hiryū*, left behind when the ship was abandoned and sunk. They are on their way to Midway Island, the only members of the Japanese fleet to set foot there, *en route* to Pearl Harbor for internment. (National Archives, via Naval Historical Foundation, Washington DC)

(86) The Texas Hero! Ensign George Gay, the only survivor from Waldron's doomed TBDs of VT-8, is pictured recovering at Pearl Harbor Naval Hospital in June 1942. He was to become a celebrity back in the USA, while other survivors from the Avenger section of his squadron were ignored. After the war his story of what he witnessed, like Topsy, 'just kept growing'. Historians and colleagues alike have largely discredited his memoirs, written shortly before his death. (US Navy, via Naval Historical Foundation, Washington DC)

(87) Ensign Clayton E. Fisher of the *Hornet*'s VS-8, relaxing at Pearl Habor immediately after the battle. (Clayton Fisher)

(88) Veteran. The author in discussion with dive-bomber exponent Lieutenant-Commander Zenji Abe at the Yasukuni Shrine, central Tokyo, 21 April 1998. (Copyright Peter C. Smith)

(89) Veterans. Signed photograph showing, from right to left: B5N2 Pilot Taisuke Maruyama from the *Hiryū*, who torpedoed the carrier *Yorktown* on 4 June, W. G. Roy, who filmed the battle from the deck of the *Yorktown* and who was part of the salvage party; Lieutenant-Commander Richard H. Best, SBD-3 pilot of VB-6, who helped to sink two Japanese carriers at Midway. (Copyright William G .Roy, Naples, FL)

(90) Veterans. Takeshi Maeda, Honorary President of Unabarakai, the veteran IJN pilot's association, at an interview with the author in the Dai-Ichi Hotel, Shinbashi, Central Tokyo on 4 November 2005. As a young lieutenant he flew a Kate torpedo bomber from the aircraft carrier *Kaga* and was aboard her at the Battle of Midway. (Copyright Peter C. Smith)

(91) Historian Ray Wagner, seated in the boardroom of the San Diego Aerospace Museum, during a meeting with the author and Clayton Fisher to discuss the influence of Ed Heinemann and the SBD on the outcome of Midway, on 28 March 2006. (Copyright Peter C. Smith)

(92) Veterans. Lieutenant-Commander Iyozo Fujita, during an interview with the author at his home on 5 November 2005. Fujita was an ace Zero pilot from the carrier *Soryū,* who flew with the CAP over the 1st *Kidō Butai* at Midway, and was shot down by 'friendly fire' during that battle, being rescued by the destroyer *Nowaki*. A leading IJN ace, he later wrote of his exploits in the book *Zero Fighter.* (Copyright Peter C. Smith)

(93) Veterans. Commander Clayton E. Fisher, outside the San Diego Aerospace Museum during one of his interviews with the author on 28 March 2006 (Copyright Peter C. Smith)

(94) Veterans. Captain N. Jack 'Dusty' Kleiss Sr, at his home in San Antonio, Texas, during an interview with the author on 1 April 2006. (Copyright Peter C. Smith)

(95) Veterans. Commander Mitsuo Fuchida. Fêted as the hero of Pearl Harbor and other battles, Fuchida was reduced to an observer's role at Midway due to illness. However, he subsequently became far more famous for his eyewitness account of the battle, which for many decades was taken as the only true and worthwhile Japanese viewpoint. His account has been increasingly criticized in recent years and he, just like the American Professor Samuel Eliot Morison, is now vilified by some American historians and researchers. (Author's Collection)

(96) George J. Walsh, with his SB2C Air Group Eighty aboard the carrier *Ticonderoga* (CV-14) in the Pacific. This former dive-bomber pilot has been a tireless campaigner for what he perceives as lack of recognition of the dive bomber's role at Midway. (George J. Walsh)

(97) The Victor of Midway! In a classic dive-bombing configuration an SBD releases a bomb from the swinging crutch, with the perforated dive flaps extended and her twin 303s watching the skies astern. The true victor of the Battle of Midway. (Copyright US Navy via Clayton Fisher)

Maps

1:   Battleground Pacific. Based upon a contemporary map of the area.   55

2:   A possible Nimitz attack plan for US task forces on the morning of 4 June 1942. This would have resulted in a combined earlier attack, and at shorter range by all three US carriers, than the attacks ultimately conducted by Task Force Sixteen and Task Force Seventeen. (Copyright George Walsh 2007)   294

3:   The map of the battle as plotted by Spruance's flagship, the USS *Enterprise*. (NARA)   298

Tables

1.	American and Japanese Seagoing Forces at the Midway and Aleutian Operations, June 1942.	11
2.	TF-16 and TF-17 First Strike 4 June 1942.	77
3.	USMC SBD-2 attack, 4 June 1942.	87
4.	US Submarine Force at Midway (Task Force 7).	90
5.	USMC SB2U-3 attack, 4 June 1942.	94
6.	Comparison Between USN and IJN Torpedo Bombers at Midway.	95
7.	Ineffectual attacks on 1 *Kido Būtai* on the morning of 4 June 1942.	99
8.	Midway SBD launch 1st attack 4 June 1942.	105
9.	The first SBD Strike from *Enterprise, Yorktown* and *Hornet*, 4 June 1942.	106
10.	Comparison between Skua and Dauntless.	125
11.	Fire Distribution (for an Eighteen strong SBD Group).	130
12.	SBD Target Designation.	130
13.	Call Signs and Voice Communications for the use of Fighter Unit (fc TAI) Control.	158
14.	SBD Losses in 1st attack at Midway, 4 June 1942.	168
15.	*Hiryū*'s First (Dive-Bomber) attack on *Yorktown,* 4 June 1942.	174
16.	*Hiryū*'s Second (Torpedo-Bomber) attack on *Yorktown,* 4 June 1942.	189
17.	Fighter Escorts for *Hiryū*'s Tomonaga Strike.	189
18.	Composition of the Afternoon SBD Strikes Against *Hiryū*, 4 June 1942.	205
19.	VB-8's SBD attack on *Tanikaze,* 5 June 1942.	225
20.	VS-6's and VB-6's SBD attack on *Tanikaze,* 5 June 1942.	225
21.	First VB-8 attack on Cruisers, 6 June 1942.	233
22.	First VS-8 attack on Cruisers, 6 June 1942.	234
23.	VS-6 attack on Cruisers, 6 June 1942.	236
24.	VB-6 attack on Cruisers, 6 June 1942.	236
25.	VB-3 attack on Cruisers, 6 June 1942.	237
26.	VS-5 (VB-5) attack on Cruisers, 6 June 1942.	237
27.	Second VB-8 attack on Cruisers, 6 June 1942.	238
28.	Second VS-8 attack on Cruisers, 6 June 1942.	239
29.	Comparison of IJN/USN Dive-bombing Attacks on Heavy Cruisers.	241
30.	NID Estimate of IJN Building Programme 1942.	303
31.	Distribution of Allied War Materials Supplied to the Soviet Union 1941–5.	324

Diagrams

1   Diagram of the May 1942 Combined Fleet's War Game of the Battle of Midway. The printed annotations are those of Rear-Admiral Edwin T. Layton, USN (Rtd), Nimitz's Intelligence Officer at Pearl Harbor in June 1942. (*Senshi Sosho,* Tokyo)   113

2   Japanese Carrier operations – Details of Carrier Landing Circle. (US Naval Technical Mission)   160

3   Japanese carrier operation – Navy Type OO Carrier-borne Fighter Arresting Hook. (US Naval Technical Mission)   160

4   Japanese carriers – Diagramatic Sketch of Typical Gasoline Supply Arrangements, based on *Unryū* class ships: (US Naval Technical Mission)   149

5   Japanese Carriers – Diagramatic Sketch of Typical Hangar Ventilation Arrangements, (based on *Shōkaku* class ships.) (US Naval Technical Mission)   150

6   US Carrier Air Group Rendezvous Prior to Departure   54

7   Cut-away Detail of the Douglas SBD Dauntless Dive-bomber   126

8   US Carrier Operations – Even Sector Number Scouting Units   127

9   US Carrier Operations – Odd Sector Number Scouting Units   127

10   1st SBD attack 4 June 1942. As recorded at the time by J. R. Penland, Lieutenant US Navy, Commander, VB-6   145

11   General Plan of Dive-bombing and Torpedo Hits on *Yorktown* (CV-5) of 4 June 1942. (Originally presented at FAST 1999, Seattle, August 99. Reprinted with the permission of the Society of Naval Architects and Marine Engineers, New Jersey)   183

12   Cross-sections of Aircraft Torpedo Damage to *Yorktown* (CV-5) on 4 June 1942. (Originally presented at FAST 99, Seattle, August 1999. Reprinted with the permission of the Society of Naval Architects and Marine Engineers, New Jersey)   194

13   Flooding from Aircraft Torpedo Hits on *Yorktown* (CV-5) on 4 June 1942. (Originally presented at FAST 99, Seattle, August 1999. Reprinted with the permission of the Society of Naval Architects and Marine Engineers, New Jersey)   195

14   General Plan of Attack by *I-168* on *Yorktown* (CV-5) on 6 June 1942. (Originally presented at FAST 99, Seattle, August 1999. Reprinted with the permission of the Society of Naval Architects and Marine Engineers New Jersey)   245

Author's Note

The Battle of Midway has proved a fascinating study of the unpredictability of war and the frailty of the exercise of 'control' over a battlefield. Rarely has the old adage that no plan survives first contact with the enemy been more vividly demonstrated than at Midway. All battles tend to lose cohesion once joined, but Midway was a confusing battle in new ways. It was a three-dimensional battle, fought on, above and below the sea; as if that was not enough it was fought across the International Date Line, with American forces using one time zone and Japanese using another. Not only were battles fought between opponents but there was conflict and tension between commanders and officers on both sides; once initiated by the admirals the battle was actually fought and won by men of relatively junior ranks, young ensigns, lieutenant (jg) and Lieutenants as well as NCOs. There was courage aplenty, the battle was filled with self-sacrifice and truly noble effort; there were tragedies galore, horrendous sacrifices by men on both sides of the conflict; high drama also, with unbelievable twists of fate that would not be contemplated for a work of fiction, so bizarre were they. There were ugly scenes among the heroism, as in any war; men were tortured and men were murdered, men were abandoned and left to die; there were tragic, lonely and unrecorded deaths as aircraft ran out of fuel in the middle of the largest ocean in the world; but the overwhelming images are those of courage and incredible fortitude. Midway has all these, and more; not surprisingly many aspects of these dramas have reverberated down the decades since it was fought, and continue to do so.

One thing about Midway is incontestable: its outcome – the winner is not in doubt! But who achieved that result, and why and how it was achieved continue to be the subject of hot debate. This book attempts to take a neutral and unbiased look at the battle. I have many friends in both America and Japan, and love both countries and peoples. But, being British, I can sometimes look objectively at events or incidents that are still highly charged and subject to intense partisan feelings in both countries. So it is with a detached eye, and a different viewpoint, that many facets of the battle are analysed here, for good or bad. And not just the battle itself; I have tried to place the battle in perspective, to give it a place in the overall scheme of things.

Did Midway affect Normandy, and therefore post-war European history, as some would have it? What of the new myth of the so-called Operation Orient, a product of revisionist and television documentary makers suddenly given undeserved prominence? Who really gained and lost by the outcome of Midway?

Three things I have sought to bring out – three simple basic truths that have tended to be underplayed or even deliberately and disgracefully ignored by the Western media since 1942. Two of them are the pivotal role of pre-battle intelligence (COMINT) and the crucial and decisive role of the dive-bombers in determining the outcome of the battle when all other methods had failed. This book tries to correct this sixty-year-old travesty of justice and in doing so, expose the third – the inaccuracy of film and TV documentaries, something that also still continues. So Rochefort, McClusky and Best get their just prominence and due in these pages, while, in terms of hardware, it is the SBD which emerges the true heroine of the story, not the TBD, nor the F4F and certainly not, as was widely proclaimed at the time, the B-17. Certain beliefs sincerely held by veterans are included, not necessarily because I subscribe to them or believe them to be true, but because every veteran has the right to have their own particular memory on record, whether misguided or not.

It is now fashionable to follow the civilian Japanese practice of placing the family name first and the given name second in books on the Imperial Japanese Navy (IJN). This is certainly accurate from the general Japanese perspective and courteous as well. Despite my favourable views, however, I have decided, in general, not to adopt this policy. Firstly, when formally listing the various *Shotaicho, Buntaicho* and *Hikotaicho*, the IJN presented their names in the Western manner, with surnames last. This was a formal left-over from their Royal Navy mentors and was normal or traditional *Kaigun* practice. Secondly, many Western readers find the practice of surnames first, given names second, rather confusing, and, as this book is originally written for a Western audience, I have followed our own practice. I have consulted with my Japanese friends on this and found only wry humour and complete understanding. I trust this will extend to my readership, even if not my critics!

Acknowledgements

My thanks go to: Susan Ring Keith, daughter of Commander Stanhope Cotton Ring, for her kind assistance and permission to quote from her late father's full letter; Takashi Doi, Yokohama WW-2 Japanese Military Radio Museum, Yokohama; Hazel Jones, The IEE Library, London; Ronald M. Bulatoff, Hoover Institution Library and Archives, Stanford University, California for the *Official History of the United States Naval Group China* file in the Milton Miles Papers (Box 5); Caroline Herbert, Churchill Archives Centre, Churchill College, Cambridge, for access to the papers of Admiral Sir James Somerville; Jonathan Parshall co-author of *The Shattered Sword* for his views on IJN Fighter Control; Mike Wenger, authority on Japanese naval air operations, for sharing some of his knowledge with me; Mark R. Peattie, Stanford University, California, author of *Sunburst* and co-author of *Kaigun*, for his help with regard to IJN Fighter Control; Lieutenant-Commander Iyozo Fujuta, Zero pilot aboard the *Sōryū* at Midway; Lieutenant Takeshi Maeda, Honorary President *Unabaraki*, Kate pilot aboard the *Kaga* at Midway; Dr Toshimasa Egusa, second son of Captain Takashige Egusa; Mr Hiroyuki Egusa, elder son of Captain Egusa; Mrs Haruko Kitamura, eldest daughter of Captain Egusa; military historian Mitsuharu Uehara; the late Lieutenant-Commander Zenji Abe; Rear-Admiral Taemi Ichikawa; Matsudo City, Assistant Communications Officer aboard *Akagi* at Midway; Sadao Seno; Captain Masato Shimada; Rear-Admiral Kazuo Takahashi, Chief-of-Staff, Commandant Kure District; Rear-Admiral Sadayoshi Matsioka, Superintendent of the Officer Candidate School, Etajima; Commander Sadamu Takahashi, author of *Flying Clouds*; Commander Iyōzō Fujita, for kind hospitality at his home in Daizawa, Setagaya-ku, Tokyo; Mr and Mrs Shuzo Inaba, for their hospitality at Kure; Tohru Kizu, Editor-in-Chief, *Ships of the World*, Tokyo; Mr Tetsuya Nakama, Hankyu Togo Group, Tokyo: Mr Kohji Ishiwata, Honorary President and founder, *Ships of the World*, Tokyo, for plans of the *Sōryū*; Lieutenant Takashi Miura, who rescued Lieutenant Ichikawa, survivor of *Akagi*; Mr Hitoshi Hasegawa, journalist, *Ships of the World*; Rear-Admiral Sadayoshi Matsuoka; Rear-Admiral Hideshi Koyayashi; Miss Misa Matsugi, daughter of Mr Fujio Matsugi; Vice-Admiral Kazunari Doke, Commandant, Kure District, and later Commander-in-Chief Self Defense Fleet; Ensign Kazutaka Abe; Rear-Admiral Katsutoshi Kawano, Director of the Administration Department, Maritime Staff Office, Etajima, who kindly made arrangements via Rear-Admiral Kobayashi for the author's visit to Etajima, by which the author was treated, not as an historian, but as an admiral; J. N. Hans Houterman at Middelburg, The Netherlands, for his very special assistance; Alan Parker, Frank Smith Maritime & Aviation, Newcastle-upon-Tyne; Kengo Yamamoto, Hyogo; Captain Hatsuhiko Watanabe; Mr Ryunosuke Valentine Megumi; Colonel Shogo Hattori; Mr Kunio Kosemoto; Commander Noritaka Kitazawa, Military History Department, National Institute for Defense Studies, Tokyo, for continuous courteous help and assistance down the years; Professor Akira Nakamura, Dokkyo University; Nakamise Suzuya, Tokyo; my good friend Tetsukuni Watanabe, and to his wife and daughter, formerly of Aichi Machine Industry, Nagoya, for all his kindness and assistance during my visits there; Seizaburou Hoshino, from Sizuoka Prefecture, Etajima classmate of Lieutenant Michio Kobayashi; Norman Polmar for refreshing views over breakfast in New York; dearest Peggy Olds, my good friend and widow of Robert Olds, for making her home at Santa Barbara ours for our extended stay and research base while in California and allowing me to use Bob's books and papers; Clayton E. Fisher, former SBD pilot aboard the *Hornet* at Midway, who has conducted much research himself which he freely shared with me and for extended interviews, also to his wife Anne, for her kind hospitality to my wife and myself at their home, and for invaluable practical help over many days during my researches while at Coronado, California; Robert McLean, National Air & Space Museum, Paul E. Gerber Facility, Suitland, Maryland; Jennifer A. Bryan, PhD, Head, Special Collections and Archives Division, Nimitz Library, US Naval Academy; Barry L Zerby, Modern Military Records, (NWCTM), Textual Archives Services Division, NARA; Ray Wagner for his ever welcome views and guidance at our meeting in the board room of the San Diego Aerospace Museum, and for making available to me certain original documentation on the development and design of the SBD;

Captain N. J. 'Dusty' Kleiss, formerly of VS-6 aboard *Enterprise* at Midway, who has allowed me to quote from his own record, *VS-6: Log of the War*, which is his personal diary, as well as allowing me to interview him at length, also to the memory of his late wife, Jean, for entertaining me and my wife at their home in San Antonio, Texas; the late Lieutenant-Commander Richard H Best, for his memories of the battle; the International Midway Memorial Foundation, for permission to reproduce part of Richard Best's separate narrative of the battle; Lieutenant-Commander William G Roy, for his great kindness and courtesy and for allowing me to use some of the incredible photographs he took of the battle when he was the official photographer aboard the *Yorktown*; Denise Duke, Historian, *Waves National*; Peter E. 'Flags' Karetka, for granting me permission to quote from his memories of the last moments of the gallant *Yorktown*, his daughter Gail Morin, and to Kelly Lewis for her drawing interpretation of *Yorktown*; Lena Kaljot, Reference Historian, Marine Corpse History Division, USMC HQ; Dr Peter Dowling, National Trust of Australia (ACT), the late Colonel Elmer Glidden, for his memories of the action; the late Admiral Paul Holmberg, for his eyewitness accounts of the battle; Evelyn M. Cherpak, PhD, Head, Naval Historical Collection, Naval War College, and her assistant, Theresa Clements, for making my visits and research so pleasant and rewarding; Captain Charles 'Chuck' Downey, former dive-bomber pilot and now aviation consultant, for so freely allowing me to interview him at his home at Poplar Grove, Illinois, and his valued friendship, also for showing me his extraordinary aviation museum at the airfield and his own vintage aircraft collection; John Vernon and Patrick Osborne, Modern Navy Records, Textual Archives Services Division, the National Archives, for so efficiently making available all the documentation on Midway for my study; Peter Bobroff, whose sources on IJN officers are invaluable; Heidi Myers, Reference Librarian, Navy Department Library, Naval Historical Center, for her unfailing help and enthusiasm during my visit; Timothy T. Pettit, Archivist, Naval Historical Center, History and Archives Division, Operational Archives Branch, for his outstanding assistance and advice in tracking down records and reports during my visit there, which proved most valuable; Mark E Horan of Toledo, one of the co-authors of *A Glorious Page in Our History*, and always a veritable fount of knowledge on carrier aircraft and operations, who kindly volunteered some of his specific knowledge; Ronald W. Russell, editor and moderator of the *Battle of Midway Roundtable* and author of *No Right to Win*, for his kindness and help; Hugh Bicheno, author of *Midway*, for kindly and unreservedly responding to my queries; Jaime Anderson, South Dakota Hall of Fame, for generously supplying documents and photographs appertaining to the early life of Lieutenant-Commander Waldron; Laura Waayers, Historical Services Manager, Naval Historical Foundation, for unfailingly coming up trumps with my every request promptly and efficiently; David M. Hays, Archivist, University of Colorado at Boulder Libraries; Lieutenant-Commander George J. Walsh, dive-bomber pilot and friend for his hospitality at his home in Darien, Connecticut – a diligent researcher himself he made many of his own notes available to me, and also produced the CDs *Dive Bombers, Smart Bombs and Suicide Aircraft* and *Battle of Midway: Twist of Fate* (Octogenarian Productions) and the *Dive Bombing WWII* DVD with me – also his charming wife, Anne, and Ione, for making my stay such a delight; Paul Simon, Archives Technician, National Personnel Records Center, Military Personnel Records; Tom Howard and Kristi Angel, editor of *The Billings Gazette*, for permission to reproduce the interview with Jim Muri; Giovanni Volpi of Venice; in Russia, my old friend Alexander Bolnykh at Ekaterinburg (Ural) and Colonel Miroslav Morozov at the Moscow Military History Institute, for guiding me through the torturous labyrinth of Soviet-Japanese relations; Ms Debbie Stockford and Mrs Catherine Rounsfell, Fleet Air Arm Museum, Yeovilton, for making my visits so pleasant and productive; Hugh Alexandria at The National Archives, Kew, London; Susan Evans, Publications Manager, the Society of Naval Architects and Marine Engineers (SNAME), New Jersey, for permission to reproduce some of their diagrams illustrating the damage to USS *Yorktown* (CV-5), which were originally presented at FAST 99, Seattle, August 1999. Mr Soukei Yamaguchi, for permission to use photographs of his late father, Rear Admiral Tamon Yamaguchi.

Peter C. Smith
June, 2007.

Part One

Build-up

Chapter One

Intelligence 1 – Seeking

On 28 April 1942, the largest battleship ever built, the 67,123-ton[1] *Yamato,* flagship of the Combined Fleet, lay at anchor at Hashirajima. She was playing host to an assembly of victorious Japanese naval commanders and planners who had led various fleets and forces during the first phase of Japan's war operations. These men had seen that phase completed with unprecedented speed ahead of schedule and with minimal loss, while their achievements had been stunning. Against the two most powerful maritime nations on the planet at that time, Great Britain and the United States (who had been aided by a doughty ally with an equally proud naval heritage, the Netherlands) the Imperial Japanese Navy (IJN) triumphed beyond the wildest imagination. From the carrier aircraft and submarine attacks on the main American naval base at Pearl Harbor and the land-based naval aircraft attacks on American airfields in the Philippines and against the British capital ships in the South China Sea, and by way of a succession of surface and sea battles across the southwest Pacific, Japan had crushed her enemies' fleets and swept away all their garrisons and possessions; from Hong Kong to Singapore, Manila to Mandalay, the flag of the Rising Sun flew triumphant.

It is difficult, looking back more than sixty years, to grasp the enormity of this victorious campaign and place it in its historical perspective. Not only did the Japanese conquests include hugely important and seemingly 'invincible' fortresses and bases, but also areas rich in the essentials that Japan so lacked: oil, rubber, tin, bauxite. But it was not just these huge acquisitions to her war and industrial bases that made the impact, it was the *manner*, the very ease, with which it was done, triumphing over the three white nations in an era when, for orientals to even dream of overcoming Western power, seemed inconceivable. It was a great awakening in the east; similarly, it was to herald the doom of empire, and of European domination of the east. Although the so-called Great East Asia Co-Prosperity Sphere turned out to be not much more than a cynical slogan, a rallying cry for the 'oppressed' nations to unite against their foreign rulers, but actually used to replace Western rule with an even harsher Japanese rule, the long-term effects turned out to be exactly as the lofty aims and ideals it professed to epitomise had predicted.

The first phase had, for the *Nihon Kaigun* (IJN), been finished with a final flourish, a series of incursions or raids by the spearhead of their victories, the now famous and much-feared 1st *Kidō Butai* (Mobile Force), centred upon five of the six big aircraft carriers that were the core of that unit[2], and under the command of Vice-Admiral Chūichi Nagumo[3]. They had hit the only port in northern Australia

---

1. Displacement on her trials which exceeded design displacement of 62,315 tons but which increased to 69,990 tons at full war-loading.
2. One carrier, *Kaga,* had been damaged by grounding at Palau on 9 February, and, after the Darwin attack, was sent home to repair at Sasebo at the end of March.
3. Vice-Admiral Chūichi Nagumo (1887–1944). b. 25 March 1887. Graduated from Naval Academy 36th Class (eighth out of 191) in 1908. Midshipman aboard former Russian cruiser *Soya.* 1909 sea service aboard armoured cruiser *Nisshin* and protected cruiser *Niitaka.* 1910 Sub-Lieutenant served aboard armoured cruiser *Asama.* 1911 Basic courses in Gunnery and Torpedoes, promoted to lieutenant (jg),

served aboard battleship *Aki.* 1913 served on destroyer *Hatsuyuki* then attended Naval College B Course. 1914 torpedo College Advanced Course and then as full lieutenant, he specialized in torpedo warfare. In 1914–15 served aboard battle-cruiser *Kirishima,* then destroyer *Sugi* before staff appointment with 4th Squadron. In 1917 staff, 3rd Special Task Fleet, before being appointed in command of the destroyer *Kisaragi.* 1918 Navy College A Course. 1920 Lieutenant-Commander 1924–6, captain of destroyer *Momi.* Taught at Naval College between extensive periods of sea duty. 1927–9 sent abroad and travelled extensively in Europe and the USA. 1926 commanded the Chinese river gunboat *Saga* and then another, the *Uji.* 1927–9 Naval War

capable of supplying the Allied forces trying to stem the flood of Japanese troops southward, Darwin, leaving its harbour full of wrecked shipping and its airports littered with smashed Allied aircraft. They had then sortied west, into the Indian Ocean, where the demoralized British were desperately trying to scrape together a second fleet to offer some bulwark to shore up their Indian Empire. In a series of carrier-launched strikes the British base ports of Colombo and Trincomalee were hit, and their scattered naval forces taught an object lesson in the correct use of naval air power. The Royal Navy lost an aircraft carrier, two heavy cruisers and two destroyers, plus many lesser vessels and a large number of aircraft, and was forced to withdraw

their surviving forces from the area. Meanwhile another Japanese naval force, with a carrier and cruiser squadron, ran riot unhindered in the Bay of Bengal, sinking shipping and bombing Calcutta. As well as the further loss of face inflicted upon the Royal Navy, the panic caused to the local populations by the quite modest air attacks on the three ports was an ominous portent of how brittle and fragile was the morale of the Indian sub-continent.

As the officers from the assembled fleet climbed the gangway up to the *Yamato*'s mighty quarterdeck that April day and saluted the flag of their C-in-C, Admiral Isoroku Yamamoto[4], who can blame them if they felt pride at what they accomplished. The term *shōribyō* ('victory fever') has

College. 1929 Captain, commanded the light cruiser *Naka*, 1930 then the 11th Destroyer Flotilla. 1931-3 various staff appointments. 1933 appointed in command new heavy cruiser *Takao*. 1934 appointed in command battleship *Yamashiro*. 1935 promoted to Rear-Admiral, commanding 1st Battle Squadron 1937, head of Torpedo School. 1939 promoted to Vice-Admiral. 1940 Director of Naval College, up to that point very much a traditional officer of the 'old school', not enamoured of Yamamoto himself, or the latters style of leadership and nor indeed of radical policies, nonetheless he was appointed in command of the *Kidō Butai* in April 1941, perhaps as some sort of check or balance, and led it through its period of greatest victories and to its ultimate destruction at Midway. Despite many and increasing calls for his removal, he served through two subsequent carrier battles in 1942, at Eastern Solomons in August and Santa Cruz in October. Finally edged out and, after brief periods commanding at Sasebo and Kure Naval Dockyards, became C-in-C 1st Fleet on 20 October 1943. 1944 on 4 March was appointed C-in-C 14th Air Fleet and placed in command of naval forces in the Marianas. When Saipan fell on 6 July 1944, he committed ritual *hari kiri* at the age of 57 to atone for its loss. Was posthumously promoted to full admiral and awarded 1st Medal on 8 July 1944.

4. Admiral Isoroku Yamamoto (1884-1943). Nicknamed 'The Razor'. b. 4 April 1894, and named Takano in Nagaoka, Niigata, changed and named Yamamoto via adoption in 1916. 1904 graduated from Naval Academy, 32 class, eleventh of 192, on 14 November as midshipman aboard submarine tender *Karasaki-maru*. 1905 served aboard armoured cruiser *Nisshin* in Russo-Japanese war, in which he was wounded. 1905 Sub-Lieutenant at Yokosuka. 1906 served successively aboard protected cruiser *Suma*, battleship *Kashima* and the old coastal defence battleship *Mishima*. 1907-08 served aboard destroyer *Kagero*, then attended basic gunnery and torpedo courses, followed by service aboard destroyer *Harusame* and cruiser *Aso*. 1909 aboard cruiser *Soya*, promoted to lieutenant. 1910 Navy College B Course. 1911 Advanced Course Gunnery School and then Instructor. 1912 on staff of Reserve Fleet. 1913 Chief Gunnery Officer protected cruiser *Niitaka*. 1914 Yokosuka and then Naval College A Course. 1915 Lieutenant-Commander. 1916-17 various Staff appoint-

ments. 1919-21 Commander and resident in USA with a period at Harvard University. 1921 XO of light cruiser *Kitakami*, then Instructor at Naval War College. 1923-24 Captain; visited Europe and USA. 1924 XO and Chief Instructor then in command Kasumigaura Naval Aviation College became a pro-air devotee, encouraging the navy's adoption of long-range bombers and torpedo-bombers. 1925-27 Naval Attaché in Washington DC which gave him a unique insight into the industrial potential of the USA. 1928 in command of light cruiser *Isuzu* and then captain of aircraft carrier *Akagi*. 1929-30 attended London Naval Conference promoted to Rear-Admiral. 1933 commanded 1st Striking Force. 1934-5, as Vice-Admiral, at London Naval Conference. Opposed the war with China and the joining of the Axis, as well as construction of new battleships, and finally of entering a war with America, all of which earned the enmity of many nationalists and 'big navy' colleagues. 1936-8 Desk jobs to keep him safe as threatened with assassination, but appointed to command Combined Fleet on 30 August 1939. Was equally ruthless himself in gaining his own way by frequent threats of resignation, to which the Naval General Staff and Admiral Osami Nagano, gave way. 1940 Admiral. Pearl Harbor and early expansion. Made careful preparations to draw out the remaining American fleet at Midway but failures of his warning systems, lack of early-warning technology, coupled with brilliant cryptology and on-the-spot decisions by his opponents, brought crushing defeat. Lost considerable face, but remained in command and oversaw the Solomons campaign which turned into a war of attrition which, although producing some stunning naval victories, ultimately sapped both the air and surface strength of the IJN. On an inspection flight again fell foul of US code-breaking and, ignoring warnings of possible interception, his aircraft was ambushed and shot down on 18 April 1943 north of Buin. Posthumously promoted to Fleet Admiral at age of 59 on 18 April 1943 and awarded 1st Medal. There have been several indifferent biographies down the years, but the definitive one to date is Hiroyuki Agawa and John Bester (translator) *The Reluctant Admiral*, Kodansha, 1979. See also Carroll V Glines, *Attack on Yamamoto*, Crown, New York, 1990, which gives a detailed account of the ambush and subsequent controversy known as the 'Navy kō incident'.

been the retrospective but widespread accusation, a rebuke and a lofty admonishment thrown at these men by friend and foe alike, but what nation on earth would not have been so affected after such an unprecedented five months? If that was indeed the mood of the day, the worldly-wise Admiral Yamamoto, who had all along warned of what they were up against, moved quickly to disabuse them of any illusions that the job was done. Far from it, he told his assembled officers, and he proceeded to spell out in detail what they must now expect.

The Second Phase Operations will be entirely different from the First Phase Operations. From now on the enemy will be an alert and prepared enemy. The Combined Fleet cannot assume a long, drawn out defensive; on the contrary, we – the Navy – absolutely must take the offensive; we must strike the enemy with effective blows, hitting him where it hurts! The enemy's power is from 5 to 10 times ours; against this we must increase the intensity of our attacks, hitting the enemy's vital places, one after the other! For this purpose our naval armaments require many skilled workmen; the previous trend must be changed; it is essential that our armaments must obtain the highest priority so that our equipment and material be sufficient to avoid defeat. For these reasons, it is absolutely necessary that our naval air

power overpower the enemy. Naval power is the protector of our Great Co-prosperity Sphere.[5]

In one sense, Yamamoto had already won his own personal victory before that conference in forcing his plan through against formidable opposition in the first place. If we go back to the beginning of the year, another conference had taken place, which had revealed a wide diversity of views in the Japanese High Command of how best to proceed. The Naval General Staff was hopelessly divided on the policy most suitable to exploit what they had gained so cheaply. There was talk about invading Hawaii or even occupying Australia and even New Zealand, while one faction advocated a push westward to seize Ceylon and eventually join forces with the Germans in the Near East.

According to Rear-Admiral Matome Ugaki[6], on 5 January 1942, a similar assembly aboard the fleet flagship had been called to give commanding officers guidance for the Phase Two Operation, but it turned out to be 'surprisingly' a study of an attack through the Indian Ocean.[7] This concept of a move westward had the allure of bringing about the final collapse of the British Empire by aiding Indian independence[8] and even held out the possibility, however remote, of the Axis powers linking hands in the Middle East. This idea was presented to the conference by Commander Yasuji Watanabe[9], the Staff Logistics Officer, and between 20 and 22 February was table-top manoeuvred

5. Japan Defense Agency Historical Division, Tokyo, *Senshi Sōsho* (War History Publications Series), Volume 43, *The Midway Operations, May–June 1942*, Tokyo, 1971, pp 87.

6. Matome Ugaki and Masataka Chihaya (translator), Donald M. Goldstein and Katherine V. Dillon (editors) *Fading Victory: The Diary of Admiral Matome Ugaki, 1941–45*. University of Pittsburgh Press, 1991. Admiral Matome Ugaki, (1890–1945) was Yamamoto's Chief of Staff and survived the air ambush. He commanded the 5th Air Fleet at Kanoya and organised *kikusui* suicide attacks. On learning of the intended Japanese surrender he took off on a final suicide mission in the rear seat of a Suisei dive-bomber.

7. The subsequent sortie by the *Kidō Butai* into that same area during April, the 'C' Operation, had no real connection with this plan, but was mounted to keep the Royal Navy subdued and protect the army's existing flanks. This fact is confirmed in the official Japanese Staff History, *Bōeichō Bōeikenshūjō Senshihu*. 'The Navy Staff Section Imperial Headquarters and the Staff of the Combined Fleet – anticipating that the British Eastern Fleet would move into the area during the Japanese occupation of the Andaman Islands and the invasion of Burma [in particular the advance on Rangoon and on to Mandalay] – decided to have the *Kidō Butai*, which had been incorporated in the Southern Forces, carry out a surprise attack against Colombo.' Admiral Yamamoto himself elaborated this pre-emptive strike to shield the

army's flank into a mission of annihilation, ordering his subordinate commander, Vice-Admiral Nobutake Kondō, to – 'destroy the enemy fleet in the Ceylon area by surprise attack'. The addition of the Malayan Force, under Vice-Admiral Jisaburō Ozawa, to make a commerce-raiding sortie into the Bay of Bengal, was an equally opportunistic extension of the same basic concept, preferably to destroy, but at the very least to neutralize any possible threat from Somerville's fleet, and this was done.

8. See Joyce Lebra (Editor), *Japan's Great East Asia Co-Prosperity Sphere,* Oxford University Press, 1953, and W. Etisbree, *Japan's Role in Southeast Asian National Movements 1940–1945*, Cambridge University Press, 1953.

9. Captain Yasuji Watanabe (1903–70). b. 26 June 1903 in Hyogo Prefecture. Graduated with 51st Class, Etajima. A gunnery specialist, who served as an Instructor at the Gunnery College, Yokosuka 1937–8 and then as Gunnery Officer on the staff of Cruiser Squadron 7, 1938–9 and of Second Fleet 1939–40 before becoming Staff Gunnery Officer, Combined Fleet under Admiral Yamamoto, 1940–3. Later he became Landing Force Officer, Combined Fleet. Between 1943 and 1945 he was a Member of Council, Military Affairs, Navy Department, Tokyo, and ended the war on the Staff of Supreme Headquarters, Tokyo. A fluent English speaker, he was in demand after the war as story consultant on such Hollywood versions of history as *Tora*,

aboard *Yamato* with the assistance of Captain Kameto Kuroshima[10] of Operations, in front of representatives from the Army General Staff.[11] There was no immediate opposition raised at this time, but the army had no taste whatsoever for the idea and soon submitted their reasons in writing. Prime Minister Hibeka Tojo[12] killed off any such notions as totally impracticable on the grounds that the 'costs were prohibitive for the advantage gained.'[13] A fanatical anti-communist, Tojo always favoured the North Strike Group against the Soviet Union.

The western operation was officially dropped on 7 March. The navy's other ambitious plan, an invasion and occupation of Hawaii,[14] was similarly rejected out of hand (it would require a minimum of four divisions and there were not sufficient transports to carry such a force to the islands, nor could they be held and supplied without a prohibitive drain on resources). In fairness, an alternative army plan to finish off the Chinese Nationalists by an advance on and capture of their capital, Chungking, was also rejected on logistical grounds.

Another section of the Naval General Staff accepted that while invading and holding all, or even just the northern part, of the huge Asian land mass, was beyond their means, a modified plan was presented, Operation FS (Fiji–Samoa), to isolate Australia from American help by taking Port Moresby in the Australian mandated territory of Papua and New Guinea, and then extend their garrisons and airstrips down through Tulagi in the Solomon Islands, New Caledonia, Samoa, and Fiji.[15] Starved of food, arms and most contacts, it was believed Australia would throw in the towel. The first part of this plan, Operation MO (Moresby), was given qualified approval on 15 March by Imperial General HQ, and Vice-Admiral Inouye Shigeyoshi[16], commanding Japanese forces at newly occupied Rabaul was commander-designate.

Yamamoto still wanted to fight the 'decisive battle' while

Tora, Tora (1970) and he also contributed the chapter 'Teitoku Yamamoto Isoroku no saigo – angō was kaidoku sareteita? (End of Admiral Yamamoto Isoroku – ciphers decoded?) to *Shōgen Watashi no Shōwashi dai 4 kan (Evidence – My History of Showa, Vol. 4)*, Tokyo, Gakugei Shorin, 1969. He passed away on 27 March 1970.

10. Rear-Admiral Kameto Kuroshima (1893–1965). Graduated Etajima 44th Class. Captain 1941, promoted to Rear-Admiral November 1944. Known as 'the God of Operations'. He apparently modelled himself on the warrior-priest Musashi, being the supreme acetic (and was nicknamed 'Ghandi'). When planning he drank sake, burnt incense and chain-smoked. A stern bachelor, he was a master swordsman and duellist, and was also reputed to have never washed (cf Hugh Bichento, *Midway*, Cassell, London, 2001). He viewed warfare as a cunning matching of wits for a noble and idealistic end, where battles, campaigns, and manoeuvring all led to an almost spiritualistic culmination of victory. He exerted enormous influence over his contemporaries. See R. Gowan, *Kameto Kuroshima: The Man Behind Yamamoto,* ECU Press, 1973, pp 110.

11. Allegations that Commander Prince Takamatsu Nobuhito, being on the Naval General Staff at this time, was also present as a 'representative of the Court', do not appear to be substantiated. However, on the day of the meeting, 25 May, he was scheduled to fly from Haneda airport, Tokyo, to Dairen (Dalny) in Manchukuo to fulfil a long-standing visit according to his diary. The trip had to be cancelled due to bad weather at Dalny, but he flew there from Haneda via Kisarazu Naval Air Base, Chiba Prefecture. It therefore seems clear that he was never scheduled to attend the war game analysis on 25 May.

12. General Hideki Tojo (1884–1948). b. Tokyo, son of an army officer. Graduated from the Military Academy in 1905. Graduated from the Army College in 1915. Teacher at War College and Infantry Officer. Politicized and joined the ultra-national *Tōsei-Ha* (Control Group) of the Double Leaf Society in 1920. Became Chief of Staff in the Kwantung Army in Manchukuo 1937. Joined the *Kodoha*. Vice-Minister of War in 1938 and Inspector-General Army Aviation to 1940, but secretly in charge of Japanese Secret Service. Appointed Prime Minister 1941 on removal of Premier Konoe and overall military commander. Resigned in July 1944 on the fall of Saipan and retired. Attempted suicide in 1945, but survived. Tried and sentenced to death for war crimes, he was hanged on Christmas Eve. His tomb is at Hazu, Aichi.

13. This kernel of a plan is discussed in more depth in succeeding pages.

14. See also Dr. J J Stephan, *Hawaii under the Rising Sun*, University of Hawaii Press, 1984, for a fuller discussion of the practicality of this option. Professor Stephan is fluent in Japanese and lived there for many years, was a Harvard MA in East Asian studies, has a PhD in Japanese history from the University of London School of Oriental and African Studies, and is a lecturer at Waseda University and the National Defense College in Tokyo as well as being Professor of Japanese History at the University of Hawaii, so commands respect. A brief reference to Combined Fleet Secret Order Number One, Section 14, dated 1 November 1941, mentions that Hawaii was scheduled for occupation in October 1942, but that same document gave the seizure of Midway as 'early 1942' so too much should not be read into what was just a 'best-case' scenario. Stephan's main keystone is Captain Shigenori Kami's exploratory proposal for the First Section of the First Bureau of the (IJN, a group that Chihaya Masataka called, 'the brain of the Imperial Navy', in January 1942. This study was sober and realistic and concluded that, although the taking of Hawaii was feasible, holding and supply it was highly improbable, given Japanese maritime resources and their already existing over-stretch.

15. Henry F. Schorreck, *Battle of Midway: 4–7 June 1942: The Role of COMINT in the Battle of Midway*, Naval Historical Center (SRH-230).

16. Admiral Inouye Shigeyoshi (1889–1975). b. Miyagi

he had a reasonable chance of winning it, however, and although he went along with the Port Moresby operation to the extent of detaching two of his fleet carriers, *Shōkaku* and *Zuikaku* of Carrier Division (CarDiv) 5, to provide air support and protection from Allied interference, it was with the proviso that they rejoin his flag in time for that long-sort-after showdown, Operation MI (Midway). No doubt he was to rue this decision for, in the ensuing Battle of the Coral Sea, the former vessel was hit by three bombs and badly damaged, while the latter had her carrier air group decimated in the fighting; thus neither carrier was available for Midway, where their presence would have been invaluable if not decisive. Two further carriers, albeit not front-line vessels, which might have provided useful replacements, *Junyō* and *Ryūjō* were hived off for a subsidiary operation, AL (Aleutians), the Aleutians, with an attack on Dutch Harbour and the occupation of Adak and Kiska. Although this operation was conceived as an entirely separate mission to AF, Yamamoto's operation, and not a feint or lure[17], nonetheless a potential eight available carriers with which to fight the decisive battle, had now been reduced to just four. More, the Aleutian mission further complicated an already complex plan, aptly described by Gordon Prange as 'a monster with two heads'[18], when what was required was a total and dedicated concentration on the main objective, the defeat of the American fleet.

Operation MI

MI as Yamamoto and Ugaki conceived it, would involve the reduction and the occupation of Midway (comprising Eastern and Sand Islets), which, while having little intrinsic value themselves other than an airstrip, were so positioned as both to extend Japanese outer-warning barrier many hundreds of miles eastward and offer a potential jumping off place should the long-term eastern operation against Hawaii ever prove a practical proposition. Regardless of the latter, it was assumed by the two originators, (and some critics felt that it was wishful thinking[19],) that the American's would not just sit back and let it happen; they would probably come out and dispute with all the force remaining to them, which is what Yamamoto badly wanted. Of course some starry-eyed Japanese had even dizzier visions and loftier ambitions, and dreamt of somehow invading (and holding) Hawaii as well!

However, not every senior Japanese officer saw merit in Yamamoto's reasoning. Some, like Commander Tatsukichi Miyo[20], who in April 1942 was serving in the First Section

---

Prefecture on 9 December 1889. 1909 graduated Etajima, 37th Class, 2nd out of 179. Joined *Soya* as midshipman. 1910 Served aboard battleship *Mikasa* and then armoured cruiser *Kasuga*, promoted to sub-lieutenant.1911, joined battle-cruiser *Kurama*. 1912 Gunnery and Torpedo Schools basic courses. 1913, lieutenant (jg) aboard protected cruiser *Takachiho* and then stood by the new battle-cruiser *Hiei*. 1915 lieutenant aboard battleship *Fuso*. 1916–17 Naval College B and Major courses. 1917 Chief Navigator aboard small cruiser *Yodo*. 1918–20, detached duties Switzerland and then France. 1921 lieutenant-commander. 1922 Chief Navigator aboard light cruiser *Kuma*. 1924 graduated Naval Staff College (22nd). 1925 commander. 1927–9 Naval Attaché Rome. 1929 captain.1930–31 Instructor Naval College 1932–33 various staff appointments. 1933–35 commanding officer battle-cruiser *Hiei*. 1935–36 rear-admiral at Yokosuka. 1937–39, served ashore as a rear-admiral in the Naval Affairs Bureau. 1939 vice-admiral, C-of-S China Area Fleet. 1940, Chief Naval Affairs Department, Naval Air Command, where he remained until September 1941. Being outspoken against surface fleet expansions, he was transferred. On outbreak of the war he commanded the Fourth Fleet, Truk. 1941 Guam and Wake operations. 1942 at Rabaul, from which in 1942 he conducted Operation MO and the Battle of the Coral Sea, followed by the Solomons campaign. In October 1942, due to the way things were going in the Solomons, he was recalled and given a back-room job as Director, Naval Academy.1943 recalled to Tokyo to head the vital Naval Shipbuilding Command and ordered to speed the completion of more

aircraft carriers. In November 1944 became XO at the Navy Ministry. Superintendent Naval Academy. His final wartime posting was a brief return to Naval Air Command at the beginning of May 1945. He later was appointed Vice-Minister of the Navy and chief of the Navy Technical Department as full admiral. After the war he became an English music teacher at a school established at his home at Yokosuka City. He died, aged 86, on 15 December 1975 and his memorial is at Fuchu, Tokyo.

17. As the whole point of AF was to entice the American fleet into battle and then destroy it, then luring it northward with AL, *away* from Yamamoto's main forces, would have been pointless for, if successful, it would have defeated the desired objective of the plan. As originally conceived both attacks were to have taken place simultaneously. However, Frederick Parker maintained otherwise and wrote: 'The centrepiece of their Midway plan was an armed feint toward Alaska followed by the assault on Midway.'

18. Gordon Prange, *Miracle at Midway*. Penguin Books, London, 1982.

19. Rear-Admiral Osamai Nagano and the Naval General Staff remained luke warm, but, as always, gave way in the end; the Army were opposed on practical grounds, but chiefly because they simply did not wish to become sucked into an open-ended commitment of precious troop resources out in the Pacific wastes.

20. Tatsukichi Miyo was the post-war author of *'Taidan Kōbō Raburu kōkūtai (Offensive and defensive battle by the Rabaul Flying Corps)*, an article in *Maru* magazine, Vol 9, No. 8, Ushio Shobo, Tokyo, 1956, pp 80–94.

(Operations Section) of the Planning Division at Naval GHQ in Tokyo, made detailed criticisms, pointing out what he felt to be a risky reliance on fairly skimpy search-plane coverage to prevent the hunters unwittingly becoming the hunted, which is what actually happened. Others, like Baron Sadatoshi Tomioka[21], also in the First Section of Plans Division, and a senior captain in the navy, thought that Midway was itself of such insignificance that the Americans would not bother risking their remaining fleet to defend it, thus erasing the basic premise of the whole plan. But their concerns were brushed aside. If the Americans came, then let them, that is exactly what was wished!

Whatever naval force the Americans chose to send to contest the issue, long-range reconnaissance by seaplanes and submarines would be in place to warn of their reaction, and they would be engaged and badly damaged by the 1st *Kidō Butai* and then finished off at leisure by the pulverizing firepower of the whole battleship force, all eleven of which were to participate[22]. Yamamoto might well be a radical airman in most respects, but it was to be the 18.1-and 16-inch barrels of traditional heavy naval guns that were expected to put the final seal on his masterpiece! If the scenario came off as confidently expected, the Americans would, it was hoped, be even further demoralized, and might even sue for a peace that would leave Japan holding most of her spoils. The fierce opposition of both the General Naval Staff and the army (who were to supply the invasion troops) was finally overcome courtesy of a combination of another resignation threat and the shock of two pieces of American aggressive action: Vice-Admiral Wilson Brown's[23] carrier strike against Lae and Salamaua on 10 March and Lieutenant-General James Doolittle's[24] raid on the homeland on 18 April.

Captain Yoshitake Miwa[25], who was the Commander-in-

21. Rear-Admiral Baron Sadatoshi Tomioka (1897–1970). b. 8 March 1897. 1917 Graduated Etajima Naval Academy (45th Class), 21 out of 89 as midshipman. 1917 Training cruise aboard armoured cruiser *Iwate*. 1918 to cruiser *Aso* and Sub-Lieutenant. 1919 to the battleship *Asahi*, then torpedo basic course. 1920 Gunnery School basic course, lieutenant (jg), to battleship *Suwo*. 1921 to destroyer *Hagi*. 1922, Naval College Navigation Course.1923 lieutenant, appointed Chief Navigator destroyer *Hokaze*. 1924 Chief Navigator destroyer *Tachikaze* and then *Shirva*. 1926, staff, 2nd Fleet. 1927, appointed in command destroyer *Matsu*, then to destroyer *Sugi*. 1927 Naval College A course, to lieutenant-commander. 1929 resident in France and Assistant Naval Attaché, staff Naval General Staff. 1931, attendant to plenipotentiary at Geneva disarmament conference. 1932, appointed Chief Navigator new heavy cruiser *Kinugasa*. 1933, to Yokosuka, Naval General Staff. 1934 commander. 1935 on staff 7th Squadron. 1936 staff duties. 1938 captain. Naval General Staff and 2nd Fleet. 1939 Instructor, Naval College. 1940 Naval General Staff, various staff duties, including Rabaul. 1943, in command light cruiser *Oyodo*, then assistant staff and Vice CoS, promoted to Rear-Admiral. 1944, Naval General Staff. 1945 Department of Navy, Tokyo, then Chief, Department of Historical Research. 1946 Demobilized. 1970 died 7 December.

22. Even so their firepower was spread over all the various units, rather than being decisively concentrated in a single battle-line. *Haruna* and *Kirishima* Battleship Division (BatDiv) 3/2 with Nagumo's Support Group; *Yamato, Nagato* and *Mutsu* (BatDiv 1) with Yamamoto's main body; *Hyūga, Ise, Fusō* and *Yamashiro* (BatDiv 2) with Vice-Admiral Shirō Takasu's guard force; *Kongō* and *Hiei* (BatDiv 3/1) with Vice-Admiral Nobutake Kondō's Midway Invasion Force.

23. Vice-Admiral Wilson Brown, Jr (1885–1955). Captain of the battleship *California*. Graduated Annapolis 1902, youngest of his class. Naval aide to Presidents Woodrow Wilson and Calvin Coolidge 1926–9, and commander of the Presidential yacht *Mayflower*; and again to Franklin Roosevelt 1934–6.

Commander, Training Detachment, flagship battleship *Wyoming* (BB-32) April-June 1937. Superintendent of US Naval Academy, June 1938–February 1941. Commander CruDiv 4 aboard heavy cruiser *Indianapolis* (CA-35) at Pearl Harbor; Commander Force Baker and Commander Scouting Force to April 1942. Naval aide to Presidents Roosevelt and Truman 1943–5. Contributed article, 'Aide *to 4 President*'s, in *American Heritage*, February 1951, Vol 6. Issue 2.

24. Lieutenant-Colonel (later General) James Harold Doolittle, US Army Air Corps (1896–1993). b. Alamdea, California. Enlisted as flying cadet in Army Signal Corps Aviation Section in 1917, and served as a flying instructor once commissioned as a lieutenant in March 1918. Continued army career, obtaining BA degree and masters and doctors degrees in science from MIT in 1924. Winner of the Schneider Cup seaplane race in 1925. Resigned in 1930 but retained as a major in the Specialist Reserve Corps, joined Shell Oil's Aviation Department as manager. 1932 set the world record for high-speed land planes and several prestigious prizes. After leave of absence returned to active duties in July 1940 and went to England in 1941 to study aerial warfare. Promoted to Lieutenant-Colonel January 1942 and personally planned and led the dramatic air attack on Japan by flying sixteen twin-engined B-25 bombers from the deck of the carrier *Hornet*, surviving bailing out over China, for which he received the Medal of Honor. As Major-General took part in the North African and Mediteranean campaigns between 1943 and 1944, and commanded 8th Air Force in Europe and Pacific between 1944 and the end of the war. Returned to Shell after the war, but continued as special assistant to the Air Force CoS (CoS), acted as advise in ballistic missile and space programmes. Retired in 1959. Advanced to General in 1989. Buried at Arlington.

25. Rear-Admiral Yoshitake Miwa (1899–1944). b. Gifu, 26 April 1899. 1917 joined Naval Academy. 1920 graduated from Etajima, 48th Class, (31 out of 171) as midshipman. Training cruise aboard armoured cruiser *Iwate*. 1921 assigned to battle-cruiser *Kongo*.1921, June, sub-lieutenant.

Chief's (C-in-C's) Fleet Air Officer, confided in his diary that, to ensure that no further American intrusions over the homeland took place, 'there would be no other way but to make a landing on Hawaii'. He added: 'This makes landing on Midway a prerequisite. This is the very reason why the Combined Fleet urges a Midway operation.'

The labyrinthine meshing of all the various forces Yamamoto deployed was to all come together in a massive trap for the American carriers and remaining battleships that were expected to rush out from Pearl Harbor once they were aware of Midway's fate. (See Diagram 1). It called for a complex timetable to be adhered to by widely dispersed forces, which was difficult to achieve. What it also called for, unfortunately for the Japanese, was for the US Navy to follow the scenario prepared for them on the games table aboard the *Yamato*. What if, the Americans did not conform as they were required and expected to? This was briefly considered and dismissed with contempt. The gaming situation threw up an awkward scenario at one point; American aircraft carriers 'appeared' on the flanks of Nagumo's force while that force's aircraft were attacking Midway. What would happen, asked Yamamoto of Nagumo, should that occur? Nagumo, who although opposed to the whole plan, had not offered a single criticism throughout, did not reply. The answer, as usual, was given by Captain Kameto Kuroshima, Senior Staff Officer of the Combined Fleet. But it was hardly the deeply reasoned answer of a master battle tactician; instead came

the traditional response of a gung-ho medieval warrior: '*Gaishu Isshoku!*'[26] And with that they had to be content – it all seemed a foregone conclusion. Nonetheless, Yamamoto was disturbed enough to caution Nagumo, pointedly in front of the rest, to keep half his air striking force back from the strike on Midway so as to be readily available in case of the unthinkable. This instruction never appears to have been followed up or committed to paper.

The war games, so weighted and biased towards the attackers as to be almost meaningless, were thus concluded on the afternoon of 23 May and were followed by a critique, which dragged on until midnight and was resumed on the morning of the following day. The academic discussion, such as it was, was interrupted by news of the American carrier strikes against the Japanese invasion fleet off Tulagi in the Solomon Islands, and, as we have seen, acted as another spur to implementing Yamamoto's master plan. The Imperial GHQ, having adopted the plan almost in its entirety now, gave it their sanction on 5 May with the issuing of Order No. 18, which ordered Yamamoto to 'carry out the occupation of Midway Island and key points in the western Aleutians in cooperation with the army.' Combined Fleet HQ then issued Operational Order 12, which was based on the original plan. However, the various modifications and revisions that had arisen during the map manoeuvres and war games, and the discussion that had followed it, were not finally sent to the participating units until 8 May, when

---

1921–2, Torpedo and Gunnery Schools base courses, sea service aboard *Kisaragi*. 1923 to Kasumigaura for flight training. 1923, lieutenant (jg) at Kasumigaura Air Course and retained as an instructor until 1925. 1925 lieutenant, to carrier *Hosho*. 1926–8, Assistant Air Attaché, USA. 1929 resumed flying instruction duties at Yokosuka and Kasumigaura. 1931 Naval College, A course, graduated 31st with honour. 1932 Lieutenant-Commander. 1933 to carrier *Akagi*, 1934–35 Staff duties 1936, Instructor flying at Yokosuka, Instructor at Gunnery, Torpedo and Navigation Schools. 1937 Staff of Naval Gunnery School. 1937, commander, appointed Chief Air, Kisarazu, then aboard carrier *Kaga*. 1938 Staff 5th Fleet, then Chief Air, Yokosuka. 1930 Naval General Staff. 1941, XO and Chief Instructor Kasumigaura. 1941, captain, to staff of Yamamoto as Chief Air Officer. 1942, staff 11th Air Fleet. 1943, Yokosuka then CoS 1st Air Fleet. 1944, killed in action on 2nd August 1944, posthumously promoted to Rear-Admiral.

26. Captain Tasuku Nakazawa, CoS of Fifth Fleet, attended the war games on 23 May. He left a written record about what took place and related that, after Admiral Yamamoto's greeting, Rear-Admiral Matome Ugaki, CoS of Combined Fleet and Captain Kameto Kuroshima, Senior Staff Officer of the Combined Fleet explained. 'We will destroy the enemy fleet at a stroke, by *gaishu isshoku* ("one touch of the

armoured gauntlet") *if* they turn up'. Misquoted in Hisashi Oide, *Hanagata Sanbo Genda Minoru* (*Star Staff Officer Minoru Genda*), and certainly *not* (as asserted by Gordon Prange in his book *Miracle at Midway*, and others since), by Genda himself. Vice-Admiral Tasuku Nakazawa (1894–1977). b. 28 June 1894. Graduated Etajima 43rd Class, Naval College 26th Class. Midshipman aboard armoured cruiser *Adzuma* 1915 and then the old protected cruiser *Chikuma*, 1916. Sub-lieutenant on battleship *Ise* 1918, then as lieutenant (jg) attended Torpedo and Gunnery schools 1918–19, joining armoured cruiser *Tokiwa* 1919 then the destroyers *Kashi* and *Sugi* 1920. Promoted to lieutenant 1921 aboard the destroyer *Hishi* 1922, then the armoured cruiser *Asama* 1923 and destroyer *Asanagi* 1924. Naval College A course in 1925 promoted to lieutenant-commander 1927, commanding officer destroyer *Asagao*, on staffs of 2nd and 1st Fleets 1928–30. Naval Gunnery School 1931, resided in USA 1932–34. As commander returned to Naval General Staff in 1934, promoted to captain 1936, staff work until 1940 when appointed in command heavy cruiser *Ashigara*. Naval Gunnery School 1941 then Chief-of-Staff 5th Fleet. Rear-Admiral November 1942, at Naval Gunnery School to 1943. Assistant Staff Officer 2nd Air Fleet in December 1944, and finished war as CoS 1st Air Fleet as Vice-Admiral. Died 22nd December 1977 aged 83.

Secret Radio Broadcast 29 was transmitted. It read as follows[27]:

> Revise organization of forces and make additions to Second Phase Second Period Operation as follows (documents will be forwarded): A: Invasion Force: (1) Remove *Shoho*[28], add *Mikasuki*[29]; (2) Invasion of Kure Island will be on 'N' minus one day. B. Striking Force: (1) Remove *Shokaku*, add one destroyer from DesRon [Destroyer Squadron] 10; (2) Air attack on Midway will commence on N-3 days. C: Naval Shore-based Air: Conduct air reconnaissance of Pearl Harbor in late May (or by 3 June) to ascertain enemy forces there, using Type-2 flying boats. D: Northern Force: (1) Add SubRon 1 [Submarine Squadron], *Shokaku*[30] and one destroyer of DesRon10; (2) Air attack on Dutch Harbor will commence on N-3 days; (3) One part of SubRon 1, after making a reconnaissance of the Aleutian Islands area, will conduct observation patrols off Seattle by N-5 days. The other part will cruise ahead of CarDiv 4 as van screen. E: Submarine Forces; (1) Delete SubRon 1; (2) One submarine will reconnoitre Midway and Kure Islands and from N-5 days onward make weather reports to the east of Midway[31]; (3) Two submarines of SubDiv 13 will be stationed at French Frigate Shoals, and one from that same unit will be stationed at Laysan Island, with the duties of refuelling flying boats and float planes at these anchorages.

With this, the die was cast!

In addition to the eleven battleships and the four big carriers of the 1st Mobile Force (*Kidō Butai*), a large percentage of the IJN's total strength was to be utilized, with a further four smaller carriers, thirteen heavy and nine light cruisers, sixty-seven destroyers and sixteen submarines, plus lesser warships like seaplane tenders, auxiliary cruisers, minelayers, minesweepers, patrol boats, as well as replenishment ships, tankers and cargo ships and troop transports, all sailing to participate. In contrast, the Americans were not to commit every ship they had available for the defence; notably the battleships that had survived Pearl Harbor and formed Task Force 1 at San Francisco, were kept in the background, despite strong attempts by their commander to get them into the fight.

On the other hand all previous analyses of the battle, while including the Japanese forces assigned to the Aleutians part of the operation, always omit the American forces assigned to their defence in the grand total (presumably because it thus makes the odds look all that much more heavily weighted in Japan's favour). If the Japanese Aleutian Force is added to the balance in assessing Midway, then so should the defending American squadron, Task Force 8. The breakdown of the various forces is as Table 1.

Impressive as this mass of shipping was, the outcome of the battle was to be decided by a fraction of that force, with the majority of warships never firing a shot or sighting the enemy. The Aleutians part of the combined mission was in fact carried out pretty much to plan and was a success, in a limited way. But it diverted forces, especially the carriers, which would have been priceless at Midway, and also ensured that some powerful battleships and heavy cruisers were so distant from the fight as to be powerless to intervene once the main battle was joined. So we can ignore the Aleutians force as irrelevant to our story on both sides.

The large submarine force was to have played an essential, indeed a vital part in the battle. These ships were to have given ample warning of the sailing of the American fleet into the prepared trap, and also to have whittled down its strength prior to actual combat. In fact, they did neither, and the failure of the underwater arm to carry out what was expected of them, was the third, after the loss of one-third of the 1st *Kidō Butai* a nd the wide dispersal of forces on non-essential tasks, in a series of disappointing lapses by the Japanese.

The Japanese Plan Begins to Break Down

The importance of the dual reconnaissance and 'trip-wire' missions for the flying boats and submarines of the 6th Fleet to conduct what can be termed the Second K-Operation[32] deserves more attention than has been given to them by most historians.[33] Admiral Fletcher's[34] air strike in

---

27. *Senshi Sōsho*, Vol 43, pp 96.
28. *Sōshō*, light carrier sunk at Battle of Coral Sea.
29. *Mikasuki*, destroyer.
30. *Shokaku*, heavy carrier, damaged by three bomb hits at Coral Sea and not available, (but note, even if she had been she was *not* to have rejoined Nagumo's force.)
31. The submarine selected was *I-168*, and she was to have an important role in the battle's final outcome, which some what redeemed the failure of the rest of the submarine force.

32. See Rear-Admiral Tsuneo Hitsuji, *Reflections of the Great Skies*, Anzen Zeppo, Tokyo, 1998.
33. One notable exception was Rear-Admiral Layton, who submitted an article on it to the Naval Institute Proceedings in May 1953. He suggested that the Japanese scheme might have been based on a pre-war two-part fictional story, titled *Rendezvous*, which had been written by Captain W. J. 'Jasper' Holmes, AOIC (Assistant Officer in Charge) Japanese Intelligence Centre Pacific Ocean Area (JICPOA) under his pseudonym 'Alec Hudson'. This story was actually run in

Table 1: American and Japanese Seagoing Forces at the Midway and Aleutians Operations, June 1942

1: American

Operation or Area	Force	Commander	Type	Ships
Point Luck	Task Force 17	Rear-Admiral Frank Jack Fletcher	Carrier	Yorktown (Flag)
			Heavy cruisers	Astoria
				Portland
			Destroyers	Hammann
				Hughes
				Morris
				Anderson
				Russell
				Gwin
	Task Force 16	Rear-Admiral Raymond A. Spruance	Carriers	Enterprise (Flag)
				Hornet
			Heavy cruisers	New Orleans
				Minneapolis
				Vincennes
				Northampton
				Pensacola
			Anti-aircraft cruiser	Atlanta
			Destroyers	Phelps
				Worden
				Monaghan
				Aylwin
				Balch
				Conyngham
				Benham
				Ellet
				Maury

the Solomons had prompted the addition of the submarine reconnaissance and early-warning patrol scheme, which was asked for another long-range search by the only available means of carrying it out, a pair of Kawasaki 'Emily' flying boats. They were again to make a long-range sortie over Pearl Harbor immediately before the Midway operation, to ascertain whether the US carriers had returned north or stayed in southern waters. Radio

the *Saturday Evening Post* in August 1941, after at first being suppressed by the Office of Naval Intelligence in 1940, and later appeared in the anthology *Up Periscope* (Macmillan, New York, 1956). Captain Holmes was an ex-submariner, who, when in the late-1920s certain medical problems precluded him from serving underwater, became a Naval Intelligence Officer. From 1929 to 1947 he served with Communications Intelligence Unit, Pearl Harbor. As a lieutenant he was actually Combat Intelligence Officer from June 1941 and was working at the Central Intelligence Unit (CIU) with Rochefort on the night of the 3 March 1942 attack. Thus, if Layton's allegation was true, the whole thing had an ironic twist to it. Holmes later became Nimitz's Intelligence Officer and, after his post-war retirement, became Senior Professor Emeritus of Engineering and Mathematics and First Dean of the University of Hawaii's Engineering Department. The College of Engineering, built between 1969 and 1972, was named Holmes Hall in his honour.

Under his own name Holmes authored some early post-war classic histories, *Undersea Victory* and *Double-Edged Secrets: US Naval Intelligence Operations in the Pacific during World War II*, as well as the official history of JICPOA (SRH020). With regard to Layton's theory, Holmes himself dismissed it in a response article, also published in the *Proceedings*, in August 1953. Layton later submitted a paper on it, *The 2nd K Operation*, to Vice-Admiral Julien J. LeBourgeois, President of the Naval War College, Newport, R.I., in September 1975.

34. Admiral Frank Jack Fletcher (1885–1973). b. Marshalltown, Iowa, graduated from US Naval Academy, Annapolis, in 1906. Spent two years at sea and commissioned as ensign in 1908. He served aboard the battleships *Rhode Island* (BB-17), *Ohio* (BB-12) and *Maine* (BB-10), and, in 1909 the destroyer *Chauncey* (DD-3) in the Asiatic Fleet. His first command was the destroyer *Dale* (DD-4) in 1910, and he later took over command of the *Chauncey*. He was awarded

Operation or Area	Force	Commander	Type	Ships
	Oiler Group	Commander Russell M. Ihrig	Oilers	Cimarron
				Platte
			Destroyers	Dewey
				Monssen
French Frigate Shoals	Seaplane Tender Force	Commander Myron T. Richardson	Seaplane Tenders	Ballard
				Thornton
			Destroyer	Clark
			Oiler	Kaloli
			Tug	Vireo
	Relief Fuelling Unit	Commander Harry R. Thurber	Oiler	Guadalupe
			Destroyers	Blue
				Ralph Talbot
Aleutians Defence	Task Force 8	Rear Admiral Robert A. Theobald	Heavy cruisers	Louisville
				Indianapolis
			Light cruisers	Nashville (Flag)
				Honolulu
				St. Louis
			Destroyers	McCall
				Gridley
				Humphreys
				Gilmer
				Vase
				Reid
				Sands
				King
				Kane
				Brooks
				Dent
				Waters
				Talbot

the Medal of Honor for distinguished conduct aboard the battleship *Florida* (BB-30) at Vera Cruz, Mexico, in 1914. He was aide and Flag Lieutenant of the C-in-C, Atlantic Fleet in 1941, and in 1915 held a position in the Executive Department of the Naval Academy. When America entered the First World War in 1917, he was serving as Gunner Officer aboard the *Kearsarge* (BB-5). Further destroyer commands followed with the *Allen* (DD-66) in February 1918 and the *Benham* (DD-49) in May, during which time he earned the Navy Cross. 1918–19 he stood by the new destroyer *Crane* (DD-109) at San Francisco and then assumed command of the *Gridley* (DD-92). A shore appointment as Head of the Detail Section, Enlisted Personnel Division in Washington DC followed between 1919 and 1922. Back on the Asiatic Station he commanded the destroyer *Whipple* (DD-217), the gunboat *Sacramento* (AG-19) and the Submarine Base at Cavite, before moving on to the Washington Navy Yard between 1925 and 1927. His next sea going appointment was as XO of the battleship *Colorado* (BB-45) and then he undertook the Senior Course at the Naval War College, Newport RI. in 1930. He became CoS to the C-in-C, Atlantic Fleet in 1931 then transferred to the Office of the Chief of Naval Operations. Between 1933 and 1936 he was aide to the Secretary for the Navy, Claude A. Swanson, before taking command of the battleship *New*

Mexico (BB-40) in 1936. In 1938 he was Assistant Chief of the Bureau of Navigation. Promoted to Rear-Admiral. Between 1939 and 1942 he commanded Cruiser Division (CruDiv) 3, CruDiv 6, Cruiser Scouting Force and CruDiv 4 in succession. Was aboard the *Minneapolis* (CA-36) at the time of Pearl Harbor. In April 1942, he was appointed in command cruisers, Pacific Fleet, and in May took part in the Battle of the Coral Sea. Senior Task Force Commander aboard the carrier *Yorktown* (CV-5) he was in command at Midway in June 1942. As Vice-Admiral he commanded at the carrier battle of the Eastern Solomons in August 1942 and earned the Distinguished Service Medal. However, his perceived caution off Guadalcanal and at the Eastern Solomons told against him and he was moved from carrier operations. Appointed in command 13th Naval District and Commander Northwestern Sea Frontier at Seattle in November 1942, he commanded at the bombardment of the Kurile Islands in 1944 and again in 1945. He later commanded the whole Northern Pacific area until the end of the war in 1945. Became Chairman of the General Board and advanced to Admiral when he retired in May 1947. He died at Bethesda, Maryland, on 25 April 1973, and is buried at Arlington National Cemetery. See Stephen D. Regan, *In Bitter Tempest: The Biography of Admiral Frank Jack Fletcher*.

Operation or Area	Force	Commander	Type	Ships
	Oiler Group	Captain Houston L. Maples	Oilers	*Sabine*
				Brazos
				Comet
	Submarine Group	Commander Burton G. Lakes	Submarines	*S-18*
				S-23
				S-27
				S-28
				S-34
				S-35
Kodiak	Local Defense Force	Captain Ralph C. Parker	Gunboat	*Charleston*
			Coast guard cutters	*Aurora*
				Bonham
				Cyane
				Haida
				Onondaga
2: Japanese.				
Midway (MI)	1st Carrier Striking Force	Vice-Admiral Chūichi Nagumo	Carriers	*Akagi* (Flag)
				Kaga
				Hiryū
				Soryū
	BatDiv 3	Rear-Admiral Tamotsu Takama	Battleships	*Haruna* (Flag)
				Kirishima
	CruDiv 8	Rear-Admiral Hiroaki Abe	Heavy cruisers	*Tone* (Flag)
				Chikuma

Message 29, when it was received at the Headquarters of Vice-Admiral Teruhishi Komatsu[35], aboard his flagship, the light cruiser *Katori,* along with the submarine depot ship *Rio De Janeiro Maru*[36]*,* probably caused considerable dismay. Unlike the majority of the recipients, neither Admiral Komatsu at Kwajalein Atoll nor any of his representatives aboard the *Rio de Janeiro Maru,* had been ordered to attend the war gaming aboard the *Yamato,* nor had the 6th Fleet received a single copy of Combined Fleet Operation Order 12. Consequently, *nobody* in the 6th Fleet had any prior inkling of what was afoot! It was a classic result of Yamamoto making up policy 'on the hoof'. This oversight was doubly unfortunate in view of the importance of the missions to which the submariners and

35. Vice-Admiral the Marquis Teruhisa Komatsu (1888–1970). b. 2nd August 1882 at Kitashirakawa as Prince Teruhisa, the third son of Prince Kitashirakawa Nagahisa, a member of the Royal Household. The House of Komatsu reverted to its original title of Highashi Fushimi after the death of Prince Komatsu Akhito on 1905. Joined the IJN as a midshipman 1909. Became a marquis (vassalized) and served aboard the battleship *Satsuma* in 1910. Attended Gunnery and Torpedo Schools in 1911, before joining the battleship *Kawachi* and being promoted to lieutenant (jg) in 1912. Between 1913 and the outbreak of the Great War served aboard cruiser *Soya* and battle-cruiser *Kurama,* then attended the Naval College (20th) and Gunnery School Advanced course, joining the battlecruiser *Kongo* in 1916. Saw war service with the destroyers *Yugure* and *Urakaze* in 1917–18. After the war he served aboard the battleship *Yamashiro.* Promoted to lieutenant-commander in 1921 after a further Naval College Advanced course various staff appointments. Promotion to commander in 1925 was followed by a period of study in England using his own finances until 1927. Commanded destroyer *Hokaze* 1927, then served as XO of light cruiser *Isuzu* and battleship *Nagato* to 1929. Commanded the minelayer *Itsukushima,* submarine depot ship *Jingei,* light cruiser *Kiso* and heavy cruiser *Nachi* between 1931 and 1935. Rear-Admiral in 1936, commanded 1st Submarine School. Chief Instructor, Naval College, in 1938 and Vice-Admiral in 1940. Commanded the *Ryojun* Graving Dock, and then became C-in-C 1 Combined Fleet (CF) in 1941. Appointed C-in-C 6th Fleet 16 March 1942. In 1943 became C-in-C Sasebo Naval Dockyard. In 1944 Director of Naval Academy. Was at Naval Gunnery School in 1945 and in Reserve at end of war. He died on 5 November 1970 at age of 82.

36. *Rio de Janeiro Maru,* was a 9,627-ton converted liner used as a submarine tender. Built in 1930 by Mitsubishi Zosen Kaisha at Nagasaki, she was requisitioned by the IJN on 8 October 1940 and converted at the Sasebo navy base. She was finally sunk by carrier aircraft from the USS *Bunker Hill* and USS *Yorktown II* at Truk Lagoon on 17 February 1944, and claimed, by some post-war American divers to have been an aircraft carrier!

Operation or Area	Force	Commander	Type	Ships
	DesRon 10	Rear-Admiral Susumu Kimura	Light cruiser Destroyers	Nagara Nowaki Arashi Hagikaze Maikaze Kazagumo Yūgumo Makigumo Harakaze Isokaze Tanikaze Hamakaze
	Supply Group	Captain Masanao Ota	Tankers	Kyokutō Maru Shinkoku Maru Tōhō Maru Nippon Maru Kokuyō Maru
			Destroyer	Akigumo
	Main Body	Admiral Isoku Yamamoto, C-in-C	Battleships	Yamato (Flag) Nagato Mutsu
			Carrier	Hōshō
			Light Cruiser	Sendai
			Seaplane carriers acting as specialist transports	Chiyōda Nisshin
			Destroyers	Yūkaze Fubuki Shirayuki Murakkumo Hatsuyuki Isonami Uranami Shikinami Ayanami

flying-boat crews suddenly found themselves entrusted.

Far from being a peripheral operation, which Komatsu's young captains could adapt themselves to and catch up on (given sufficient time), they were in fact expected to act as the vanguard, the very spearhead of the operation. Consequently the 6th Fleet were expected to start later than everyone else, but would still have to be ready and in place *ahead* of everyone else if they were to be effective. Not surprisingly, despite their best efforts, this just did not happen. Moreover, the fleet was expected to be in place in areas as far apart as Midway Island, Kure Island, the Aleutian Islands and Dutch Harbour and Seattle simultaneously!

While Komatsu's team tore their hair out and burnt up the airwaves with requests for some rapid elucidation, preliminary moves were started. However, it was not until 12 May that Commander Takayasu Arima[37], who was

---

37. Captain Takayasu Arima (1905–57) b. Kagoshima City, Kyushu, 15 August 1905. Graduated Etajima 52nd Class. He specialized in submarine warfare early in his career and among his commands before the war were the *Ro-28*, *I-3*, *I-74* and *I-122*. In between his underwater duties, he also served as a Staff Officer on the China Area Fleet, the Combined Fleet, the Eighth Squadron, the Fourth Destroyer Squadron, the Third Fleet and the Navy General Staff. He survived the war, and enjoyed a long retirement. He died on 20 June 1957.

Operation or Area	Force	Commander	Type	Ships
			Tankers	Narutō
				Tōei Maru
	Guard Force – BatDiv 2	Vice-Admiral Shirō Takasu	Battleships	Hyūga (Flag)
				Ise
				Fusō
				Yamashiro
			Light cruisers	Kitakami
				Oi
			Destroyers	Asagiri
				Yūgiri
				Shirakumo
				Amagiri
				Umikaze
				Yamakaze
				Kawakaze
				Suzukaze
				Ariake
				Yūgure
				Shigure
				Shiratsuyu
			Tankers	San Clemente Maru
				Tōa Maru
Midway Invasion Force	Main Body	Vice-Admiral Nobutake Kondō	Battleships	Kongō
				Hiei
			Carrier	Zuihō
			Heavy cruisers	Atago (Flag)
				Chōkai
				Myōkō
				Haguro
			Light cruiser	Yura
			Destroyers	Murasame
				Samidare
				Harusame
				Yūdachi
				Asagumo
				Minegumo
				Natsugumo
				Mikasuki
			Tankers	Sata
				Tsurumo
				Genyō Maru
				Kenyō Maru
			Repair ship	Akashi
	Close Support Group	Vice-Admiral Takeo Kurita	Heavy Cruisers	Kumano (Flag)
				Suzuya
				Mikuma
				Mogami
			Destroyers	Asashio
				Arashio
			Tanker	Nichiei Maru

Operation or Area	Force	Commander	Type	Ships
	Transport Group for Ichiki Brigade	Rear-Admiral Raizō Tanaka	Troopships	Kiyozumi Maru
				Keiyō Maru
				Zenyō Maru
				Goshu Maru II
				Tōa Maru
				Kano Maru
				Argentina Maru
				Hokuriku Maru
				Brazil Maru
				Kirishima Maru
				Azuma Maru
				Nankai Maru
				Akebono Maru
				Patrol Boat 1
				Patrol Boat 2
				Patrol Boat 34
			Light cruiser	Jintsū (Flag)
			Destroyers	Kuroshio
				Oyashio
				Yukikaze
				Amatsukaze
				Tokitsukaze
				Hatsukaze
				Shiranuhi
				Kasumi
				Kagerō
				Arare
	Seaplane Support Group	Rear-Admiral Ryūtarō	Seaplane tenders	Chitose
				Kamikawa Maru
			Destroyer	Hayashio
			Transport	Patrol Boat 35
	Minesweeping Force	Captain Sadatomo Miyamoto	Minesweepers	Tama Maru 3
				Tama Maru 5
				Shōnan Maru 7
				Shōnan Maru 8
			Subchasers	Ch-16
				Ch-17
				Ch-18
			Support ships	Sōya
				Meiyō Maru
				Yamafuku Maru
Advance Force	6th Fleet	Vice-Admiral Teruhishi Komatsu	Depot ship, Kwajalein	Rio De Janeiro Maru
			Submarines	I-156
				I-157
				I-158
				I-159
				I-162
				I-165
				I-166
				I-212
				I-122
				I-123

Operation or Area	Force	Commander	Type	Ships
Aleutians (AL)	CarDiv 4	Rear-Admiral Kakuji Kakuta	Carriers	Ryūjō (Flag)
				Junyō
			Heavy cruisers	Maya
				Takao
			Destroyers	Akebono
				Ushio
				Sazanami
			Tanker	Teiyō Maru
	Main Body	Vice-Admiral Moshirō Hosogaya	Heavy cruiser	Nachi (Flag)
			Destroyers	Inazuma
				Ikazuchi
			Tankers	Fujisan Maru
				Nissan Maru
			Freighters	3
	Attu-Adak Invasion Force	Rear-Admiral Sentarō Ōmori	Light cruiser	Abukuma (Flag)
			Destroyers	Wakaba
				Nenohi
				Hatsuharu
				Hatsushimo
			Minelayer	Magane Maru
			Troopship (for Hozumi Brigade)	Kinugasa Maru
	Kiska Invasion Force	Captain Takeji Ono	Light cruisers	Kiso (Flag)
				Tama
			Auxilliary cruisers	Aska Maru
				Awata Maru
			Destroyers	Hibiki
				Akatsuki
				Hokaze
			Troopships (for Mukai Brigade)	Hakusan Maru
				Kamagawa Maru
			Minesweepers	Hakuhō Maru
				Kaihō Maru
				Shinkotsu Maru
			Submarines	I-9
				I-15
				I-17
				I-19
				I-25
				I-26
	Seaplane Force	Captain Keiichi Ujuko	Seaplane tender	Kimikawa Maru
			Destroyer	Shiokaze

Torpedo and Submarine Staff Officer for the Combined Fleet, finally arrived at Kwajalein in person aboard the training cruiser *Kashima* with the actual copies of the 5 May order for the combined MI-AL mission under his arm. Moreover, Arima also presented yet another additional and totally fresh order, No. 14 dated that same day, with details of what air-search missions were required, the deployment times for the submarines and what was known of the enemy's engagement methods.

An emergency meeting was held aboard *Kashima* with Komatsu's available staff and representatives of the 24th Air Flotilla, including Goto Eiji who was the senior naval shore-based air commander in the Marshall Islands. A study of these plans revealed that yet three further duties had been added to the submarines' assignments: to act as a radio beacon; to act as life guard to rescue downed aircrew off Hawaii; and to act as Oahu weather reporter. Submarines *I-171*, *I-174* and *I-175* (SubRon 3) were allocated those tasks. The agreed date of reconnaissance (P-Day, Pearl) was 31 May, the date of the full moon. If conditions proved unfavourable then this could be postponed, but after 3 June the operation would be cancelled. The two Type-2 flying boats (W-45 and W-46) and submarines of SubDiv 3, SubDiv 13 and SubRon 3 were all to be utilized.

The plan called for the Emilys to leave Wotje at 0000 on P-Day, refuel with 10 tons of aviation fuel at French Frigate Shoals from 1430 and depart from there at 1600. Arriving over Oahu around 2045, they would conduct their study of the fleet anchorage, paying particular heed to the presence or otherwise of American carriers, and arrive back at Wotje around 0930 on P+1.

The submarines were disposed as follows. The Refuelling Group, *I-124*, *I-123* with *I-122* as the stand-by reserve vessel, would be in positions 330°, 1.7 miles; 170°, 2.5 miles and 260° 6.5 miles respectively from La Perouse Pinnacle in the Shoals. *I-171*, as the beacon vessel, would position herself at Point M, in Latitude 19° north, Longitude 174° west. From here she would transmit radio beacon signals half an hour before and half an hour after 0380, the time the Emilys were due to pass overhead; the lifeguard submarine, *I-174* would be in place at Point N, some 200 miles 200° from Keahole Point, about midway along the west coast of Hawaii Island in case either Emily had to ditch. Finally, the weather station unit, *I-175*, would place herself about 80 miles south-west of Oahu. She would transmit changes in the weather, conditions, wind force and direction, type and height of waves etc. back to the CO 24th Air Flotilla. It was stated that 'should the enemy's patrol of French Frigate Shoal be vigilant' and there proved to be no prospect of refuelling, then the whole operation would be aborted.

Having decided that Commander Arima had to radio the CoS, Combined Fleet, that these new arrangements would necessarily compromise the original submarine plan to intercept, report and attack the American fleet as it sortied out. The three submarines of SubRon 3, would just 'not be able to reach the designated picket line by date scheduled'. There was worse to come. Following discussions it soon became clear that SubRon 5 would not be able to complete their preparations in time, and therefore would not be on station by the due date either! Finally, they had worked out that the two Emily flying boats, fully laden, would be unable to take off from Wake Island due to the shoals, and would have to leave from Wotje, returning to Wake when they would be higher in the water. The CO 24th Air Flotilla therefore had to modify Search Sector I by reducing the outward reach by 200 miles. The two flying boats and their tender, *Kamoi*[38], duly moved base to Wotje. On 27 May a message was received from the Combined Fleet CoS instructing that the mission was to be conducted during bright moonlight and in the utmost secrecy, thus negating earlier instructions to attack targets with 250 kg bombs at the Navy Yard.

Misfortunes continued. The *I-122* suffered a breakdown, which delayed her arrival at Laysan Island until 4 June, making her mission pointless. Then *I-123* arriving off French Frigate Shoals on 29 May, found a startling revelation. Far from the area being deserted, two American seaplane tenders[39] were on station and their aircraft were making regular patrols throughout the day. Mortified, she radioed this unpalatable news back to Kwajalein the next day, which brought about first a postponement of the 'Second K' sortie and, when on on 31st she reported continued American activity, its outright cancellation. It was decided to use the Emilys to reconnoitre Midway instead, but even this failed, 'neither crew having any night-landing experience in that type of aircraft'[40].

The post-war summary of the failure of the 'Second K' operation was terse and sombre. 'Thus, a means of obtaining intelligence of the enemy, which had been highly regarded, collapsed . . .'[41]

Aboard the fleet flagship *Yamato*, the feeling probably was that this did not matter too much. They thought they knew exactly where at least some of the US carriers were, and it was not at Pearl. The CoS, Rear-Admiral Matome Ugaki, was writing in his diary:

For several days past, there have been reports from Communications Intelligence of increased enemy activity in the Noumea-Suva area. Transmissions from 0000 today have placed by direction-finding bearings some 400 miles, bearing 155° from Tulagi. In the judgement of Commander 8th Communications Unit at Rabaul, these transmissions are

---

38. *Kamoi,* a 17,000 ton former US tanker built in 1922 by the New York Shipbuilding Company at Camden in 1922. She was converted into a seaplane carrier in 1933. Reconverted to a tanker again in 1943 due to shortages of such vessels, she was sunk by carrier attack at Hong Kong on 5 April 1945.

39. These were the USS *Ballard* (AVD 10) USS *Thornton* (AVD 11) a pair of old 'flush-decker' destroyers which had been converted into fast seaplane tenders in 1940.

40. *Senshi Sōsho*, Vol 43, pp 257

41. *Ibid,* pp 254–5.

from enemy carriers. For this reason the eighteen land bombers that have been training at Tinian have been ordered back to Rabaul. It is now estimated that the American carrier force is now in the South Pacific area.[42]

The fact that the Americans were patrolling French Frigate Shoals, and the fact that the US carriers were nowhere near the South Seas, were both due to Intelligence schemes set in train through the reading of Japanese signals. The USS *Tangier* (AV-12)[43] and the heavy cruiser *Salt Lake City* (CA-25) had been employed since 24 May broadcasting decoy signals to each other and to various shore stations, from various parts of the Coral Sea as part of Admiral Nimitz's radio deception plan, based on a suggestion from General Douglas MacArthur. The fact that all this convenient signals traffic might be a set-up does not appeared to have percolated through to the Japanese at this stage, however. A morose summary in the official history makes plain their chargin at the failure of the 'Second K'[44].

We were not able to ascertain by air reconnaissance that the American aircraft carriers *were* at Pearl Harbor, the value of which would have been tremendous. Had we been able to determine that the enemy carriers were *not* at Pearl Harbor, we would have had to decide whether (a) they had not yet returned from the South Pacific or whether (b) they had returned and had departed Pearl Harbor for a counter-attack against our forces. Either of these judgements (from our navy's estimate of the situation for the period end of May to beginning of June), of such a confirmation of an absence of enemy carriers from Pearl Harbor, would have deepened our conviction at that time that they were still operating in the South Pacific.[45]

Meanwhile the three submarines were sent off to take their places on their original designated picket line A[46], but again, far to late to catch the US task forces which had already moved through and beyond that area.

So American intelligence work, backed by quick action by the new C-in-C of the Pacific Fleet, Admiral Chester W. Nimitz[47], and the commander of the Hawaiian Sea Frontier in sending forces to the Shoals, had proved its value in both scuppering Japanese efforts at their own prying, and also fooled their Japanese opposite numbers. This was a stunning blow to Japanese plans, but that was just the beginning. Even more devastating than these Japanese failures was the fact that their American opponents had a pretty shrewd idea of where, when and to some degree how Yamamoto's MI operation was to develop. Of this breakthrough the Japanese remained blissfully unaware!

Midway provides an interesting contrast to the land battle and seminal victory of the British 8th Army at El Alamein later that same year. In the latter, the part played by the ULTRA intelligence was paramount, equal to the part played by MAGIC at Midway, but there was one big difference. At El Alamein, the victorious British commander, General Bernard Montgomery[48], *knew* full well that he had overwhelming superiority in numbers and equipment, and

---

42. Ugaki, *Fading Victory*.
43. USS *Tangier*, the 11,700 -ton cargo ship ss *Sea Arrow*, acquired from owners and taken into USN service and converted to a seaplane tender.
44. Although in one way even the abortive 'Second K' *did* work in Japan's favour, in that it influenced many in the US Communications Intelligence (COMINT) world, Station Negat in particular, and even Layton initially, that Hawaii might well be the main target, rather than Midway. Admiral Redman to Murphy, 15 May 1942, HC IV W.3.25.
45. *Senshi Sōsho*, Vol 43, p 244
46. *Senshi Sōsho*, Vol 43, p 255.
47. Fleet Admiral Chester William Nimitz (1885–1966) b. Fredericksburg, Texas graduated seventh in his class from the US Naval Academy, Annapolis, in 1905. Served aboard the battleship *Ohio* (BB-12) and, as an ensign, commanded the captured Spanish gunboat *Panay* in the Philippines. While in command of the destroyer *Decatur* (DD-5) she ran aground leading to Nimitz's court martial and reprimand. He was transferred to submarine service commanding four different vessels. In 1913 he was sent to Germany and Belgium to learn about diesel engines and supervised the building of first such vessel for the US Navy, the oiler

Maumee (AO-2) at Brooklyn Navy Yard, becoming her Chief Engineer. As lieutenant-commander he returned to submarines and then became XO of the cruiser *South Dakota* (ACR-9). In 1920 he supervised the building of the submarine base at Pearl Harbor, which was followed by study at the Naval War College where he specialized in afloat logistics. In 1923 he was aide to Commander, Battle Force. As captain in 1929 he became commander Submarines and in 1931 was OIC Reserve Fleet Destroyers, San Diego. Commanded heavy cruiser *Augusta* (CA-31) in the Pacific, then served three years at the Bureau of Navigation, Washington DC, promoted to Rear-Admiral 1938. Commanded CruDiv 2 and BatDiv 1 before becoming Chief of the Bureau of Navigation. Assumed command of Pacific Fleet after Pearl Harbor but kept most of his predecessor staff. Commanded the Pacific Fleet right through the war, being promoted to Fleet Admiral in 1944. After the war, as Chief of Naval Operations he oversaw the run-down of the fleet to peacetime establishment. He retired in 1947, serving at the United Nations 1949–52. He suffered a stroke and died on 20 February 1966.
48. Viscount Montgomey of Alamein, KG, GCB, DSO, PC, Bernard Law Montgomery ('Monty') (1887-1976), victor of

planned a deliberate and methodical battle of attrition accordingly; at Midway, Admiral Chester W. Nimitz, the C-in-C, Pacific Fleet, as a matter of policy, actually restricted the size of his forces and set broad limitations on their usage. His was an ambush strategy designed to inflict the maximum damage while keeping his own losses to a minimum.[49] Nimitz wanted to keep the fight flexible, with the options for his commanders to stop, and even withdraw, should the fight not develop favourably. Montgomery had no qualms about accepting heavy losses, so long as the payback meant his enemy was totally crushed; withdrawal or defeat was never considered as an acceptable option.

Both men were conscious of the legacy of defeat that their forces had hanging around their necks, and the price of failure. At Midway and El Alamein foreknowledge was an essential element, and for both the stakes were high. Both men were constrained by the need for secrecy as to their sources, of course, but, in a seeming reversal of stereotyping, while the American kept a close lip and his thoughts to himself, refusing even to allow the vainglorious exaggeration, bragging and boasting of the Army Air Force typified by Billy Mitchell to provoke him into revealing the truth, the British recipient seemed to revel in the secrecy. 'Monty' appeared to welcome the silence in order to build up a reputation for sagacity and wisdom and his place in history, which any subsequent revelations of the intelligence sources to which he owed his success came far too late to temper.

The Japanese victims of the outstanding codebreaking,

of course, were very muted, both from the shame of failure and the overriding need to keep the truth from the public. Even today, there is a marked reluctance among many to discuss the overall battle or even facets of it. To a generation instilled with a philosophy of death rather defeat, the ignominity of the withdrawal in the face of the enemy was almost unbearable, and for many has remained so, while all around them post-war Japan changed radically.

The Ace in the Hole

The supreme importance of intelligence gathering has rarely been put to such spectacular use as in the months preceding the Battle of Midway. The word 'spectacular' can fairly be used to describe both the Allied and the Japanese methods of figuratively peeking over the shoulder of the enemy. In the case of the Japanese, 'spectacular failure' would describe the total bankruptcy of their methods, while in the American camp 'spectacular success' is an almost inadequate phase; the more apt description 'priceless advantage' given by Frederick D. Parker is totally fitting.[50]

The origins of American cryptology are usually traced back to the recruitment of a remarkable naval officer from the obscurity of commanding a minesweeper up the Yangstze River to a desk in the newly created Code and Signal Section of the Office of Naval Communications (ONC). That officer was one Lieutenant Laurance F. Safford.[51] The *raison d'etre* for the new post and the new

El Alamein. b. Kennington, London. Educated at St Paul's School and Royal Military College, Sandhurst. Commissioned in 1908 in Royal Warwickshire Regiment. Served on the Western Front in the First World War and survived being shot through the lung by a sniper. Between the wars served at home and in India. 1939 major-general and commanded 3rd Division in British Expeditionary Force in France and Belgium 1940. Came out via Dunkirk. Replaced General Auchinleck as Commander British 8th Army ('The Desert Rats') in North Africa in 1942 after the loss of Tobruk. Adopted idiosyncratic uniform and lifestyle that endeared him to his troops, living in a caravan instead of at HQ. Teetotal and non-smoking. After defeat of German and Italian armies in North Africa he took part in invasions of Sicily and Italy in 1943, then commanded British and Canadian armies at the invasion of Normandy (D-Day) in 1944. Promoted to Field Marshal in September. Liberated Holland, Belgium and Denmark, and took the surrender of northern German armies in the west on 4 May 1945 at Lunenburg Heath. Was created a viscount and became Chief of Imperial General Staff 1946–48 and Deputy Supreme Commander of NATO Forces Europe, 1951 to 1958. Wrote several controversial war memoirs. Died in 1976

49. Nimitz instructed his task force commanders: 'You will be governed by the principle of calculated risk, which you will interpret to mean the avoidance of exposure of your force to attack by superior enemy forces without prospect of inflicting, as a result of such exposure, greater damage to the enemy.'

50. Frederick D. Parker, *A Priceless Advantage: U. S. Navy Communications Intelligence and the Battles of Coral Sea, Midway, and the Aleutians. Part Two: The Battles for Midway and the Aleutians.*

51. Captain Laurance F. Safford (1890–1973). b. Massachusetts. Graduated from Annapolis in 1916. Appointed to crack the Japanese codebook as the first naval cryptologist, establishing the Research Desk of the Code and Signal Section, ONC between 1924 and 1926, and actively recruiting equally talented agents (Joseph Rochefort, Joseph Wenger, Agnes Meyer Driscoll among them) to OP-20-G (Combat Intelligence). Safford was handicapped in his efforts by periodically being assigned other duties (in 1926–9 and 1932–6) but eventually created a system of direction finding 'Intercept' stations to read IJN signals and co-ordinate a dedicated assault on deciphering them. With the forward-minded adoption of modern equipment in conjunction with IBM, he mechanized the system for speed. Unusually, during a period of intense inter-service rivalry for limited funding, he established a rapport with his army counterpart, Frank Rowlett, and between them they devel-

assignment was the secret photographing by the Division of Naval Intelligence (DNI) of the IJN's 'Red' codebook during a succession of break-ins at the Japanese Consulate in New York in 1924.[52] This coup was carried out in the immediate aftermath of the Washington Treaty, which had put strict limitations on naval rearmament. Although they had ultimately signed the treaty, its arbitrary freezing of the IJN's battleship strength at 60 per cent of that of the Royal Navy and the USN had not played well in Japan. Their much-cherished 'Eight-Eight' building programme had been ruined and their avidly pursued policy of achieving equality with the other two major naval powers had been smashed. The Japanese made no secret of their discontent with the treaty, which they felt they had been coerced into signing, and the acquisition of the code book by the Americans was seen by the purloiners as a legitimate step to ensure that they were keeping to the letter of the document, and not attempting to evade it.

Among those whom Safford recruited was a 'mustang', an ex-enlisted officer who had not attended the Naval Academy but who had graduated from the Stevens Institute of Technology and then been commissioned into the service as an ensign in 1918, one Joseph John Rochefort.[53]

His original intention was to become a naval aviator but this never happened. Instead, pure chance led him down a very different road. The XO[54] of the battleship *Arizona*, was a crossword fanatic and Rochefort shared this pastime while aboard her. When that officer was later appointed to Navy Department HQ in Washington DC in 1925, and when a vacancy occurred for someone to fill the not very glamorous post of decoder as an aide to Safford at the Research Desk in Room 1621 in the Mall Navy Building, Rochefort was recommended. A six-month crash course in cryptanalysis followed. Destined to become one of the most famous crypt-analysts of the twentieth century, he proved a natural talent. When Safford's turn for sea duty took him back to the fleet in February 1926, Rochefort filled his seat as Officer in Charge (OIC). The job became a personal challenge, and the young officer showed the compulsive obsession that was to mark him out in later life, indeed so much so that he developed an ulcer before he again resumed sea-going duties for a spell in 1927.

The original teams had been painfully put together on a shoestring over three decades, the US Navy sending two 1906 Annapolis graduates to Tokyo in 1910, with a new officer being assigned each year after that.[55] One of the

---

oped a secure cipher system for their own national defence, the Sigaba machine, which remained inviolate throughout the war. The Japanese diplomatic codes (encrypted via the J or *97-shiki O-bun In-ji-ki* (Alphabetical Typewriter 97 – PURPLE) were also penetrated by a team under William F. Friedman, Chief Cryptanalyst of the Army Signal Corps. However the Naval Communications Service Director, Rear-Admiral Leigh Noyes was not convinced by Safford's warnings. Later, after Midway, and despite the outstanding success in breaking JN-25, both Safford and Rochefort were removed from their posts. Safford later returned to intelligence work with the ONC and he was a key witness into the hearings into both Pearl Harbor, where he defended Admiral Kimmel, and the fall of Corregidor. He retired from the service in 1953, and died in May 1973. His surviving papers are in the Safford-Hile Archive at Laramie.

52. This code was solved by the Black Chamber team lead by Herbert O. Yardley, under the combined auspices of the State Department and the army. Despite their success Secretary of State Henry L. Stimpson deemed such work 'unethical' and withdrew funding!

53. Captain Joseph John Rochefort (1898–1976). 1918–25 Fleet School including sea-going service aboard the battle-ship *Arizona* (BB-39). 1925–9 OP-20-G. Between normal sea-going duties Rochefort was picked by Captain Safford to join OP-20-G in 1925 and was tutored by Safford himself and Driscoll, becoming second-in-command until 1929. 1929–32 Japanese Language Training; underwent an intensive Japanese language course. 1932–3 ONI. 1933–6 battleship *Maryland* (BB-46). 1936–8 11th Naval District (ONI). Resuming intelligence work he showed a natural flair for the work. 1936–9 *New Orleans* (CA-32). 1939–41

fleet (staff Scouting Force, Pacific fleet, aboard *Indianapolis* (CA-35). 1941–42 OIC 14 Radio Intelligence (RI) Unit. Safford again selected Rochefort when setting up the CIU at Pearl Harbor. The work of Rochefort and his team was outstanding, but when Safford was eased out of OP-20-G Rochefort lost his protection. He was removed from intelligence work. (See Frederick D. Packer, 'How OP-20-G got rid of Joe Rochefort', article in *Cryptologia*.) Even Admiral Nimitz could not reverse this decision. After turning down a fighting command, (he was offered a destroyer), he ended up in command of a dry-dock on the West Coast. Nor did Rochefort ever receive a promotion to Rear-Admiral, although few men deserved it more. It would appear that he was a maverick whose face did not fit, added to which he had the enormous misfortune of being right and proving his superiors wrong, a fatal combination for any career, naval or otherwise! (The insubstantial entry for Rochefort on the NSA (National Security Agency) web site *Hall of Honor* makes absolutely no mention of these discreditable machinations.) Ten years after his death some measure of justice was finally metered out to his memory, when he was posthumously awarded the Presidential Medal of Freedom, which is the highest American peace-time award for military personnel. The former editor of the *Honolulu Advertiser*, Elliott Carlson, has promised us additional startling revelations about Rochefort's life in a planned biography.

54. Commander Chester C. Jersey.

55. For a fascinating insight into the origins of US Naval Intelligence in Japan, based on first-hand interviews, see Richard Bradford, 'Learning the Enemy's Language'.

original pair, Lieutenant Frederick Rogers[56], in 1913 influenced another young ensign then serving aboard the battleship *Virginia*, Ellis P. Zacharias[57] into joining, and he would eventually turn out to be a leading light in the service.

Although the illegal entry had got the DNI the 'Red' code, that was only part of the solution; what they lacked, and what Rochefort had laboriously to construct, was the key to that code, the 'Additive' book.[58] As this latter document was continually being changed to keep the code secure, this proved to be an enormous task. Meanwhile, in June 1939, the IJN had introduced a new main operation code, *Kaigun Ango-sho D, Ransuhyo nana* (Navy Code Book D, Random Numbers Table Seven). This was attacked by the redoubtable Ms Agnes Driscoll[59], who almost immediately made a breakthrough.[60]

By 1941 the two men had reunited in their task when

---

56. Captain Frederick Fremont Rogers (1884–1952) b. Clinton, Illinois, on 21 September 1884 and educated at Clinton Grade and High Schools. Entered U S Naval Academy, Annapolis, in 1902. Graduated as a midshipman in February 1906 and ordered to the Asiatic Station aboard the battleship *Wisconsin* (BB-9), followed by service aboard the ex-Spanish gunboats *Quiros* (PG-40) and *Samar* (PG-41) and the battleship *Alabama* (BB-8). 1908 promoted to ensign and assigned to the despatch vessel (former unarmoured cruiser) *Dolphin* in which he served until 1910, including the cruise to Venezuela in 1908 conveying American Ambassador Buchanan to negotiate the Venezuelan foreign loans settlement. Rogers became the first US naval officer ordered to Tokyo for study of the Japanese tongue, becoming Attaché at the American Embassy between April 1910 and May 1913. 1913, June, joined the battleship *Virginia* (BB-13) as watch officer and first lieutenant during the Mexican campaign. 1916, March, transferred to patrol gunboat *Castine* (PG-6) as XO and Navigator, and served in the Dominica Campaign. 1917, January, First World War service with the *Illinois* (BB-7) and then the *Oklahoma* (BB-37) as Navigator, serving with the British Grand Fleet at Scapa Flow. 1919–21, at the ONI. 1921–2 Fleet Intelligence Officer, Asiatic Fleet at time of Washington Treaty. 1922, August, appointed in command of destroyer *Barker* (DD-213). 1923, June, attended Senior Course at the Naval War College, Newport, and from May 1924 served on the College staff to September 1926, when he assumed command of the navy transport ship *Sirius* (AK-15). 1927, October, transferred to the light cruiser *Concord* (CL-10) as XO. 1928, again on the staff of the Naval War College. 1931–1933, Commander, DesDiv8, Scouting Force before resuming duties briefly in May 1933 in ONI. 1933, September, returned to Tokyo as Naval Attaché until September 1936, attending the funeral of Admiral Togo in 1934. 1936, November, commanded the battleship *Texas* (BB-35). 1938, completed the Advanced Course at Naval War College. 1939, June to November, Naval Examining Board, Navy Department, Washington, DC. Was on the Navy's selection committee for language instruction. 1940, helped establish the US Navy Japanese Language School, at the University of Colorado, at Boulder, after the earlier shift from Tokyo to University of California at Berkeley in 1940 was considered necessary due to deteriorating relations. Transferred to Retired List on 1 February 1942. May, recalled to active duty, as CO of Advanced Base Depot, Davisville, RI and Commander of Naval Construction Training Center (NCTC). On 26 October 1942, relieved of command of the Base Depot and continued duty as Commander, NCRT, Davisville, RI. Awards included Mexican Service Medal,

Dominican Campaign Medal, Victoria Medal, Grand Fleet Clasp, Portuguese Commander of the Military Order of Avis and Venezuelan Bust of Bolivar 1945, finally retired on 13 August. He spent his retirement at his home in Newport, RI where he died on 3 November 1952, age 66. One of the unsung Intelligence men of his day, he was 'unknown' to the Midway generation who followed him but his groundwork gave all who followed the firm base from which the Japanese defeat was ultimately to stem. His collected papers from 1924 to1960, MS Collection 46 is held in a box at the Naval War College Archive, Newport, RI.

57. Rear-Admiral Ellis Mark Zacharias (1890–1961). b. 1 January 1890 at Jacksonville, Florida, graduated from US Naval Academy Annapolis, 1912. He served aboard the battleship *Virginia* (BB-13) and during the First World War served as a line officer aboard the *Pittsburgh* (CA-4). In 1942, as a captain, he commanded the heavy cruiser *Salt Lake City* (CA-25) during the Wake Island attacks and the Doolittle raid. He conducted a radio psychological warfare programme aimed at the Japanese High Command. Became Deputy Chief of Naval Intelligence later in the war and retired from the navy in 1946 following a heart attack. He later became a radio narrator for the programme *Secret Missions*, and later did the same on television for the programme *Behind Closed Doors*, both taking their names from two best-selling books. Died after a second heart seizure age 71 and was interred at Arlington National Cemetery, Washington DC on 3 July 1961.

58. Like most secret codes of the time the Japanese 'Red' was enciphered, with the substitution of a numeric value for every likely word or syllable. Prior to transmission, an 'additive' set of numbers, selected at random from a second book, were tacked onto each code group in any message, with a hidden indicator which enabled the proper recipient to remove these again prior to de-coding.

59. Agnes Meyer Driscoll (1889–1971). b. at Genesco, Illinois, 1889. 1907–09 Otterbein University, Columbus, OH. 1910–11, Ohio State University earning an AB degree in maths, physics, foreign languages (Japanese, German, French and Latin) and music. On graduation appointed Director of Music at the Lowry Phillips Military Academy then, in 1914 appointed Chairwoman of local High School Mathematics Department, Amarillo, TX. 1918, June, enlisted as Chief Yeoman in USNR assigned to Department of Cyphers, Riverbank Laboratories, Chicago, IL., seconded from the Officer of the Director of Naval Communications. Helped develop the Cypher Machine (CM) for the navy with Lieutenant-Commander William F. Gresham, winning the Senate prize in 1937 for their work. Served until 1949 with a short interlude in private employment. 1923, left navy and

Safford, again OIC Communication Security Section, Naval Communications[61], working from Room 1649 of the Navy Department Building on Constitution Avenue in Washington DC, was selecting key personnel to man the main intelligence units that had been established around the Pacific. The system had three of these core units, the main one being in the Navy Department itself, with subsidiary direction-finder (D/F) and intercept stations covering the Atlantic. Washington also had responsibility for monitoring foreign government traffic and was the training centre for all other intelligence units. Consequently it had both the largest number of the most experienced staff, those of more than ten years experience, and the largest number of inexperienced personnel.[62]

The equivalent intelligence network for the Pacific Theatre was based at Pearl Harbor, and had intercept and D/F stations at Oahu, on Midway Island, in Samoa and at Dutch Harbour in the Aleutians.[63] The third and final core

became technical advisor of Edward Hebern's Electric Code Company (whose 'unbreakable code' she had broken in 1921), working on rotor technology. 1924, married Washington lawyer Michael Driscoll, and returned to navy employment in the DNC again when the Hebern company failed. Became the navy's leading cryptologist breaking IJN 'Red' book code in the 1920s; 'Blue' book code in the 1930s (which necessitated the simultaneous breaking of both the code and its overlaying cypher) and led work on M-1 Grand Naval Maneuvers cypher machine (Orange), then began penetrating Operational Fleet Code JN-25 in 1940s before moving on to tackling the German Enigma machine up to 1942. 1950, December, joined Armed Forces Security Agency. 1952, joined National Security Agency. 1959, July, retired from federal service. 1971, died, and interred at Arlington National Cemetery, Washington, DC. Biography is Susan M. Lujan, 'Agnes Meyer Driscoll', article in *Cryptologia*, Vol XV, Issue 1 (dated January 1991), pp 47–56, republished in *Selections from Cryptologia: History, People, and Technology*, Cipher Deavors, Editor, Artech House, 1998, pp 269–78.

60. Among those Agnes Driscoll tutored in its secrets during 1940–1 was Lieutenant John M. Lietwiler, and he was packed off to the Philippines once he had mastered it to put his knowledge to work. Another protégé of hers was Lieutenant Lee W. Parke, who came up with an automatic decoding machine that could unravel the columns of additive/subtractive tables. Parke's secure unit designator was GYP and he wryly christened his mechanical pet Jeep IV. The Acting Chief of Naval Operations, Rear-Admiral Royal Ingersoll, enthusiastically backed the project in a memo dated 4 October 1940, in which he stated that the current time taken to recover the additive key cipher for each message could be anything from one hour to several days. Jeep IV should speed things up, although he warned that, even so, immediate results would seldom be possible. This device was built and duly shipped out to Lietwiler in the Philippines aboard the ancient navy transport *Henderson* (AP-1), arriving on 6 October 1941, just two months before Pearl Harbor.

61. Safford himself described what this title meant thus: 'The words "Communication Security" were a covering title to mask Communication Intelligence, although we also performed security duties in the design and preparation of naval codes and ciphers and general communications security duties; that is, surveillance over their use.' Captain Stafford testifying at the proceedings of the Hart Inquiry, Saturday, April 29 1944. Navy Department, Washington DC.

62. The chronology of the US Navy intelligence organization was as follows. Confidential Publications Section (Op-58) established January 1917 in Division of Operations, OCNO, (Office of the Chief of Naval Operations) OpNav absorbing the cryptographic functions vested since at least 1848 in the Signal Office, Bureau of Navigation. Renamed the Code and Signal Section, 10 October, 1917, and placed (as Op-18) under the authority of the Director of Naval Communications, 15 January, 1920. Op-18 established a Research Desk, responsible for cryptanalysis, in January 1924, thereby creating a unified naval cryptological activity.

The Code and Signal Section was formally made a part of the Division of Naval Communications (DNC), as OP-20-G, on 1 July, 1922. Successively redesignated Communications Security Group (OP-20-G), DNC, OCNO, 11 March, 1935; Radio Intelligence Section (OP-20-G), DNC, OCNO, 15 March, 1939; and Communications Security Section (OP-20-G), DNC, OCNO, 1 October, 1939.

Op-20-G was reorganized as an exclusively cryptanalytic operation, the Radio Intelligence Section (Op-20-G), DNC, OCNO, 12 February, 1942, with former cryptographic and security functions assigned to separate sections, designated as OP-20-Q and OP-20-Y, respectively. Renamed, 20 October, 1942, the Communications Intelligence Organization (OP-20-G), DNC, OCNO. Naval communications intelligence elements collectively designated Communications Supplementary Activities (OP-20-2), DNC, OCNO, 10 July, 1946.

63. The CIU became the Fleet Radio Unit Pacific (FRUPAC). The chronology of this unit, as itemised in *Frupac History*; by Supplementary Radio Unit, Commandant, Navy 128, CO Fleet Post Office, San Francisco, Calif, Secret Letter JSH/J1 File A-3 (I) Serial Z-006094 of 8 January 1946, was: Major Decrypt Unit Honolulu proposed CNO 1929. Communications Intelligence Unit established, Commandant 14th Naval District, Headquarters Building, Naval Shipyard, Pearl Harbor. Lieutenant Thomas M. Dyer, July 1936 – July 1938; Lieutenant Thomas B. Birtley, July 1938 – June 1941; Lieutenant-Commander Joseph J. Rochefort, from June 1941. Commandant 14th Naval District, Combat Intelligence Unit form; Lieutenant W. J. Holmes, CIC Officer, June 1941. Communications Intelligence Unit absorbs Combat Intelligence Unit in June 1941. Communications Intelligence Unit becomes Combat Intelligence Unit, Lieutenant-Commander Joseph J. Rochefort, from June 1941–July 1942. Radio Intelligence Unit 14th Naval District, Captain W. B. Goggins, July 1942–8 September 1943. Pacific Fleet Radio Unit (FRUPAC), from 8 September 1943.

unit was temporarily located at Cavite Naval Base, in 1936, then moved to Mariveles, Bataan and finally, in October 1940, relocated to Corregidor, all in the Philippines. The cryptology centre was based in the Manila Tunnel, an underground complex hewn out of solid rock. In the phonetic alphabet C for Cast was applied for Cavite then Corregidor, and this morphed into the appellation Station Cast commonly assigned to this facility. There were also subsidiary units at Guam and, initially, from the fourth floor of the American Consulate in Shanghai monitoring the Sino-Japanese conflict, but this had been forced to evacuate to the Philippines in December 1940. In addition there were intercept and D/F stations on the west coast, but the former fed direct to Washington rather than Pearl. Safford described Pearl's duties as restricted to 'the dispositions and plans of naval forces in the Pacific Ocean and to surveillance over Japanese naval communications'. He added, perhaps with a tinge of irony, 'We expected that this would prevent the Fleet being surprised as the Russians had been at Port Arthur.'[64] Their duties excluded any diplomatic traffic[65], but the personnel had, on average, about four or five years of CI experience, and Safford stated unequivocally, 'The officers included our best, and six or seven had had previous CI duty in the Asiatic CI Unit.' In fact, Safford had hand-picked Station Head Rochefort in May 1941, digging him out from his mundane post as Intelligence Officer aboard the heavy cruiser *Indianapolis* (CA-35), and giving him pretty much *carte blanche* to select the rest of the

Hypo[66] team, which had the daily task of taking in the intercepts of Japanese signals traffic, translating them, decrypting them, slotting them into the mosaic of developing events and reporting their analysis and reviews upward, along with recommendations.

Rochefort's team was, housed in the unhealthy atmosphere of basement offices, (known to their inmates as 'the Dungeon') under the Administration Building. There was an original staff of ten officers and thirty enlisted men. The team initially only had the IJN Flag Officer's code assigned to them to work on. The CIU network included the outstations at He'eia and in the Naval Magazine at Lualualei in the Lualualei Valley in the Waianae Mountains on Oahu.[67] It was not until after Pearl Harbor that the team started to get their teeth into the difficult JN-25B code, with CIU making the first decrypt in January 1942. Its security only really began to crumble in any depth from March 1942. To lever open this initial crack in the system the team that were working round-the-clock shifts[68] included Joseph Finnegan, a language officer in Tokyo between 1934 and 1937; Lieutenant Thomas H. Dyer, USNA (United States Naval Academy) 1924; Major Alva B. 'Red' Lasswell, US Marine Corps (USMC), a Japanese linguist; Lieutenant Wesley A. Wright, USNA 1926, a code breaker; Lieutenant-Commander Thomas A. Huckins, USNA 1924, a radio traffic analyst; Lieutenant-Commander Jack S. Williams, USNA 1927, who ran the IBM machines; and Wilfred Jasper Holmes.[69] CIU also worked with the British

64. Proceedings of the Hart Committee.
65. As prescribed by the War Plans then in force, WPDNC-8: Appendix IV; Art. 4–25).
66. Station H was the name allocated to the Intercept Station, which had been established at the US Coast guard site at He'eia, off the Ha'iku Valley, on the north-western coast of the island of Oahu. Rather appropriately for the Battle of Midway, the name in Hawaiian is a compound one, *he'e* and *'ia*, which can translate as 'washed away', a symbolic reference to an ancient battle in which victory was achieved by the local populace with the aid of an opportune tsunami which washed away the enemy. Station H certainly helped 'wash away' Nagumo's threat. The US Navy phonetic alphabet allocation was H for Hypo. He'eia thereby became Station Hypo. Although on rare occasions during 1942 the term Station Hypo was unofficially used to denote all Hawaiian intelligence, the correct title for the 14th Naval District's Communications Intelligence office in the islands was the Combat Intelligence Unit, Pearl Harbor, usually shortened simply to CIU. It is only post-war that Hypo has generically been universally (and misleadingly) applied to CIU.
67. The Naval Communication Facility at Lualualei replaced the old Hospital Point installation of 1916 and was set up to support the 1920-built receiver station at Wailupe. Work commenced in 1933 and the main antennes were completed

two years later, the Lualualei facility becoming fully operational in 1936.
68. For a detail account see speech, by Captain Forrest R. 'Tex' Biard, to the National Cryptologic Museum Foundation, Dallas, on 12 July 2002.
69. One young intelligence analyst ensign (and later lieutenant) on the CIU team was the now Rear-Admiral Donald M. McCollister 'Mac' Showers, (25 August 1919 in Iowa City). Destined to rise to great heights in the naval intelligence field he was educated at the University of Iowa, majoring in journalism and political science. 1940 joined the US Naval Reserve (USNR). 1941, September, commissioned as ensign, USNR and assigned to 13th Naval District HQ (Com 13), Seattle, on the district intelligence officer's staff. 1942, February, transferred to Pearl Harbor to join staff of CIU under Rochefort, working as an intelligence analyst with the unit cryptanalysts and Japanese speakers, with specific responsibility for extracting key data from intercepts, plotting IJN ship movements prior to Midway, and preparing graphic presentations for Nimitz. Showers remained with Fleet Intelligence for the duration of the war. ICPOA (Intelligence Center Pacific Ocean Area) Estimates Section and Photo-Reconnaissance section, establishment of JICPOA. Weekly Intelligence Bulletin, casualty estimates for proposed Operation *Olympic*. 1947, transferred to the US Navy as a regular officer at Pentagon. 1962–6 CinCpacFlt tour; 1965

sigint (Signals Intelligence) team (which, perforce, had been withdrawn in quick succession from Hong Kong, then Singapore to just outside Colombo and finally, right back to Kilindini, in East Africa under a new leader, Commander, Bruce Keith) and, while they lasted, the Dutch in Java. Some of the British Singapore Sigint team managed to escape to Australia and were incorporated in Captain Eric Nave's Royal Australian Navy (RAN's)[70]

cryptology unit at Melbourne, including three British Foreign Office linguists Henry Archer, Hubert Graves and Arthur Cooper. Also on Nave's unit were Lieutenant-Commander Jamieson, Professor Dale Trendall, Major Athanasius Treweek from Sydney University's Greek Department, Eric Barnes, Jack Davies and Corporal Ronald Bond. Later, in time for Midway, another US intelligence section of decoders was established at Melbourne[71],

---

Promoted to Rear-Admiral. 1966–71 Vietnam War, CoS, Plans and Programmes, DIA (Defence Intelligence Agency). Showers retired from the navy in 1971 as a Rear-Admiral, but then worked as DIA for a further twelve years, retiring in 1983. He originated the Rear-Admiral Donald M. Showers Award at the Navy Marine Corps Intelligence Training Center (NMITC) at Dam Neck, in 1999. 1986 was instrumental in securing the posthumous Distinguished Service Medal for Rochefort. His memories, 'ULTRA. The Navy's COMINT *weapon in the Pacific*', Spring/Summer edition, Vol 15, gives an excellent insight on the work of CIU at that vital 1942 period. See also Oral History interview with William J. Alexander 13 March 1998, OH1257.

70. Commander Theodore Eric Nave, OBE, RN, (1899–1993). b. 18 March 1899 Adelaide, South Australia. He was described as 'secretive and mysterious' and soon got on the wrong side of most of his contemporaries. Transferred to the Solutions Division of the Central Intelligence Bureau soon after. On 1 March 1917, Nave, who had resigned from South African Railways, joined the navy as a Paymaster Clerk and spent the greater part of his 35-year naval career on loan to the Royal Navy. A fluent and natural Japanese linguist, he was ready-made to pioneer the 1921 decision by the RAN to copy and read all Japanese naval wireless traffic. He served in Japan and then at the Admiralty in London, who detached him to the China Fleet. His work there led the Royal Navy to make his transfer permanent in 1930, and, although Australian, he remained officially a Royal Navy officer until he retired in1949. He made significant contributions to intelligence-gathering and was among the first to break into Japanese naval telegraph and codes, but remained largely anonymous. He was based at Hong Kong in 1936–7 and saw Japanese expansion policy at close range. He was at Singapore until February 1940 when, his health wrecked by the tropical climate, he returned to Australia to recover. He almost single-handedly organized Australia's SigInt. After leaving Melbourne he was recruited by Mic Sandford to work under American command at General Douglas McArthur's Combined Bureau in Brisbane. He did not mix well, describing the various labyrinthine American army and navy systems, seemingly working more against each other than against the Japanese, as 'dysfunctional'. At wars end he compiled a comprehensive crib on how the Japanese codes were broken. Discharged from the RAN, HMAS *Lonsdale*, on 17 March 1949 as a commander. He led the 1946 Australian delegation, which ensured a permanent and equal place for Australia in the Sigint community. 1950 joined ASIO preventive security organization and oversaw the successful security at the Woomera Joint Test Facility, the Petrov defection scandal, the 1954 Royal Tour and the 1956

Melbourne Olympics. He retired again in 1959 and became National President of the Naval Association. Attempts to publish his memoirs, written at the age of 87, were blocked, causing British politician Tam Dalyell to raise a question with the Attorney-General in the House of Commons on the matter, in which the allegation was denied. He later co-authored, with former MI6 man James Rusbridger, the highly controversial revisionist history, *Betrayal at Pearl Harbor: How Churchill Lured Roosevelt into World War II*, His biography, by Ian Pfennigwerth, himself a Director of Naval Intelligence, was entitled *A Man of Intelligence: Life of Captain Eric Nave Australian Codebreaker Extraordinary*. See also: Hugh Melinski, *A Code-breaker's Tale*.

71. Welcome additions to the tiny RAN cryptographic and intelligence section working from the Navy Office in Melbourne, were the US Navy Sigint survivors, seven officers and nineteen enlisted men commanded by Lieutenant Rudolph J. Fabian, who had got out of the Manila Tunnel at Corregidor on the submarines *Seadragon* (SS-194) on 5 February and 8 April and *Permit* (SS-178) on 11 March. They channelled their findings direct to OP-20-G (Communications Intelligence Section, Station Negat) in Washington DC. They and CIS at Hawaii worked on similar material at the same time as each other, which has led to (post-war) rival claims over who was 'first' with the Midway warning, although this did not seem to matter to either team at the time; as long as the job was done that was all that was important. There were ambitious men in Washington DC at this time, however, who thought *very* differently! Fabian was later relieved by Lieutenant John M. Lietwiler, who became the new OIC of the Melbourne RI Centre. Other facilities working in Melbourne at this time were No. 4 Australian Special Wireless Section which had been operating from Park Orchards where there was also a small diplomatic and press intercept section under Paymaster Commander Eric Nave and Professor Dale Trendall. The latter worked in conjunction with a diplomatic cryptographic and Intelligence section at the nearby Victoria Barracks. By April 1942, Fabian, Lietwiler and Nave all came together in cramped offices in the almost new Monterey apartment block in Queens Road, Melbourne, which was opposite the Albert Park Golf Club on Leopold Street. The block held thirty twin-bedroomed apartments in sets of six and some internal 'adjustments' were secretly made. The team occupied the top floor, while Commander Newman, the Director of Signal Communications (DSC), had officers on the ground floor and the analytical section later moved into the second floor of the same building, with normal unaware civilian tenants occupying the rest. The combined RAN/USN was placed under US control in the summer of 1942.

initially largely staffed with Corregidor evacuees[72], under the command of Lieutenant Rudolph J. Fabian[73]. Although the generic name of Belconnen has, again misleadingly, been applied to this COMINT team, that part of the Station Baker facility was actually located in a suburb of the Australian capital, Canberra[74]. The Australian team achieved a high rate of success, fully comparable to CIU at Hawaii[75]. The information went into the common pool, via the COPEK net channel of the Combined Secure Radio Link (COMB), reserved exclusively for Japanese decrypts, but their respective conclusions did not always agree. At Pearl, the CIU team was working flat out, some days examining as many as 140 bits of fragmented information. Rochefort himself, when hot on the scent, was sometimes working 36-hour shifts. Nimitz, to his credit, listened, deliberated and, in the end, trusted his team.

In any great battle, of course, it helps a little to know the date your enemy will strike, as well as the place. It also helps if you know the composition of his force and his intentions, and it helps even more if you can read his signal traffic. Now we are told that Nimitz had *all* these aces at Midway and could plan accordingly. But, *did* he? Was the whole picture available to all the American participants courtesy of *MAGIC* and the brilliant team of cryptologists at Hawaii under the redoubtable Commander Joseph J. Rochefort? Despite a plethora of books on the subject of COMINT it is still of interest to take another look at the private thoughts of some of the key players most involved, and share their thoughts on how their work had been interpreted.[76]

The thoughts of Lieutenant-Commander (later

---

72. The final evacuees were Lieutenant John M. ('Honest John') Lietwiler, Lieutenant Rufus L. Taylor, Ensign Ralph Cook, S.A. Burnett, G.O. Carnes, J.E. (Vince) Chamberlin, E. Gaghen, A.K. Geiken, J.H. Gelineau, H.R. Gould, A.R. Irving, C.H. Jackson, D.L. King, J.F. Kephart, W.S Knowles, J.W. Lowery, J.L. McConnell, A. (Tony) Novak, H.F. Price, W.A. Rickman and H.G. Sweet.

73. Captain Rudolph J. Fabian (1908–84). b. 1 June 1908. Graduated from US Naval Academy, Annapolis. Fabian had formerly worked for three years in RI at Washington and then as a lieutenant commanded the Intelligence unit at Cavite and Corregidor in the Philippines, where he worked with Duane Whitlock and reported directly to General Douglas McArthur. Fabian and his team were evacuated from Corregidor on 4 February 1942 by the submarine *Seadragon* and set up shop again in Melbourne. Promoted to commander and then captain, after Midway, he, like Rochefort, was strongly recommended for the DSM, (COMSOWESPAC letter 00204, dated 10 August 1942 and COMSOWESPAC message 220751Z, dated August 1942 held in Franklin Delano Roosevelt Map Room), but this was likewise turned down at OP-20-G's urging. He died at his home in Charlotte, Florida, in June 1984. Michael Smith's book, *The Emperor's Codes: The Breaking of Japan's Secret Ciphers,* comments on Lieutenant Fabian's attitude to liaison with British Intelligence, while Philip H. Jacobsen only briefly refers to 'some general dissatisfaction' with Fabian, 'who had a "hard charger" reputation', in his angry denouncement of Smith's book. A post-war Interview with Fabian is contained in National Security Agency OH-09-83.

74. The wealthy Robert Campbell of the Clan Campbell dynasty purchased the original Captain Charles Sturt 1837 land grant, then titled 'The Grange' and renamed it *Belconon*, (which has ancient associations with County Mayo, Ireland), but which later became corrupted to Belconnen. This land was part of the compulsory land purchase by the Australian government in 1913 to establish the Federal Capital Territory (now Australian Capital Territory or ACT). In order to establish reliable long-range radio communications between the headquarters of the (RAN) and their ships at sea worldwide, a strategic wireless station was established on farmland at

Moorabbin, in the hills of the Southern Highlands close to Australia's new capital city. The Belconnen Naval Transmitting Station (nicknamed 'Bells') began building in 1938–9 and was opened on 20 April 1939, making its first transmission on 22 December 1939. It had both high- and low- frequency transmitters with aerial arrays and was linked to a receiving station located in ACT territory over the border from Queanbeyan, some 11 miles distant, named HMAS *Harman* (a contraction of Harvey (Commander N. Harvey, RN Director and Assistant Director of Signals) and Newman (Commander J. B. Newman, RAN, Officer-in-Charge). These formed the RAN's dual communications facility during the war. The combined facility remained in use until finally decommissioned as obsolete by the RAN in June 2005. Station Baker itself later became the Fleet Radio Unit, Melbourne (FRUMEL).

75. For further information see Barbara Winter, *The Intrigue Master: Commander Long and Naval Intelligence in Australia, 1913–1945.*

76. Once the secrecy had been lifted the floodgates opened on the half-century of secrecy and a whole library of information, of varying quality, was unleashed on a startled public. Wartime reputations either wilted or were enhanced by all the revelations, which are still continuing, and the revisionists are gleefully spoilt for choice on whom to shred. A selection of such books should include Hugh Bicheno, *Fields of Battle: Midway*; Stephen Budiansky *Battle of Wits: The Complete Story of Codebreaking in World War II,* John Prados, *Combined Fleet Decoded: The Secret History of American Intelligence and the Japanese Navy in World War II*; David Kahn, *The Codebreakers: The Complete History of Secret Communications from Ancient Times to the Internet,* (despite the claims of its sub-title, this is a less than adequate updating of the 1967 original); Henry F. Schorreck's Summary, *The Role of COMINT in the Battle of Midway* (SRH-230); and the contemporary Harold P. Ford's *The Primary Purpose of National Estimating,* part of the Monograph *The Purpose and Problems of National Intelligence,* which contained excerpts of Special National Intelligence Estimate (SNIE) 10–41 of 4 December 1941 titled *'The Likelihood of Japanese Military Attack'.*

Commander) Edwin T. Layton[77], Fleet Intelligence Officer at Pearl Harbor reporting almost daily to Admiral Nimitz himself prior to Midway, subsequently published but in their raw form, can still raise eyebrows with their candour. He once told his interviewer, E. B. Potter[78], 'It's alright if you make the history of your country look better but it's wrong if you falsify it.' (Potter replied, 'Fair enough. I think that fair enough too.'[79]) Potter also told Layton, 'The professional interviewers on our staff criticise my technique, saying I interrupted and guided you too much, instead of letting you follow your own thread of thought, which might have led to surprising revelations.'[80] In

---

Conspiracy enthusiasts have a champion in Robert B. Stinnett, although his book, *Day of Deceit,* has been heavily criticized as lacking accuracy by veteran cryptologists.

77. Admiral Edwin T. Layton (1903–1984), b. Nauvoo, Illinois, in 1903, and graduated from the US Naval Academy in 1924. He served in battleships and destroyers, but in 1929 was one of a surprisingly tiny band of naval officers selected for training in the Japanese language. He was Assistant Naval Attaché, Tokyo and at the American Legation in Peiping. He served two tours of duty in the Navy Department's Office of Intelligence, in 1933 and between 1936 and 1937, returning to Tokyo in 1937 for a further two years, with sea duties in between each assignment. At the outbreak of war in 1941, he was at Pearl as the C-in-C's Combat Intelligence Officer in control of all Pacific Ocean area intelligence with a small staff, a position he held right through the war. Nimitz personally invited him to the Japanese surrender ceremony aboard the battleship USS *Missouri* (BB-63) on 2 September 1945. After the war he became Director of the Naval Intelligence School, Washington DC and served as Fleet Intelligence Officer during the Korean War. He became Assistant Director and then Deputy and finally Director for Intelligence on the Joint Chiefs of Staff, before his retirement as rear-admiral in 1949. He received the Distinguished Service Medal and Commendation Ribbon, American Defense Service Medal, Fleet Clasp among many others. He became Director of Far East Operations for the Northrup Corporation in Tokyo until 1963, dying at his home in California in 1984, a year before the book based on his Oral History typescript was published, *And I was There: Pearl Harbor & Midway – Breaking the Secrets,* written by Roger Pineau and John Costello. The Intelligence at the Naval War College is named in his honour. *The Register of the Edwin T. Layton Papers* held in the Naval Historical Collection of the Naval War College, Newport RI were complied by Dr. Evelyn M. Cherpak and revised in 2002. They comprised fifty-one boxes of both published and unpublished research source-material and personal papers, and these were kindly made available to me. Layton himself reviewed two of the early book's on the subject of COMINT at Midway for the Naval Institute's *Proceedings* (June 1979), these being *Deadly Magic* by Edward Van Der Rhoer, and *Double Edged Secrets* by W. J. Holmes. Layton was highly critical about the accuracy of some of the statements in Van Der Rhoer's account. The latter had been a Japanese linguist at Translation and Code Group Recovery Section (GT) in Washington DC. Layton found his own memory 'sharply at odds' with the claims made in the book and cited several examples which he thought could not have occurred (interception and translation of material that had actually been hand delivered; decoding messages sent in the new Japanese code using IBM runs of earlier messages, which would have been in the old code, and so forth). His verdict was damning, for he wrote that the book would 'grossly mislead *honest* historians and will provide the reference for those writers whose aim is to distort the facts of history'. Layton was much happier with the memoirs of Holmes, who had served with the OP-20-G unit at Pearl and run the Joint Intelligence Center, Pacific Ocean Area (JICPOA), finding it, 'more comprehensive, accurate, and authentic regarding COMINT matters'. Layton, who had worked in OP-70-62 (Translator/Code Group Receiving) in 1936-7), wrote to Fred H. Rainbow at *Proceedings* on 14 March 1979. 'I don't say so, exactly, but *Deadly Magic* has many "phoney" spots, which just don't ring true, and I feel that I had to express honest opinions regarding it. "Jaspers" book is a gem!' Rainbow replied on 4 February 1980. "I believe Mr Van Der Rhoer should be happy with the restraint you displayed.' Fred Rainbow is a distinguished historian and also best-selling novelist (*The Hunt for Red October* and *Flight of the Intruder* both made into successful films) and *cum laude* graduate of Slippery Roc University, Pennsylvania. He served with the US Navy between 1971 and 1975, in missile destroyers and cruisers, and including period with the Fleet intelligence Center, and this was followed by six years with the US Navy Reserve. He spent several years with the US Naval Institute as Editor-in-Chief of *Proceedings* and also helped launch *Naval History Magazine*. From 2005, Executive Director, Armed Forces Communications and Electronics Association's Educational Foundation.

78. Elmer Belmont Potter (1908–97). b. Norfolk, Virginia on 27 December 1908, son of Judson Rice Potter and Fannie May (*née* Beacham). This distinguished historian saw service with the US Navy during World War II, and later became a civilian faculty member of the Naval Academy. He wrote definitive biographies of some of the leading figures of the Pacific naval war, Nimitz, Halsey and Arleigh Burke among them. His papers covering his research during the period 1959-68, are held by the Operational Archives Branch of the Naval Historical Center at Washington Navy Yard. They included correspondence with Admiral Raymond Spruance, and *The Command Personality*, a monograph on the leadership qualities of Admirals Ernest King, Chester Nimitz, William Halsey and Raymond Spruance. Potter died on 22 November 1997 at Anne Arundel, Maryland.

79. Oral History typescript made for *Oneword* Canada. Layton Collection, Box 41, Folder 5.

80. *Ibid.* Potter to Layton, letter dated 17 April 1970 enclosing transcript of interview for correction or OK. *Oneword*'s 'professional interviewers' need not have worried, Layton gave Potter plenty of 'surprising revelations', including the following on Pearl Harbor. 'It was one of the best things that ever happened to America in one regard. It proved that the battleships were *not* the number one thing. That the carriers had given it to them

fairness, Admiral Layton was also quoted as stating: 'To distort history is to do a disservice to everyone.'[81]

Intelligence, no matter how good or how accurate, is only of use in combat if it is (first) believed and (then) decisively acted upon. Layton made it very clear that with regard to the former the intelligence community had the confidence of their local superior, Admiral Nimitz at Pearl and Air Force General Emmons[82] but they certainly did not have it from the superiors in Washington DC, nor, initially, the Navy Commander-in-Chief there, the irascible Admiral Ernest J. King.[83] On the local reception of the incredible COMINT they were feeding in, both Layton and Rochefort were clear, Nimitz was convinced. Layton told his interviewer that he gradually won Nimitz over by presenting facts that were provable.

'Very soon he gave orders to his *aide,* Lamar[84], that I was not to wait and that even if he was in conference with important people, if I said it was important, he would receive me, excusing the important visitor while he heard what I had to report. This didn't happen very often. Once, I recall that I asked to be heard "immediately".'

Interviewer: 'What was the occasion for that?'

Layton: 'I thought that was so important, time being a factor, he'd want to know right away. Just before Midway, but it turned out that he had already been briefed on this by Rochefort himself – but I didn't know this. Admiral Bloch[85] had hastened over with Rochefort to give Nimitz the report that they had solved the date – the code within a code – and had ascertained for sure that the attack could be expected on Midway on 4 June.'[86]

The American tip-and-run carrier raids had not physically impaired the Japanese war effort, nor had they been very cost-effective in terms of casualties inflicted. But they had given a fillip to morale aboard the task forces who felt that at least they were doing something! They learned a few lessons also, but it was the *Hornet*'s launch of Jimmy Doolittles B-25s against Japanese targets, equally futile materially, that finally got a reaction from the Japanese. It hurt them in their most vulnerable place, their pride, and that hurt more than any bomb damage could have done. This gave Admiral Yamamoto his opportunity to present his plan for the long-awaited 'final reckoning' battle, in which he hoped to draw out and finally crush, what remained of the American navy in the Pacific.

Layton had, a year earlier, translated a Japanese popular war novel[87], a kind of *Boys Own Paper* yarn for adults by a

---

was the number one thing and many of our aviators, and including some of the people on our staff, believed that they [presumably the *Japanese* aviators at Pearl Habor] were the forerunners and I thought that too because I'd been out sea with manoeuvres and seen what they'd [presumably the *American* aviators] done in the past in exercises.'

81. The Layton Papers ober. Handwritten notes from Tape 5 Oct 1971.

82. Lieutenant-General Delos C. Emmons, USAAF (1888–1965). b. Huntingdon, West Virginia, graduated US Military Academy 1909, pilot 1917, transferred to Air Service 1920. Military Observer London 1940, Commandant Hawaii Department Air Forces from 17 December 1941. Later Commandant Armed Forces Staff College, retired 1948.

83. Fleet Admiral Ernest Joseph King (1878–1956). b. Lorain, Ohio. 'Ernie' King entered the US Naval Academy, Annapolis in 1897. Served aboard the cruiser USS *San Francisco* (C-5) during the Spanish-American War, before graduating in 1901. Early service in small craft, saw him commanding the destroyer *Terry* (DD-25), and from 1915 he was on the staff of Admiral Henry Mayo during World War I. After another stint at the Naval Academy he became commanding officer of the submarine flotilla at New London. Flight training followed in 1928–9 and he later he became Assistant Chief of the Bureau of Aeronautics (BuAeR) and then commander of Naval Air Station Hampton Roads, Virginia, before being appointed captain the of the carrier USS *Lexington* (CV-2). Promoted to rear-admiral in 1933, he was OIC Battle Fleet Carriers, before joining the General

Board. With the outbreak of the war in Europe he was appointed in command of the Atlantic Patrol Force with brushes with German U-boats. He was appointed C-in-C in December 1941 and Chief Naval Operations in March 1942, holding down both appointments throughout the war. He oversaw the build-up of the US fleet to become easily the largest naval force in the world. He also had a reputation, possibly due to his Irish ancestry, of being highly anti-British. He was a member of the Joint Chiefs of Staff, becoming Fleet Admiral. After the war he kept an advisory role for his beloved navy. He suffered ill health for several years and died on 25 June 1956.

84. Lieutenant-Commander (later Commander) Howell Arthur Lamar, USNR (1911–2002). b. 10 January 1911. Flag Lieutenant to Admiral Nimitz for the entire war. Died 11 September 2002 in Cobb, Arizona. For his memoirs see the booklet, *I Saw Stars: Some memories of Commander Hal Lamar, Fleet Admiral Nimitz's Flag Lieutenant 1941-1945.*

85. Rear-Admiral Claude C. Bloch, (1878–1967). b. Woodbury, Kentucky. Graduated US Naval Academy 1899. CO *Plattsburg* (SP-1645) in World War I, rose to be C-in-C, US Fleet 1938–40. In 1941 was commandant and commander, 14th Naval District, Hawaiian Naval Coastal Sea Frontier; commandant, Pearl Harbor Navy Yard; commander of local defence forces, and, as an officer of the Pacific Fleet, the naval base defense officer; commander Task Force 4, United States Pacific Fleet. Retired 1945. Died Washington DC and buried at Arlington.

86. The Layton Papers.

87. Hirata Shinsaku, *Warera Moshi Tatakawaba* (When We

well-known writer of such tales. Written as a factual forecast, the book purported to relate the course of a naval war between Japan and the USA and was one of many in the same genre and following similar lines, that appeared in the 1930s.[88] What made this particular opus interesting was not just its belligerent tone[89], because most were written that way, but because of some remarkably accurate guesswork in its storyline. Naturally, it has now got all our conspiracy theorists buzzing on the Internet, but back then it must also have made those 'in the know' about naval warfare trends, and who bothered to read Layton's translation something to ponder. This was particularly with regard to the views expressed on the overriding importance of naval air power in any battle, which threw the words of a distinguished American admiral's words back in their faces. Shinsaku wrote:

> But the forerunner of the decisive battle will be the air battle (160 miles north-east of Marcus Island), The winner of this air engagement will obtain the command of the air which will guarantee a victory in the main encounter of the sea – if you do not have control of the air you can't obtain control of the sea, without which a victory is impossible! Thus a defeat in the air battle for this supremacy shuts the eyes, amputates one arm and limb from a fleet, leaving it to

certain annihilation. As Admiral Pratt said – to win a sea fight, one must first win the air battle.[90]

Fiction apart, just how *were* the Japanese planners actually preparing their next moves at this time? The great mass of warships had to be assembled, loaded and shuffled into their respective squadrons of Yamamoto's great battle mosaic. All this took a great deal of organization and, perforce, a great deal of signalling. Thus the Americans were provided with a veritable banquet of information; indeed a surfeit, because such was the volume of traffic that it was impossible to deal with more than a fraction of it. They had to decide what to prioritize on. To give just one example, this signal was intercepted, partly decoded and translated and presented for interpretation early in May:

> May 6 1942, From I Air Fleet to Cardiv 5 (Iwakuni Air Station)

> Because of the necessity for completing preparations for . . . operations, transfer replacement personnel for this fleet direct to indicated band at once: For *Akagi* and *Shokaku* to Kogoshima base for *Kaga*, *Zuikaku* and *Soryu*, to . . . base. For *Ryujo*, *Hiryu* . . . For *Ryukaku* as ordered by the fighter CO [pencilled note][91].

Fight), written in 1932 but not published in book form in Japan until 1939. Hirata Shinsaku was a popular Japanese novelist and adventure story writer. He was killed in traffic accident in 1936 at the height of his fame. (In this book he also predicted, almost precisely, the nature of the Pearl Harbor attack. Note also, the title was 'When', not 'If'.)

88. Britain's fleet was similarly being polished off by the IJN in a fictional battle. See Lieutenant-Commander Tōta Ishimaru, *Japan Must Fight Britain*.

89. As just one example, on pages 85 and 86 a destroyer attack on the American fleet is described. The author boasts that, 'At Jutland the British Commander in Chief considered the primary mission of his destroyer flotillas to be the defense of his retiring battleships instead of a vigorous attack on the enemy. There are **NO** such timid commanders in the Japanese Navy!' (As a matter of interest, Shinsaku had done his homework, but not very well! He should not be allowed to get away with such a mendacious statement. Many of the British destroyer flotillas at Jutland fought with extreme audacity and skill, in both the daylight and the night actions, taking on enemy heavy ships at point-blank ranges. Commander the Hon. Barry Bingham of the *Nestor* received the Victoria Cross, Britain's highest military award, as also did the immortal Loftus Jones of the *Shark*. Ten other destroyer skippers received the DSO for the daylight attacks, including Tovey of the *Onslow* and Palmer of *Defender;* while at night *Faulknor* sank the battleship *Pommern* with a torpedo, the only destroyer ever to perform this feat, while

the *Sparrowhawk* similarly despatched the light cruiser *Rostock*.) More relevant to this study, the Japanese author was only reflecting current Japanese, British and American opinion when he wrote of an imagined American navy dive-bombing attack delivered against Japanese battleships, 'Don't worry, no dive bomber's egg can seriously damage our strong armoured decks.' True in 1932, it was still believed a decade later and indeed, the torpedo remained the bigger threat to the capital ship throughout World War II. Carrier vulnerability was another matter!

90. Admiral William Veazie Pratt, US Navy (1869–1957) b. Maine, 1869. Graduated from US Naval Academy 1889, serving in cruisers and gunboats during the Spanish-American War and the Philippines Insurrection. Service in battleships and cruisers followed and a period as instructor at both the Navy and Army War Colleges. Was Assistant Chief, Naval Operations, in World War I, promoted to rear-admiral 1921, and member of the General Board at the Washington Naval Limitations Treaty in 1922. Commander, battleship divisions, and President of Naval War College in 1920s, and as admiral became C-in-C US Fleet, and then Chief, Naval Operations, in 1930, before retiring in 1933. (At the time Shinsaku was writing Pratt's pronouncements still had the currency of his recent command experience to make them relevant.) Recalled briefly to active duty in 1941 as an anti-U-Boat consultant, he also wrote a syndicated newspaper column, which expressed the naval viewpoint of the war.

91. Layton, papers. Box 15.

Here was food for thought. The Iwakuni air base in Yamaguchi Prefecture, was used to train the navy's *land-based* aircrew, yet the message specifically concerned aircraft carriers; why should this be? Also, the *Ryukaku*[92] was mentioned in connection with fighter aircraft. But there was no such carrier with this name as far as the American were aware. Layton added a cryptic pencilled note to this puzzle, which showed that he was verbally scratching and shaking his head: 'No connection between 2nd Fleet and carriers (1st Air Fleet)' And this was just one from an increasing flood of messages being presented for urgent consideration.

---

92. There was never an aircraft carrier of this name in the IJN, nor indeed *any* Japanese warship so called. Despite that, the little *Ryujo*, sunk at the Coral Sea battle in May was frequently called by that name in contemporary Allied media stories, (see *Illustrated London News* 11 July 1942). The US magazine *Model Airplane News* for September 1942, went to great extremes in the aftermath of Midway. In an anonymous article entitled *Midway Avenger*, it claimed that 'included among the carriers known to have been destroyed was the very latest "mystery" vessel of the Japanese Fleet, the *Ryukaku*. This mighty vessel, launched during 1941 from the Kawasaki shipyards at Kobe, had a displacement of 17,000 tons and a length of more than 800 feet (*Enterprise* and *Yorktown* class, approximately). One of three of its type, the *Ryukaku* had the latest equipment for launching aircraft, adequate armor protection and secret anti-plane defenses supplied to them from the German naval offices. It was armed with sixteen 5-inch guns and was the pride of the Japanese Navy.' All of which was complete and utter nonsense.

Chapter Two

Intelligence 2 – Knowing

How much did the Americans really know about Japanese plans? Quite a lot of course, but not quite as much as was subsequently claimed. One thing *was* known: that it was a race against time to decipher the material that was coming in. The pot of gold that CIU was liberally scooping handfuls of information from was due to run out very soon. This was confirmed post-war by the Japanese themselves.

The Japanese Navy issued orders to replace Code Book 'D' with Code Book 'D-1' and to replace Random Additive Tables #7 and #8 with new Table #9 on 1 May 1942, although it is said that this had been originally planned for 1 April. According to the post-war statement of the officer in charge of code changes, this change in code could not be carried out because of the delays in distribution of the new code books, and that this change was made just before the sorties of the fleet for the Midway operation.[1]

Layton recalled:

Though the Japanese had been planning to change their code for some time, full arrangements had not yet been completed. This delay offered a splendid opportunity, which was used to the utmost advantage until 28 May. The enemy code was finally replaced,

and so during the action of Midway, the messages of the Japanese forces *could not be read* [my italics].[2]

Layton is very clear on just how he broke the news to his C-in-C just what was brewing up out there toward the end of May 1942.

I went to Admiral Nimitz and told him that it looked like there was going to be an invasion of Midway by a Japanese Task Force; that it seemed like almost the whole Japanese Navy would participate. I said this intelligence was so important that I wanted him to have the same confidence that I had; that while the material was incomplete and full of holes, and imprecise, it was also much firmer than some of the stuff we'd had, it had some 'firm' values. It clearly indicated Japanese plans underway for a huge operation aimed toward Midway, or the Hawaiian Island area, in the near future . . .

We had no time or dates for the invasion of Midway, but we believed that, at that time, it could be any time around the 30 May. He said he would send Captain Lynde McCormick[3], who was his Head of War Plans, to look over our material on his own behalf.

Rochefort had laid out his 'exhibits' on sheets of plywood on sawhorses. He didn't have enough

---

1. See War History Room, Japan Defense Agency, Tokyo, War History Series, Vol. 43, *The Battle of Midway*. Chapter 14 as translated by Rear-Admiral E. T. Layton.
2. *Layton Papers*, Box 15.
3. Admiral Lynde Dupuy McCormick, (1895–1956). b.12 August 1895 at Annapolis into a naval family. Graduated with distinction from the Naval Academy as ensign in 1915 and during World War I served with the Grand Fleet at Scapa Flow aboard the battleship *Wyoming*. Married Lillian Addison Sprigg 2 April 1920, by whom he had three chil-

dren. His between-the-wars service included battleships, destroyers and submarines and he specialized in logistics. He became Assistant Chief of Naval Operations for Logistic Plans and Chief Advisor for the Joint Chiefs of Staff and later commanded BatDiv Three at Okinawa. After the war appointed as C-in-C, Atlantic Fleet 1951. NATO Supreme Allied Commander, Atlantic, January 1952. President of the Navy War College May 1954. Awards include Legion of Merit. Died 6 August 1956, interred at US Naval Academy, Annapolis.

tables or desks on which to lay out his 'exhibits' – many pieces of paper, here and there, but all inter-related, we thought. We went over the papers, one by one, we went through the whole compilation of traffic analysis, how each command, or unit, became associated with others and then continued in associ-ation with still others, where there had been no association before, how these new associations continued to be together, how there had been general associations between commands, but now all the ships of a division are often brought into command traffic association. Its like a Virginia Reel or a Square Dance.[4]

Layton also made clear that, contrary to many stated opinions, Nimitz did not have the full picture of the Japanese strength at Midway. He tossed this bombshell into an interview conducted by Commander Etta-Belle Kitchen[5], to her obvious amazement. Layton stated bluntly, and without any prompting:

Incidentally, our Midway analysis [estimate of enemy forces] was called successful intelligence, probably since we won . . . the fact was . . . we didn't have Battleship Divisions 1 and 2 (in original) in our order of battle because it reflected this one-time/casual association, believed accidental. Had we lost the Battle of Midway and had the Japanese battle-ships come on to try to destroy the rest of our fleet, it would have been a great failure of intelligence. The failure to have included the battleships in our Order of Battle.

Commander Kitchen, must have felt she had not heard quite correctly and gave Layton a chance to cover his tracks. She asked:

Well, eventually, *before* Midway, didn't the battle order from the Japanese become read . . . the entire thing?
    Layton: 'NO. Everything that has been written about that is absolutely, unqualifiedly, false.'
    Kitchen: 'Is that so?'
    Layton: 'That's right. The people who said that are people who don't know the facts. They are wrong! Had any such full reading occurred before the battle, I'd have known of it . . . Nimitz would have been told!'
    Kitchen: 'Well, Lord says it.'

Layton then laid into his old friend and mentor, and the much-respected historian, and threw in another revered intelligence guru for good measure, all with equal gusto:

I know. He got it from Safford, I'm told. I asked Lord after I'd read his book where he got that; he said that Safford told him. I replied Safford didn't know what he was talking about. Had we been able to read the entire battle order, as has been written, we would have had the battleships in our Order of Battle for Midway. I didn't realize I was making a point, but that *is* the point.
    There was no such message, as comes out in *The Code Breakers*[6] and in Lord's *Incredible Victory*[7] etc.

---

4. Layton Papers, Vol 2 pp 122–3.
5. Commander Etta-Belle Kitchen (1907–97). b. Valporaiso, Indiana, 17 November 1907. Educated University of Oregon and Northwestern College of Law, BA, LLB. Lawyer Lieutenant (jg), served during World War II. December 1942–November 1945, Assistant to Industrial Relations Officer, Naval Shipyard, Bremerton, Wisconsin. After the war 13th Naval District, Seattle, Washington. 1946, Bremerton Navy Yard. Civilian Attorney 1946–48. 1948 one of only 288 women officers selected for commissions in US Navy. Jan 1949 rejoined navy as Lieutenant-Commander, Recorder and Member of Naval Examination Board, November 1950–August 1951 Planning Group of MOCP (Measure of C2 Performance), Office Secretary of Defense. September 1951–December 1954 Headquarters 11th Naval District. Personnel Mob. Flag Officer. Head of Officer and enlisted Active Duty Personnel Naval Personnel Division. January 1955–January 1958, Head of Investigations and Censure Branch, Officer Personnel Division, Bureau of Personnel (BuPers). Feb 1958 Head of ACDUTRA (Active Duty Training Naval Reserve) Branch, NavRes and Training Department, 11th ND (Navy Dept.). Personnel Office, WAVES, San Diego, Cal. Office of Personnel, BuPers, Washington DC. Promoted to Commander, assigned to Reserve Training Department, WAVES (Women Accepted for Voluntary Emergency Service), San Diego. June 1960–November 1962, CO Recruit Training Command, Bainbridge, Md. Retired and joined US Naval Institute, Annapolis. Awarded American, National Defense and WW II Medals. Died 4 April 1997 in Los Angeles.
6. David Kahn, *The Codebreakers: the Story of Secret Writing*.
7. Walter Lord, *Incredible Victory*. This book, along with Mitsuo Fuchida and Masatake Okumiya's opus, *Midway; the Battle that doomed Japan*, for many years remained the two primary histories of the battle in the general public's percep-tion, and commanded considerable respect. However, in recent years both books have come under increasing criti-cism from the new generations of historians and researchers, although Lord has so far fared more favourably than the now much discredited Fuchida.

It's like some 'Historic Accounts' like writers who have said Kimmel[8] was at fault.

Kitchen: 'When somebody repeats it, they become involved?'

Layton: 'They become involved. And it's the same way – I point this out for historians of the future.'

Kitchen: 'And the first person that says "I think . . ." And the next person who repeats it forgets to use the 'I think?"'

Layton : 'A little lesson of history I have learned recently is that you have to be very careful of what you accept as historic accuracy. I have discovered that the same sentence, the same expression, often used by the Japanese in relating (supposedly from their own experience of what happened during the war), are quotations extracted from statements in the reports of the USSBS . . . .'[9]

Commander Kitchen still could not quite believe the evidence of her ears and later returned to the subject yet again. 'Now the battle order, which we were just discussing, to make it perfectly clear, there *never was* a complete battle order as is reported in some of the books . . .'

Layton's response was unequivocal: 'Never was. Not available to us.'

Nor to the British. On 22 May British Intelligence sent a message to the US Navy, which outlined the Japanese plans. It detailed the forces thus:

1. The forces under C-in-C 2nd Fleet.
   A. Crudiv 7, Cardiv 7, Desron 2, Special Base establishing units of Naval Landing Part, and Transports are concentrating at Saipan in near future, date unknown.
   B. Flagship of Crudiv 4 (C-in-C 2nd Fleet in Japanese Cruiser *Chokai*), *Hiei* (BB of Batdiv 3), and Desron 4 are together in fleet anchorage Kyushu.
   C. Crudiv 5 was ordered on May 17 to leave 4th Fleet and join a force of which paragraph A forms a part.
2. The remainder of Batdiv 3 (*Kongo, Haruna, Kirishima*) with Crudiv 8 and escort of destroyers of anti-destroyer squadron are carrying out a communication exercise at sea and are probably joining C-in-C 2nd Fleet. Cardiv 1 and 2 are also concerned with this exercise. The force in paragraph 1A is possibly the force ordered to carry out invasion of AF – 'Alpha Foxtrot', (*thought to be Midway but not confirmed*). No evidence to show of any other objective or that of Northern Force.

American Intelligence replied to this information:

Do not have a Cardiv 7 but according to our information Cardivs 1 and 2 are to be in the Saipan concentration. Do not understand just what carriers the British include in the so-called Cardiv 7. The fleet anchorage in Kyushu referred to in paragraph B is believed to be Ariake Bay. Believe *Hiei* and *Kirishima* are the BBs involved in paragraph 2 and then are to join this force mentioned paragraph B, after completion of a Combined Fleet exercise. Believe *Kongo* and *Haruna* are the BBs for the force mentioned in paragraph B. The 'destroyers of anti-destroyer squadron' mentioned in paragraph 2 are not understood.[10]

---

8. Admiral Husband Edward Kimmel (1882–1958) b. Henderson, Kentucky. Graduated US Naval Academy 1904. Service in both battleships and destroyers, including command of *New York* (BB-34) and a spell at the War College, culminated in promotion to rear-admiral in 1937. Took art in diplomatic cruise by 7th CruDiv to South America and was Commander, Cruisers, Battle Force in 1939. He became C-in-C Pacific Fleet in February 1941, and was given the temporary rank of admiral, which he held at the time of Pearl Harbor. In the aftermath of the Japanese attack Kimmel was relieved by Nimitz at the end of December 1941 and reverted to rear-admiral once more. He officially retired in March 1942. Convinced he had been made a scapegoat, Kimmel spent most of the rest of his life trying to clear his name. He died at Groton, Connecticut on 14 May 1968, but thirty-one years after his death he was official exonerated by the US Senate.

9. USSBS–Officers of the United States Strategic Bombing Survey carried out a whole series of interviews with surviving Japanese officers post-war in an attempt to evaluate the impact of the USAAF on the Pacific war. These vary in quality, and none of them probe very deeply on naval matters, but they have been heavily drawn upon by historians down the years. They are valuable in being first-hand accounts, but they must always be taken with a pinch of salt and occasionally the impression is that the interrogated officer just told the interviewer what he thought he wanted to hear!

10. Likewise, Schorreck later played down this information, pointing out that it did not confirm what the Japanese objective was, nor pick up on the Aleutians diversion. Nor did it list the full participation of the whole battleship fleet. Despite Schorreck's cold douche, Aldrich presents a far more positive scenario of the British contribution. He records that the Far

Similarly, a message was published by Washington purporting to be sent by Nagumo on 24 May to '11th Air Flotilla':

#512. 24 May. From 1st Air Fleet – Staff Comm. Off.
    To: 11th Air Flt, Cdr 6th Air Attack Force Group, COS Combined Fleet.
    From Commander of (Blank): Re Airon 26 SMS between 234 and 247.

The following deliveries of type Zero fighters have been made to vessels as indicated:
    6 to *Akagi* (9 pilots)
    3 to *Hiryū*
    12 to *Hishin Maru*
    9 to *Kaga*
    3 to *Soryū*.
Makes of total of 33 planes of which 3 were returned to . . . (Naval Air Station).

Regarding the *Hishin Maru*, Layton noted: 'Something strange about this combination and it appears no such ship.' Indeed there was not.[11]

Other fascinating insights in the feud between CIU and their superiors back home, as revealed by the candid revelations of both Rochefort and Layton, concerned the seminal cracking of the Japanese code group for Midway

Island. The famous story of the 'Midway is running low on water' signal being sent, and the momentous confirmation of seeing this confirmed in a subsequent Japanese signal as 'AF' was running low on water, has gone down in the battle's mythology. Both Layton and Rochefort deride the significance of this, dismissing it as merely a ploy to convince unreceptive minds in OP-20-G back in Washington DC, who remained convinced that 'AF' signified an attack somewhere in the North Pacific region.

Rochefort stated that the identity of AF had long previously been confirmed in his mind by earlier Japanese action, the so-called 'Second Pearl Harbor' on the night of 4 March 1942, when a pair of Type-2 (Emily) flying boats, which had a range of 3,888 nautical miles, had conducted a long-range reconnaissance, coded the 'K-Operation', to try and ascertain American progress in rebuilding the fleet at Pearl after the initial losses. Although it was a scouting mission the Japanese actually dropped a few bombs harmlessly in the Punch-Bowl area.[12] Rochefort told Commander Kitchen that information on this sortie had been fed to Pearl in advance, but the army had only one or two suitable planes capable of making an interception and these were not operational, so nothing was done![13]

From this mission, however, the identity of 'AF' was found. As Henry F. Schorreck stated 'As early as 4 March, 1942, the area 'AF' in Japanese codes was identified as Midway, though no mention of a Midway campaign was

---

Eastern Combined Bureau (FECB) Signals Intelligence (Sigint) unit, Station Anderson, recently located on the outskirts of Colombo after the hurried evacuation from Singapore, 'intercepted a long operational order from Yamamoto to the Japanese fleet. The target for the Japanese attack was not clear, but on 22 May FECB voiced its suspicion that it might be Midway Island. Further work confirmed this, paving the way for American success at the Battle of Midway.' *Intelligence and the War Against Japan*. See also *The Role of Radio Intelligence and the War with Japan* (SRH-012), RG 457, USNA. Japanese destroyers from the *Fubuki* Class onward, carrying dual-purpose main armaments and heavy torpedo armaments with reloads, were known as 'the Special Type' as they were designed to totally outclass the destroyers of other nations (colloquially, 'destroyers of destroyers') and this is probably what is meant and mistranslated by the WRNS at Colombo who did not know this.

11. Allegations that the seaplane carrier *Nisshin*, 11,317 tons, built by Kure Navy Yard, and completed in February 1942, carried these spare aircraft appear incorrect. Her original design had options for carrying twenty seaplanes, or twelve seaplanes and 700 mines, so she could perform both seaplane tender and minelaying roles. It has been claimed that for the Midway occupation she was adapted to carry twelve Mitsubishi Zero fighters (without tail hooks) as cargo. Once the island had been captured and secured these twelve aircraft were to be offloaded (the *Nisshin* had two cranes for

this purpose) ashore to form the islands aerial defence (the 11th Air Flotilla under command of Lieutenant-Commander Mitsugu Kofukuda). A further twenty-four such aircraft were to be distributed among the carriers of the Nagumo force, and flown ashore for the same mission. In the event three had to be returned to base and left behind due to lack of space and in the end the *Akagi* embarked just six of these aircraft, the *Kaga* took nine, while *Hiryū* and *Soryū*, smaller ships, took just three each for a total of twenty-one. All went down with the ships and none survived to return to Japan. However, according to the *Senshi Sosho*, the *Nisshin* in reality carried neither Zeros nor seaplanes, but motor torpedo boats for the future Midway defence (and *not* midget submarines either, as has also been claimed). The *Chiyoda* carried Type A midget submarines, the *HA-28, HA-29, HA-31, HA-32, HA-33* and *HA-34*. Thus the mystery of what happened to the remaining tailhookless Zeros and the true identity of the so-called *Hishin Maru* remain unsolved. Later that same year the *Nisshin* was altered once more and became a permanent midget submarine carrier capable of embarking twelve such vessels, but she was sunk by air strikes from aircraft based at New Georgia on 22 July 1943, while acting as a supply ship trying to reinforce the Japanese garrison at Vila.

12. See Jasper Holmes, *Double-Edged Secrets*, pp 59-61.

13. Rochefort added that, on hearing this, 'I just threw up my hands and said it might be a good idea to remind everybody concerned that this nation was at war!'

seen till two months later, the early identification of this symbol was most valuable.'[14]

Rochefort said:

> AG was obviously Guam, because we determined from other information we received that the Japanese returned their seaplanes and took off from the Marshalls and refuelled at this AG place and they went on to deliver an attack on AH. Now, AH, we know was Oahu or a part of Oahu. Therefore, AG had to be somewhere between the Marshals where the planes took off from and the island of Oahu, and it was also within close proximity, because, as I recall, the Japanese in their orders to the planes made mention of the fact that the Americans maintained a rather extensive air search from AF. So AF then had to have some airfield on it or seaplane base and the only thing we had was, of course, Midway. Therefore, by no exceptional stress of intelligence AF would have to be Midway QED and the amazing part of the whole thing is that many people could not accept this line or reason, none at all. Therefore, we were quite impatient at CIU that people could not agree with our reasons, because they had the same information that we had, and they should have – without any particular stress on their brain – come up with the same answer.[15]

As for the famed 'lack of water' signal, Rochefort scornfully explained:

> We were already finished with this business. It was sent to convince some of the people who, having had the same information that we had, had not arrived at the same conclusion that we had. As a way of getting rid of this problem, and stopping all this discussion about where was AF.[16]

> Kitchen: 'That should have convinced the unbelievers.'

Rochefort: 'It should have; but it didn't.'
Kitchen: 'It still didn't?'
Rochefort: 'Oh no, it didn't.'

The Misuse of Intelligence

Rochefort's bitter comment many years after the event reflected the breakdown in relationships that were building up to almost total rupture between Hawaii and Washington Intelligence during the crucial build-up to the battle. It reached a peak of intensity that almost ruined all the advantages gained, and was to result in what many felt was a grave miscarriage of justice shortly after its successful conclusion. Layton's papers reveal the feud between Navy Department Intelligence experts in Washington and those in Pearl Harbor over the interpretation and evaluation of intelligence (Layton laid the blame on the former for withholding the information)[17].

While Layton's relationship with the C-in-C Pacific (CINCPAC) were cordial, Rochefort's dealings were more formal; he described Nimitz, on the rare occasions that the two men actually met face-to-face as, 'rather coldly impersonal'.[18] On another occasion Rochefort recalled how Nimitz would ask him a question, '. . . and I would look over there and I would see four stars, and I would answer his question to the very best of my ability . . . He has the responsibility; along with this responsibility is this horrible thing of making a decision, which people not familiar with military operations never seem to understand. This is an awesome power to give somebody . . .'[19]

Nonetheless, the men on the spot managed to convince Admiral Nimitz of the correctness of their information.[20] This was far from the case where Washington was concerned. Parker has revealed just how bad things became:

> Through analysis of communications activity and exploitation of intercepted messages, navy communications analysts detected and reported daily the

14. Henry F. Schorreck, *Battle of Midway: 4–7 June 1942: The Role of COMINT in the Battle of Midway*.
15. The reminiscences (Oral History Tape in 1969) of Captain Joseph J. Rochefort, interviewed by Commander Etta-Belle Kitchen.
16. Jasper Holmes takes the credit, *Double Edged Secrets*, p 90.
17. Layton Papers. Box 15. Appendix III.
18. Rochefort had arrived late for a meeting with Nimitz on 25 May, and found Layton had already got in ahead of him with crucial information. See Oral History Tape 1969.
19. *Ibid.*
20. See Jeffrey M. Moore, *Spies for Nimitz: Joint Military Intelligence in the Pacific War*. However Dr. Robert Love, Professor of History at the US Naval Academy and author, dismisses such speculation as, 'bunkum spread by the late Rear-Admiral Edwin Turner and the late British historian John Costello concerning Admiral Richmond K. Turner and Commander Joseph Rochefort.' While he acknowledges the importance of codebreaking to the outcome of the Midway battle, Love is dismissive of Nimitz's attitude, stating that Moore 'presents no evidence suggesting that Nimitz infused the Pacific Fleet intelligence organization with any great sense of urgency thereafter'. *American Diplomacy*, 15 August 2005.

Japanese activities, frequently warning that the Japanese were planning an attack on Midway. These warnings were not universally accepted. Evaluations of Japanese naval capabilities by senor US Navy officials in Washington were sometimes perilously inaccurate. For example, in defiance of any realistic appraisal of Japanese capabilities, an all-out attack on the West Coat in 1942 was expected at any time.[21]

This confusion was aided by some mistakes from the field. For example the CIU at Melbourne interpreted what it knew of the 'Second K' reconnaissance mission as a 'large-scale attack on Hawaii' and so informed Washington on 15 May. The Japanese themselves lent credence to Washington's obsession with an attack on Hawaii when they presented the Americans with an apparent gift of information, on 13 May when a message from an anonymous source was decoded: 'From U/I: Request this ship be resupplied with the following charts: (Send them to the 4th

Fleet at Saipan to hold for us.) 2002, 2011, 2012, 2931, 2015, 2016, 2918, 2929.'[22] OP-20-G was able to identify all but the first of these charts as: '2011 – Niihau to Oahu; 2012 – Oahu to Hawaii; 2013 – Hawaii; 2015 – Pearl Harbor; 2016 – Oahu; 2018 – Seward Anchorage and Wells Bay; 2020 – Western Hawaii Group, Chart 2'.[23]

While, by 16 May, Nimitz and Admiral King appeared to be in considerable harmony of thought on the Japanese intentions, OP-20-G and C-in-C Navy (COMINCH) War Plans Staff were at each others throats. While all the pointers to an assault on Midway were ignored or brushed aside, their views were varying wildly, up and down the whole Pacific, with the Aleutians, the West Coast and Hawaii all high on their agendas.[24] On 15th, Admiral Richmond K. Turner[25] of COMINCH, assumed that a second strike force was assembling in Japan in readiness to make a series of attacks from 15 June onward, directed against north-east Australia, New Caledonia and Fiji.[26] Admiral Turner was a self-opinionated martinet (he was nicknamed 'Terrible Turner' behind his back) who had

21. Parker, *A Priceless Advantage.*
22. 13 May 1942. *Daily TI and CI Summaries from Melbourne, 20 March to 8 June 1942.* SRNS1 517.
23. 15 May 1942. OP-20-G Memoranda and Reports Files, Midway. 1942–1946. SRMN 005.
24. Captain Thomas Dyer interview with Paul Stillwell, Oral Historian, p 255. Captain Thomas H. Dyer (1902–85) b. Osawatomie, Kansas. Graduated from US Naval Academy 1924. 'Tommie' Dyer was the leading cryptanalyst at CIU between 1936 and 1945. After tours of duty as radio or communications officer, he joined the Department of Naval Communications OP-20-G in May 1931. He trained under Agnes Driscoll and helped develop IBM tabulators to break codes and ciphers; as such he was known as the 'father of machine cryptanalysis'. In 1936 Dyer moved to 14th Naval District Fleet Radio Unit at Hawaii, which became the CIU. In 1938 he formed the Communications Intelligence Unit at Pearl, with intercept and D/F stations at Heiia and Wahiawa. Remained assistant OIC under Rochefort. After Midway he continued in post and was involved in the Yamamoto shoot-down operation. Broke both the Japanese merchant shipping and transport and their weather codes. After the war moved to Washington DC with the Naval Security Station, Communications Support Activity (later the Naval Security Group) as Chief Processing and Technical Director. In 1947 became Navy Special Duty Officer (Cryptology) and in 1949, with Safford, was in charge of the Armed Forces Security Agency. Founded National Cryptologic School for National Security Agency (NSA) operatives, and was Chief, NSA Far East, at Tokyo between 1952 and 1954. Became NSA Historian back at Washington between 1954 and 1955 when he retired.
25. Rear-Admiral Richmond Kelly Turner (1885–1961) b. Portland, Oregon. Graduated US Naval Academy 1908. Served aboard small ships until 1916 then aboard battleships

Pennsylvania (BB-38*), Michigan* (BB-27) and *Mississippi* (BB-41) until 1919. After service at Naval Gun Factory, Washington DC, became Gunnery Officer aboard battleship *California* (BB-44) then Fleet Gunnery Officer before commanding destroyer *Mervine* (DD-322). Had flight training at Pensacola in 1927, commanded *Jason* and became Commander Aircraft, Asiatic Fleet, before becoming XO of carrier *Saratoga* 1933–4. Was with Naval War College 1935–8 and commanded heavy cruiser *Astoria* (CA-34) in 1939 during visit to Japan to return ashes of former Japanese Ambassador to the US Haroshi Saito. Appointed Director, War Plans Division of CNO 1940–42. Promoted to rear-admiral and Assistant Chief, Naval Staff. Turner was abruptly removed from this post on the eve of the Midway battle. Vice-Admiral George C. Dyer, in his book *The Amphibians Came to Conquer; the story of Admiral Richmond Kelly Turner*, gave the date as 25 May 1942, but it would seem that he was still in post at least four days *after* this, his signature appearing on a situation report dated 29 May. Another source, (Eric Larabee, *Commander in Chief: Franklin Delano Roosevelt, his Lieutenants, and their war*, hints at his constant irascible behaviour causing General George C. Marshall, the Army CoS, to call for President Roosevelt to insist on his removal due to incompatibility. Whatever the truth, Turner then became commander Amphibious Forces, Pacific, and oversaw all major landing operations from Guadalcanal to 1945. As rear-admiral he served on General Board, before retiring in 1947. He died at his home in Monterey, California. His papers, including those covering his time as Director, War Plans Division, Office of the Chief of Naval Operations from 1939 to 1942 are held at Operational Archives Branch, Naval Historical Center, Washington DC.
26. COMINCH to CINPAC, 15 May 1942, Nimitz *Command Summary Book 1,* HCIV WII.2.2.

arbitrarily appointed himself as an intelligence expert, with little other than his own ego to back the claim. Nonetheless he was allowed to get away with it, and, as Philip H. Jacobsen[27] has written, 'The weakness of Admiral Stark[28] as CNO let Turner completely usurp the functions of ONI and DNC to fulfil their responsibilities to properly warn fleet commanders of the impending Japanese actions based on the *Purple*[29] diplomatic decrypts and other indicators.' This had been the case prior to Pearl Harbor, when, 'more serious war warning messages and a more accurate picture of the current situation as indicated by Japanese decrypts that were advocated by Captain Laurence Safford as OP-20-G Admiral Noyes DNC[30], and the Acting Director of Intelligence (DNI) Captain Kirk[31], were forestalled or

27. Philip Hans Jacobsen (1924–2002). b.15 March 1924 in Madera, son of Danish immigrants. Graduated high school aged seventeen in June 1941. Enlisted in US Navy and served for twenty-eight years. Selected for OP-20-G, Washington, DC. Was assigned Kaneohe Bay, Oahu, Intelligence Monitoring Station under Rochefort. Volunteered for combat duty and attached to 1st Marine Division, Guadalcanal. Served at Guam later in the war and then based at Imperial Beach 1945. Met and married Bessie Le Blanc of Naval Security Group. Post-war naval service included intelligence officer aboard the heavy cruiser *Salem* (CA-139) flagship 6th Fleet. Later served aboard nuclear-powered submarine *Nautilus* (SSN-1). Proficient Japanese and Russian speaker. Retired from navy in 1969. Bachelor's degree in political science University of Nebraska at Omaha and law degree at University of San Diego. Assistant Attorney-General at Guam, becoming Attorney-General. Became Chief Deputy Tax Collector for San Diego County in 1982 and retired in 1992. Mounted sustained attacks on Pearl Harbor revisionist writings, especially Robert Stinnett's *Day of Deceit* in 1999. He stated: "These revisionist claims are fraught with a wide range of serious errors that render them baseless." Died on 22 August 2006, aged 82, at his home in Otay Mesa, California, while still working on his book on navy cryptology.

28. Admiral Harold Rainsford Stark (1880–1972). b. Wilkes-Barre, Pennsylvania. Graduated from US Naval Academy, Annapolis, 1903. Was aboard the battleship *Minnesota* (BB-22) during the Atlantic Fleet's round-the-world cruise, before serving in torpedo boats and destroyers, his war service included an epic destroyer voyage from the Philippines to the Mediterranean in 1917 and service on the staff of Commander, US Naval Forces European Waters, between 1917 and 1919. After the war he became XO of the battleships *North Dakota* (BB-29) and *West Virginia* (BB-48), and this was followed by a period at the Naval War College, and then with Naval Ordnance, including command of the 10,600 ton ammunition ship *Nitro* (AE-2). Promoted to captain he became CoS, Commander Destroyer Squadrons Battle Fleet in the late 1920s early 1930s and returned to the battleship *West Virginia* again as her commanding officer from 1934 to 1937. As rear-admiral he was appointed Chief, Bureau of Ordnance, then commanded CruDiv 3 and became Commander, Cruisers, Battle Force in 1938. The following year he was promoted to full admiral and he became Chief of Naval Operations between 1940 and 1941, but was somewhat out of his depth in that position. He relinquished the post to Admiral Ernie King and was sent to London as Commander US Force, Europe, where his diplomatic skills were more appreciated, and the title Commander 12th Fleet was added in 1943. He was involved in the US naval side of the Normandy landings (D-Day) in 1944. He

returned to Washington DC in 1946 and retired in 1947. See Harold P. Stark, *Commanding the Fleet*.

29. The Japanese diplomatic codes had been broken about a year prior to Pearl Harbor. See Lieutenant-Commander P. R. Gardella, Thesis *A Certain Grandeur: U. S. Communications Intelligence in the Pacific War, 1941-1945*.

30. Rear-Admiral Leigh Noyes (1885–1961). b. 15 December 1885 at St Johnsbury, Caledonia, Vermont. Graduated US Naval Academy Annapolis, 1906 and commissioned 1908. Commanded the destroyer *Biddle* (DD-151) 1919-20. Graduated Naval War College 1923. Member of US Naval Mission to Brazil 1926-9. Commanded the light cruiser *Richmond* (C-9) August 1934 to March 1936. Flight training and won wings as naval aviator March 1937. Commanded carrier *Lexington* (CV-2) 1937-8. CofS to Commander Aircraft, Battle Force 1938-9. Promoted to rear-admiral July 1939. Chief ONC, Navy Department 1939-42. Commander of Task Force *Negat* (Air Support Force) at the landings in Solomon Islands August 1942. At the Battle of Eastern Solomons in command of Task Force 61.3 had the carrier *Wasp* (CV-7) as his flagship, with Task 18. She was torpedoed and sunk from under him on 15 September 1942. Senior Member of Board of Inspection and Survey 1942-6. Decorations included Navy Cross, Legion of Merit and Purple Heart. Retired as vice-admiral November 1946. Died on 24 March 1961.

31. Vice-Admiral Alan Goodrich Kirk (1888–1963). b. Philadelphia. Graduated from US Naval Academy, Annapolis, 1909. Served in World War I. Naval Attaché, London, 1939–41. Director of OCI March October 1941, marred by continual interference from Turner. Promoted to rear-admiral and again naval Attaché, London, between 1941 and 1943. He then commanded the Amphibious Forces Feb-October 1943, and was at the invasion of Sicily in 1943, for which he received the Legion of Merit. Commanded the Western Task Force from command ship *Ancon* (AGC-4) at the Normandy Landings (D-Day) in 1944 and was promoted to vice-admiral. Retired as full Admiral in February 1946. After the war was appointed US Ambassador to Belgium and Minister to Luxembourg (1946-9), US representative on UN Special Committee on Balkans, 1947-8; US Ambassador to the Soviet Union (1949-2) and finally Taiwan (1962). President of American Committee for the Liberation of Russian Peoples (Amcomlib) in 1952 resigned due to poor health. Chairman of Board Mereast Corp. 1954-8; Director of New York World's Fair. Died on 15 October 1963, and buried at Arlington National Cemetery. See also Oral History transcript of *Interview* conducted by the Columbia University Oral History Research Office, 1961, held at the John F. Kennedy Presidential Library Museum Archives.

greatly watered down by Turner.[32]' This policy Turner had not modified and blithely carried it on into the Midway period.

Despite this, King, sagely advised that there were indications that, while CarDivs 1 and 2, BatDiv3, CruDivs 4 and 8 and two DesRons, plus a landing force, would assault Midway', 'remainder of 1st Fleet may take up a supporting position west of Midway, which he assumed was, 'in order to trap and destroy the US Pacific Fleet'.[33]

On 18 May Admiral Nagumo obligingly gave further details 'within the framework of a ubiquitous 10 May request for weather information that may account for the seven-day delay in translation'.[34] His message included the interesting tit-bit that, 'since we plan to make attacks roughly from the north-west from N minus 2 days until N day, request you furnish us with weather reports three

hours prior to the time of take-off on said days . . .[35]' The Melbourne intelligence team also came up with another fragment from the same messages which revealed that the Japanese air strike force would be launched 50 miles north-west of 'AF'.[36]

On the basis of this Layton submitted 'a masterful summary' which pinpointed Midway as one of the principal objectives of the Japanese operations. However, far from being received with enthusiasm in Washington DC, his report arrived in the capital exactly at the time when the simmering interdepartmental 'war' between OP-20-G and Admiral Turner finally reached breaking point, Layton's brief becoming the straw that broke the camel's back. None of this was helped by Joseph R. Redman's[37] increasingly hostile attitude towards CIU. Parker describes the scenario thus:

32. Lieutenant-Commander Philip H. Jacobsen spent twenty-seven of his twenty-eight years of naval service with the Naval Security Group. On retirement in 1969 he became Attorney-General of the Territory of Guam. He is a staff member of *Cryptolog*, the Naval Cryptologic Veterans Association magazine. See *Naval Intelligence as of Pearl Harbor, – Intelligence, Stemming the Tide of Japanese Expansion.*

33. Parker, *A Priceless Advantage.*

34. *Ibid.*

35. 18 May 1942. SRNS1 517, Record Group 457, National Archives, Washington DC.

36. 18 May 1942. Com 14 to COMB 020934Z June 1942.

37. Admiral Joseph Reasor Redman (1891–1968). b. Grass Valley, California 17 April 1891, son of Joseph Reasor a physician, (who as a lad of fifteen had run away to become a drummer boy in the Union Army and had been wounded five times) and Mabel Katherine Dwight. Entered US Naval Academy Annapolis, 1910, a midshipman, to sea aboard armoured cruiser *South Dakota* (ACR-9) in 1914; Commissioned as ensign 1914. August 1914 armoured cruiser *West Virginia* (ACR-5) in Vera Cruz operation, awarded Mexican Medal. January 1915 to St Louis. April 1915 to battleship *Oregon* (BB-3). June 1915 to gunboat *Yorktown* (PG-1). December 1915 to the repair ship (a former collier) *Prometheus* (AR-3), then to battleship *Maine* (BB-10), then June 1916 to old armoured cruiser *Montana* (ACR-13) for torpedo instruction. November to submarine tender *Fulton* (AS-1) ex-*Niagara*, for submarine instruction. Specialized in submarines. June 1917 Lieutenant (jg) to submarine *C-3* (*SS-14*). August 1917 Lieutenant (T). December 1917 commanded the submarine C-5 (SS-16) based at the Panama Canal. November 1918 to *O-14*. May 1919 Third Naval District, Receiving Ship at New York. WWI Victory Medal (submarine clasp). May 1919 Postgraduate instruction Marine Engineering, USNA, Annapolis. 1919 lieutenant-commander (T). MS Columbia University and General Electrics, Schenectady, New York 1920–1 postgraduate studies. July 1921 Submarine Base, New London, Connecticutt, and Exide Storage Battery Co

Philadelphia. September 1921 Electrical Officer battleship *New Mexico* (BB-40) fleet electrical and aide Vice-Admiral H. A. Wiley, Battle Fleet, and Divisional Radio Officer 1921–4. October 1924 to battleship *West Virginia* (BB-48). Lieutenant-Commander Bureau of Engineering 1924–7. Fleet duties 1927–30. 1929 to light cruiser *Detroit* (CL-8) as Navigation Officer. Chief of Frequencies Section, Naval War Center 1930–3 and again 1937–9. Married Marion Smith 1932. Technical advisor to US Delegation International Radio Telegraphy Conference, Madrid, 1932 and at Cairo 1938. March 1933 to battleship *Colorado* (BB-45) as Engineer Officer. August 1934 commander. Asiatic Fleet in command of submarine tender *Canopus* (AS-9) 1934–6. XO of heavy cruiser *Tuscaloosa (*CA-37) December 1939 to May 1940. June 1940 to March 1941 in command of the old troop transport *Henderson (AP-1)* which cruised between the Philippines and China, ostensibly carrying US Marines between garrisons, but thought by some to be clandestinely engaged in monitoring Japanese radio traffic. July 1940, as captain, was Assistant Chief to Rear-Admiral Leigh Noyes, Communications Division (ACNO). Deputy Director Naval Communications 1942. February–September 1942, replaced Noyes. July 1942, rear-admiral. Commanded the light cruiser *Phoenix* (CL-44) between October 1942 and April 1943 in Coral Sea and with 7th Fleet. Resumed duties as Director of Naval Communications again between April 1943 and August 1945. Became Nimitz's Intelligence Chief and promoted to vice-admiral. Many awards US and foreign, including DSM and appointed an Honorary Commander of the Military Division from Great Britain 'for distinguished services to the Allied cause'. Retired from active duty January 1946. Member of Board of War Communications Bureau, Joint Communications Board and Combined Communications Board, State Department. After the war Companion of the Naval Order. Vice-President Western Union Telegraph Co, plant and engineering until 1965 and second retirement. Lived at Westmoreland Hills, Maryland. Died after choking on food at a dinner at Crystal Towers apartments, Arlington, on 2 September 1968, aged 77. Interred at Arlington Cemetery.

The relationship, already far from harmonious, had deteriorated steadily since early March. At that time, newly formed OP-20-GI (Combat Intelligence) and OP-20-GZ (Translation) began to produce 'current' intelligence reports based on the output of the Pacific centers and current translations after 13 March 1942, based on the work of OP-20-GY (Cryptanalysis). The final breakdown stemmed from a series of minor disagreements between the analysts in War Plans and their counterparts in OP-20-G concerning Japanese preparations for the Midway/Aleutians campaign.

The available record of the dialogue between War Plans and OP-20-G reveals a very active and sometimes acrimonious relationship, touching on virtually every Japanese Navy initiative between 14 March and 27 May 1942. Disagreements were often so profound that the head of OP-20-G, Commander John R.

Redman[38], frequently had to rewrite the intemperate comments of the analysts who prepared responses to the questions from Admiral Turner and his staff. The record, unfortunately, also reveals that analysts in both War Plans and Negat were often unaware of the decisions and actions emanating from both Admiral King and Admiral Nimitz, particularly during the critical period between 8 and 23 May. In addition, the record suggests that the analysts in OP-20-G (unofficially known as Station *Negat*) and War Plans were so engrossed in their own activities that they sometimes overlooked vital information concerning the Imperial Fleet readily obtainable from translations from OP-20-GZ and the daily reports from the Pacific centers.[39]

What was described as, 'a face-to-face confrontation' duly ensued, with Turner and Redman exchanging

---

38. Vice-Admiral John Roland Redman (1898–1970). b. Reno, 31 January 1898, after his father, mother and elder brother Joseph had moved to Nevada from Grass Valley. Graduated from Reno High in 1915. June 1915 midshipman. May 1917 joined battleship *South Carolina* (BB-26) for cruise until August. May 1918 detached from US Navy Academy, Annapolis, to Europe. June 1918 aboard battleship *Texas* (BB-35) Grand Fleet, to April 1920. Victory Medal. Ensign. September 1918 lieutenant (jg). University of Nevada. Graduated from US Naval Academy, Annapolis, 1919. Specialized in sports activities: football, lacrosse and wrestling. Captain of US wrestling team at Antwerp, Belgium 1920 Olympics. 1920 joined battleship *New York* (BB-34). 1921 lieutenant. July 1921 duty aboard destroyer *Paul Hamilton* (DD-307*)*, then destroyer *Tattnall* (DD-125) and in October the destroyer *La Vallette* (DD-315). Specialized in radio communications, Postgraduate course in radio engineering. 1924 duties aboard battleship *Wyoming* (BB-32). Old gunboat *Sacramento* (PG-19) as Radio & Communications Officer Destroyer Squadron Asiatic Fleet. October 1926 – June 1927 battleship *Arizona* (BB-39). 1927–9 12th Naval District. 1929 destroyer *Zeilin* (DD-313) as XO. Represented US at various international conferences between the wars. 1930 destroyer *Claxton* (DD-140) as XO. 1931 XO of destroyer *Evans* (DD-78), escorting Japanese Emperor and Empress on US tour. Asiatic Fleet with China service in mid-1930s. February 1932 ONC, Naval Operations, Navy Dept Washington DC to May 1934. 1934 lieutenant-commander. Radio officer Destroyers, Battle Force 1935 Commas [Communications Assistant] and RO Scouting Force aboard heavy cruiser *Indianapolis* (CA-35) March 1936 Comms Officer on staff C-in-C Pacific Fleet. December 1937–December 1938,Commanding Officer *Dale* (DD-353) December 1938 January 1939 Office of CNO, Washington DC, Interdepartmental Communication Liaison Division. July 1939 commander. July–August 1941 Naval Hospital Washington DC. On the departure of Captain Laurence Safford as Head of the Communications Security Unit, Joseph Redman's younger brother, Captain

John R. Redman, who had been at OP-20-G from 1938, took his place, becoming Pacific Fleet Communications Officer 14 August 1942 until April 1945. September 1942 captain and was promoted to rear-admiral in March 1944. The two Redmans thus became the first brothers to hold that rank simultaneously. May 1945 – January 1946 commanded the battleship *Massachusetts* (BB-59), including bombardment of Kamaishi, Hamamatsu and Kamaishi again in 1945. Wartime decorations included Legion of Merit with two gold stars, Navy Unit Commendation ribbon and various other honours. After the war John Redman commanded Naval Receiving Station, Treasure Island, San Francisco March 1946–January 1947. January 1947 Deputy Commander and CofS Western Sea Frontier, until July 1949. Chief of Naval Communications from August 1949 to 1951, and had the same post for the Joint Chiefs of Staff between 1951 and 1953. Last appointment was as Commandant of 12th Naval District at San Francisco. Launched nuclear submarine *Sargo* (SSN-583) at Mare Island in February1956. Retired from navy in October 1957 after forty-three years service. Twice married, one daughter, Mary from first marriage (1924) to Elizabeth Clemons (d.1955) and Lillian Peterson. Died in San Francisco in May 1970, aged 72 and buried at Arlington National Cemetery.

By stark contrast, in October 1942 Joe Rochefort had followed his old chief into obscurity, ending up in command of a floating dock until the war was almost over. It is said that the reason Rochefort was never subsequently promoted was because, due to his intelligence work, he lacked the sufficient sea-time; others have alleged that inter-departmental politics led by the Redman brothers, was behind this apparent snub. Even Nimitz's efforts to secure a Distinguished Service Medal for Rochefort's outstanding achievements were blocked on two separate occasions. For more details, see Stephen Budiansky, *Battle of Wits: The Complete Story of Codebreaking in World War II,* also Herb Kugel, *America's Code Breaker,* in *Military History* and especially, Frederick D. Parker, *How OP-20-G got rid of Joe Rochefort.*

39. Parker, *A Priceless Advantage.*

viewpoints. The admiral told Redman that he was 'seriously dissatisfied' with reports from both OP-20-G and the Hawaiian stations. His main thrust was that neither groups had differentiated between the Japanese AF and K campaigns; he also complained that they did not understand that C-in-C 5th Fleet was 'merely' a sea frontier commander, and thus did not control the units that passed through his area. At the end of this harangue, during which the word Midway was never once uttered, Redman was left in absolutely no doubt that, other than new contradictory evidence becoming known, every COMINT centre was to refrain from any comments which elevated C-in-C 5th Fleet to command of any of the units currently, 'concentrating in Northern Empire Waters', but was automatically to follow Turner's views as being 'correct'. Fortunately, 'events' overtook Turner's *diktat*.

That Midway was far from being the agreed AF target for the expected Japanese thrust was manifest in Washington DC, even though it was agreed this was case by Nimitz, King and the COMINT stations. As we have seen, neither Turner's Plans staff nor the analysts in the Negat Station subscribed to the theory, with Hawaii, Samoa or the West Coast competing for that 'honour'. Even the man charged

with defence of the Aleutians, Admiral Robert A. Theobald[40], commanding Task Force 8, remained among the doubters and omitted details of the enemy plans and dates from his own preparatory plans. King's team, while agreed that Midway was the target, were still at the late date of 2nd June, insisting that 'BatDivs 1 and 2, CarDiv4 and DesRon3' were in the 'Bonins-Home Waters'[41] area, when, in truth, all these warships were approaching Midway from the north-west. It was a serious omission that might have had fatal consequences had a different admiral been in command of the American forces three days later. At the opposite extreme ONI also reported this day that the carrier *Zuikaku* was present when she was not! Fortunately, Nimitz chose to carry on with his plans, despite this further piece of misinformation from Washington DC.

Nonetheless, on 25 May CIU cracked the date cipher and could now apply themselves to filling in the final details by going back over the older decoded signals and adding this new information, which revealed to Rochefort that the Midway attack was scheduled for 4 June. Again, there was opposition from his own staff but Nimitz made the decision and the next day American preparations went into high gear with the return to Pearl of Admiral William F. Halsey's[42]

40. Rear-Admiral Robert Alfred Theobald (1884–1957). b. San Francisco, 25 January 1885. University of California 1902–03 and US Naval Academy 1903–06. Commissioned ensign 1908. Specialized in gunnery and became Gunnery Office of Battleship *New York* (BB-34), flagship of US Squadron with Grand Fleet 1917–18, promoted to commander by the end of the war. 1919–24, XO, Naval Postgraduate School, 1922–4, commanded a destroyer in the Asiatic Fleet. XO battleship *West Virginia* (BB-48) 1927–9, followed by Senior Class, Naval War College 1929–30. Secretary, War Plans, 1930–2 and promoted to captain. 1932–4 CoS, Pacific Fleet Destroyers. Naval War College again Seminar Study of Japan and Pacific War, followed by OIC Strategy Division, Naval War College. Commanding the Battleship *Nevada* (BB-36) 1937–9, and CoS, US Fleet, 1939–40. Promoted to rear-admiral June 1940, and Commander CruDiv 3. 1940–1 Commander Flotilla One and then Battle Force, light cruiser *Raleigh* (CL-7) as flagship, then Pacific Fleet Destroyers at the time of Pearl Harbor until May 1942. Commander, Northern Pacific Force 1942–3, Kodiak, flagship light cruiser *Nashville* (CL-43) to hold Dutch Harbor, but unable to bring the Japanese squadron to battle. Commandant 1st Naval District and Navy Yard Boston, 1943–4, at launches of aircraft carrier *Wasp (II)* (CV-48), light cruiser *Topeka* (CL-67) and destroyer escort *John M. Bermingham* (DE-530) opening of Wind Tunnel and US Naval Flight Preparatory School at Williamstown, Massachusetts in 1943. Retired 1945. Theobald went on to become one of the first 'conspiracy theory' advocates, with his book *Final Secret of Pearl Harbor*. Selected papers 1908–57 held at Hoover Archives at Stanford University (94305-6010).

41. 2 June 1942 – OPNAV to CINCPAC (timed 2231Z), CINCPAC's Message File, National Archives, RG38.

42. Fleet Admiral William Frederick Halsey, Jr (1882–1959). "Bull" Halsey was the archetypical US naval admiral who acquired a legendary reputation as a master of carrier warfare. Aggressive and impetuous, always eager to 'steer for the sound of the guns', he took big risks and sometimes, as at Leyte Gulf, made rash decisions, but his men adored him. b. Elizabeth, New Jersey, son of a naval officer, Halsey graduated from the US Naval Academy in 1904. His early service was in both battleships and torpedo craft, but small ships were his first love. He commanded the Atlantic Fleets Torpedo Flotilla 1912–13 and was captain of several destroyers (including war service aboard the *Shaw* (DD-68) in 1918) and torpedo boats in the 1920, as he rose up the ranks. A period as Naval Attaché, Berlin, in 1922–5 was followed by more of the same when he commanded the destroyer *Dale* (DD-290) in European waters. He attended the Naval College in the mid-1930s and trained as a naval air observer, becoming converted to flying operations. He gained his 'wings' at the age of fifty-two and went on to command the carrier *Saratoga* (CV-3), and then NAS Pensacola. Promoted to rear-admiral Halsey was in his element commanding various carrier divisions, and then, as vice-admiral, as Commander, Aircraft Battle Forces, where he wrote the navy's air doctrine manuals by which the Battle of the Coral Sea and Midway were successfully fought. Fortunately, when the attack on Pearl Harbor took place, Halsey was at sea in his flagship, the USS *Enterprise* (CV-6), but he conducted daring carrier raids with limited forces for the first months of the war, taking the fight to the enemy as best he could. Hospitalized during Midway. (A totally

Task Force 16 built around the carriers *Enterprise* and *Hornet*, which were joined by the damaged *Yorktown* on the 27th. She immediately went into the dockyard where round-the-clock work commenced to get her ready in time for the battle.[43]

It was on this day that the Japanese finally got around to the code change they had decided upon earlier, and with the introduction of this new cipher, 'Baker-9' replacing 'Baker-8', all the wonderful source messages immediately became unreadable. Nevertheless enough was now known and American plans went ahead. The radio D/F stations were still able to keep tabs on the known Japanese forces for although their carriers maintained strict radio silence throughout the next two days, they received a message from Tokyo, which identified them, and their destroyer escorts squadrons were also identified. On the 29th the *Akagi* broke radio silence, which was picked up, although the exact location of the Striking Force could not be ascertained.[44]

But now it was the American's turn to generate radio traffic as their task groups sortied out from Pearl, to alert the listening Japanese radio traffic analysts. They duly reported that they had intercepted no fewer than 180 such messages and that seventy-two of them were urgent. Not surprisingly they were highly suspicious. They deduced that the US carriers were not only in the Hawaiian area but were on the move; a hunch reinforced by Wake Island's reports of increased aerial patrols being flown from Midway Island itself. Although these reports were speculative they were hugely important. Parker stated:

Incredibly, all of the discoveries concerning US activities made by Japanese COMINT in Tokyo or in the *Yamato*, were withheld from the Midway Strike Force by Admiral Yamamoto. They were not reported to these key subordinates either because he assumed they had heard the Tokyo broadcasts or because he refused to break the radio silence that he ordered be strictly maintained when they had departed home waters.

Even when the *Yorktown,* patched up enough to fight, sailed with Task Force 17 on 30 May, to join the other two American carriers, this movement, although 'probably' also detected by *Yamato*'s COMINT detachment, this momentous news was also withheld. To paraphrase Dallas Isom many years later[45], it seemed that, in the end, everyone on the Japanese side knew the American carriers were out, except Admiral Nagumo!

However, Parshall and Tully's recent excellent analysis[46] is on firm ground when they state that, notwithstanding Yamamoto remaining mute on such important information, Nagumo, with all the modern communications available to him via his own carriers and his escorting battleships and cruisers, which were very well equipped in this respect, should have been in possession of certain vital pieces of news transmitted by the First Communications Unit back in Tokyo and available to all who cared to tune in. These were that patrol activity from Midway had greatly increased; that there had been a huge increase in American signals from the Hawaiian area, which indicated they were on the move; and finally that, with the collapse of the 'Second K' he did not know for certain whether the American carriers had been present at Hawaii or not; in which case he really ought to act on the conservative assumption in conjunction with the other two bits of information, that they *might* very well have been. Nor could he assume that, just because the Japanese submarines (too late on station as it happened) had not reported any enemy, therefore no movement had occurred.

Layton wrote:

The messages, intercepted on June 5, 6 and 7, were worthless. The Battle of Midway had already begun,

---

opposite personality to Admiral Frank Fletcher, revisionist and alternate history 'Internet Anoraks' have made hay with the 'What if Halsey had been in charge at Midway' scenario ever since!) Halsey was back in harness off the Solomons from October 1942 onward and from then until the end of the Pacific War he was in the thick of the fighting and commanded the Third Fleet during the closing stages. The Japanese surrender took place aboard his flagship, the battleship *Missouri* (BB-63) on 2 September 1945. Shortly afterward he was promoted to fleet admiral, but retired from active duty in 1947. He died in 1959.

43. The naval dockyard at Pearl worked wonders and got an estimated ninety days' work done in seventy-two hours by working round the clock full-out. The Air Group became a very mixed bag and eventually the reinvigorated *Yorktown* sailed to war with eleven F4F-4 Wildcats from VF-3, and

nineteen more from VF-42, the latter still fiercely independent and led by Lieutenant (jg) William N. Leonard, but all temporarily operating under the overall control of Commander John S. Thach; eighteen SBD-3s of VB-3, with aircraft maintained by the old VS-5 personnel and eighteen SBDs of VB-5, operating for this mission (and much to their disgust) as VS-5; and thirteen TBD-1 Devastators of VT-3, with again, the aircraft maintained by VT-5 personnel.

44. CINPC to COMINCH 29 May 0419Z, and CINCPAC to all task forces, 29 May, 1409Z both CINCPAC Message File, Record Group 28 National Archives, Washington DC.

45. Dallas W. Isom, '*The Battle of Midway: Why the Japanese Lost*'.

46. Parshall and Tully, *The Shattered Sword: the Untold Story of the Battle of Midway*.

and though radio intelligence could not read the current Japan despatches, bulletins for US naval forces at Hawaii were confirming the value of radio intelligence reports, issued some weeks before the action began.[47] But he also recalled: 'We had another kind of "combat intelligence unit"' which had been organized by Rochefort from personnel from his communication intelligence unit. On Admiral Nimitz's authority, our senior task force commanders like Admiral Raymond A. Spruance[48] and Admiral Fletcher, were given a special radio intelligence unit called: 'Combat Intelligence Unit.'[49] Each unit consisted of trained Navy intercept operators from Rochefort's unit, plus a Japanese linguist, a former Japanese Language Officer. These units stood intercept watches on the Japanese short-range circuits used by their air-reconnaissance and air-scouting networks; they performed Air Early Warning func-

tion. During action, all tuned in their voice radios, on the enemy's air-defense commander, air-commander and leaders of their fight squadrons, torpedo squadrons or dive-bomber squadron (we knew the frequencies they used) and reported all activity heard, which would be passed to Admiral Fletcher, or Spruance, by the language officer. The intercepted enemy voice commands to attack, or to assemble or move further on and prepare to attack, were thus made immediately available to [our] own Task Force Commanders.[50]

In fact only the *Yorktown* and the *Enterprise* had mobile detachments aboard at the Midway battle. The *Hornet* did not embark any such team, which may, but may not, have been a contributory factor in her poor showing on 4 June. Admiral Fletcher's team was led by Commander Ranson Fullenwider[51], a linguist, and included Captain Forrest

47. Layton Papers, Box 15.
48. Admiral Raymond Ames Spruance (1886–1969). b. Baltimore, Maryland. Graduated from US Naval Academy, Annapolis, in 1906. He immediately took part in the voyage of the 'Great White Fleet'. Further sea service followed with promotion first to ensign (1908), then lieutenant jg (1911) with appointment to his first command, the US Navy's very first destroyer, the *Bainbridge* (DD-1) by then an old, run-down part of the Asiatic Fleet. He became a lieutenant in 1913, lieutenant-commander in 1917 and commander in 1918. In the interim he undertook further education in electrical engineering, which became his speciality. After World War I Spruance commanded the destroyers *Aaron Ward* (DD-132), *Percival* (DD-298), *Dale* (DD-290) and *Osborne* (DD-295) between 1919 and 1932, and, as a captain, commanded the battleship *Mississippi* (BB-41). Also served in intelligence and staff roles between the wars and at the Naval War College. Commanded the Caribbean Sea Frontier. As a rear-admiral, he was appointed in command of CruDiv 3, which led from the heavy cruiser *Northampton* (CA-26). Due to Admiral Halsey's incapacitaty at the time of Midway, he was appointed in command of Task Force 16. Appointed CoS to the Commander US Pacific Fleet and Pacific Ocean area 1942–3, and then became Deputy Commander in Chief. From August 1943, commanded the Central Pacific Force and in April 1944 the 5th Fleet and won the Battle of the Philippines Sea in June 1944. He has been heavily criticized by the 'brown shoe' faction for his decisions at both Midway and Philippines Sea. He oversaw the Gilbert, Marshal, Marianas, Iwo Jima and Okinawa landings, with the heavy cruiser *Indianapolis* (CA-35) as his flagship. After the war, he commanded the Pacific Fleet 1945–6, and then became President of the Naval War College. He retired from the navy in July 1948. His last official appointment was as US Ambassador to the Philippines between 1952 and 1955. He died at Pebble Beach, California in December 1969. The best biography of him by far still

remains Thomas B. Buell's, *The Quiet Warrior: A biography of Admiral Raymond A. Spruance.*
49. The very first mobile radio intelligence unit (RIU) was established aboard the carrier *Enterprise*, on 31 January 1942, and comprised Captain Bankson T. Holcomb, Jr USMC and three radio operators. The first carrier-to-carrier combat operation that had featured shipborne RIUs was the Coral Sea encounter, where such units had been in place aboard the carriers *Yorktown* (under Lieutenant-Commander Forrest R. Biard) and *Lexington* (under Lieutenant-Commander Ranson Fullenwider) at the Battle of the Coral Sea, but Admiral Fletcher had not been enamoured of them and placed little faith in the accuracy of their reporting unfortunately. See Forrest R. Biard, *Some Notes on Radio Intercept Work in the Coral Sea Action*, unpublished MSS dated 20 June 1984. Brigadier General Bankson T. Holcomb, USMC (1908). b. Wilmington, Delaware 1908. Enlisted USMC 1925, served at the American Legation in Peking (Beijing), American High School. Naval Academy, Annapolis 1929, graduated 1931 and commissioned second lieutenant. Full lieutenant 1934, captain 1939, major 1942, brigadier-general 1943. Fluent Chinese and Japanese speaker. 4th Marines Shanghai 1932, Chinese language course at American Embassy and Japanese language course at American Embassy, Tokyo. US Naval Advisory Group, Chungking. At Hawaii at the time of Pearl Habor. Special Intelligence Officer US Pacific Fleet 1941–3. Later fought at Iwo Jima and Okinawa post-war occupation of Japan. CoS Pacific Fleet Marines, Guam. 1st Marine Division Korea, at Pusan, Chosin Reservoir engagement and Chongjin. Assistant CoS G-2 (Intelligence). See Oral History Typescript of Interview by Richard D. Alexander, OR 315, 1970.
50. Layton Papers, Vol 2.
51. Rear-Admiral Ranson Fullenwider (1905–69). b. 23 October 1905, in Washington DC, son of Simon Peter Fullenwider and Bettie née Gaines. His brother, Edwin G. Fullenwider, also made rear-admiral and survived him.

Biard.[52] The latter was later to comment that the team 'provided valuable information after contact was made, through interception of Japanese plain language reports'. Admiral Spruance aboard the *Enterprise* was supported by a COMINT detachment for which the linguist was Captain Gilven Slonim.[53]

The overwhelming importance of RI was to be acknowledged by Nimitz himself, who wrote: 'Had we lacked early

Educated Swavely's Army and Navy Preparatory School. June 1922 entered US Naval Academy, Annapolis, as midshipman and graduated as ensign with class of 1926. 1929 lieutenant (jg). On Asiatic Station served with Yangtze River patrols and received Award. Attended US Navy Japanese Language School in Tokyo July 1932-September 1935. 1936 lieutenant. After nine-month tour in Office of CNO.1926–27 served aboard the battleship *New Mexico* (BB-40). 1927–8 fleet oiler *Ramapo* (AO-12). 1928–32 aboard the destroyer *Borie* (DD-215) on the Yangtze River. 1932 USNA, then CNO, Washington DC. September 1932– September 1935 Office Naval Attaché, American Embassy, Tokyo. 1935–6 CNO Office, Washington DC. 1936–9 sea service aboard battleship *New Mexico* again. Married Gabie Marie DeLores of Seattle. Served at HQ 14th naval District, Pearl Harbor, May 1939–March 1943. As a lieutenant (O-3) was one of only two Japanese language officers at CIU in 1940. January 1941 lieutenant-commander, was the RIU officer aboard the carrier *Lexington* (CV-2) at the Battle of the Coral Sea. After her sinking he took passage aboard *Yorktown* (CV-5) from Tongatabu to Pearl and remained aboard as Fletcher's RI officer after Biard had stormed off. Transferred to heavy cruiser *Astoria* (CA-34) with Fletcher when *Yorktown* was damaged. December 1942 commander (TS). April 1943–September 1944 CNO, Navy Department. 1944 captain (TS). November 1944–September 1945, US Pacific Fleet, Radio Unit. 1947 full commander. 1945–6 Commanding officer of the attack transport *Bosque* (APA-135). March–July 1946 CNO, Navy Dept. August 1946–8 was Naval Attaché and Naval Attaché for Air, American Embassy, Buenos Aires. June 1949, Captain, to HQ Ninth Naval District; 1952 US Navy War College course in Strategy and Tactics. August 1953 in Naval Hospital Bethesda. November 1953 Office of the Naval Attaché, Karachi, Pakistan, for one year, Military Assistance Advisory Group, Lisbon, and Madrid. HQ Potomac River Naval Command, Washington DC. July 1956 retired as captain, advanced to rear-admiral on the basis of combat service. Temporary Disability Retired List. Decorations included Navy Commendation Ribbon with 'V', Order of the Liberator, San Martin (Knight Commander Argentina), the Paraguayan Award, Navy Unit Commendation, American Defense Medal; Asiatic-Pacific Campaign Medal etc. Retired to Fort Lauderdale. Suffered a stroke while driving with his wife from Florida to his brother's house in Washington DC. Died at Highlands Community Hospital, Macon County, North Carolina, 6 September 1969, age 63. Interred at Arlington National Cemetery. 10 September 1969. Also see – *Fabian interview*, National Security Agency, Oral History, OH 09-8.3 and *Discrete Records of Historical Cryptologic Import: US Navy*, SRMN-005, OP-20-G – *File of Memoranda & Reports Relating to Battle of Midway May 20th 1942 – 30th June 1942*, 27 pps. (Navy Department Library).

52. Captain Forrest R. 'Tex' Biard (1912) b. November 1912,

Dallas, Texas. Attended the US Naval Academy, Annapolis 1930–4, graduated 24th. As a young lieutenant he studied Japanese in Tokyo for two years between July 1938 and August 1941, leaving in the nick of time in August 1941. From November 1941 at CIU as a linguist (not a code-breaker) at the time of Pearl Harbor. Famously quarrelled with Fletcher, who did not believe in RI's validity, while aboard *Yorktown* (CV-5) at Battle of Coral Sea in May 1942. Transferred to the Intelligence unit at Melbourne as a captain in November 1943, before returning to CIU later in the war. Biard worked with many of the leading code-breakers of his era: William Friedman, Frank Rowlett, Joseph Rochefort and Abraham Sinkov. Graduate of Ohio State University, masters degree in nuclear physics. Witnessed the H-bomb tests at Eniwetok and finally retired from the navy as a captain in 1952. Studied astrophysics at CalTech. Spent the next twenty-three years teaching university level nuclear physics at various colleges. Honoured in 2001 as the last of the twelve CIU operatives. Lives at Highland Park and still actively pursues his studies of the Japanese language, Japanese military and general history, as well as conducting lectures and tours. See Oral History file OH877, NSA. See also Forrest R. Biard, 'The Pacific War: Through the Eyes of Forrest R. Biard', and Forrest R. Biard, 'Breaking of Japanese Naval Codes: Pre-Pearl Harbor to Midway'.

53. Captain Gilven M. Slonim (1913–2000). b. at St Paul, Minnesota, on 29 September 1913. Educated at Central High School and Duluth Junior College. 1931, enlisted in USNR on 9 June, serving until 1932, when he was appointed to the US Naval Academy, Annapolis. He graduated on 4 June 1936, 138th in his class, and was commissioned as an ensign. 1936–7 served aboard the battleship *Maryland* (BB-46). 1938, transferred to the destroyer *Barry* (DD-248) in May. 1939, from July, attended Japanese language school attached to the US Embassy in Tokyo. In 1941 transferred to CIU, in time for Pearl Harbor. Assigned to Admiral Halsey's intelligence staff aboard *Enterprise* (CV-6), and, at Midway, stayed when Admiral Spruance took over command. His obituary states that he, 'provided critical intelligence that contributed directly to the Navy's victory'. Also involved in the Admiral Yamamoto assassination in 1943. Served at every major naval battle except Leyte Gulf. By the end of the war Slonim was the senior Japanese interpreter to Fleet Admiral Nimitz aboard the battleship *Missouri* (BB-63) being present at the surrender on 2 September 1945. Among many awards were the Legion of Merit, Bronze Star, Gold Star in lieu of second Bronze Star Commendation Ribbon. After the war Slonim returned to sea duty and became a well-known destroyer skipper, commanding *Jarvis* (DD-799) in January 1946 and then the Gearing-Class destroyer *Vogelgesang* (DD-862) from July the same year, until June 1947. 1947–8 Naval War College Newport, then Strategic Planner at OCNO, Navy Department, Washington, DC. 1950–1, Command and General Staff College, Fort Leavenworth, then Executive

information of the Japanese movement, and had we been caught with Carrier Task Forces dispersed, possibly as far away as the Coral Sea, the Battle of Midway would have ended far differently.'[54] Indeed, it is possible that it would not have taken place at all.

Even the taciturn, hard-to-please Ernie King was forced to acknowledge the fact, on 23 June 1942 he sent to the RI Section a two-word signal, that, for him, spoke reams. 'Well Done.'

Halsey Drops Out

Admiral Halsey, on his return to Pearl, was a sick man; he was suffering from dermatitis, accentuated by his frustration at lack of positive action for his command. Ironically at the very moment action beckoned, he needed immediate hospital treatment. He was forced to lie in bed completely naked save for a single sheet, with his entire body smeared with ointment to sooth the affected skin. This was all totally unexpected and hush-hush. Spruance's Flag Lieutenant aboard the heavy cruiser *Northampton* (CA-26), Robert J. Oliver, later revealed that he and Spruance only found out when they went to pay a visit to Halsey on docking at Pearl, only to be informed he was in hospital and that Spruance was to report to the submarine base to see Nimitz. Spruance was also informed, 'You have to take the Task Force out.' While Spruance went to CINCPAC's office, Oliver talked to Layton, who told him: 'Good luck and give them hell!' Afterwards both men met up again and on the way back to the ship Oliver told Spruance what had been revealed. According to Oliver's memory of things, Spruance answered in this way.

Very well. Now, this is what I have. It appears that I am one of those commanders who have two sets of orders.

I have written orders to meet and defeat the Japanese. My oral orders are not to lose my force. If things go badly, I am to withdraw and let them have the place because they can't hold it and we will get it back.

On leaving *Northampton* to join the *Enterprise,* one of his staff asked Spruance whether he had any concerns about commanding a carrier task force. 'Spruance replied that he did not because he would have all the technical brains of Bill Halsey's staff at his elbow.' Spruance called on Halsey but what passed between them was never revealed. Oliver recorded that on taking over command Spruance dramatically changed his style from an extreme 'hands-on' man to a 'hands-off' man. This only lasted until disillusionment set in early in the battle, when he reverted more to type.[55]

Halsey considered Spruance to be 'the only man for the job', but no two men could have been more dissimilar. That the Battle of Midway would have been a vastly different battle had the 'Bull' been in charge, as we are constantly told, there can be no doubt whatsoever, but historians will argue to eternity whether that would have been a good thing or a bad thing!

The situation on the American side on the eve of the battle was a rather strange one. Nimitz, with confidence in his intelligence, was sure he had a good opportunity to inflict a defeat on the Japanese and take out some of their carriers. It was not a 'massive risk' as is so often claimed, nor a breathtaking gamble, for he had a pretty shrewd idea he could make the enemy pay but still preserve his own ships and pull them out to fight another day if things did not pan out. So Midway was to be a carefully calculated play by Nimitz. He was to exercise caution ('Don't lose my carriers!' he cautioned his subordinates before sending them out to battle) for he did not know everything that Yamamoto had out there, nor during the course of the battle did he *ever* know the *whole*

Assistant Deputy CofS, Plans and Operations, Eastern Atlantic and Mediterranean. 1952, in July appointed in command of the destroyer *Irwin* (DD-794), seeing combat service off North Korea, for which he earned a Gold Star. 1954, in June was on staff of C-in-C Atlantic Fleet as Special Plans Officer. 1956, in September commanded DesDiv 162 to September 1957 and in June 1961 became CofS and Aide to Commander A/S (Anti Submarine) Defense Force, Pacific Fleet. 1958–9 General Planning Group, OCNO, he was appointed in command of the destroyer tender *Everglades* (AD-24). 1957, promoted to captain on 1 July. 1960 in March he became Commander DesRon 28. 1963, assigned to Office of the CNO once more in September. In 1965 he took retirement, and resided at Jefferson Street, Duluth, but his son, Richard, had joined the Navy and became a cryptology specialist, just like his father. Max Slonim retired to Falls Church, VA and died on 22 November 2000 in the Inova Fairfax Hospital. On his death his ashes were scattered at sea from the Guided Missile Destroyer *Hopper* (DDG-70) on 30 May 2001. On 16 May 1989, Slonim advised Frederick Parker, that he was preparing a book about his experiences in the RI detachments that he plans to have published 'in time for the 50th anniversary of the Battle of Midway'. His promised book on his experiences has not appeared at the time of writing, but his papers, including PhD dissertation; *Speeches on World Ocean, Pearl Harbor* and miscellaneous letters and exerts from the Congressional Record 1983–1998 are held in a box at the Naval War College.

54. CINCPAC (Nimitz) to COMINCH (King), A16, Ser. 01849, dated 28 June 1942, PP24, para 69.

55. Letter, Oliver to Thomas B. Buell, dated 5 August 1971, Naval War College archives. It is noteworthy that even almost thirty years on, Oliver makes not a single mention of Jack Fletcher, Spruance's commanding officer.

enemy picture, as is often stated. With Halsey out of the picture and the only other out-and-out naval aviator on station, Rear-Admiral Leigh Noyes, acting as Nimitz's aviation planning advisor ashore, the great carrier duel was orchestrated by a submariner[56], Nimitz, and played out by two cruiser specialists, Fletcher and Spruance!

All three American leaders apparently shared one common belief about their enemy, that the Japanese would operate their carriers in two separate groups, one attacking Midway directly the other acting in support. Fletcher's obsession with this *idée fixe* seems to have stemmed, rather naturally, from his bitter experience at the Coral Sea fight; Spruance's adherence to it appears to have resulted from the fact that, initially, only two Japanese carriers were reported when there were actually four present, but quite where Nimitz's similar fixation originated is less clear for, up to now, at Pearl Harbor, at Port Darwin and in the Indian Ocean foray, Nagumo had run all six of his carriers together as a unit perfectly successfully, other than when damage or necessary maintenance had reduced the force to five. The Coral Sea foray had been an exception, not the rule, and only came about because Yamamoto had (mistakenly) conceded the hiving off of one carrier division in what he hoped was only a 'temporary' measure.

The Heavy Bombers Move Up

Among the doubters as to whether the Intelligence that Nimitz was basing his whole defensive preparation on was

in fact sound, were the Army Air Corps. Brigadier-General Clarence L. Tinker[57] of the 7th Air Force was present at the combined service meetings and was reluctant to commit his whole force of Boeing B-17 four-engined heavy bombers to the dubious safety of the exposed runway at Midway. These great machines, with their 'incredible' Norden bomb sights and commanding presence, were the very epitome of Army Air Corps thinking for the previous two decades. Their aircrews as well as their leaders were supremely confident that they could easily deal with the whole Japanese fleet unaided and finally vindicate the 'Victory through Air Power' theorists who had been stridently forecasting such a thing for years. The B-17s had the range to mount sorties from Pearl itself, albeit with reduced bomb loads, hence the reluctance to commit them closer the enemy. Finally, however, Tinker was cajoled and persuaded to move at least *some* of this force up, so that they could make attacks at maximum range. Thus, during 30 and 31 May, in two groups of eight and nine respectively, the Boeings[58] finally arrived at the island. Here they were subordinated to the local commanders.[59]

On arrival at Midway the Air Corps personnel found much to their distaste.

Servicing and maintenance conditions, as well as the general living conditions on small Eastern Island at Midway were poor, due to lack of provision for greatly augmented airplane strength. Combat crews consistently flew long, gruelling

---

56. Nimitz it was who actually laid down the ground rules, this being the key part of exercising his interpretation of retaining 'general tactical command'. It was Nimitz who ordained that the two carrier groups, Task Force 16 and Task Force 17, should operate as separate entities. Fletcher and Spruance were blamed by the 'brown shoe' school for this arrangement, but the decision had been Nimitz's, and he had even briefed his two task force commanders quite separately and apart from each other, prior to the battle, almost as if to emphasize this separation.

57. Brigadier-General Clarence Leonard Tinker, USAAC (1887-1942). b. 21 November 1887, eldest son of George E. Tinker and Sarah A. Schwagerte, in Osage County, Oklahoma. This was the former Osage Nation Indian Territory and Tinker was one-eighth Osage Indian. Educated at Catholic schools in Hominy and Pawhuska, Oklahoma, and at Elgin public school, Kansas, and from 1900 at Haskell Institute, Lawrence, Kansas. 1906 enrolled Wentworth Military Academy, Lexington, Missouri, graduated 1908 and commissioned as third lieutenant in Philippine Constabulary. 1912, commissioned as second lieutenant, USA, as Infantry officer assigned 25th Infantry Division, Fort George Wright, Spokane, Washington, then Hawaii. Married Madeline Doyle of Halifax, Nova Scotia.

World War I served at home and promoted to major. 1919 commenced flying lessons and transferred to Army Air Corps. Flight duty from 1 July 1922 serving at various USAAC bases in south-east. Awarded Soldier's Medal in 1931. Was the first of American Indian blood to reach rank of major-general in the history of US Army and commanded MacDill Field, Tampa, Florida. Further promoted to brigadier-general 1 October 1940. Concerned with planning defence of Panama Canal and Caribbean area before the war. After 7 December 1941, appointed in command Hawaiian Department and promoted to major-general early 1942. Commander 7th Air Force, with HQ at Hickham Field. After Midway volunteered personally to lead a four-plane attack with Consolidated Liberator heavy bombers on Wake Island on 5 June. Tinker's aircraft crashed over the sea, and all on board were killed; his body was never recovered. Posthumously awarded DSM. Tinker AFB, Oklahoma City was named in his honour. Biography by James L. Crowder, Jr, *Osage General: Major General Clarence L. Tinker*.

58. These fifteen machines were from two separate bombing groups, the 5th, represented by the 31st, 72nd and 294th Squadrons; and the 11th, with 431st squadron.

59. Commander Cyril T. Simard, USN and Lieutenant-Colonel Harold Shannon, USMC.

missions daily, and were forced to do their own servicing and necessary maintenance to a large extent. As a result of this condition, and because of continuous search missions before the beginning of the attack, many of the combat crews fought missions in an exhausted physical condition. Only damaged aircraft were returned to Oahu during the battle, and many crews were used continuously throughout the operations.[60]

Despite these difficulties the Fortresses made their first combat sortie later that day. Armed with four 600 lb bombs and fitted with extra fuel tanks carried in their bomb bays, which reduced their offensive ordnance to just four 600 lb bombs, fifteen of them took off between 1330 and 1350 that afternoon. They were directed to search an area some 700 miles west of Midway, as agreed with the navy, to fit in with the latter's own PBY sweeps. The leader[61] was forced to abort his own mission, returning to base at 2000 that evening. The others returned in straggling gaggles rather than as a unit, having sighted nothing whatsoever, some experiencing great difficulty in locating the island at all. This was due, according the report by the Naval Operations Officer on the spot[62], to, 'inferior flight and communications discipline'.

The PBYs Find – and Strike

The Consolidated Model 28, whose designer[63] opted for performance rather than aesthetics, was perhaps the most ungainly looking aircraft of World War II; rating only after the British Fairey Swordfish and Albacore TSRs for obvious antiqueness and sharing their distinct lack of speed; yet she was to prove among the most versatile, useful and endearing of combat planes. A monoplane seaplane, itself revolutionary, the concept was adopted to keep the big twin Pratt & Whitney R-1830 radial engines as far above wave-level as possible. By 1939 an amphibious version had also appeared on the scene.

The PBY first appeared in the mid-1930s and was initially identified by the US Navy as the P3Y (P for Patrol, 3 for Type, Y for Consolidated), who envisaged her role solely as a search-and-rescue plane. The inbuilt ability to carry a bomb load – a maximum of 1,000 lb could be carried on wing-racks – saw her designation changed to PBY (Patrol Bomber Consolidated). But it was for her reconnaissance and rescue roles that she was initially commissioned into the service with sixty ordered in 1935 and joining the fleet two years later.

The PBY-1 was followed by improved variants[64], also ordered in small batches, but the arrival of the PBY-5 coincided with an emergency requirement for long-range maritime reconnaissance aircraft by Great Britain with the opening of World War II, and Consolidated was swamped with UK orders. Subcontracting followed to keep pace with requirements.[65] Indeed it was actually the British who dubbed the PBY-5 the Catalina and the US Navy merely followed suit.[66] To the young aircrew that flew this lumbering monster into action she was affectionately known simply as 'Cat', and when radar later gave her the ability to 'see in the dark'[67], this naturally transmogrified into the Black Cat whose exploits in the South Pacific and elsewhere became legendary.[68] At Midway the 'Cat' proved indispensable[69], not only in her Search and Rescue (SAR) role, but in new configurations.

By 20 May there were thirty-two of the Navy's PBY-5s

---

60. Brigadier-General, H. C. Davidson, A.US Commanding Confidential Report, *Incidents and Conclusions reached which should be of Value to Training Establishments*, contained in CINCPAC File A16, *Battle of Midway*, ADM 199/1302, held at National Archives, Kew, London.
61. Lieutenant-Colonel Walter C. Sweeney, USAAC.
62. Captain Logan C. Ramsey, USN.
63. Isaac Laddon.
64. PBY-2 (forty aircraft); PBY-3 (sixty-six aircraft) and PBY-4, the latter featuring for the first time the distinctive large dorsal observation 'blisters' (thirty-three aircraft).
65. Includes batches built by the Canadian subsidiaries of the American firm Boeing and the British firm Vickers, as well as by Boeing (PB2B) and the Naval Aircraft Factory (PBN-1 Nomad) in the States itself. Later developments included the PBY6-A and PB2B-2 while those that served with the USAAF were designated as the OA-10.
66. For reasons probably connected with asserting their national independence, the Royal Canadian Air Force named their PBY-5 as the Canso, but this name never really took hold.

67. In the United States airborne radar was slow in coming, but the PBY was among the first US aircraft to feature it. The earliest combat worthy sets were of the metric wave type with dipole antenna arrays fitted to the wings, but this was followed by the installation of centimetric radar in its own fairing added atop the pilot/navigators cockpit.
68. See Richard Knott, *Black Cat Raiders of World War II*. In Great Britain, under the then existing convoluted and bizarre division of responsibilities, it was the RAF and not the navy, which operated the Catalina for British maritime operations. They flew one over the German battleship *Bismarck* during her one-and-only foray, thus adding to the Cats fame while keeping the true locator, the ULTRA intercepts of her signals, safely concealed under the resulting press ballyhoo.
69. As just one example, over the whole ten-day period of the battle, 27 May–5 June 1942, the twelve crews of VP-44 averaged 88.5 hours combat duty. Four crews exceeded 100 hours each, one notching up 114 hours. (source – *VP-44 Golden Pelicans WW2 History*).

and 5As established at Midway[70] and they began their 700 mile search legs. They were divided into two components, with twenty-two based on Sand Island and the remaining ten working out of Eastern. None of these were equipped with radar, but four were being so fitted back at Ford Island and were due to join them as soon as they were ready.[71] Like their B-17 counterparts, the navy VP aircrews did not find life on Midway a bed of roses. They had fairly good sleeping quarters at first, then a Japanese submarine lobbed a few shells ashore, one of which detonated right among their bunks. Thereafter they had to make do with sleeping in dugouts that were both musty and full of bugs. It was generally agreed that any PBY that did spot the Japanese fleet by daylight, just as the British PBY had done two months earlier off Ceylon, had very little chance of surviving that sighting. The crews started a fund among themselves to provide money for the unlucky aircrew's families back home.

The fatigue of the aircrew themselves was an important factor. Vice-Admiral Bellinger, who was in command of the VP (Patrol Squadron) units[72], himself stated, in another context:

There is always a question of the life of the planes versus the physical fatigue of the crew. The planes now stand up and can operate continually more and to a greater extent than can the crews. Therefore, the question of number of planes and number of crews for these planes, in order to place them in the air each day . . . becomes a matter of adjustment and not a concrete statement as regards to the actual number of planes required.

Bellinger was also to say that the PBY was 'the only type of plane the navy had,' to conduct such searches, 'and 800 miles was considered about the maximum length of leg that could be carried out by the PBY plane'. And to give another estimate for the PBY on the basis of 25 miles visibility, I quote the following: 'Radius of delay search, 800 miles; number of searching planes daily, 25 mile visibility, 50; flight times per search plane, 16½ hours; total planes hours per month, 24,750; total number of planes required, 150; number of flight crews required, 225, engine changes per month, average, 82½; spare engines required, 182; fuel consumption per month, gallons of gasoline, 1,980,000; search effectiveness estimate at 50 per cent. When asked whether the PBY patrol bombers were equipped with radar prior to the time of the Pearl Harbor attack, Bellinger answered 'No.'[73]

The PBYs commenced those long journeys, taking off around 0415 each morning, so close that they could wave to the pilots on either side of them according to one veteran, but, by the time they reached the end of their leg each would be about 60 miles apart. They continued this unrewarding toil for a week, but, on 3 June, things dramatically changed. That morning twenty-two search planes took to the air, covering sectors 200 to 020. The NAS Midway War Diary logged. 'Coverage excellent beyond 450 miles to NNW.'[74]

The first contact was made at 0845, when a VP-23 Catalina, 6V55[75], reported, 'Investigating suspicious vessel.' This report was followed at 0904 by a second signal reporting two Japanese cargo vessels, bearing 267, distance 470 miles.[76] At 0923 this PBY reported being fired upon by the Japanese ships and requested instructions. The ships sighted were in fact two Japanese minesweepers, *Tama Maru No.3* and *Tama Maru No. 5*, which had sailed from Wake Island on 31 May and had got ahead of the invasion force in error. Their being mistaken for troop transports led to some unnecessary confusion back at Midway, but fortunately, a more accurate and pertinent report was soon being received from another scouting plane.

That morning 27 year-old Ensign Jack Reid[77] of VP-21

---

70. Units from VP-14, 23, 24, 44, 51, 72 and 91 were present.
71. In the event, due to the time factor, only two of the four that eventually arrived, had their radar sets installed.
72. Bellinger's many titles included Commander Patrol Wing 2; he also commanded Patrol Wing 1; Commander Fleet Air Detachment, Ford Island and Commander Task Force Nine.
73. Vice-Admiral Patrick Bellinger, Testimony at the Proceedings of the Hart Inquiry, Wednesday March 15 1944 before Admiral Thomas C Hart, Navy Department, Washington DC,
74. NAS Midway, *War Diary, 1942-May-30 to 1942-June-07.* Record Group 313-58-3456, Box 1, Folder 25, pp 7, held at NARA, San Bruno.
75. Piloted by Ensign James Palmer O'Neil Lyle, A-V(N), USN. It is stated in *A Glorious Page in our History,* p 52, that Lyle reported, 'transmitted another message, that he had spotted two Japanese converted minesweepers', but this appears *not* to have been the case, as the entry in the NAS Midway War Diary record makes clear.
76. NAS Midway, *War Diary, 1942-May-30 to 1942-June-07.*
77. Captain Jewell Harmon "Jack" Reid, (1914–2003). b. Paducah, Bandana, Kentucky 1914. Moved to Aptos in 1907. Educated local high school. Joined navy in 1933. In 1937 commenced flight training at Pensacola Naval Air Station (NAS), Florida, graduating as pilot in 1938. Assigned San Point NAS, Washington, and attained University of Washington. Attained a degree in aeronautical engineering from LaSalle Extension University, Chicago. Ensign with VP-21 1942-3 then served with VP-44. DFC for Midway. Flew many VIPs as passengers, including Admirals Halsey and Radford, Madame Chiang Kai-sheik and the Secretary of the Navy. Served in the Korean War and was on

had left earlier than usual and had pushed Catalina *8V55* as far out as she would go.[78] Just before 0900 the Catalina had droned over the usual empty sea to the limit of their search once more but, just before they were ready to haul about, the radioman aboard picked up muzzy radio chatter that seemed rather close to their position. He consulted the navigator and he, in turn, told Reid that they would like to push out a little bit further to check this out. Knowing the fuel situation was normally tight, Reid checked with his engineer, Chief T. J. DeRoin, a married man with two children, and was informed that that worthy had topped up with an extra 50 gallons of fuel for each member of his family as insurance, before they had left. With a 150 gallon bonus sloshing around in their tanks it was agreed they should keep going beyond the limit.[79] They were duly rewarded with a sighting. Many years later Reid was to recall the next tense moments.

It looked like it would be another empty trip, when – just as they were about to turn back – Reid spotted a few specks on the horizon. At first he thought they were dirt spots on the windshield. 'Pick up the binoculars and see what's out there,' he told his co-pilot, Ensign Gerald Hardeman, 'I think I see some ships.' Hardeman lifted the glasses to his eyes. Reid remembers the moment exactly. 'He said, 'Jack, you're damned right. Those are ships out there' ''. Reid and his crew had run into Japanese Adm. Nobutake Kondo's attack force. 'I had three options,' Reid says, ticking them off his fingers. ' I could stay at that altitude and fly in close and probably be spotted, or I could climb to 2,000–3,000 feet and see what was back of them.' But Reid knew both options would probably earn his crew that widow's fund. He decided to go with the plan he had thought up the night before. ' I immediately cut the power on my engines and dropped down to 500 feet,' Reid says.

Skimming over the ocean, he flew the PBY 30 miles north, then 30 miles toward Tokyo. 'I figured we were abreast of the ships, so I climbed back up to 1,000 feet,' Reid remembers. Like poking his head over a fence, Reid spotted six large ships and radioed back what he had seen. Then he ducked back down to 500 feet and did something no Japanese had expected an American plane to do. He flew in behind the fleet.[80]

Reid's sighting signal, timed at 0925, simply read 'Main body', but to all those that received it those two words meant that they had hit the jackpot; the Japanese were coming in right on schedule just as CIU had said they would. All the plans in place had rested on that assumption, now it was known that Rochefort's predictions and Nimitz's faith, were sound. At 0927 Reid sent an amplification signal, 'Bearing 262 – distance 700.' Reid counted some eleven ships in columns, on a course of 090 degrees, speed 19 knots.

Despite being fired on by the escorting cruiser and destroyers, Reid and his team made it back to Midway after a fourteen-hour flight, with just enough fuel, 'Our engines quit just as we landed,' he was to recall.

On receipt of positive information the Army Air Corps commander at once despatched Flight 92, a striking force of B-17s of the 431st Bombardment Squadron, to attend to the matter. Nine of the big four-engined aircraft took off at 1230, seven carrying four 600 lb demolition bombs apiece, the other two laden with four 500 lb demolition bombs. They found their quarry at 1623 (local) on a bearing of 261° from Midway Island, at a distance of 570 miles. They estimated that the Japanese force comprised five battleships or heavy cruisers, plus forty other ships, including destroyers and transports.[81] They attacked in three groups of three, stacked at 8,000 feet, 10,000 feet and 12,000 feet.

The bombs duly detonated far below and jubilantly the

the staff of Com-FloWingPac and that of Admiral Radford, C-in-C, Pacific Fleet. Married Ina Mae, and they had two sons. Retired from navy 1961 and moved to San Francisco area, new career as real estate broker and developer. Became life member of California Alumni Association and attended University of California, Berkeley. Retired second time to Rio del Mar area, Served as panellist at two symposiums, National Air and Space Museum in 1990 for fiftieth anniversary of Midway and also re-visited Midway in 1995 to erect granite memorial. Died aged 90 in a Santa Cruz, convalescent hospital.

78. Reid's aircrew were Ensign Gerald H. Hardeman (co-pilot), Ensign Robert A. 'Bob' Swan (pilot/navigator), Aviation Mechanic Mate Second Class (AMM2c) R. J. De Roin, plane captain, AMM1c J. F. Gammell, (AP gunner) AMM3c J.

Goovers, who was on his indoctrination flight, AMM3c P. A .Fitzpatrick, (ordnanceman and gunner), and Aviation Chief Radioman (ACRM) Francis Musser, (chief radioman and gunner).

79. The basic facts of this incident were confirmed by Bob Swan at the PBY Catalina Foundation 1994 reunion at Santa Rosa: Just how DeRoin obtained an extra 150 gallons from Midway where the fuel situation was tight, or how they managed to stow it, was unfortunately *not* explained!

80. Jack Reid, to Peggy Townsend, '*Memories of war: He changed history*', article in *Santa Cruz Sentinel*, 26 May, 2002.

81. See CINCPAC Report, *Battle of Midway* – Appendix II, *Analysis of Attacks*, in ADM199/1302 held National Archives, Kew, London.

airman reported that enormous damage was done to the enemy. They claimed to have severely damaged a battleship or heavy cruiser, which fell out of the column. Another heavy cruiser and one transport 'of the *Normandie* class'[82], was possibly damaged. Two of their victims were described as 'out of column', and 'motionless' and both were 'issuing huge clouds of dark smoke which mushroomed above them'[83].

While the B-17s were still droning their way back to Midway, back on the island four navy PBY-5A volunteer aircrew[84] were being briefed by Ramsey to locate and attack the Japanese troop transports with torpedoes. Three aircraft of amphibious type (two of them radar-equipped[85]) from VP-24 and one from VP-51 were selected as suitable for this task even though they had only arrived at Eastern Island after their ten-hour flight from NAS Ford Island, Hawaii, that afternoon. Each Catalina was fitted with a single Mk XIII, Model 1 torpedo for this ground-breaking night mission. They were to be led by the (XO) of VP-44[86], who was already in the picture, and who would take passage aboard one of the aircraft.

The quartet took their departure at 2115, pulling up into clear skies, with broken cumulus cloud at 1,000 feet. The clouds thickened and between midnight and 0100 on the 4th, the rear two aircraft lost contact with the two leaders, and as neither of them was radar-equipped, they never regained it. One, Rothenberg, failed to find the enemy and eventually turned back; the other, Propst, made an independent attack. At 0115 the airborne radar of the leading PBY, Richards, picked up an echo which, on analysis, indicated some ten large vessels at 10–12 miles range. Pushing in closer the Japanese ships silhouettes were made out and it was estimated that there were ten transports in two columns flanked by six destroyers.

The attack was conducted so as to achieve maximum surprise and minimum warning to the enemy, for the lumbering seaplanes were sitting ducks for the anti-aircraft gunners once spotted. With the planes darkened, the switching off of the taillight of Richards's aircraft being a silent indication of the commencement of the attack, and in a glide approach with engines throttled back, the two PBYs selected the nearest large ship as their target. Descending to the requisite 100 feet altitude for launching the torpedo, as they had been instructed, Richards released at a range of approximately 800 yards and then turned away, climbing as he did so. The crew reported a hit and an explosion. Davis, in the second PBY, aborted his attack due to a flawed approach and calmly went around and tried a second time. Then he attacked up the path of the moon against a brilliantly silhouetted target, working both the rudder and the torpedo director himself. He continued his descent down to just 40 feet above the water, under considerable fire from several of the enemy convoy and escorting destroyers. The Japanese captain made the standard avoidance turn-away to starboard, thus presenting his stern to the attacker. The ship's screws and rudders were reported as being 'clearly visible' and Davis was forced to drop from dead astern, but even at the point-blank range of 200 yards, with such a narrow target the torpedo ran wide.

Despite receiving many hits, smashing the Norden bombsight and even shooting off the goggles of one of the aircrew leaving the man intact, Davis coolly circled once more at 1,500 feet to observe the effects of the two attacks.

The third PBY, Probst, also located the convoy later and similarly tracked his target up the path of the moon, releasing straight and true, although by now the Japanese were fully alert and engaged him with gunfire. He also reported the flash of a direct hit but could not verify it for he was immediately attacked in his turn by a defending fighter, only avoiding destruction by taking refuge in a convenient cloud bank.

Their return path to Midway was taken individually, but long before they got near they picked up radio warnings that their base was under attack, and most changed course toward Lisianski. Eventually one landed offshore there due to fuel shortage, and they were stranded at sea for fifty-three hours before being picked up. Davis hugged the deck and avoided the attentions of the Japanese then ran into a

82. Action Report of First Lieutenant Robert B. Andrews, USAAC to Commanding General VII Bomber Command, *Special Mission*, dated 6 June 1942, in ADM199/1302 held National Archives, Kew, London. The French Transatlantic liner *Normandie* (71,300 tons) was the world's largest ship when built, and, although surpassed by 1942 by the British liners *Queen Mary* and *Queen Elizabeth* in tonnage, was still the longest vessel afloat at 1,029 feet overall. The *Argentina Maru*, *Kiyozumi Maru* and *Nankai Maru*, the three transports that any bombs came remotely near were 13,000 tonners and less than half the length. Nor were there any battleships or heavy cruisers with the convoy the largest warship present was

the 5,195-ton light cruiser *Jintsu*, flagship of Rear-Admiral Raizo Tanaka.

83. Action Report of Lieutenant-Colonel Walter C. Sweeney, Jr, USAAC, *AAC Action with the Enemy*, in ADM199/1302 held National Archives, Kew, London.

84. The four pilots were Lieutenant (jg) Charles P. Hibberd, Lieutenant (jg) Douglas C. Davis aviator-volunteer (naval), (A-V(N)), Ensign Allan Rothenberg, USN of VP-24 and Ensign Gaylord D. Propst of VP-51.

85. As they were carrying torpedoes these four could claim to be the first-ever PTYs, had such a designation existed.

86. Lieutenant William L. 'Red' Richards, XO of VP-44, who embarked with Hibberd's crew.

tropical storm, 'ceiling and visibility zero and a 30-knot wind', which did not help the onboard repairs being effected. They eventually put down with five minutes fuel remaining, at Alyson Island, east of Midway. Meanwhile the other two Catalinas individually made landfall at Laysan, finally returning to Hawaii on the 5th.

It was a very brave effort and had struck the first blow of the battle. It deserved better results than it actually achieved. The only actual hit scored was on the bow of the tanker *Akebono Maru*, which had been steaming in the vulnerable rear position in the more northerly of the two columns. The detonation was fierce and resulted in the deaths of eleven of her crew, with a further thirteen being wounded, mostly from burns. The aircrew in the waist of the PBY later reported that it was, 'as if the whole ship had blown up'[87]. The official analysis of the attacks claimed that one attack transport or attack cargo ship (AP or AK) was considered sunk and one severely damaged.

However, the actual damage inflicted on the ship herself was minimal and did not affect her speed, which she reported was still good for 12–14 knots, more than sufficient to enable her to continue on with the convoy. Davis's target was the troop transport *Kiyozumi Maru*, and she was practically unscathed, although machine-gun fire sweeping her deck had wounded eight of the SNLF (Special Naval Landing Force) men of the Kure unit taking passage aboard her. Propst may have attacked the same target later, but, whichever ship he did attack, the flash he reported was not a hit, but probably that of one of her responding guns, because she also remained untouched. All these ships ploughed doggedly on toward Midway undeterred. Alas for the Americans, the failure of the single hit that they did achieve was to be but a depressing foretaste of the miserable performance of their torpedoes throughout the battle.

Despite this, the PBY had opened the battle and taken the fight to the Japanese. There could no longer be any justification for Yamamoto's cosy illusions, either that the Americans would not fight, or, that his complex operation could develop in the manner he had decreed and expected. That torpedo strike on the *Akebone Maru* was just the first of many such disillusionments that were to burst over the Japanese forces during the course of the next few days.

---

87. Action Report, CO VP-44 to Commander Task Force (dated 25 June 1942), *Midway*, held in Archives II, College Park, Maryland.

Chapter Three

Preparing The Ambushes

Intelligence work was now reaching a climax, but not all of it had been as totally flawless as has been claimed. Nimitz had previously advised the Midway defenders that according to interpretations at Pearl, the Japanese were due to carry out simultaneous invasions at both Midway and in the Aleutians on 5 June. He therefore warned them to expect preliminary attacks on the night of 2/3 June or the early morning of the 3 June. But nothing had happened.[1] Despite this, Mitscher was later to claim: 'On the night of May 30 a CINCPAC intelligence report, giving an accurate estimate of the Japanese Midway force organization, was received.[2]

Both sides had now moved up into position, and at this stage both were secure in the knowledge that they had the drop on the other. One fleet was soon to be bitterly disillusioned.

Early call on 4 June meant an 0330 breakfast for the SBD pilots before they stumbled their way to their respective squadron ready rooms. Then the waiting began, interrupted only by two false alarms which sent the men to their aircraft, only to have the mission aborted each time. Third time lucky? There was a hint of *déjà vu* about the whole scenario, which, as Richard Best was to recall, followed almost exactly that of the briefing that Spruance and his team had laid on for them shortly after leaving Pearl Harbor.[3]

At 0500 local Midway time on 4 June, back at Pearl the clocks were showing 0730 and tension was mounting to breaking point. Lieutenant-Commander Layton was brimming with confidence. He predicted to Nimitz that, within an hour, one of the search aircraft from the island would locate the enemy about 175 miles distant on a bearing of 325 degrees. He was absolutely right.[4]

Day One 4 June 1942

In anticipation of surprising the Japanese carriers once they had committed at least part of their main strength in attacking the fully alerted Midway defences, Fletcher moved his two task forces carefully from the Point Luck waiting position and into an ambush position. The waiting area intended by Nimitz was to be some 200 miles to the north of Midway itself at dawn on 4 June, for the carriers of the 1st *Kidō Butai* were expected to make their initial launch from a position north-east of the island. This would have placed the Task Forces 16 and 17 nicely within 180 miles of their opponents. Thus positioned, Fletcher could reasonable hope to outflank his enemy and get in a heavy blow when the Japanese carriers were at their most vulnerable. So much for theory, but the actual placing of the American carriers required rather fine judgement, a balance of not being too close and thereby risking early detection by the longer-legged Japanese reconnaissance patrols, but close enough for the Americans to launch as quickly as possible, and within range, once the enemy had been pinpointed. The advantage of surprise Fletcher certainly had, but in naval combat, and especially carrier-to-carrier combat, one had to expect the unexpected. Unlike

---

1. Secret and confidential Message 310357, CINCPAC to NAS Midway, (and repeated to the commanders Task Forces 4, 9,16, 17 and COMINCH) held on microfilm RG-313, Reel 13.
2. CO *Hornet* to CINCPAC, CV8/A16–3, Ser. 0018, dated June 13, 1942, p 1, para 2.
3. Best to Buell, Interview dated 15 May 1966.
4. But Layton was *not* as much of a prophet as some historians like to maintain. Both E. B. Potter in his book *Nimitz,* and Gordon Prange in his book *Miracle at Midway,* date this forecast as being made many days earlier, late in May! This, apparently, despite the fact that Layton deliberately told Prange that his prediction was actually *not* made until the morning of 4 June.

conventional surface battles, things would happen very quickly once the two sides made contact with each other, and there would be no time for leisurely second-guessing. The old Civil War maxim of being 'the fustest with the mostest'[5] never felt more aptly applicable than in those tense, waiting hours just before first light on 4 June.

Some twenty-two PBYs had left on the morning search, eleven amphibians from the lagoon and eleven from Eastern Island. The first contact was from Midway-based Catalina PBY of 23 Squadron[6] piloted by Lieutenant Howard P. Ady, Jr[7], who, at 0503, sighted a solitary aircraft heading for Midway. He made the very first contact report of the day, the laconic single word, 'Aircraft.' He then sighted the Nagumo force itself and broadcast an amplification report at 0534, 'Enemy Carriers.' At 0540 Ady signed 'ED [Enemy Detected] 180 sight 320' and at 0552, he finally gave all the information the waiting task force commanders were waiting for 'Two carriers and main body of ships, carriers in front, course 135, speed 25.'

The second report came from Midway-based Catalina PBY of 23 Squadron piloted by Lieutenant (jg) William E. Chase, who sighted the airborne striking force heading for Midway and signalled in plain language at 0544; 'Many planes heading Midway.' He in turn, sighted the *Kidō Butai* soon after and signalling the fact at 0552, but only reported *two*, not the actual four, Japanese carriers present.

Unfortunately Ady's report, which certainly confirmed that the Japanese were right on schedule and approaching from the prevailing upwind position, actually contained a sizeable positional error, placing the 1st *Kidō Butai* about 40 miles nearer in to Midway than was actually the case. This error was compounded by the fact that Fletcher failed to close his attacking carriers to within the 200 mile striking range the plan called for. In fact, at dawn, the American carriers were some 260 miles from Nagumo, or 90 miles east of Nimitz's desired position at 0600.[8] According to one source, the US task forces had made good a course of 210 degrees true during the preceding hours of darkness, when in fact, to close the enemy carriers, they ought to have made good a course of 230 degrees. They had been steaming at the best economical speed of the escorting destroyers, 15 knots, but had been constantly zigzagging so were actually only making a forward progression of 12.5 knots.[9] At that speed they should have made 75 miles by 0600 on 4 June, and dawn found them about 80 miles east of Nimitz's 'desired position.'

---

5. This famous, perhaps apocryphal, comment on how to win battles is usually attributed to the brilliant Confederate General Nathan Bedford Forrest (1821–77), an outstanding Tennessee cavalry officer during the Civil War, who remained undefeated in a series of actions against superior Union forces until almost the end. However, it may be typical 'yellow press' journalese, for it first appeared in print in a 1917 edition of the *New York Times*.
6. The strange designation term 'Strawberry 5' is still used to describe Ady's aircraft, but Ady stated he had never heard such a term being applied. It was actually just a typical piece of Hollywood fiction from the Charlton Heston film packed with such nonsense, but which has distorted factual history. Ady also complained that in the film he was called 'Howie' but, again, nobody ever did call him that!
7. Captain Howard Parmele Ady, Jr, (1917–98) b. Texas, 25 July 1917. Originally wanted to join the Army Air Corps, but bowed to his mother's wishes to join the navy instead. 1939 graduated US Naval Academy Annapolis. With VP-23 in 1941 Pearl Harbor. 1942 Midway. Post-war Commander, Air Group aboard the carrier *Kearsarge* (CVG-101) during Korean War. Onboard carrier *Hornet* (CVA-12), CO VFAW-3 at NAS North Island. CofS, Western Sea Frontier, Treasure Island, California. Teacher and coach at US Naval Academy. Retired as captain in 1963 after twenty-eight years in the navy. Decorations included DFC, Air Medal and DVC for Korea. Died from heart attack at home Sun City West, Arizona, 23 April 1998, aged 80.
8. Commander Richard C. Epps, served aboard the destroyer *Aylwin* (DD355) of DesRon 1, screening Task Force 16 and acted as plane guard for *Enterprise,* thereby strictly conforming to all her movements during the battle. He informed George Walsh that he plotted data from the *Aylwin*'s position reports for the evening of 3 June and the morning of 4 June 1942, for these results. The positions he used were:

Midway Atoll position-	Lat 28–13 Long 177–22
3 June 1942 2000-	Lat 33–17 Long 175–42
4 June sunrise- (about 0600)	Lat 31–40 Long 176–04
TF16/17 should have- been at by 0600	Lat 31–35 Long 177–22

Commander Richard C. Epps to George Walsh, 29 August 2006, reproduced by permission of George Walsh.
9. *Ibid.* Commander Epps believes that Fletcher was not ignoring Nimitz's direction and that he was trying to reach that point before sighting reports started arriving. The reason why the two task forces were not proceeding at higher speeds in order to achieve this, Epps puts down to the need for Fletcher to conserve the destroyers' oil stocks for a pitched battle the next day. Fletcher might not have known much about aircraft, but, as a surface ship commander he was well aware of the limitations of his ships. Using the destroyers' cruising turbines only in order to achieve the minimum fuel consumption limited their top speed to 15 knots. Epps wrote: 'When speed is cranked up to 25 to 30 knots, a destroyer uses an unbelievable amount of oil. He knew that he would not be able to refuel his screening ships

Had Nimitz's intentions been followed to the letter, some naval aviators maintain, a much better scenario would have developed as far as the morning strikes were concerned. 'Nimitz would have probably relied on the expertise of Admiral Pat Bellinger[10] and Captain Arthur Davis[11], both of whom were experience aviators, in working out this positioning.'[12] Certainly no finer minds could have been applied to the problem. Bellinger was the doyen of naval aviators, who had been among the seven such pioneers[13] deployed at the Naval Aviation Camp at Guantanamo Bay, Cuba, in early 1913 with their Curtiss 'A' aircraft, and had also been among the group that set up the US Navy Flying School at Pensacola in March 1914.[14] Davis was one of the earliest exponents of dive-bombing with VB-2 in the late 1920s and had led the epoch-making January 1929 dive-bombing attack on the Miraflores locks on the Panama

Canal, when during exercises the *Saratoga*'s air group had totally surprised the defending US Army's defending fighters and US naval aviation had come of age. Davis knew the supreme importance of positioning and timing and any plan he had a hand in would be perfectly honed to achieve the maximum surprise and effect.

Davis had developed the dive-bomber tactic further while at the Bureau of Aeronautics and Ordnance, even applying himself to the creation of a dive-bombing sight. His credentials were impeccable and he was marked down for early promotion to rear-admiral and a carrier command.

Nimitz tasked Bellinger with organizing search patterns by his PBYs, which resulted in dawn reconnaissance missions out to 700 miles, in order that the Japanese could be located before they could launch their strike. Davis was instructed to predict as best he could the Japanese

after the action started.' Even so, however much the 'tin-can' sailors can understand this argument it still cuts very little ice with the aviators because that decision, which ultimately led to an extended range attack, was strictly a matter of life or death for them.

10. Vice-Admiral Patrick Nielson Lynch Bellinger (1885–1962). b. Cheraw, South Carolina, on 8 October1885. Graduated from US Naval Academy, Annapolis, 1907. Initially served in submarines but, along with contemporaries Ted Ellyson and Ken Whiting, made the total switch to aviation in 1912 becoming Naval Air Pilot No. 4. First US Navy pilot to use a catapult at sea and first in combat, operating from battleship *Mississippi* (BB-23), when his Curtiss 'A' flying boat was fired upon during the Vera Cruz, Mexico, campaign in 1914, for which he received the Medal of Honor. Set two altitude records in June 1913 and April 1915. During World War I commanded NAS Hampton Roads, Virginia. Commanded the navy's first transatlantic Seaplane crossing attempt in May 1919, flying NC-1, along with Marc Mitscher, which although he did not complete, won him the Navy Cross. 1940 rear-admiral, commanding Patrol Wing 2, Honolulu, and Senior Naval Air Officer at Pearl Harbor on 7 December 1941. He sent the famous signal, 'Air Raid, Pearl Harbor – this is no drill'. In May 1942, in command of both Pacific Fleet Patrol Wings as Captain Task Force 9 August 1942 CoS to C-in-C, Ernie King. March 1943 in command of Atlantic Fleet Air Force for anti-submarine operations and 14th Naval District. October 1943. Medals include DSM, the French Legion of Honour and Croix de Guerre, Italian Order of Saints Maurice and Lazarus and Portuguese Military Order of Tower & Sword. Retired as vice-admiral 7 July 1947. Lived at Covington and Clifton Forge, Virginia until his death on 30 May 1962. Interred at Arlington National Cemetery. See Paolo E. Coletta, *Patrick N. L. Bellinger and US Naval Aviation*. The collected Bellinger Papers 1903–62, are held at the National Personnel Records Centre, St Louis, Missouri, and copies were donated by Captain Paolo E. Coletta, Professor Emeritus of History at USNA in 1985, and these are held at the Operational

Archives Branch, Naval Historical Center, Washington DC.
11. Captain Arthur Cayley 'Art' Davis (1893–1965). b.14 March 1893, in Columbia, South Carolina. University of Nebraska 1909–11. Cadet at US Naval Academy, Annapolis, 1911–15. Commissioned 1915. Qualified as naval aviator 1923. Bureau of Aeronautics and Bureau of Ordnance from 1925. 1929 Commanded VB-2 aboard carrier *Saratoga* (CV-3) carried out pioneering dive-bomber experiments including attacks on Miraflores and Pedro Miguel Locks, Panama Canal. Head, Plans Division, Bureau of Aeronautics (BuAer) 1936–9. CO seaplane tender *Langley* (AV-3) 1939–40. CINCPAC Staff Aviation Officer 1940–2. Commanded CarDiv 5 aboard the carrier *Enterprise* (CV-6) at the Guadalcanal landings. Battle of the Eastern Solomons 1942. Commander, Carrier Replacement Squadron, Atlantic Fleet 1942. Rear-Admiral 1942. Commander, Fleet Air Atlantic 1942–3. Assistant CoS, US Atlantic Fleet 1943–4. On staff C-in-C, Washington DC 1943–4. Relieved Charles J. Moore as Spruance's CoS Fifth Fleet, aboard heavy cruiser *Indianapolis* (CA-35) July 1944–45. Vice-admiral 1951. Deputy US Military Representative to NATO Military Staff Committee then Director, Joints Chiefs of Staff 1949–52. Deputy Assistant Secretary of Defense (International Security Affairs) 1952–5. Promoted admiral on retirement 1955. Died 1965 and interred at Arlington National Cemetery. Married three times, third wife Eunice W, died 1974. Awards include three Navy Crosses, two DSMs, three Legions of Merit with Gold Star.
12. George Walsh to the author 3 October 2006.
13. These were First Lieutenant Bernard L. Smith, USMC, First Lieutenant Alfred A. Cunningham, USMC, Lieutenant John H. Towers, USN, Lieutenant (jg) Patrick N. L. Bellinger, USN, Ensign Victor D. Herbster, USN, Ensign William D. Billingsley, USN and Ensign Godfrey de C. Chevalier, USN.
14. These were Lieutenant-Commander H. C. Mustin, USN, Lieutenant Victor D. Herbster, USN, Lieutenant W. M. McIlvain, USN, Lieutenant Patrick N. L. Bellinger, USN, Lieutenant R. C. Saufley, USN, Lieutenant John H. Towers, USN, Lieutenant B. L. Smith, USMC, Ensign Godfrey de C. Chevalier, USN, and Ensign M. L. Stolz, USN.

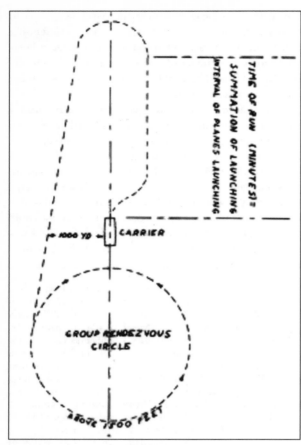

Inside the diagram:
TIME OF RUN (MINUTES)?
SUMMATION OF LAUNCHING
INTERVAL OF PLANES LAUNCHING
1000 YD
CARRIER
GROUP RENDEZVOUS CIRCLE
ABOUT 1700 FEET

Diagram 6. US Carrier Air Group Rendezvous Prior to Departure

intentions and methods of operation, and advise how the American task forces could most successfully counter them. As Lundstrom acknowledges, 'It was vital to determine the best initial position for the US carriers.'[15] Davis duly advised that, with Bellinger's search patterns in place, there would be 'an excellent flanking area northeast of Midway for our carriers' . Davis also stressed that the best chance of success was with 'prompt action' and indeed placed added emphasis on the fact that the carriers should attack, 'at the earliest possible moment.'[16]

Those who believe that Nimitz's plan would have been ideal if it had been strictly followed also claim that it would have been logical for the two task forces to continue to move southward until 0700, at which time they would have been 120–150 miles from the *Kidō Butai*.

Launching a full-strength attack from that position would have enabled proper group rendezvous and coordinated attacks. It would have allowed plenty of fuel for search, combat and return for all elements of the attacking force. It would have placed Task Force 16's aircraft over the target closer to the time of the attacking forces from the island of Midway. The Japanese defenses would have been overwhelmed. While there is no way of knowing how many American lives would have been saved, it can be assumed that there would have been no losses to the sea for lack of fuel, The return flight for all the US Navy pilots would have been shortened along with the outgoing leg.[17]

Whatever the reason, Fletcher's placing actually put the three American carriers way off beam from their four Japanese opposite numbers, who had themselves begun flying off the first of the 108-plane striking force against Midway Island at 0426. By 0445 all these aircraft had formed up and headed out toward the target, a strike reach of about 240 miles, way beyond anything the US carrier air groups were capable of. It was a model of professionalism to assemble and despatch such a fully synchronized force with elements from all four carriers gelling as one unit, and all achieved in less than twenty minutes. In this respect the Japanese were still far in advance of their American counterparts.

A combat air patrol (CAP) of eleven Zeros was also launched and took station at two levels (6,500 and 13,000 feet) over their charges and their relief *shotai* (a group of three aircraft) were already being spotted on the flight decks. Mindful of his instructions Nagumo had kept back at least half his available striking force in case of emergencies. The seven scouting planes from the two heavy cruisers *Chikuma* and *Tone* were catapulted off at intervals between 0435 and 0500 and droned off to cover their sectors. They were not expected to sight any enemy force this early in the operation, but they covered a wide sector from the north through the east to the south of the Japanese force, covering an arc from 031degrees down to 181 degrees. At the end of their outward leg they were to turn north at 0700 for half an hour and then commence the return track. One of those aircraft, Scout No. 4 searching out along the100 degrees vector, was late in launching and consequently, in order to comply with her timetable for the turn, did not reach out as far as her compatriots.

---

15. Lundstrom, *Black Shoe Carrier Admiral: Frank Jack Fletcher at Coral Sea, Midway, and Guadalcanal.*
16. Davis to Nimitz, dated 26 Mary 1942, contained in NAS Midway Unit History, Appendix D2.
17. George Walsh to the author, 3 October 2006.

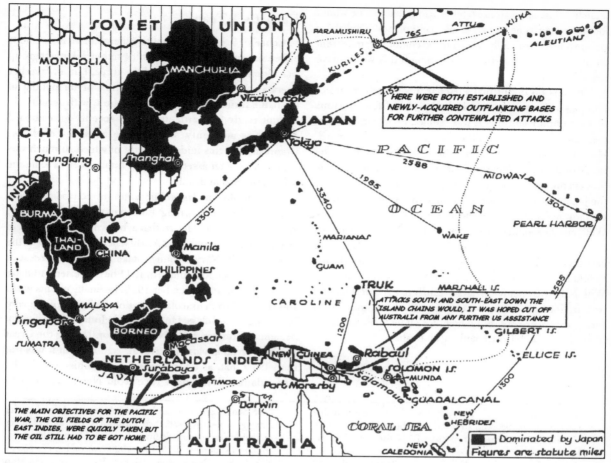

Map 1: Battleground Pacific. Based upon a contemporary map of the area.

Meanwhile, still unaware of the Nagumo force's precise location, Fletcher, always cautious, flew off his own scouting force at precisely the same time. This consisted of ten Douglas SBD Dauntless dive-bombers from the temporary Scouting Five (VS-5)[18] under the command of Lieutenant Wallace C. Short, which were provided with an escort of six Grumman F4F-4 Wildcats from Fighting Three (VF-3). Their mission was to cover a sector 100 miles out to the north of the American task forces, which were then just over 200 miles north of Midway. They commenced flying off from *Yorktown* at 0431 and, once they had vanished over the early-dawn horizon, Fletcher turned his two groups of ships

north-eastward at a speed of 13.5 knots, with the two task forces just barely in visual contact with each other, and continued the patient waiting. So while Fletcher cast north with one carrier, Spruance was forced to conform his task force to that of his senior officer and also led off to the north-east. It remained so until 0607, when Fletcher finally ordered Spruance to turn south-west and attack, but still kept him on a rein, for the order contained the qualification 'as soon as definitely located'. Still, this release order at least gave Spruance the go-ahead to turn back toward the desired optimal launch position[19], but it was at a range of about 215 miles from the target that the Americans finally started to

---

18. VB-5 had been forced to change its designation to VS-5, at least for the duration of the battle, to avoid confusion aboard *Yorktown* when the original Scouting Five, decimated at the Coral Sea encounter, was replaced at Pearl by VB-3. This decision, made by Rear-Admiral Leigh Noyes, the shore representative of Commander, Carriers, Pacific Battle Force

at Pearl, did not sit very well with the personnel of VB-5.

19. Fletcher's principal champion says: 'In fact Spruance changed course at 0600 simply to maintain relative position on TF-17. He did not turn toward the enemy until he received Fletcher's order.' Lundstrom, *Black Shoe Admiral*, p 243. Lundstrom uses this to reinforce the fact

launch[20]. The order from Fletcher also stated that he would follow as soon as he recovered his scout planes. Thus there was no question of a fully co-ordinated combined strike from all three American carriers, even though this would have been desirable.

There is no doubt that Fletcher was acutely aware of Nimitz's stricture not to risk the US fleets' few precious carriers unduly and that it was Nimitz, in 'general tactical command'[21] who directed the change of course on the 3rd. However, many contend that the best way to ensure the safety of the three American carriers was to knock out the four enemy carriers as quickly as possible and that, because the Japanese would *always* outrange the Americans, to get the blow in fast. So why the delay and temporary turn away? Well, another influencing factor on Fletcher, following his experience at the Coral Sea battle when the Japanese carriers had caught him on the hop, was that he did not wish to find himself in the same unenviable position at Midway. With only two enemy carriers *actually confirmed*, Fletcher was anxious about the other pair, which he knew from Intelligence were out, but which, for all he knew might be operating separately in a flanking ambush.

Hornet's A Team

Mitscher's[22] flagship was sent to general quarters one hour before sun-up according to his biographer[23]. Her air group was, nominally, the weakest of the three, but, in fact, her operational complement on the morning of the first day of the battle turned out to be the strongest, with seventy-six aircraft ready for battle as against seventy-four aboard *Enterprise* and only seventy-one aboard *Yorktown*. Unfortunately, this initial strength, of which so much was expected, was an asset that failed totally. Let us examine what happened in detail.

Superficially, the *Hornet* air group seemed to hold many aces that calm, still morning. For a start there was the fact to gladden any aviator's heart, that a 'brown shoe' man was in charge. Rear-Admiral Marc A. Mitscher had been one of the first of the US Navy's young intake to take an interest in flying, and, as a midshipman in 1911 he requested a transfer to aeronautics. In September 1915, he finally got his wish, and reported to Pensacola as part of the intake of the very first flying school class. He qualified in June 1916, officially becoming Thirteenth US Naval Aviator. During the Great War he served at various naval air stations, but it was not until 1919 that, as a lieutenant, he made his mark in the transatlantic flying boat race from Newfoundland to

that Fletcher, and not Spruance, was in command at this stage of the battle. And so it did, but therefore the responsibility for this misplacement of his force had to be Fletcher's.

20. *Aylwin*'s Navigator logged her position as 31° 38' north; 176° 04 west at 0800 on the 4th, about 180–190 miles to the *Kidō Butai*.

21. Nimitz, *OpPlan 29–42*.

22. Admiral Marc Andrew 'Pete' Mitscher (1887–1947). Born Hillsboro, Wisconsin. Graduated US Naval Academy, Annapolis, 1910. Served at sea for two years and commissioned ensign 1912. Served aboard the cruiser *California* (ACR-6) 1913 on the West Coast during the Mexican Campaign, then served aboard the destroyers *Whipple* (DD-15) and *Stewart* (DD-13). Joined the cruiser *North Carolina* (ACR-12) fitted with a flying-off catapult at Pensacola Naval Aeronautical Station for pilot training and qualified 2 June 1916. Retained at Pensacola for duties and further training. Great War April 1917 catapult training experiments aboard the armoured cruiser *Huntingdon* (CA-5). February 1919 Aviation Section, Chief of Naval Operations. Commanded Naval Air Stations Rockaway, Long Island and Miami in 1918. Post-war promoted to lieutenant-commander and took part in a Flying Boat race across Atlantic from Newfoundland to Plymouth in May 1919. Awarded first (of three) Navy Cross. Joined the old minelayer *Aroostook* (CM-4), then being utilized as the Pacific Fleet Aviation Tender, 1920–1, and commanded a Detachment of air forces at Fleet Air Base, San Diego. In 1922 to Plans Division, Bureau of Aeronautics, Washington DC, and at

NAS San Diego, commanded NAS Anacostia. Joined carrier *Langley* (CV-1) in 1926, then *Saratoga* (CV-3) as Air Officer on maiden voyage, made first take-off and landing from that ship on 11 January 1928. June 1929 returned to *Langley* as XO. CoS to Commander Aircraft, Base Force, non-stop flight between San Francisco and Honolulu, January 1934. Became XO of *Saratoga* between 1934–5, then commanded seaplane tender *Wright* (AV-1) and Patrol Wing One. Further service in 1938–40 as Assistant Chief, BuAer July 1941 appointed to command carrier *Hornet* (CV-7) fitting out at Norfolk, Virginia, and remained her captain for Doolittle raid, Midway and Solomon Islands campaign 1941–2. Commanded Patrol Wing Two then December 1942, Commander Fleet Wing, Noumea. Rear-admiral in April 1943 as Commander Air, Solomon Islands. January 1944 commander CarDiv3 then in February 1944 commanded TF-58 as vice-admiral for Marshall's campaign. June 1944 Battle of Philippine Sea from flagship carrier *Lexington* (CV-16) and October 1944 Battle of Leyte Gulf. 1945 Okinawa operations, having two carrier flagships under him hit by kamikazes , *Bunker Hill* (CV-17) and *Enterprise* (CV-6), before hoisting his flag aboard the carrier *Randolph* (CV-15). After the war rejected post of Chief, Naval Operations, after serving as deputy from July 1945, as admiral. Appointed to command Eighth Fleet March 1946 and subsequently C-in-C US Atlantic Fleet September 1946, from flagship carrier *Franklin D. Roosevelt* (CVB-42). Died of heart attack 3 February 1947. Buried at Arlington National Cemetery.

23. Theodor Taylor, *The Magnificent Mitscher*.

Plymouth, for which he received the Navy Cross. He served at the Bureau of Aeronautics (BuAeR) during the turbulent era that almost saw the demise of naval aviation as a separate entity. But it was his work in the late 1920s aboard the carriers *Langley* and *Saratoga* that as Air Officer, Mitscher, then a lieutenant-commander, laid the sure foundations of carrier operating techniques and the promotion of the dive-bomber type for future requirements. As a commander he headed the Flight Division at BuAer from 1935 to 1937 then commanded the tender *Wright*, before promotion to captain and command of Patrol Wing One. He returned to Washington as Assistant Chief of BuAer in 1938, before being appointed to command *Hornet* in May 1941. Mitscher brought a wealth of aviation experience to his new command and much was expected of her.

But the presence of veteran pilot Mitscher in command was but one 'ace-in-the-hole' for the *Hornet*; there were many others, not the least of which was the CHAG himself, Commander Stanhope C. Ring.[24] Here at least, it must have been thought, the right man was in the right place at the right time. No US Navy aviator could claim such a wealth and depth of experience and expertise as Ring, and few of his contemporaries had such a glittering background in naval aviation, nor his qualifications to lead a dive-bombing mission against the IJN's elite carrier force; it was exactly the mission that Ring had been planning and training for almost since he first set foot in an aeroplane back in the 1920s. As the US Navy's competence and growth as the major naval dive-bombing force in the world had been initiated, carefully nurtured and subsequently grown and blossomed, so Ring had been present at each step and his reputation had grown with each advance until it stood very high indeed in the fleet.

Commander Ring had been born into a naval family,

being the son of Commodore James Andrew Ring, who had first served aboard the frigate *Guerrierre* in 1867. Stanhope Ring was destined to follow his father's footsteps and graduated from the US Naval Academy, Annapolis, in 1923. After an initial period as a fresh young ensign seeing sea service aboard the battleship *Colorado*, he concentrated his career on aviation. After flight training at Pensacola, he joined VS-5, which had been attached initially to the aircraft tender *Wright* and then taken aboard the newly converted and completed carrier *Lexington* when she was first commissioned.

On completion of his first tour of duty as a pilot, Ring had been placed at the very centre of US naval aviation development, becoming Aide to Rear-Admiral William A. Moffett himself, the very first Chief of the BuAeR. Ring's charm and natural presence also saw him appointed as Naval Aide to the White House during President Herbert Hoover's term of office. A string of influential appointments followed for the dashing young aviator, which saw another tour of duty with VS-3 aboard the carrier *Langley*, followed by a term as Assistant Operations Officer on the staff of Commander, Aircraft, Battle Force, before he was transferred to NAS San Diego, where he flew with VF-3B, who were the innovators and perfectors of dive-bombing in the US Navy, bringing the 'helldiver' technique to the forefront of attention. Just prior to his marriage, he survived a horrific aviation accident when his aircraft caught fire over east San Diego. He circled for half an hour trying to avoid a crash, controlling his aircraft despite the flames, but although his leather gloves protected his hands and arms, and his goggles his eyes, he suffered second-degree burns that left permanent marks to his face, and he eventually had to parachute to safety.

This experience did not deter him and he continued to

24. Vice-Admiral Stanhope Cotton 'Slim' Ring (1902–63). b. Norfolk, Virginia 1902. Graduated from US Naval Academy, Annapolis, 1923. Ensign aboard battleship *Colorado* (BB-45). Flight training Pensacola, gaining his wings in 1927, then VF-5 with aircraft tender *Wright* (AV-1) and carrier *Lexington* (CV-2). As lieutenant was Aide to Chief of BuAer, Rear-Admiral William A. Moffett and Naval Aide to White House. Appointed to VF-3 aboard carrier *Langley* (CV-1), then Assistant Operations Officer, Commander, Aircraft, Battle Force before joining NAS San Diego with VF-3B developing dive-bomber techniques there and embarked aboard carrier *Saratoga* (CV-3). June 1937 appointed XO, then CO of Patrol Squadron (VP)17, Alaska, 1938–9. In1940 as lieutenant-commander, Assistant Naval Attaché, London, then Naval Liaison Officer, Force H, embarked aboard British carrier *Ark Royal* operating from Gibraltar 1940–1. Awarded CBE by British. October 1941 as commander, appointed CHAG aboard *Hornet*. 1942

Doolittle Raid, Midway then Solomons campaign on staff of Admiral Marc Mitscher. Director Aviation Training for Deputy Director Chief of Naval Operations (Air) 1943–4. CO escort carrier *Siboney* (CVE-112) from May 1945. Post-war commanded *Saratoga* between March and June 1946; then appointed in command carrier *Boxer* (CV-21) between July 1947 and July 1948. Promoted to rear-admiral, then vice-admiral. Commander, Naval Operating Base and NAS Kwajalein, and *de facto* Governor of Marshall Islands. As such he hosted Lieutenant-General 'Pete' Quesada, USAF, the Commander of the Atomic Task Force undertaking Operation *Greenhouse* at Eniwetok between 8 April and 25 May 1951.Deputy CoS, Allied Forces, Southern Europe. Commander, Carrier Division One and finally Vice-Commander, Military Air Transport Service. Retired prematurely due to a debilitating illness, 'apparently some form of muscular dystrophy', and lived at Coronado, California until his death in 1963.

play a part in the expansion of dive-bombing as a viable technique to revolutionize sea warfare, flying from the carrier *Langley* and then *Saratoga* during the 1930s. After a short spell with a patrol squadron in Alaska, as XO and then commander between 1938 and 1939, he was sent to back to the BuAer again in Washington DC, as head of the Administrative Division. On the outbreak of war in Europe, Ring was sent over to London as Assistant Naval Attaché and later became one of several US Navy 'observers' aboard the British aircraft carrier *Ark Royal*. This famous ship was serving with Admiral Sir James Somerville's Force 'H', based at Gibraltar and operating into both the Mediterranean and eastern and southern Atlantic. She had spearheaded Royal Navy air operations in the period 1940–1 and pioneered the effective use of radar to co-ordinate air defence against superior land-based

opposition, both German and Italian. Ring absorbed these lessons and reported back to Washington DC on their effectiveness. The British thought highly of him, awarding him the CBE in recognition of this liaison work.

On return to the States in October 1941 Ring was appointed to the new carrier *Hornet*, then completing for sea and took charge of her air group as CHAG, a plum job. Air Group Eight (AG-8) itself comprised twenty-seven operational Grumman F4F-4 Wildcat fighters; fifteen operational Douglas TBD-1 Devastator torpedo bombers and no fewer than twenty-four operational Douglas SBD-3 Dauntless dive-bombers; these latter belonging to VB-8, commanded by Lieutenant-Commander Robert R 'Ruff' Johnson[25] (nineteen aircraft, of which one was commandeered by Ring as his personal mount) and VS-8, led by Lieutenant-Commander Walter F. Rodee[26].

---

25. Rear-Admiral Robert Ruffin 'Ruff' Johnson. (1902–70). b. Detroit, Michigan, 15 July 1902. Educated Northwestern High School, Detroit, graduating June 1918. Detroit Junior College 1991–21. June 1922 midshipman 13th Michigan District. May 1926 U S Naval Academy, Annapolis, instruction in aviation. Commissioned as ensign. September 1926–August 1927 aboard light cruiser *Milwaukee* (CL-5). Six months participating in Nicaraguan Campaign. September 1927–June 1928 service aboard repair ship *Vestal* (AR-4). July 1928–March 1929 aboard destroyer *Brooks* (DD-232). March–May 1929 aboard destroyer *Hopkins* (DD-249). May 1929 NAS Pensacola, for instruction. November lieutenant (jg). Won wings 1930. February 1930 to VO-2-S, aboard battleship *Arkansas* (BB-33), at Guantanamo Bay to June 1931. June 1931 VP-8S, embarked heavy cruiser *Augusta* (CA-31) 1932 USNA July–August. 1932 Married Helen M. Roux. Two sons Jack Roux and Robert R. Jr. 1934 –36 VF-2B, High Hats, aboard carrier *Saratoga* (CV-3). 1936 VP-5F, Coco Solo, Canal Zone. 1937 lieutenant, VP-5. 1939 Fleet Air Detachment, NAS Norfolk. 1939–September 1941 CO of VS-72, relieving Captain D. E. Wilcox, embarked carrier *Wasp* (CV-7). October 1940 lieutenant-commander. September 1941 CO VB-8 embarked carrier *Hornet* (CV-8) Doolittle Raid and Midway. July 1942–July 1944 Superintendent of Training and XO, NAS Jacksonville. September 1942 commander. August 1944 CO of training carrier *Charger* (CVE-30). August 1945 aboard amphibious warfare command ship *Eldorado* (ACG-11) as CO Air Support Control Units, Amphibious Forces, and then Tactical Air Control Group, Pacific to April 1947. May 1947 Staff, Commandant, Armed Forces Staff College, Norfolk. 1950–51 CofS CarDiv 4. 1951–53 staff of Joint Chiefs of Staff, Washington DC, 1953. Commander Naval Air Training Command, Norman. 1954 CoS and Aide, Commander Fleet Air, Whidbey. Retired as captain January 1956, advanced to rear-admiral on basis of combat service. Awarded DFC. Resided Mill Valley, California. Died 9 July 1970.

26. Rear-Admiral Walter Fred Rodee (1904–2003). b. Milwaukee, Wisconsin, 29 May 1904, but raised in Tucson,

Arizona. Educated Tucson High School class of 1922. Early interest in flying after watching barnstorming pilots at Tucson airport in 1922. Graduated from US Naval Academy, Annapolis, June 1926 as ensign. Spent mandatory sea time aboard the battleship *West Virginia* (BB-48) June 1926–February 1929. At Long Beach in 1927 where he met his wife Virginia. Married her at Yuma in 1928, two sons, Walter and Donald, three daughters, Mary, Carolyn and Virginia. March 1928 reported to Pensacola for flight training. April 1929 gained wings. May 1929 joined VF-3 aboard the carrier *Lexington* (CV-2) until May1931. June 1931 joined VF-2, FAB, Coco Solo, Canal Zone, Ferry Detachment at Hampton Roads, Virginia, flying Martin patrol boats from Baltimore. 1929 lieutenant (jg). 1933–June 1936 Line post-graduate school, Annapolis, followed by a Masters Degree in Aeronautical Engineering from the California Institute of Technology. June 1936 Lieutenant, Air Department carrier *Ranger* (CV-4). Feb 1939 NAS San Diego. September 1940 lieutenant-commander. Assigned to *Hornet* (CV-7) in 1941 as CO VS-8. Fought at Midway, and Air Group Commander at Battle of Santa Cruz Island in 1942. September 1942 commander (TS). When *Hornet* was sunk in October, Rodee flew his aircraft to Espiritu Santu and crash-landed, joining up with a US Marine detachment on the island for a while. January 1943 NAS Astoria. To escort carrier *Pybus* (CVE-34) XO until it was handed over to the Royal Navy as *Emperor* (D98). *Wake Island* (CVE-65) as XO. October 1943–June 1944 light carrier *Independence* (CVL-22) XO.1944, including Rabaul attack November 1943, Gilbert Islands. Captain (TS). Office of CNO, Navy Dept, Washington DC Fleet Maintenance Division. December 1945–August 1946 commanding carrier *Puget Sound* (CVE-113). After the war served as the BuAer representative at the Consolidated-Vultee Aircraft Company. August 1947, commander. November captain. During Korean War, as Commander CarDiv 15 served aboard the carriers *Valley Forge* (CV-45) and *Boxer* (CV-21), was aboard the destroyer *Mansfield* (DD-728) for the Inchon Assault. Was awarded the Legion of Merit while CoS and Aide to the Commander, CarDiv3. Appointed in command

In view of the almost universal disapprobation Ring was to suffer, from both his colleagues and historians, it might restore the balance of his memory if some contrasting viewpoints were put on record here for the first time. One historian described Ring as 'inexperienced'[27], which, considering his aviation career, and the part he had played in the development of dive-bombing techniques since the mid-1930s, especially with VF-3B and aboard *Saratoga*, is surely bizarre. Another critic devoted several pages of analysis to Ring, describing him disparagingly as a 'naval *beau ideal*', but one who despite all his advantages ('handsome, charismatic, popular with women and easy with his superiors') was also 'a martinet' and 'not a successful leader.'[28]

On 28 March 1946, Ring was to compose a 22-page handwritten letter describing events at Midway as he saw them. Discovered by his daughter, Susan Ring Keith some fifty-three years later after his death, tucked away in a sea chest in his Coronado home and never read, this missive was partially published in the USNI *Proceedings* in August 1999, thanks to the intervention of Captain Bruce Linder.[29] The magazine saddled this document with the journalistic title *Lost Letter of Midway* but at least gave it the belatedly public hearing it deserved. Susan Ring Keith kindly made a copy available to me following my research visit to Coronado in 2006.

Clayton Fisher, who was to be Ring's reluctant wingman at Midway, took me across the road from his home at Coronado during my visit, and pointed out the Ring home in Tolita Avenue. It is just a few hundred yards away, obliquely across the street from the Clayton residence, and, ironically the two houses might have been SBDs in formation, wingman and leader, but he told me: 'I never visited with Stanhope Ring and had no social contact with him.'[30]

Susan Keith Ring was kindness itself. She recalled that, after her father finished his stint aboard HMS *Ark Royal* and returned home he brought with him 'a collection of wooden dolls from Portugal, each one representing a different industry of Portugal, and an ashtray made out of the deck of the *Ark Royal*, all of which are permanently displayed in my living room.'[31]

Ring's old friend from his *Ark Royal* days was Admiral Sir James Somerville, and he recorded in his Report of Proceedings that: 'Lieutenant-Commander Ring, US Navy, US Naval Observer, joined *Ark Royal* on 24 March 1941[32], just before his command, Force H, sailed from Gibraltar for a long stint of patrolling in the Bay of Biscay between Ushant and Lisbon.' Much later in the war, on 18 December 1944, long after the *Ark* had been sunk by a German U-boat and Somerville had moved on to become the British Admiralty Delegation (BAD) representative in Washington DC, he recorded his delight that Ring had the thoughtfulness to look him up and they had a chat about 'the old days'. This appears a considerate thing to have done and in my opinion gives a measure of the man. Somerville wrote in his desk diary:

Captain Ring, USN, who had served in the rank of Lt-Cdr as Observer in the *Ark Royal* in 1940 and '41, called on me and said he had been at pains to impress on people in his service the great achievements of the British Navy in the early years of the war when they had practically no reserves and were fighting single-handed. He referred in particular to the magnificent work of the *Ark Royal* and her handful of fighters who would make sortie after sortie and work under conditions which would be regarded as quite unacceptable nowadays; he said that people were inclined to forget this great achievement and he felt highly privileged that he had been there himself to see what could be done . . . [33]

Others have equally agreeable memories of Ring, in contrast to the picture presented in the history books. Lieutenant-Colonel Rufus B. Thompson, Jr, USMC, knew

---

of carrier *Essex* (CV-9) at Yokosuka in June 1952, but prematurely relieved in September of that year, being awarded a second Legion of Merit. July 1954 rear-admiral (TS). May 1957 rear-admiral. July 1957 Commander Continental Air Defense Command, ENT AFB, Colorado Springs. Appointed commander of North Island NAS, San Diego, and Eleventh Naval District fields, and ended his career overseeing the merging of naval air bases during the cutbacks of the late 1950s. Retired from the service in July 1961. In civilian life lived at Coronado, California. Joined the Air Logistics Corporation at Pasenda for five years before a final retirement in 1967. Awards included Distinguished Flying Cross and Navy Cross. His role in jet aircraft development off Korea was portrayed in John H. Auer's film *The Eternal Sea* (1955) by the actor Louis Jean Heydt. Died at his home

at San Pedro on New Year's Day 2003, after complications from a stroke.

27. Thomas Wildenberg, *Destined for Glory; Dive Bombing, Midway, and the Evolution of Carrier Airpower.*
28. Alvin Kernan, *The Unknown Battle of Midway: The Destruction of the American Torpedo Squadrons.*
29. Captain Bruce Linder. Commanded a guided-missile frigate and two major shore bases while in active service, and wrote the history book, *San Diego's Navy.*
30. Clayton Fisher to the author, 24 April 2006.
31. Susan Keith Ring to the author 15 May 2006.
32. Report of Proceedings, Force H, 24–31 March 1941 (SMVL 7/7, Churchill College Archive Centre, Cambridge).
33. BAD desk diary, 18–29 December 1944 (SMVL 2/3, Churchill College Archive Centre, Cambridge).

Ring well when the latter was CO, Naval Operating Base, Kwajalein Island, Marshall Islands in 1950–1. He told me:

> In my capacity as Commanding Officer of the Marines, and Provost Officer of the Island, I reported directly to him resulting in almost daily contact. He was a fine officer and a real gentleman, maybe a little aloof to some, but very approachable and a good leader. He was tall, very distinguished looking and reserved in his mannerisms. Under several emergency conditions and personnel crises, he remained cool in his demeanour, making quick and well thought out decisions.[34]

Thompson's daughter also recalled Ring this way. When her parents were carrying out very necessary repair work to their house, Rear-Admiral Stanhope C. Ring spotted Betty on the roof one day. He asked, 'Is that you Mrs Thompson?' She replied, 'Yes sir.' He asked, 'What are you doing up there?' She said, 'Repairing the roof.' He replied, ' Probably only a Marine's wife would do that.'[35]

These small glimpses tend to show a rather different from the one hitherto presented as, 'rigid and overbearing'.

We shall return in detail to Ring's letter, described by himself as 'an attempt, almost four years after the action, to set down in black and white my best recollections of what occurred', but by Kernan as an attempt 'to exculpate himself from failures he had never been publicly charged with'.[36] Ring's opening line is worthwhile recording here however: 'There has been much written about the Battle of Midway,' he wrote, one senses wearily, 'and in many respects there has been a startling lack of accuracy.' He wrote those words in 1946. He was not to know the half of it!

Begging to Differ – Carrier Operations in 1942

The Japanese had only recently developed the art of working many carriers together to form one formidable force. The war in China had seen the *Kaigun* take a strategical approach with their air power, not only through the adoption of long-range, land-based bombers, itself a unique innovation for a strictly naval air force, but in the use of their carrier-borne aircraft also.

The China experience seems to have been partly responsible for the IJN's development of a very significant doctrinal innovation in carrier warfare – concentration of carriers in a single formation. In order to mass aircraft for strikes, carriers operated in company off China. Wargaming also suggested that concentration of carriers could be valuable in fleet actions. Ultimately, the IJN shifted from dispersed to concentrated carrier operations just before the outbreak of war. Its 'First Air Fleet' of six carriers provided it with the strongest mobile air striking force anywhere and contributed greatly to IJN success in the first six months of war.[37]

However, the China operations were against land targets, of little use for training naval pilots. It was the flexibility of the carrier that made its use so attractive; they were able to range up and down the whole coast of China wherever needed. But the actual blows they could inflict were minimal in terms of bomb tonnage dropped; this was not so important as it seems, for naval precision attacks on Chinese airfields could cause more damage than dispersed high-level bombing, a point the German Junkers Ju.87 Stukas were making at the same time in Spain. Still, the need to bring greater numbers to bear was always a major consideration.

Operating over a continent, weather was a major factor also. It is perhaps no coincidence that one of the leading Japanese aviation planners at the time, Lieutenant-Commander Jō Eiichirō[38], was also an enthusiastic amateur meteorologist. Eiichirō's work in planning the first IJN air offensive of the China Incident, from late 1937 onward, involving the carrier *Kaga*, was ground-breaking. The US

34. Lieutenant-Colonel Rufus B. Thompson, to the author, 18 June 2006.
35. Sue and Mike Sanders to the author, 29 June 2006.
36. Alvin Kernan, *Unknown Battle of Midway*.
37. William D. O'Neil, *Military Transformation as a Competitive Systemic Process: The Case of Japan and the United States Between the World Wars*.
38. Rear-Admiral Jō Eiichirō, (1898–1944). Graduated Etajima, 47th Class. 9 October 1919–31 May 1920, served aboard the training ship (former armoured cruiser) *Adzuma*. 13 May 1921–1 November 1921, as warrant officer first class, served aboard the old protected cruiser *Akashi*. 1 April 1928–10 December 1929, XO of the carrier *Akagi*. 16 November 1936–1 December 1937 staff of 2 Air Fleet. 1937–8, Operations Planning Officer, 1st Air Fleet, carrier *Kaga*. 1939–40, Navy General Staff, also taught at Navy and Army War Colleges. 1940–1, 13th Air Fleet, China. 1941–3, Naval Aide-de-camp to Emperor Hirohito. 1943 appointed in command as captain of the carrier *Chiyoda*. August 1943, was said to have originally postulated the concept of the *tokko* or *kamikaze* attack, later developed by Onishi Takijiro, and Oikawa Koshiro. 25 October 1944, killed in action (KIA) when *Chiyoda* was sunk with all hands at the Battle of Leyte Gulf, going down in 18° 37'N, 126° 45'E. Posthumously ranked rear-admiral.

Navy had launched 'in-bash-out' type air strikes against ground targets in exercises against army interceptors, notably at Panama, but Eiichirō's missions were sustained campaigns and the navy learned a lot about long-range operations and sustaining carriers at sea for long periods. Despite this, up until 1940, Japan still operated her carriers in two-ship divisions

Hitherto all navies with carriers had, from time-to-time, operated two carriers in concert for specific exercises; the Royal Navy had even experimented with a three-carrier unit in the 1930s, and in actual combat off Norway in June 1940 the *Ark Royal* and the *Glorious*, escorted by the fast battleship *Valiant,* heavy cruiser *Berwick* and eight destroyers, had formed what was, in fact, the world's first task force as we now use the word, and during the *Pedestal* convoy to Malta in August 1942 they employed three carriers working together – *Victorious, Indomitable* and *Eagle* – with a fourth, *Furious,* operating in an aircraft-ferrying role. But in all these cases the carriers had operated in conjunction with the others, and not as part of an integral and integrated team. The Japanese concept was different, in that during 1941 they were operating their carriers in two-ship divisions that trained together as a fighting unit, so that the two carriers acted in concert as one powerful group. Fighters from one carrier had no problem combining strikes with dive-bombers or torpedo-bombers from another. This was extended logically, by a similar combining of divisions, and the 1st *Kidō Butai* eventually comprised three two-carrier divisions.[39] This gave the Japanese great flexibility and enormous punch. Not all the aircraft could be launched in one wave, but a strike that combined half the available total

of all types from six carriers was a massive – and cohesive – force that could crush any likely Allied opponent it was likely to encounter at sea.

It should be remembered, when considering this revolution in naval power, that it was still experimental, subject to slow, almost creeping change, and remained very much so into the war.[40] The new doctrine was not set in stone. Midway was to prove that, as well as the advantages of overwhelming striking power, there were also basic inherent risks in operating four to six carriers together, the most obvious one being that all the eggs were very much in one basket; find one carrier and you found them all! IJN aviation experts were divided on the subject, and were to remain so. Also, even among those who wholeheartedly embraced the new philosophy, there was more interest in the offensive advantages than in any possible defensive paybacks.

American doctrine was very different and did not approach the Japanese style, either in power or in co-operation until much later in the war; indeed operating more than one carrier in a screen was at first frowned upon although it was eventually done. This experiment in concentration, with two carriers operating together inside a single screen, was conducted by Carrier TF-11 during the successful carrier attack on the Japanese invasion fleets at Lae and Salamaua, New Guineas, on 10 March 1942. This revolutionary tactic was instigated, despite howls of protest from traditionalist, by Vice-Admiral Wilson Brown, with the proactive input of the captain of the *Lexington*, the impetuous Frederick C Sherman.[41]

The attack itself was only modest in its achievement, and

---

39. This did not happen until the very eve of the Pacific War. Mike Wenger among others, whose field this is, ascertained that, although the 1st Air Fleet was set up in April 1941, full multi-air-group operations were only finally adopted in October 1941. Even then it appears to have been, 'pushed through by enthusiasts, like Genda and Onishi, against the strenuous objections of individual carrier captains and air officers' – Jon Parshall to the author, 10 March 2006. In my own opinion, the IJN's addiction to offence, above all else, probably helped carry the day; whereas the defensive penalties that could (and ultimately were) exacted, were probably not treated with the priority that they warranted, and for much the same reason.

40. Minoru Genda, '*Evolution of Aircraft Carrier Tactics of the Imperial Japanese Navy*'.

41. Vice-Admiral Frederick Carl 'Ted' Sherman (1888–1957) b. Port Huron, Michigan, 1888. Graduated from US Naval Academy, Annapolis, 1910. Commanded the submarines *H-2* (SS-29) and *O-2* (SS-63) during World War I. Transferred to flying training and served as XO of *Saratoga* (CV-3) in 1937. To NAS San Diego 1938 before being appointed in command *Lexington* (CV-2) in 1940 until she was sunk at

Coral Sea in 1942. As rear-admiral replaced Admiral Kinkaid aboard *Enterprise* (CV-6) but when she was replaced by HMS *Victorious* in April 1943, served with ComAirSopac [Commander Air, South Pacific] under Vice-Admiral Aubrey Fitch. Later to only remaining operational carrier, *Saratoga* (CV-3) as Commander CarDiv1 raided Rabaul in November. Joined new carrier *Essex* (CV-9) as Commander, CarDiv 2 in June 1943. March–August 1944, ashore with Commander, Fleet Air, West Coast, then back to sea with Task Group 38.3 from 1944, flying his flag in *Bunker Hill* (CV-17) under Rear-Admiral Montgomery as Commander Task Group 58.1. Attacked Formosa and was at Battle of Leyte Gulf. At Iwo Jima in 1945, then attacks on Japanese mainland under Mitscher. Vice-admiral in June 1945, Commander 1st Fast Carrier Task Force. Awarded three Navy Crosses. Post-war Commander, 5th Fleet in 1946, flying his flag aboard battleship *Iowa* (BB-61) until May, and then light cruiser *Vicksburg* (CL-86). Retired from Navy in 1947. Wrote the book *Combat Command; The American Aircraft Carriers in the Pacific War*. He died on 27 July 1957, at San Diego, California. The airfield at San Clemente Island was named Frederick C. Sherman Field in his honour.

greatly over rated by the Americans[42], but it was a successful raid at a time when such operations, however tiny, had seemed beyond the Allies. This might have seemed to justify Brown's daring innovation on the use of carriers, but it proved a one-off. Despite receiving a grandstand greeting and the Distinguished Service Medal for his perceived 'great victory' on his return to Pearl Harbor at the end of the month, Brown was relieved of his command and packed off to become Amphibious Warfare Commander, Pacific Fleet.[43]

'Black Jack' Fletcher had though that the Brown model was a good idea, bringing the maximum defensive capability, both airborne and shipborne, together. He used a slightly amended version of it during the Coral Sea encounter, also adjudged reasonably successful. Thereafter, the American carrier groups reverted back to their own independent screens, acting in loose cohesion but each as a separate entity, The reversion to standard practice subsequently remained in place in time for Midway, where, once again, each carrier's air group acted independently, albeit with a common objective. At Midway there seemed to be little enthusiasm among the American commanders for the combining of attacks and the overwhelming application of mass which characterized the new Japanese style, and it was only by luck that some carrier groups arrived over the target at the same time; most, unfortunately for them, arrived in sequence in small, isolated and therefore easily dealt with squadrons. Of course, to be fair, time was at a premium for the Americans prior to Midway; just getting the badly damaged *Yorktown* up and running in order to take part took a lot of work, and was magnificently done, but

even so it is perhaps salutatory that it was *Yorktown*'s scratch air group that was by far the most well organized of the three US air teams and out-performed both the *Hornet* and *Enterprise* on 4 June.

US Navy carrier doctrine had gradually evolved during the 1920s and 1930s but for much of that period had been centred on just two very large carriers, *Lexington* and *Saratoga*, and a smaller one, the former collier *Jupiter*, renamed *Langley*. Right from the start the US Navy adopted a very different approach from the Royal Navy; the aim of the pioneering US aviators[44] was cram as many aircraft into their ships as possible, and this led to the development of deck parks. Obviously the emphasis for the US Navy carriers was on offence, albeit still as a single-carrier strike force; whereas the Royal Navy, with the exception of the *Ark Royal*, only embarked small numbers of aircraft in penny packets.

This divergence of ideas was made sharper by the immediate pre-war building programmes of the respective nations, the American ships, even the first keel-up built *Ranger* of 14,500 tons displacement (completed in 1934) being capable of carrying seventy-two aircraft, while the 22,000-ton *Ark* (1938) could only field sixty. This gap in capability widened with the introduction by the British of the armoured deck, adopted with the likelihood of having to withstand heavy land-based bombing attacks from the German and Italian air forces – a type of threat the US Navy never contemplated as part of Plan Orange. This led to a further reduction of British carrier capability from sixty to a mere thirty-three in the three 23,000 ton *Illustrious* class ships, which was only partially remedied by the *Indomitable*

---

42. The returning US carrier pilots claimed to have destroyed five transports, two heavy cruisers, a light cruiser and a destroyer but, in truth, only actually sank three attack transports and a converted minelayer. Such overestimation of results by attacking airmen was commonplace in all nations' air forces throughout the war, but in 1942, desperate for some positive achievement, the Americans had perhaps not yet begun to discount the wilder claims, as they did later in the war when less starry-eyed and more hard-nose analysis was done.

43. Lundstrom states that Brown's selection, given his past record in amphibious planning, was a totally 'logical' choice and certainly not a penalty for his presumptuousness in throwing out the tactical book on carrier operations. Be that as it may, after Fletcher's modified adoption of it during the Coral Sea battle, the Brown experiment was not to be repeated by the Americans for a very long while. Whether it was a good thing or a bad thing is still the subject of heated debate. The advantage of concentration of aerial fire power, it is said, could still be achieved without placing the carriers adjacent to each other, with its inherent risk of putting all one's eggs in one basket. Both viewpoints had their merits and de-merits amply demonstrated at Midway – the

Japanese, waiting to deliver the full concentrated blow, had all their carriers located and destroyed; while the Americans, separated, avoided that disaster, both Japanese strikes concentrating on *Yorktown* and ignoring the other carriers. On the other hand, as we shall see, there was very little co-ordination, and a lot of confusion, in the American attacks, only luck and the good sound sense of junior commanders achieving the desired objective.

44. Among these were the outstanding advocates of naval air power William A. Moffett, Joseph Mason Reeves and John H. Towers. Although the men had violent disagreements the expansion and the development of naval air power remained their mutual goals, while their younger protégé Halsey, Mitscher and at squadron command level, Miles R. Browning, Patrick N. Bellinger and Donald B. Duncan, worked out detail. Recommended reading on this aspect are: Paulo Coletta and Bernarr B Coletta, *Admiral William A. Moffett and United States Naval Aviation*, Clark G. Reynolds, *Admiral John H. Towers; The Struggle for Naval Air Supremacy*, Thomas Wildenberg, *All the Factors of Victory; Admiral Joseph Mason Reeves and the Origins of Carrier Airpower*, and Charles M. Melhorn, *Two Block Fox: The Rise of the Aircraft Carrier 1911–1929*.

(forty-five aircraft) and two *Implacable* class ships (sixty aircraft once more). Meanwhile the three similarly sized American *Yorktown* class increased their aircraft complements to ninety-six machines (eighteen fighters, thirty-seven dive-bombers, thirty-six torpedo bombers and five utility planes in 1938) and even the smaller *Wasp*, (14,700 tons, completed 1940) could tote seventy-six aircraft into combat.

During the war (and after) there was a tendency, by politicians like Churchill and Roosevelt as well as the media, to count naval air power in relation to the number of carriers deployed, but it can be seen that this is false accounting; what really counted was the number of *aircraft* that could be deployed against a given target. Thus a *Yorktown* could deploy for battle three times as many aircraft as an *Illustrious*. In April 1942, Somerville's three carriers in the Indian Ocean could only offer about one-sixth of the aircraft embarked in Nagumo's five vessels of the same type, and even those aircraft were of decidedly inferior performance.[45] The new American *Essex* class went for ninety aircraft and even the 10,600-ton light carriers of the *Independence* class, converted from *Cleveland* light cruiser hulls, could carry into battle as many aircraft as an *Illustrious*. This American superiority in numbers of usable aircraft per individual carrier, to a large extent, dictated the original pre-war carrier doctrine.

US Navy Carrier Doctrine 1942

The parameters which controlled to a large extent the handling of the US carrier forces at Midway, rested still on guidelines drawn up by Commander Aircraft Battle Force (ComAirBatFor), none other than Vice-Admiral William F. 'Bull' Halsey himself, fifteen months earlier, but modified by recent war experience. Whereas 'Wild Bill' had made his name as a destroyer man, he had made a late conversion to

the flying navy, qualifying as an aviator in 1935. Since then his rise had been meteoric and his influence enormous.

There had been a tendency among an earlier generation of naval aviators to look rather scornfully on any kind of laid-down 'rules' on air fighting at sea. Aviators tended, by their very nature, to be improvisers, 'doers rather than scholars'. One of the earliest attempts to get a form of written manual to the complicated circus that was naval flying air tactics had been made by Commander Frank D. Wagner, who commanded VF-2 at North Island airfield in 1926. He received little encouragement from his peers, Reeves being scathing, telling him that once anything was printed up 'in hard covers' everyone would treat it as 'gospel'. His point was that situations were rarely the same twice and any such guidelines would be restricting rather than enlightening. 'They won't be able to act until they find the book reference.'[46] One can see what Reeves was concerned might result from such a seemingly binding set of rules being applied to such unpredictable and fast-moving scenarios. Examples of 'going by the book' to the exclusion of good practical original thinking are to be found all over the Midway battle, and carried out not just by the unfortunate Ring. And yet all military organizations had, and continue to have with increasing complexity, such 'guiding principles'[47]. The important thing was that such basics provided a firm base to the shifting structure of a battle, and an air battle at that, the most difficult combat to keep any sort of handle on. The danger was, as Reeves foresaw only too well, that it could stifle initiative if taken too far.

Despite some deep-rooted or gut-feeling opposition to their introduction, the pre-war bureaucracy of the navy, for both practical training and operational needs, ensured that those 'hard-cover' guidelines duly appeared. They were titled *Current Tactical Orders and Doctrine* (USF-74)[48] and the March 1941 edition was a revision of the earlier one.[49]

---

45. Admiral Layton told Somerville on 9 April 1942 that Fleet Air Arm aircraft were, 'an embarrassment' – The Papers of Admiral Sir Ralph Edwards (Churchill Archives Centre, Churchill College, Cambridge – File No. REDW 2/9).
46. Adolphus Andrews Jr, *Admirals with Wings: The Career of Joseph Mason Reeves*, unpublished thesis, Princeton University, 1943. (Copy held Navy Library, Naval Historical Centre, Washington Navy Yard, DC)
47. Wayne P. Hughes, *Fleet Tactics: Theory and Practice*.
48. In full, confidential document *Current Tactical Orders and Doctrine U S Fleet Aircraft: Volume One Carrier Aircraft (USF-74 (Revised)*, dated March 1941. Held in *Command File World War II*, Naval Historical Center, Washington Navy Yard, DC, copy in authors collection. (Hereafter referred to as *Doctrine*)
49. Changes were naturally ongoing as experience increased in an actual battle, as opposed to a peacetime theoretical, envi-

ronment. Admiral Ernest J. King, who was appointed C-in-C, US Fleet, (COMINCH) and who won his wings as early as 1927, approved a later foreword to a temporary change to USF-74 which saw most of Part II and some sections of Part III substituted with 'new material based on *combat* (my italics) experience'. More revisions were to follow but were not deemed the most urgent, which meant that, 'for the present' many outdated or outmoded sections 'which will not be in harmony with the material presented in this proposed change' would continue to be retained for a while. 'For example, the majority of the diagrams and many sections of the text of the original Parts I and III indicate that the standard squadron organization is based on the 9-plane division, whereas current carrier squadrons doctrine points strongly to the adoption as standard of the 4-plane division in the VF, 4 or 6-plane divisions in VT squadrons, and the 6-plane division in VSB squadrons.'

They were not universally rigid instructions, however, for Chapter 3, which applied to the VF component, said: 'The tactical situations which may confront the fighting squadron are so numerous and varied that definite tactical rules of procedure cannot be set down to cover them.' In this book we are principally concerned with the doctrine as applied at the time of the Midway battle to the dive-bombers (VB and VS) and we will study them in considerable detail later, but overall positioning of the carriers themselves relevant to the enemy and individual air-group launch procedures both so influenced the outcome of the battle that they command some attention.

After eleven minutes of steering east at 15 knots on course 330 degrees TF 16 had finally been released to attack, but only once the enemy had been 'definitely located'. Leaving Fletcher far astern and still ploughing diligently east, *away* from the enemy, in order to facilitate the recovery of his scouting aircraft, Spruance took TF 16 onto a new course of 240 degrees and worked up to a speed of 25 knots. Two at least of Nagumo's carriers were then thought to be roughly 180 miles distant, (due to the faulty PBY data transmitted), which, even if true, was still a bit too far to start the launching of Spruance' s two striking forces, (*two* striking forces, because although *Enterprise* and *Hornet* were in the same task force, they still continued to act as individual ships and not as one whole division, as the Japanese would have done).

The splitting of the American carriers in this way, whatever the motives behind it, did not go down well with many of the aviators. One of those who disapproved was Lieutenant-Commander John S. 'Jimmy' Thach[50], leader of *Yorktown*'s VF-3, and destined to achieve fame that day by taking on the hitherto 'invincible' A6M *Reisen*'s and beating them at their own game via his inventive manoeuvre named the 'Thach Weave'.

Many years later, in 1971, he was interviewed five times by the redoubtable Etta-Belle Kitchen and his remarks later incorporated into a book.[51] He told her that he did not have time to talk to Fletcher, 'but I did go to Murr Arnold.[52] I said I was appalled that the *Yorktown* was in one task group

50. Admiral John Smith 'Jimmie' Thach (1906–81). b. 19 April 1906 in Pine Bluff, Jefferson County, Arkansas, the younger of two sons, with brother James, of school teachers James H. and Jo Bocage Thach who were destined to become US admirals. Graduated from US Naval Academy, Annapolis, 1927. Served two years on battleships *Mississippi* (BB-41) and *California* (BB-44). Volunteered for flight training 1929, received his wings in 1930. Served with VF-1, High Hats in 1931 and they 'starred' in the 1931 Clark Gable movie *Hell Divers* which did so much to influence Japanese and German thinking on the subject. Set endurance record with the XP2H seaplane from Norfolk, Virginia to Panama, and became well known as a test pilot, flying with such luminaries as Butch O'Hare, instructor and aerial gunnery specialist. Commanded VF-3 aboard first the *Lexington* (CV-2) until her loss at Coral Sea, then the *Yorktown* (CV-5) until her loss at Midway. Originated the 'Thach Weave' aerial fighting tactic that helped redress the balance between the Wildcat and the Zeke a little. Post-Midway went home to NAS Jacksonville, to instruct other pilots and make combat films to illustrate this tactic before being appointed Operations Officer to Vice-Admiral John S. McCain in the fast carrier task forces in the Pacific and was present aboard the battleship *Missouri* (BB-63) at the Japanese surrender ceremony on 2 September 1945. After the war continued in Air Training Staff assignments, principally as Director of Training at NAS Pensacola and Special Aide to Vice-Admiral 'Black Jack' Reeves during the USAF onslaught on the navy's aircraft carrier fleet. Thach then became captain of the escort carrier *Sicily* (CVE-118) with USMC Corsair ground support aircraft embarked during the early days of the Korean War, sinking a North Korean submarine and capturing a Soviet MiG-15 jet fighter in his 'Pinch-a-MiG' operation on 9–10 July 1950.
Thach moved on to Senior Naval Aide to Assistant

Secretary of the Navy for Air, John Floberg. This was followed by command of the carrier *Franklin D. Roosevelt* (CVA-42) in the Mediterranean between 1953 and 1954. Promoted to rear-admiral in 1955, he was Commander of Naval Air Bases, 6th Naval District, then served with the Weapons Systems Evaluation Group. Later he flew his flag aboard the carrier *Valley Forge* (CVS-45) as commander of the Anti-Submarine Development Unit, Task Force Alpha and CarDiv 16 in 1958–9. Promoted to vice-admiral he commanded Anti-Submarine Warfare Force, Pacific Fleet, and then became Deputy Chief of Naval Operations (Air) and fought through the adoption of the A-7 Corsair II medium bomber for the carrier force, despite fierce opposition by the anti-navy Secretary of Defense, Robert McNamara. On attaining the rank of Admiral he became C-in-C US Naval Forces Europe, between March 1965 until his retirement in May 1967. He passed away at his Coronado, home on 15 April 1981. In 1984 the guided missile frigate, *Thach* (FFG-43) was named in his honour. See Steve Ewing, *Thach Weave: The Life of Jimmie Thach*. Also 'The Goblin Killers', article in Time magazine, 1 September 1958 edition.

51. Admiral John S Thach, *Reminiscences of Admiral John Smith Thach, U.S Navy (Retired)*.

52. Rear-Admiral Murr E. Arnold (1900–91) b. 12 December 1900 at Shubonier, Illinois. Educated at State Normal School at Durant, Oklahoma and Albion, Iowa. 1919 appointed to US Naval Academy, Annapolis, and graduated on 4 June, 1923, 305th in his class. 1923 commissioned as an ensign. Served aboard the Navy Transport *Argonne* (AP-4), and then the gunboat *Huron* up the Yangtze River in China as part of the Asiatic Fleet, during which he participated in rescue work during the Yokohama earthquake. 1925, in May transferred to the *Smith Thompson* (DD-212). 1925, returned to the United States and received flight training at NAS Pensacola, being designated naval aviator on 24 April 1926. July 1926

separated from the *Enterprise* and the *Hornet*.' He thought that they would 'stick very close together, so that it would be close enough for mutual defensive support. But the next morning, we were separated by at least 20 or 30 miles.' He continued:

I'm sure that the people who made the decisions to have two task groups, separate, expected that they would remain close enough for mutual support, but it didn't work out that way. Thach then came to the crunch of the 'black-shoe, brown-shoe argument'. 'Neither Fletcher nor Spruance were naval aviators – they had not grown up in carrier-based squadrons or had command of an aircraft carrier, where all the experience and knowledge is absorbed which would qualify one to command a carrier task force.'

Kitchen: Who made the decision that they should stay that far apart? Do you know?

Thach: Rear-Admiral Fletcher directed Rear-Admiral Spruance, Task Force 16, to proceed toward the enemy and launch a strike saying he would follow with Task Force 17 as soon as *Yorktown* recovered her scouts. So Frank Jack Fletcher caused the initial separation. Did he realize he was violating one of the basic principles of warfare? That they should be in two task groups, it was obviously Admiral Nimitz. The failure to keep them together is obviously the man in charge, the admiral and his staff. You can say Fletcher or Spruance, but, of course, Fletcher didn't have an aviation staff, and they had no real background of experience in operating carriers. Spruance had Halsey's staff, but they were ordered to proceed south-west and launch a strike. Spruance was junior to Fletcher. The *Yorktown* had sent out scouts and she had to land them aboard, but I know the wind was such that we could have kept them closer together and could have kept the same speed of advance if they had paid more attention to it and realized how im-portant it was. Later, I'll point how this can be done. It'll be much later, though, when I was operations officer of the fast carrier task force. We operated five carriers inside of a screen and kept them together, and took planes aboard, and the wind was from the wrong direction. But you can do it, if you insist on it being done, and if you look ahead a few hours, you can do it. We operated three and four separate task groups making continuous strikes yet remaining within mutual support distance.

Kitchen: Have you ever read anything on that point?

Thach: And I was very bitter about this and was for a long time. I think one of the basic principles of warfare was violated, not intentionally, I presume. Of course, I was only a lieutenant-commander then, and I couldn't fuss at anybody very much, and I'd had only about fifteen years' experience in studying warfare, plus four years at the Naval Academy, where they taught us the basic principles of warfare, and

---

assigned to Torpedo Two, the first carrier-based torpedo-bomber unit, aboard the carrier *Langley* (CV-1), serving until January 1928. 1928, staff duty as Personnel Officer, Commander Aircraft, Battle Fleet. 1928, appointed to VS-2 until October 1929, during which period he took part in the National Air Race at Cleveland, Ohio. 1929, joined VP-2 at NAS Coco Solo, until May 1931. 1931–2, Aircraft Squadron, Battle Fleet, and in October 1932, joined the 'Top Hatters', VS-1 aboard the carrier *Saratoga* (CV-3). 1932–4, served with Utility Squadron One, Aircraft Base Force. 1934–6 BuAer, Washington DC, with Aviation Procurement Division. 1936, in June joined VS-5 (later Cruiser Scouting Squadron Two) aboard the cruiser *Trenton* (CL-11). 1938 appointed in command of Naval Reserve Aviation Base, Detroit. 1940, in May appointed in command VB-5. As Commander Air aboard *Yorktown* (CV-5) advised Fletcher at all major operations until her loss. Among many combat honours were Silver and Bronze Stars and Commendation Ribbon. July 1942–27 May 1944, Director of Personnel and Training, Commander Fleet Air, West Coast, for which he received the Legion of Merit. 1944, between July and October, special secret mission into the interior of China, journeying via Africa and Burma. 1944 Officer of CNO, Washington, DC, then with Naval Group 196 in Pacific Theatre and staff of C-in-C, Pacific Fleet. 1945, on 10 January, appointed in command of the escort carrier *Fanshaw Bay* (CVE-70) seeing combat in the closing stages of the Pacific Campaign and earning the Presidential Unit Citation. September 1945 to BurPer, Washington DC. 1948, in January appointed in command of the carrier *Princeton* (CV-37). 1949, again at BurPer from March to May 1951. and Assistant Chief. 1951–2, CO NAS Kwajalaein. 1952, October, appointed in command of CarDiv 15, being promoted to rear-admiral on 1 July. 1953, on 1 August became Deputy Chief, BurPer until 1956. To the command of CarDiv 4, commanding 6th Fleet carriers from *Forrestal* (CVA-59) in the Mediterranean, Atlantic and North Sea. 1958, on 30 April appointed Commander, Fleet Air, Alameda. 1959 Commander Naval Air Bases, 12th Naval District, Pacific. 1960 Commandant 11th Naval District, San Diego. He earned the Legion of Merit, Yangtze Service Medal. In retirement resided at Kimberly, Iolaho, with his wife, *née* Gala Franklin, by whom he had three daughters, Dona, Patricia and Binney. He died on 13 April 1991, aged 90.

they made sense. It wasn't just an edict or Bible, because the basic principles of warfare weren't invented, they were discovered. They exist as a law of nature, and the law of strategy and tactics, and people who violate any one of them are at a disadvantage, and people who exploit one of the principles, such as concentration of forces, usually do better that the other fellow, if he doesn't.

Kitchen: Were you bitter at anyone in particular at the time?

Thach: Well, yes, Admiral Nimitz, Rear-Admiral Fletcher, Rear-Admiral Spruance and Captain Buckmaster.[53] As I said, I was a young lieutenant-commander, then, and since then having grown up and gotten to be a captain with more experience in task group, task forces and fleet operations and had command of two carriers, then rear-admiral of a task group, and a vice-admiral of a task force, and finally a four-star admiral of forces in Europe, I haven't changed my mind one damned bit!

Kitchen: I can tell from your comments that you

haven't, but I wondered if you were bitter at anybody at the time.

Thach: Well, not anybody in particular, but a group of people, including all the people who were in charge of the thing.

Kitchen: You didn't say, 'This man should have known better,' or did you pinpoint any particular person?

Thach: It was too late to say anything at that point.

Kitchen: I know it, but in your mind did you feel that there was a person who was responsible?

Thach: Well, again, we went into this battle with inexperienced commanders to fight the kind of battle that we were fighting, Admiral Fletcher and Admiral Spruance, they didn't grow up in aircraft carriers, they'd never operated aircraft carriers tactically. So, maybe, they're not to blame. Maybe, it's Nimitz. Maybe it's somebody in Washington. Whoever assigned these two admirals to operate aircraft

---

53. Vice-Admiral Elliott Buckmaster (1889–1976) b. Brooklyn, New York, 19 October, 1889. Educated at Woodberry Forest, Virginia, Switzerland and Columbus, Ohio. 1908 entered US Naval Academy, Annapolis, and graduated as ensign on 7 June1912. Appointed briefly to the battleships *South Carolina* (BB-26) and *Kentucky* (BB-6), then the new battleship *Wyoming* (BB-32). 1913, from April, served aboard the battleship *New Jersey* (BB-16) at the occupation of Vera Cruz in 1914 leading the 1st Company of the battleships landing battalion, for which he was awarded the Navy and Marine Corps Medal. 1916, between May and November served as Watch and Division Officer aboard the battleship *Vermont* (BB-20), and then the *Tacoma* (C-18) on Atlantic convoy duties, as Gunnery Officer, Navigator and XO until December 1919. After six months at the Naval Academy, Annapolis, Gunnery Department, appointed In temporary command gunboat *Asheville* (PG-21) on 20 July 1920; 1922 CO, Receiving Ship, Boston. 1924, from July to July 1926 Repair Officer aboard the destroyer tender *Black Hawk* (AD-9) on the Asiatic Station. 1926-7, Squadron Engineer, on staff of Commander, DesRon 14, Scouting Fleet. Aide to the commandant Portsmouth Navy Yard 1927-9. Subsequently served mainly in destroyers, commanding the *MacFarland* (DD-237) 1929-31. 1931-2, Engineering Officer of the battleship *Arizona* (BB-39). 1932-4, Shop Superintendent, Boston, then as a full commander, commissioning and commanding the new destroyer *Farragut* (DD-348) at Charleston in 1934 for service in Caribbean and then DesRon 20 in Pacific until 1936. Transferred to flight

training as the very last JCL ('Johnny Come Lately') in June 1936, qualifying in May 1937. XO Fleet Air Base Coco Soto, 1938. June 1938– August 1939, carrier *Lexington* (CV-2) and then NAS Pearl Harbor, August 1939. Assumed command of *Yorktown* (CV-5) in February 1941, took part in island raids, Coral Sea and Midway. Was awarded Distinguished Service Medal and Gold Star, but after loss of ship, for which he was never forgiven despite all his efforts to save her, sent to NAS Norfolk from July to October 1942 and promoted to rear-admiral on 10 October. 1942–4 served as commander Navy Air, Primary Training Command, NAS Kansas City. At launching of new *Yorktown* (CV-10) at Newport News by President Roosevelt in February 1943. Commandant Naval Air Center, December 1943–January 1945. Returned to Pacific as Commander Western Carolines Subordinate Area with HQ at Peleliu and was involved in the search for survivors from the heavy cruiser *Indianapolis* (CA-35) in 1945. August 1945, left to become Commander Naval Forces, South China, with the messy business of clearing up French Indo-China, moving Chinese 52nd Army to Taiwan in October 1945 and other 'tidying up' duties. As part of 7th Fleet his flagship was the Coast Guard Cutter *Ingham* (WPG-35) until November 1945, then the *Charleston* (PG-51) at Shanghai and Hong Kong, then back to Haiphong. Decorations included two DSMs. 1946, May hospitalized in 11th Naval District and relieved of active duty. Retired as vice-admiral on 1 November 1946. Took part in the US Antarctic Expedition to the Bay of Whales 1947-8. Died 10 October 1976, at home in Coronado, California.

carriers when they had no experience in aircraft or aircraft carriers.[54]

However Thach and kindred spirits felt about it, the die was now cast. All through the morning of 4 June, Admiral Nagumo's carrier force was to be almost continually engaged fighting off a succession of attacks. There was hardly any pause or let-up; the Zero CAP had to be maintained, and their operations kept the flight decks occupied. This is the reason that currently holds favour among historians as to why no Japanese strike, even partial, was able to be mounted against the Americans. Conversely, Spruance and Fletcher had, for most of the morning and early afternoon, absolutely no enemy action to contend with whatsoever. They had the leisure to pick their time and place and launch without disturbance. They even had a choice of options as to the method with which to send their aircraft away.

Nonetheless, Buell was later to state: 'The action of the US carrier air groups is almost as varied as is that of the two opposing commanders. Throughout the battle there was never a sign of a real co-ordinated attack. Losses were undoubtedly higher because the commanders did not, or would not, co-ordinate their attacks.'[55]

Admiral Frederick Sherman alleged that Mitscher proposed heading west at high speed overnight to get well within range by dawn but Spruance warned him off and instructed him to steer east, adding 'Beware an end run'.

4 June – *Enterprise*

On the bridge of the *Enterprise* the ball temporary passed to Spruance although Fletcher was still technically the overall commander and would remain so throughout that day.[56] Spruance relied heavily on Halsey's old staff of course; they in turn had to deal with a largely unknown factor and found him a very different character from their old boss. Buell[57] caught the difference between the men nicely describing Halsey as 'ebullient' while Spruance was 'a chilling contrast'.[58] However, at Midway, Spruance initially had enough faith in Halsey's team to follow their recommendations to the letter.[59]

Naturally it was upon his CoS, Captain Miles R. Browning[60] that the admiral most heavily relied and

---

54. Thach interviewed by Kitchen, Oral History Series, Interview #3.
55. Buell, transcript, Vol, 2.
56. This fact has been the subject of much dispute, principally by the Morison, Bates and Buell, but also by Spruance's Flag Lieutenant, Robert J Oliver, and Operations Officer, Commander William H. Buracker, (both letter and statement being contained in Collection 37, the Spruance Papers at the Naval War College, Newport). Admiral Spruance himself never claimed to have assumed total control and his TBS (talk between ships) signal of 1811 to Fletcher asked, 'Have you any instructions for further operations?', which seems to indicate that Fletcher was still his superior officer. Not until Fletcher's reply to the effect that he had no such orders and would merely, 'conform to your movements' did Spruance assume overall control of events. In fact Spruance subsequently made his understanding of this matter scrupulously clear.
57. Thomas Bingham Buell (1936–2002). b. Detroit 1936. Raised in northern Michigan. 1954 entered US Naval Academy, Annapolis, specializing in naval history. 1958 graduated and served as first lieutenant aboard destroyer *Hamner* (DD-718) on Taiwan patrols during the Quemoy-Matsu crisis with China. Detached for duty to commission the guided missile destroyer leader *Ernest J. King* (DLG-10). Naval Postgraduate School. Appointed Weapons Officer aboard the frigate *Brooke* (FFG-1). Service at Norfolk Naval Shipyard followed by XO of guided missile destroyer *John King* (DDG-3) which took part in the blockade during the Cuban missile crisis. 1971 Honor Graduate from College of Naval Command and Staff, then a member of Naval War College faculty. 1973 appointed in command of the frigate *Joseph Hewes* (FF 1078) in Atlantic Fleet then Indian Ocean

and Mediterranean. 1976 military history teacher at US Military Academy, West Point. 1979 retired from navy and joined Honeywell International in Minneapolis. Author of many USNI *Proceedings* articles and respected historical studies, notably *The Quiet Warrior*, the impeccable biography of Spruance; but also *Master of Sea Power: A Biography of Fleet Admiral King*, and *The Warrior Generals: Combat Leadership in the Civil War*, *Naval Leadership in Korea: The First Six Months*. Died in Wake County, North Carolina, aged 66, on 26 June 2002. The Thomas B. Buell papers, correspondence and typescripts relevant to Midway (2 Vols) are held in boxes at the Naval War College.
58. Thomas B. Buell, *The Quiet Warrior*.
59. *Ibid.*
60. Rear-Admiral Miles Rutherford Browning (1897-1954). b. 10 April 1897 Perth Amboy, New Jersey, son of New York stockbroker and a poet descended from Mohawk Indians. Educated public schools and appointed to US Naval Academy, Annapolis, 1914. Ensign 1917, Served aboard battleship *Oklahoma* (BB-37) to 1918, then stood by battleship *New Mexico* (BB-40). War service aboard French auxiliary cruiser *Lutetia* attached US Naval forces until the end of World War I. Post-war served with battleship *Pennsylvania* (BB-38), destroyer *McKean* (DD-90) and as Engineering Officer of *Crane* (DD-109) and *Howard* (DD-179) in the Pacific Fleet. In 1920 joined destroyer *Badger* (DD-126) at Mare Island Navy Yard as XO, transferring to the 'four-stacker' *Kidder* (DD-319). Married Catharine Isabella Parker 1922. From 1922 Senior Patrol Officer with the old protected cruiser *Charleston* (C-22) and then the destroyer *Thompson* (DD-305) at San Diego until January 1924. Transferred to NAS Pensacola for flight training. Natural flyer and qualified as a naval aviator 1924, assigned to *Langley* (CV-1). Served with

although he did not know him very well, he knew of his reputation. Browning was regarded by Halsey as an outstandingly intelligent man with a fine, clear mind for planning detailed aviation operations based on years of experience. He was to write of his 'temperamental' subordinate, 'Miles has an uncanny knack of sizing up a situation and coming out with an answer.'[61] Lundstrom described Browning mildly as 'intelligent but erratic,'[62] but others who actually knew him showered less complimentary epithets upon him.[63] Harold Buell labelled him a 'emotionally unstable and evil tempered', a man who at the slightest provocation could become, 'angry, excited and irrational'. He had been credited with the planning and successful execution of the raid on the Marshall Islands a few months before, for which this passed-over commander was given promotion to captain, awarded the Distinguish Service Medal and feted as a 'hero' by *Life* magazine.

However, as was once stated, Spruance was fighting a war not running a charm school and what counted for him was Browning's vast experience and mental capabilities for decision making with regard air operations. Although Spruance was to be quickly disillusioned during the course of the Midway fighting, at the start he placed enormous faith in what Browning had to say.

Certainly, as in the case of Ring, Browning's aviation pedigree was very impressive. While undergoing flight training at Pensacola in 1924, he exhibited natural skills and incisive judgement, which saw him qualify as a naval aviator easily within nine months. He built up his operational expertise while serving in a humdrum unit, VO-2, and honed his organizational skills with a two-year stint as Operations Officer at NAS Norfolk. This was followed by a further stint from the summer of 1929 with VS-5S. But his true worth came to the fore when he was assigned to the BuAer in Washington, DC, where he helped shape the future design of US Navy fighter aircraft. Serving with VF-3B aboard the carriers *Langley* and *Ranger* from 1936, he applied his undoubtedly sharp mind to the tactical problems connected with carrier operations, and produced his own dense and thought-provoking thesis on the subject.[64] Although only twenty-nine, Browning had the intelligence to foresee the classic dilemma, made awful reality for Nagumo six years later, the remorseless equation of finite resources and time imposed upon carrier commanders. His

---

VO-2 between 1925 and 1927, first with the old minelayer being used as the Pacific Fleet aviation tender *Aroostook* (CM-4), then the battleship *Idaho* (BB-42). Participated in Curtiss Marine Trophy Race. Operations Officer at NAS Norfolk. Assigned VS-5S aboard light cruiser *Trenton* (C-11) from 1929 to 1931, then BuAer, Material Division (Design) to 1934. Commanded VF-3B aboard first *Langley* then *Ranger* (CV-4), before Naval War College, Newport. Became Navy Instructor at USAAC Tactical School, Maxwell Field 1937–8. Joined staff of Admiral Halsey as Air Tactical Officer, before becoming Air Wing CO aboard *Yorktown* (CV-5) until 1941. Moved with Halsey as his CofS aboard *Enterprise* (CV-6). Awarded Navy Cross, Distinguished Service Medal, Presidential Unit Citation and American Campaign Medal. Feted (in some quarters) as the brain behind the Midway victory. Returned to counsel Halsey for Guadalcanal campaign. Appointed in command of *Hornet* (CV-12) in July 1943. Promoted to rear-admiral. Took part in raids on Palau, Truk and Ponape and the softening up of the Philippines. Dismissed from *Hornet* after a succession of bad command decisions, assigned to NAS Leavenworth, Kansas. Later served at Command and General Staff College. Toured Japan after the war and retired 1 January 1947, at the early age of 49. Contracted systemic lupus erythematosus and died at Chelsea, Massachusetts. 29 September 1954.

61. Quoted in Samuel Eliot Morison, *The Two-Ocean War: A Short History of the United States Navy in the Second World War.*
62. John B. Lundstrom *Black Shoe Carrier Admiral.*
63. Commander Harold L. Buell, (no relation to Thomas Buell but a dive-bomber pilot who later served under Browning) delivered a slashing exposé of Browning in the February 1986 edition of the US Naval Institute magazine *Proceedings*,

for its '*Leadership Forum*' section, entitled '*Death of a Captain*'. His memory of Browning was of, 'a scowling, chain-smoking martinet who prowled the bridge of the *Hornet* like a caged animal. Every order was a snarl, and his subordinates reacted to him with fear and hatred.' Buell listed the, 'imposing list of adjectives' he had compiled that had been used to describe the man – 'irascible, unstable, intemperate, irrational, insulting, profane, erratic, unreliable, testy, dogmatic, vicious, insubordinate, negligent, temperamental and saturnine'. In a letter commending the article Major F. G. Sandford, Jr, USMC, found a few more to add to the list including, 'caustic' and 'tyrannical', adding that it was Brownings, 'frenzied approach to fanatical obsessions' that could, if unchecked, 'destroy the cohesion and teamwork essential to the accomplishment of his own goals. Such a captain eventually destroys himself.' (Letter, USNI *Proceedings*, April 1986). Browning commanded by bullying and intimidation and one adjective that did not appear on any list used by his fellow officers to describe him was 'bland'; perhaps because he went behind the back of one such compatriot and seduced his wife, Jane Matthews, taboo for any self-respecting officer in those far-off days of standards. Browning's 'slide-rule' brain let him down here for Matthews was former middleweight fleet boxing champion and, when he caught the pair in the act, he gave Browning a deserved full thrashing before suing for divorce. None of this had any effect of Halsey who relied heavily on Browning's expertise and could 'manage' him. Even Spruance thought him 'smart and quick'.

64. Typescript Memorandum, Miles Browning to Admiral J. M. Reeves, *A Short Discussion of Shipbased Aircraft Operations in the Fleet,* dated 1 June 1936, contained in Papers of Robert P. Molten 1911–1940.

most quoted comment from that early paper cut to the heart of the dilemma:

> Every carrier captain has known the bitter experience of rushing his aircraft up and down the deck to meet changing probabilities in the situation and to care for the impending return of a scouting flight, just as the situation was becoming crucial. Every carrier we have knows what it means to be 'bopped' with all planes on deck, because her hands were tied by uncertainty as to her next move.[65]

When Browning joined the staff of Admiral William F. Halsey in 1936 as Air Tactical Officer (ATO), the two very different men worked well together and formed a team that honed and refined operations, and put their stamp on American naval air power as it existed in 1941. Halsey came to rely on Browning, moving him with him as Operations and War Plans Officer with the Air Battle Forces post. This was the man whom Spruance had inherited, and in whom he placed his trust that fateful morning of 4 June 1942. Just how much depended on which account one reads. As in most aspects of Midway, there is wide leeway on which to make an 'informed' choice.

Spruance's biographer stated that, earlier that day, the admiral had risen and joined the small group already assembled in the flag shelter very early that morning.[66] They sat and waited for the radio loudspeaker tuned in to the Midway PBY's radio frequency. Following the receipt of the 0603 message, the other three men exploded into action and 'lunged in a body toward the navigation chart, all grabbing for the single measuring dividers'. In contrast to this keyed-up excitement, Oliver said that Spruance adopted the policy that would characterize his subsequent demeanour throughout the battle. Calmly rising he picked up his measuring board, unrolled it and stood quietly behind the frantic group while they plotted the estimated position, then requested ranges and bearings from Midway to both his force and the enemy. He plotted these on the board. Spruance then used the rough-and ready way of estimating the range to his target 'using thumb and index fingers as dividers', he came up with a distance of 175 miles (which happened to be the maximum range for his torpedo-bombers), and made an instant decision, 'Launch the attack'.[67]

Much of this is surely pure hokum for it was not until four minutes later that Fletcher released Spruance; until then, although the aircrew were standing by in the ready rooms and the aircraft were spotted on the flight decks ready to launch, Spruance was still on a course *away* from the enemy; changing course at 0600 had merely been to conform to *Yorktown*'s steering toward 'Point Option' to recover her scouts. Thus it was not until 0614 that *Hornet* and *Enterprise* came round to course 240 degrees and steered to close with Nagumo, who was bearing 247 degrees true calculated range 175 miles. As for launching immediately as Buell has it, this was hardly sensible, for, with a 6 knot wind from the south-east the carriers would have had to turn away from the enemy again at high speed to get the planes airborne, thus increasing the already maximum distance the F4F and TBDs were capable of by an extra 20 miles, even had 175 miles been an accurate estimate which, as we have seen, it was not.

Here was where Browning's experience and knowledge came into their own. He counselled delaying the launch until 0700, by which time the theoretical gap between the two carrier groups, providing the Japanese held on toward Midway, would have reduced by 20 miles, and turning into the wind to launch would result in the 175 mile base line being conformed to. He accepted this advice and, at 0638, so signalled to *Hornet*. He was praised by Bates for this 'excellent demonstration of the will of the Commander; that quality which, in conjunction with the mental ability to understand what is required, enables the Commander to ensure for his command every possible advantage which can be obtained'.[68] However, Spruance later admitted that he just wanted to hit the enemy with everything he had as quickly as possible[69]; so it was surely his deferring to Browning's judgement which was the real 'courageous decision'.[70]

Another version, by Sam Morison[71], is that Spruance far from ordering a immediate launch and being talked out of it by Browning, actually wanted to delay the launch until 0900. This is just as much patent nonsense as Buell's assertion the other way and was brought about because Morison had not taken into consideration the fact that the Zone + 10 time [local time plus ten hours] recorded in the TF-16's logs meant that 0900 actually translated into 0700. One wonders why this was not picked up for Morison and Bates

65. *Ibid.*
66. Buell listed these as Browning, Commander William H. Buracker (Operations Officer), Robert J. Oliver (Flag Lieutenant) and an unnamed staff watch-officer.
67. Buell, *Quiet Warrior*.
68. Bates Report.
69. Confirmed in a letter Spruance wrote to the former Under Secretary of the Navy James V. Forrestal, dated 14 December 1962, and contained in the Spruance Papers, Coll. 37, box 7, held at Naval War College, Newport.
70. Bates Report.
71. Morison, *United States Naval Operations, Vol 4*.

co-operated closely on their respective histories and Bates is clear enough on the matter.

In the interval Spruance and his team were no doubt hoping for further confirmation and updates on the progress, course and speed of the 1st *Kidō Butai* so they could fine-tune their air strikes, but the minutes ticked away and no such confirmation or amplification was received. TF-16 therefore had to calculate their best course of attack on information that was now very cold. Nagumo could have been 20 miles in any direction from the last sighting, but the general consensus was that he would continue in toward Midway to recover his first-strike aircraft. That being so, the estimate on *Enterprise*'s bridge was that, at 0700 the enemy were on a bearing of 239 degrees true, and a distance of 150 miles. In fact the 1st *Kidō Butai* were far more efficient at carrier operations than the Americans gave them credit for, and Nagumo scooped in his aircraft steering into the wind as predicted, but then did a hard turn to the north-east to close with his enemy. This change of course, which of course made nonsense of the projected position of intended movement (PIM) of the Japanese carriers, on which the Americans based their actions[72], was not picked up by scouting aircraft between the 0603 signal and the 0803 departure of the American air groups, which also, once committed, were supposed to be operating under 'strict' radio silence.

Just before the agreed deadline, at 0648, TF-16, speeding up to 28 knots to generate enough wind over their decks, broke up into two separate groups once more, following the standing instructions still in place. Once split they remained separated by distances that varied from a few thousand yards to 20 miles, and steering slightly deviating courses, until late in the evening. This made the close co-ordination of strikes even more difficult, for the invaluable TBS[73] system was essentially a short-range tool and radio silence was deemed essential for the American carriers to remain cloaked from the enemy to avoid counter-strikes.

Five minutes after the agreed deadline the *Enterprise* began her launch; and here too the two carriers, belonging to the same task force and on the same mission, differed in their methods. As Browning's plan gave each captain *carte blanche* on how each organized their own aircraft it was at their respective captains' bidding that the air groups were sent away again according to standing doctrine. Thus, Captain George D. Murray, the CO of the *Enterprise*[74] ordered the standard and well-rehearsed 'deferred departure' option. By this 'by the book' method, each squadron would take off and circle the carrier waiting for the rest of the air group to join them. Only when all the squadrons had left the deck and attained the required altitude and formed up, would the Air Group Commander lead them off against the enemy on the already agreed outward course. On the way to the target they were instructed by Browning to employ the standard 'search-attack' deployment, with at least one SBD squadron deploying into line abreast in the likelihood that the actual positioning of the enemy was inaccurate, (as indeed it certainly was). Once the enemy had been located the Air Group Commander would, in theory, direct them onto the target as a cohesive whole[75], which meant that aircraft of widely varying abilities had not only

---

72. Except for Waldron of course, whose 'gut feeling' convinced him that this was what would occur, but who failed to persuade Ring, or anyone else.

73. TBS – Talk Between Ships. This was a VHF radio network communication system brought in as a more convenient system to signal lamps and flags over short ranges. The transmissions were in 'clear'. Prior to its introduction VHF transmission were rarely used for fear of giving away one's own position to the listening enemy. Specialist 'talkers' were employed on the ship's bridge, and they used a standard encoded terminology using simple code words (e.g. fish = torpedo) to build up short sentences. For messages containing numerals, as for example courses and speeds, an alpha-numeric was introduced, termed a 'shackle code', whereby the word 'shackle' preceded a numeric sequence where a series of numbers would be represented by a series of letters; at the end of each series the word 'unshackle' would indicate the end of that particular numeric group. They used long bronze-wire antennae, which could be spliced with silver solder when cut by over-enthusiastic AA gunners!

74. Captain George D. Murray, (1889–1956). b. 6 July 1889 at Boston. Graduated from US Naval Academy, Annapolis. 1914-5 NAS Pensacola, qualified as a naval aviator.

Commanded the carrier *Enterprise* (CV-6) from March 1941 to June 1942. Commander Western Sea Frontier. Commander, Mariana Islands. Accepted Japanese surrender aboard his flagship, the heavy cruiser *Portland* (CA-33). Commandant 9th Naval District 1946-7. Retired as vice-admiral 1951. Joined Pacific Telephone & Telegraph Company. President of California Branch of the English-Speaking Union. Died age 66, on 18 June 1956 in San Francisco. Interred at Arlington National Cemetery. Posthumously designated as third recipient of Gray Eagle Award for most senior active naval aviator from 1947–51.

75. An alternative option from the 'manual', which could be employed where more than one carrier was operating against the same target, was available. This was for the adoption of 'wing' tactics, whereby the senior air group commander assumed control of all the air groups as they arrived and directed them *in succession*, so that no target was left uncovered and not everyone concentrated on the same one. This type of attack took an incredible amount of organizing, and was fraught with complications. Indeed such an attack would take far more organization than the Americans were capable of at this stage of the war and Browning, sagely, opted for independent, but simultaneous attacks by the air groups,

to leave together, but, in order to maximize their effect, *arrive* together.

First up were eight Wildcats to maintain the carrier's own CAP; the next group to be launched were the thirty-seven longer-ranged SBDs, which, having by far the longest reach (over 200 miles), could be sent off ahead of the shorter-legged F4Fs and Devastators knowing they had sufficient fuel to linger while the air group formed up. This was a long process for the Americans at this stage of the war. Whereas Nagumo had lofted 108 aircraft in seven minutes to attack Midway, and this was purely routine, the two American carriers took an hour to get 117 aircraft airborne.

Following the Dauntless launch, the *Enterprise*'s order of preference was a small force of ten Wildcats as strike defenders and, finally the fourteen old TBDs staggered into the air heavily penalized with their torpedoes slung at an angle below their tubby bellies. Because the heavily-laden SBDs required the maximum take-off run, it meant that the *Enterprise* strike had to be sent off in two separate deck loadings. Bringing up the second wave entailed yet more delay. This achingly tense time factor was not helped by the fact that four SBDs aborted the mission and had to be man-handled out of the way before the second spot could be flown off.

Although most historians agree that Spruance, at this stage of the proceedings at least, left all this specialized avia-tion planning and execution to the experts, he could not help but be worried by the time all this elaborate aerial ballet was taking, when, at any time Japanese dive-and torpedo-bombers might suddenly appear on his radar screens. It was a worry the meticulous Browning shared – although prob-ably more obviously than the placid Spruance – and he finally had enough of the shilly-shallying when a the carrier's radio intelligence officer notified him that his team had intercepted an enemy sighting report, sent uncoded, which revealed 'the speed and composition' of TF-16.[76]

At 0745 CEHAG patiently orbiting at 20,000 feet above the toiling *Enterprise*, received curt instructions by signal lamp to 'proceed'. McClusky recorded his feelings on how this strike was put together, and they were not favourable.

My orders were to make a group attack on the enemy striking force. Radio silence was to be maintained until sight contact with the enemy was made. That was the extent of my instructions. The *Hornet* group was likewise to be launched and, although the *Hornet* group commander was senior, no command relationship or co-ordination was prescribed. No information was received to indicate how the *Yorktown* group was to participate. So, with this meagre information, we manned our planes[77].

At 0945, by flashing light signal, I was ordered to 'proceed on mission assigned'. No information was given as to why the torpedo planes and fighters were delayed. This meant we would be without fighter protection – a serious predicament.[78]

Another *Enterprise* pilot recalled the frustrations of that launch many years later.

I believe the most important question concerning the [American] leaders of Battle of Midway was the apparent lack of Commanders sending orders, or their intentions, to their subordinates. VS-6 and VB-6 circled the *Yorktown* for almost half an hour, expecting their SBDs to join us. That waste of time and gas caused LOTS of serious problems. Communications by flags or searchlight could have avoided that big flaw; *that* information was more important than all other items . . . .[79]

each under the direction of their own group commanders. See ComAirBatFor *Current Tactical Orders, Aircraft Carriers, U.S. Fleet*, USF-77, Revised in March 1941.

76. Lieutenant Gilven M. Slonim. For his account see ' A Flagship View of Command Decisions'. This message, timed 0728, originated from Petty Officer First Class Yōji Amari piloting the heavy cruiser *Tone*'s No. 4 search plane. It read: 'Sight what appears to be ten enemy surface ships, in position bearing 010 degrees distance 240 miles from Midway. Course 150 degrees, speed over 20 knots.' Station Hypo at Pearl Harbor picked this up also, but seven minutes later than Slonim, but Fullenwider's team apparently did not pick it up at all. Although oddly it made no mention of American carriers, never has one message made so many people jump as Amari's; it certainly upset Nagumo's serene apple-cart, and likewise turned Spruance's cool detachment into understandable anger, being the straw that broke the hitherto imperturbable admirals back.

77. In 1987 Lundstrom stated in a footnote to Buell's revised edition of *Quiet Warrior* that: 'Spruance actually did not know his task force had been spotted by the enemy until nine minutes after the last planes left the *Enterprise*'s flight deck. He became impatient with the slowness of the *Enterprise* takeoffs, because he could see the *Hornet* had already launched all her planes.' Yet in 2007, thirty years later, in *Black Shoe Carrier Admiral*, Lundstrom seemingly contra-dicts himself, for he confirms that the last torpedo bomber, 'lifted off the *Enterprise*' at 0806, while at the beginning of the same paragraph he confirms Slonim's alerting of Spruance to the sighting report as 0740! If the *Quiet Warrior* footnote were taken as correct, Slonim would have had to sit on Amari's signal for almost half an hour before taking it up to the flag bridge!

78. McClusky, '*Historical Commentary*'.

79. Jack Kleiss to George Walsh, e-mail Wednesday, 27 September 2006.

On receiving the Go from Spruance, McClusky gathered the two dive-bomber squadrons under his wing, and the SBDs droned away at 0752, unescorted and unaided. McClusky recorded of the enemy that, at his departure time, ' they were believed to bear about 240 degrees, distance 155 miles and heading toward Midway at 25 knots.'[80] The launching of VF-6 had meanwhile finally been accomplished at 0749, but when they reached the assembly height, their commander, Lieutenant James S. Gray, confused the departing torpedo bombers of VT-8, already airborne, for the Devastators from his own ship and left with them on a very different course from VB-6 and VS-6, thus giving top cover to the wrong squadron. By the time VT-6 had been brought up on deck and launched the rest of the *Enterprise* air group had long gone and, at 0806, the TBDs belatedly took their departure, but on a different heading to either the F4F's or the SBDs, 240 degrees.

How then had *Enterprise* fared? Not very well. Instead of one co-ordinated air group, the dive-bombers, by Spruance's personal intervention[81], had gone off on their own; the fighters had left with another carrier's aircraft and the torpedo bombers had launched late, about eleven minutes after the rest of TF-16's aircraft. All three components had become split up, steering slightly different courses. As if this was not enough of a shambles, the super-efficient Browning had initially neglected to inform *Hornet* of his intentions, causing Mitscher's team some frustration

as they alternatively sent the aircrews up from the ready rooms and then recalled them again.

This was all bad enough, but unfortunately, far from the situation being redeemed by her fellow carrier with her own team of aviation experts, the *Hornet*'s experience was, if anything, ultimately to prove to be even more disappointing than the messy fumble by *Enterprise*.

4 June – *Hornet*

Captain Marc Mitscher, pacing *Hornet*'s flag bridge, was getting rather impatient after a few false starts and irritated at the lack of information coming over from the *Enterprise*. He was eager to launch his air group as soon as possible and was more than ready to go by the time he finally received Spruance's instructions to launch at 0700, take independent deferred departure and adopt a 'search and attack' mode, all contained in a belated signal from Miles Browning at 0653.

In contrast to Spruance, Mitscher was quite at ease with naval flying operations, and had ample confidence in his team. Ring he had served with previously, and knowing him from way back[82], counted on him to apply himself with meticulous care to the task in hand. The *Hornet*'s Air and XO, Commander Apollo Soucek[83], also had a highly distinguished background in naval aviation. In the 1920s and 1930s he and his brother Zeus had broken a series of world

---

80. McClusky, *Midway Battle Manual*.
81. With Browning's blessing ('concurrence') according to Lundstrom (*Black Shoe Carrier Admiral*), but Buell has Spruance personally abandoning 'his' agreed plan, 'consciously and deliberately' (*Quiet Warrior*,) and the same line is taken by Parshall and Tully (*Shattered Sword*). For once Bates quits fawning on Spruance and questions the wisdom of this decision. 'The advisability of this move is open to question, as the plan for the attack called for each carrier attack group to make a coordinated bombing and torpedo attack.' Spruance's decision, Bates noted cautiously, 'made such coordination much more difficult'. In truth, combined with all the others mistakes it made it impossible. Bates of course gave Spruance an 'out', and considered that he may have assumed that 'the planes which had attacked Midway were now due back at the Mobile Force and could soon be relaunched' . (Bates Report).
82. Many years later one of the pilots of VB-8, Roy Gee, was to aver that their friendship was of 'the "good ole boy"' variety. However, this opinion must be tempered by the acknowledged fact that Gee and many other AG-8 aircrew, smarting under Ring's rigorous regime designed to lick them into shape before battle, 'had little respect for CHAG'. Quoted in Kernan, *Unknown Battle*. The easy and obvious mutual admiration between Mitscher and Ring might well have irritated some junior officers under such circumstances.
83. Vice-Admiral Apollo 'Sockem' Soucek (1897–1955). b.

Lamont, Oklahoma on 24 February 1897, into a Czech immigrant family he was among the earliest of young officers to volunteer for flying. Educated at Medford Primary and Werntz Preparatory School, Annapolis. Entered the US Naval Academy on 9 June 1917 as a midshipman, serving aboard the battleship *Missouri* (BB-11) in Atlantic Fleet in 1918. Graduated and commissioned as ensign 3 June 1921. Served aboard the battleship *Mississippi* (BB-41) in the Pacific Fleet. 1924, February, to NAS Pensacola for flight training. He almost killed himself when his parachute failed on one of his first flights, but survived and designated naval aviator October 1924. November, joined the carrier *Langley* (CV-1), then to VO-2, as Assistant Flight Officer. He subsequently excelled as a flyer, becoming a noted test pilot. Along with his brother he became famous for setting, and then exceeding, several world altitude records. He received many trophies and honours for this work in the 1920s and 1930s, including the Spartan Award in June 1929. 1925 aboard the battleship *Maryland* (BB-46) as Junior Aviation Officer, VO-1, then Assistant Navigator. He married Agnes Eleanor O'Connor in May 1930 and a month later, on 4 June 1930, broke the world altitude record again with an altitude of 43,166 feet. Soucek was among the early, and largely forgotten, pioneers. 1930–2, served successively as Flight Officer VF-3 aboard the carrier *Lexington* (CV-2), and then VF-1 aboard carrier *Saratoga* (CV-3). 1932–5 Naval Aircraft Factory Assistant Superintendent Aeronautical Engineering

---

records. Apollo was principally famed for regaining the height record on 8 May 1929, when, as a young lieutenant, and flying a Wright F3W-1 Apache powered by a 425 horse power -Pratt & Whitney Wasp engine, he had set the new world record for a class C landplane of 39,140 feet over NAS Anacostia, a ceiling he exceeded by almost 5,000 feet later in a seaplane. He had also been a noted test pilot in that pioneering period of his life. And even the two officers most diametrically opposite in their viewpoints, Ring and Waldron, had been at Pensacola at the same time in the early 'twenties.

So, there was no shortage of expertise aboard the *Hornet* that morning. What there was, however, was a total lack of *combat* experience coupled with a distinct lack of harmony. With a relatively untested air group, Mitscher opted for the simplest and most familiar launch routine.

Because Browning had offered no Point Option[84], Mitscher sent for Ring and his four squadron commanders[85]; these, together with Apollo Soucek, tried to reach agreement on the best outward course to take from the very limited information they had before them, plus their own expertise. This decision was crucial because, once airborne, strict radio silence was to be maintained until the enemy was sighted. So they talked, but it seems they came to little or no consensus. Once they had lofted their strikes

into the wind, the two task groups would turn back on a south-west course of 240 degrees to close the range once more; this was a known factor. The last-known plotted position of the enemy was another. The wild card of course, was whether the Japanese carriers would have continued on their last reported course toward Midway to recover their first strike aircraft, or, if they had indeed sighted TF-16 and 17, have turned away from Midway and begun to close the range to hit the American ships. Also they could have increased their speed, and some time had already elapsed and more would tick by while the American strikes were *en route*. The area of possibilities was increasing by the minute.

All seven men had exactly the same minimal information on which to base their calculations (albeit that some of it turned out to be inaccurate) and had individually worked out their solutions; apparently none tallied.

Ring therefore, as CHAG and ultimately responsible, made the decision that they would follow the course he had computed. That should have been the end of the matter, but the CO of VT-8 continued to express strong disagreement. Mitscher however, authorized Ring's decision and the group leaders dispersed to join their pilots, many of whom were already in their aircraft waiting to launch.

What *exactly* Ring's decision was remains unknown.

Laboratory 1935, June, Hangar Deck Officer, Flight Deck Officer aboard the carrier *Ranger* (CV-4). 1937, June, CO VF-2 aboard *Lexington* again, then BuAer, Washington DC. May 1940–June 1941, Navigator aboard carrier *Yorktown* (CV-5). He later filled the post of CoS, Air Intermediate Training. On the eve of the Pacific war had been appointed to stand by the new carrier *Hornet* (CV-8) as her Air Officer and liased with Major General James Doolittle during the Tokyo Raid in 1942. Soucek had to explain to the army aviators just how a carrier operated aircraft and was rewarded with no failures when it came to the launch of the B-24s. After Midway he served with *Hornet* as her XO until her loss at Santa Cruz on 26 October 1942, finding and rolling overboard an unexploded bomb before being taken off. He was awarded both Silver and Bronze Stars. 1942–June 1943, Assistant CofS, Operations, US Pacific Fleet, awarded Gold Star and second Legion of Merit. 1943, July, NAS Pensacola, as CofS Naval Air Intermediate Training Command.1944, 23 June, promoted to rear-admiral. He ended the war standing-by as Captain-designate of the big new battle carrier *Franklin D. Roosevelt* (CVB-42), which he commissioned in front of President Harry S Truman on 25 October 1945. After her shake-down cruise in the Caribbean she underwent alterations at New York, before becoming the flagship of Admiral March Mitscher where the two old Midway veterans were reunited. Soucek captained her through the spring manoeuvres of the Atlantic Fleet in 1946 and became the US Navy's first carrier captain to welcome aboard Sikorsky H03S helicopters. 1946, August, Commander Fleet Air Wing One then, in 1947, CO Naval Air Test Center,

Patuxent River. 1949, April, Director of Aviation Plans and Program Division, then in 1951, US Naval Attaché, London. In July 1952 Commander, US Naval Forces in the Formosa Strait during the difficult time when Communist China threatened the offshore islands and war was a distinct possibility. He saw further active service in Korea where he commanded CarDiv 3 earning the Distinguished Service Medal. Became Chief of the BuAer between 30 June 1953 and 4 March 1955 and his naval career continued and he headed up the Missile Force, before becoming Assistant Chief of Naval Operations. His retirement came early, on 4 March 1955, following a spell in Bethesda Naval Hospital. He passed away on 25 July 1955. The NAS at Oceana, Virginia Beach, was named Apollo Soucek Field in his honour on 4 June 1957. The Lieutenant Apollo Soucek Collection (1920–60) is held at The Fred E. Anderson Collection, History of Aviation Collection, Specials Collections Department, McDermott Library, The University of Texas at Dallas, 10–81, collection number CA 10–81.

84. Point Option was defined as 'an imaginary point moving on a specified course and speed such that at any instant it represents the predicted position of the carrier'. It was the vital piece of information for aircrew of course representing the predicted location of 'home' in the vast empty expanse of the Pacific Ocean.

85. Lieutenant-Commander J. C. Waldron (VT-8); Lieutenant-Commander F. Rodee (VS 8); Lieutenant-Commander R. R. Johnson, (VB-9) and Lieutenant-Commander S. G. Mitchell (VF-8).

Cressman *et al* state unequivocally, almost as if they were present that day, that the course selected was 265 degrees true.[86] Lundstrom also opted for the same course, but less dogmatically, stressing that 'the evidence seems to suggest' that this was the heading chosen[87], although thirty years on he seemed more certain, offering no such qualification[88]. However, he did attribute to a more directly westerly sortie, reaching out to an extreme distance of 225 miles, as evidence that Mitscher was conducting a search-and-strike mission hoping to locate the phantom 'second group' containing the two missing Japanese carriers. On what facts or documentation this is inferred is not clear. There is nothing in the Mitscher report to suggest such was the case, although of course that is now widely discredited as a reliable source. Wildenberg accepts that theory as fact without question.[89] Mitscher's biographer offers no confirmation that this was the plan, indeed he emphasised that the original sighting remained his air group's target. 'Last-minute teletype instructions to the *Hornet*'s air group placed the enemy at a distance of 155 miles.'[90] Parshall and Tully at least offer evidence, stating, 'The fact that Waldron subsequently closed 1st *Kidō Butai* from almost dead ahead (i.e. from the north-east) is further indication that Ring's flight path was headed due west, and thus missed Nagumo to the north.'[91] This theory of course presumes that the Japanese force *was* heading north-west at that particular moment after their convoluted twisting and turning to evade previous attacks.

So much for the historians, what of the participants? Ring, in his unpublished account, could have clarified the whole matter decades ago, but he only stated that he led off on a 'predetermined interception course' without saying what it was. Nor did he say anything to lend credence to the claim that he was looking for an, as yet unsighted 'second' Japanese carrier division. Far from believing he had led his group too far north, Ring clearly felt that, if anything, he had led them too far to the *south,* and blamed lack of updated information about Nagumo's turn north which, he alleged, was given to Commander Enterprise Air-Group (CEAG) ('*Enterprise* Group was favored with later information of the whereabouts of the enemy'), but not himself.[92] Taylor stated that 'Stanhope Ring kept the air group travelling south-west.' He also claimed that, far from

the CO of VT-8 veering off to port, he 'rolled the torpedo squadron northward on a strong hunch,' which, if true, would have meant making a *starboard* turn away from a course south of the enemy.[93] However, Taylor's allegation, again presented as fact, is unsubstantiated, for he offers no source or evidence.

The greatest research into this mystery was, of course, conducted by Major Bowen P. Weisheit.[94] He shared his knowledge with Lundstrom and his findings have been widely (but not quite universally) accepted as correct ever since. Weisheit made a powerful case for assuming that Ring adopted a heading of 265 degrees true, by asserting that they were so 'tracked by the ship's radar for 50 miles'. His interview with seven surviving participants brought mixed responses[95]. Tappan could not remember the heading; Mitchell did not elucidate either; Gray was clear that the heading was 'about' 304 degrees true; Talbot apparently failed to contribute that information; nor apparently did McInerny although he stated he saw smoke to the South; Foster, the ship's Air Officer, confirmed that *Hornet*'s radar had tracked the group on a heading of almost due west for at least 50 miles. Rodee, in a somewhat incoherent taped phone conversation made a number of comments on the heading, that they had the bearing of the enemy (240 degrees) and flew down it; and that VF-8 flew approximately 15 degrees apart from VT-8 (Weisheit prompted him that he went to the south of Waldron, but Rodee's reply was ambiguous on that part of it). He repeated that the Wildcats took the given bearing and course and when asked if they could recall what that had been started to respond but was again prompted by Weisheit who suggested 240. Rodee, however, responded that it was about 265, which figure Weishart repeated to be sure he had heard aright. Rodee came back slightly hedging his bet with 260–5, concluding it was almost due west. Guillory was another who apparently proffered no information of the heading but, from his position at the rear of the formation, was able to confirm that VT-8 turned to port some 50 miles from departure (inconveniently and frustratingly, just beyond the range of the *Hornet*'s radar reach), which would have confirmed a turn south from a bearing north of Nagumo, rather than a turn north from a bearing south of the Japanese force.

86. Cressman *et al., A Glorious Page.*
87. Lundstrom, *The First Team.*
88. Lundstrom, *Black Shoe Carrier Admiral.*
89. Wildenberg, *Destined for Glory.*
90. Taylor, *Magnificent Mitscher.*
91. Parshall and Tully, *Shattered Sword.*
92. Ring, *Lost Letter.*
93. Taylor, *Magnificent Mitscher.*

94. Major Bowen P. Weisheit, *The Last Flight of Ensign C Markland Kelly, Junior, USNR: with a new, corrected charting of the flight of VF-8 from USS* Hornet *during the Battle of Midway.*
95. Ensign B. Tappan, USNR, Ensign T. T. Guillory, USNR, Ensign H. L. Tallman, USNR, Lieutenant-Commander S. G. Mitchell, USN, Ensign J. E. McInerny, USNR and Lieutenant R. Gray, USN.

The *Hornet*'s Navigation Officer's report, cited by Weisheit, admitted that the ship's magnetic compass had not been swung during her February working-up period and Weisheit postulates that, if this had never been corrected, all subsequent calculated headings were between 20 degrees and 28 degrees too high.

One important dissenting voice is that of one of the last survivors, Clayton E. Fisher, who was Ring's wing-man on this mission, and with whom I spent several very interesting days in detailed discussions. Clayton has vigorously conducted his own research and remains in dispute with those who claim Ring took them too far north. It should be noted that Fisher holds no affection for Ring whatsoever, so he is not influenced in his beliefs by any loyalty to his former CHAG. However, he told me quite clearly, and repeated it in a follow-up e-mail so there should be no doubt:

> This brings up the statement of Rodee that the *Hornet* attack force flew at 265 degrees. I have always had the greatest respect for Rodee for his leadership etc. but I strongly believe we flew a southwest course of about 235 to 240 degrees. I do remember when we plotted our course to the reported position of the enemy task force it was to the southwest. I stand on my belief we were between Midway and the enemy task force.[96]

Finally, it is noteworthy to record that Bates in his analysis seemingly ignored *Hornet*'s radar plotting, for he wrote that when Ring had failed to sight the Japanese forces at 0920, he, 'continued' (not 'turned', notice) to the southwest.[97]

Hornet's aircraft were flown off her flight deck into the wind, the ships' heading 158 degrees true according to her log entry; but the escorting heavy cruiser *Minneapolis* plotted a 130 degree heading, revealing that 28 degree difference again. The air group was launched in two batches but, inexplicably, Mitscher chose to spot the ten short-range F4F's of the escort in the first range, and, moreover, ahead of everything else in that range other than the task group CAP. The subsequent launch cycle was VS-8, CHAG and two wingmen and then VB-8. Last away in the first wave were six of the TBDs, presumably because the *Hornet*'s captain thought these heavily laden aircraft would require the maximum deck length in order to get airborne. Nine further TBDs remained in the hangar, and, while these were laboriously brought up on deck and formed the second launch, their companions spent their time gaining altitude and being marshalled by Ring into the regimented and precise parade-ground formation decided upon. Ring himself recalled that, 'almost one and a half hours were consumed in Group rendezvous after launching. All airplanes maintained moderate altitude (below 5,000 feet) until after rendezvous of the Group was effected.' Once the second wave was aloft, and had in turn been marshalled into place by Ring, (who appears to have formed up his air group with all the due deliberation and precision of George Pickett dressing his line before the charge on the afternoon of 3 July 1873 at Gettysburg[98]), the air group took their stately and impressive departure. The time was 0806.

Whatever the heading they actually took, the first launch had been burning up vital fuel as they waited overhead and this preyed on the minds of the fighter pilots in particular. This already critical fuel situation was compounded by the 'speed regulation' Ring imposed on the force, in order to keep in step with the slow TBDs and kept the group together. It was to lead to fateful decisions later, but at least Ring got his air group away ahead of the *Enterprise*'s, and, initially at least, as one organised entity.

4 June – *Yorktown*

Having steamed for some considerable time away from TF-16, much to Thach's anger, Fletcher finally recovered his scouting aircraft (which, naturally, had seen nothing whatsoever) and Captain Buckmaster had then respotted his strike force by 0645. During the long interval word had come in of the first Japanese strike on Midway Island itself from Nagumo's carriers[99], which were at that time positioned some 225 miles distant from *Yorktown*. Fletcher, although still edgy that he might be ambushed from the missing two enemy carriers he had failed to locate, was spurred to join in the carrier duel, and left further searches to the north-east to the Midway PBYs, something he could have done anyway. The plan was now for TF-17 to deliver a follow-up blow to finish off what he hoped TF-16 had started to deliver. Course was set south-west once more, on a heading of 225 degrees and *Yorktown* cranked up to 25 knots to try and make up some of the lost time and distance. Fletcher's experts advised a launch at a comfortable distance of 160 miles from the enemy, which TF-17 hoped

---

96. Fisher to the author, e-mail 10 May 2006.
97. Bates Report.
98. Major General George Pickett (1825–75). Commanded the Confederate Army's elite Virginia Division at Gettysburg. During the final afternoon Pickett led it to virtual annihilation in a vain uphill attack on an entrenched and unbroken Union force, suffering more than 60 per cent casualties.
99. The first bomb hit Midway at 0633 delivered in a horizontal attack. CinCPac Report, 116.

to be in a position to do by around 0830 and advised Spruance accordingly[100].

While awaiting for the clock to crawl round, Fletcher's airmen, who as well as Buckmaster and Arnold, included the Commander *Yorktown* Air Group (CYAG), Lieutenant-Commander Oscar Pedeson[101] of VF-42, an 'old-timer' who to his fury had been forcibly grounded as Fighter Direction Officer, had ample time to think out the best attack plan. They would expect the advantage of at least part of TF-16's air groups flushing out the enemy, but could not be certain. Fletcher was still hedging his bets; spurred on by various sightings of enemy snoopers between 0810 and 0821, he deducted the seventeen dive-bombers of VS-5 from the strike force and, when its commander[102] protested, he got very short shrift.

Likewise, Thach, whose new plan required the Wildcats to work in groups of four, was incensed to learn that his force had been reduced to a paltry six machines! Thach blamed Buckmaster. 'He wanted to keep as many as possible back to defend the *Yorktown*,' he was later to complain.[103] Not notified of the superior's change until 0838 he tried to get a hearing but Arnold fended him off with the news that 'they' had decided and that was that! Thach had only a few brief minutes with his pilots to cobble up a modified scheme, which he did 'on the hoof', retaining one four-plane unit high, with the odd pair of F4Fs dropped down astern of the TBDs. The assertion therefore, that everybody concerned 'all agreed' can be taken as a rather dewy-eyed memory of what took place, as well as that, 'all of them carried out this exactly'[104]; at least two squadron commanders did not, but, unlike Waldron, such objectors held their peace, obeyed and simply got on with it.

However much Thach might have disliked what was being done in detail, the overall attack plan proved to be a much better constructed affair than either of those sent away by TF-6. Strangely, one part of the plan that Thach might have been expected to 'kick' against, the range of the strike, 175 miles, he accepted with good grace. Arnold, while accepting as had Spruance's teams, that the 1st *Kidō Butai* would continued toward Midway to recover its striking force into the wind, was not convinced that it would hold that course for long, and was certain a competent Japanese commander would not risk his valuable ships too close to Midway's airfield. This meant the Nagumo force, on reaching roughly an imaginary red line which was assumed to be drawn 120 miles out from Midway, would turn, and most probably that turn would be toward the Americans, which it was felt from all the attention that TF-17 was now receiving, must surely to be firmly fixed on Nagumo's plotting table.

Estimating that the enemy would be found on a bearing of 230 degrees from the point at which Fletcher planned to launch and that by then the range would be down to about 150 miles, well within TF-17's air group capabilities,

---

100. Fletcher's signal, timed 0648 advising TF-16 of his new intentions, still revealed Frank Jack's continued concern, almost an obsession, about whether he was yet about to be 'suckered' by an ambush, as at Coral Sea: 'Two carriers unaccounted for.' Did this postscript possibly influence Mitscher and lead to the *Hornet* striking force adopting that alleged 265 degree heading? One can only speculate.

101. Rear-Admiral Oscar 'Pete' Pederson, (1904–94). b. New York City, on 10 July 1904. Educated at various New York schools. Entered the US Naval Academy, Annapolis, on 21 June 1922, and graduated as ensign on 3 June in 1926, 187th in class. 1929, January, transferred to flight training to NAS Pensacola, and awarded his wings as a naval aviator in March 1930. 1930 joined VT-9-S (later VP-10-S) with Aircraft Squadrons, Scouting Fleet. Initially he flew flying boats and seaplanes. 1932, back to Annapolis, for Aeronautical Engineering course, Naval Postgraduate School, and attended University of Michigan at Ann Arbor, graduating with Master of Science in Engineering, June 1935. 1935–6, served with VS-4B aboard carrier *Langley* (CV-1). June 1936–June 1938, ship's officer aboard the carrier *Lexington* (CV-2). 1938–40 NAS, Naval Operating Base, Norfolk. Joined VS-41 (later VF-42) in June 1940 and became CO in May 1941 until April 1942. Saw combat between January and March 1942 and was awarded the Air Medal and the Distinguished Flying Cross. 1942 from April to June, Air Group Commander aboard the carrier *Yorktown* (CV-5), and Fighter Director at Midway for which he received the Bronze Star. 1942, June–October on staff of Commander, TF-16 and from November 1942 to July 1943, Navigator of the carrier *Enterprise* (CV-6). 1943–5 was a student at the Army and Navy Staff College, Washington, DC. 1945, February, appointed in command of the escort carrier *Prince William* (CVE-31), until May 1946. After the war OIC Naval Air Reserve Training Unit, and then CO between August 1946 and January 1949. 1949, appointed CO NAS Guantanamo Bay, Cuba, and then Assistant Operations Officer (Air) on staff of Commandant Naval Operating Base, and for TF-64. 1950, Naval War College Strategy and Tactics course. 1951, appointed in command of the carrier *Valley Forge* (CV-45) and in action off Korea, for which he received the Legion of Merit. 1952, staff Naval War College, Newport, as Head of Strategy and Tactics Department and November 1953–May 1954 CoS. 1954, June, Commander, Naval Air Bases, 4th Naval District, Atlantic City, and CO NAS Atlantic City. Retired from the navy on 1 July 1956, lived New York City then North Carolina with his wife Dorothy née Robertson, by whom he had three daughters, Cecil Aileen, Dorothy and Pamela. Died on 22nd October 1994, at Whispering Pines, North Carolina.

102. Lieutenant Wallace C. Short.

103. Thach to Kitchen, 3rd Interview.

104. As quoted in Lundstrom, *Black Shoe Carrier Admiral*.

1. The Commander-in-Chief of the Combined Fleet, Admiral Isoroku Yamamoto. (*Courtesy Library of War History Department, National Institute for Defense Studies, Tokyo*)

2. The Commander of the First Air Fleet, Vice Admiral Chuichi Nagumo. (*Courtesy Library of War History Department, National Institute for Defense Studies, Tokyo*)

3. The Chief of Naval General Staff Admiral Osami Nagno. (*Courtesy Library of War History Department, National Institute for Defense Studies, Tokyo*)

4. The Chief of Staff, Combined Fleet, Rear Admiral Matome Ugaki (*Courtesy Library of War History Department, National Institute for Defense Studies, Tokyo*)

第二列左から　新宮（暗）、有馬、市吉、永田、和田、磯部、藤井、佐々木、渡邉、田口（医）、京谷（主）、福崎（副）

聯合艦隊司令部職員

5. The Commander and staff of the Combined Fleet. (*Courtesy Library of War History Department, National Institute for Defense Studies, Tokyo*)

6. The Commander and staff of the First Air Fleet. (*Courtesy Library of War History Department, National Institute for Defense Studies, Tokyo*)

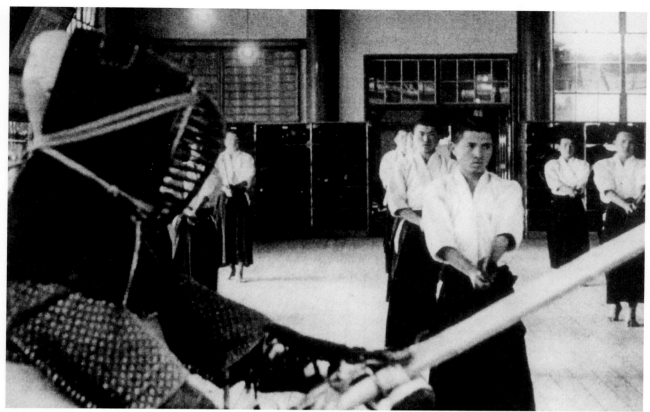

7. The young officer cadets of the Imperial Japanese Navy trained hard to fight hard. Here a kendo class is underway at the Etajima Training College across the bay from Kure. They were highly disciplined and taught that a superior spirit and better weapons would obviate the numerical advantage held by the United States and Great Britain. (*This photograph was part of a series taken in the 1930s by famous photographer Matsugu. Reproduced by courtesy of his daughter Miss Mitsa Matsugu.*)

8. Here the young officer cadets of the Imerial Japanese Navy move from one classroom to another with their books and notes, in strict file and always at the double. Fiercely proud and ruthless in combat, many declared even then that to die in combat was their avowed aim. With such an inbuilt attitude, the Western Allies found them more than a handful when talk changed to action in the Pacific. (*This photograph was part of a series taken in the 1930s by famous photographer Matsugu. Reproduced by courtesy of his daughter Miss Mitsa Matsugu.*)

9. Captain Joseph John Rochefort, an unorthodox maverick, whose work in Station *Hypo* gave the Americans unrivalled insight into the war plans and intentions of their enemy and gave them a 'priceless advantage' in the ensuing naval battle. He outthought his opposite numbers in Washington DC, but they quickly got their revenge and Rochefort was recalled and kicked out of Intelligence ('They don't think like we do', said one of his detractors, – too right he didn't, for he got it right and they got it mainly wrong!). He turned down a destroyer command and ended up in charge of a floating dock on the west coast. (*Naval Historical Center, Washington DC*).

10. Captain John Redman, pictured at Tarawa in November 1943. The younger of the two brothers. Rochefort was consigned to years in the wilderness after his brilliant deduction on Japanese intentions before Midway negated Washington's incorrect diagnosis of the evidence. 'Not the most glorious episode in the history of the US Navy', was one historian's verdict on what took place. (*Naval Historical Center, Washington DC*).

11. Rear Admiral Joseph R. Redman, seen here in 1957 with Fleet Admiral Nimitz. The elder of the two brothers who extended their control over Navy Intelligence after Midway, despite making an incorrect diagnosis. (*Naval Historical Center, Washington DC*).

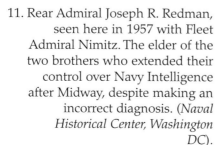

12. Aerial view of the Japanese aircraft carrier *Akagi*, sunk at Midway. (*Courtesy Library of War History Department, National Institute for Defense Studies, Tokyo*).

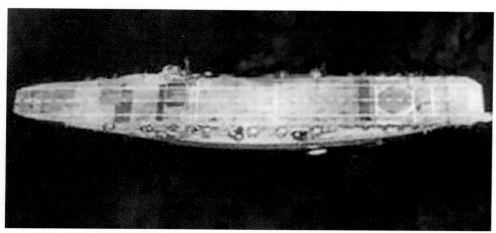

13. Overhead view of the Japanese aircraft carrier *Kaga*, sunk at Midway. (*Courtesy Library of War History Department, National Institute for Defense Studies, Tokyo*).

14. Starboard-side view of the Japanese aircraft carrier *Soryū* sunk at Midway. (*Courtesy Library of War History Department, National Institute for Defense Studies, Tokyo*).

15. Port-side view of the Japanese aircraft carrier *Hiryū*, sunk at Midway. (*Courtesy Library of War History Department, National Institute for Defense Studies, Tokyo*).

16. Nakajima B5N (Type 97)
Kate torpedo-bomber.
(*Courtesy Library of War
History Department,
National Institute for
Defense Studies, Tokyo*).

17. Lieutenant Commander Zenji
Abe, with his Aichi D3A/1 Val
dive-bomber, aboard the aircraft
carrier *Akagi* in 1941. Abe took
part in the Pearl Harbor attack
that December and served right
through the war in dive-bombers,
his final action being at the Battle
of the Philippine Sea in June 1944,
when, piloting a Yokasuka D4Y
Comet (code-named Judy), he
scored a very near miss on the
aircraft carrier *Bunker Hill* (CV-17)
and escaped to Rota Island.
(*Zenji Abe*)

18. Aichi D3A (Type 99) Val carrier-(dive-)bomber. (*Courtesy Library of War History Department, National Institute for Defense Studies, Tokyo*).

19. The A6M3 (Type 0) Reisen (code-named Zeke by the Allies but more commonly known as Zero, after the Japanese year of manufacture, 2,600) was the best combat fighter in the Pacific Theatre in 1942. Here a Zero is cheered on as she takes off from the deck of a carrier to attack. (*Courtesy Library of War History Department, National Institute for Defense Studies, Tokyo*).

20. Some of the top American officers involved in the Midway encounter. From left to right, Admiral Raymond A. Spruance, Admiral Ernest J. King and Admiral Chester W. Nimitz. They are seen here later in the war at Saipan with Brigadier-General Sanderford Jarman (far right). (*National Archives via Naval Historical Foundation, Washington DC*).

21. Captain Arthur C. Davis, Aviation Officer at Hawaii, one of a small group of experienced naval aviators who gave advice to former submariner Nimitz before and during the course of the battle. (*Naval Historical Center, Washington DC*).

22. Frank Jack Fletcher, as a Vice-Admiral later in the war. The senior naval officer on the spot and the tactical commander of the US forces at the Battle of Midway. (*Courtesy of Mr George Fletcher, donated 1976, via Naval Historical Foundation, Washington DC*).

23. Japanese ace Zero pilot Iyozo Fujita during the war. He stacked up a heavy count of 'kills' and even lost track of just how many in the end, assigning his later victims to his squadron rather than himself. (*Iyozo Fujita*).

24. The *Hikōchō's* domain. The small size and fragility of the bridge structure of Japanese aircraft carriers, when compared with American or British ships of the same vintage, is made clear in this view of the *Soryū*. She is undertaking her sea trials in the Bungo Suido Channel. This much smaller profile was due to the fact that, instead of incorporating single upright funnels into the structure, with trunked uptakes leading to a single vent, Japanese carriers often had their uptakes curved over outboard to take the fumes and smoke away from the flight decks. The actual air defence station can be seen atop the compass bridge, and a direction-finding loop antenna, a 60cm signal lamp, signal flag hoists, ratio aerials and a 1/5 m rangefinder can all be seen. (*Author's collection via* Ships of the World).

25. Lieutenant-Commander John C. Waldron. Commander of torpedo-bomber squadron VT-8 from the carrier *Hornet* (CV-8). Waldron disagreed with the Air Group plan on the morning of 4 June 1942, and led his unit to their destruction in a gallant but hopeless attack, alone and unaided. This rather fuzzy photograph was taken before the war.
(*Courtesy of South Dakota Hall of Fame*).

26. The ill-fated Douglas TBD-1 Devastator torpedo-bomber. Here seen before the war, a TBD-1 ended up in the catwalk abaft the bridge of the USS *Yorktown* on 3 September 1940 following a landing accident. This particular aircraft was subsequently repaired and assigned to Torpedo Eight, and was one of the many such aircraft lost during the Battle of Midway on 4 June 1942. (*Naval Historical Foundation*).

27. *Top*: Date: 13 June 1940. Location: deck of the British aircraft carrier *Ark Royal* off the coast of Norway. Aircraft: fifteen Blackburn Skua dive-bombers. Mission: attack on German battle-cruiser *Scharnhorst* at Trondheim. Result: fighter escort failed to show up, defending German fighters in the air waiting for them, eight Skuas lost. (*Author's collection via Dickie Rolph*).

Déjà vu

28. *Bottom*: Date: 4 June 1942. Location: deck of the American aircraft carrier *Enterprise* off Midway Island. Aircraft: fourteen Devastator torpedo-bombers. Mission: attack on Japanese aircraft carriers off Midway. Result: fighter escort failed to intervene, defending Japanese fighters in the air waiting for them, ten Devastators lost. (*US Navy Official*).

29. The ill-fated Torpedo Eight, led by Waldron, forms up prior to departure from the USS *Hornet* on the morning of 4 June 1942. The last known photograph of the unit in battle formation, taken by the official *Hornet* photographer, William B. Gibson (*Copyright William B. Gibson*).

30. The US Army Air Force employed four of their new twin-engined Martin B-26 Marauder medium bombers as makeshift torpedo-bombers at Midway. Fast and brand new, they were no sitting ducks like the Devastators, but for the loss of half their number they were equally unsuccessful, despite the usual claims to the contrary. Here the crew of Lieutenant James Muri pose for the cameras on their return to Midway, with more than 500 bullet holes in their aircraft. (*US Air Force via Naval Historical Foundation, Washington DC*).

31. A famous still from the John Ford film of the battle showing US Marine Corps SB2U-3 Vindicator dive-bombers of Scout-Bombing 241 taking off from Midway Island airstrip to strike the Japanese fleet on the morning of 4 June 1942. Known derisively as the 'wind indicator' (because one could judge wind direction by the way the sealing tapes used to patch up the old machines were blowing), the Vindicator saw her first and last major action at Midway. (*NARA, Washington DC*).

32. Not even close! Bomb patterns well clear of the circling carrier *Hiryū* during the opening engagements of the battle. The US Army Air Corps B-17s never justifing the boastful propaganda of the air force top brass and the baying headlings of the *New York Times*. Not once, in the entire Pacific War, did an altitude bombing attack score a hit on any carrier or battleship of the Imperial Japanese Navy. The photograph is significant in other ways also, for it shows the carrier's flight deck almost bare of aircraft: only two Zero's can be seen, and there is no sign of a massed 'spotting' of any counter-attack force, at least at this time. (*Naval Archives via Naval Historical Foundation, Washington DC*).

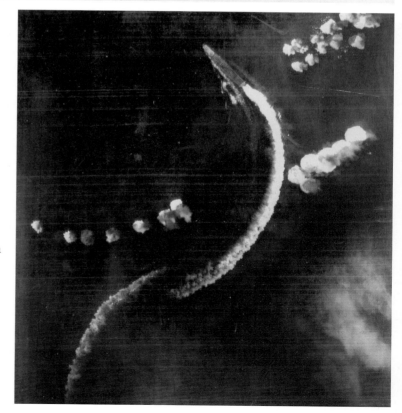

33. The author seated in the cockpit of the preserved Mitsubishi Zero fighter at the Mitsubishi Heavy industries factory in Nagoya, Japan. This particular aircraft is a salvaged and rebuilt Model 52, serial number 4708, of a later type of Zeke than those used at Midway. (*Copyright Peter C. Smith*).

34. The starboard-side view of the cockpit of a captured Mitsubishi A6M Zero fighter (AI-154) that was recovered after the Pearl Harbor attack and examined at Hickham Field. The Type 96-Ku-1 radio control box can be seen in the centre with the transmitter on the shelf below and astern of it. (*Hickham Base Photograph Laboratory via LRA*).

35. The black box on the right-hand side of the cockpit of the preserved Mitsubishi Zero fighter at the Mitsubishi Heavy Industies factory in Nagoya is a replica of the Type 3-Mark 1 radio set used at Midway. (*Copyright Peter C. Smith*).

36. The USS *Enterprise* (CV-6) steaming at high speed during the Battle of Midway. Two SBDs can be seen 'spotted' aft, and on the right. In the distance, is the heavy cruiser USS *Pensacola* (CA-24), one of here screening escorts. (*Naval Archives via Naval Historical Foundation, Washington DC*).

37. The bridge structure of the carrier *Hornet* (CV-8) (the *Yorktown* and *Enterprise* were near-sister ships and just about identical with similar camouflage-pattern paintwork). The Union Flag can be seen at the gaff, with radar atop her foremast in front of the large funnel and the HA director atop the three-tier bridge. The large bridge island makes a stark contrast to the scanty upperworks of the Japanese carrier *Soryū* of roughly the same vintage (*see Illustration 22*).

38. The SBDs of VS-6 in immaculate formation. This is an obviously posed shot as the bomb crutches are empty and they rarely used this type of stacked-up *en echelon* formation in combat conditions. The old-type Gunsight can clearly be seen and the pre-war markings are plain. (*Norman J. 'Dusty' Kleiss*).

Arnold briefed his squadron commanders. Importantly, he added the mandatory caveat that, should the Japanese force *not* be located at that point, then they were positively not to turn to port (south-eastward), but, instead to turn to starboard (the north-west) on a bearing of 010 degrees. Thus CYAG was given firm instructions[105] on precisely how to conduct himself and was spared the classic '50-50' decision that was to face Ring, who was left to make that tortuous decision unaided by his peers. Indeed the paucity of information provided to the TF-16 airmen by Miles Browning, who was to be eulogized in print as, 'one of the most brilliant tacticians of carrier air warfare before and during World War II',[106] was remarkable. As well as no Point Option (which Browning felt was unnecessary as it was 'obvious') TF-6's aviators were given no target designations and no group course.

The *Yorktown* team also worked hard to ensure that their aircraft could be recovered after the strike. Arnold considered that Browning's advocacy and Spruance's acceptance, of a Point Option course of 240 degrees and a speed of 25 knots was highly unlikely to be attainable and was too optimistic by half. From his experience of flying operations, coupled with the current wind conditions, Arnold considered a more realistic and attainable overall rate of advance would be more like 10–12 knots. After some arguments back and forth Fletcher agreed to a compromise of 18 which became the official figure duly conveyed to the air group, but Arnold also informed the squadron commanders 'off the record' during the final briefing that they should allow the speed of the fleet to be 12 knots.

Launching now got underway from *Yorktown*'s deck, with the seventeen SBDs of VB-3, followed by the twelve lumbering TBDs of VT-3[107] and soon the whole air group was airborne, the last aircraft being the six F4Fs of the air group's depleted fighter cover, which departed at 0907. Massey and the slow TBDs were already well on their way, having departed at seventeen minutes earlier. Incredibly, Leslie, who had been circling awaiting his fighter cover, had absolutely no idea that VS-5's seventeen further Dauntless dive-bombers would not now be following him out as planned. Once the aircraft were airborne, Captain Buckmaster set *Yorktown* off at a brisk gallop, 25 knots, but

Table 2: – TF16 and TF17 First Strike 4 June 1942

Carrier	F4F	SBD	TBD	Total
Hornet	10	34	15	59
Enterprise	10	32	14	56
Yorktown	6	18	12	36
Total	26	84	41	151

on a heading of 225 degrees· Fletcher duly informed Spruance that TF-17 was attacking the same target as TF-6, but with only 'three-fourths' of its total strength.

Now all three American air groups were committed and the outcome of the battle vanished from the control of the admirals to rest in the hands of the young aviators. In total, Fletcher's carriers had put 151 aircraft into the air, broken down as in Table 2.

This was a force of sufficient power to bring grief to the enemy, providing they could locate him. But it was not a concentrated force. The *Enterprise*'s aircraft had flown off in dribs and drabs and were all over the place; the *Hornet*'s had left together but within thirty minutes Waldron had had a final row with Ring over the radio (ignoring the strict silence command)[108] and virtually mutinied at 0825 by turning his squadron away on a totally different bearing toward the known enemy, a course which was to prove only too tragically accurate. Gradually, beset by fuel worries, Ring's painfully assembled 'group parade formation' unravelled piece by piece as fighter pilots also rebelled, gave up the ghost and turned back, again, in groups rather than together. Eventually, even the dive-bombers split up, and as a last blow, Ring's two wingmen also left him. Only the *Yorktown*'s formation held steady as the only truly integrated striking force until almost the end. Then, right at the last minute, they likewise faltered and failed to coordinate their attack fully.

How the hitherto invincible 1st *Kidō Butai* coped with these disparate forces would decide the outcome of the battle and, to a large extent, the course of the Pacific war.

---

105. Rear-Admiral Oscar Pederson, Papers held at Emil Buhler Library, National Museum of Naval Aviation, NAS Pensacola.
106. Clark G. Reynolds, 'The Truth about Miles Browning', in *A Glorious Page in our History*. Indeed he probably was, but not *this* day!
107. The sequence was thus adopted due to the fact that several of the TBDs with tired old engines needed every spare foot of flight deck they could get in order to get the necessary

speed and lift to get airborne. Launching the Devastators last helped in this but even so one 1st Division machine, T-3 piloted by Mach Harry Lee Corl, with Lloyd Fred Childers, ARM3c as his rear gunner, almost failed to clear the water as she clawed her way over the carrier's prow.
108. This was independently asserted by two of pilots, Guillory and Tappan ('emphatically'), who gave taped interviews to Weisheit for his *Last Flight of Ensign Kelly*.

Part Two

The Battle Commences

Chapter Four

The 1st *Kidō Butai* Under Siege

The defenders of Midway now threw everything they had at the Nagumo force. The attacks came, not in one organized, concerted and overwhelmingly powerful blow, but in waves. And soon the first carrier attackers joined in, dashing themselves against the CAP and the flak one upon another as the hours crawled by.

The Collins Attack

In the American armed services before the war, aerial torpedo attack had always been the exclusive prerogative of the US Navy, with little or no interest from the USAAC. However, the success of the Italian *Regia Aeronautica* tri-

motor Savoia-Marchetti Sm.79 *Spaverio* (Sparrow) as a torpedo carrying aircraft, in 1940–1, coupled with the startling demonstration of what could be done by land-based twin-engined bombers with the IJN's simple destruction of the battleship *Prince of Wales* and the battle-cruiser *Repulse* off Malaya on 10 December 1941, forced a rethink.[1]

Lieutenant-General H. H. 'Hap' Arnold[2] immediately demanded that the air force be allocated at least 150 of the navy's standard 18-inch (*sic*) torpedoes and trials were planned once stocks became sufficient, to equip several units with this weapon for deployment in Australia for use in stemming the Japanese tide in the South Pacific.

By 12 February 1942, Arnold was despatching a memo

---

1. For a full outline history of the development and war usage of aerial torpedoes see-Peter C Smith, *Ship Strike. The History of Air-to-Sea Weapon Systems*.
2. General of the Air Force, Henry Harley 'Hap' Arnold (1886–1950). b. 25 June 1886 at Gladwyne, Pennsylvania, son of a physician. Entered US Military Academy in 1903, aged seventeen. Commissioned 1907 as an infantry second lieutenant and joined the 29th Infantry initially in Philippines and later at Fort Jay, New York. Volunteered for military surveying under Captain Arthur S. Cowan until 1909. Volunteered as aviator in Aeronautical Division of the US Signal Corps 1911 and attended Wright brothers' flight training school, Simms Station, Ohio, qualifying as a pilot in 1911. Survived one air crash and almost lost his life in a second in 1912. Promoted first lieutenant 1913, and married Eleanor Pool in 1913, returning to the Philippines as infantry officer with 13th Division until 1916. Promoted to captain and returned to aviation once more at Rockwell Field. Transferred to the Panama Canal Zone and, on outbreak of war with Germany, became major in Information Division in Washington DC. Colonel in 1917, XO Aviation Section, unsuccessful in efforts to expand air arm. In charge of demobilization Rockwell 1918. Army Industrial College 1924, threatened with court martial over Billy Mitchell affair, Arnold was instead transferred to 16th Observation Squadron, Fort Riley, Kansas, well out of harm's way! Army

Command and General Staff School, Leavenworth 1928–9. Air Material Division 1931, Commandant March Field, California 1931–3. Brigadier-general 1935, and Assistant Chief of Air Corps 1935, then Chief Air Corps on General Westover's death. When USAAF formed in June 1941, Arnold made Chief and developed the AWPD-1 air strategy plan that called for expansion to 60,000 aircraft. Created Eighth Air Force in England. Lieutenant-general 1941, Commanding General of autonomous USAAF, and Joint CoS. Initially supported unsupported strategic bombing until it proved too costly, then – helped introduce long-range fuel tanks for fighter escorts, as well as B-29 development. Four heart attacks 1943–5. General in 1943 and remained fiercely anti-navy. Touring Europe in 1945, and also founded what became the RAND Corporation the same year. Retired from Air Force in 1946, retired to Sonoma ranch, in California, suffering a fifth heart attack in 1948. General of the Air Force in 1949 and died on 15 January 1950.

3. Henry Lewis Stimson (1867–1950). b. New York into a firmly Republican family, and educated Phillips Academy, Andover, Massachusetts, and Yale, receiving his BA in 1888. Graduated Harvard Law School 1890, joined Root & Clark 1891, partner in 1893. Appointed US Attorney in 1906, but defeated as Republican contender for Governor, New York 1910. Made Secretary of State for War by President Taft in 1911. In Great War served as colonel in Artillery in France

to the US Secretary for War, Henry L. Stimson[3], advising him of the latest update on how this programme was progressing. He listed the actual torpedoes on hand thus:

Estimated number in Australia	20
Arrived on the *President Polk*[4]	60
En route to Australia on other vessels	20
Scheduled to be shipped in February	30

Arnold told Stimson that, once the promised accelerated production of aerial torpedoes got underway in April, 'we should be able to get greater deliveries'. He revealed that adapters had been made for the new Martin fast light bomber, 'so that all B-26s can carry torpedoes. There will be a total of 115 operating B-26s in the ABDA [American-British-Dutch Area Command] area capable of carrying torpedoes.' He continued, outlining the extent to which he hoped the air force could adapt to using this new form of anti-shipping weapon: 'Our total torpedo requirement as furnished to the Navy is for 150 torpedoes immediately and 5,000 additional for delivery as soon as possible. The type of torpedo desired is the Navy aerial torpedo M XIII Mod-1.'[5]

In view of Arnold's anxiety to get the exact type of torpedo, it might be thought that the M XIII was some sort of modern wonder weapon. In fact, compared with Japanese, British and Italian aerial torpedoes then currently in use, this weapon was a relatively short-range missile of undesirable fragility. Furthermore, even if it had been supreme at its job, which proved to be very far from the case in practice, in view of the very limited production facilities at the antiquated Naval Torpedo Factory situated at Goat Island, Narragansett Bay, near Newport, Rhode Island, and the hugely increased demand of the navy's own carrier-born torpedo bombers, about to undergo an huge expansion, meeting the army's demands was out of the question.

In any event, at the crucial time of Midway, only a mere five B-26-B and -S aircraft were actually available to carry this weapon, and these were equipped at NAS Ford Island. Once the appropriate torpedo-lifting shackles were installed their totally novice aircrews had to be taught the bare rudiments of how to operate the equipment. It transpired that the only training that the five crews received was from attending a lecture given by personnel from VT-6 at the base on 27 May. Before the five aircraft flew on to Midway Island, one was damaged and thus only four remained to carry out the mission, two from the 18th Reconnaissance Squadron, Medium, and two from the 69th Bombardment Squadron, Medium.

At dawn on the 4th, the four Martin B-26 Marauders that had been standing by on runway alert immediately took off, then adopted a loose diamond formation, led by Captain James F Collins, Jr, USAAC.[6] According to one source, Collins totally failed to notify his crews that they were taking

---

in 1918. 1927 to Nicaragua as plenipotentiary; Governor-General Philippines 1927–9. Secretary of State to President Herbert Hoover 1929–33, infamously and naively closing down all Intelligence-gathering and decoding work as 'unethical'. In US delegation London Naval Conference 1930–1, also Geneva Disarmament Conference. Adopted anti-Japanese attitude after Manchurian episode. Appointed Head of War Department for second time by President F. D. Roosevelt in 1940, oversaw expansion of US forces and also development of atom bomb. Also instigated the Nuremberg war trials 1945–6. Died 20 October 1950. The Henry Stimson Center for furtherance of the study of international relations, was founded in Washington DC in his honour.

4.   The 10,496-ton *President Polk* (ex-*Grand State*) was a cargo liner taken over the by US Government as a war transport. She and the *President Coolidge* had been hastily combat-loaded at San Francisco with US Army fighters, bombers and their aircrew as well as much-needed ammunition and parts (including the sixty Mk XIII aerial torpedoes). The *Polk* (by then yet again renamed as the *President Taylor*), ran aground on the reef at Canton Island (Abariringa Island) of the Phoenix Group, halfway between Hawaii and Fiji, jointly occupied by Great Britain and the United States, where the wreck remained for many months and proved an irresistible target for raiding Japanese aircraft.

5.   Memorandum, Lieutenant General H. H. Arnold, US Army, Deputy CoS for Air, War Department, Office of the CoS,

Washington, DC to Secretary of State for War, dated 12 February 1942. (Copy Franklin Delano Roosevelt Library, PSF, Box 1.)

6.   Major James Francis 'Jim' Collins, USAAF (1917–96). b. Meridian, Mississippi on 23 November 1917. Was no stranger to dangerous situations, having walked away from an accident in a little Curtiss P-12E trainer at Mitchell Field when he was with the 5th Bomb Group in 1940. Two years on from that, in May 1942, he joined 69th Squadron, 38th Bombardment Group equipped with the new Martin B-26S Marauder, based at Patterson Field AFB, which was part of the force planned to be transferred from the USA to Australia. In response to the emergency Collins led a flight of four B-26s diverted to Hickham Field, Hawaii, were they were hastily equipped for torpedo dropping, given the bare outlines of the method the navy used and despatched on to Midway Island 1,200 miles away, on 29 May. Surviving the mission, Collins took passage back to Hawaii in a B-17 to get another aircraft but the battle was over by the time he arrived at Hickham Field once more. This attack constituted the first ever torpedo-bomber attack mounted by the USAAF and Collins was awarded the Distinguished Service Cross. He later rejoined his unit and at the end of June 1942 they moved to the South Pacific combat zone with four fresh B-26s, also converted to carry torpedoes to resume operations. They were based initially at Tontouta, the Plains de Giac. Here they waited for the call to action, having lectures by

---

part in a combat mission.[7] If true, this only added to the confusion when the four sleek aircraft burst out of cloud over the Japanese fleet. Collins took his quartet in a circuit to select his targets, thus exposing his force to the Zero CAP and defensive flak from the screen for a fatal length of time. Two of the Marauders were shot into the sea[8], before they could reach launch positions, the other two were damaged. Collins reported that his own five defensive guns 'balked and hung up, making them virtually unusable"'[9], his aircraft having had her hydraulic system shot up and received an estimated 500 bullet holes in just one side, from both flak and fighter fire, including some in the propeller blades themselves! The American survivors claimed that about fifty Zeros engaged them, but a calmer analysis of *shōtai* sorties revealed that some thirty fighters became engaged at this time, some straight from the carriers flight decks and through the defending flak. They divided their attentions between the Marauders and the slower Avengers which, by pure coincidence, made their attacks simultaneously.

Like their navy counterparts, who had given them what brief insight they had had on torpedo dropping, the fast, twin-engined B-26s planned to make a low-level approach, but, in the end, Collins made his drop from a height of 200 feet at a range of 800 feet. The only other Marauder to launch her torpedo was 'Susie-Q', commanded by First Lieutenant James P. Muri[10], while a third, piloted by First Lieutenant Herbert C. 'Herbie' Mayes, was according to Lord, alleged to have made a near-suicidal run at the bridge of the *Akagi*, missing wiping out Nagumo and his entire staff by mere feet before crashing into the sea. Muri later recorded that directly his torpedo was released, at a distance of approximately 450 yards according to some sources[11], he turned sharply to clear the deck of his target, 'nearly grazing the bridge'. He continued, 'I swung over the bow and then raced back the length of the deck, climbing as I went.'[12]

Muri's mount (No. 1391) was similarly heavily hit[13]; the hydraulic system was damaged, one wheel was shot off,

---

navy torpedo experts on launching and dropping techniques and also practised low-level bombing on a wreck on the reef. The units had a few alerts as the months passed but no action. Collins assumed command on 21 July 1942. Promoted to major, Collins finally took his three aircraft up to Henderson Field, Guadalcanal on 18 November 1942 with the 70th Squadron similarly equipped, but saw little action other than a sortie on 24 November 1942, and the unit returned first to New Caledonia to convert to skip-bombing, returning to Guadalcanal on 1 January 1943. Died aged 78, on 15 November 1996 at Portland, Cumberland, Maine.

7. Gilbert Cant, *America's Navy in World War II*. This was repeated by Kernan in *The Unknown*. However, Muri himself both confirms this and refutes this in the same article. On the one hand it is stated that *Battle of Midway* Liaison Officer Joe Warner informed them that the target was 'the inbound Japanese fleet, 320 degrees, 150 miles out', while a little later the report has Melo asking 'What's the target?' and receiving the response from Muri,' 'Probably some freighter.' See Jonathan Abbott, 'The Last Ride of Susie-Q'.

8. These B-26s were piloted by First Lieutenant Herbert C. Mayes and Second Lieutenant William S. Watson. There were no survivors.

9. See Jennifer King and Timothy Rollins, 'Sixty Years Ago . . . .', article in *The American Partisan*, 10 June 2002.

10. Lieutenant-Colonel James P. Muri. b.1918 west of Miles City and raised on the family ranch in Carterville, near Billings, Montana. Enlisted in USAAC in 1938. With 22nd Bomb Group he travelled to Hawaii via Langley Field, Muroc Field and March Field, then via Sacramento and San Francisco. Assigned as pilot to one of two 22nd B-26s held back at Hickham and joined by two more from 38th Bomb Group converted to torpedo carrying with single 18 inch, 2000 pound standard navy aerial torpedo. After Midway transferred to Florida as squadron commander for the B-26 training squadron. When the USAAF abandoned torpedo

dropping Muri became commandant of an AFB in South Dakota. After the war sent to Japan and became US Air Attaché at the American Embassy in Brussels. Retired to his ranch in Reedpoint, Montana, where he carved out a new career in real estate. On second retirement moved to Billings and continued ranching with cattle and pigs. Aged 88, Muri was still actively giving interviews in 2005.

11. According to the official USAAF figures the first torpedo was released at an altitude of 200 feet and a speed of 210 miles per hour, while the second was released at an altitude of 150 feet and a speed of 195 miles per hour, both at a range of 700–800 yards and both with a depth setting of 12 feet, both running 'true towards target'. See Confidential Report, *4 B-26s Attack Early 4 June 1942*, contained in CINCPAC File, held National Archives II, College Park, Maryland.

12. Cant, *America's Navy in World War II*. One Marauder aircrew from the 18th Recon, 22nd Bomber Group, Charles Lowe, who is described as 'an aerial photographer and tail gunner', has had his diary published on an Internet site. Although he did not fly the Midway mission, Sergeant Frank L. Mellow, Jr, Muri's radioman, who did and was wounded, apparently told him that this attack had been witnessed by the crew of a high-flying B-17 who saw their torpedo hit the *Akagi*. This piece of pure hokum ignores the fact that the B-17s did not even arrive over the *Kidō Butai* until half an hour after the B-26s' attack; also that, from 15,000 feet, even if they had been there and not 100 miles away, it would have been impossible to make out such detail. Some even go as far to claim it was Muri's 'beat-up' (at 200 feet!) that caused Nagumo to decide to make a second strike on Midway, with disastrous results. While serious historians dismiss such claims as the ridiculous nonsense they are, some people still desperately seem to want to believe such yarns, and so they continue to have currency among the gullible.

13. Muri told one interviewer in 2005, 'We stopped counting the bullet holes after 500' see Jon Gutman, *'Marauder at Midway'*.

the rear gun mounting, along with the gunner, was obliterated. The army flyers claimed two 'probable' hits on carrier targets and two or three Zeros destroyed. Like many of the colourful descriptions given to the press soon after, this was all good copy of course, but mainly fantasy[14]. No hits were scored on any Japanese ship, but one Zero was confirmed shot down by the B-26s; this kill subsequently turned out to be the sole contribution of the whole USAAF to the battle.

The two surviving B-26s managed to evade further damage by taking advantage of cloud cover, and the pair got back to Midway, but were so damaged that both machines were write-offs. Both Collins and Muri were later awarded the Distinguished Service Cross for their sortie, which was the first time army aircraft had attacked with torpedoes. They were interviewed by radio reporters on their return to Midway; 'We got three out of four hits,' Collins proclaimed to the world and the *Honolulu Advertiser* ran with it, but alas, it was just not so.

The Fieberling Attack

Meanwhile Lieutenant Langdon K. Fieberling,[15] had been leading the VT-8 detachment to its rendezvous with death. By coincidence the slower Grumman TBF Avenger naval torpedo aircraft from the *Hornet*'s VT-8 detachment flying from the Midway runway, arrived over the *Kidō Butai* at the same time as the B-26s. They hit the force further north and thus took the *Hiryū*, leading the port-hand of the two carrier columns, as their target. This marked the debut in combat of the Avenger, an aircraft on which high hopes had been pinned by the navy, but whose first mission was a catastrophe.

The Grumman Aircraft Engineering Corporation had a reputation for turning out strong and robust aircraft, ideally suited for the rough and tumble of deck operations. The F4F Wildcat might not have been the fastest or most

manoeuvrable naval fighter in the world, but it could absorb punishment better than most. Likewise then, coming from the same designer and stable, with many strong resemblances ('A scaled-up Wildcat' was how one Royal Navy test pilot described her[16]) the Avenger was a rugged aircraft. The TBF was the result of a 1939 design competition in which the Bethpage, Long Island, company's engineering team had worked in every modern innovation capable of being absorbed by her tubby hull, including a large internal weapons bay able to accommodate a 22 inch aerial torpedo or as many as four 500 pound bombs or a load of depth-charges – making her versatile in every role – and a power-operated rear turret housing a 0.5 machine-gun and two smaller machine-guns. In addition, and much envied by all other naval aircrews, the TBM could install a long-range fuel tank with 275 US gallons of extra fuel to increase her 1,105 mile range. She had armour protection for her three-man crew[17] and self-sealing fuel tanks. Some early models even featured the Type B (ASB) radar. She was also faster, if not by very much, than the Devastator, her 1,700 horse power Wright R-2600 radial engine giving her 249 units per hour flat out, and she cruised at 153 mph, as against the Devastator's more sedate perambulations at 118 miles per hour.

The VT-8 section, who had begun to familiarize themselves with their big, sturdy new mount at NAS Norfolk, were quite impressed. They had flown the six available aircraft to Pearl, missing the sailing of the *Hornet* by a single day, and so had proceeded on to Midway. They were scrambled away at 0615, just ahead of the B-26s, with the intention of making a combined attack with the marine dive-bombers, but, instead flew off alone and unescorted directly toward the enemy.

On their way out on course 320 degrees at 4,000 feet altitude, the half-dozen TBMs passed the incoming Japanese strike, and two of the less disciplined of the Zeros[18] were tempted, breaking off to make a quick attack pass at the

14. More responsibily, see, Martin Caidin's account in *The Ragged Rugged Warriors*.
15. Lieutenant Langdon Kellogg Fieberling (1910–42). b. 3 January 1910 in Oakland, California. Enlisted in Naval Reserve 7 October 1935. Trained and served as an aviation cadet and commissioned as an ensign, 1 March 1937. From 26 July 1941, assisted in the establishment and training of VT-8 in readiness for the commissioning of the USS *Hornet* (CV-8). Leader of a group of six volunteer pilots for the conversion of VT-8 from the Douglas TBD Devastator to the Grumman TBF-1 Avenger, they collected them at Norfolk, Virginia. On 8 May they were ordered to fly their new aircraft back to the West Coast and then were ferried out to Pearl Harbor on 29 May, the day after *Hornet* sailed. On 1 June they flew out to Midway Island for operations and were

placed under the Marine Air Group Commander, Lieutenant-Colonel Ira E. Kimes, USMC. Fieberling was KIA on 4 June 1942, and posthumously awarded the Navy Cross. The Destroyer Escort USS *Fieberling* (DE-640) was named in his honour by his mother, Mrs C. A. Fieberling, in 1944.
16. Eric Brown, *Wings of the Navy: Flying Allied Carrier Aircraft of World War Two*.
17. Pilot, radio operator/gunner, bombardier/radar operator.
18. Incredible as it seems, the Americans identified the radial-engined Zekes as German Messerschmitt 109s, an in-line-engined fighter of quite different profile and wing form. This elementary recognition error was to be repeated several times during the course of the battle. In the heat of combat such an apparently basic mistake was understand-

lumbering torpedo-bombers but no damage was taken. This might have given the green crews some feeling of elation or even immunity, but, if so, it did not last very long. At 0710 the six Avengers started to let down into their attack mode but were met, initially in some cases head-on, by at least six Zeros from *Hiryū*'s CAP, which were soon joined by others, including that of Petty Officer Ichiro Sakai, who abandoned his landing mode to rejoin the defence.

One by one the TBM's were overwhelmed as they continued steadily in, half of them being shot into the sea, to the accompaniment of applause from the Japanese ships' crews watching the slaughter. These three were chopped down before they even had time to launch their torpedoes. As they went to their deaths the remaining trio of Avenger crews tried desperately to fight back – indeed one Zero was claimed destroyed – but most were disorientated, dropping their torpedoes at such distances that *Hiryū* had ample time merely to reverse her course and outpace the pair launched against her until they stopped on reaching the end of their runs and sank. One damaged and already doomed TBM, in desperation dropped at the light cruiser *Nagara*, leading the fleet, but the lithe little vessel had even less difficulty in avoiding the torpedo. Her attacker was Ensign Albert K. Earnest[19] and the fact that he managed an attack at all was an achievement.

Earnest was cool-headed enough during the nightmare approach to appreciate that he was going to be hit, and hit hard. He therefore opened his bomb-bay doors while he still could, and before the hydraulic controls were shot away which, shortly afterwards, they were. His tail-wheel dropped, his red wing folding alert tabs displayed, indicating that the mechanism had unlocked. The radio was out, and so was the compass. The ball turret gunner was killed almost immediately[20], and the radio operator,[21] also wounded, could not fire the ventral rear machine gun as the dangling tail wheel obscured his line of sight. Earnest himself was hit in the wrist and head and temporarily concussed.

Despite his wounds, he came to and not only managed to lift the nose of his aircraft, (Bu.#00380) and so prevent her plunging into the ocean, but toggled the torpedo release as *Nagara* crossed his vision, before somehow clawing his way out from the fighters and flak into the safety of the clouds. Somehow he managed to nurse his battered aircraft back to Midway Island and land in one piece[22].

---

able from aircrews that had not been in aerial combat before. Apparently, although a captured A6M in good condition had been examined in China as early as 1940, fully reported on by General Claire Chennault, and a completely intact Zero (V-172, s/n 3372) salvaged from a beach at Qian Shan (Teitsan) on the Leich Peninsula after a forced landing there, and even test flown before being shipped to the USA where it was again test flown at Eglin Field and Wright Fields, two years later, and with scores of combat experiences from Pearl Harbor and the Philippines to the Coral Sea to go by, it had still not been included in US Navy aircraft recognition books! Nor were the Americans in any way alone in this misidentification charade. The British in Malaya and Singapore in December 1941 might very well have had up-to-date information on the Zero fighter from intelligence sources, but it was not disseminated to the fighting units. Air Commodore Stanley Jackson Marchbank, who was on the Air Staff HQ Far East from 1938 to 1943, told Sir George Nevile Maltby of the Foreign Office, on 21 September 1954, that such details were kept at Air HQ and not passed down to the RAF squadrons (who were flying Brewster Buffalo sorties against the Zero on almost suicidal missions). See CAB101/160, held at National Archives, Kew, London. In April 1942 Admiral Somerville had reported the Japanese Navy Aichi D3A1 Val dive-bombers variously as Junkers Ju 87 Stukas, and also, (as a result of their totally out-manoeuvring the British Fairey Fulmar fighters that they encountered and shooting down two of them for no loss to themselves), as 'fighter-bombers'! It was as if the Western nations even now could not change their old fixed mind-sets of automatic superiority and just could not believe that the Japanese could both build and fight superior aircraft to their own, but had to have assistance from their European allies. The long-exploded myth that the first Zero to be captured intact was the one that crashed in the Aleutians in 1942 still somehow persists to this day. See James F. Lansdale, *War Prize: The Capture of the First Japanese Zero Fighter in 1940*, www.j-aircraft.com/research/War Prizes.htm

19. Ensign (later Captain) Albert K. 'Bert' Earnest, USNR.
20. Seaman First Class Jay D. Manning.
21. Radioman 3rd Class (later Commander) Harry H. Ferrier.
22. Earnest and Farrier were thus two of only three survivors from VT-8, although they received none of the overwhelming publicity given to the third survivor, Ensign George Gay. Both men received awards, Earnest two Navy Crosses and Farrier the Distinguished Flying Cross, for this action. While Earnest stayed with VT-8, which re-formed with Avenger TBFs aboard the *Saratoga* (CV-3), Farrier was transferred to VT-3 aboard *Enterprise* (CV-6) for the subsequent operations off Guadalcanal. When the *Enterprise* was hit and damaged on 24 August, a section of VT-3 was flown off ashore to support the marines in the New Hebrides, while when *Saratoga* was torpedoed and also damaged the same month, VT-8 was sent ashore to serve with the Cactus Air Force at Henderson Field. Farrier rejoined his old unit and the two men were reunited. They remained together until VT-8 was relieved in November and sent back to San Diego, where it was decommissioned on 12 December 1942. Farrier went on to transfer to dive-bombers and flew SBD-5s aboard the new carrier *Yorktown II* (CV-10) in 1943-4 and retired as a full commander. He later wrote of his experiences, see H. H. Ferrier, '*Torpedo Squadron Eight, the Other Chapter*'. Bert Earnest also survived the war and retired as a full captain, moving to Sarasota, Florida.

Not surprisingly, neither survivor could enlighten the debriefing team on either the result of the attack or what had happened to the rest of the detachment. However, that ubiquitous B-17, flying reconnaissance, reported seeing one torpedo-bomber score a hit and so they were credited with a 'probable'. Alas, no hits whatsoever were made. The subsequent analysis of their valiant action came to the not very surprising conclusion that: 'Although the TBF is a well-armed plane, it is obvious that it cannot go through fighter opposition without fighter protection'.[23]

The Henderson Attack

The dive-bombers of the Marines Scout Bomber Squadron (VMSB-241), which could have co-ordinated their attacks with the TBMs, perhaps to the advantage of both groups, were sent off in two separate units. The first group, consisting of sixteen Dauntless SBD-2s, was led by Major Lofton R. 'Joe' Henderson, USMC.[24] Both groups were airborne when Lieutenant-Colonel Ira L. Kimes[25], having received the 0552 visual contact signal of Japanese carriers, sent off an urgent broadcast to the two divisions: 'Attack enemy carriers bearing 320 degrees distant 180 miles course 135 degrees speed 20 knots.'

Kimes never received any acknowledgement from the units that they had received this signal, so it was re-transmitted at intervals thereafter. In fact the dive-bombers received the first signal and both groups immediately acknowledged receipt[26]. The SBDs formed up at the rendezvous position on bearing 90 degrees 20 miles out around 0630, and began the flight out to the target.

Shortly after 0755 Henderson's First Division, flying at an altitude of 9,500 feet and divided into two boxes, broke through the cloud cover above Nagumo's ships. Henderson broadcast 'Attack two enemy CVs on port bow' and began a wide circle to shed some height in readiness for the final attack run which he intended should be a glide-bombing attack from 4,000 feet. As the SBD was an out-and-out dive bomber designed to plunge in at 70 degrees plus, the adoption of the shallower approach meant much longer exposure to enemy fire and fighters and less accuracy from a slanting rather than near vertical bombing run.

Henderson's reason for throwing away the prized advantages of a full dive was that his young pilots had received little or no training in this highly specialized form of attack. Fuel on Midway had been strictly rationed, which prevented even rudimentary practice, and few of the aircrew had really got to grips with the capabilities and limitations of their new mounts. Although VMSB-241 could muster a strength of thirty-four aircraft, Henderson only had twenty-nine pilots, so a pilot from VMF-221 was drafted in.[27] Eventually, the best machines were selected for operations, twelve SB2Us out of seventeen, and sixteen SBDs from the

---

23. C-in-C's Report, (ADM 199/1302).
24. Major Lofton R. 'Joe' Henderson, USMC (1903–42). b. 24 May 1903 in Lorain, a suburb of Cleveland, Ohio, at the mouth of the Black River on Lake Erie. Graduated from US Naval Academy, Annapolis, 1926. In 1927 he was posted to the Asiatic Fleet and in 1928 served as a marine officer with the Third Brigade in China before volunteering for flight training and becoming an aviator. He commenced his aviation career at Pensacola in October 1928 and qualified in September 1929. He flew from the carriers *Langley* (CV-1), *Ranger* (CV-4) and *Saratoga* (CV-3) and saw combat with the Aviation Detachment of the Second Marine Brigade against insurgent forces in Nicaragua from January 1930 to September 1931, being awarded the Cross of Valor by the Nicaraguan President. From 1931 to 1933 He was a flying instructor at NAS Pensacola, while his family home was in Gary, Indiana. He then served with Navy Observation Squadron VO 8-M based at NAS San Diego, as well as at Quantico, Virginia and Parris Island, South Carolina. He participated in the National Air Races in Los Angeles in 1936 and his unit won the Herbert Schiff Trophy in 1936. Appointed in command of VMSB-241 of Marine Air Group 22 (MAG-22) he flew their newly-delivered SBD-2s, transported by the *Kitty Hawk* (APV-1) to NAS Midway Island in March. KIA on 4 June and posthumously awarded the Navy Cross. The Japanese landing strip captured by the US Marines on Guadalcanal Island later that year was named in

his honour by Marine General Vandergrift on 18 August 1942, as also was subsequently the 1945 *Gearing* class destroyer *Henderson* (DD-785). Also named in his honour was the Lofton Henderson Memorial Bridge, a high-level crossing in Lorain County.
25. Brigadier-General Ira L. Kimes, USMC (1899–1949). As a major he had commanded the utility squadron VMJ-2 at MCAS [Marine Corps Air Station] Ewa in 1940, and this became VMJ-252 on 1 July 1941. His promotion and the command of MAG-22 followed and with his staff he worked indefatigably to prepare the base for the coming ordeal. In his subsequent personal account he recorded the telling fact that: 'some of the young pilots who came out with the SBDs and F4F-3s on the USS *Kitty Hawk* had not had as much as four hours' flying time since completing the final stages of flight training. They arrived on Midway on 26 May and on 4 June were called upon to face the cream of Japanese naval aviation.' He was awarded the Distinguished Service Cross for his work at Midway, and his inspiration was used on USMC recruitment scripts thereafter. (See State Historical Society of Missouri's document collection item #716). Died age just 49 of coronary thrombosis at Bethseda Naval Hospital, Maryland, on 14 February 1949.
26. According to Captain Marshall A. Tyler, USMC, senior surviving officer VMSB-241. (See Report of CO, VMSB-241, dated 7 June 1942).
27. Second Lieutenant Daniel L. Cummings, USMCR.

Table 3: – USMC SBD-2 attack, 4 June 1942

Section	Pilot	Aircrew
First Division		
Command	Maj. Loften R. Henderson	Pfc Lee W. Reininger
	Capt. Richard E. Fleming	Corp. Eugene T. Card
	Top Sgt Clyde H. Stamps	Pfc Horace B. Thomas
First	Capt. Elmer G. Glidden, Jr	Corp. Meade T. Johnson
	2nd Lt Thomas J. Gratzek	Sgt Charles W. Recke
Second	1st Lt Daniel Iverson Jr	Pfc Wallace J. Reid
	2nd Lt Robert J. Bear	Pfc Truell L. Sidebottom
Third	Capt. Armond H. DeLalio	Corp. John A. Moore
	2nd Lt Maurice A. Ward	Pfc Harry M. Radford
Fourth	2nd Lt Albert W. Tweedy	Sgt Elza L. Raymond
	2nd Lt Bruno P. Hagedorn	Pfc Joseph T. Piraneo
Second Division		
First	2nd Lt Richard L. Blain	Pfc Gordon R. McFeely
	2nd Lt Bruce Ek	Pfc Raymond R. Brown
	2nd Lt Jesse D. Rollow, Jr	Pfc Reed T. Ramsey
Second	2nd Lt Thomas F. Moore, Jr	Pvt Charles W. Huber
	2nd Lt Harold G. Schlendering	Pfc Edward O. Smith

nineteen on hand. Two Vindicators had ground looped on 28 May, but one of them was back in service by the 4th.

However understandable the reason for the glide approach selection, the cost was high as the CO unhesitatingly led his force toward the nearest carrier.

The Marine flyers, most of them green as grass, later identified their target as the *Akagi* but it now appears that it was the *Hiryū* that was once more the subject of their attentions. To reach her they had to cross the leading ships of the destroyer screen and brave the anti-aircraft fire of the battleship *Haruna*, but for six of the SBDs, including that of the commanding officer himself, this was academic for once more the Zeros of the CAP were on them and scoring devastatingly fatal hits well before then. An eyewitness recounted:

As we approached the Japanese fleet and their carriers it was a beautiful day with scattered broken layers of clouds below us. Before we could reach them we were attacked by the shipboard fighters and I was amazed at the ease with which they flew rings around us. Their gunnery wasn't the best though as they could and should have blown us out of the sky. I was in the number three position on the squadron commander's wing and after a few runs both he and the other wingman were gone.[28]

Henderson was obviously the leader and two or three of the defending fighters took him as their initial target; after two passes the SBD began to burn and Captain Elmer Glidden[29] realized from the movements that the

28. Colonel Elmer Glidden to the author; see Peter C. Smith, *Into the Assault: Famous Dive-Bomber Aces of the Second World War*.
29. Colonel Elmer George 'Iron Man' Glidden, USMC (1915–97). b. Hyde Park, Massachusetts, on 1 December 1915, later moving to West Roxbury, then to Scituate. Graduated from Mechanic Arts High School in 1934, then spent four years at Rensselaer Polytechnic Institute, Troy, New York, and in 1938 achieved a Bachelor of Aeronautical Engineering. Meanwhile had joined the US Marine Corps Reserve in April 1938 at Quantico, Virginia. Spent a year in the cotton industry then enlisted in the USMC in October 1939, requesting flight training. Appointed an aviation cadet at Squantum, and sent to Pensacola for instruction. Survived a crash which killed his instructor. On qualification in September 1940 was commissioned Second Lieutenant and

sent to Miami for dive-bomber training. On completion of training assigned to VMS-2 in January 1941, and ferried first long-range Vought SB2U-3 aircraft to NAS San Diego with VMB-231. Transferred to Hawaii in May and was at sea *en route* to Midway at the time of Pearl Harbor. Finally flew out to Midway in his first long range flight. Awarded Navy Cross at Midway then MAG-22 returned to Ewa and re-equipped with SBD-3s, and Glidden became XO of VMSB-231. Served at Guadalcanal from August to October 1942, earning second Navy Cross and promotion to major. From December at USMCAS (United States Marine Corps Air Station) El Toro, rebuilding squadron with SBD-4s. July–December 1943 back at Midway, then moved to Tarawa then Majuro with MAG-4 attacking targets in the Marshall Islands. Completed 104th dive-bombing mission in August 1944, and awarded Air Medal and promoted to leader had been hit and was out of the fight. He wrote in his report:

I was leader of the second box immediately behind the Major. As soon as it was apparent that the Major was out of action I took over the lead and continued the attack. Fighter attacks were heavy so I led the squadron down through a protecting layer of clouds and gave the signal to attack. On emerging from the cloud-bank the enemy carrier was directly below the squadron and all planes made their runs. The diving interval was about five seconds.

Immediately after coming out from the protection of the clouds the squadron was attacked again by fighter planes and heavy[30] AA. After making my run I kept heading on for the water, and I headed on an approximate bearing home. Looking back I saw two hits and one miss that was right alongside the bow. The carrier was starting to smoke.

Glidden told me that when they emerged from the protection of the clouds they were at a height of about 2000 feet and two carriers with destroyer escorts were immediately below them. The enemy carriers were steaming on parallel courses, surrounded by other fleet units and easily identified by the Rising Sun painted on their flight decks. The surviving SBDs pushed hard down and released their 500 pound bombs at heights between 600 feet and 400 feet, losing two more of their number in the process as the Zeros followed them all the way down. Even when they had delivered their bombs the Zeros continued persistently to follow them well out from the fleet. Fighting back Corporal Johnson was killed and many hits were taken.

We headed for the fleet in a long let-down rather than a dive and dropped our bombs. I don't think we accomplished much but we did our best and turned to reorganize for return to base. The Jap fighters

followed us down and away from the Jap fleet having at us at will. We staggered back to base in bad shape.[31]

The Marine SBDs had taken a pasting; in return, despite their optimistic reports of three direct hits on *Soryū*, which they 'left afire'[32], and two near misses on *Hiryū*, plus the destruction of four 'certain' and two 'probable' enemy fighters. In truth not a single bomb had struck any Japanese vessel, and the rear gunners had accounted for a single Zero. Like other survivors who made it back to Midway, most of the dive-bombers were badly shot about, one machine having been riddled with over 200 bullet holes[33] and still getting back. The pilot of this aircraft had his throat microphone shot from his neck and made a emergency landing on one wheel with no flaps, but still his only comment in his subsequent report was 'My plane was hit several times.' Only two aircraft remained fit for service. In his report Glidden noted the following salient points from the mission.

1: Glide-bombing was more hazardous than dive-bombing in the absence of protecting fighters. ('This has been known for a long time,' Kimes wrote in the margin).

2: There was a need to co-ordinate attacks by different units. (The First Division had gone in alone and unaided, piecemeal attacks were easily countered).

3: On sighting the target units should proceed to attack as rapidly as possible, any delay was fatal. (Kimes scribbled, 'And no circling!'')

4: The Japanese Zero CAP operated at two or three different levels, with the fighters working in pairs, 'with excellent teamwork' and their subsequent attacks were 'heavy and persistent'.

lieutenant-colonel. Assistant Operations Officer MAW-4 (Marine Air Wing Four) Kwajalein. May 1945 returned to duty with Aviation Division, Marine HQ, Washington DC. Married Phyllis, by whom he had two children. Amphibious Warfare School, Quantico in 1948 and again in 1954. Commanded VMF-323 1949–50. Flew with MAG-32 in Korea and in Japan as Combined Operations Officer. 1957–9 Commanding Officer, Marine Air Division, Memphis, Tennessee. Special Weapons Command, Albuquerque as Colonel 1958, Assistant CoS, El Toro. Student National War College 1961–2. Action Officer, Joint Chiefs of Staff at Pentagon. Then AC/S (Assistant Chief of Staff) G-5 and G-3 MAW-3 HQ and Deputy CoS G-6 in

Vietnam, flying non-combat missions. CoS COMCAB-WEST (Commander Marine Air Corps Bases, Western Area) 1966, then CO Marine Barracks, Panama. 1969 retired from service with two Navy Crosses, Legion of Merit, three DFCs and twelve Air Medals. Set up print company before retiring for second time in 1976 at Canton, Norfolk, Massachusetts. Died at Boston, aged 81, on 11 June 1997.

30. Glidden, Battle Report dated 7 June 1942.
31. Glidden, in *Into the Assault*.
32. CINCPAC Secret Report A16 (in National Archives ADM199/1302).
33. First Lieutenant Daniel Iverson, Jr. Report on the action of 4 July 1942 dated 7 June 1942, MAG-22 Report.

The Sweeney Attack

Colonel Walter C Sweeney, USAAC[34] led the heavy bomber units. The B-17 attacks were pretty much a repeat of those of the day before. Fourteen aircraft were despatched at 0415 local time and sent to attack what was assumed to be 'the same body bombed the previous afternoon.' While on their way and still at a distance of about 200 miles, a message was received 'in the clear', diverting them against 'another enemy task force complete with many carriers, which was approaching Midway from 325 degrees true at a distance of 145 miles. All the Fortresses swung round to a new interception course, climbing up to 20,000 feet as they did so. They were rewarded with sight of the enemy formation at 0732, and, thirty-eight minutes later, they identified two aircraft carriers emerging from beneath the broken clouds.

The first two flights attacked these vessels, dropping a total of forty-four 500 pound demolition bombs. They claimed to have obtained one direct hit on the stern of their carrier target by the second element, which they said was confirmed by photographs. The third flight of three B-17s also stated that they scored no less than two direct hits, one on the carrier's port bow the other on the waterline amidships, with one further possible hit and two near misses. The fourth wave of another three B-17s bombed a third carrier, 'obtaining one hit and two near misses', leaving all three enemy carriers, *Akagi*, *Sōryū* and *Hiryū*, on fire. They reported that anti-aircraft fire from the enemy fleet was heavy and detonating at the correct altitude, but was generally exploding astern of the B-17 formations. While a recent

account claims that 'the Americans were never in any great danger'[35] from the anti-aircraft fire, and that, 'the Japanese antiaircraft fire was none too good'[36], however Sweeney's co-pilot reported that 'the very first round exploded just to the right' and smashed the co-pilot's window.[37] As for the protecting fighters, the Fortress crews reported that these 'were not anxious to close', but of those that did, two were shot down[38].

Davidson concluded that 'no great difficulty was experienced in hitting surface ships' at altitudes of up to 25,000 feet.

Lieutenant W. A. Smith of the 394th, attached to the 31st, took off at 0400 with no bombs as none were available for his aircraft, nor were there any bomb shackles, even if bombs had been available. He took off with the striking force, 'to do nothing more than observe and take pictures of the bombing'. He was therefore entirely free to concentrate on the accuracy of his companions with no distractions. He reported that the enemy fleet was located 135 miles out from Midway on a bearing 320 degrees magnetic.

He reported that there were two or three carriers, many cruisers, destroyers and battleships 'impossible to count'. The enemy carriers took avoiding action mostly by turning in individual circles. Smith took up position astern of one formation of three B17s, which attacked one carrier from astern. 'We saw one train of bombs string across the aft end of a carrier and a torpedo plane (Marine) torpedo the same carrier'. Smith reported that, despite being over the enemy fleet for an hour, he only saw this one action before he left for to start back on the long journey to Hickham Field.[39]

---

34. General Walter Campbell Sweeney (1909–65). b. Wheeling, West Virginia 23 July 1909 into a military family. Graduated from US Military Academy and commissioned as second lieutenant of Infantry, June 1930. Entered Primary Flying School, Randolph Field, Texas, October 1934. Advanced Flight Training at Kelly Field, Texas, graduating October 1935 as first lieutenant. Assigned to the Eighth Attack Squadron, Third Attack Group, Barksdale Field, Louisiana. Joined Fifth Bomb Group, Hawaii, in June 1939, then became CO 431st Bomb Squadron, 11th Bomb Group. Promoted to captain in June 1940, major in July 1941 and lieutenant-colonel in January 1942. Commanded the USAAC Task Group at Midway in June, returning to Washington DC in July as colonel to be Air Officer, Theatre Group, Operations Division of the War Department General Staff. July 1944 assigned to 73rd Bomb Wing Colorado Springs and then Pacific area as CoS, then Deputy Commander in Marianas. Took part in the first attack by B-29 Super Fortresses against Japanese targets. Shot down into the sea on another mission he survived and paddled ashore on a life raft. July 1945 appointed first Director of Plans, Pacific Ocean Area at Guam. After the war returned to Washington on Joint War Plans Committee for Army Air Force. July 1946 instructor at National War College. Office of the Assistant Secretary of the Air Force in October 1947, and in 1948 at Strategic Air Command, Omaha, Nebraska. Commanded Fifteenth Air Force at March AFB, April 1953 and in 1954 commanded the three Stratojets which made first non-stop crossing of Pacific. Commanded Eight Air Force, Westover AFB, between August 1955 and September 1961. Promoted to four-star general October 1961 and took command of Tactical Air Command at Langley AFB. Awards included DSC, DSM, Silver Star, Legion of Merit with oak leafs, DFC and Air Medal. Retired on 1 August 1965 and died on 22 December of the same year. Buried at Arlington National Cemetery.

35. Parshall & Tully, *Shattered Sword*.

36. *Ibid.*

37. Colonel Everett C. Wessman, USAF (Ret) to Walter Lord.

38. Brigadier General H. C. Davidson, Confidential Report (contained in ADM199/1302, National Archives, Kew, London).

39. Lieutenant W. A. Smith, Midway Mission Reports, first report dated 6 June; second report dated 12 June 1942, (contained in ADM199/1302, National Archives, Kew, London).

Table 4: – US Submarine Forces at Midway (Task Force 7)

Task Group 7.1 Midway Patrol Group	Task Group 7.2 Roving "Short-Stop" Patrols	Task Group 7.3 Local Patrol north of Oahu
Cachalot (SS-170)	Narwhal (SS-167)	Tarpon (SS-175)
Flying Fish (SS-229)	Plunger (SS-179)	Finback (SS-173)
Tambor (SS–198)	Trigger (SS-237)	Pike (SS-230)
Trout (SS-202)		Growler (SS-215)
Grayling (SS-209)		
Nautilus (SS-168)		
Grouper (SS-214)		
Dolphin (SS-169)		
Gato (SS-212)		
Cuttlefish (SS-171)		
Gudgeon (SS-211)		
Grenadier (SS-210)		

The Brockman Attack

The American submarine patrol lines were established according to the hastily concocted plan laid down by their CO, Rear-Admiral Robert H. English[40], Commander, Submarine Force, Pacific Fleet, at his HQ at Pearl. The plan was worked out under the gimlet eye and basilisk scrutiny of Nimitz, himself a submariner of long standing. This placed fifteen submarines in two task groups along two arcs respectively 200 miles and 150 miles out from Midway Island. To back these up the large, new submarine tender *Fulton* (AS-11), moored at Pier S-13, looked after most of the needs of SubRow 8.[41] The forces at the disposal of English, TF-7, were divided into three patrol lines, as shown in Table 4:

In contrast to the Japanese submarines, the American underwater screen was in position in an arc well to the west of Midway well in time to intercept the expected Japanese invasion convoy. However, this punctuality in contrast to their Japanese opposite numbers' tardiness was about the only facet of the underwater conflict in which the Americans could claim superiority.

The philosophy of the US Navy submarine service for a projected naval war in the Western Pacific was 'the maximum number of potential torpedo hits and the maximum service of information to the Commander-in-Chief'. At Midway they totally failed to deliver either. This non-performance is even more remarkable as pre-war submarine training was almost identical to that of the Japanese in that the underwater craft were treated as another arm of the main fleet, and Midway was exactly the type of battle they had trained for.

Of all the submarines deployed by English, 'only two or three got off a torpedo, and none hit anything. One sent an incomplete contact report that misled Admiral Spruance and prevented the possible sinking of more major Japanese ships. The skippers blamed Bob English's plan; Bob English blamed the skippers.'[42]

Clay Blair, himself an ex-submariner, goes on to claim that there were many causes for this poor showing. Many

---

40. Rear-Admiral Robert Henry English (1888–1943). b. 16 January 1888 Warrenton, Georgia. Graduated from the Naval Academy Annapolis, 1911. Transferred to the Submarine Branch in 1914 and his first command was the gasoline-driven *D-3*. When America joined the war in 1917 he stood by and then commanded the new *O-4* (SS-65). Was awarded the Navy Cross for the rescue of an officer who became trapped in a sister ship, *O-5* (SS-66). Between the wars he held various submarine commands and was a divisional commander. Commanded the light cruiser *Helena* (CL-50) at Pearl Habor on 7 December 1941, during which she was damaged. Later In December he was Commander SubRon 4 and Commanding Officer of the Submarine Base, Pearl Harbor. May 1942 relieved Rear-Admiral Thomas Withers as Commander, Submarines Pacific just in time for Midway.

Between 14 May and 20 September 1942 he was Commander, Submarine Force, Pacific, at Honolulu and between 21 September 1942 and 21st January 1943, ComSubPac. Rear-Admiral English, along with several of his staff officers, was killed in a plane crash in the California mountains on their way to a conference. Posthumously awarded the Distinguished Service Medal. The destroyer *English* (DD-696), launched by his daughter, was named in his honour and more recently the Tactical Training facility at the US Naval Submarine Base, New London, Connecticut, was named English Hall to commemorate his memory.

41. USS *Fulton*, War Diary, 1–30 June 1942 Location and General Activities, (1 June, 1942).

42. Clay Blair, Jr, *Silent Victory: The US Submarine War Against Japan.*

submarine skippers who had excelled in the pre-war service and exercises made poor showings under the harsh conditions of actual combat; the emphasis on range and surface cruising was justified given the vast distances involved in Pacific Ocean warfare, but this made the boats unhandy and unwieldy. Moreover, those employed at Midway were not the best in service in many cases; for example the *Dolphin* (SS-169) was almost a decade old, having been launched in March 1932. She was only equipped with six torpedo tubes, carried eighteen torpedoes and had a top surface speed of only 18 knots. After Midway she was quickly relegated to training duties. The *Cachalot* (SS-170) and the *Cuttlefish* (SS-171) were far smaller vessels with no stern tubes, slower speed and less endurance. The sister boats *Narwhal* (SS-167) and *Nautilus* (SS-168), were even more ancient[43], dating from 1927, but, at 2,987 tons and a length of 355feet, were actually the largest American submarines built for fifty years.

But of course even had men and machines been up to the high standard they were ultimately to achieve in 1944–5, all their efforts would have foundered, like those of their compatriots in the torpedo-bombers, on the inadequacy of their main weapon, the torpedo. The Mk XIV (described before the war as a 'wonder weapon') was abysmal, and not until 1943, when English's successor[44] as COMSUBPAC got to grips with the arming mechanism did things start to improve.

A more recent critique claims that the problems ran deeper than mere material failure. 'The operation failure at Midway resulted from the failure to abide by the operation art factors of synergy, simultaneity and depth, anticipation, and leverage.' Further: 'These failures were a consequence of the submarine force, and the Navy, not adequately

addressing and training on operational art during the interwar years.'[45]

At least one submariner proved a worthy exception to the general mediocrity on display at Midway, and that was 'fresher' Lieutenant-Commander William H. Brockman, Jr.[46] His command, his first, was the old, large but refurbished *Nautilus,* which was hastened out of dry dock for a refit and sent off to battle, sailing at 0900 on 24 May and reaching her appointed station four days later at 1000 on the 28th. He had a crew of ninety-one officers and men, many equally inexperienced in combat. After taking up her patrol station Brockman and his crew spent the time in active preparation and further familiarization, making routine dives. He sagely got his radio teams to beam in to the Midway Catalina search frequency well ahead of schedule and was duly rewarded.

At 0420 on 4 June, Brockman was submerged on course 040 degrees true when *Nautilus* picked up the PBY clear voice transmission of the sighting of enemy aircraft at 0544, the only American submarine to do so[47], and set off at her best submerged speed of 7 knots toward the northern section of her search area. Fortunately for Brockman, Nagumo assisted things by steering a course that conveniently closed the gap at a much higher pace and, at 0710, in position 30° 00' N, 179° 25' W, anti-aircraft flak bursts and smoke were sighted to the north-west through the periscope. Brockman swung the *Nautilus* round to a course of 340degrees true and went to full submerged battle condition, and at 0755, when mastheads appeared, he continued to approach at a depth of 100 feet. Five minutes later he had managed to penetrate the 1st *Kidō Butai*'s outer defensive screen.[48] Another snap viewing revealed an *Ise* class battleship, a *Jintsū* class light cruiser and two *Yūbari* class light cruisers.[49]

---

43. Although, in fairness, both boats had been given completely new Fairbanks-Morse diesel engines in refits during 1940–1.
44. Rear-Admiral Charles Lockwood.
45. Thomas G. Hunnicitt, *The Operational Failure of US Submarines at the Battle of Midway – and implications for Today.*
46. Rear-Admiral William Herman 'Bob' Brockman, Jr, (1904–79). b. Baltimore, Maryland, 18 November 1904. Enlisted in the Naval Reserve in 1922. 1923 entered US Naval Academy Annapolis and graduated in 1927. Specialized in submarines from 1929, interspersed with surface and office duties. 1938–39 was Captain of the submarine rescue ship *Mallard* (ASR-4). In command of the submarine *Nautilus* (SS-168) during the Midway battle. For his work there and subsequent patrols, including the raid on Makin Island in August 1942, was awarded the Navy Cross with two Gold Stars, while his command was awarded the Presidential Unit Citation. 1943 served with Submarine Force, Atlantic, before becoming a submarine division commander between September 1944 and December 1945. Promoted to captain

March 1945. After the war commanded the *Cahaba* (AO-82). February 1946 served on the staff of the Seventh Fleet and at Navy HQ. Retired from the navy in November 1947 with the rank of rear-admiral. Began a second career in business. Died at Boca Raton, Florida on 2 January 1979.
47. The whole submarine force was not required by COMSUBPAC directive to monitor aircraft clear voice radio circuits before 0730 each day; nor was it likely that the submarines had been issued with the code to monitor these aircrafts secure transmissions either, even though they were mainly running surfaced at night and at periscope depth from dawn.
48. Confidential, USS *Nautilus – Report of first War Patrol* (including FB5-42/A16-3. Submarine Division Forty Two. Serial 025, dated 13 July 1942, USS *Nautilus* (SS168) – *Report of First War Patrol*). Archives Division, US Naval Submarine Base, New London, Connecticut.
49. The battleship was probably *Kirishima*, the light cruiser was the *Nagara*, but the other two 'light cruisers' were in fact large destroyers of the *Kagerō* class.

He reported being strafed by a Mitsubishi and depth-charged by a float plane and cruiser, none of which inflicted any damage nor prevented his continued penetration into the heart of the Japanese fleet. At 0825 the *Nautilus,* by some miracle, found herself the centre of attraction, with ships seemingly swirling all around. Brockman's own graphic report is a submarine classic, of course, but is well worthwhile repeating once more. 'Ships were on all sides moving across the field at high speed and circling away to avoid the submarine's position. Ranges were above 3,000 yards. The *Jintsū*-class cruiser had passed over and was now astern. The battleship was on our port bow and firing her whole starboard broadside battery at the periscope!'[50]

At 0825, taking a snap sighting, Brockman fired two torpedoes at the starboard side of the huge battleship target, which was steering west at high speed, a range of about 4,500 yards. He considered he could hardly miss, but miss he did with the only torpedo that actually left the tube (the other ran hot and failed to fire). The one missile that did run left behind its unique signature of a bubble trail, which a hard-a-port turn by the battleship easily avoided, but down which another cruiser appeared to be homing on the *Nautilus* at high speed. Brockman took his command down to 150 feet and awaited the inevitable depth-charging, which soon materialized.

Undeterred by the counter-attack and the failure of his first strike, and still unharmed even if shaken[51], Brockman, rather than cutting his losses and sneaking away while he could, resumed his probing, risking raising his periscope once more at 0900. Brockman sighted a Japanese carrier of the *Soryū* class about 16,000 yards off, manoeuvring at high speed, before further anti-submarine measures forced him to fight back. At 0910 he took a pot-shot at his chief tormentor, the light cruiser *Nagara*, which was closing at speed to less that 3,000 yards. Once again his torpedo was avoided and *Nautilus* was rigged for depth-charges. Nor was she disappointed as after *Nagara* had had her fill she appointed one of her flotilla, the destroyer *Arashi*, to remain behind and either finish off the audacious American intruder for good, or at least keep her so fully occupied that

the heavy ships could move away without further molestation. The *Arashi*'s commanding officer[52] took his job very seriously and despite evasive action and even a dive down to 200 feet depth Brockman failed to shake the persistent terrier off. Two depth-charges were released which detonated very close indeed to the old submarines hull at 0933. Although she had come close to a kill, *Arashi* felt she could tarry no longer and made haste to catch up with the rest of her force, now long departed the scene of the hunt. Thankful to be spared, Brockman took *Nautilus* back to periscope depth just before 1000 and then surfaced and began patiently chugging along the route of the vanished Japanese fleet. He was persistent too!

We have not heard the last of Brockman and his intrepid command, but for the moment in the morning sequence of attacks, his two torpedo launches had also failed to inflict any damage on the enemy at all.

The Norris Attack

Then it was the turn of the Vought SB2U-3 Vindicators, led by the unit's XO, Major Benjamin W. Norris, USMCR.[53] Their aircraft were the long-range 3s, built especially for the Marine Corps, giving them the flexibility that island-hopping in the Pacific would require, but that, alas, was about their only asset. Its history was very similar to the British Blackburn Skua in that when the Vought company brought out the design in 1934 it was highly innovative, being the first monoplane dive-bomber to join the US Navy, having folding wings to facilitate hangar storage and, for its day, quite fast at 257 miles per hour, (which was actually a knot or so speedier than the early SBDs!).

The XSB2U-1 prototype first flew in January 1935 and reflected the technology of the day in that she was of composite design (like the Hawker Hurricane) with the wings, rear fuselage and all movable tail surface still being fabric-covered.[54] Also like the Skua, teething problems delayed her entry into service. The experimental reversible propeller, which the navy introduced to restrict diving speed, was fitted, but never worked correctly in practice

50. USS *Nautilus – Report of First War Patrol Report.*
51. Brockman in his report noted: 'Damage caused by depth charging was negligible, two soft patches are now weeping as a result. After starboard group hydraulic supply line silver soldered connection ruptured allowing leakage into engine room. Controller for forward battery blowers was thrown out.' However, he also commented that 'depth charging, especially if accurate, has a decided effect on personnel and it is considered a good idea to proceed to a quiet area for a day or so after depth charging.'
52. Commander Yasamusa Watanabe.
53. Major Benjamin White 'Ben' Norris, (1907–42). b. Callao, Peru, 15 May 1907. Educated at high schools in Maryland and New Hampshire before settling in New York City. Princeton University, graduating in 1928 with a BA degree. Joined USMC, serving as VMSB-241 of MAG-22 at NAS Midway, where he led the long-range Vought SB2U-3 Vindicators, which had made the record-breaking nine hours forty-five minutes flight from MCAS Ewa on 1 March. KIA 4 June 1942, and posthumously awarded the Navy Cross on 10 November 1942.
54. Lee M. Parson, *Dive Bombers: The Pre-War Years.*

and was consequently not used. The fitting of slatted dive-brakes under the wings, which opened at right angles like a Venetian blind and prevented the aircraft from diving too fast, was, conversely, just too efficient, slowing the SB2U so much that even in level flight full engine power had to be used to overcome the drag effect. This led to a distinctly makeshift solution, which was to lower the landing gear to provide the drag and restrict attacks to shallow angles, thus negating the rationale of the Vindicator. Finally the power plant selected, the Pratt & Whitney R-1535-94 radial, although powerful, repeatedly failed while in the dive, with the master rod bearings unable to take the stress. It was not until March 1938 that the adoption of silver-lead bearings overcame this problem.[55]

The Vindicator, as she was named, served as the main carrier bomber with the fleet between 1938 and 1941, and, elderly though she was by the time of Pearl Harbor, there were still sixty-two in front-line carrier service aboard the *Lexington*, the *Ranger*, the *Saratoga* and the *Wasp*. Foreign orders included a batch for the French navy, some of which were taken over by the Royal Navy and dubbed the Chesapeake, but they were never used operationally. The SB2U-3s were a special batch of fifty-seven Vindicators for USMC land-based usage, and they had additional armour protection worked in, which decreased their speed, and extra fuel tanks were fitted in any available nook and cranny, which led to them being dubbed, 'a flying fuel tank'.[56] The cynical aircrew awarded them other epithets including 'Vibrator' and 'Wind Indicator', as they were allegedly shuddered and jolted so much in flight as they aged. Nonetheless VMSB-241s flight to Midway was to break the record for the longest non-stop, overwater mass flight by a single-engined aircraft.

The Vindicators were also organized in two groups and made their approach at 13,500 feet. When still some 165 miles away, at 0820, the eleven dive-bombers caught a glimpse of the Japanese fleet through what was described as 'almost solid cloud cover'. Despite this, a *shōtai* of Zeros from *Akagi* were soon in among them and causing havoc. Even before the SB2Us could commence their initial 'drop-down' approach three of their number had been hit, although they claimed to have destroyed one Zero with return fire. But additional Zeros were continually joining in the slaughter until there were some fourteen snapping at the

heels of the Vindicators. Despite this, and severe damage to several of the dive-bombers, the whole marine force was able to form into column for the standard 'shallow dive' glide-bombing approach at 240 knots. This temporary immunity might have been down to the attitude of the defending fighters, if one eyewitness account is to be taken at face value. One of the marine pilots later recalled, with envy and awe, 'The amazing nonchalance of Zero pilots who did vertical rolls right throughout formation . . . .' However, he commented that although this was an enormously impressive demonstration of superiority, it was, 'very good for us since more attention to business might easily have wiped out eleven of the slowest and most obsolete planes ever to be used in the war.'[57]

Even so, Norris sought temporary refuge back in the clouds and when they re-emerged they found themselves at 2,000 feet, 'almost on top of' a screening battleship. He only had seconds to make his mind up and, because the carriers were still some distance off and he was sorely beset, concluded he would never make it if he tried to close the gap. He elected instead to concentrate his attack on the Japanese capital ship, which turned out to be the *Haruna*, which was as surprised as they were. The CO therefore banked hard to starboard and led his SB2Us down in a concentrated glide attack against this veteran, but thoughtfully, in case he personnaly failed to survive, radioed the homeward course to get any survivors back to Midway. His wingman, Second Lieutenant George Lumpkin, graphically described the attack in his later report.

Lieutenant Campion, who was No. 3 man, followed him and I dove third. Anti-aircraft fire from the Jap battleship was very close. In fact the air was so rough from the fire it was practically impossible to hold the ship in a true dive. The Jap battleship zigzagged frantically. I tried to release my bomb but the mechanism did not work. I pulled out of my dive and headed slightly south to keep from coming too close to a Japanese transport following the battleship. They were still shooting at me with anti-aircraft, probably 3-inch shells.[58]

Between the flak and the fighters, Norris lost three of his Vindicators in this attack, and, once more, the Zeros stayed

55. BuAer report, *Model SB2U-1 and SB2U-2 airplanes – conversion to permit dive-bombing operations*, BuAer Washington DC, dated 16 November 1939.

56. Boone T. Guyton, Vought test pilot, in '*Dive-Bomber for Sale'* by Beaucham, 'Flying the Vought SB2U', in *Wings* magazine, May 1975.

57. Major Allan H. Ringblom, narrative submitted to USMC

Historical Section, 'Dive-Bomber Pilot's Narrative, Battle of Midway'.

58. Major George T. Lumpkin, USMCR (1918–91). b. 10 February 1918, at Youngsville, North Carolina, and resided in nearby Louisburg. Served in 113th Field Artillery, North Carolina National Guard for three years from 1938. Enlisted July 1941 and in August appointed aviation cadet. On

Table 5: – USMC SB2U-3 Attack 4 June 1942

Group	Pilot	Aircrew
One	Maj. Benjamin W. Norris	Pfc Arthur B. Whittington
	2nd Lt George T. Lumpkin	Pfc George A. Toms
	2nd Lt Kenneth O. Campion	Pvt Anthony J. Maday
	2nd Lt George E. Koutelas	Pfc Warren H. VanKirk
	2nd Lt Orvin H. Ramlo	Pvt Teman Wilhite
Two	Capt Leon M. Williamson	Pfc Duane L. Rhodes
	2nd Lt James H. Marmande	Pfc Edby M. Colvin
	2nd Lt Jack Cosley	Pfc Charles E. Cayer
	2nd Lt Allan H. Ringblom	Pvt Eugene L. Webb
	2nd Lt Sumner H. Whitten	Sgt Frank E. Zelnis
	2nd Lt Daniel L. Cummings	Pvt Henry I. Starks

with the retreating dive-bombers for quite a while as the surviving eight machines made their way out to safety. As another VMSB-241 pilot was to record, he was 'surrounded' by Zeros and although he released his bomb, was unable to see the results as survival dominated.

For the next fifteen minutes I had nothing to do except try to get away from five fighters that were concentrating on me. In the hit and run dog fighting, which was my initiation to real war, my old, obsolete SB2U-3 was almost shot out from under me. I finally made my escape in the clouds. I flew back to Midway using full right rudder, right aileron and my elevator controls were frozen, and my instruments shot away. About five miles from Midway my gasoline gave out and I made a crash landing in the water.[59]

Cincpac credited the SB2Us with scoring two hits on *Haruna*. 'When last seen the battleship was smoking and listed.'[60] Actually she was listing because she was violently manoeuvred by her captain, with smoke from her funnels through forcing her engines flat out at top speed! However much the Marine Corps resists the facts, the sad truth was that, although there were five or six near misses, no hits at all were scored on *Haruna*, and she escaped without so much as her paintwork being scratched![61] The two Zeros claimed as shot down, plus the two 'probables,' were also largely figments of imagination.

The Waldron Attack

Lieutenant-Commander John Charles 'Johnny' Waldron[62] was by reputation a hard taskmaster who had whipped his

---

gaining his wings he was commissioned as second lieutenant in Marine Corps for aviation duty, March 1942. May 1942 transferred to Pacific War Zone with VMSB-241. He survived Midway and was awarded the Navy Cross. Served at Guadalcanal with the Cactus Air Force. Awarded Air Medal. Promoted to first lieutenant in December 1942. Married Hollywood actress Marjorie Riordan (real name Marjorie Shoresman). Promoted to major. Lumpkin's quoted statement is enclosed in the report on the action of 4 July 1942, XO MAG-22 to CO MAG-22, *Executive Officer's Report of the Battle of Midway, June 3, 4, 5,6, 1942 with Preliminary Phase from May 22, 1942,* dated 7 June 1942. Also CO VMSB-241 to CO MAG-22, *Report of Activities of VMSB-241 during June 4 and June 5, 1942,* dated 12 June 1942. Major Lumpkin died on 29 January 1991 in California.

59. Second Lieutenant Daniel L. Cummings, *Report on action of 4 July 1942,* MAG-22 Report.
60. CINCPAC, Secret Report, A16.
61. *Haruna* was the Japanese capital ship that bore a charmed life. Designed originally as a battle-cruiser, hence her high speed, 30.5 knots, to accompany and protect the Kidō

Butai's carriers, she and her two sisters had been reconstructed as fast battleships between 1927 and 1928, and again modernized with new engines in 1933–4. *Haruna* shared roughly the same symbolic status as the Royal Navy's carrier *Ark Royal*, in that they were both claimed sunk by enemy bombers time and time again. The B-17s had already claimed to have sunk her off the Philippines in February 1942 and were, incongruously, to claim her again at Midway. Again at Leyte Gulf she was claimed destroyed, but the doughty old warrior survived it all. She was finally rendered inoperational due to lack of fuel; she was sunk in shallow water with her upperworks and gun turrets above the surface in a series of carrier strikes on 28 July 1945, just a few days before the war ended.

62. Lieutenant-Commander John Charles 'Johnny' Waldron (1900–42). b. 21 August 1900 at Fort Pierre, South Dakota, youngest of five children of a farmer and horse-dealer in a Catholic family, whose great-grandmother on his mother's side, was an Oglala Sioux (as Waldron himself confirmed in his last letter to his wife although Parshall and Tully claim Cherokee) by whom Colonel Dixon had a daughter, Mary Aungie. Educated Rapid City High School and then at Ferris

94

Table 6: Comparison Between USN and IJN Torpedo Bombers at Midway

	Douglas TBD-1 Devastator	Nakajima B5N2 Kate
Designation	Carrier torpedo-bomber	Carrier attack bomber
Mission	Carrier-borne torpedo-bomber and level bomber	Carrier-borne torpedo-bomber and level bomber
Crew	3 (pilot, torpedo officer/navigator, radioman/gunner)	3 (pilot, navigator/bomb aimer, radio operator/gunner)
Configuration	Single-engined, all-metal monoplane	Single-engined, all-metal monoplane
Power Plant	Pratt & Whitney R-1830-64 Twin Wasp double-row radial, rated 900 hp for take-off.	Nakajima NK1B Sakae 11 14-cylinder air-cooled radial, rated 1,000 hp for take-off, driving a three-bladed propellor.
Speed	Max – 206 mph at 8,000 ft	Max – 235 mph at 11,810 ft.
	Cruising – 128 mph	Cruising – 161 mph at 11,810 ft
	Climb – 720 ft/min	Climb – 9,845 ft in 7 min 40 secs.
Service Ceiling	19,500 ft	27,100ft
Armament	Two .30 mgs (one forward-firing fixed, one on flexible mounting aft)	1 rear-firing 7.7 mm Type 72 mg on a flexible mounting aft.
Fuel Capacity	Max – 180 gallons (818 litres)	Max – 317 gallons (1,441 litres)
Range	716 nautical miles	528 nautical miles (1,075 nautical miles max.)
Offensive Capability	1 x 1,949 lb Mk XIII torpedo or 1,500 (3 x 500 lb) free-falling bombs.	1 x 1,746 lb torpedo or equivalent weight of free-falling bombs.
Dimensions	Span – 50 ft (15.2m) Length – 35 ft (10.6m) Height – 15 ft 1 in (4.6m) Wing area – 422 sq ft (39.2sq m)	Span – 50 ft 10 in (15.45m) Length – 33 ft 9 in (10.28m) Height – 12ft 1in (3.68m) Wing area – 405.8 sq ft (37.69sq m)
Weight	Empty – 5,600 lb (2,539 Kg) Laden – 9,444 lb (4,723 Kg)	Empty – 5,024 lb (2,289 Kg) Laden – 8,378 lb (3,900 Kg)

new squadron into fine shape by the time of Midway, but who freely mixed with his aircrew when off duty. Kernan described him as a 'perfectionist' but added that he had 'manic streak'.[63] He had not distinguished himself at Pensacola but had built up a hard-earned reputation as a more than competent pilot and, more relevantly, navigator, during his years of flying. He exuded self-confidence and many are the stories of his exhortations to his crews prior the battle. He 'knew' where the enemy was, and even if it meant disobeying the orders of his flight commander,

would take them there. He was also sagacious, having enough of his great-grandmother's 'savvy' in him to perfectly understand that their chances of survival were slender, and to urge that, even if only one aircraft was left she was to go in and hit the enemy. It may be argued that, in abandoning his air group and fighter cover to 'go it alone', he made a high probability of death for his squadron pretty much a guaranteed certainty. That decision does not detract one jot from Waldron's bravery, but it does give pause for thought on his temperament. To that might be

Institute, Big Rapids, Michigan. Graduated US Naval Academy, 1924. Served aboard the old armoured cruiser *Seattle* (CA-11), formerly *Washington*, the flagship of the C-in-C, US Fleet in the Pacific. After this commission Waldron applied for flying training and, in 1926, attended Flight School at Pensacola. Qualified as a naval aviator 1927. Also met and married Abigail Wentworth by whom he had two daughters. Studied law and admitted to the California Bar but never practised. Served in several air units, at the BuOrd, Washington DC, and was an instructor at the Naval Academy

and at Pensacola. For a period appointed Naval Observer at Norden Bomb-Sight Factory when the navy expressed interest in what was principally an army contract. In July 1941 appointed in command of VT-8 assigned to *Hornet* (CV-8), which he led at Midway. Awarded the posthumous Navy Cross exactly one year after his death. The destroyer *Waldron* (DD-699) was named in his honour. See Nancy Waldron LeDrew, handwritten document on her father in South Dakota Hall of Fame, Chamberlain, South Dakota.

63. Kernan, *The Unknown Battle of Midway*.

added the assertion by one of the few who survived the ordeal, that Waldron 'certainly knew we were flying beyond our endurance to get back to our ship".[64]

The Douglas TBD-1 Devastator was a single-engined, all-metal monoplane which, when she first joined the fleet back in the late–1930s, had been a cutting-edge aircraft, but that was more than four years earlier. Certainly, while the Royal Navy still flew obsolete biplanes like the antiquated Swordfish and her even more ineffective replacement, the Albacore, in 1942, the Devastator still appeared positively sleek by comparison. This was deceptive, however, for her speed, her fuel capacity and her defensive armament all spoke of yesteryear to an expert. For a more realistic and serious comparison than the British wire-and-fabric anachronisms, the Devastator should be compared with the Japanese navy's Nakajima B5N2 Type 97 (christened 'Kate' by the Allies); then the stark inadequacy of the TBD-1 becomes 'devastatingly' apparent.

As we have seen, the TBD-1's replacement, which made her debut in the same battle, fared no better.

To the obsolescence of the aircraft, and the almost complete uselessness of the torpedo she carried into battle, must be added the fact that many of the aircrews went into action on 4 June, without having dropped an aerial torpedo in their lives, not even practice ones![65]

Once Waldron had made his turn away from CHAG's course with his fifteen TBD-1s they were on their own.

In the immediate post-battle analysis, VT-8's attack is regarded not as foolhardy but as 'heroic', but it acknowledges that 'overwhelming fighter opposition' was encountered some 8 miles, from three enemy carriers. They estimated that ten torpedoes had been successfully launched, with five aircraft being destroyed before they could make their drops. A single hit on the carrier *Kaga* was

credited to them, probably on Gay's flawed observations, with several 'possible hits' on other enemy carriers.[66] Some sixty years later this erroneous belief is still being cited on the Internet, but it is total fiction.

In the first place VT-8's target was never the *Kaga*, but the *Soryū*. The 1st *Kidō Butai*, steaming south-east in two columns, had been turned on to a new course, east-north-east, 070 degrees, to close and engage the newly sighted American carrier. Each carrier turned individually, maintaining their relative formation positions and locations. The four carriers were in a slanted parallelogram, or 'stretched' box formation with *Hiryū*, the latter to the south-east of *Soryū* leading the columns; the heavy cruiser *Tone* beyond her and the battleship *Haruna* extending the front to the north-west. The fifteen aircraft of VT-8 approached on a reciprocal course of 234 degrees from the north-east and sighted the Japanese force dead ahead; they were simultaneously sighted by the *Tone* at 0918. She opened fire and started to lay smoke to draw the CAP's attention to their approach.

Initially Waldron selected the *Hiryū* for the target as by turning to port they would have been able to make a broadside launch against her port side, but, as she was further away than *Soryū*, and because already some twenty-plus Zeros had gleefully begun swarming in, he changed to take the nearest carrier instead. Both *Soryū* and *Hiryū* turned sharply to port in reaction to the torpedo threat and reversed course, thus presenting their sterns rather than their bows or broadsides to the Devastators trundling painfully along at a mere 100 knots when the attack broke at 0930. Neither the *Kaga* (at 1000) nor the *Hiryū* (at 1035) was attacked at this time.[67]

Calling in vain for fighter support[68] which never came[69], all fifteen Devastators where clinically chopped down in a bloody fifteen minutes, leaving but one solitary survivor

64. George Gay, 'The Skipper – Torpedo 8'.
65. Many people even today just refuse to believe (or do not want to know) this incredible fact, but it was confirmed long ago by the navy itself. 'For many of the pilots of torpedo eight, it was their first flight with a torpedo or "pickle" as they called it.' See Naval Press Release, *Decoration of Torpedo Squadron Eight* (Official Naval Transcript), Navy Department, Washington DC, 4 June 1943.
66. CinCPac report, *Battle of Midway*, Appendix II, *Analysis of Attacks*.
67. *Senshi Sōsho*.
68. Gay recalled that Waldron had called Stanhope Ring, 'From John E. One, answer.' Gay commented, 'We received no answer from the air groups. I don't know whether they even heard us or not, but I've always had a feeling that they did hear us and that was one of the things that caused them to turn *north* (My italics).' This would imply that Ring was to the *south* of VT-8. See *Battle of Midway: Oral History;* narrative of Lieutenant George Gay given to Lieutenant Porter in

Room 1827 Main Navy Building, 12 October 1943, compiled and formatted by Patrick Clancey, http://www.ibiblio.org/hyperwar/USN/ships/logs/CV/cv-8-EnsGay.html.
69. Lieutenant James S. Gray's ten F4F-4's from VF-6 were orbiting above during the massacre at a height of 22,000 feet. They heard nothing, and, as they did not venture below the overcast, also saw nothing. They remained for an hour thus, in splendid isolation, without a sign of friend nor foe, and then went home as fuel was running low. Moreover, it was not until 0956, just as they were leaving the battlefield, that they finally bothered to inform their carrier that they were over the enemy fleet Even then, after an hour, they only reported two carriers! As they left a *shotai* of Zeros was climbing to engage them but were too late. However, the fact that a strong force of American aircraft could circle the *Kidō Butai* undetected for an hour gives the strongest indication of the basic weakness of the Japanese-style air defence, and they ignored even this late lesson to their ultimate cost.

famously hiding beneath his floating seat cushion as the battle roared past him.[70] Sadly for posterity, instead of three hits, there were none whatsoever, although *Soryū* was forced into another S-turn when the last three TBDs seemed to be getting close enough to launch, but she was never endangered.

Thus the bulk of VT-8 passed into immortality, all twenty-nine casualties posthumously, but deservedly, receiving the Presidential Unit Citation, 'the highest award that can be conferred upon any group in the armed forces of the United States'.[71] They were certainly brave; the Japanese also thought they were amateurish. They achieved one thing about fifteen minutes' delay in recovering or replenishing the CAP, which was not possible on the westerly course, and Nagumo had to get his carriers turned back into the wind. He was not granted the opportunity for, almost immediately, at 0938, another string of wave-clipping Devastators were seen clawing up from the south.

The Lindsey Attack

This new 'threat' was posed by VT-6, led Lieutenant-Commander Eugene 'Gene' E. Lindsey.[72] If Waldron had any premonition of his fate, then Lindsey, too, was pushing his luck to the absolute limit. As well as being 'taped from the navel to the armpits,' having injured his back in an accidental ditching from *Enterprise* just a few days earlier, he had for some time been suffering problems with his eyesight, something he kept from the unit doctor. Despite this he determined to take part in his squadron's attack, and left his bunk in sickbay to do so. When one of his pilots remonstrated with him that he was unfit for combat duty, he was disdainful. 'I will lead my squadron in.' He also knew that fighter cover was essential and had made a scheme of his own to ensure he got protection when he needed it. The squadron XO knew VF-6 would fly out to the enemy at high altitude, but agreed with Gray that when he radioed 'Come on down, Jim', the Wildcats would swoop to their rescue, using the height advantage they

would have over the more nimble and deadly Zeros.

Thus prepared and very determined, Lindsey led the fourteen Devastators of VT-6 on a 240 degree approach course and, at 0931 they saw the remains of smoke trails laid by *Tone* and *Chikuma* during the Waldron attack some 30 miles distant. Lindsey therefore turned his whole force to starboard to take a closer look and split it into two groups[73] to make a classic pincer attack on the closest carrier, which, as they approached from the south, turned out to be the *Kaga*. As usual the heavy cruiser *Tone* was on the ball and opened fire on them with her four twin 8 inch guns, all concentrated forward, at 0940. Meanwhile the twenty-seven strong CAP was hastily reinforced by a further seven Zeros, but there was really no need, for another slaughter quickly unfolded.

Both Lindsey and Ely made radio requests for fighter assistance as they slowly clawed their way toward their target, but none materialized as Gray was now heading back to base oblivious of their fate. Following standard Japanese procedure *Kaga* again presented her rear to the attackers and cracked on speed, so that closing that gap was a long, slow business, too long and too slow for most of the attackers. This gave time for the Zeros to return from polishing off the remnants of VT-8 to the north-east. There was still the escorting cruiser's and destroyers' flak to brave and then the close-in fire-power of their target, but soon the CAP arrived hot-foot fresh from their earlier killing spree and began the process all over again. Ely's division, being closer to the returning Japanese fighters, initially took the brunt of the attack, only two managing to reach their drop points, but their torpedoes were easily evaded by a sharp turn to port by *Kaga*, which then turned back in a looping run to starboard to again throw off Lindsey's team. This expert ship-handling served its purpose well, as ruefully acknowledged in the detailed post-action report on the torpedo-bombers by the senior surviving officer from VT-6, who stated that *Kaga*'s violent manoeuvrings 'were so timed that it was impossible to obtain an advantageous point from which to drop'.[74]

70. Ensign George Henry Gay, a Texan who alleged that, from sea level and beneath his seat cushion, he had managed, to witness, and in considerable detail, most of the rest of the battle. See George Gay, '*Torpedo 8: One Man's Story*', in *Frontier* magazine, California, July 1981. He became an overnight national hero on the strength of it.

71. *Decoration of Torpedo Squadron Eight.*

72. Lieutenant-Commander Eugene 'Gene' E. Lindsey (1905–1942). b. Sprague, Washington, 2 July 1905. Graduated from the US Naval Academy in 1927. Volunteered for flight training and completed it as a lieutenant (jg), in 1929. Served in a variety of units in the 1930s and was placed in command of VT-6 in 1940. Took part in the early carrier raids from the *Enterprise* (CV-6), including

the Marshall Islands in February 1942. On 28th May his TBD-1 crashed astern of the carrier in an accident and Lindsey and his crew members, Thomas E. Schaeffer and Charles T. Granat, were rescued by the destroyer *Monaghan* (DD-354) and, despite some severe back injuries, insisted on taking part in the action of 4 May. The destroyer-minelayer USS *Lindsey* (DM-32) was later named in his honour.

73. The 2nd Division being led by the XO, Lieutenant Arthur V. 'Art' Ely.

74. See Lieutenant (jg) Robert E. Laub, *Attack on Japanese Task Force, 4 June, 1942*, VT-6/A5-2/ECA (029), dated 4 June, 1942 and Acting CO VT-6 R E Laub to COMINCH, *Torpedo Plane Operations in the Air Battle of Midway, 4 June, 1942*, dated 21 June 1942.

Lindsey overhauled her from the port quarter and began an attack run but was met almost head-on by a freshly-launched and fully armed force of nine further Zeros. He was the first to go, and three more TBD-1s followed him into the ocean in short order. Three torpedo-bombers dropped at extreme range but *Kaga* disdainfully made another turn and easily avoided these. The few survivors from VT-6 now had to find sanctuary and the only way out was to fly through the Nagumo force, assailed on all sides. Fortunately for these few, once they had dropped their torpedoes, the Japanese fighter pilots, sensing their stings had been drawn, seemed less inclined to waste their time and ammunition on them.

In total six of the *Enterprise*'s torpedo-bombers lost before they could launch their torpedoes, and a further three were hacked down before they could get clear. Of the eight torpedoes dropped it was claimed that two were hits on one carrier. In fact, yet again, there were no hits, indeed no torpedo passed even remotely close to *Kaga*. On the credit side, the Devastators are credited with one definite Zero scalp. On the way back one heavily shot-up torpedo-bomber succumbed to her damage and had to ditch.[75] Just four Devastators finally managed to stagger back to base.

Not surprisingly some of these survivors were traumatized by the experience and, like the British 'Tommies' on the beaches at Dunkirk, were seething at being left bereft of any fighter support throughout their ordeal. According to one account on landing back aboard *Enterprise* one survivor had to be held back from storming the ship's bridge, Colt 45 in hand, to find Gray and kill him, so incensed was he at the latter's conduct.[76]

The Massey Attack

Yet another torpedo bomber attack now developed as more TBD-1s arrived to be fed into the maw of the Zero CAP mincing machine. Lieutenant-Commander Lance E. 'Lem' Massey[77] arrived with VT-3. The *Yorktown* had finally

recovered her scouts and launched a belated strike which in contrast to those from *Hornet* and the *Enterprise,* were reasonably co-ordinated. Steering course 240 degrees the whole of CYAG's force had stayed close together throughout their passage at 1,500 feet echeloned starboard in two divisions[78], and when, at 1003, they glimpsed smoke on the horizon some 25 miles off, the whole force turned towards it as one unit. The TBDs were initially at an altitude of 2,600 feet and climbed slightly as they approached the enemy. They were, in turn, spotted by the Japanese at 1006 and the already powerful CAP of thirty-six machines was topped up by another half-dozen, which the heavy cruiser *Chikuma* directed towards the TBD-1s with well-aimed main battery fire. Thus once more fixated on the low-level danger, the Japanese lookouts failed to spot the rest of CYAG's team and torpedo-and-dive attacks developed, if not simultaneously, in close approximation. The official American verdict on VT-3's attack was that 'the torpedo bomber attacks were *almost* co-ordinated[79] with the SBD attacks, but large losses would have been suffered even had there been perfect co-ordination because of lack of adequate fighter protection. Throughout the Midway operations, the Japanese concentrated both fighter and AA fire on the TBs.' [80]

Unfortunately for VT-3, almost was not quite enough to save them from sharing the fate of their predecessors, which was almost total annihilation. Zero attacks started some 16 miles out, first a pair, then at 10 miles, another couple and then eight, until thirty or more had joined the feeding frenzy.[81] The usual Japanese carrier tactic of turning sharply away from the torpedo threat was followed, with all four ships executing a hard port taking them on a north-westerly course in staggered line abreast with the battleship *Haruna* in between the two divisions. Fighter protection in the form of six VF-3 Wildcats was divided, with just two providing close cover, but at least it offered a modicum of support initially, one Zero being splashed. All too soon, however, the F4-Fs were fighting for their own existence and lost

---

75. This was T-8 (BuNo. 0367) the mount of Machinist Albert Walter 'Walt' Winschell and his rear gunner Douglas M. Cossitt ARM3c. Happily both men managed to survive seventeen days afloat in their rubber boat before being rescued by a PBY.
76. This was Chief Machinist Stephen B. Smith according to Steve Ewing, or Steven Smith according to Alvin Kernan.
77. Lieutenant-Commander Lance Edward 'Lem' Massey, (1902–42). b. Syracuse, New York, on 20 September 1909. Graduated from the US Naval Academy in 1930 and, as naval aviator in 1932. Service under Lindsey as the XO of VT-6 aboard the *Enterprise* during the early actions of the Pacific War, and he was credited with sinking a Japanese vessel at Kwajalein on 1 February 1942. Assigned to command the

scratch VT-3 formed at NAS Kaneohie, Hawaii, late in May 1942, then based aboard the hastily repaired *Yorktown* (CV-5) at Pearl in time for Midway. Massey was KIA on 4 June and later the destroyer *Massey* (DD-728) was named in his honour.
78. Second Division led by Lieutenant Patrick H. Hart.
79. My italics.
80. CinCPac Report, *Battle of Midway*, Appendix II, *Analysis of Attacks.*
81. Not an exaggeration. One of the few American survivors, rear gunner and radioman Lloyd F. Childers, ARM3c, wrote in his after-action report that the Mitsubishi's attack was 'a melee' and that the Japanese fighters were, 'going crazy', while their methods he described as 'the most undisciplined, uncoordinated attack that could be imagined'.

Table 7: – Ineffectual Attacks on 1st *Kidō Butai* on the morning of 4 June 1942

No.	Time	Service	Commander	Attackers	Type	No.	Lost	Damaged	Hits Claimed	Hits Scored
1	0710	USAAF	Collins	B-26	Torpedo-bomber	4	2	2	2	0
2	0710	USN	Fieberling	TBF-1	Torpedo-bomber	6	5	1	1	0
3	0755	USMC	Henderson	SBD-2	Glide-bomber	16	8	6	2	0
4	0814	USAAF	Sweeney	B-17E/F	Heavy-bomber	0	0	0	3	0
5	0825	USN	Brockman	*Nautilus*	Submarine	1	0	1	3	1*
6	0820	USMC	Norris	SB2U-3	Glide-bomber	11	3	2	2	0
7	0920	USN	Waldron	TBD-1	Torpedo-bomber	15	15	0	3	0
8	1020	USN	Lindsey	TBD-1	Torpedo-bomber	14	10	0	2	0
9	1025	USN	Massey	TBD-1	Torpedo-bomber	12	12+	0	2	0
					Totals:	79	55	12	20	1**

* Two damaged aircraft ditched on reaching the US Task Force on return.
** Hit by dud torpedo, no damage inflicted on enemy.

touch as the torpedo-bombers descended through the overcast to deliver their attacks.

Once more the Devastators entered the crucible alone, with Massey diving his group down at 1020 with the loss of just one of their number, the rear machine being picked off. The jinking of the 1st *Kidō Butai* forced Massey to re-evaluate his chances and he switched his attack away from the most northerly of the carriers, which was the *Hiryū*, and turned toward a closer and more immediately attainable target, the *Soryū*, letting down to 50 feet in preparation. Even so the plodding bombers ran out of time – and luck. While some A6M2s duelled with the Wildcats above, the majority of the *shotai* concentrated on the task in hand, and with a vengeance! One Japanese pilot alone, Lieutenant Iyōzō Fujita, was credited with the destruction of a whole quartet of TBDs[82], others joined in enthusiastically and within minutes Massey had gone, still a mile from the carrier. All but one of his division quickly shared his fate.

---

82. Commander Iōyzō Fujita (b. 1917) b. 26 November 1917, at Tienchin, China (south-east of Beijing). Etajima 66th Class. Entered the navy in 1940. A veteran Zero pilot. He qualified as a pilot in the Oita *Kokutai* and served in combat with the Mihoro *Kokutai* (a force of eighteen to twenty-seven aircraft) based at Shanghai, China, from April 1941. In September 1941 he was appointed to the *Soryū*. At Pearl Harbor, as a lieutenant (jg) where he led the *2nd Shotai*, he took over command of Iida's unit on the latter's death and took part in the Indian Ocean raid. At Midway as divisional leader (*Buntaichō*) he was to suffer the indignity of being shot down by his own screens anti-aircraft (AA) fire during the battle. He was fished from the sea onto the deck of the destroyer *Akagi* by two former Etajima classmates, none the worse for wear. Later in 1942 he was appointed Flight Commander of Hidaka *Buntai* (a group of two or three *shotai*) at Rabaul, and at Kendari, Celebes, flying missions against both Guadalcanal and New Guinea. In November 1943 he joined the 301st *Kokutai* until March 1944, when he became CO of the 601st *Chutai* (a small group or medium-sized group) flying the new Yokosuka D4Y2 Suisei Model 22 'Judy' dive-bomber, and took part in the Mono Island operations. In 1945 was commander of the 402nd *Chutai* of the 341st *Kokutai* based at Clark Field, near Manila, which carried out raids against American forces in the Philippines. He survived the war as a commander and as fighter ace had forty-two claimed and eleven confirmed victories. He became President of *Unabarakai* the Zero Pilots Association, for a time after the war. I had the great pleasure of being the guest of himself and his family in his home in Daizawa, Setagaya-ku, Tokyo in November 2005, and found him lively and alert still but in September 2006 his wife reported his physical condition had not been good. He contributed to the book *Zero Fighter* by Akira Yoshimura. Some relevant documents, letters, press cuttings etc. can be found in the Joseph Gervais Papers, H118-05, Series I, Box 3, folder 4. (Specials Collections Department, McDermot Library, University of Texas, Dallas, Texas).

The 2nd Division also took casualties in short order, leaving just four TBD-1s left to make their torpedo drops.

Again the US analysis credits VT-3 with making five drops against their targets, of which two were successful against one Japanese carrier. Once more it was all illusion; the self-sacrifice of the Devastators was unrewarded and no hit was made. At 1000 the 1st *Kidō Butai* seemed to be again emerging unscathed from a succession of amateurish assaults. One point that has been made relating to the lack of CAP vigilance at altitude is that the Vindicators and Dauntless aircraft from Midway were both usually carrier-borne dive-bombers, and that this might possibly have misled the Japanese into thinking the Americans had shot their bolt in this respect, as they clearly had with their torpedo-bombers. This might have led to a feeling that they had nothing to fear. However, in my view this does not wash, and certainly Nagumo himself does not appear to have been fooled because in a signal he sent at 1000 he clearly stated: 'Many enemy *shore-based*[83] planes attacked.'[84] So then, where *were* the dive-bombers from the American carriers that should obviously have accompanied the fighters and torpedo-bombers encountered? *Someone* on the Japanese side ought surely to have been asking that question even as Massey's men followed Waldron's and Lindsey's to their fiery, watery death.

Wasted Sacrifice – the Naval Torpedo Disgrace

Fifty-one torpedo-bombers had been despatched against the Japanese carrier force, seven had survived. Whether such heavy losses had been caused by failure to integrate the attacks; failure to wait for or seek fighter protection – or indeed failure to provide it – obsolete aircraft; or just plain bad tactics, can be debated *ad infinitum*. What is in no doubt is that, even had these gallant men been able to score any hits on their targets, the probability is that they would have inflicted no damage whatsoever. As Alvin Kernan pithily comments, American torpedoes were 'duds'.

The standard US aerial torpedo used throughout the Pacific War was the 22.4 inch Bliss-Leavitt Mk XIII[85]. Developed from 1930 and first entered into service in 1935, it had a length of 13 feet 5 inches, and at this stage of the war was equipped with a 401 pound TNT warhead. Its all-up weight was 1,927 pounds[86], which made it among the heaviest carried by any of the world's torpedo-bombers in 1942. The usual dropping height of this weapon, from a straight and steady approach at a maximum of 110 knots, was between about 50 feet and 110 feet – certainly no higher due to its fragility.[87] Any higher and the Mk XIII would suffer damage, run off course or even disintegrate! Alternatively, the torpedo would strike a wave crest and cartwheel over and over; to prevent this a square plywood tail device called a Slater vane was fitted. The usual launching distance from the target was 800 yards, which of course was well within the reach of the innumerable long-range and even some close-range anti-aircraft guns with which warships were liberally supplied. If this temperamental weapon could be eased into the water without any of the foregoing hazards being initiated, then it would run at a speed of 33.5 knots (about the same speed as most Japanese carriers were capable of), being propelled by twin counter-rotation propellers and kept on course by control fins and at the correct depth by inbuilt gyroscopes.[88]

The Mk XIII had a range of 6,300 yards. As the torpedo made its way toward its target it obligingly left an easily detected trail of hydrogen bubbles to assist in location and evasion.[89] Even if the aircraft survived long enough to make the drop, and the torpedo held together and entered the water at the right height and speed, and even if by some chance it stayed on course without veering off[90], and if it was not outrun or avoided by its target, the missile had to strike the hull of the target ship almost at a 90 degree angle in order for the inbuilt Mk 4 exploder to function correctly and trigger the detonation of the warhead. Often the exploder device armed itself while still airborne, resulting in the warhead detonating when it hit the water.[91]

Despite all this, one authority claimed that these torpe-

---

83. My italics
84. *Senshi Sosho.*
85. Developed from a 1925 concept Project G-6 and re-designated in 1930. See Lieutenant-Commander Buford Rowland, *US Navy Bureau of Ordnance in World War II.*
86. Kernan says 2,216 pounds, but that was the later model with a 600 pounds Torpex warhead, not generally in service at the time of Midway.
87. This was squadron usage. Officially, the Mk. XIII was a 'reliable' weapon with 80 per cent reliability when dropped from a height of 140 feet.
88. Depth-keeping was unreliable and pre-settings were often

way off mark. Early tests indicated a 4 foot error but subsequent tests by US forces in Australia, hotly disputed by Goat Island, indicated 11 foot errors. They compromised on 10 feet!
89. H. A. Eggers, *Wake Survey of the Mark 13 Torpedo.*
90. Among the Mk XIII array of endearing faults was a tendency to adopt a marked left deflection of its rudders.
91. Lieutenant-Commander Richard H. Best spent two years specializing in torpedo-bomber tactics before the war, and he told me that, in 1940, when it was obvious to him that war was coming, he had volunteered to get back to sea in readiness for it. 'I had asked for assignment to a torpedo squadron believing that was where we would win the forthcoming

does were excellent weapons and had long service lives, Mk.13 remained in service until 1950.[92] However, that same source went on to admit that they 'had significant problems that were only fixed after wartime use began.' The Newport Torpedo Station was still testing this device in 1943, long after Midway was a memory. They dropped 105 Mk. XIIIs in these tests of which 36 per cent ran cold; 20 per cent sank outright; 20 per cent showed poor deflection performance and 18 per cent were unsatisfactory at depth-keeping. Just 31 per cent of the torpedoes actually performed as they should have done, while many had combinations of all these faults. In all the BuOrd listed twelve major faults. It was not until after they had called in the National Defense Research Committee to help in developing a brand-new Mk XXVI aircraft torpedo, and adopted the drag ring (known as the 'pickle barrel') for the nose, and the California Institute of Technology's shroud ring over the tail of the existing Mk XIII that things began to get better.[93] By 1945, with the war almost over, the situation had been transformed, with Mk XIIIs being dropped regularly from heights of 800 feet at speeds approaching 300 knots. There were even trial drops from altitudes of between 5,000 and 7,000 feet, five of the six Mk XIII's thus launched running 'straight and true', which would have been totally unbelievable to Waldron, Fieberling and all their gallant, doomed companions just three years earlier.

Midway Hit

While these American attacks had been breaking over Nagumo, the *Kidō Butai*'s own first strike had gone about its business methodically and professionally. The launch had commenced at 0426, at a mere 40-mile range, and had gone in from just before 0630, relatively smoothly[94]. While Lieutenant Jōichi Tomonaga, was in overall command due to Fuchida's incapacity, he also led the high-level bombers, which comprised eighteen Nakajima B5N2 Type 97s from *Hiryū*, most of which hit the Sand Island defences[95] eighteen more from *Soryū*, under Heijiro Abe, struck Eastern Island. They lost eight of their number to the defenders, five from *Hiryū* and three of the *Soryū kanko* (carrier-based torpedo-bombers).

In a like manner the *Akagi* and *Kaga* contributed eighteen *kanbaku* (carrier-based dive-bombers) apiece, with Lieutenant Shōhei Yamada leading the D1A1s from the former ship, and Lieutenant Shōichi Ogawa the latter, as well as being the principal dive-bomber leader. The Vals lost one plane from each carrier, with others damaged, two badly.

The fighter cover was similarly mixed, with nine A6Ms from each of the four Japanese carriers providing top cover. *Kaga*'s fighters were led by Lieutenant Iizuka Masao, *Akagi*'s by Lieutenant Shirane Ayao, *Soryū*'s by Lieutenant Suganami Masaji and *Hiryū*'s by Lieutenant Yasuhiro Shigematsu. All of *Soryū* and *Hiryū*'s fighters got back safely but two of the latter were virtual write-offs. *Akagi* lost one A6M2 as did *Kaga,* while four other fighters were damaged in varying degrees.

These losses, eleven aircraft, were far less than claimed by the American defenders, but every one could ill be spared. In return they had decimated the defending aircraft, destroying fifteen of the twenty-five Brewster F2A-3 Buffalo and Grumman F4F-3 Marine Corps fighters and leaving only two of the ten survivors fit to fly again. A second Japanese strike would not find much left to oppose it in the air.

The actual physical destruction wrought was, however, strictly limited – indeed it could hardly be otherwise. The main achievements of previous Japanese air strikes, from December 1941 onward, had been to wipe out the enemy air force on the ground by surprising them; this had been the pattern repeated from Pearl Harbor, to the Philippines and had usually worked. This time they found no aircraft conveniently lined up awaiting their attention – the planes they were supposed to torch were actively engaged against their home carriers. There was not much left of interest; the artillery batteries to be sure, command posts, power plants, the oil tanks to limit further American ripostes. But such a small bombing force was never going to neutralize Midway in one blow. They could bomb hangars without planes

---

battle. I was not then aware of the shortcomings of our notorious Mark XIII torpedo.' Lieutenant-Commander Best to the author, 15 October 1996. The navy being the navy, it was perhaps inevitable that the ex-fighter pilot with torpedo-bomber specialist experience, who volunteered for torpedo-bomber duty, was actually sent to a dive-bomber unit! In the end, of course, the US Navy got full value from Best, as we shall see, but his experience does illustrate that the fact that American torpedoes were a scandal was not obvious before hostilities.

92. Frederick J. Milford, 'US Navy Torpedoes, Part Two: The Great Torpedo Scandal, 1941–42.

93. Also the Arma Division of American Bosch Arma Corporation devised a gyroscopic computer. Even Albert Einstein was drafted in to assist. See Records of Bureau of Ordnance, Division of Research and Development, correspondence relating to his participation in the Navy's torpedo research programme. BuOrd File 4.4 – *Records of Subordinate Units 1900–44*, National Archives, Washington DC.

94. NB: The Japanese were running on Tokyo time; see *Sensei Shōsho*, Vol 43, *Midooei kaisen*.

95. One Kate was forced to abort the mission due to engine trouble.

inside them, or barrack blocks when the soldiers were safe in slit trenches, but committing highly skilled anti-carrier experts on such secondary tasks was a risky, and wasteful, option, and the Japanese losses of such men and machines achieved, in return frustratingly sparse results.

Although Lieutenant Ogawa was to report at 0640 that his force had obtained 'great results', Nagumo had earlier (0520) alerted his carriers that a second strike would most likely be necessary, and had confirmed this fact at 0715. Aircraft which he had wisely held back in case American carriers showed up, following Yamamoto's earlier stricture, were now to be struck down back into their hangars, in order to have their ordnance changed in readiness for *Kaga*'s flight operations officer (*hikōchō*)[96] to lead the follow-up attack.

This change-over of ordnance was not the simple thing it appeared on the face of it. The Kate was a versatile naval attack aircraft and performed both the level-bombing and torpedo-bombing roles assigned to it with consummate skill. The hangar ordnance crews were, likewise, professionals at the top of their game; if any team could carry out the complicated process of striking down the forty-three Nakajima's, removing the torpedoes and rearming them all with 800 kg HE bombs instead, in the minimum time, they could. But, was it wise? Nagumo was still waiting for the

searching cruiser floatplanes from *Chikuma* and *Tone* to report back. One had still failed to do so, because of a late launch. By 0715, Nagumo decided he could wait no longer; disregarding Yamamoto's caution back at the briefing, the order went out to rearm the strike force and down on the lifts of the *Akagi* and *Kaga* went the first of the B5N2s.[97]

Indecision

Less than half and hour after this fateful decision there was consternation on the bridge of the Japanese flagship. As we have seen, the *Tone*'s No. 4 search plane, call-sign *Meku* 4, piloted by Petty Officer First Class Yōji Amari[98], which was delayed by a fault on the launching catapult, had contacted an enemy force! Had he searched his assigned route, he would not have made contact at all; that he did find the Americans was highly providential, but in the end that one piece of good fortune was thrown away by the dilatory actions and reporting of the excruciatingly vague Amari during the subsequent hours. His report spoke only of 'ten surface ships'[99], on a bearing of 010 degrees some 240 miles from Midway. This put them on a bearing of 052 degrees from *Akagi* and at 200 miles' range.[100] Amari must have been aware that the crucial information was whether there

---

96. Captain Takahisa Amagai (1902–83). b. 15 July 1902 in Ibaragi Prefecture. 1920 entered Etajima 26 August. 1923 graduated as midshipman 14 July. 1941, Chief Air Officer aboard carrier *Hiryū*. 1942, April, became Chief Air Officer carrier *Kaga*. June segregated at Kanoya Air Base. August, appointed Technical Officer, Air Staff, Aviation HQ. 1944, May, appointed in command 634 *Chūtai*. November transferred to command of 765 *Chūtai*. 1945, on staff of CarDiv 1. 1945, became the second Team Chief of Education Section at Aviation HQ. July retired from IJN. Died on 1 December 1983 age 81.

97. The D3A1 dive-bombers on the other two carriers could be rearmed with 242 kg land bombs up on deck rather more easily.

98. Ensign Yōji Amari (1921–45) b. 31 March 1921, in the Nagano Prefecture. 1938, 1 April joined the *Kousyu Yokaren* (Naval Aviation School), which had only been established the year before, as one of the first entries. November, promoted to petty officer 3rd Class. 1940, graduated on 30 March and assigned Ooita NAS for pilot training. To Kure NAS, Hiroshima prefecture on 1 July. Assigned to seaplane carrier *Mizuho* on 23 October. Promoted petty officer 2nd Class 1 November. From December engaged in combat duties from *Mizuho* during landing operations in the Philippines invasion. 1942, took part in Manado Sulawesi island landing operation. 1 May *Mizuho* sunk by US submarine, Amari survived as assigned to Tateyama NAS, Chiba Prefecture. Assigned to heavy cruiser *Tone* on 21 May and fought at Midway. Combat duties at Second Battle of the Eastern Solomons on 24 August and on 25 October at the

Battle of Santa Cruz. 1942 pilot at Atugi NAS, Kanagawa Prefecture on 28 August, and promoted to chief petty officer on 1 November. 1944, 20 February, the Atugi unit was re-organized as 208 *Butai*. March unit moved to Thitose AB in Hokkaydou then send to Shumshu Island AB, near Kamchatka carrying out daily reconnaissance flights. Engaged and destroyed enemy aircraft on 3 May. In January 1945 was serving with 131 *Butai* when the unit was reorganized with Zeke fighters and the Suisei dive-bomber as a night-fighting outfit, renamed as *Hyuoy Butai*. April promoted to ensign. On 13 May he was on a mission when communications with him faded out. It transpired he was shot down when he was about 95 miles from Toimisaki Capa in Miyazaki. His body survived the crash and was taken by the current of the Black Stream, being washed ashore at Kouchi.

99. Captain James M 'Boob' Steele, Nimitz's Head of War Plans Section, ran a daily analysis log, the CINCPAC Greybook, independent of the CIU. The translated de-crypts of the increasingly impatient signals between Nagumo (call-sign *Mari*) and the obtuse Amari on the morning of 4 June are contained in File SRMN-012, held at Naval Historical Center, Kidder Breese Street, Washington Navy Yard, DC.

100. Amari was a graduate of the *Kō* 2 Flight Reserve Enlisted Trainee Class of April 1938–December 1939, on observation aircraft. He was diligent and persistent, taking great risks and skilfully avoiding the angry probing of the American fighter defenders trying to locate him and knock him down. The cloud banks made the task of avoidance easier, but complicated his attempts to get a clear view of his target.

were any carriers among the force he sighted, but he did not specify one way or the other.[101]

Nagumo ordered the rearming of the Kates to cease. To rearm them again with the discarded torpedoes would take much longer than replacing the torpedoes with bombs had done. As torpedo-bomber pilot Takeshi Maeda explained to me:

Not all the mechanics aboard had the special training for this job. There were special technical petty officers and ratings trained for this. Only certain hangar teams had the expertise to mount torpedoes on aircraft, which was different than loading bombs. A different number and type of bolts were required, the depth-settings on the torpedoes had to be pre-set according to expected target type, which called for expertise and fine-adjustment under pressure. With up to eighteen aircraft requiring this very special attention it could not be hurried, it might take up to three hours.[102]

Historians have since argued that Nagumo, and certainly his aviation advisors Genda and Kusaka, should have reasoned that for an enemy force to be out, surely must have at least one carrier; what purpose would they have in going out without one? It is felt, then the Japanese should therefore have acted instantly and, as advocated by at least one carrier commander, Yamaguchi, immediately launched everything they had, armed with whatever they had. Japanese naval aviators shared the long-held wisdom of their American counterparts about getting in the first blow. Instead there were arguments on the best action to take – go now or hold off and go *en masse* by the book. And all the while the clock ticked remorselessly on.

---

101. One officer, Lieutenant Makoto Kuroda Makoto, *hikōchō* aboard the *Chikuma,* and chief officer of the flight group, took the failure of the search planes to find the Americans very badly and never forgave himself, taking his deep remorse to the grave. He is alleged to have stated, 'I am responsible for the Japanese defeat', just three months before he died – Takeshi Maeda, interview with the author, Tokyo, 4 November 2005. Another Japanese source, Ryunosuke Megumi told the author, that he discovered 'the terrible fact' that Amari was made a scapegoat. The real failure of the scouting planes that morning was made by the *Chikuma*'s No.1's pilot, Lieutenant Chuma, who overflew the American force without sighting them, and broke off his mission due to bad weather. This failure, by an Etajima graduate, was covered up in the official history, which itself was written by the elite IJN alumni, at least according to this theory. Ryunsuke Megumi to the author, 17 December 2006.

102. Takeshi Maeda, interview with the author, Tokyo, 4 November 2005. But also see especially Dallas Woodbury Isom's detailed breakdown in '*The Rearming Operation*', in '*The Battle of Midway: Why the Japanese Lost*'.

Chapter Five

The Wide Blue Yonder

The Dive Bombers

The combined strengths of the American dive-bomber force put into the air on the morning of 4 June, were considerable, as the following tables indicate.

The order of battle for the first SBD attack on 4 June was as opposite.

Not every Dauntless attacked. From VS-6, Ensign E. E. Rodenburg (S-9) was forced to abort the mission, while Lieutenant F. A. Patriarca (S-13) was a non-starter; from VB-6 Ensign T. F. Schneider ran out of fuel before finding the enemy and had to ditch, while Lieutenant L. A. Smith (B-4), Lieutenant H. P. Lanham (B-10) and Ensign A. L. Rausch (B-17) were not launched. The VB-3 pilots Lieutenant-Commander M. F. Leslie (B-1), Ensign P. W. Cobb (B-9), Ensign C. S. Lane (B-11), and Ensign M. A. Merrill (B-17) suffered faulty bomb-release and they were unarmed.[1]

The Flight to Nowhere

According to the USS *Hornet*'s Report of Action, her air group comprised twenty-seven Grumman F4F Wildcat fighters, thirty-five Douglas SBD Dauntless dive-bombers and fifteen Douglas TBD Devastator torpedo-bombers, 'which aircraft strength was maintained until contact was made with the enemy'[2]. By 1 June her TF-17 had reached the holding position, Point Luck, and had already received CincPac's intelligence reports, which gave precise details of the large Japanese fleet they were going up against. They had also taken in various sightings of Japanese aircraft operating to the north-west of Midway Island. Rendezvous was made with the *Enterprise* group, TF-16, on the afternoon of 2 June, but the two units continued to operate apart, though usually within visual range of each other, until 3 June. Incoming sighting reports of the Japanese 'main body' placed them some 700 miles from Midway itself, on a bearing of 261 degrees true and the *Hornet* steered south-west to engage.[3]

The first indication Mitscher says he had of the Japanese strike against Midway itself, was at 0810[4] on 4 June. This was report from a PBY of the enemy bearing 320 degrees true, 100 miles from the island.[5] However, this vague sighting was soon followed by others that left no doubt the Japanese attack was taking place as predicted.[6] The famous 'many planes' report followed within two minutes and the

1 Radio-gunner Lloyd Childers, the rear-seat man with Harry Corl of VT-3, was to claim that it was the bomb splashes caused by these premature releases that caused him to assume they were under attack and that, as a result, he scanned the horizon and saw the smoke screen laid down by the screening destroyers of Nagumo's force and that this in turn, is what led VT-3 to the enemy. However, the faulty bomb-release incident took place within a short time of launch, long before they were anywhere near visual range of the enemy, so this claim has to be treated with extreme caution.

2 Commanding Officer, USS *Hornet*, Serial 0018 of 13 June 1942, Report of Action 4-6 June 1942. Hereafter cited as Mitscher Official Report.

3 Mitscher was critical of the fact that many despatches that he received were in High Command ciphers, which his staff could not read, not having, 'a class 5 cryptographic allowance'. He had to rely on what *Enterprise* team deigned to pass over to him, which entailed both delay and selection, and even this supply of information would have dried up totally should the two groups become separated during battle.

4 Mitscher's report times were given in Zone +10.

5 CincPac 041807.

6 Lieutenant Stephen Jurika, Jr, one of the few really fluent Japanese linguists (he had spent a year in Japan 1939–40) actually at sea for the battle, was embarked aboard the *Hornet*. Barde recorded that, 'while much of the Japanese radio traffic was in code, Jurika could report certain events to his commanding officer'. Captain Jurika to Barde 20 May 1966.

Table 8 Midway SBD Launch First Attack, 4 June 1942[7]

	Enterprise (CV-6)		
CEAG	Lieutenant-Commander Clarence Wade McClusky, Jr.	SBD-3	1
VB6	Lieutenant Richard Halsey Best	SBD-2/-3	15
VS6	Lieutenant William Earl Gallaher	SBD-3	17
	Hornet (CV-8)		
CHAG	Commander Stanhope Cotton Ring	SBD-3	1
VB-8	Lieutenant-Commander Robert Ruffin Johnson	SBD-3	18
VS-8	Lieutenant-Commander Walter Fred Rodee	SBD-3	15
	Yorktown (CV-5)		
CYAG	Lieutenant-Commander Oscar Pederson	SBD-3	1
VB-3	Lieutenant-Commander Maxwell Franklin Leslie	SBD-3	17

[7] Held in reserve were the 16 SBD-3s of Lt Wallace C. Short's VS-5 (the former VB-5) which had the change of designation forced upon them by Rear Admiral Leigh on 21 May.

First	S-1	Lieutenant Wallace Clark Short, Jr. (CO)	John W. Trott, ACRM (PA)
	S-2	Lieutenant Harlan Rockey Dickson	Joseph Michael Lynch, Jr, ARM2c
	S-3	Ensign Carl Herman Horenburger	Lynn Raymond Forshee, ARM3c
	S-4	Lieutenant (jg) Nels Luther A. Berger	Otto Russell Phelps, ACRM (PA)
	S-5	Ensign Leif Walther Larsen	John F. Gardner, ARM3c
	S-6	Ensign John David Bridgers	William Johnson, ARM3c
Second	S-7	Lieutenant Sam Adams	Joseph John Karrol, ARM1c
	S-8	Lieutenant (jg) David Render Berry	Earnest A. Clegg, ARM2c
	S-9	Ensign John N. Ammen, Jr	John Iacovazzi, ARM3c
	S-10	Lieutenant (jg) Charles Neal Conatser	Henry P. McGowan, Jr, ARM2c
	S-11	Ensign Benjamin Gifford Preston	Harold R. Cowden, ARM1c
	S-12	Ensign Robert D. Gibson	Wilburn D. Harp, ARM3c
Third	S-13	Lieutenant (jg) William Francis Christie	Alvin A. Sobel, ARM1c
	S-14	Lieutenant (jg) Henry Martin McDowell	Eugene C. Strickland, ARM2c
	S-15	Ensign Liston R. Comer	Harold J. Wilger, ARM3c
	S-16	Lieutenant Johnn Ludwig Nielsen	Walter Dean Straub, ACRNM (PA)
	S-17	Lieutenant (jg) Raymond Phillip Kline	Norbert A. Fives, ARM3c
	S-18	Ensign Richard Frederick Wolfe	Leon L. Getz, ARM3c

first sight of two enemy carriers at 180 miles' range followed at 0826, galvanizing the waiting US fleet into action. General quarters was sounded off and aboard the *Hornet* (the '*Horny Maru*' to her aircrew) all the pilots and crewmen of AE-8 went to their ready rooms at flight quarters. Information on the enemy's estimated location, heading and speed as received from the scouting aircraft was fed to the assembled pilots via the ship's teletype, along with the same details of *Hornet*'s force. To this was added the latest wind speeds at sea level and at a range of altitudes, and the latitude and longitudinal co-ordinates, plus their magnetic compass vari-

ations. The pilots transcribed this data via their crayons to their individual chart boards and then calculated their own relative motion course out to the target and back. [8]

The five airborne commanders were doing much the same thing but while Lieutenant-Commander Mitchell of VF-8 stated he would go with the final decision, the other four had a sharp difference of opinion as to the correct outward course to adopt.

Mitscher's own report makes absolutely no comment on the divergence of opinions among the airborne commanders, and states that the position of the enemy carriers

---

7.   Held in reserve were the sixteen SBD-3s of Lieutenant Wallace C. Short's VS-5 (the former VB-5 which had the change of designation forced upon them by Rear-Admiral

Leigh Noyes on 21 May).

8.   Based on the memory of Captain Roy Gee, *Remembering Midway*.

Table 9 – 1st SBD Strikes from USS *Enterprise*, *Yorktown* and *Hornet*, 4 June 1942

Division	Aircraft	Pilot	Rear Seat
USS Enterprise			
CEAG		Lieutenant-Commander Clarence Wade McClusky, Jr.	W. G. Chochalousek, ARM1c
	S-8	Ensign William Robinson Pittman, A-V (N)	Floyd Delbert Adkins, AMM2c
	S-11	Ensign Richard Alonzo Jaccard, A-V (N)	Porter William Pixley, RM3c
VS-6			
First	S-1	Lieutenant William Earl Gallaher (CO)	Thomas Edward Merritt, ACRM (AA)
	S-2	Ensign Ried Wentworth Stone, A-V (N)	William Hart Bergin, RM1c
	S-3	Ensign John Quincy Roberts, A-V (N)	Thurman Randolph Swindell, AOM1c
	S-7	Lieutenant (jg) Norman Jack Kleiss	John Warren Snowden, ARM3c
	S-9	Ensign Eldor E. Rodenburg	Thomas James Bruce, Sea2c
	S-18	Ensign James Campbell Dexter, A-V (N)	Donald L. Hoff, RM3c
Second	S-10	Lieutenant Clarence Earle Dickinson, Jr (XO)	Joseph Ferdinand DeLuca, ARM1c
	S-15	Ensign John Reginald McCarthy, A-V (N)	Earl Edward Howell, ARM2c
	S-12	Ensign Carl David Pfeiffer, A-V (N)	Frederick Charles Jeck, ARM3c
	S-16	Lieutenant (jg) John Norman West	Alfred R. Stitzelberger, ARM2c
	S-17	Ensign Vernon Larsen Micheel, A-V (N)	John Dewey Dance, RM3c
	S-14	Ensign John Cady Lough	Louis Dale Hansen, RM2c
Third	S-4	Lieutenant Charles Rollins Ware (FO)	William Henry Stambaugh, ARM1c
	S-5	Ensign Frank Woodrow O'Flaherty, A-V (N)	Bruno Peter Gaido, AMM1c
	S-6	Ensign James Arnold Shelton A-V (N)	David Bruce Craig, RM3c
	S-8	Ensign William Robinson Pittman	Floyd Delbert Adkins, AMM2c
	S-11	Ensign Richard Alonzo Jaccard	Porter William Pixley, RM3c
VB-6			
First	B-1	Lieutenant Richard Halsey Best (CO)	James Frances Murray, ACRM (PA)
	B-2	Lieutenant (jg) Edwin John Kroeger	Gail Wayne Halterman, RM3c
	B-3	Ensign Frederick Thomas Weber, A-V (N)	Ernest Lenard Hilbert, AOM3c
	B-5	Lieutenant (jg) Wilbur Edison Roberts, A-V (N)	William Burr Steinman, AMM1c
	B-6	Ensign Delbert Wayne Halsey, A-V (N)	Jay William Jenkins, RM3c
Second	B-7	Lieutenant Joe Robert Penland (FO)	Harold French Heard, ARM2c
	B-8	Ensign Tony Frederick Schneider, A-V (N)	Glenn Lester Holden, ARM2c
	B-9	Ensign Eugene Allen Greene, A-V (N)	Samuel Andrew Muntean, RM3c
	B-11	Ensign Thomas Wesley Ramsay, A-V (N)	Sherman Lee Duncan, ARM2c
	B-12	Ensign Lewis Alexander Hopkins, A-V (N)	Edward Rutledge Anderson, RM3c
Third	B-13	Lieutenant (jg) John James Van Buren	Harry William Nelson, Jr, ARM1c
	B-14	Ensign Norman Francis Vandivier, A-V (N)	Lee Edward John Keaney, Sea1c
	B-15	Ensign George Hale Goldsmith, A-V (N)	James William Patterson, Jr, ARM3c
	B-16	Lieutenant (jg) Edward Lee Anderson	Stuart James Mason, Jr, ARM2c
	B-18	Ensign Bertram Stetson Varian, Jr., A-V (N)	Charles Robert Young, ARM3c
USS Yorktown			
CYAG		Lieutenant-Commander Oscar Pederson	
VB-3			
First	B-1	Lieutenant-Commander Maxwell Franklin Leslie	William Earl Gallagher, ARM1c
	B-2	Lieutenant (jg) Paul Algodte Holmberg (ADO)	George Albert LaPlant, AMM2c
	B-3	Ensign Paul Wahl Schlegel	Jack Alvan Shropshire, ARM3c
	B-4	Ensign Robert Keith Campbell (GO)	Horace Henry Craig, AMM1c
	B-5	Ensign Aldon W. Hanson	Joseph Vernon Godfrey, ARM3c
	B-6	Ensign Robert Haines Benson	Frederick Paul Bergeron, ARM3c
Second	B-7	Lieutenant (jg) Gordon Alvin Sherwood (EO)	Harmon Donald Bennett, ARM2c

Division	Aircraft	Pilot	Rear Seat
	B-8	Ensign Roy Maurice Isaman	Sidney Kay Weaver, ARM3c
	B-9	Ensign Phillip Walker Cobb	Clarence E. Zimmershead, ARM2c
	B-10	Lieutenant Harold Sydney Bottomley, Jr. (FO)	David Frederick Johnson, AMM2c
	B-11	Ensign Charles S. Lane	Jack Charles Henning, ARM2c
	B-12	Ensign John Clarence Butler	David Donald Berg, ARM3c
Third	B-13	Lieutenant DeWitt Wood Shumway (XO)	Ray Edgar Coons, ARM1c
	B-14	Ensign Robert Martin Elder	Leslie Alan Till, RM3c
	B-15	Ensign Bunyon Randolph Cooner	Clifton R. Bassett, AOM2c
	B-16	Lieutenant (jg) Osborne Beeman Wiseman (PO)	Grant Ulysses Dawn, ARM3c
	B-17	Ensign Milford Austin Merrill	Dallas Joseph Bergeron, ARM3c

USS Hornet

CHAG   Commander Stanhope Cotton Ring   Arthur M. Parker, ARM2c

VS-8

		Pilot	Rear Seat
		Lieutenant-Commander Walter F. Rodee (CO)	John L. Clanton, ACRM (PA)
		Lieutenant John Widhelm (XO)	George D. Stokely, ARM1c
		Lieutenant Ray S. Davis (FO)	Ralph Phillips, ARM1c
		Lieutenant Erwin Stebbins (EO)	Ervin R. Hillhouse, ARM2c
		Lieutenant Ben Moore, Jr (PO)	Richard C. McEwen, ARM2c
		Lieutenant Laurens Adin Whitney (MO)	Angus D. Gilles, ARM2c
		Lieutenant Orman Griffith Sexton III (GO)	William L. Payne, ARM2c
		Lieutenant (jg) James M. Forbes	Ronald H. Arenth, ARM3c
		Lieutenant (jg) Ralph B. Hovind	Charles B. Lufburrow, ARM3c
		Lieutenant (jg) Donald Kirkpatrick, Jr.	Harman L. Brendle, ARM2c
		Lieutenant (jg) Albert Harold Wood	Richard T. Woodson, ARM2c
		Ensign Phil J. Rusk, (NO)	John Louis Tereskerz, ARM3c
		Ensign Stanley Robert Holm	John H. Honeycutt, ARM2c
		Ensign Benjamin Tappan, Jr	James H. Black, Jr, ARM2c
		Ensign Paul E. Tepas	Earnest R. Johnston, ARM3c
		Ensign Helmuth E. Hoerner	Moley J. Boutwell, ARM3c
		Ensign William E. Woodman	David T Manus, ARM3c
		Ensign Harold H. White	Gerald A. McAffee, ARM2c
		Ensign Augustus A. Devoe	John S. Urban, ARM3c

VB-8

Division	Pilot	Rear Seat
First	Lieutenant-Commander Robert Ruffin Johnson (CO)	Joseph G. McCoy, ACRM
	Ensign William Douglas Carter	Oral L. Moore, ARM2c
	Ensign Phillip F. Grant	Robert H. Rider, ARM2c
	Lieutenant James Everett Vose, Jr. (FO)	Joseph Yewonishon, ARM2c
	Ensign Roy Phillip Gee	Donald L. Canfield, ARM1c
	Ensign Joe Wiley King	Thomas M Walsh, ARM3c
	Lieutenant (jg) Fred Leeson Bates (EO)	Clyde S Montensen, ARM1c
	Ensign Arthur Caldwell Cason Jr.	Alfred D Wells, ARM3c
	Ensign Clayton Evan Fisher	George E. Ferguson, ARM3c
Second	Lieutenant Alfred Bland Tucker III (XO)	Champ T. Stuart, ARM1c
	Ensign Gus G Bebas	Alfred W. Ringressy, Jr, RM3c
	Ensign Don Dee Adams	John B. Broughton, Jr, ARM2c
	Lieutenant John Joseph Lynch (MO)	Wilbur L. Woods, ARM1c
	Lieutenant James Austin Riner, Jr	Floyd A. Kilmer, ARM2c
	Ensign Troy Tilman Guillory	Billy Rex Cottrell, ARM2c
	Ensign Kenneth B White (GO)	Leroy Quillen, ARM3c
	Ensign Thomas Junior Wood (PO)	George F. Martz, ARM3c
	Ensign Forrester Clinton Auman	Samuel P. McLean, ARM3c

'was calculated to be 155 miles distant, bearing 239 degrees true.'[9]

The *Hornet*'s battle action report gave the actual launch time as 0900, with the ship steering a course of 120 degrees at 25 knots. Barde stated that Ring's air group finally departed on a heading of 240 degrees.[10]

To help understand why a good half of Spruance's initial striking force failed to even find the enemy, let alone inflict damage up on them, it is necessary to examine the unpredictability of airborne navigation for naval carrier aircrew in 1942. To those who live in the cushioned world of the Global Positioning System (GPS) which takes you reliably to and from anywhere, the uncertainties and unreliability of the primitive navigation systems of the time might appear quaint, but they were state-of-the-art then, and people's lives depended on them.

As we have seen, pre-launch the known data was given out to the pilots in the ready room, but these essentials would be minimal: the known position of the carrier at time of launch; the last reported position (latitude and longitude), heading and speed of the target; the wind direction and other weather factors that might be encountered on the way; the agreed speed and height of their own force; and the predicted position (Point Option) of their carrier by the time they had located the enemy, attacked, survived to rendezvous again and returned. The carrier crew could deduce a reasonable estimate of the aircraft from foreknowledge of its search pattern and time of flight, backed up to a limited extent by the ship's own radar plot for part of the way. But of course once in the air things were not so simple. The enemy was also moving, and unpredictably; his original location as originally supplied might be (and at Midway, *was*) incorrect; the wind might change direction and strength; they would be subject to variations in speed due to cloud cover and avoidance of defensive measures, and so on. All of which would only compound the fact that they were working this out under the stress of combat conditions and with primitive equipment.

Navigation – Getting out There

The SBD pilot heading out in search of the Japanese fleet that June morning would have as his basic instrument of computation a chart plotting board (Mark III or Mark IV). It was just that – a large rectangular stowable board which was tucked away below the instrument panel when not in use and hauled out when required for updating and balanced on the pilot's knees as the aeroplane flew a steady course on instruments. It was clumsy, got in the way of stick movements and took away vital concentration while flying in formation.

The board comprised a clear-plastic overlaid compass rose, backed by a circular, centrally-pivoted, disc.[11] This had the virtue of being simple, there being only a solitary moving part. The overlay had tabs for lifting and was marked with concentric rings from the centre and cross-gridded lines to subdivide it into squares. These covered a distance of about 200–300 miles from the carrier itself. The pilot marked his data onto the plastic overlay with a wax pencil (the thickness of which represented at least a mile in either direction!).

Because it was laid down that enemy contact reports had to be made in latitude and longitude, with the board came a geographical template, in effect a circular slide-rule, the US Navy Aircraft Navigational Computer Mk 8-A (FSSC No. 88-C-1151). This was formatted to assist with time/distance calculations, air temperature, pressure, altitude etc., and included corrected altitude only (not density altitude). The aircraft's true airspeed could be worked out – very necessary for high-altitude flying, which was to prove particularly pertinent to the fighter escort as conducted on Midway missions.

The board was used to compute either a geographic plot or a relative plot thus:

(a) Utilizing latitude and longitude the pilot input his known information, as above for the carrier. From this he did his calculus by rotating the gridded disk, inputting variations in wind speed and other corrections as he went along.

(b) For a relative plot, the carrier would always be central, and the pilot would mark the grid with his course, any alterations to that, and the distance he had flown since leaving the ship. Once he was ready to return he could work out a suitable bearing from the last plot. In theory this would be sufficient to get him back to within what was hoped would be visual contact with the carrier, or at least the friendly force. But it did not always happen, and the further out he had gone, the remoter the chances of it happening.

9. Mitscher Official Report.
10. Robert Elmer Barde, *The Battle of Midway: A Study in Leadership*.
11. These boards came with an Instruction booklet and the more detailed *Tactical Graphics for Aircraft Operations*, issued by the US Navy Hydrographic Office, Washington, DC.

Dive-bomber veteran George Walsh gave one of the best descriptions of this device.

You have to appreciate the difficulty of navigating over the open expanse of the Pacific Ocean. Picture the two opposing fleets steaming at 20 to 30 knots and changing direction frequently as they turned into the wind for takeoff and recovery of aircraft.

Pilots navigated with the aid of a plotting board which was about two feet square which slid in and out of the instrument panel, a tray which held a circular plastic grid for plotting position of the aircraft, the target and the carrier. A small circular calculator aided computations.

On takeoff our pilots were given the last known position, course and speed of the Japanese fleet and the estimated course and speed of our own fleet. A simple line could be drawn between the two indicating the compass direction to take and the distance to be flown outbound. Assuming 150 miles at a speed of 100 knots the pilot would adjust for the move of the target after an hour and a half, approximately 30 to 45 miles, hoping that the target maintained the last course reported.

Now the calculator is used to adjust the ground speed. An indicated air speed on the instrument panel gives the ground speed at sea level, but in the thinner air at altitude the ground speed increases. For instance, and indicated air speed (IAS) of 120 knots would be 172 knots true air speed [True or T] at 19,000 feet. The pilots use the calculator to compute his ground speed at various altitudes. He plots an elapsed time and the distances on his plotting board, along with the compass heading.

Finally, another vector would be entered on the plotting board to account for the wind affecting his true path over the ocean. Navy pilots were trained to estimate the speed and direction of the wind by observing the white caps on the surface of the sea. However, the wind at various altitudes might be completely different both in force and direction, introducing another unpredictable factor in plotting an interception course. The wind would be different for the high flying dive bombers than it would be for the sea level torpedo bombers. Once the flights lost sight of one another there was no way they would arrive at a designated position at the same time.

Each pilot maintained his own plotting board while flying formation to the target area. If separated from the leaders he had to be able to find his way back to the estimated position of his home carrier. The Japanese had planned their Midway attack position perfectly. Their pilots flew directly into the wind to the target and downwind to return. The American pilots had to contend with cross winds flying in both directions.[12]

Navigation – Getting Back Again

A radio homing beacon to guide home strike aircraft the last 50 miles or so to the carrier after a mission had long been a requirement once basic carrier air attack techniques had been developed by the US Navy. Exercises had revealed that lack of such a 'gathering-in' device tended to inhibit carrier commanders from committing their aircraft *en masse* at the ever-lengthening ranges they were theoretically capable of. Just an ordinary rotating long frequency (LF) broadcast signal coupled with basic aerial direction finding (ADF) equipment was, of course, not the answer for that would also 'home in' the enemy from a considerable range, with disastrous consequences. What was wanted was a system that was efficient and easy to use, but which would conceal the home base from all but friendly aircraft.

The problem was first addressed by the Naval Research Laboratory (NRL) in 1935[13] and three years later they came up with a short-range homing receiver.[14] The first experimental model was installed on the carrier *Ranger* (CV-4) in 1938 and flight-tested by the pilots of VF-4.[15] This was Model YE and it was an immediate and outstanding success. The Commander, Aircraft Battle Force's[16] flagship was the aircraft carrier *Saratoga* (CV-3) in May 1938 and, although never one to go overboard on anything, King was moved to write to the Navy Department on 29 August, 'Adopt the system for primary means of homing radio aircraft.' Such a firm recommendation was implemented at once[17] and as the YE-ZB (as the production carrier/aircraft combination was christened), it became

---

12. George Walsh, unpublished research paper, *Searching for the Truth about the Battle of Midway*.
13. Naval Research Laboratory, Homing Devices for Aircraft, NRL File F42-1/25, 1935–38, held in National Archives, College Park, Maryland.
14. L. A. Gebhard, *Evolution of Naval Radio-Electronics and Contributions of the Naval Research Laboratory*.
15. ComAirBatFor to Chf BuEng, *Preliminary Report of VF-4 Tests of XAD Equipment*, dated 29 August 1938, BuEng CF File F42-1/69H.
16. Admiral Ernest L. King.
17. Naval Research Laboratory, *Aircraft Homing Devices*, NRL File F42-1/69H, held in National Archives, College Park, Maryland; NRL CRMO.

a standard installation.[18] The YE-1 homing beacon antenna equipment was manufactured by the RCA Victor Division of the Radio Corporation of America (RCA), New Jersey, as the transmitting part of the set-up.[19] The YE (and its follow-on system, the YG) used a directional antenna to reduce the possibilities of the enemy locking on to its signal. The YE signal carried coded information to identify the ship itself via a two- or three-letter Morse code identifier.

The system was, in essence, a UHF converter, which was connected to the existing communications receiver. They termed this the YE/ZB receiver. The YE part of it applied to carriers and also to fixed shore-based stations. The carriers had the YE stations installed, and these sent out a double-modulated, line-of-sight (i.e. short-range) UHF signal in the range 234–258 MHz, which carried an LF signal in the range 800–1000 KHz. The latter was tone modulated with letters from the standard Morse code.[20] The SBDs 12-inch antenna, mounted on the underside of the aircraft, received the signal and used the radio unit (RU) to convert this for the crew to understand.

The 'Hayrake'

The aircraft carrier's transmitter antenna was a flat, circular plate, from the perimeter of which twelve vertical antennae projected. When this device first appeared aloft on the masts of carriers, its outlandish appearance soon earned it the nickname 'hayrake'.[21] When the carrier's air group was due to be within range returning from a strike, then (and only then) the 'Hayrake' was switched on and via a gyro repeater it automatically sequentially transmitted a different, preselected, code letter from each of the twelve antennae.

Each carrier decided on its own pattern of letters of the day for an operation and these were marked on a special circular pattern, in which, again, a circle was subdivided into twelve equal segments marked with the whole 360 degrees of the compass. Each segment would be allocated its own letter and each pilot supplied with a copy of the day's pattern, which they usually affixed to the bottom of their plotting board.

On the way back to the carrier after a mission, the aircraft's Zed-Baker receiver was switched on, the carrier's channel was selected[22], and the volume cranked up to maximum. In theory, depending on conditions, altitude and the efficiency of the carrier's transmitting equipment, at ranges of 50 up to a maximum of 100 miles, but more usually at 25 miles[23], (the range depended on the aircraft's altitude) the Morse signal would be heard, hopefully increasing in volume as the range came down. Whichever letter the pilot received would indicate the carrier's course. He would need to steer the reciprocal heading to reach his home base. If the ship changed course (as it well might if itself under attack[24]) then the code letter received would change and the pilot would adjust his own heading accordingly. Should the code change dramatically to a reciprocal letter on the pattern to the one required, this would indicate that for some reason – bad visibility perhaps – he had overshot the carrier, and this warning would be reinforced by a steady weakening of the signal.[25]

In practice, the YE coding became an essential part of the aircrews briefing before any mission. As one veteran dive-bomber pilot told me:

After your early call and chow you headed to the squadron ready room. You get your chart board out. The first thing you'd do is get the YE code for that twelve-hour period. Make sure its not left over from the day before, or know if its gonna change while you are on the strike. That's the first thing you did – the YE. You'd get that from the briefing officer, it would

18. *Ibid.*
19. Restricted Manual, *Antenna Equipment: Model YE-1,* RCA CRV-23263.
20. See Naval Research Laboratory, *The US Naval Research Laboratory; Fulfilling the Roosevelt's' Vision for American Navy Power (1923–2005),* 30 June 2006, NRL/MR/1001=06=8951, NRL, Washington DC.
21. The Royal Navy's equivalent device was the Transmitter Type 72X, developed from 1934 onward, with trials held at Southsea Castle. It was first fitted aboard the new aircraft carrier *Ark Royal* when she ran her trials in May 1938. As it was fully enclosed, rather than exposed as in the case of the American equipment, the British tars dubbed it the 'Pepperpot'.
22. The aircraft were fitted with the ZBX receiver, which later became the ARR-1.
23. Which may account for the fact that the Japanese never developed any counter-equipment to lock onto the UHF signal itself. They usually adopted the far simpler solution of just trailing the returning American strike back to its base.
24. Unfortunately, due to the state of the art, if the ships manoeuvring were too violent, then often the gyro stabilization could not always adjust quickly enough.
25. 'The homing system used two frequencies that confused the Japanese admirals, who realized that US aircraft were successful in returning to their carriers but did not understand how this was accomplished.' At the Battle of the Philippines Sea in 1944, 'the device was also credited with saving many pilots by homing back to their carriers in the dark with this equipment.' A. H. Taylor, *Radio Reminiscences: A Half Century, Naval Research Laboratory.*

be published in front of you. He'd remind you to be sure you got the YE, and make sure it wasn't going to change before you got home. It was a good aid. That was why a lotta guys at the battle of Midway got lost; they didn't have that, didn't have the signal. They just didn't get it. So they were using dead reckoning. Now you have gotta be a pretty good navigator to dead-reckon your way home without it.

You had a briefing officer who would tell you pretty much what it was. What it is, what was the target, how far is the target, what is the course. What is Point Option (or Point Oboe, they changed the phonetic alphabet part-way through the war) our 'where are you when I come home' information. Well, they are never there. You have a reference point. Fortunately, the task force distribution covers a lot of square miles of the ocean. In the screen, the stereotype picture is like a circle. So, lets say, if you had had twelve destroyers and the diameter of 35 miles, well, you're pretty much bound to find a destroyer somewhere, or you gonna hit some cruisers, oh and there's the carriers. Well, make sure it's your carrier. Well you knew your own ships code numbers. First you'd have a number, say nineteen, if in doubt, then, nuts, go somewhere else. Then you'd also have the task group point code, TF16.1 or TF 16.2 etc.[26]

Hornet's Misfortunes

The Zed-Baker homer device is central to the saga of *Hornet*'s aborted mission of course, as Ring's 'lost letter' made clear. But his handwritten notes turned out to be frustratingly vague on many important points. Many people have analysed them according to whether they reinforce or oppose their own prejudices, but the vital facts, such as the departure heading, are just not there. However, if we cannot glean the story from Ring, what about the man who flew with him, tucked in close to CHAG for the whole outward leg, his wingman Clay Fisher?[27] He has given his version of events many times but, it seems, 'nobody's buying'. Why not? Clayton is an alert, active man, I can readily attest and has, moreover, undertaken considerable research on the subject, as well as having an excellent memory. He agreed to supply me with his version of events again, but this time in conjunction with Ring's account, not all of which he agrees with.[28]

Ring/Fisher – The Outward Leg

Ring: Departure from *Hornet* was taken on pre-estimated interception course, Group Commander leading. High altitude elements commenced their climb.[29]

---

26. Captain Charles Downey USN (Rtd), taped interview with the author at his home in Poplar Grove, Illinois, 17 April 2006.
27. Clayton Evan 'Clay' Fisher (b. 1919). b. Janesville, Wisconsin, 14 January 1919. Educated High School, Janesville, Seventh Day Advent College, Milton, Wisconsin and University of Wisconsin, majoring in chemical engineering. Applied twice for Naval Aviation Flight Program, accepted in January 1941 and sent to NAS Jacksonville, for primary and basic flight training. Completed carrier operational flight training at NAS Opa Locke, received wings and commissioned as a naval reserve ensign 8 August 1941. Married Annie, 18 February 1942. Assigned to Bombing Squadron Eight, *Hornet* Air Group. After Midway promoted to lieutenant (jg), and fought at Battle of Santa Cruz, when *Hornet* (CV-8) was sunk on 26 October 1942. Wounded, 20 mm shrapnel wound in right arm, treated at Balboa Naval Hospital. Promoted to lieutenant February 1943. NAS Fort Lauderdale, retrained as landing signal officer (LSO or 'Batsman'), assigned to Lake Michigan paddle training carriers *Sable* (IX-81) and *Wolverine* (IX-64). Then NAS Vero Beach, as dive-bomber flight Instructor and, from 1944, as night-fighter pilot training with Grumman F6F-5N Hellcats until end of war. Promoted to lieutenant-commander 1945 and transferred to regular navy. 1946 NAS Kodiak, flying amphibians, then 1948 General Line School, Monterey. 1949 BurOrd, Washington DC, Aviation Procurement Branch. Managed to get back to flying as XO of an F4U-4B Corsair fighter squadron flying from carrier *Essex* (CV-9) Korean War. Flew eighty combat air support and deep interdiction missions over North Korea. Promoted to commander. 1952/53 NAS North Island in Personnel Division, ComAirPac, followed by Basic Instrument Training Squadron at NAS Pensacola for two years. Appointed CO VU-3 at NAS Miramar, San Diego, providing F6G target drones for fighter training. Air Operations Officer at NAS Miramar, three years as XO and then as CO. Passed over for promotion as part of the 'hump' and resigned from navy in June, 1961. Awards included Navy Cross for Midway, DFC for Korea, Purple Heart for Santa Cruz and three Air Medals for Korea.1961–5, stockbroker on New York Stock Exchange, then joined Beckman Instrument Company supervising installation of ultra high-speed centrifuges in West Coast Universities. Joined real estate company, San Diego, and finally established own reality company in Coronado. 1981 sold business and retired. Currently resides at Coronado and is writing memoirs, provisionally titled *The Tales and Adventures of a Naval Aviator*.
28. Clayton Fisher to author, 18 March 2006.
29. Ring, Lost Letter. Reproduced by the kind permission of his daughter, Susan Ring Keith.

Fisher: Our navigation course was plotted by all the SBD pilots to the last reported position of the enemy carriers. Ring did not consider that the enemy carriers would need to change course to recover aircraft that had attacked Midway. Waldron correctly assumed that the enemy carriers *would* change course. To have a co-ordinated attack all the *Hornet* squadrons had to fly basically the same course, adjust airspeeds of different types of aircraft and launch the slowest and shorter-range aircraft last and have radio communications between squadron commanders. Later on in WWII during carrier operations trying to practice successful co-ordinated air group attacks the results were jokingly referred to as 'Group Gropes'. They were always tough to execute.

Ring: VB-8, VS-8, accompanying fighters of VF-8 and the Group Commander were to proceed at (20,000 feet). Nearly one and a half hours were consumed in group rendezvous after launch. All airplanes maintained moderate altitude (below 5,000 feet) until after rendezvous of the Group was affected.

Fisher: Due to the SBD deck spot I was the first SBD launched followed by the Group Commander. I flew the left wingman position on the Group Commander. We did circle but I think we kept climbing after the SBDs effected a rendezvous. I don't think the SBD ever climbed above about 14,000 feet. Just getting to 14,000 feet burned a lot of extra fuel. The SBD did not have a single-stage engine blower, to enable us to climb effectively to 20,000 feet[30]. The oxygen system and pilots' oxygen masks were crude compared to the fighter pilots' masks. My mask collected ice from my breath and I had to take it off occasionally to remove the ice. We all wore summer flight suits and it was pretty cold. Frankly, I never could see why the SBDs needed to get to 20,000 to commence dives. All dive-bombing training dives were done from around 8 to 10 thousand feet. At 14,000 feet I don't think AA was a threat to the dive-bombers.

I remember trying to spot the VT-8 aircraft below us but we encountered various layers of clouds and I never could see the VT-8 aircraft.

Ring: Upon arrival at the line between the last reported position of the enemy and Midway Island, since the high element had made no contact, I decided that I should proceed on the assumption that the enemy was closing Midway and directed the course of the high element accordingly.

Fisher: Flying the left wing position I flew a loose position and was able to observe a vertical column of black smoke at my 10 o'clock position, which gradually appeared at my 8 o'clock position. I assumed the smoke was from a fuel storage tank on Midway. We had unlimited visibility at this time. Ring gave me a hand signal to form a scouting line and pointed down at the VS-8 formation. We had unlimited visibility and forming a scouting line was going to break up our tactical defensive formation. A 'scouting line' was a pre-war relic. I don't remember ever changing course before Ring's command to me. I have researched a time line of the *Enterprise* and *Yorktown* dive-bombers and have always been convinced that the enemy aircraft carriers had not been hit when I observed the column of black smoke. Also, all the photographs I have seen of the burning fuel tank and the resulting column of smoke I observed were very similar.[31] I was always positive any enemy fighters would hit us from the north. I was devastated when I was assigned to fly wing to Ring and knew he intended to fly above and ahead of the dive-bombers.

30. Apparently, the F4F-4s were stacked at 22,000 feet and the SBDs at 20,000 feet. Pat Mitchell placed the Wildcats behind and *above* Ring ready to dive to their aid if intercepted. The maximum official climb rate accredited to the Wildcat was 1,950 feet per minute, but the then current doctrine restricted them to 500 feet per minute, which meant that it would have taken them half an hour to reach the desired height. Fuel of course was gobbled up at a worrying rate while this was being done, and then they had to circle and wait for the TBDs to get airborne. The SBDs maximum climb rate was 1,190 feet per minute, but, with a thousand-pounder slung under their belly and also limited by the same doctrine, they would need twenty-six minutes to reach 18,000 feet. After much discussion, it had been Mitscher and his operations officer, Lieutenant Stanley E. Ruehlow, who made the final decision to put the fighter escort with the SBDs rather than the TBDs. Ruehlow to Barde, interview dated 25 May 1966.

31. Clayton Fisher was flying at approximately 12,000 feet at the time; he had taken off his oxygen mask because they had descended from the former higher altitude, the visibility was unlimited and the column of smoke was fairly large. Given these facts one naval officer stated recently that the smoke must have been 20 miles away. In relating these facts Clayton told me, 'I strongly believe our flight must have been at least under 50 miles from Midway. If our flight was north of the Japanese carriers how could I see the Midway smoke column? I think a key fact would be how far could I see an object as large as the smoke column from 12,000 feet.' E-mail, Fisher to the author, dated 15 September 2006.

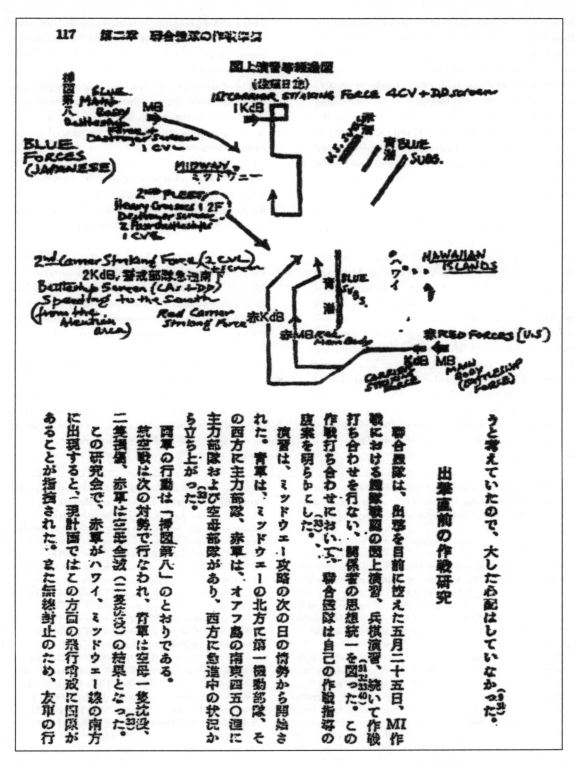

うと考えていたので、大した心配はしていなかった。

出撃直前の作戦研究

聯合艦隊は、出撃を目前に控えた五月二十五日、MI作戦における図艦隊戦図の図上演習、兵棋演習、続いて作戦打ち合わせを行ない、関係者の思想統一を図った。この作戦打ち合わせにおいて、聯合艦隊は自己の作戦指導の成案を明らかにした。

演習は、ミッドウェー攻略の次の日の情勢から開始された。青軍は、ミッドウェーの北方に第一機動部隊、その西方に主力部隊、赤軍は、オアフ島の南東四五〇浬に主力部隊および空母部隊があり、西方に急進中の状況から立ち上がった。

両軍の行動は「捕図第八」のとおりである。航空戦は次の対勢で行なわれ、青軍に空母一隻沈没、二隻損傷、赤軍は空母全滅（二隻沈没）の結果となった。

この研究会で、赤軍がハワイ、ミッドウェーの南方に出現すると、一男計画ではこの方面の飛行哨戒に間隙があることが指摘された。また無線封止のため、友軍の行

Diagram 1. Diagram of the May 1942 Combined Fleet's War Game of the Battle of Midway. The printed annotations are those of Rear-Admiral Edwin T. Layton, USN (Rtd), Nimitz's Intelligence Officer at Pearl Harbor in June 1942. (Senshi Sosho, Tokyo)

If we had encountered enemy fighters we would have been hit first to take out the leader. The *Enterprise* Group Commander, McClusky, flew as the flight leader of his group's SBD formation.

When I tried to join on the flight leader of VS-8 to pass on Ring's order, the formation was commencing a 180 degree turn to the reciprocal course to the *Hornet*. I turned back to try and locate Ring. All I saw was an empty sky so I turned back and followed VS-8. I didn't want to burn excessive fuel so I never did catch up to the formation I could faintly see ahead of me.

Ring: It is appropriate at this time to interject my understanding that the *Enterprise* Group was favored with later information of the whereabouts of the enemy than the *Hornet* Group. Although communications in 1942 were most unreliable between air and surface craft, even though *Hornet* might have broken radio silence to keep the Group informed of the latest developments, there was no assurance that such information would have been received by the Group. As a matter of fact, I do not believe that *Hornet* received the reported new position of the enemy.[32] Therefore my change of Air Group course to the south was based entirely on my estimate of the situation (which proved faulty) and not on definite information of the enemy movements.[33]

Fisher: All my research indicated that McClusky had the same information as Ring and McClusky flew approximately the same course as Ring. McClusky also flew to the end of his navigation leg and finally changed course to the north-east after sighting an enemy destroyer on a north-east course. I believe the *Yorktown* Group which launched last, did have updated information on the estimated enemy carrier's location.

Ring: *Hornet* Group proceeded south until smoke of Midway was sighted. At that time it was apparent that immediate return to the carrier was necessary if landings aboard were to be effected, since fuel supply was running low.

Fisher: I estimated I observed the smoke from Midway[34] at least fifteen to thirty minutes before Ring decided he wanted VS-8 and VB-8 to form a scouting line. I never changed course to the south. It was obvious the enemy had to be north to north-west.

[Backing for Ring's and Fisher's contentions were long ago given by Walter Lord. He interviewed one of the VF-8 pilots, Lieutenant Stan Ruehlow[35] while researching his book, and wrote the following: 'About half an hour earlier [1030 local] Ruehlow had *looked to the north*[36] and seen in the distance what he had spent all morning searching for: the Japanese fleet.'[37]]

---

32. Kernan interprets these two sentences thus: 'He confusedly blames the ship for not updating him, and then says that he doubts they knew about the enemy's change of course.' (*Unknown Battle*).

33. Barde was to comment: 'The time of Ring's launch, radio silence by the *Hornet* and the differences of frequencies between his planes and those from Midway attacking the Japanese, combined to keep him ignorant of the attacks that were going on while he was looking for the enemy carriers.'

34. The smoke from the burning oil tank on Midway was visible from a distance of 50 nautical miles according to the reports of the various returning and departing land-based aircraft.

35. Captain Stanley Erdman Ruehlow. (1912–81). b. Brodhead, Wisconsin, 1912. Graduated Brodhead High School 1929. Enlisted US Navy 1931. Recruit training and radio school course at NTS (Naval Training School) San Diego, served aboard carrier *Saratoga* (CV-3). Married Marjorie Lucille Dodge, hometown sweetheart, one daughter, Nancy. Selected for Naval Academy Preparatory School, Norfolk. Passed interview and entered US Naval Academy, Annapolis, June 1931. 1935 Graduated as ensign, served in carrier *Ranger* (CV-4). 1937 Flight Training at NAS Pensacola. 1939 to carrier *Yorktown* (CV-5*)* with VF-5. 1941 transferred to VF-8 as Operations and XO, aboard carrier *Hornet* (CV-8). Doolittle raid and

Midway. Led section of ten VF-8 F4Fs back and ditched, rescued by VP after five days adrift and shark attacks. October 1942 XO of VF-10 aboard *Enterprise* (CV-6), Santa Cruz, and sent to join marines ashore at Guadalcanal, three confirmed kills for which he was awarded DFC. July 1943 Training and Operations Officer, Staff Fleet Air, NAS Alameda. July 1945 commanded FAG-8 aboard carrier *Bennington* (CV-20) and at surrender of Japan. January 1946 XO and then Commander 7 April 1948, FH-1 as one of the first jet fighter pilots in navy. CO *Chenango* (CVE-23) then *Suwannee* (CVE-27) and *Santee* (CVE-29). May 1949 Staff CNO, Washington DC, November 1952 Operations Officer, Staff Commander CarDiv 4. July 1954 Assistant for Plans, OCNO. June 1956 Staff Commander 7th Fleet, Western Pacific. July 1957 commanding seaplane tender *Onslow* (AVP-48). June 1958 Head, Air Weapons Systems Analysis, OCNO. June 1959–July 1960 commanded carrier *Lexington* (CV-16). July 1960 Joint Staff, Strategic Target Planning, Offut AFB. September 1962 CofS and Aide to Commander 2nd Fleet Norfolk. September 1964 CofS Commandant 12th Naval District, San Francisco. Retired from Navy 1965 as captain. Died of cancer 3 June 1981.

36. My italics

37. Walker Lord, *Incredible Victory*.

Ring: Great reliance was placed on the YE homing beacon. I switched radio at the time to the homing frequency but *Enterprise* was all that could be heard. The letter signal received, compared to the YE letter chart furnished us by *Hornet* prior to takeoff, convinced me that something was wrong. It later developed that the *Enterprise* and *Hornet* were on different YE homing codes and that the change in code prescribed by CTF [Task Force Commander – Spruance] in *Enterprise* had not been received by the *Hornet*. Because of the obvious discrepancy in *Enterprise* YE signal received as applied to the YE homing chart of *Hornet,* I disregarded the YE signal and attempted to change course of the group toward the dead reckoning position of *Hornet.* VS-8 under Lt-Cdr Rodee followed me in my change. VB-8 under Lt-Cdr Johnson appeared to follow the false course indicated by YE signal and was followed by VF-8, Lt-Cdr Samuel Mitchell. I left VS-8 and attempted to rally the departing aircraft of VB-8 and VF-8 in order to lead them back to *Hornet* but I could not catch them. When I finally gave up the chase VS-8 had disappeared from sight and VB-8 was apparently headed for Midway. I then resumed my dead reckoning course to intercept *Hornet,* proceeding singly at 20,000 feet. Since oxygen supply was failing and I began to notice the effects of lack of oxygen, I dropped gradually to 10,000ft.[38]

Fisher: 'This entire paragraph is a little confusing. The YE radio signal was a line-of-sight signal and was not normally needed until the aircraft were probably fifty miles from the *Hornet*. The SBDs did not follow false courses, VS-8 flew directly back to the *Hornet*. Rodee, CO of VS-8, probably may have made a small course direction indicated by the YE signal as they approached the *Hornet*. Tucker[39], the XO of VB-8 elected to return his flight division back to the *Hornet* without incident. Ruff Johnson the CO of VB-8 made his decision to lead his division to Midway due to his concern about his fuel status.[40] I think if we had been too far north Johnson would never have decided to go to Midway. I never knew what Ring did after the SBDs leaders made their decisions. Also Ben Tappan[41], a VS-8 pilot flew the right wing position on Ring. He must have been directed by Ring to have VB-8 form a scouting line and must have finally joined on a VB-8 flight to return to the *Hornet*. Ring was the last SBD to return to *Hornet* long after the SBDs had landed. We thought he had probably ditched.

The VF-8 pilots had flown beyond their point of no return and simply did not have enough fuel to reach the *Hornet*. VT-8 had changed course to the right from the course the SBDs flew. I have no idea why the VF-8 pilots did not just fly the reciprocal course they flew above the SBDs to try to return to the *Hornet*.[42]

---

38. It is interesting to note that, more than forty years after Ring's comment, Weisheit raised the question of the oxygen supply at high altitudes as possibly contributing to some of the odd decisions made by VF-8 pilots that morning. He even cites both American and British research facilities that separately found, 'excessive concentrations of carbon monoxide gas,' under certain operating conditions. (*Last Flight)*.
39. Lieutenant Alfred Bland Tucker.
40. One SBD, crewed by Ensign Troy Tilman Guillory and Billy Rex Cotrell, ARM2c, was forced to ditch due to problems with the reduction gear, but both men were later rescued by a PBY unharmed. A second dive-bomber, crewed by Ensign Thomas Junior Wood, A-V (N) and George F. Martz, ARM3c, ran out of fuel well short of Midway and also had to pancake. Johnson ordered his remaining aircraft to jettison their bombs, and carried out the correct recognition procedure agreed beforehand for even days, which was a left turn with two over-emphasized wing-dips, but this did not save them from Midway's trigger-happy marine AA gunners who blasted the SBDs, hitting three of them in yet another exhibition of terrible aircraft recognition. Yet a third SBD's fuel gave out, forcing them to ditch in the lagoon, the crew, Ensign Forrester Clinton Auman A-V (N) and Samuel P. McLean, ARM3c, being rescued by the *PT-28*. The eleven surviving VS-8 dive-bombers subsequently refuelled and later flew back to the *Hornet* at 1527. Fisher also told me that

'Lieutenant Robert "Ruff" Johnson was my first squadron commander. He commanded VB-8 from it's commissioning in September of 1941 until the squadron returned to Pearl Harbor after the Battle of Midway. He made his decision to take his flight division to Midway and his XO, Lieutenant Alfred Bland Tucker, elected to lead his flight division back to the *Hornet*. Sort of strange decisions. I felt Ruff probably flew more by his gut feelings and "AB" Tucker was probably a better navigator and knew he could make it back to the *Hornet*. We later lost "AB" on his first flight as our new "Skipper" flying a 200 miles search mission on our deployment to the south Pacific after Midway. The plane developed a cockpit fire and he and his gunner had to bale out and we didn't have the parachute packs with a life raft in 1942. The two man raft was stowed in the aircraft. Ruff lasted the war and then some, and was 68 when he died.'
41. Ensign Benjamin Tappen, Jr.
42. Clayton later told me: 'According to the official accounts, *Hornet* resumed a course of 240 degrees true after launching all her aircraft. I am sure that is the course I plotted to the enemy position on my plotting board. If Ring took on the 270 course I sure as hell would have been aware of it. I absolutely do not buy the 270 degree theory. Also I have read Weisheit's book many times and I feel like he was trying to fit a piece of a jigsaw puzzle into a space that it did not quite fit in. Ruff Johnson stated after not sighting the enemy carriers

Ring: Eventually, I sighted aircraft below me and noticed water landings of at least two airplanes. After about 4.5 hours in the air (and having assured Parker[43], my radioman, that a water landing could be easily effected), I sighted the white wakes of a Task Force at high speed. Further investigation revealed it to be our own force. I made a wide approach to arrive within the 'recognition sector'. *Hornet* turned into the wind and received me aboard. VS-8 had landed: VB-8, VT-8 and VF-8 were missing. It later developed that VT-8 had, with the exception of Ens. Gay, been lost in an attack on the Japanese carriers. Lt-Cdr Waldron leading the squadron had courageously and in the face of certain destruction, led his command in a torpedo attack against the enemy. VB-8 had (with the loss of two planes) landed at Midway. VF-8 had apparently landed at sea, out of fuel.

I was shaken at the realization of such losses and will admit that I was in poor condition to take the air in a renewed attack on the Japanese carriers which had, by then, been located. About one hour after my landing the remaining aircraft of the Group were ordered launched for the next attack.

Fisher summation: I realize that the *Hornet* had to launch a CAP of fighters first but I have never understood why the shorter range torpedo aircraft and the fighters of the escort were not launched last. To me it defied all logic. The Group Commander should have been leading one of the SBD squadrons. The SBDs fast firing twin mounted 30 caliber guns were a very effective weapon when you had an entire formation firing together. The concept of a Group Commander flying off the formations was a prewar concept. With complete radio silences what was there to direct?

The Pearl Harbor attack and the early deployment of the *Hornet* to the Pacific disrupted a normal training cycle for a newly formed Air Group. The Doolittle mission eliminated the very badly needed dive concentrated bombing practice on moving target boats for all the SBD pilots. I flew thirty-seven single plane, two hundred mile searches before the Battle of Midway. Usually we had to circle the task force waiting for the last search plane to return, had sufficient fuel to climb to at least 10,000 feet and to a dry dive-bombing run on a screening destroyer. We did carry charges but you could dive with ordnance load but would have needed to pull of the dive a little higher. I asked our CO about getting permission to make those practice dives and nothing happened. Most of the *Hornet*'s dive bomber pilots got their dive bombing practice at the Battle of Midway in combat!

One commentator even claimed: 'Ring's analysis, that failed communication and an inexperienced crew caused the planes [F4Fs] to run out of fuel and ditch at sea, corroborated the evaluation Nimitz gave in his official report of the battle.'[44]

North or South

So the argument continues. We have already touched on the continuing differences of opinion, but they need further examination. While the majority of those who have studied the battle have come down on the side of the 265 degrees heading for *Hornet*'s air group that day[45], others apart than Clayton Fisher still claim it was 240 degrees. Ring himself claims the course adopted was aligned to the DR track of the target, which he considered he would intercept at around 0900. Unfortunately, and unavoidably, this of course was based on the only available information, the erroneous PBY report. However, due to the long wait between the launch and the departure of the air group (ninety minutes), Ring later readjusted his course by a few degrees to compensate for this because, at 30 knots, the enemy would have traversed almost another 50 miles. Ring then expected to sight the enemy around 0930.

If the heading was indeed 265 degrees, was this Ring's decision alone, as many claim, or did he bow to his old friend Mitscher's wish to try and find the two carriers of the undiscovered, or at least "unreported", second Japanese carrier division that so dominated Admiral Fletcher's thinking that morning? Why did *Hornet* launch the

---

he turned south toward Midway. After reaching Kure Island he made the decision to head for Midway and his XO "AB" Tucker, headed for the *Hornet*. Why wouldn't Tucker have seen the enemy carriers on his return to the *Hornet*? I'm convinced I could not have seen the smoke from Midway if we were as far north as we would have been had we flown a 270 degree course.' (Fisher to the author, 27 September 2006.)

43. Arthur M Parker.
44. Ken Biggs, Lone Star Internet Inc, Famous Texans – Chester W. Nimitz, The Handbook of Texas Online, http://www.famoustexans,com/chesternimitz.htm.
45. The much-respected Mark E. Horan, for example, stated quite firmly that 'contrary to the *Hornet*'s written action report' they adopted a course 'well north of the bearing to *Kidō Butai*', and that VT-8, 'turned to port on 234°'.

shortest-legged aircraft first? The pre-war (and still at the time of Midway) US doctrine on aircraft launching stated clearly: 'Commanding Officers are responsible for prescribing the condition that will be assumed by his flight deck and his vessel as a whole, and the order of spot of airplanes that will best insure compliance with orders and the needs of the tactical situation.'[46]

This surely places the onus on Mitscher (still a captain although earmarked and confirmed for promotion to admiral, as the presence of his relief, Captain Charles P. Mason aboard emphasized) rather than Ring. At any event, the actual launch sequence ignored the doctrine and became solely concerned with the restrictions of flight deck length on the heavily laden TBDs and the need to get as many aircraft into the air as quickly as possible. This made local sense but the rule book was tossed out of the window right at the start.

One must question the standing doctrine in the light of its inability to cope with this (in retrospect) obvious limitation. But in other respects, which applied equally to the other American carriers and not just *Hornet*, the rules were found wanting and pre-war experience did not match actual combat reality. Again 'the book' loftily assumed an overall launch time for a full air group of seventy-four aircraft of twenty minutes, or one aircraft airborne every sixteen seconds. The Japanese had worked hard at this for two years and for them it was achievable. *Hornet*, which had never been in action, but equally the combat-tested *Enterprise* and *Yorktown*, were never to match such a peace-time achievement during the battle. A detailed study was subsequently

made[47], based on the time recorded by Ensign George Gay[48], the first TBD pilot to leave *Hornet*'s flight deck. His watch showed a lift-off time of 0915 (0715 Local).[49]

A total of 44 aircraft launched prior to ENS Gay's launch at 0715. This averages one aircraft every 20 seconds. From 0715 to 0806 a total of 14 aircraft launched, equating to one aircraft every 3 minutes 38 seconds. Recall that nine aircraft of VT squadron were still below in the hangar waiting to be brought up to the flight deck, prepared for launch (unfolding wings), spotted and launched. Assuming that it only took 20 seconds to launch each of the five VT-8 aircraft that were spotted on the flight deck, then it took approximately 5 minutes 25 seconds for the remaining aircraft to be brought from below and launched. This delay accounts for the hour taken to launch the entire group, but the group did not take their departure from until almost an-hour-and-a-half after CDR Ring launched at 0713.[50]

As for the actual air group departure sequence, doctrine allowed for three options:

1: Normal – No fighter opposition to the attack anticipated and the target at such a distance that an *en route* rendezvous could be effected. Scouts (VS) departed 'by sections', followed by the various squadrons to a rendezvous position prior to departure.

---

46. US Navy, *Current Tactical Orders and Doctrine, US Fleet Aircraft, Volume One, Carrier Aircraft* (USF-74), March 1941 edition.)
47. Lieutenant-Commander Brian G. Falke, Research Report, *Battle of Midway: USS* Hornet *(CV-8) Air Group*, submitted to the Faculty Air Command and Staff College, Air University, Maxwell AFB, Alabama, April 2000. (AU/ACSC/2000–04). Hereafter cited as Falke, Report.
48. Ensign George Henry 'Tex' Gay (1917–94). b. Waco, Texas on 8 March 1917. Served in army's Reserve Officer Training Corps (ROTC) 1936–8 at Texas Agricultural & Mechanical University. Joined navy as air cadet on 3 April 1941. Completed flight training at Jacksonville and commissioned as ensign on 22 September, then assigned to VT-8 in time for Midway. After his rescue by a PBY he was feted by Nimitz, no less, and featured on the cover of *Life* magazine. His battle report, written in hospital, where he was undergoing treatment to wounds in his left hand, was the only account of gallant end of Waldron's unit. When fully recovered he returned to operations with VT-11 during the Guadalcanal campaign, then was shipped home to become an instructor back at NAS Jacksonville. For the rest of the war Gay was also used as a valuable recruitment asset by the navy, touring from coast-to-coast to relate his tale. On 20 March 1945 he was at the launch of the new carrier *Midway* (CVB-41) at Newport News. After the war he remained in the naval reserve until the 1950s but as a civilian he joined the airline TWA as a pilot and was with that company for thirty years. His wrote his memoirs in 1979. Upon his death on 21 October 1994 he was cremated and his ashes were subsequently scattered, on 31 August 1995, close to the spot where all his old colleagues had gone to their deaths more than fifty-three years earlier. Chuck Downey gave further insight into Gay's later thinking, telling me in a recent interview. 'I had the privilege of meeting with George Gay on several occasions. We had drinks together. He always felt he got a bad press. One of the things he was upset about, post-war, was that he had wanted to stay in the Navy Reserve, but he couldn't because *they* wouldn't permit because he was an airline pilot. In Chicago he was honoured. And he was piped in every Pearl Harbor Day. He felt bitter that we were not better prepared for that, and felt things were heading the same way again.'
49. He had not adjusted his watch from Hawaiian time; misleading Sam Morison among others!
50. Falke Report. But note that Fisher, and *not* Ring, was first aloft.

2: Urgent – Target at close range, and its exact location positively known. All aircraft departed by sections, and squadrons effected an *en route* rendezvous.

3: Deferred – When determined fighter opposition was expected. All squadrons to rendezvous prior to departure with the aim of mutual protection and a combined and coordinated attack.

There was little doubt in anyone's mind that the A6Ms, with their awesome reputation, would be waiting for them and they would probably have to fight their way in. Ring's choice of deferred departure was therefore hardly surprising. The penalty for this was initially a delayed departure, and the *Hornet* air group did not finally leave until 0843, one and a half hours from the initial launch.

Clayton Fisher gives this very vivid account of what this complicated aerial quadrille of a rendezvous meant to the pilots themselves.

As I was going to fly a wing position on the CHAG I turned down-wind until he flew past me and then I closed in on his aircraft. All the SBDs were joining their formations behind and below us so I wasn't aware of the respective positions of the SBD squadrons except they were behind us. I never did see the VF-8 formation. I was just trying to hang in my wing position.

He commented on the official histories of the battle using true headings in their accounts.

We all flew magnetic heading readings from our aircraft compasses. In the South Pacific the compass variation was 10 degrees East. That was a huge variation but in the Midway area the variation is 2 degrees, East ('the compass is least') you subtracted the 2 degree variation from 'true' for your magnetic headings so that there is little difference between a 'true' and our magnetic compass headings. So, at the Battle of Midway flying your compass headings would be pretty close to your true headings.

He noted that Walt Rodee claimed in his conversation with Weisheit, that he flew 265 degrees true that morning.[51]

He flew his magnetic heading but that heading had been adjusted for magnetic variation to give a true heading course (track). The only time the SBD pilots ever used true headings was when working out our 200 mile navigation problems, but we flew those navigational legs using magnetic headings adjusted magnetic variation. You set your directional gyro from your aircraft compass. I don't think navigation was a problem. The problem was the estimated location of the enemy task force.

He also made reference to the fact that the *Hornet*'s launch, recovery and attack tracks were reported to be 20–30 degrees too high due to incorrect compass calibration.

This seems strange to me because if the *Hornet*'s magnetic compass was that far off I probably would not be writing these comments, I would have been lost on a 200-mile search mission long before the Battle of Midway. I flew a 200-mile search on June 1st and had no trouble with my navigation not checking out.

Respected historian Bill Vickrey, who conducted exhausted research and interviews with Midway veterans down the years, told Fisher:

I am convinced that Ring flew a path similar to the one flown by McClusky. George Gay says that Waldron veered off to the right of CHAG and logic points to this being true. If you, Ivan[52] and others saw smoke at Midway before you made your turn then you were most certainly south of the IJN fleet – and I think you were.[53]

It will be recalled that, due to the hiatus caused by marshalling his group to his satisfaction, Ring had assumed an estimated time of arrival (ETA) with the 1st *Kidō Butai* around 0930. In fact, due to the need to achieve the desired co-ordination, the F4Fs and the SBDs had to throttle back and perform a series of convoluted S turns in order to hold formation with the stately TBDs ('flying box cars with a star on the side') staggering along below at 110 knots. This manoeuvre extended the actual flight

---

51. Additionally, Rodee told Lundstrom researcher James Sawruk that 265 degrees was the course he had entered in his flight log. See Ronald Russell, 'Changing Course: The *Hornet*'s Air Group at Midway. However, as Ronald Russell told me, 'As for Rodee, it's interesting that he declined to provide a copy of his log with the purported 'course 265' entry

to another researcher (one of the best).' (R. W. Russell to the author, 3 January 2007.) Rodee's 265° thus remains *Ipse dixit*.

52. Lieutenant (jg) Ivan L. Swope of VS-8.

53. Bill Vickrey e-mail to Clayton Fisher 6 September, 2004. Reproduced by permission of Clayton Fisher.

54. In the case of the Wildcats from 140 to 165 nautical miles.

distance[54], and therefore used up yet more precious fuel. Moreover, it increased yet again the expected ETA, which went up to 0959.

How long this speed adjustment continued is a moot point. Ring makes no mention of the blazing row conducted over the airwaves with Waldron that others have commented upon. If indeed Waldron really did tell CHAG to, 'go to hell', as Kernan asserts[55], then from that point there was no need to hold back the rest of the air group. Cressman discreetly states that, at 0820, Waldron broke radio silence. 'The two strongly disagreed over the course to follow, and Waldron eventually told Ring, in effect, that he would lead his squadron to the enemy even if he had to do so alone.' VT-8 then headed off to the south-west.[56] Cressman does not cite a source for this statement but Ensign George H. Gay had made the allegation in his book *Sole Survivor* some years earlier[57], and this book was listed in the Cressman account's Bibliography.

Gay's book is highly suspect in many of its allegations and most historians give it little credence.[58] However, if it is held up to prove one side of the argument in one respect, then, for balance, the same source can be used to give the opposite viewpoint on another. Thus as the even-handed Ronald Russell also recorded, Gay's comment that, prior to take-off, that Waldron had said that CHAG was going to take the whole bunch, 'down there' but that he, Waldron, 'was going more to the north' surely implies a 240 degree heading. But for every recollection one way, one can readily produce an opposite memoir, and Russell also mentions

Captain Roy P. Gee's pre-launch memory as an example of this. 'He particularly recalls plotting the enemy's position himself before the call came to man aircraft, and noted the drastic difference in the solution he and his fellow VB-8 pilots had calculated compared to that ordered by Ring.'[59] Gee also asserted that while Ring had his own navigation solution, so also did Johnson, Rodee and Waldron, and they were all different. Exceptionally, the CO of VF-8[60] stated that he would go with whatever course was decided upon.

If the subsequent slight change of course was to prove the straw that broke Waldron's back (he had already lost the right to fighter cover which was allocated to the dive-bombers against his recommendation) was it sufficient for him to deliberately disobey orders, not once, but twice (once to break radio silence and once to break ranks) after becoming airborne? Mitscher's own subsequent official report, describes Waldron as 'a highly aggressive officer leading a well-trained squadron'. We now know that the latter assertion was open to doubt, Gay and others assert very little actual torpedo dropping was done – but how about the first? Did Mitscher mean 'aggressive' as in his attitude toward the enemy, or was the term a broad hint as to why he had flaunted standing orders? Certainly Waldron's native instinct, was cited as to the reason for his conviction where the enemy lay, and his courage in following his feelings through, no matter what.[61] Mitscher could hardly publicly disparage such devotion to duty and bravery, so perhaps this was a hint to his superiors as

---

55. Kernan, *Unknown Battle*.
56. Cressman, *et al*, *Glorious Page*.
57. George Gay, *Sole Survivor: The Battle of Midway and Its Effect on His Life*. Gay makes no mention of any such conversation during his 1943 interview (or it might have been edited out prior to release). All Gay said in 1943 was that 'before we left the ship, Lt Comdr Waldron told us that he thought the Japanese Task Force would swing together when they found out that our Navy was there and that they would either make a retirement in just far enough so that they could again retrieve their planes that went in on the attack and he did not think that they'd go on into the Island of Midway *as most of the Squadron commanders and air Group commanders figured* [my italics] and he told us when he left not to worry about our navigation but to follow him as he knew where he was going, and it turned out just exactly that way. He went just as straight to the Jap Fleet as if he'd had a string tied to them.' Gay Narrative.
58. Weisheit is a notable exception, and he cites as evidence Gay's memory of having the 'pale moon' clearly showing in 'the centre of his windshield' as proof of a bearing of 234 degrees true, (*Last Flight*). This is all reasonable and fine, unless, of course, Gay actually saw this graphic reference point *before* VT-8 broke away rather than after it had done so. Gay's accounts were 'flexible' enough on other matters

down the years for the timing of this event to be, at the very least, open to question.
59. Russell, *Changing Course*.
60. Lieutenant-Commander Samuel Gavid Mitchell.
61. His eldest daughter, Nancy Wentworth Waldron LeDew, although only thirteen at the time of her father's death, remembered him as, 'a calm, easy-going person', adding, 'He was especially proud of being part-Sioux and instilled in his daughters that same pride.' She recorded that her grandmother was part-Sioux Indian and taught Indian children, as there were no organized schools for Indians at that time. She recalled it was stated that her father used his Sioux Indian instinct to find the enemy. The South Dakota Historical Collections compiled by the State Historical Society (Volume XXII, 1946) also has records showing that his mother fought for the rights of people of part-Indian blood to Indian benefits in the early 1900s and that her father, Henry Aungie, was a son of Augustin Aungie and an Indian woman, and that her mother was Mary Aungie, a daughter of Colonel Dixon a, a famous Indian trader of the early 1800s, and an Indian woman. 'It would be hard to find a native-born South Dakotan with roots more firmly in the region of those of John C. Waldron.' I am grateful to the custodians of the South Dakota Hall of Fame at Chamberlain, for supplying me with copies and allowing me to quote from these papers.

to why VT-8 had rebelled and gone its own way to immortality.[62]

Whether there was an argument over the radio or not, Waldron had almost certainly made up his mind before he left the *Hornet*'s flight deck. If his quoted comment *was* actually made, then the subsequent dispute (breaking the sacred radio silence to do so and so compromising the whole force to the enemy, surely unthinkable) would have been superfluous.[63] But then again, we might apply Pierre Bosquet's famous words to the whole concept of Waldron's lone attack, 'C'est magnifique, mais ce n'est pas la guerre.'[64]

Ring himself makes no reference whatsoever to any such airborne argument, indeed he only mentions Waldron at all in order to pay tribute to his courage, but he *does* confirm Fisher's account that the higher-flying aircraft, verbal disagreement or not, soon lost all visual contact with the Devastators.

If Ring is to be censured for taking too northerly a course to make contact with the enemy, then he cannot be criticized for turning south at the end of it. He took the right decision there, but had gone too far west. What Lundstrom called 'Mitscher's great gamble' (note, not Ring's) did indeed end in disaster, but Ring did not, at the end of the 225 mile outward leg merely 'reverse course straight to the *Hornet*'[65], he turned south, albeit in vain. If, on the other hand, Ring had really taken the same course as McClusky, but turned south toward Midway at the end of it, and had guessed wrong by so doing (which he fully admitted to), in contrast to McClusky who guessed correctly and turned north (but it must be recalled, had not been so *instructed* to do before he left his carrier) then Ring can be censured for that mistake; but he cannot be censured for *both*!

Moreover, if Ring's wrong call led to a large part of the American dive-bomber force not making contact with the enemy, and thereby not subjecting *Hiryū* to attack along with the other Japanese carriers, then why is Fletcher's sudden and arbitrary decision (made at the very last minute and which changed an already fully agreed plan), to hold back Wally Short's SBDs aboard *Yorktown*, not similarly criticized? Short wanted to go with the rest of the air group but was overruled. So last-minute was Fletcher's intervention that even as Leslie's VB-3 attack was later developing, he was still radioing to Short on target allocation, believing him still to be in position astern of him. And what use were Short's retained dive-bombers put to. After three hours of kicking their heels on deck, just ten of them were despatched on another futile reconnaissance, while the other seven were struck down back in to the hangars. True, two of Short's men *did* eventually find the *Hiryū*, and were able to update her position, but by that time of course *Hiryū* had already launched her first counter-strike. Had Fletcher let the original launch plan stand, Short's squadron might possible have inflicted earlier damage on *Hiryū* and pre-empted any such strikes, thus ensuring total immunity for the *Yorktown* from retaliation. Of course, even had he gone as planned, Short might still have not have spotted *Hiryū* in the overcast, but, again, the same argument can hold good for Ring.

It has to be remembered that, for all their pre-war experience, Ring, like most of the men he led, had no previous experience of actual combat conditions. Experienced as he was in peace-time manoeuvres, he was to discover that, going rigidly by the book, a book which he had done much to compile, was no substitute for battle experience; for in battle, things rarely, if ever, followed the 'rules'.[66] The old saw that any battle plan never survives first contact with the enemy, was to hold as true for Midway as for any other combat, except that, with aerial air/sea combat, the range of things that could go wrong had vastly expanded in all

62. Mitscher, *Report of Action – 4–6 June 1942*, dated 13 June, 1942 (OF10/Ld, CV8/A16-3, Serial 0018.
63. Walter Lord has Waldron giving his men 'a few final words' in the ready room. 'He said he thought the Japanese ships would swing around once they discovered US carriers present; they would not go on to Midway as everyone seemed to think. So don't worry about navigation; he knew where he was going. 'Just follow me, I'll take you to "'em." (*Incredible Victory*). Others have it rather differently. 'We will strike of course, regardless of consequences. I wouldn't be surprised if they should change their course. If I seem to be wandering off, don't get worried. Just follow me and we'll get there.' (South Dakota Historical Collections, Vol. XXII, 1946). But the gist is the same; Waldron was going his own route!
64. Marshal Pierre Francois Joseph Bosquet (1810–61). These words, 'It is magnificent, but it is not war', are attributed to him as he witnessed the Charge of the Light Brigade during the Crimean War in 1854.
65. Lundstrom, *Black Shoe Carrier Admiral*.
66. Ring was criticized for his, 'leadership style', which, it is claimed, 'exacerbated' the already critical time factor when assembling the *Hornet*'s air group. This style 'forced the pilot not to question his orders or authority and follow doctrine to the letter'. (Falke Report). While agreeing that many found Ring's leadership strict and unbending, I find this reasoning hard to follow in that no air group leader was subjected to such mass disobedience, or perhaps non-compliance with his orders, as was Ring that morning. First the entire VT squadron left to go it alone, then, unit by unit, he was progressively deserted until he was left entirely on his own. In practice, every pilot questioned his orders and authority and, for whatever reasons, not one of them in the end followed his doctrine-driven plan 'to the letter'.

three dimensions, and everything happened at a far faster rate than the stately land campaigns of even recent years. The German Panzer/Stuka combination had turned conventional warfare on its head in Europe just two years earlier[67], but at Midway, there were the added complications of sea-borne warfare to throw into the dizzy mix. Air/sea battles, and Midway was only the second such to be fought, featured constantly changing mobile and vulnerable air bases, the unpredictability of the weather and vast, featureless, distances. A lost Stuka pilot over Poland or France could soon find a railway line or river to guide him home; a disorientated F4F or SBD pilot, unable to raise his companions or his base, and having no idea in the vastness his carrier home might be, had no such lifelines to cling to.

Nowhere was this lack of exact science more keenly felt than in the reconnaissance reports of both sides. Both the catapulted float planes from the Japanese heavy ships and the long-reaching PBYs and B-17s from Midway constantly came up with inadequate, incomplete and just plain wrong information time after time. If Nagumo was puzzled and irritated by the vagueness of search teams' reports, then a similar paucity of information dogged the Americans, and the most crucial information, the sighting report of the morning, was so inaccurate as to lead all TF-16's flyers astray, not just Ring. No one could say that reconnaissance was easy; these lumbering floatplanes were, after all, sitting ducks once spotted, they had no speed to escape and not much to fight back with. There was no glamour to the job; it was mind-numbingly boring most of the time, and suicidally dangerous during the rare times they succeeded in finding what they were searching for. Nobody could envy the scouting aircrews with their slow aircraft and indifferent communications equipment. Even so, that *was* their role, and, after all, that was what these crews had been trained to do. Their only mission was to collect and transmit accurate information, but few seemed capable of doing either with any fullness or clarity when it came to it.

It is ironic that Weisheit's search for a different scenario from that presented officially by the *Hornet* air group's history, should have been triggered by a latitude and longitude written on a ten-dollar bill by a crew member of a rescuing PBY[68], which might well have been a perfectly accu-

rate record but, which, given the track record of other such aircraft at Midway, might just possibly have been erroneous.

The post-war Naval War College study comes down heavily on Ring for his decisions at the end of the outward leg of his search. Bates was to write scathingly:

It must have been apparent to him that if the enemy initial position was considerably in error – he could see 25 miles – then the possibility of his finding them was poor. If the enemy course and speed were radically incorrect or if he had excessive drift then the possibility of finding them was also poor. However, if the course and speed were not seriously incorrect, or the drift was slight he should be able to locate them by the employment of the expanding square. This expanding square was the method prescribed for locating own carrier when not sighted upon return form a mission with no radio aids available.[69] Its employment would assist not only in searching the areas for slight errors in course and speed or for sight navigation errors due to drift, but as the square expanded, would also assist in searching the area for incorrect position and for larger errors in course and speed.

However, to Bates's obvious irritation, Ring 'did not employ the expanding square but headed in a southerly direction.'[70]

Barde is equally scathing. Ring's mistakes were numerous.

His air group was slow in forming and in departing from the *Hornet*. He allowed his fighters to remain with him far longer than it was safe for them. His insistence on a parade formation that wasted valuable fuel, while not increasing the effectiveness of the search, was inexcusable. Moreover, he allowed his air group to scatter without any explicit instructions from the commander.

However, he softened this list of criticisms by adding:

These criticisms of Ring's leadership are, of course, evaluated in the light of a calm detachment far

---

67. Peter C. Smith, *Junkers Ju.87 Stuka*, Crowood Press.
68. The PBY-5B was No. 7 of VP-51, gallantly flown by Lieutenant (jg) Frank M. Fisler, A-V (N), and his crew, who saved many lives after the battle. They rescued three F4F-4 pilots on 9 June and another 'near the spot we found the other three' on 10 May. Their course from Midway was printed on the bill as being 047 degrees true, 134 miles distant from latitude 28 degrees 23' longitude 177 degrees 21'.
69. US Navy, *Current Tactical Orders and Doctrine*, USF-74 (Revised).
70. Bates Report.

removed from the scene of conflict. The situation that prevailed that night of 4 June on the *Hornet* was hardly different. The air group was bitterly disappointed and rightly or not, the men placed the blame for failing to find the enemy squarely on Ring. Although he would lead his air group throughout the battle it was apparent to all that Ring had lost the confidence of those he led.[71]

It was Captain A. F. Brassfield[72], from VF-3, who made the often misquoted, and rarely correctly attributed, comment that, when the air group had returned to Ewa, 'no one would associate with the air group commander, particularly during social times at the Club'.

In Ring's defence against Bates, Barde and later critics, Falke makes the following very pertinent points.

> CDR Ring has been criticized for not executing an expanding square search even though doctrine does not address this method for search of a surface vessel. But this begs the question: which direction should he have started the expanding square search, to the south-east or north-west? Either direction, and his group would soon have been critically low on fuel, possibly resulting in more unnecessary losses due to fuel exhaustion. Thus, by not finding the Japanese and returning to the carriers without attacking and not mounting a credible protracted search, CDR Ring ensured that those aircraft and pilots would be available for subsequent attacks.[73]

One final word on this disappointing, and, to many, tragic mission. Ring is still held accountable today for the massacre of VT-8 and the loss of so many VF-8 pilots. Is this fair? It was Waldron, not Ring, who broke away and, no matter how gallantly and bravely, led his squadron to their destruction. CHAG might well have done better to follow Waldron's 'hunch' of course, but that is pure hindsight. All Waldron's undoubted skill and self-sacrifice, in the end, achieved naught, however hard that may be to accept. And the fighter pilots? Ring states he tried to catch

them in order to guide them back along the correct track to *Hornet*, but they had too big a lead. In fact, starting with Ensign John Edward McInerny, Jr. A-V(N), around 0910, they had all already taken unilateral action due to their fuel situation, overriding their skipper[74] and then, some 160 miles out, being followed by the rest, and those SBD pilots who saw them go, figured they were heading south to try and make Midway. In fact the fighters, now in two separate groups[75], headed off on slightly different courses that both diverged south-east of a straightforward reciprocal course to their outward journey.

Lundstrom explains that almost none of the F4F pilots, other than their squadron leader, knew the headings anyway and relied, as was commonplace, on the bombers to find the way out and back, while they 'tagged along'. On turning back while both McInerny and Magda picked up on the Zed Baker homing signal from *Hornet*, only one pilot[76] from Mitchell's group managed it, and he was placed in the lead. The other pilots were 'unfamiliar' with the device. Tragically Mitchell's more northerly group actually sighted the smoke of TF16 but assumed they were the enemy and kept going. The duo steering somewhat south of them failed to notice it at all, and likewise continued heading into infinity. Inevitably their fuel began to reach exhaustion and one by one they were forced to ditch until all ten were down, but widely separated, and two of them had died.[77]

Again doctrine decreed that, in the case of a mass ditching, the squadron leader was to alight the aircraft together, so that they could provide mutual assistance to each other and be easier to find as a group. Instead each plane struggled on to its own final resting place according to how each pilot could eke out his fuel. Doctrine also stated:

> Each plane is at all times responsible for its own navigation and will continually fix its own position as accurately as its facilities permit. Even when flying in formation, each plane must, to the best of its ability, record its successive positions in order that it may be able at any time to operate independently. If any pilot believe that his formation commander is flying on an

71. Barde, *The Battle of Midway: A Study In Command*. Barde interviewed both Captain Edgar Erwin Stebbins, then Commander, Fleet Air, NAS Alameda, and Captain A. J. Brassfield, the latter on 6 November 1966.
72. Captain Arthur James Brassfield, USN (1910–76). b. Browning. Montana on 21 September 1910. Enlisted in US Navy 1937. 1942, as lieutenant (jg) was the Engineering Officer VF-3 at Midway. Ace fighter pilot credited with over six 'kills'. Awarded two Navy Crosses and Gold Star. 1963–5, captain of the aircraft carrier *Hancock* (CV-19).

Retired in post as captain, July 1969. Died, Arlington in January 1976.
73. Falke Report.
74. Lieutenant-Commander Samuel Gavid 'Pat' Mitchell.
75. McInerny and his wingman Ensign John J. Magda as one group, and Mitchell with the rest of VF-8 as the other.
76. Lieutenant Stanley Erdman Ruehlow.
77. Ensign George Russell Hill, AV-(N) and Ensign Charles Markland Kelly, Jr, USNR.

incorrect course he may fly alongside the leader and indicate what he considers to be the correct course, but he shall then rejoin the formation and continue to follow his commander.[78]

Falke concludes:

From the inaction by any other pilot it appears that CDR Ring was the only pilot maintaining an accurate navigation picture. When CDR Ring disregarded the erroneous YE-ZB beacon signal, the fighters and bombers continued on the same course leading to an open ocean.[79]

78. US Navy, *Current Tactical Orders and Doctrine,* (Revised). 79. Falke Report.

Chapter Six

The 'Barge' Saves the Day

Out of all the mass of ships and weapons committed to battle that fateful 4 June, one aeroplane turned the disastrous tide for the Americans and changed a potential damaging defeat into the US Navy's proudest victory of World War II. Denied her true glory by the air force, the press and the radio communiqués of the day, and airbrushed from history ever since by Hollywood and the TV documentary makers[1], it is high time the true victor of Midway received her due.

The Aeroplane

The Douglas SBD-3 Dauntless ('Slow But Deadly') was one of the most famous and versatile dive-bombers of World War II – and this was in company with such outstandingly successful aircraft as the German Junkers Ju87 Stuka, everyone's concept of the ideal dive-bomber, the Japanese Aichi D3A1/2 Val and the British Blackburn Skua. All were single-engined dive-bombers produced for a specific precision task, and all appeared on the scene around the same period. I have written the definitive histories of all four of these famous aircraft[2] and for *naval* warfare requirements the SBD undoubtedly was the best of the quartet. She carried a heavier bomb load than the D3A1/2, had a longer ranger than the standard Junkers Ju87B and outpaced and out-reached the British Skua. Each aircraft had its particular merits but, for the top all-round perfor-

mance at sea, Ed Heinemann's product had to be rated the highest.[3]

The basic design, that of a low-wing, single-engined all-metal monoplane, represented the state-of-the-art transition from the fabric-covered biplanes of an earlier era which had not changed much since World War I. As has been recorded:

To understand how the Douglas Dauntless happened to be the Navy's primary carrier-based dive-bomber at Midway, it is necessary to return to the year 1934. In that year the Navy Bureau of Aeronautics (BuAer) solicited proposals from the Aviation Industry for both scout-bombers and dive-bombers, and ended up awarding contracts for the design and construction of seven prototype aircraft. One of these aircraft was the Ed Heinemann designed Northrop XBT-1. A later derivative of this aircraft became the Douglas XSBD-1 Dauntless.[4]

The XBT-1 had her maiden flight in August 1935, and first featured the big, hinged split-flaps attached to the trailing edges of the wings. These were later modified to eliminate the air flow 'vortex' problem by having a series of 3 inch diameter circular holes cut into them, and this distinctive design became the hallmark of subsequent US

---

1. The only time the SBD is shown on TV nowadays is by the BBC, Discovery and History channels, which invariably depict them *attacking* Pearl Harbor on 7 December 1941!

2. Peter C. Smith; *Douglas SBD Dauntless, Junkers Ju 87 Stuka, Aichi D3A1/2 Val,* and *Skua: the Royal Navy's Dive Bomber*.

3. The renowned naval test pilot, Eric 'Winkle' Brown, who flew almost every type of dive-bomber, including the earlier vintage Vought Vindicator/Chesapeake and the Curtiss

SB2c Helldiver and Vultee V-72 Vengeance, actually rated the Ju 87 the best in its designed role; with the modified Vultee Vengeance running it a close second. However, the Vultee; flown in combat by land-based units of the RAF, RAAF and Indian Air Force in Burma and New Guinea as well as by the French air force in North Africa and also by the Brazilian air force as an anti-submarine aircraft, was a land-based aircraft and of a later generation.

4. Edward H. Heinemann and Glenn E. Smith, Jr, *Sugar Baker Dog: The Victor at Midway*.

dive-bombers. Developed as the BT-1 a handful of these aircraft joined the fleet in 1937–8 and were still in service as late as 1940.

When Douglas took over Northrop in 1937, Ed Heinemann continued on as Chief Designer and considerable improvements and a new power-plant resulted in the XBT-2 which had metamorphosed into the XSBD-1 by the time it was accepted into service in February 1939. In April 1939, the BuAer placed orders for 144 SBD-1s and bestowed upon her the name Dauntless. Meanwhile another Douglas variant, the DB-19, had been sold (with, it should be noted, an export licence granted by the US Government, indicating tacit approval of the deal) to Japan, who designated her the DXD-1. Fortunately, the Japanese were also evaluating the German Heinkel He118 at the same time, and Aichi followed up a long line of original design rather than copy the Douglas example.

The SBD had been progressively improved through the Dash-2 into the Dash-3 model, spurred on by the fall of France in June 1940, brought about in large part by the use of the Junkers Ju87 Stuka dive-bomber. Orders for 174 Dash 3s were placed in September of that year, and they featured improvements like the Wright R-1820–52 radial engine, new larger and self-sealing fuel tanks, steel armour for the aircrew along with a bullet-proof windshield and a new, twin .50 calibre rear gun. The first SBD-3 joined the fleet in March 1941, just in time, and by the time of Midway was the standard equipment of all the VB and VS units on all three US carriers present. With a maximum speed of only 250 miles per hour the US Navy's phonetic translation of the new dive-bombers initials, 'Sugar Baker Dog', was soon replaced by wry commentary of her potential by the young pilots themselves. 'Clunk' was one, the ironic 'Speedy' was another, while yet a third was simply 'the Barge.'[5] But, when push came to shove, it was 'The Barge' that was to save the day at Midway.

One veteran of the SBD gave me this personal critique of the aircraft.

The Dauntless was a charm; rock steady in a vertical dive, completely responsive to the controls (unlike the Curtiss SBC and SB2C) and ready to absorb punishment and still get you home. I was worked over by two Japanese Type 97 fighters over Maloelap on the afternoon of 1 February 1942, and came out of it unconcerned with fifty holes through the tail surfaces and left wing tip (not enough lead), a hole in the gas tank in the root of my right wing (good lead but probably out of range) and one small calibre that broke apart when it hit the back of my armoured seat. None of our planes had the glass chins of the Japanese. They had the manoeuvrability, but at what a cost.

Our greatest vulnerability was the inadequate armour protection for the rear seat gunner. At Midway a good number of our torpedo plane losses must have come after the gunner was killed. At that point the dive-bomber or torpedo plane is dead unless he is not too badly outnumbered and is able to use effective single plane evasion tactics. It was my observation that as long as the tail gunner was firing, the attacking fighter tended to break off the attack before getting in killing range. For the defending plane a nose-down hard turn becoming a vertically-banked turn as the fighter came in range caused the fighter to break off early. He is a no deflection target for the gunner and at the same time finds his target a full deflection target. As he gets close if he gives the target the proper lead, he finds himself flying blind and into the cockpit of the bomber at the kill stage. The ones I saw were *not* kamikazes![6]

The Method

American doctrine, as we have seen, allocated both the scouting and the dive-bombing duties of a carrier force to the same aircraft, although both VB and VS squadrons were

Table 10: Comparison Between Skua and Dauntless

Aircraft	Span	Length	Speed MPH	Range	Weight empty	Weight Loaded	Engine	Wing Area	Ordnance
Skua	46 ft 2in	35 ft 7 in	225	760	5,490 lb	8,228 lb	890 hp	500 sq feet	740 lb
Dauntless	41 ft 6 in	32 ft 8 in	250	1,345	6,345 lb	10,400 lb	1,000 hp	325 sq feet	1,200 lb

5. Actually the SBD came out well in comparison with the Royal Navy's very similar single-engined, all-metal, monoplane dive-bomber, the Blackburn Skua, as table 10 indicates:

6. Lieutenant-Commander Richard H. Best to the author, 15 October 1996.

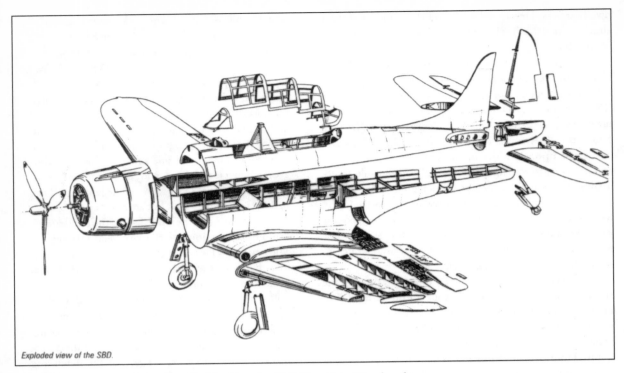

Exploded view of the SBD.

Diagram 7. Exploded view Detail of the Douglas SBD Dauntless Dive-bomber

given the leeway to make attacks as the opportunity arose, and therefore in practice the scouting squadrons allocated to each carrier were, actually, VSB units, fulfilling a combined mission brief. Let us examine the scouting mission first.

The then current doctrine laid down that the VSB tactical organization was, in fact, based upon the normal bombing unit, the six-plane division[7], but emphasized that the two-plane section was the normal scouting unit and was considered 'more effective than a single plane unit'. The single scout method was used but only when the considerations of conservation of material, reduction of workload on pilots and number of planes held back to form a striking force, predominated. There were also a variety of subsidiary missions which the VSB aircraft could be utilized for, including relief spotting (taking over from battleships and cruisers' own observation floatplanes (VO) during protracted shore bombardments), carrying out reconnaissance ashore if called upon, (but this was very much a rarity in 1942), patrol (usually anti-submarine sorties in areas adjacent to the task force), smoke laying (rarely employed, as this task was more normally left to the destroyers of the screen) and combat patrol (as an 'emer-

gency' additional airborne screen against incoming enemy attacks, and so used at both Coral Sea and Midway).

But their basic task was scouting out the enemy, a job which, as we have seen, the Japanese relegated to the catapult-launched seaplanes of escorting battleships and heavy cruisers. In the IJN these heavy ships usually carried two or three scouting aircraft, but two heavy cruisers, *Tone* and *Chikuma,* which routinely accompanied the 1st *Kidō Butai*, were designed to carry six[8], and had their four 8 inch main gun armament turrets deliberately concentrated forward to leave the quarterdeck entirely clear for such operations. Each system had its merits and its faults: the Japanese method left the whole complement of each carrier free to concentrate on its main task, the attack; the Americans could afford to devote a percentage of their aircraft quota to scouting because the scouts could also act simultaneously as dive-bombers and being the same aircraft, fitted in harmoniously and because they utilized deck-parking rather than hangar stowage and could always carry ten to a dozen more aircraft than their Japanese opposite numbers and thus could partially compensate for the use of this many aircraft as other than strike planes.

For scouting the VSB squadrons usually employed the

---

7.   US Navy *Current Tactical Orders and Doctrine* (Revised).

8.   Although, in practice, they normally only embarked five.

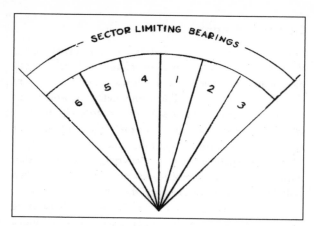

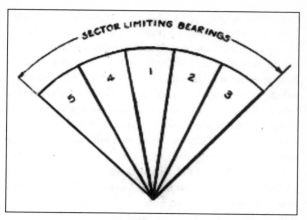

Diagram 8. US Carrier Operations – Even Sector Number Scouting Units

Diagram 9. US Carrier Operations – Odd Sector Number Scouting Units

'sector search', by which a given sector would be divided into sub-sectors assigned to each two-(or single-) plane unit to scour. These sub-sectors were of equal arc and if there happened to be an odd number of scouts available for whatever reason, the squadron commander, or the senior section leader, would be assigned the central sub-sector. When an even number of units was available then the squadron commander was usually assigned the first sub-sector to the right (starboard) of the median of any squadron sector. In peacetime practice the First Division would be assigned the sub-sector to the right of the squadron commander in numerical order of sections, and the Second Division would align to the left of the commander.

Once the enemy was found their principal duty was to report back accurately on what they had located, its position in latitude and longitude, its composition, its speed, its course and then track it, using any cloud cover to avoid detection and retaliation, for as long as endurance permitted or as directed. However, at Coral Sea the opportunity to attack was also an option, and one that was taken with excellent results on at least one occasion.[9]

Eliminating the Opposition

The dive-bombing doctrine had, as we have seen, been the subject of intense study in the US Navy for more than a decade, and had been honed and perfected to a high degree of regimentation, despite the earlier fears expressed by Reeves and his fellow pioneers that this might stifle initiative. The rules were detailed but the main mission objective was quite clear, obvious and to the point; in essence, 'the rapid and effective delivery of heavy bombs on enemy objectives' (in fact, the enemy carriers). The pre-emptive strike was the key to success and had long been known to be so – and not just by the American and Japanese navies, the Royal Navy had encapsulated this main principle in March 1936, stating that: 'the primary duty of naval aircraft is the destruction of the enemy carrier'. It was unequivocally placed on record that 'a fleet without carriers cannot with any hope of success, sustain major naval operations against a fleet with carriers'.[10] The Battle of Midway was to confirm that wisdom totally and completely.

The US Navy was equally convinced and declared that 'carrier based aircraft are essentially offensive weapons' and

9. Air navigation definitions as applied at Midway were:
   Bearing – The direction of one object from another, expressed as an angle measured clockwise from true north. Bearing is true unless otherwise designated.
   Heading – The angular direction of the longitudinal axis of the aircraft with respect to true north. In other words it is the course with the drift correction applied. It is true heading unless otherwise designated.
   Course – The direction over the surface of the earth, expressed as an angle, with respect to true north, that an aircraft is intended to be flown. It is the course laid out on the chart or

   map and is always the true course unless otherwise designated.
   Track – The actual path of an aircraft over the surface of the earth. Track is the path that *has* been flown. Course is the path *intended* to be flown.
   Point option – A point moving on a specified course and speed such that at any instant it represents the predicted position of the carrier, with an allowable error of less than half the radius of visibility.

10. Admiralty, *Memorandum on Naval Air Policy, Volume 1*, Director of Naval Air Division Naval Staff, dated 13 March 1936, contained in National Archive File ADM 116/4030.

that 'their major offensive power is the heavy bomb'. Moreover they stated as a matter of basic faith, 'Once the enemy is located all other considerations are secondary to the delivery of heavy bombing and torpedo attacks.' As we have seen, Admiral Fletcher for one did not fully subscribe to that view, preferring to hold back the scouting part of his 'offensive capability' as insurance against surprise. If control of the air was all-important in the naval battle of the 1940s then those 'Brown Shoe' men who drew up policy were clear on how it was to be achieved. 'It is highly improbable that control of the air can be gained by employing aircraft to shoot down enemy aircraft. The surest and quickest means of gaining control of the air is the destruction of enemy carriers . . . by bombing attacks.'[11]

How best to go about this? The doctrine was that once the enemy had been located and was within striking distance, '*all*[12] enemy carriers must be put out of operation at the earliest practicable moment'. This key point was reiterated and re-emphasized (and one can almost see Halsey's jaw squaring up as he dictated the words): 'The attack group should be of such strength and their fire so distributed that *all*[13] enemy flight decks are damaged, at least to the extent that their aircraft cannot be operated therefrom.' It was fully conceded that this was new thinking and; 'a departure from our previous idea of concentration "to sink" rather than "to disable"'. Nonetheless it was now considered that, 'even if just one enemy carrier is left undamaged' then the consequences for the American force 'may well be disastrous'. Again, the fate of the *Yorktown* was to demonstrate just how accurate this forecast was. Other guiding principles depended on this desirable state being imposed on the enemy. Once done, the sinking or complete disabling of individual enemy vessels was achievable. As to which would be the best ordnance for the job in hand – armour-piercing (AP – usually reserved for battleships), semi-armour piercing (SAP – generally against carriers and heavy cruisers) or general purpose (GP – for unarmoured vessels like destroyers or mercantile-type hulls which the AP and SAP bomb would merely pass through), that would naturally depend on the type of ships under attack and was left to the officers in tactical command. (However, it was to be found that, even here, the choice was not so simple, and was, indeed, to lead to dispute, because weight of ordnance restricted the range of the aircraft toting it.)

Getting Through

Once the enemy was found and the attacking force in place, the next problem was how to overcome the hazards, both natural and man-made, that might restrict or even prevent the desired outcome. 1: The enemy defences, which subdivided into aerial defence CAP or how to avoid the Zero cloud; 2: anti-aircraft fire from the target ship and her screening vessels (both long range and close range), and 3: the high-speed evasive manoeuvring of the target ship itself (which, as we have seen, was not to be scorned when skilfully done, as it had thwarted the TBDs almost totally).

It was considered that, once the SBDs were within striking range of the target, providing they kept closed up for mutual defence, enemy fighters would find it difficult to stop an attack developing. The best defensive formation for a six-plane division was considered to be two sections of three-plane Vs, with the rear section under and slightly astern of the leading three. This would concentrate maximum defensive fire on the attackers. If the attacking force was set upon prior to commencement of the dive, 'the attack must be pressed home in spite of opposition'. Once the dive had commenced however, 'there is little to fear from fighters', as the speed-retarding devices (dive-brakes), 'cause enemy fighters to overshoot so rapidly' that effective gunnery by them would be rendered almost impossible. Once the bomb was released then the best defence was considered to be two SBDs acting in concert, laterally separated by about 200–300 yards. Trying to run from a Zeke just offered up a nil-deflection shoot with the inevitable result.

As for anti-aircraft fire, that was best overcome by conducting 'a vigorous, coordinated and speedy attack, starting from at least 20,000 feet'. In other words offence was the best form of defence for a dive-bomber. Time in the enemy gunsights was minimal and the effect of the first few bombs 'have a destructive effect on enemy morale and especially if one or two are direct hits'. As in pre-war exercises, so in actual combat conditions up to that date, 'experience seems to indicate that anti-aircraft fire is very ineffective against dive bombers'.

Various alternatives were offered to offset the effects of target manoeuvres but basically it came down to whether the skill of the pilots exceeded that of the captain of the ship. We shall see examples of both coming out on top in this battle. Great store was set by surprise, which the dive-bomber, above all types, was expected to achieve. Surprise not only gave the dive-bomber immunity, it produced an instant lowering of morale among the defenders, especially

---

11. US Navy, *Current Tactical Orders and Doctrine,* (Revised). Part II.

12. Emphasis in the original.

13. Emphasis in the original.

those on the target vessel. The weather conditions could be favourable for this, cloud cover concealed an approach until it was too late; attacking out of the sun was a standard ploy which hindered anti-aircraft fire. It was felt a high-altitude approach aided surprise and it was for this reason that Ring, among others, had adopted it. However, this was a limited asset; it certainly proved crucial at Midway for the Americans as the Japanese had no radar, but it was more and more difficult to achieve once they started to install air-warning sets from 1943 onward.

For the actual dive attack, (always assuming that the dive-bombers had overcome or evaded all defences to enable them the luxury of choice) a fore-and-aft attack from directly ahead produced a steep dive and offered the maximum aiming space in range, combined with the minimum deflection, but this was an ideal. Attacking from astern offered a similar scenario but if the speed of the target vessel herself was greater than the wind at the 'bombs off' height, it made it an upwind dive. Dives tended to 'flatten out' and overshoots were more common. In both these cases to correct a pre-selected point of aim was comparatively simple compared to a similar correction for deflection. Thus, although beam attacks gave the most aiming area in deflection it was hard to achieve in practice and exposed the attacker to the maximum defensive gunfire.

As to the form of the attack, it was concluded that the single-plane attack, which resulted in 'a continuous rain of bombs at intervals of 2 to 8 seconds' was the best approach, giving the enemy gunners 'a confusing multiplicity of targets'. It was spelt out clearly that the standard angle of dive employed by the US Navy dive-bombers was not, as often presented, a screaming 90 degree approach, but was delivered at angles between 65 and 70 degrees. This was described as 'the standard dive'. It was, in fact, exactly the same as that employed by the Royal Navy Skuas and the Japanese Vals, although the German Ju87s often went into far steeper dives, sometimes hauling over onto their backs and going in almost vertical, as evidenced by numerous photographs. Low cloud conditions tended to preclude high dives and neutralized the effect of the dive brakes, in which case the SBDs conducted attacks at angles of between 45 and 50 degrees, and such an approach was described as 'glide-bombing'.[14]

Co-ordinating attacks with the low-flying TBDs was never going to be easy, even though it was the much-sought-after, but rarely-achieved, ideal. Maintaining sight contact between the two groups was considered vital, which meant a maximum altitude difference of 10,000 feet between the squadrons.

The SBD's 'final approach' scenario was divided into two forms: the initial (shallow) dive commencing at 20,000 feet (or higher), and the final (steep) dive being initiated at between 15,000 and 12,000 feet. The first phase had the squadron closed up against fighter attack and deploying at a distance of about 10 miles from the target on signal from the leader. With the aircraft spread at 400 feet intervals from one another in column, and with succeeding planes slightly stepped down, there was room to manoeuvre and the desired bombing interval. The final push for the attack commenced at around 12,000 feet. An alternative final approach had the defensive formation maintained until within 5 miles of the target and in the attack the second and following divisions diverted slightly to the right and to the left. The description of the final dive was:

(1)   The section leader wobbles wings, points to the side on which the target lies, pulls up directly over the wingman on side toward the target, cracks his diving flaps, and pushes over into the final dive.

(2)   The number two and number three men in the section continue as before, the wingman on the target side assuming the guide, and the other wingman flying laterally on him.

(3)   After about two seconds the guide wingman wobbles wings, pulls out radially and follows leader down.

(4)   Successive planes continue to break off in the same manner to enter the final dive. Care must be exercised that the attacking planes break off radially and that the pilots assuming the lead fly on a straight course in taking their interval. Planes must stay closed up.[15]

No minimum release height was specified, as this depended on the type of bomb carried and what terminal velocity (TV) it required to do its assigned job. The manual merely stated that, in order to increase the accuracy of bombing, 'the dive should be continued to the minimum altitude of release consistent with recovery above the danger space of the bombs carried and with pull-out restriction upon the airplane'. It was stated that using the sight as a rangefinder would greatly assist, but this ignored the fact, discovered in combat in the Coral Sea and elsewhere before Midway, that the telescopic sight tended to mist up as the

14. *Ibid.*

15. *Ibid.*

129

altimeter wound down and different densities of atmosphere were encountered.

The earlier practice of the rear-seat man calling out the altitude to the pilot over the interphone, thus leaving him free to concentrate on accuracy 'is unsound and must be discontinued'.[16]

When committing full squadrons to an attack on an enemy fleet the question of fire distribution was important. In practice, the enemy carrier was the only real target that any SBD skipper actually cared about; they were his principal enemy and, moreover, the biggest target and the one he could hurt the most. As an alternative a plump battleship was tempting, but they knew they could never sink one outright.

The recommended fire distribution for a squadron of eighteen SBDs, armed with heavy bombs, was suggested as in Table 11:

It was emphasized that this was just a guide, showing the optimum; the actual fire distribution naturally depended on such factors as number of aircraft available to the strike group, number of suitable targets and the tactical situation. 'As an example, it would be most unsound to concentrate 18 bombers on one carrier and to leave another in the [enemy] disposition untouched'.[17]

To maximize effect, and to avoid confusion, target designation at the start of the dive-bombing attack was vital. Again, doctrine laid down just how this was to be conducted.

In a mass attack, with every pilot concentrating on getting a hit on his selected target, the potential was there for aerial collision. It was therefore duly noted that when bombing four ships, the direction of the dive must not coincide with the line of bearing. 'This precaution is necessary in order to avoid pulling out directly toward and over the target of following airplanes'.[18]

Table 11: Fire Distribution (For an Eighteen-strong SBD Squadron)

Type of target	Number of SBDs to concentrate on
Aircraft Carrier (CV)	All 18
Battleship (BB)	All 18
Heavy Cruiser (CA)	9 against each
Light Cruiser (CL)	6 against each
Destroyer (DD)	3 against each
Submarine (SS)	3 against each

The Men

What was it like to be an SBD pilot in 1942. Here is one splendid account from a Midway veteran[19], well worth recording.

When I boarded the CV-6 USS *Enterprise* in May 1941, I entered into the best of all worlds. The ship had all of the latest features and equipment available at that time, yet it had made a 'shakedown' cruise to correct the problems always encountered with a new ship and its new crew. They knew this ship would be their home for years. After six months in the Pacific, this ship would return to its home port and to overhaul. The squadrons would practice elsewhere, but in a few months they would fly back to their friends on board.

The ship's company knew our needs and our limitations. They may have regarded aviators as oddballs, but not as condescending elite. The problem of 'brown shoe' vs 'black shoe' did not exist. The decisions of Captain Murray and his Executive, Commander Jeter, in regarding actions and justices for discipline and infractions, were only

Table 12: SBD Target Designation

No. of ships to be bombed	Target Assigned Each Section					
	1st Sec	2nd Sec	3rd Sec	4th Sec	5th Sec	6th Sec
1	1	1	1	1	1	1
2	1	1	1	2	2	2
3	1	3	1	2	3	2
4	1	2	3	4	3	4
5	1	2	3	4	5	5
6	1	2	3	4	5	6

16. *Ibid.*
17. *Ibid.*
18. *Ibid.*
19. Lieutenant (jg) N. J. Kleiss, *VS-6 Log of the War. Personal Diary* and *USS* Enterprise *Orders, of a Scouting Six SBD Dive Bomber Pilot. Pearl Habor Attack through the Battle of Midway.*

out-classed by the Ten Commandments.

Court-martials were rare, but decisions usually found the offender guilty in 99/100% of the cases. Punishment fitted the crime. The lawyers had not yet taken over.

Gender bias and other problems prevalent with today's Navy were not tolerated. A December 1941 court-martial was scheduled for an *Enterprise* officer who reportedly patted a waitress on her derriere. It was cancelled only because the officer was killed in the 7 of December attack.

An officer was expected to be a gentleman and his promise was a bond.[20] A bad check or drunkenness on duty and your career was at a dead end. On the other hand, the demonstration of unusual skill or effort moved an officer to the top. Political appointments by the President were rare.

Officers and enlisted men respected each other. The enlisted men respected officers for their knowledge and experience. The officers respected the enlisted men for their skills, perseverance and abilities. Our picnic at Barber's Point, before the war, exhibited the camaraderie between officers and enlisted. We were a family.[21]

The new SBDs which replaced the ancient SBCs brought in a new social problem. The old SBC had an oxygen pipe stem (held in the aviator's mouth), which could be easily cleaned. The new oxygen face mask of the SBD was not so easily cleaned. Slobber from the previous individual was a consideration.

Senior officers recalled the routine periodic 'short arm' inspections made of all enlisted men. They also recalled the substantial percentage of venereal disease found in homosexuals and certain racial groups.

The air group flight surgeon was not only a physician, but also a confidant. He 'grounded' aviators who had stopped up ears. Eardrums must be able to 'equalize' quickly. The 240-knot downward dive, from four miles high, took less than a minute. Air pressure doubled.

The flight surgeon would also check the pilot's ability to withstand the normal 'g' encountered in ending his dive. The force against the seat, for the normal pilot and equipment of 200 pounds, resulted in a load of 1,600 pounds. The SBD could withstand 13 'g'. Most pilots would probably become unconscious beyond 10 'g.'

At a later date, the flight surgeon would watch aviators as they returned from a harrowing day of combat. Occasionally, he would dispense white paper cups of USN bourbon to ensure pilots would sleep soundly for an early morning flight. Lt J. M. Jordan, MD, was a great help to us.

The new SBDs required new knowledge. A new pilot was blindfolded and required to locate 80 different controls and indicate up/down and on/off positions. Pilots were warned to turn automatic pilot gradually from 'off' to 'on' and be prepared to overpower unexpected gyrations as it warmed up.

The pilot's two .50 caliber guns firing through the SBD propeller seldom gave any problems. The original single .30 caliber gun operated by the rear seat man also worked well. A twin .30 caliber machine gun later replaced it and worked even better. Frequent practice runs by pilots and by rear gunners were fired against a sleeve towed by another airplane. Various colors of paints on projectiles showed who made holes on the sleeves. Competition was intense.

Radio silence required to conceal our locations was not a problem for older aviators who had flown aircraft before radios were added. Hand signals, light signals, aircraft wiggles or motions and Morse code 'dits and daws' displayed by hand movement or flashlights served us well. Hand signals between aircraft were close enough to be read at night.

Eighteen-plane formations at night without any lights were standard, with a few exceptions. Colored position lights, unique to each aircraft, were lit as they departed from the aircraft carrier. They were lit until the last plane had found and arrived in its assigned position. Then all lights were turned out.

Another exception was joining up on night flights after making practice bombs on flares used as targets

---

20. This even held good for those who had broken the unwritten 'code'; Miles Browning, for example, given the opportunity by Halsey, 'to do the right thing', very quickly married his paramour once she had become divorced.

21. This may, however, seem like a very 'rose-tinted' viewpoint to many. Contrast Kleiss's memory with that of an enlisted seaman, an ordnance man aboard the same *Enterprise*. Alvin Kernan's tart reflections on exactly the same theme make for a totally different point-of-view. 'The officers called us by our last names and we called them "Sir". Few enlisted men knew an officer as a person, which meant that the deaths of the pilots when they came were not felt very personally. We felt them as fans feel the loss of a game by their football team. There was always a lot of tension between the enlisted men and the officers, largely based on the enlisted men's real fear of officers, who looked down on them, and the officers' reciprocal fear that their orders would not be obeyed by men they never quite trusted.' (Kernan, *Unknown Midway*.)

on the open sea. Night flights were made with 45° dives rather than vertical flights. We frequently did these night bombing practices and we never lost a plane or pilot by accident, and considered ourselves super.

One thing we lacked (initially at least, it was gradually phased in) on our SBDs was the YE-ZB homing device. With this assistance, we could easily have found the *Enterprise* when we returned from a 500-mile scouting mission. Its line-of-sight capability would have given us signals without giving information to the enemy. Lacking it, we were dependent on determining wind directions and speed by watching ocean waves. An error distance of five miles (or ⅛ inch error on your chat board) meant deep trouble. Fortunately, that seldom happened.

Our goal on landing our 18 airplanes on the *Enterprise* was three minutes. From the ten seconds between 'cuts', the following items must occur: the pilot lands the aircraft and then, having it stopped by a 1⅛ inch cable, the cable jerking back the aircraft to give slack to the cable, two men releasing the cable from the landing hook, the pilot raising the hook, the barrier/barricades being lowered to the deck, the pilot scurrying the plane to the 'park' on the bow, the barrier/barricade being raised, the landing signal officer seeing that all this had been done, then giving the next plane a 'cut'. All of this in 10 seconds.

We generally did this on schedule, unless the ship was rolling and heaving.

Our squadron Scouting Six was a well-oiled, practiced, experienced machine ready for anything. We older officers knew that an almost certain war was not far away.

Our F4F aircraft and squadron were in great shape – not as good as Scouting Six, but still great.

Our ancient TBDs and their poor torpedoes were not in great shape. Several Scouting Six pilots were assigned to watch TBFs fire their torpedoes against a target. We plotted their course and put smoke markers where the torpedoes stopped so they could be picked up and reused. For practice, the warhead was replaced by water, which then was expelled by air when the torpedo stopped. Then the empty nose held the torpedo afloat.

Unfortunately, most of the torpedoes I followed did not go straight. Some even circled. They had to be dropped at 100 feet and a maximum speed of 100 knots (Japanese torpedoes were much better).

Being of a curious nature, I flew on possibly the first TBF which landed on Ford Island, Oahu. I flew alone and had no problem. Sometime later, another pilot flew it with a passenger. When he landed the passenger had died of carbon monoxide [poisoning]. Perhaps this glitch in design correction delayed the arrival of TBF's to Torpedo Squadron Six.

Pre-Launch

Another veteran dive-bomber pilot also gave me his personal recollections.[22]

The routine would be, you'd be called early. First you're gonna get chow, and you'd muster in the ready room. Each squadron had a ready room for the officers and another for the enlisted men, each had their own ready room. You had your own chair, your place where you'd keep your helmet and your weapon, everything locked up in your own bailiwick, and that chair would be secured by four little cups to the deck, to prevent it swaying back and forth. The ready room was just below the teak flight deck. That was your domain aboard ship, you were either in that chair or in your own state room or you could be about the ship.

During the briefing you would want to know what kind of bomb load have you got, what's the disposition of the enemy, what do you look for i.e. type of ship.

You'd gear on your weapon, your Mae West, we would carry our flight suits and hang 'em in our rooms because there were the smells, you know, I don't recall that they always went to the laundry. A lotta times you just wore your khaki pants, your shirt with your rank insignia and you'd take sensible shoes, and you'd pull the flight suit over. That could either stay in your drawer or hanging on the wall, that's where they were put. Then you had a lot of airflow in the ready room but it had its own smell, of bodies. It wasn't exactly like, a shade off a gym locker room maybe, We had cleaners on the ship, some enlisted men, the lesser ratings, would have been assigned to bomber ready room for cleaning, maybe once a week swab the deck or something. But we tried to keep it nice, you know its where you live and you were not gonna live in a pig-pen or be untidy. It wasn't spick-and-polish *every* day, it's where you worked.

---

22. Chuck Downey, taped interview.

You used grease pencil on the lighted back-boards; that's were you used the grease pencil, I don't recall using those in the airplane. Your duty officer would be assigned to the back-lighted board for putting up the essential stuff, the specific highlights. You'd take notes, you wanted enough information, bearing, distance, what to expect at the target, the rendezvous, techniques, all of which were pretty much squadron doctrine all the time, unless there was a minor change. Talk to your buddy, check parachutes. You had a similar thing when you got back, an 'un-brief'. You had a young, intelligent, educated officer who had been through college, assigned as Air Combat intelligence, who would have been to intelligence school. He was assigned to do the debriefing for you and he would take copious notes from you after you came back.

Sometimes the Skipper would give the briefing; the Flight Leader will give the briefing or the Air Combat Intelligence officer could give the briefing. So we had three sources, and assessing all three together would collaborate the strands of information. The Air Combat Intelligence Officer was a function for a senior lieutenant, knowledgeable, sort of like the eyes and ears for the effort going back to the admiral's staff – what happened? – what happened here? – who saw what? Photo assessment, some aircraft were equipped with K20 cameras and you could use them for overviews. The K20 camera was hand-held by the rear-seat man and a fairly big camera. There were some pictures of the ship that was destroyed there [the cruiser *Mikuma*]. The gun-camera film was taken, developed and hidden forever, nobody ever saw it. George (Walsh) is very suspicious of that fact. He and I, and others, felt that the dive-bombing tactic was sufficiently proven to get by without that proof for our own satisfaction; but we feel it was not sufficiently advertised or explained to the public at the time, or ever since.

Once briefed you manned your allocated airplane. You'd come out of the ready room, you just climbed up a short ladder and you were on the flight deck. Your rear-seat man, he would have had a briefing separately. He'd meet you at the airplane, you'd shake and say 'How ya doing?' All the airplane

checks would already have been done for you. You had a division or unit assigned to the ship for the care and maintenance of each type of airplane. So you'd have special mechanics that did fighters, special mechanics that did dive-bombers and torpedo-bombers. So they'd check 'em out and note any discrepancies, they wrote them up in report sheets and they would correct them and render the airplane 'ready for service'. So you didn't have your own crew chief like you did in the air force. You never had your own airplane; you had whatever airplane was spotted, say number thirty-four, number ten, whatever it was. That would be allocated to you at the briefing and be already spotted on the deck.[23] It'd often be dark for pre-dawn launches, and you couldn't find it; so 'where the hell is it', and you couldn't use a flashlight up on deck naturally.

You also had no opinion on the ordnance you carried. You had an ordnance officer on the ship who decided that according to mission/target-type and the planes were bombed up and ready to go. The armourers did all that on the flight deck, contrary to the Japanese below decks:

So we are in our airplanes and we suit-up and strap in, slip your chart board in underneath the instrument panel check the cockpit all over, put on your flying helmet and wait to start engines. Of course you are placed at the stern of the ship, relatively, to give you a long take-off run; the fighters are being shot off forward of you, they can take off in 300 feet. On a long-range strike, in the air for hours, well your ass got sore; you had to urinate in a stainless-steel relief-tube; sometimes we had a box lunch with us on really long hauls.

Deck Routine

The following excellent account of the deck routine was given to Barde.

The men who would fly the blue aircraft were still in the depths of the ship. Others, though, scurried about the breezy deck in a variety of colored helmets and shirts. Men in brown clambered over the planes carrying out their duties as plane captains. Those

23. Dusty Kleiss recorded that there was only one occasion when he refused to take his allotted aircraft, which was poised for take-off. 'All the gauges read perfectly, but I gave a thumb's down. Chief Dodge, probably the best aircraft engine man on the ship, ran up for a look. I again gave full power and the gauges said OK, but I still downed the plane. A younger pilot replaced me and took off. His engine failed, he crash landed just ahead of the ship, and was picked up by a destroyer. To this day, I do not have the faintest idea of what was wrong. I do not believe in ESP, but I do believe in awareness of familiar things beyond normal perception.'

wearing dark blue were busily engaged in moving the planes as they respotted them for launch. Highly skilled ordnancemen inspected torpedoes, bombs and machine-guns, their bright red tops setting them apart from the others. At intervals near the catwalks, pairs of green shirted sailors indicated the presence of fuelling stations. They stood ready to drag a hose to any aircraft that needed 'topping off'. Close to the island structure was a group of men dressed in pale yellow. At the moment their duties were minimal but when the signal was executed to launch aircraft, their work would not allow a moment's rest. Some would direct pilots to start engines, unfold wings, and taxi to the proper position. Others like the flight deck officer, would signal the pilot to 'wind up' and when that proper moment arrived his arm would drop smartly toward the bow. Then, and only then, would the pilot release his hold on the brakes.[24]

Launch and Flight

After starting the engine and going through the cockpit check list the aircrew awaited their turn on the 'spot'. As each plane taxied forward to the take-off position the pilot received a 'Stop' signal and then a 'Hold Brakes' signal. The flight-deck take-off control officer (TCO) then took charge of the final launch procedure. He held his black-and-white checkered flag at the ready and, once the preceding aircraft had launched, this was raised above his head and rotated. This was the signal for the pilot to rev his engine up to full take-off power, while still holding the brakes on, and using the elevators in their fully upward position to hold the aircraft's tail down. Then the TCO caught the pilot's eye, bent forward on one knee and pointed the flag toward the bow for the 'Go' signal. The pilot released the brakes and away the SBD went over the prow of the carrier, dipping slightly with a heavy bomb load, and then climbing steadily away to her rendezvous circuit.

Chuck Downey continued:

We rarely had an oxygen problem in the dive-bombers. We didn't use radar, but IFF, always. Mostly, radio silence, initially. We had learned to fly without over-use of radios and eventually there were only four VHF channels for the whole war in the Pacific. So you stayed off it if you were a wing man, unless it was absolutely essential.

There was some contact back-and-forth with the rear-seat man. We passed cigarettes between us. We

had a little message-carrier between the cockpits, so we could pass cigarettes or matches one way or the other, we both smoked. In formation it was just as easy to fly close up as light and loose. It doesn't take any more; it's not *that* difficult to keep tucked in, because you are comfortable flying with the guys you are always with, it's how we trained. That's why you've learned to fly together all this time; you prefer to be with the same people you know and trust. If you lose someone you feel kinda bad. And you have to start up again with a new guy.

So the tactic then was two sections together for protection because if you are attacked it's better to have six weapons firing than two. Although Zeros in the second attack shot down Weber[25], amazingly not one SBD was lost in the first attack. There was just nobody there; they were down on the deck! They could have been out of ammo. The thing that I want to convey is that we were supported, not a lot maybe, but the fact that you did have *some* fighter cover made you feel better. If the enemy fighters showed up likely they'd get them off your ass.

Clay Fisher offered another view:

Our standard dive usually started from 10,000 to 14,000 feet. We rolled out of our formation in either a nose down right or left turn to start the dive and at the same time we opened our split dive flaps (dive brakes). We wanted to be able to steep the dive to where we were in a vertical aircraft position to the water or ground surface. The track (path) of the aircraft was about 70 degrees. You knew when you were in a vertical position when your butt was not pushing against your seat nor were you hanging against the safety belt.

Correcting the lead for the target's speed, wind factors and probably equally important was trying to keep the aircraft from skidding laterally. We used our left hand to adjust the rudder trim tab, a small wheel. There was a ball in the 'needle-and-ball' indicator instrument. If you were skidding the ball would be off-center either right or left.

The SBD dive bomber was a tough old bird structurally and we could do hard snap pull outs at 1,500 and still recover safely. We completely blacked out on a snap pull out but you also recovered your vision more rapidly. The SBD did not have shoulder straps

---

24. Robert E. Barde, *The Battle of Midway: A Study in Command.*

25. Ensign Frederick Thomas Weber, AVB-N of VB-6.

in 1942 and during a hard pull out I always tried to get my head down near my thighs so I would not black out as much.[26]

Return

Chuck Downey described a typical mission return after hard combat action in a dive-bomber.[27]

After the attack then it's 'So long, see you back at the ship!' Nobody's going to sit around and be a mother hen.[28] If you were unlucky enough to be hit in the power plant, and you are pumping oil out, you don't have an oil priority gauge, you just have an oil pressure gauge; when all your oil's gone your pressure will go down and you'll quit flying. And you'll go down in the water. So, OK, you are not gonna sit around and loiter, you are in Jap country and the squadron's gonna go back to the ship. So here you are. So you just keep going toward the fleet. So the chart board is out and you are doing your maths. Once you see the first destroyer you feel pretty relieved.

Dusty Kleiss related:

The British called our carrier landings 'controlled crashes', but they were not all that difficult. The pilot started downwind as he came abeam of the stern of the ship. His speed was about five knots above stalling speed and his altitude a few feet higher than the deck of the ship. He then made a semi-circle, keeping his eye on the Landing Signal Officer (LSO). Then all he had to do was watch the LSO's flags[29] and go slower, faster, higher or lower, and finally make a 'cut' [cut engine and land] or 'wave off' [rev up engine and go round for another try]. The LSO's decisions were inviolate.

On one occasion an F4F pilot was ordered to report on the *Enterprise* if he successfully made his carrier landings. His first six attempts were total fiascos. On the next try, he was given a 'wave off' but took a 'cut'. His plane bounced on the deck and over

the port side. Captain Murray was not impressed. Scuttlebutt[30] had it that he ordered the ship's log book to read: 'Lt (jg) Blank reported aboard', followed by the exact day, hour, minute and second of the incident. The next item was almost exactly identical, except it read: 'Detached. Duty completed' and the time was one second later The pilot was recovered by a destroyer and returned to Pearl.

Pilots making a landing soon learned to take a quick look at the photographer perched on the top deck of the island structure. He never wasted a film or missed an accident. If he looked bored, you were OK. If he stood up, you had better do something quickly! This area was called 'Vultures Row'. I spent some time there watching new pilots land.

A safety net perhaps ten feet wide was placed a few feet below and abaft the LSO. From Vultures Row I watched LSO Bert Harden signal a plane to take a wave off because the aircraft was too slow. The airplane responded slowly and headed directly for Bert. He dived for the safety net. He jumped so vigorously that he dived completely past the whole net and made a perfect swan dive of 65 feet. The destroyer behind the *Enterprise* picked him up unharmed.

On one occasion, I watched an airplane catch on fire as it stopped near the barrier. I was sure that the pilot would be lost since he was engulfed by flames. But, in seconds, the man in the asbestos suit had grabbed him out and he was on his way to sick bay in good shape.

On still another occasion, a fighter, probably damaged in combat, landed so flat during a crash landing that it could not be moved normally. Within a minute, dozens of men swarmed under it like ants and lifted it up on a dolly. (They were in blue suits, as I recall. Others, such as ordnance men, wore different color suits.) Meanwhile, others were taking the trigger motors from the machine guns. Within a couple of minutes the whole mess was pushed over the port side and other fighters could land. The extra trigger motors would let more of our fighters use all of its guns.

---

26. Clayton Fisher, note for the author, April 2006.
27. Describing an SB2C mission he flew off the Chinese coast later in the war, but the basics are the same.
28. But this was not always the case, as we shall see in the unselfish actions of Leslie and Holmberg in getting Bill Esders rescued after his ditching.
29. The Royal Navy used solid 'bats', much like enlarged table-tennis bats in outward appearance, which could be illuminated at night, hence the unofficial term 'Batsman' for

their LSO. The Japanese were far more sophisticated and used a system of coloured lights (*chakkan shidōtō*) to do the same job automatically.

30. Scuttlebutt – the rumour mill of any ship – instantaneous transmission throughout the vessel and invariably way ahead of official pronouncements, either confirmations or denials. Invariably 100 per cent wrong in mission predictions but all-encompassing with regard to life aboard.

The above might seem that crashes landed daily, or during night landings. This was far from the case. The 16,000th carrier landing occurred in 1941, three years after the *Enterprise* was commissioned. Only accidents get attention.[31]

So that is how it was; but already that morning at Midway *Hornet*'s dive-bombers had run out of luck. All now rested on the SBDs of *Enterprise* and *Yorktown*.

Blind Man's Bluff – the *Enterprise* Strike

Under the CEAG, Wade McClusky[32], the *Enterprise* air group had left at 0945 and had climbed to 20,000 feet on a heading of 231 degrees. McClusky himself, with his two wingmen[33], took the central position of the formation with Gallaher's three divisions stepped down to port and Best's three divisions to starboard. McClusky estimated that the anticipated interception point was 142 miles out. However, by 1120 this force had reached this point with no sign of the enemy whatsoever. Interestingly, some of the *Enterprise* pilots also reported seeing a column of smoke rising from Midway off on their distant port side. McClusky's group was almost as fragmented as Ring's had been at this point, but the dive-bomber force was still intact. McClusky's mount carried a single 500 pound bomb under her belly, plus two 100 pounders, one on each wing; the fifteen surviving VB-6 aircraft, SBD-2s and -3s, toted a single 1,000 pound bomb each fitted with 1/100 second fuses; and fourteen of the sixteen VS-6 dive-bombers carried 500 pounders. The last two VS-6 off the deck had been able to tote a single 1,000 pound bomb apiece[34]. Two SBDs equipped as photographic planes (SBD-3P's) accompanied CEAG.[35] Two more of the assigned SBDs had failed to make it thus far.[36]

Faced with the same decision as CHAG on what to do next, McClusky opted for a turn north-west with his full force, accepting the risk involved by their dwindling fuel reserves. The minutes ticked by with still no sign of the

enemy and, after about thirty-five minutes of fruitless searching, the point of no-return for many of the SBDs was fast approaching; indeed, for some, it had already passed. Here fate took a hand, for, at 1205, their course and speed brought them into visual contact with a lone warship, steering to the north-east at high speed.

This ship turned out to be the destroyer *Arashi*, which we last saw dropping depth-charges to deter the persistently troublesome submarine *Nautilus* from making any more of her bold incursions into the sea-space of the Nagumo force. Now, her duty done, her captain[37] was cracking on speed to rejoin his colleagues, and was blissfully unaware that he had company 20,000 feet above and astern of him. McClusky was no dive-bomber pilot[38] his knowledge of doctrine was what he had been able to pick up since his appointment as CEAG just a few weeks before, but he had a perfectly good brain, and now he used it. It seemed clear enough to him that any solitary destroyer was not loose about its business in the Pacific on her own, and she was obviously rejoining a larger force. He reasoned that this could be his intended target and decided to 'tag along' for a while and see what turned up. What turned up was the *1ˢᵗ Kidō Butai*, which duly hove into view at 1005[39].

Dusty Kleiss recorded:

At 0910 [0710] Scouting Six was in the air, a total of 17 planes (Pat Patriarca had a 'down'). We rendezvoused and accompanied the rest of *Enterprise* Air Group to the location. One of these 17 planes was forced to return to the ship because of engine trouble (Ensign Rodenburg 6-S-9). I was leading the second section. Rendezvous completed at 0745.

The enemy force was not easily located because it had changed course to the North, and although it was only about 140 miles distant, we did not sight this enemy force until 1200 [1000]. Many planes were very low on gas at this point and knew they could (1)

---

31. Kleiss, *Log of the War*.
32. McClusky was flying with a new radioman, Walter G. Chochalousek, ARM1c, from VB-6, after his regular back-seat man, John Murray O'Brien, ACRM, of VF-6, had broken his spectacles in a fall.
33. Ensign Richard Alonzo Jacard and Ensign William Robinson Pittman.
34. Spruance to Nimitz, Action Report of USS *Enterprise*, Battle of Midway Island, 4–6 June, 1942, dated 8 June 1942.
35. 6-S-8 piloted by Ensign William Robinson Pittman with Floyd Delbert Adkins, AMM2c in the rear seat and 6-S-11, piloted by Ensign Richard Alonzo Jacard, with backseat

man Porter William Pixley, RM3c.
36. 6-S-13 piloted by Frank Anthony Patriarca with Jack Richard Bagley, ACRM failed to start while still aboard and 6-S-9 piloted by Ensign Eldor E. Rodenburg with Thomas James J. Bruce, SEA2c who was forced to return to the carrier when he was unable to shift to higher blower.
37. Commander Yusumasa Watanabe.
38. McClusky had familiarized himself with the SBD since being appointed Air Group Commander on 15 March, but had never yet actually dropped a bomb in practice or anger.
39. The *Akagi* apparently did not notice the oncoming dive-bomber force until fourteen minutes later than this, at 1019.

jettison bombs and fly safely back to ship or (2) Bomb enemy carriers and run out of gas and take a chance of being picked up eventually, by a patrol plane – one chance in a hundred. Everyone made the attack [1027].[40]

The enemy fleet's strength was very accurately estimated to comprise four carriers, four battleships and heavy cruisers and between eight to ten destroyers. Weather was described as clear with excellent visibility. Scattered cumulus clouds stretched up from 1,500 to 2,500 feet, and the ceiling was 'unlimited'. There was a light, 5–8 knot surface wind from the south-east.

During the approach one of Best's wingmen, Lieutenant (jg) Edward J. Kroeger[41], made hand signals which indicated that his rear-seat man's[42] oxygen supply had become exhausted. Rather than detach this aircraft, which was carrying a 1,000 pound bomb, Best decided to take his whole force down to 15,000 feet. At this altitude there was no need to rely on the oxygen mask and Best removed his to indicate the fact to Kroeger. The force lost yet more SBDs around this point. Ensign Eugene A. Greene[43] had broken away earlier, but the reason for this was never established for his aircraft vanished from view for ever. Ensign Tony F. Schneider[44] of VB-6 had been nursing his aircraft with a rough-running engine for some time already. As he crossed the Japanese screen he first thought it was TF-16, but was disillusioned from thoughts of salvation by the sight of battleships, and, at this point of revelation, his fuel supply finally ceased and the engine spluttered to a halt. He had no option but to try and coast to a safe water landing away from the enemy. He warned his gunner[45] to ditch the twin 30 calibre machine gun and let down to a smooth landing. Even so, the machine gun, which had not been jettisoned, broke free, knocking the gunner out. Schneider got the raft blown up and somehow or other managed to haul his gunner to safety onto it before the plane sank beneath them.

Right on the Money – the *Yorktown* Strike

The *Yorktown*'s attack group, comprising the seventeen SBDs of VB-3, each of which carried a single 1,000 pound bomb with Mk 21 and Mk 23 fuses, approached the enemy along a track of 240 degrees true and arrived over the Nagumo force at about 1020. An enemy carrier, which was thought to have been the *Akagi*, but which is now known to have been the *Soryū*, was observed away to the north-east, leading the by now rather elongated gaggle of carriers, which was all that had been retained of their previously immaculate 'box' formation. Lieutenant-Commander Maxwell Leslie[46] led VB-3 up-sun at an altitude of 14,500 feet, losing contact with VT-3 who were dropping down to

40. Kleiss, *Log of the War.*
41. Lieutenant (jg) Edwin John Kroeger.
42. Gail Wayne Halterman, RM3c.
43. Ensign Eugene Allen Greene, with Samuel Andrew Muntean RM3c as gunner.
44. Captain Tony Frederick Schneider.
45. Glenn Lester Holden, ARM2c.
46. Rear-Admiral Maxwell F Leslie. (1902–85) b. Spokane, Washington, 24 October 1902. Educated Spokane North Central High School, Spokane, and University of Washington, Seattle. 1922 entered US Naval Academy, Annapolis, class of 1925. Graduated June 1926. 1926–7 service aboard the old 'Hog Islander' *Procyon* (AG-11), which was serving as flagship of training. Pacific Fleet. 1927–8 watch and divisional officer destroyer *McDermut* (DD-262). 1928 married Elizabeth Harris Black in Los Angeles, two sons Maxwell Franklin Jr and William Neil. 1929 Signals Officer battleship *Colorado* (BB-45). 1929–30 flight training NAS Pensacola. 1930–3 served in Observation Squadron Three aboard battleship *Oklahoma* (BB-37). 1933–5 flew with VP-4 PatRon (Patrol Squadron), Honolulu. 1935–7 aboard carrier *Ranger* (CV-4). 1937 senior naval aviator aboard heavy cruiser *Pensacola* (CA-24). Service baseball ace. 1938–40 Access Officer, NAS San Diego. 1940–2 XO then CO VB-3 aboard carrier *Saratoga* (CV-3) until torpedoed in January 1942. Shore-based Hawaii until April then embarked *Enterprise* (CV-6). 1942 CO VB-3 transferred to carrier *Yorktown* (CV-5) for Midway. June–October 1942, Commander AG 6 aboard carrier *Enterprise* again. Guadalcanal operations. October 1942–March 1943 CO NAS Daytona Beach. March–November 1943 CO NAGS (Naval Air Gunners School), Hollywood. November 1943–April 1944, graduated Army Navy Staff College. April to July 1944 instructor C&GSS Fort Leavenworth. July 1944 to January 1945 Operations Officer, Staff Commander for Land-based Air, TG 59.6, during invasion of western Carolines. January–November 1945, Air Support Control Unit officer for Peleliu, Okinawa and Iwo Jima invasions, planning invasion of Japan. November 1945–6 CO escort carrier *Windham Bay* (CVE-92). 1946–7 CO Naval Reserve Training Unit, NAS Miami then CO NAS Miami. 1947–8 Instructor Armed Forces Staff College, Norfolk. 1949 Graduated Armed Forces Staff College. 1948–50 CoS, ComFAir (Commander Fleet Air), Quonset Point. 1950–2 Head, Shore Establishment & Aviation Branch, OPNAV (Office of the Chief of Naval Operations)(412). CO NAS Barber's Point, Oahu. Detached September 1955 as member of Naval Examining Board and the Physical Disability Appeal Board, Navy Department. Retired July 1956 as captain, advanced to rank of rear-admiral on the basis of combat awards, which included the Navy Cross for Midway, Bronze Star Medal, Commendation Medal, Pacific Campaign Medal with eight stars, etc. Resided at Arlington, Virginia for a while. Served as technical advisor for the film *Battle of Midway*, although his advice would seem to have

137

make their assault on the nearer *Hiryū*. As the dive-bombers closed their target they observed that: – 'Its flight deck was covered with planes spotted aft'.[47]

Once the American dive-bombers were sighted by *Soryū*, steaming at a good speed[48] to avoid the torpedo bombers, her captain appeared to the SBD aircrews to swing her into a hard starboard turn, bringing her onto a southerly course.[49] As she did so her anti-aircraft guns opened up turning the carriers sides, 'into a veritable ring of flame'. But, oddly, despite their expectations of having to fight their way through, not a single A6M2 appeared to disturb the measured approach of Leslie's team. It was unexpected, it was eerie, but it was the opportunity of a lifetime.

Where Was the CAP?

Even at this critical juncture it would appear that at least one carrier, *Akagi*, was still landing some of her fighters to refuel and rearm as late as 1010, with the American torpedo-bombers of VT-3 actually in view. Nor was this done with much urgency.

There have been a lot of second-hand 'guesstimates' about how the Japanese air groups were working, but at least one American naval aviator gave a very precise and detailed account of *exactly* how they were operating at that critical time. Ensign Gay, from his unique viewpoint down at sea level, offers this insight into the way the Japanese CAP was conducting itself just prior the arrival of the SBDs; – if his account is considered credible evidence.

The Zeros were coming aboard and they'd circle way back behind the ship, have 1500 or 1000 feet altitude above her and coming straight in on their low gliding approach coming in straight and they weren't landing planes nearly as fast as we do. It seemed to be a slow operation. I don't know what kind of arresting gear they had aboard ships, it seemed to step them pretty well as soon as they hit the deck, must have had a number of wires because when they landed in all kinds of different places it would stop right off, but I

was a little bit interested in watching that, but I didn't care to do it at such close hand. They went right by me about 500 yards to the west of me and the cruiser that was with her [the carrier] was only a thousand yards, screen and I presume, went by about 500 yards to the east of me headed north and they circled back.[50]

Nevertheless, the 'Grand CAP' had thirty-six A6Ms aloft at 1010, which shortly afterward had been increased to forty-two. Were they *all* at nought feet chasing TBMs or at 5,500 feet duelling with Thach?

One group of three interceptors which certainly *ought* to have been at the correct altitude to intercept the SBDs were the Zeros that had been tardily launched by *Soryū* some twenty minutes earlier[51] in order to intercept the so-called 'horizontal bombing unit' which, after almost an hour, the Japanese had finally spotted orbiting aimlessly at 22,000 feet (in reality Lieutenant James S. Gray's ten impotent and now-departing F4F's of VF-6). It would have taken these three speedy Japanese fighter planes about eight minutes to reach even Gray's dizzy altitude, but Leslie was at least 7,000 feet lower than that, and the Zeros had the better part of twenty minutes to reach him. So why was there no waiting *shotai*?

This *shotai* vanishes from all American accounts of the morning battle at this stage, apparently quickly giving up the chase of the fast-disappearing Gray and turning away to deal with the threat 'developing to the south-east'[52], where Nagasawa subsequently perished in the ensuing combat.

Now, the combat in the south-east concerned the vain defence of the *Akagi* and the *Kaga* against McClusky's and Best's attentions, and that gives pause for thought. If a *Hiryū* defensive CAP had taken it upon itself, or possibly even been directed, to deal with another carrier's defence, where does that leave the prevailing wisdom that each carrier's *hikōchō* was only ever concerned with the defence of his own ship?

been mostly ignored. Died of cardiac arrest at his home in Coronado, California on 26 September 1985. Ashes scattered from the carrier *Ranger* (CV-61) off San Diego.

47. Captain Elliott Buckmaster to Admiral Chester A. Nimitz, *Report of Action for June 4, 1942 and June 6, 1942*, dated 18 June 1942. (CV5/A16-3 (CCR-10-oah).

48. Nagumo's own signal, timed at 1000, spelt it out, 'Our position is HE E A OO [the Japanese grid-coded location as they, like the Royal Navy used a grid system, which the Americans did not] course 30 degrees, speed 24 knots.'

49. Nagumo's signal.

50. Gay, *Narrative*.

51. Under the command of Petty Officer First Class Kaname Harada, with wingmen PO1c Takahashi Okamoto and PO3c Genzō Nagasawa. Harada not only survived the battle, but also the war, becoming an air ace with at least thirty 'kills' to his credit. At the age of over eighty he, a Pearl Habor as well as a Midway veteran, attended a ceremony held by the Japanese Imperial Navy Surviving Aviators Association aboard the museum ship carrier *Midway* moored at San Diego, on 21 May 2004.

52. Parshall & Tully, *Shattered Sword*.

The Attack on *Akagi*

As to the much-discussed state of the Japanese carriers at this crucial juncture, VB-3's Report of Action, is just as uncompromising as Fuchida's now much-derided account: 'Bombing Three commenced its approach from the north with the objective a very large carrier of about 25,000 tons believed to be the *Akagi*. Its flight deck was covered with planes spotted aft.[53]

The SBD attack very nearly went fatally astray at the start due to the inexperience of McClusky as a dive-bomber commander. Bill Vickrey stated:

Weber was one of Dick Best's wingmen that morning, when Dick, Bud Kroeger and Weber were the only ones to attack *Akagi*. There were some communications mix-ups in the *Enterprise* Air Group. McClusky gave an order for Gallaher to take one carrier and Best was to take the other. Dick did not get this message but sent one of his own saying, 'I am attacking according to doctrine.' McClusky had been a fighter pilot up until March (I think) of 1942[54] and did not understand dive-bomber doctrine. This made no difference, as he did not get Dick's message anyway. I have talked with most of the VB-6 pilots and rear seat men and none of them heard either message. When Dick comprehended the attack that McClusky was taking – and that he would have been taking 'according to doctrine' – it was too late for him to get his full squadron turned around so he took his own section – Best, Kroeger and Weber – and attacked *Akagi*. They got two hits (with 1,000 pound bombs) and one near miss.[55]

In his opinion, the decision-making of both Wade McClusky and Dick Best certainly deserved the Medal of Honor. They never received such acknowledgement of the part they played, although other men had received that distinction for far less.[56]

Another point made recently is that the assertion that Best radioed that he was 'attacking according to doctrine' does not ring true, as it was not a 'viable' radio message. However, it is only four words, which seems brief enough; and it may even be that in transcribing it later, a comma was misplaced and Best might have merely signalled 'Attacking', which was later described as 'Attacking, according to doctrine' – to explain it, but that the comma, or pause, was omitted.

Dick Best has left us with this detailed account of his attack.[57]

About that time, my left wingman ran out of oxygen and so informed me by hand transmitted Morse code. I started dropping down to 15,000 feet where he could be comfortable without the use of oxygen. This put me well below and ahead of the AGC [air group commander], so that when we sighted the Japanese carriers I was 5,000 feet under him. He assigned targets by radio, which I didn't receive. When abreast of the nearest carrier, I called him to say that I was attacking according to doctrine (i.e. leading aircraft take the far target and trailing planes take the nearer targets) and thus share the surprise. I turned toward the nearest carrier [*Kaga*], split to either side of my second and third divisions. When nearly over the target with my division in column, I started to open my dive flaps when right in front of me, and from above, the AGC and Scouting Six came pouring in. Furious at the foul-up, I tried to cause my squadron to rejoin, but without success, and I took my first section of three planes[58] toward the next carrier [*Akagi*].

I was at full throttle nose down so that when I

---

53. Bombing Squadron Three, *Report of Action – period 4 June 1942 to 6 June 1942, inclusive*, FVB-3/A16/nhn, dated 10 June, 1942.
54. The date of McClusky's appointment was, in fact, 21 March 1942.
55. Bill Vickrey to Clayton Fisher, 6 September 2006.
56. Vickrey revealed that Vice-Admiral Bill Houser, who had become Deputy Chief Naval Ordnance (Air) by the time he retired, had 'made a stab at getting a Medal of Honor for Best, but got nowhere'. e-mail, Vickrey to Fisher.
57. Lieutenant-Commander Richard Halsey Best (1910–2001). b. Bayonne, New Jersey. Graduated US Naval Academy Annapolis, 1932. Served aboard light cruiser *Richmond* (CL-9) 1932–4. 1934 flight training, earning wings 1935. 1936–8 with VF-2 ('Flying Chiefs'). Navy Flight School, Pensacola 1938–40, teaching instrument flying and evalu-

ating torpedo bomber tactics. Requested torpedo-bomber duty but instead was assigned to VB-6 aboard *Enterprise* (CV-6) 1940–2, serving at raids on Marshalls, Marcus and Wake and the Doolittle raid. Awarded Navy Cross for Midway also the DFC. Hospitalized at Pearl Harbor and underwent thirty-two months' treatment for TB. Retired from navy in 1944 with 100 per cent disability. He joined Douglas Aircraft for a while, and from 1947 joined the Rand Corporation, ending up as Security Manager. Between the ages of 32 and 42 spent four years in hospital. Member of the Order of Daedalians. Died 28 October 2001 at Santa Monica, aged 92. Interred at Arlington National Cemetery (Sec. 54, Lot 3192).
58. Best's wingmen were Lieutenant (jg) Edwin John Kroeger with Gail Wayne Halterman, RM3c (B-2) and Ensign Frederick Thomas Weber with Ernest Leonard Hilbert, AOM3c (B-3)

approached the push-over point, I was going too fast to open my dive flaps. Horsed up on the stick, I was at 14,000 feet before I slowed down sufficiently to open my flaps. With all of the violent manoeuvring, we were not detected and there was no AA fire or any other sign of awareness. We came in at a 70-degree dive angle released at 2,000 feet, and were cocked back at a steep climb angle to observe the bombing results. The first bomb hit forward of the bridge and tore up the deck. The second bomb hit the lead fighter on the fantail of a group of six or seven Zeros, which were in the process of launching (the first Zero ran through my bomb sight as I put my eye to the telescope at 3,500 feet).[59] The third bomb hit among the Zeros, and probably was the bomb that jammed the rudder and had the *Akagi* mindlessly circling as long as she stayed afloat.

As we exited, we flew through a covey of Zeros on the reverse course and apparently attempting to get in position ahead of a torpedo squadron still in tight formation. Our exit course was taking us directly to the carrier *Soryū* further to the east, which was under attack from Bombing Three from the *Yorktown*. The Japanese only credit four or five hits, though I thought it was nine or ten. It was completely engulfed in smoke and flames and erupting explosions as the bombs hit.

Best told me that although he considered himself a non-regular officer when the war started on 7 December 1941, he was instructed not to keep war diaries and not to take pictures in case of the loss of the *Enterprise* and a possible compromise of US operations. 'For some reason, I complied. My recollections are all from memory and not diaries or pictures,'[60] which is probably why recent re-evaluations totally discredit Best's eyewitness observations of the time.[61] Whichever version one prefers to believe,

there can be no nitpicking about the basic fact – Best's attack totally sealed the fate of Nagumo's flagship.

His wingman, Ed Kroeger[62], fixed his telescopic cross-hair right in the centre of the bright red 'meatball'[63] clearly defined against the bright yellow of the carrier's deck planking. Attacking across the target instead of along it, his aim was well off, his bomb clipping the port rim of the flight deck, just ahead of the bridge, and detonating close alongside. Weber's 1,000 pound bomb was also either a grazing hit or a very near miss on the port side, but right aft and the concussion did a lot of harm, the well-known 'water-hammer' effect causing heavy jarring and culminating in damage which brought about the subsequent jamming of the ship's port rudder thus rendering her *hors de combat*. Although they lost touch with Best, both these pilots evaded the attentions of the A6Ms and correctly used the ZB signal to find their way safely back to the *Enterprise*.

The Attack on *Kaga*

McClusky had already broken radio silence to report to *Enterprise* that he had made contact.[64] He assumed that Ring would have come to the same conclusion that he had concerning the enemy position and would soon also be attacking; he therefore thought it best to concentrate the two *Enterprise* SBD squadrons on two enemy carriers in order to ensure their destruction (he believed that the force he personally commanded could not satisfactory deal with more than two carriers, although this, as we have seen, was contrary to doctrine), leaving the others for *Hornet*'s dive-bombers to take out. McClusky therefore selected the two carriers closest to him in the line of approach and ordered VS-6 to follow the CEAG section in attacking the carrier, 'on the immediate left' and for VB-6 to deal with, 'the right-hand carrier'. McClusky commented: 'One remarkable fact

---

59. This was the aircraft of Petty Officer 1st class Koreo Kimura.
60. Lieutenant-Commander Richard H. Best to the author, 15 October 1996.
61. Parshall and Tully, *Shattered Sword*, credit Best's unit with only a single direct hit and two near misses which caused little or no damage, but the later version by Lundstrom, *Black Shoe Carrier Admiral*, upgrades this again to two 1,000 pound bomb hits and a damaging near miss.
62. Lieutenant (jg) Edwin John 'Bud' Kroeger.
63. This was the national marking, the *hinomaru*. These are the subject of endless anguished debate by modern-day modellers as to whether they were white circles blocked out with red or not. The SBD pilots seem to have had no doubts about their intensity of colour, and indeed many commented on the generosity of the Japanese in providing such perfect aiming points for them that morning.
64. Earlier, Lieutenant James S. Gray's signal that he was

returning to base with VF-3 had been mistaken on Spruance's bridge for a message from McClusky, which it was not. This led to the first of a series of hysterical outbursts from Miles Browning that were to intensify as the battle went on. He seized the microphone and, at 1008, screamed into it, 'McClusky attack, attack immediately!' He repeated this exhortation a minute later. McClusky, who had sighted the enemy at 1002, was probably nonplussed by all this, although he never actually transmitted the response attributed to him by Morison ('Wilco, as soon as I find the bastards', a typical piece of Morison journalese]. Incidentally, Lundstrom takes McClusky to task for failing to acknowledge Browning's enquiry of whether the enemy was in sight, (*Black Shoe Carrier Admiral*) citing it as an example of, 'a serious flaw'; but McClusky himself was quite clear that he *did* transmit a sighting report before attacking; 'This is McClusky. Have sighted the enemy.'

stood out as we approached the diving point – not a Jap fighter plane was there to molest us'.

CEAG then gave this account of his attack at 1022.

I started the attack, rolling in a half-roll and coming to a steep 70 degree dive. About halfway down, anti-aircraft fire began booming around us – our approach being a complete surprise up to that point. As we neared the bomb-dropping point, another stroke of luck met our eyes. Both enemy carriers had their decks full of planes, which had just returned from the attack on Midway. Later it was learned about the time we had discovered the Jap force, an enemy seaplane had detected our forces. Apparently then, the planes on deck were being refuelled and rearmed for an attack on our carriers. Supposing then we, Air Group Six, had turned southward toward Midway, as the *Hornet* group did, I can still vividly imagine the *Enterprise* and *Hornet* at the bottom of the sea as the *Yorktown* was some three days later.

In the meantime, our bombs began to hit home. I levelled off at masthead height, picked the widest opening in their screen and dropped to deck level, figuring any anti-aircraft fire aimed at me would also be aimed at their own ships. All their ships' fire must have been pretty busy because I was well through the screen before I noted bursting shells creeping up behind. With the throttle practically pushed through the instrument panel, I was fortunate in avoiding a contact with death by slight changes of altitude and varying the getaway course to right and left.[65]

Despite being set upon by a pair of enraged A6M2s as he made his escape, CEAG, by dint of good evasive flying and staunch work by his indefatigable rear-gunner[66], who managed to shoot down one of their attackers and force the other to break off, escaped intact, even though they had been hit no less than fifty-five times.

When McClusky had led the command section down, his number two wingman, Floyd Adkins, fully expected him to postpone his section's dive in order to enable them to take some good photographs of the target under attack and the results, but McClusky powered on down without hesitation at 1022 leaving Adkins out of sequence, and in the end he went in as third man after Jacard.[67] The latter, equally flummoxed, lowered his undercarriage instead of his split-flaps, but went on down anyway and Adkins followed him.

After Best's section of three aircraft had attacked *Akagi*, the rest of VB-6 followed VS-6. Lieutenant Gallaher[68] was the CO of VS-6 and he led his fourteen SBDs down following hard on McClusky. The CO risked 'hanging' his aircraft after bomb-release to observe results, something he had repeatedly warned his pilots *not* to do! He glanced astern and was rewarded with the sight of the detonation that followed his 500 pound bomb thumping fair and square into *Kaga*'s deck aft, fitting revenge, he felt, for the total destruction of his very first ship, the battleship *Arizona*, at Pearl Harbor six months earlier. Further near misses and yet more hits followed in rapid succession as *Kaga* was totally overwhelmed by the scale of the assault on her. At least five known direct hits have been recorded and there may possibly have been more.[69]

---

65. Rear-Admiral Wade C. McClusky, Jr, unpublished article, 'The Midway Story.'
66. Walter George Chochalousek, ARM1c.
67. Adkins later developed film which only revealed lots and lots of empty ocean, while Jacard's camera film was quickly taken from his aircraft after he landed safely back aboard and was never seen again! If anyone developed prints of the *Kaga* under fire, then they are still sitting on them and both the National Air and Space Museum and Naval Historical Center deny all knowledge of their whereabouts. There is a 'conspiracy' theory attached to this disappearance (as always) but to me it smacks more of incompetence. The Japanese photographs of the on-board damage to the carriers either went down with the ships or was suppressed and destroyed by the IJN censorship; and here there really was a conspiracy involved, but it was a 'face-saving' one by the navy and directed against the Imperial Japanese Army (IJA) and the Japanese public.
68. Rear-Admiral Wilmer Earl Gallaher (1907–83) b. 9 May 1907, Richardson Park, Wilmington, New Castle, Delaware. Graduated US Naval Academy, Annapolis, 1931. Initial sea-going service as ensign aboard the battleship *Arizona*

(BB-39). Commissioned as lieutenant in June 1939 and spent seventeen months aboard *Enterprise* (CV-6). Was XO of VS-6 in 1942. Awarded the Navy Cross of Midway. No further combat post-Midway due to the back sprain brought about by his attack on *Kaga*. Commander NAS Panama and NAS San Diego. 1 August 1950 promoted to commander. 1 November 1959 retired from service as rear-admiral. Resided at Kensington, Maryland. Taught NJROTC (Naval Junior Reserve Officers Training School) at Maryland High School in 1968. Died from cancer at North Bethesda, Montgomery, Maryland, 4 February 1983.

69. For example, Kleiss said that, in addition to Gallaher's hit, 'at least two more direct hits were scored by the first division', that the Second Division leader scored a direct hit and that 'at least two other hits were scored by this division'. While recording that none of the pilots of the Third Division returned from the attack, 'the second division leader stated that the third division made at last one direct hit'. (Kleiss, VS-7 *Log of the War*). Ensign John Quincy Roberts followed Gallaher down. He had the reputation of being a not-so-hot pilot and had pleaded to be included on the mission, telling Gallaher that he would land his bomb aboard an enemy

141

One telling blow was delivered by 'Dusty' Kleiss[70]. He hailed from Coffeyville, Kansas, the town whose straight-shooting citizens had unceremoniously stopped dead (literally!) the Dalton Gang back in 1892.[71] He was to demonstrate the Coffeyville tradition for accuracy[72], on the *Kaga* at Midway that morning. Kleiss was fourth in line in the dive; he recalled:

The skipper put a direct hit on the stern on a group of planes just about to be launched. By the time I was ready to drop bombs the after half of the ship was in flames 50 feet high. One more hit might have been made amidships or the fire may have spread. Anyhow the bow with a big red circle was intact. I released a 500 lb bomb at 1500 feet (instead of the usual 2500 feet) my two 100 lb incendiaries at 1000 feet. When I glanced back (I barely managed to make the pull out because I dived so low to be sure and hit) I saw an explosion in progress on the big red circle, or rather a big one and a little one of greater intensity. A second later the entire ship was a mass of flames 100 feet high.

Kleiss placed the *Kaga* at the time of his attack as in 30° 15' N, 118° 45' W.

One fighter attempted to shoot me on the pull-out but Snowden, my gunner, chased him away. Meanwhile a second carrier nearby had burst into flames after an attack by Bombing Six. They were beautiful sights, like a haystack in flames. Fires 300 feet high. The steel red hot. I circled wide around the formation; One DD fired a few ineffective shots. I continued the large circle.

One more fighter came close, took a look down Snowden's guns, and left. Then, about ten minutes after the attack, a large explosion on the *Kaga* amidships. Rockets of flame, pieces of steel bolted upward to about three or four thousand feet. I then tried to join a section of our new pilots, Michele[73], etc., but they thought I was a Jap, poured on the soup, and pulled away. I decided the protection wasn't worth the waste of gas (I had barely enough to reach the ship) so I throttled back to 110 kts and chugged toward Midway.

Both carriers were burning better than ever. The one which hadn't exploded was down by the bow or stern. One other ship – couldn't tell whether it was a CV or BB because it was a solid mass of flames[74] – was also on fire. The ship we bombed then sent up a huge brown cloud of smoke, the smoke separated itself from the ship, and I could not see the ship no longer

---

carrier, even if he had to take it aboard. He was as good as his word, but he never pulled out of his attack dive. (Gallaher to Bard, interview 30 June 1966.)

70. Captain Norman Jack 'Dusty' Kleiss, Sr. (b. 1916). b. 7 March 1916 in Coffeyville, Kansas. Aged fifteen joined the 114th Cavalry, Kansas National Guard, Fort Riley. 'In exercises the Red Team wiped us out. They had an airplane and we didn't. I decided that airplanes were the wave of the future.' Worked as an apprentice toolmaker as a young man while waiting to join the US Naval Academy. Graduated in June 1938. As a midshipman served on gunnery team aboard the battleship *Arkansas* (BB-33). Also flew military aircraft from Scott Field, at Bolling Field, Washington DC and had crewed a Martin PM-1 seaplane at Annapolis. Was handed his commission as an ensign by President Franklin D. Roosevelt himself. On leave flew a tri-motor Ford and Beechcraft stagger-wing aircraft with Inmann Brothers Flying Circus. Turret officer aboard heavy cruiser *Vincennes* (CA-44) and then aboard the destroyer *Yarnal* (DD-143), before she was handed over to the Royal Navy in 1940, then the *Goff* (DD-247) in 1940 on the Atlantic 'Neutrality' patrols, for his compulsory two year's sea-time. Flight training at NAS Pensacola followed, in N3N basic trainers, then at NAS Opra Locka, on Boeing F4B-5s. Assigned to VS-6 in May 1941, flying the Curtiss SBC biplane dive-bomber, later replaced by the SBD. Promoted to Lieutenant (jg) in June 1941. Remained aboard the *Enterprise* (CV-6) for two years, serving all through the first seven months of the Pacific War, island raids and the Doolittle raid, culminating

in Midway, where he won the Distinguished Flying Cross. Also awarded the Navy Cross. Returned to the USA in June 1942 and married Jean Mochon in July. Became instructor at NAS Cecil Field, training dive-bomber pilots. US Navy Postgraduate School and CalTech followed, obtaining masters and professional engineering degrees. Assigned aeronautical engineer with speciality in structures at BuAer, Burbank, working with Lockheed's Colonel Greenbank and Kelly Johnsons 'Skunk Works', as well as Ed Heinemann of Douglas. Served with Ship Installation Division of BuAer on Fresnel Landing Light System. Retired from Navy in 1968 after thirty years' service and started work for Hercules Powder on the Polaris missile programme two days later. Now retired and living near San Antonio, Texas, where I interviewed him in March 2006.

71. The notorious Dalton Gang attempted to rob two Coffeyville banks, the First National Bank and C. M. Condon Bank, on 5 October 1892. Led by US Marshal Connelly, the citizens of the town fought back. In the ensuing slaughter, four of the gang were killed and a fifth wounded, while the Marshal and three citizens were also killed.

72. Kleiss reminisced that as a youngster he had learned to shoot a BB gun before he could ride a bicycle. 'My best friend across the street, Earl Alfonso Rosebush, could shoot a jackrabbit, using a pistol, while driving a Chandler automobile along a country road. My Aunt Helen Ruthrauff was Women's Shotgun Champion of Kansas.'

73. Ensign Vernon Larsen Michele, A-V(N).

74. In fact, the *Hiryū*.

so presumed it was sunk. The other fires were visible at least 30 miles away.[75]

Lieutenant Harold S. Bottomley remembered first and foremost:

I was scared to death! We were at about 14,000 feet, climbing in formation, making our approach toward high-speed wakes, which gradually grew into a vast armada of carriers, battleships, cruisers and then destroyers across the horizon. The cold of the cockpit at that altitude was compounded by shivers of dread and anticipation that ran up and down my spine and made my teeth chatter.

Getting set for the attack dive 'gave me something else to think about', and soon he was lined up and ready.

The carrier is steady on course into the wind to launch aircraft. What an ideal situation! My plane is steady. My gunsight is steady, leading the red ball on the carrier's bow. Paul Holmberg's bomb explodes right smack on the forward elevator! A plane taking off just ahead of it is flipped like a matchstick. The carrier has a full deck load. I am number four in the dive!

I glance again at the altimeter passing through 3,000 feet, then back to the sight, and press the bomb release button switch, then reach and pull the manual release toggle. I know I can't miss! I pull the stick back into my gut, close the dive brakes; and as the plane starts coming out of the dive, jam on full throttle! 'Let's get the hell out of here', as I bank the plane toward open water.

Meanwhile Johnson has a perfect view. 'We got her,' he shouts into the intercom. I cannot resist sneaking a look back to see the target completely enveloped in flames as bombs explode in the pack of massed aircraft.[76]

Tenth off into the stack was Ensign McCarthy[77], and he also enjoyed a dive free from interference from defending fighters. However, that all rapidly changed once he had pulled out of his dive at around 500 feet. McCarthy was forced to abandon any attempt to rejoin the squadron XO, Lieutenant Dickinson[78], his divisional leader, at the squadron rendezvous point, by a shouted warning from his rear gunner[79] that an A6M2 was fast climbing up toward them from near sea level determined to hack them down. Abandoning laid-down section defence tactics, McCarthy hit the deck and waited until the angry Zero was lined up ready to shoot, then turned hard left on his gunner's warning, taking extreme avoiding action. Return fire from the SBD was effective, and the fighter was last seen on fire and apparently attempting to ditch up-wind. McCarthy then sought company and some sort of mutual fire protection.

Such a group was being led by Lieutenant Ware[80], the Flight Officer of VS-6 who, on completion of his own dive, had bravely made a slow-speed withdrawal to enable less experienced pilots to form up on him for the long haul back to the carrier. He drew to him four novices[81] and McCarthy joined up with this little band. They formed two sections and lowered both altitude and speed, first to 115 and then to 105 knots. Thus the dive-bombers could both concentrate their defensive fire and try to eke out their rapidly-vanishing avgas reserves. This doughty half-dozen SBDs drew vengeful Zekes down on their heads in droves, and their attacks continued for about a quarter of an hour, but they were beaten off without loss. Eventually the frustrated Japanese gave up and broke off to try and find if any deck was left for them to alight on. Ware concentrated on extracting his charges, scribing a large circle from north of the Nagumo force and gradually heading them around to the south.

En route, around 1115, the six SBDs stumbled crossed the path of *Hiryū*'s counter-strike, eighteen D3A dive-bombers escorted by six Zeros, under the command of Lieutenant Michio Kobayashi[82], which had been despatched at 1057. The site of Ware's force proved too much temptation for the aggressive Zero pilots, who mistook them for yet more TBDs, and their leader, Lieutenant Yoshuhiro

75. Kleiss, *Log of the War.*
76. Lieutenant Harold S. Bottomley, then living at Coronado, California, remembering Midway in unpublished document, *Looking Back Forty Years at the Battle of Midway 4–7 June 1942, as told by some of the men who fought for the United States of America against the Empire of Japan*, edited and compiled by Lee Fleming Reese, M.A., 1982, cited hereafter as Reese, *Looking Back.*
77. Ensign John Reginald McCarthy.
78. Lieutenant Clarence Earle Dickinson, Jr.
79. Earl E. Howell, ARM2c.
80. Lieutenant Charles Rollins Ware.
81. Ensign James Arnold Shelton, USNR, Ensign Carl David Peiffer, A-V (N), USNR, Ensign John Cady Lough, A-V (B), USNR, and Ensign Frank Woodrow O'Flaherty, A-V (N), USNR. They had been in the squadron less than four months and this sortie was their first time in action.
82. Lieutenant Michio Kobayashi (1914–42). b. 28 October 1914 at Fuirukawa, Sasebo. 1934, Naval Academy, Etajima, 23rd Class, graduated midshipman 1937. Flight training 1938. Became *buntaicho* 1st *shotai*, *Hiryū* at Midway. Killed in attack on *Yorktown* 4 June 1942.

Shigematsu[83], signalled for his *kansen* to break off and dispose of the enemy. Ware repeated the earlier successful tactic, figuratively again 'circling the wagons' and letting the angry Zekes dash themselves in succession against the twelve .50s. Two of the A6M2s were so damaged that they had to return to their carrier, the other four finally broke off to resume their escort duties and, at the end of it, yet again, not a single SBD had been lost.

All this was very well done, but now tragedy overtook the little band. McCarthy and Ware held a hand-signal conversation about the best course to adopt, which ended in the force breaking up; McCarthy turned to starboard and another pilot, Lough, also turned right on an even more radical heading while Ware continued on with Pfeiffer, O'Flaherty and Shelton. Within a quarter of an hour all three units had lost visual contact, and, sadly, only McCarthy survived the final leg home. He climbed, but could not pick up *Enterprise*'s YE until finally his rear-seat man managed to home in on that of the *Yorktown*. Even so the Dauntless was finally forced to ditch outside TF17's screen but both men were rescued by the destroyer *Hamman*. No trace was ever found of the other five SBDs who had fought so hard and bravely to survive.[84]

Meanwhile VB-6 had followed the bulk of VS-6 into action. Lieutenant Joe Penland[85] led the Second Division. He reported: 'enemy disposition sighted to northward, distance 40 miles'. They reduced altitude to 15,000 feet during their approach and the enemy turned south. 'Enemy ships scattered and circled at high speed during attack, general course southerly'. Penland reported: '2 CVs hit; each by several bombs; huge fires on both; one of these first hit by VS-6; a third CV hit by VB-3'. Pulling out at about 500 feet Penland 'Retired to NW', swinging around 'through North to a course for Midway (120°)' thence to ship'. All the time they were under heavy attack, the A6Ms engaging the dive-bombers as they pulled-out. 'Retirement was made at 500–100 feet altitude.'

Penland described his attackers: 'Fighters were khaki colored, marked with three red stripes on fuselage beside wing marking's. Tactics used by the CAP were described as 'variable'. 'The general rule was for them to gain altitude several thousand feet above and to rear of SBD formation and then to make a dive run (or nearly so), either slightly above or on our own level'. Some of the Zeros 'pulled out early when encountering free gun fire'; another made a 'lone run from astern, fired and continued past' below them. 'He was fired on by our fixed guns'. Several attacks of this type took place and continued until the SBDs were about 20 miles from the enemy fleet. While some fighters 'would not press home attacks', others 'were very aggressive'. The Zeros used .50 calibre and 20mm cannon. The Dauntless kept flying through a whole string of damaging hits; for example Penland recorded that SBD 6-B-16 received hits in propellor, elevator torque tube, fuselage frame 17, wings antennae, rubber boat, rear-seat parachute and radio; the left main fuel tank was penetrated at the after side by a machine-gun bullet, but sealed itself effectively.[86]

The disposition of the four Japanese carriers of the *Kidō Butai* at the time of this seminal attack as viewed by Lieutenant Penland, and sketched by him in his battle report, is shown in Diagram 6. This layout is considerably at variance with the many post-war interpretations; three carriers are seen heading south-west, while the fourth, VB-3's target, is steering a diametrically opposite course, north-east; one torpedo bomber group, VT-3, is seen actually under attack from the CAP. Many will dispute this observation, but this is what was actually observed by the commander of VB-3 at the time, and deserves to be preserved for posterity.

Another thing that ought to have been preserved for posterity were the photographs taken by one VB-6 SBD, about the only one with the presence of mind to use their on-board camera to record the attack. The team concerned was Lieutenant (jg) Wilbur E. Roberts[87], and W. B. Steinman, AMM1c[88]. Steinman confirmed that he took a sequence of photographs of one of the Japanese carriers, probably *Kaga*. Unfortunately, Roberts was forced to get down aboard the wrong carrier due to fuel exhaustion, smacking down on the *Yorktown*'s deck just before the she underwent the first attack by *Hiryū*'s dive-bombers. Bustled out of the way in the subsequent action, Roberts

83. Lieutenant Yosuhiro Shigematsu (1919–44). Naval Academy Etamjima, 24th Class, graduated midshipman 1938. Flight training, qualified April 1941. Assigned to *Hiryū* Air Group. January 1942 *bontaicho,* 2nd *chūtai.* Survived Midway, joined carrier *Junyō* and fought at Battle of Santa Cruz October 1942, (two missions). *Hikōtaichō* of 263rd Air Group in July 1944. Led force of six aircraft from Marianas *en route* to Palau on 8 July 1944. Intercepted by F6F Hellcats of VF-31 flying from carrier *Cabot* (CVL-28) near Yap Island and killed. He had at least ten confirmed 'kills' to his credit at the time of his death.

84. The full story of Ware's last fight was researched and later publicly posted on the Internet as *The Last Flight of Charles R. Ware* (http://216.65.20.88/midway/horan.html) by that outstanding aeronautical historian Mark Horan, and I fully acknowledge my indebtedness to him for preserving this unique facet of Midway history.

85. J. R. Penland, USN.

86. Lieutenant J. R. Penland, Combat Report, NND968133, held at National Archives, College Park, Maryland.

87. Lieutenant (jg) Wilbur Edison Roberts, A-V (N).

88. William Burr Steinman, AMM1c.

Diagram 10. 1st
SBD attack 4 June
1942. As recorded at
the time by J. R.
Penland, Lieutenant
US Navy, Commander,
VB-6

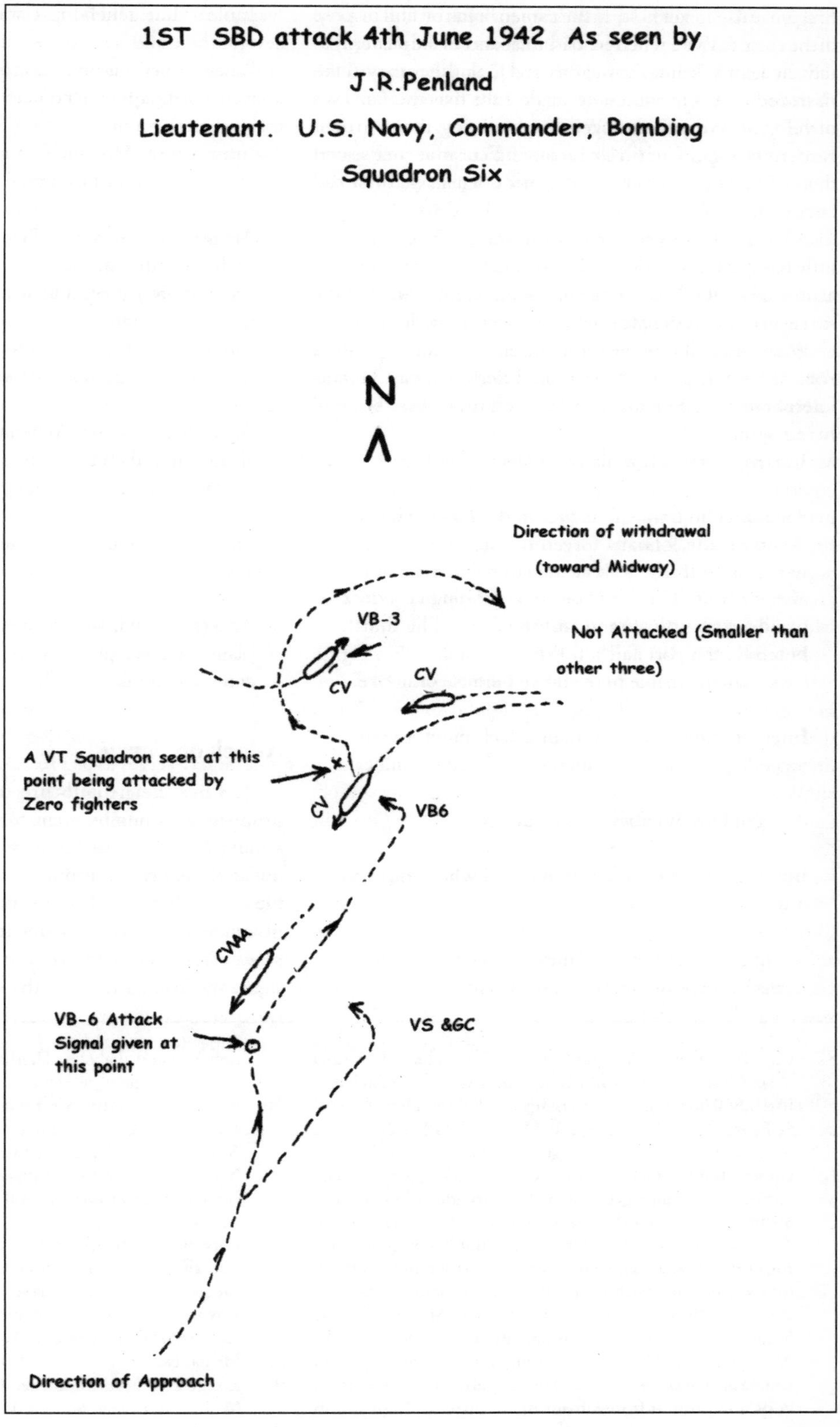

1ST SBD attack 4th June 1942 As seen by

J.R.Penland

Lieutenant. U.S. Navy, Commander, Bombing

Squadron Six

N
∧

Direction of withdrawal

(toward Midway)

VB-3

Not Attacked (Smaller than

other three)

CV

CV

A VT Squadron seen at this
point being attacked by
Zero fighters

CV

VB6

CVA

VB-6 Attack
Signal given at
this point

VS &GC

Direction of Approach

had the sense to get hold of the camera and the film to keep them secure. Even when he had to abandon ship later that day, he kept a firm hold on both and took them aboard the *Portland* (CA-45), where he made sure that the film was developed and printed. While examining these prints, Roberts was approached by a senior officer who confiscated them all! Roberts never saw the prints again, and nor did anyone else. Whoever took them and hid (or destroyed them), will probably be cursed by historians for eternity, for he was never tracked down. The resulting prints might have answered a lot of questions and saved many gallons of ink and acrimonious debate down the succeeding decades!

What was it like on the receiving end? Captain Takahisa Amagai[89] was the Air Officer aboard *Kaga* that day. He was interrogated on 6 October 1945[90] and these were some of his answers.

Interrogator[91]: 'How many bombs hit the *Kaga*?

Amagai: There were four hits on the *Kaga*. The first bomb hit the forward elevator. The second bomb went through the deck at the starboard side of the after elevator. The third bomb went through the deck on the port side abreast of the island. The fourth bomb hit the port side aft. When the bombs hit, big fires started. Unable to see much because of smoke.

Interrogator: Which type of attack most feared – torpedo plane, dive bomber, or horizontal bomber?

Amagai: Dive bomber, cannot dodge.

Interrogator: Were planes on board when ship was hit?

Amagai: Yes, about 30 planes in hangar loaded and fuelled, *remainder on deck*[92], six VF in air.

Interrogator: Did bombs sink the ship?

Amagai: Yes, gasoline and bombs caught fire. Ship sank itself, Japanese no need sink with torpedo.

Interrogator: How many protective fighters [CAP] were over carrier formation?

Amagai: Normally 28. Two carriers supplied eight each, the other two carriers provided six each. This was normal patrol, if attacked, other planes rose to meet opposition.

Interrogator; How long did fighters stay in air, and how were planes in air relieved?

Amagai: Two hours. When the waiting planes get in air up high, then the former patrolling plane comes down and lands.

Interrogator: How are fighter planes controlled in the air?

Amagai: By wireless. A special officer controls the planes. He is a pilot, in his absence the anti-aircraft commander takes his place.

Attack on *Soryū*

With VB-3, Leslie and three other pilots[93] had already dropped their bombs prematurely by using the electronic arming device. Under this new system the pilot electrically initiated the precise arming as well as the actual release of the bomb. When VB-3 pushed the button, due to faulty installation, the wrong sequence was set in train and the bomb release was triggered. For bomb release, the electrical signal was routed through the weapons system circuits to

---

89. Captain Takahisa Amagai (1902–83). Graduated Etajima (51st Class) 1924. Spent twenty-one years in the navy and had 2,500 hours' flying experience. Air Officer aboard *Hiryū* at Pearl Harbor and *Kaga* at Midway.1942–4 Naval Air Service HQ, Tokyo, in charge of the CV flight-deck installations. 1944–5 CO 634th Air Group. First Japanese naval officer to be interrogated after the surrender of Japan. His testimony has been dismissed as untrue by many modern American historians and researchers, but his original interrogators noted: 'Did not volunteer information but answered direct questions without hesitation. His statements were confirmed by subsequent interrogations.' After the war he became a successful businessman and finally retired on his 65th birthday. He then ran a mathematics and English language school, which was very popular and he remained very busy but suffered from heart disease, high blood pressure and diabetes. Died at on 15 December 1983 of a cerebrouvascular incident.

90. See United States Strategic Bombing Survey (Pacific). *Interrogations of Japanese Officials* (CPNAV-P-03–100) Naval Analysis Division, Interrogation NAV No 1. USSB No. 6 *The Battle of Midway*, Tokyo, 6 October 1945. *Interrogation of Captain AMAGAI, Takahisa, IJN, Naval Aviator*.

91. Captain C. Shands. Other Allied officers present were: Captain S. Teller, USN; Captain J. S. Russel, USN; Lieutenant-Colonel Parry, USA; Commander J. T. Hayward, USN; Commander T. H. Moorer, USN; Lieutenant-Commander J. A. Field, Jr, USNR.

92. My italics.

93. Ensign Roy Maurice Isaman (B-8), Ensign Charles S. Lane (B-11) and Ensign Milford Austin Merrill (B-17).

the bomb rack. This particular signal activated a solenoid which in turn activated the release linkage in the bomb rack. This caused the suspension hooks to open, letting the weapon fall away from the aircraft. There were thus several stages at which this delicate chain of electronics might fail but unfortunately that part worked perfectly and away went the bomb![94]

Until just prior to the Battle of Midway, bomb fuse delay (AD = 1/100 second), bomb arming, as well as bomb release, had all been done mechanically. Fortunately for the Americans, and possibly the very outcome of the battle, even when the electrical bomb release system had been fitted to the SBDs, the mechanical system was retained as a back-up.[95] The Midway experience ensured that this mechanical apparatus was retained in place for the rest of the war.

However, on the morning of 4 June, when the VB-3 pilots began to set this arming device in motion, the bombs immediately dropped. Leslie broke radio silence to yell 'Don't use the damn electronic device – arm the bombs manually', which all of the other thirteen pilots did. The outcome of the Battle of Midway might have been different if all of VB-3 had prematurely dropped their bombs. The American carriers would have had to contend with both *Hiryū* and *Soryū*, the latter sporting the incomparable Lieutenant-Commander Takashige Egusa and his dive-bomber elite, who were just raring to be unleashed.

Bomb or no bomb, Leslie determined to lead his unit into battle and started a descent to 14,500 feet. Their target had still apparently not sighted them and, at 1023, turned to starboard to bring her into the wind in readiness for launching further fighters. Two minutes later Leslie initiated a perfect dive-bombing run along the whole length of the *Soryū* fore and aft, as per the book. Leslie had to content himself with venting his frustration by strafing with his forward-firing guns from a height of 10,000 feet down to about 4,000 feet. Unfortunately he kept his button pushed

down continually the whole time and the weapons jammed.

Second off the stack behind Leslie's First Division was Lieutenant (jg) 'Lefty' Holmberg[96], and he described his method to me.

Fortunately for our dive bomber squadron, enemy fighters were remaining at low altitudes as we approached, to cope with our torpedo plane attack taking place *at the same time.*[97] Therefore, we had no air opposition while proceeding to a point over our selected target at about 24,000 feet altitude. In the initial part of our dive (down to 12,000 feet) our flight path (dive) was at about 70 degrees (20 degrees less than vertical). This tactic enabled us to expedite the attack as no enemy opposition appeared. In the vertical phase, from 12,000 feet down to bomb release, I was concentrating on adjusting the aircraft's heading to keep the cross hairs of my telescope bomb sight on a red ball painted on the forward part of the flight deck on the target ship. I concentrated on two things at this juncture; one was to watch the altimeter for 1,500 feet coming up, the other was to push the electric bomb release button, and, at the same time, pull the manual bomb release lanyard at 1,500 feet altitude. I did this to make doubly sure my bomb was released!

Next, I concentrated on pulling out of my dive so that I would be just skimming the water when I regained the horizontal flight when my gunner (my rear-seat man[98]) shouted joyously over the intercom that my bomb had struck the target and that I should look back to see. I did so with satisfaction – but just for a moment, for then I concerned myself with evading ship's gunfire that manifested itself by shell splashes in the water in my vicinity.[99]

Holmberg thought his target was the *Kaga*, and this is what he told me, but she was in fact the *Soryū*.[100] His method

---

94. Leslie commented in 1982: 'The new mechanisms were set on "safe" prior to take-off, and we believed that they released the bombs when they were set on "armed" once we were in flight. In any event, we proceeded to the target, minus four of our most effective weapons.'

95. See 'Naval Aviation in WW II', in *Naval Aviation News*, July-August 1991.

96. Rear-Admiral Paul Algodte 'Lefty' Holmberg (1915–86). b. Stanberry, Brunswick, Missouri 18 April 1915. Student at University of Missouri, graduating 1935. BS in Electrical Engineering from Massachusetts Institute of Technology (MIT). US Naval Academy, Annapolis. Graduated and commissioned as ensign 1939. Flight training and awarded wing as naval aviator 1941. Married Louise Gallagher 7 February 1942, by whom he had five children (Louise, Marty

Patricia, Carl Christopher, Kathleen Mildred and Marta Ellen). Fought at Midway and at Guadalcanal 1942. Awarded two Navy Crosses in World War II. Specialized in aeronautical engineering. MS in Aeronautical Engineering from MIT1947. Assistant Commander Research and Technical Group, Naval Air Systems Command. Advanced in rank to become rear-admiral in1965. Student Harvard Business School 1964. Retired in 1971. Naval Commemorative Medal. Died at his home in Arlington, Virginia. July 1986. Holmberg Fairways Gold Club named in his honour.

97. My italics.

98. George Albert LaPlant, AMM2c.

99. Rear-Admiral Paul A. Holmberg to the author, 5 June 1977.

100. VB-3's *Report of Action*, states that Holmberg's bomb

was followed by succeeding pilots who had bombs, while Leslie's example was followed by those who did not. An estimated five direct hits and three near misses were claimed in this devastating attack.[101]

The last of VB-3's dive-bombers were the two aircraft of the Third Division, led by the squadron's Personnel Officer, Lieutenant (jg) Osborne B. Wiseman. Seeing the carrier was well hit, Wiseman and his lone wingman, Ensign John C. Butler, turned their attentions to the battleship *Haruna*, but could only manage a near-miss which, if it ruffled the old lady's dignity a little, caused her no damage whatsoever. Another section[102], two of whom still had bombs to utilize, turned their attentions to the destroyer *Isokaze* and claimed to have hit her aft, but this was not the case and, like *Haruna*, the little ship also suffered no ill-effects from the single close miss.

Although VB-3 did not loose anyone in their morning attack on *Soryū*, they *did* lose several through fuel starvation on the way home. Both Leslie and Holmberg were forced to ditch alongside the heavy cruiser *Astoria*. They may well have made the *Enterprise*'s flight deck had they not tarried and circled over torpedoman Bill Esders, who was down in the water, in order to direct a destroyer to his location, in which they were successful.

Mass illusion?

A final thought. Conventional wisdom is now almost united that the many reports by the attacking SBD aircrew that told of the Japanese carriers' flight decks being packed with their aircraft just waiting to take off were false. Certainly Fuchida's classic account has been tossed in the dustbin of history and the man branded as, at best, a charlatan, 'a man with an agenda'.[103] Even if one accepts this reappraisal as accurate, however, how does one account for so many American eyewitness descriptions? A photograph taken by the B17s clearly showed only a few fighter aircraft on a carrier deck at 0800, but did that mean that they were not there almost two and a half hours later? Parshall and Tully have painstakingly recreated fighter aircraft movements for all four carriers in those fateful 177 minutes which seem conclusively to prove that they could not have been. But just where does that leave the veracity of the SBD aircrew that reported otherwise? Are they too, to be accused of having

'agendas' or did they, as has been suggested, just see what they expected or wanted to see?[104] Not everyone is totally convinced. Bill Vickrey for one, was to muse: – 'Too many pilots and gunners have told me that the decks were covered with aircraft which were fully loaded with fuel and that is the main reason they exploded so quickly'.[105]

And it is not just American pilots. Forget Fuchida, if he is suspect. What are we to make of Commander Hisashi Ohara, the XO of the *Soryū*, who commented: 'Our planes were being made ready for a second sortie and were all lined up on the flight deck ready to take off'. It was with just such thoughts in mind that I questioned four surviving Japanese pilots of the battle when I visited Japan in November 2005. I asked all four of them, specifically whether any of the Kates or Vals were being readied up on deck when the SBDs attacked; all seemed certain in their minds that none were. Even allowing for the long passage of years, these views have to command respect.

The Funeral Pyres of Japan's Hopes

The three Japanese carriers burned. The memory of all who witnessed their sudden and total undoing was indelibly that of overwhelming, indeed all-consuming, fire and flame.

All the nations that operated aircraft carriers were only too aware of just how vulnerable they were. Much of the distain that 'battleship admirals' had for aircraft carriers, and indeed operating aircraft from ships in general, was due to their perceived vulnerability. There was a justifiable mistrust and fear of such an obvious hazard to any ship's safety, which reinforced the other prejudices most seamen (but obviously not aviators), had. Fire at sea has for centuries been the sailor's worst fear. To a dyed-in-the-wool naval officer, obsessed with protection, aircraft were a provocation, blatantly ignoring years of hard-learned sea-lore. The aircraft carrier herself merely epitomized that danger. Huge yet fragile targets for the most part un-armoured and full of combustibles, they seemed to defy normal naval logic. Aboard these vulnerable beasts were yet more invitations to disaster, the aircraft themselves, packed wingtip-to-wingtip; bombs and torpedoes, at best a terrible concentration of destructive risk but in the midst of the confused arming and rearming fiasco of 4 June, strewn

---

'exploded directly in the midst of the spotted planes, turning the after part of the flight deck into sheets of flames. A fighter was blown over the side as it was being launched.'

101. The Japanese report, however, only credits the SBDs with three direct hits, one amidships, one just ahead of the forward elevator and one among the Zeros spotted on her after deck.

102. Ensign Robert Martin Elder (B-14), Ensign Bunyon Randolph 'Randy' Cooner (B-15) and Ensign Milford Austin Merrill (B-17).

103. Parshall and Tully, *Shattered Sword*.

104. *Ibid*, pp 231.

105. Vickrey to Fisher, 9 September 2004. Reproduced by permission of Clayton Fisher.

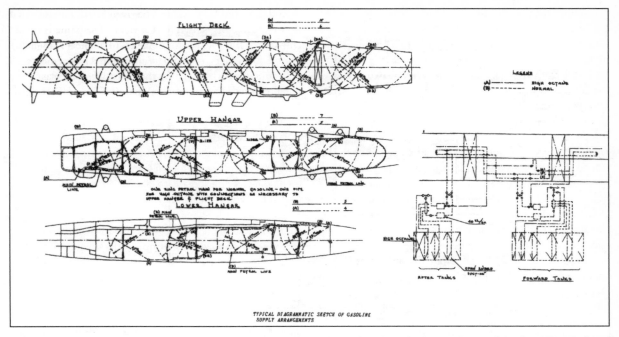

Diagram 4. Japanese carriers – Diagramatic Sketch of Typical Gasoline Supply Arrangements, based on *Unryū* class ships: (US Naval Technical Mission)

around and unsecured a major danger; and, above all, fuel and oil, a whole network of liquid dynamite needing but a spark to unleash its potency.

The aircraft carrier's overwhelming strength was that she could project power far beyond the mightiest gun, but that was her one and only function. Once her aircraft were neutered, either away on their missions, or struck down while being rearmed or refuelled, even the mightiest aircraft-carrier was impotent. The British had earlier discovered the vulnerability of these ships if caught in such a situation, which, in truth, was part and parcel of their very existence. Early in the war, in June 1940, the carrier *Glorious* was caught by the German battle-cruisers *Scharnhorst* and *Gneisenau,* with none of the scorned heavy ships in company to protect her and, once her two escorting destroyers had sacrificed themselves in vain, was quickly reduced to scrap, totally unable to defend herself. The British were extremely reluctant to allow that particular scenario to develop again. But against the dive-bomber, early warning and fighter aircraft offered some limited protection if the fighters were in the right place, which meant the right height and the right distance to knock out all the enemy attackers, for any that got through could do lethal damage. On the morning of 4 June the dive-bombers had *all* got through unopposed. The result was predictable.

If it could not be prevented then just how did the Japanese envisage coping with such an outcome? Normally, bomb and torpedo handling were afforded the safest routines that could be conceived. Both types of ordnance were stowed in separate flash-proof compartments in the ship's hold. Most carriers had bomb rooms both forward (serving the lower of the two hangar decks only) and aft, with the torpedo stowage adjacent to the aftermost one and serving the upper hangar and deck via a combined hoist. The fighter aircraft were concentrated at the extreme forward end of the upper hangar and their belted ammunition and cannon shells came up to them from the magazines via much smaller, dedicated hoists.

Both bombs and torpedoes were transferred from their storage bins onto light trolleys via hydraulic hoists, the trolley then being wheeled out to a platform, itself 3 feet above deck level. This was to permit a 3 foot high coaming around each lift shaft, to stop fuel (or gas) from running down into the bomb rooms. Hoists above this platform were used to lift the bombs or torpedoes onto dollies or carts for transportation to the aircraft. In the main, the Japanese preferred to affix heavy ordnance to the aircraft on the flight deck, but heavier bombs and torpedoes were also loaded in the hangars.

The hangars themselves followed the British practice of being fully enclosed, but whereas the Royal Navy opted for

149

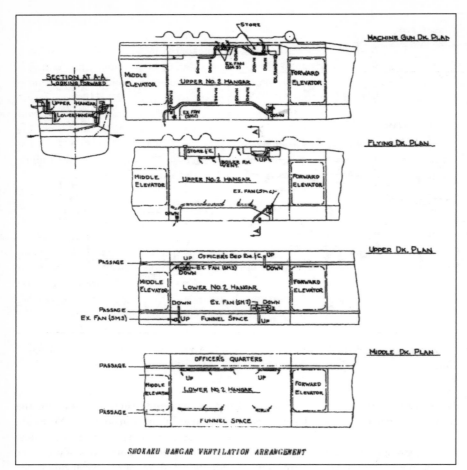

Diagram 5. Japanese Carriers – Diagramatic Sketch of Typical Hangar Ventilation Arrangements, (based on *Shōkaku* class ships). (US Naval Technical Mission)

an armoured deck in a futile attempt to keep heavy bombs out, the IJN followed the USN practice in order to attain maximum aircraft stowage for offensive power. It was, as has been commented upon many times, the worst of both worlds, for any bomb would penetrate, but its explosive power would be unable to freely vent, thus increasing its destructive force.[106] Likewise, subsidiary explosions or fire would be confined within the ship and accompanying vessels would be severely curtailed in the assistance they could bring.

The Japanese method of fire-fighting was curtailment. The design built in the capacity to subdivide the hangars into sections by the quick application of fire curtains, which were of the vertical type, constructed on a roller-blind principle for speedy use. The number of subdivisions varied from ship to ship, but usually the elevator shafts were sealed off from the rest of the hangar decks. Sprays automatically operated by the fire mains were initiated to try and keep the temperature of the curtains themselves down. Any fire that got a hold within the hangar spaces was to be tackled with foam and a double row of nozzles were built in to either side of those spaces. The lower bank delivered 22 gallons per minute to the hangar deck while the upper row projected a soap solution at twice that capacity into the upper area. The lower hangar had a system specifically meant to cope with major bomb detonations, being a

---

106. When the British armoured deck carrier *Illustrious* was dive-bombed off Malta in January 1941 by the land-based Ju 87 Stukas of the *Luftwaffe*, six bombs initially hit her. Some were instantaneously fused direction action bombs intended to destroy her defences, but her armour deck failed to keep out two of the 1,000 pound AP bombs employed, while the third and fourth bombs penetrated down into the hangar by way of the after lift well which was unfortunately open with the elevator descending with an aircraft on it. No system can design out pure chance! The resulting explosions simply shredded the in-place fire curtains. However, her engineering spaces were not violated and she was able to keep steaming.

150

blanket carbon dioxide delivery from bottles via perforated pipes that were on the undersides of the upper hangar deck. The flight deck itself was fitted with hoses with foam nozzles that were kept fully rigged during operations. In the event, all these systems were simply overwhelmed.

Their fire-fighting teams were decimated almost from the first, and the resultant fires were fuelled repeatedly, not only as fully fuelled and armed aircraft progressively 'cooked off', but by the ruptures of their avgas supply systems. Again, the system varied from carrier-to-carrier, although even the oldest ships, *Akagi* and *Kaga*, had been brought into line with their newer brethren during refits in the late 1930s.

The avgas aboard Japanese carriers was modified after the experience of Midway, but the fundamentals remained the same. This highly inflammable cargo was carried in two groups of tanks, situated forward and aft of the machinery spaces. The tanks formed part of the ship's structure and were surrounded by an air space filled with carbon dioxide and this could also be used in an emergency to fill the space above the avgas in the tanks and elsewhere.[107] Each of the groups was subdivided, one compartment carrying the Type A high-octane fuel (used for engine starts and high-speed bursts) and the other filled with a low-octane fuel for cruising, Type B. Both types were pumped out according to type required and fed through to hangar and flight deck filling positions, with mains and risers located in the middles sections of the lower hangar and the end sections of the upper hangar. Twice as many outlets were provided for the Type B fuel. Flexible copper hoses, 25 yards in length, could reach any aircraft in either hangars or the flight deck.

Another weak point in Japanese carrier design was found to be their hangar ventilation systems. The venting of dangerous and noxious fumes was conducted by means of fan supply and fan exhaust, clean air being blown in one side of the hangar at a height of 4–5 feet above the deck, with exhaust from the opposite side being at a lower level. The system could change the air inside each hangar once every ten minutes. The *Kidō Butai*'s carriers vented their funnel gases downward away from the flight deck via curved funnels located on their starboard side, and, in order to avoid pulling the funnel gases into the hangar, the supply intakes for the ventilation system had to be located on the port side, with exhausts to starboard. Unfortunately, it was found that this tended to set up a hangar flow circulation about the longitudinal axis and resulted in a mix of air and petrol vapour.[108] All these precautions were just simply overwhelmed in practice and, once the first bombs reached the avgas tanks themselves, the result was an inferno.

But it should be noted that, terrible though the destruction caused by the SBDs was, as usual bombing failed instantly to sink these ships. As with heavily armoured battleships like *Prince of Wales, Bismarck, Yamato* and *Musashi*, the torpedo still remained the decisive anti-ship weapon, and the A6M2s had certainly not been complete idiots to concentrate their attentions on the TBMs, for the torpedo bomber was then, and was to remain, the main threat[109]. So the three carriers burnt, but, for the moment at least, they still remained afloat.

---

107. Midway proved that this protection was totally inadequate and concrete was used instead as protection against bomb damage.
108. U.S. Technical Mission, *Aircraft Arrangements and Handling.*
109. Despite the almost universal post-war adulation of the bomber as the destroyer of battleships, capital ships of most nations remained relatively immune from this method, while at sea and underway. Only stationary capital ships were ever sunk by free-falling bombs alone, and even then only a few; the American *Arizona*, and the Soviet *Oktoberskaja Revolutia* were old ships, while the German *Tirpitz* and several of the old Japanese battleships at the wars end, were already badly damaged and also totally immobilized prior to their being finished off by bombs.

Chapter Seven

Inquest

The surprise achieved by the SBDs had been akin to that sprung by the British Blenheims a few weeks earlier, but the results were far more devastating. Had the Japanese learned nothing from the April scare? It was too late to change tactics now, but just how did the CAP find itself so totally out of position in those fateful five minutes? Some of the blame may lie with indiscipline, and part with the sheer relentlessness of the American assault; but for many the clues pointed to lack of communication.

Controlling the Rapier

When the replacement for the IJN's existing Mitsubishi A5M4 carrier fighter was first under consideration, the 12-Shi specifications sent to both Nakajima and Mitsubishi companies in May 1937 were updated in October of the same year. One of the key requirements for the new aircraft, which became the Mitsubishi A6M2 and A6M3 Type O Carrier Fighter (*Rei Shiki Kanjo Sentoku*) Model 11, informally the *Zero*[1] *Sentoku*, or *Zero-sen* (and sometimes *Rei-sen),* much later codenamed Zeke by the Allies but more commonly-known as *Zero* after the Japanese year of manufacture 2600, was that she be equipped with a complete *96-Ku-1*[2] airborne radio set, as well as a radio direction finder ('homer') for long-range maritime navigation.[3] It was the Model 21 Zeke that was still being used by the Japanese front-line carrier units in their three-plane *shōtai* fighter units at the Battle of Midway in June 1942.[4]

At that date the set was still in the 'experimental manu-

facture' category, with development work still being undertaken and models eventually being produced in small numbers. The Type 96, Model 1 was a voice/telegraph system, and, because of its relative simplicity compared to older systems, it soon became the standard radio system fitted in Japanese fighter aircraft of the late 1930s.[5] As with all things concerning military aviation at this time, the Japanese had the hard testing ground of the war in China to work on and improve the function of the Type 96 in combat conditions. The pressure of actual war acted as a forcing ground to speed the set quickly into the 'experimental production' phase and then into full-scale manufacture. However, it must be borne in mind that, with regard to the fitting of the 96-Ku-1 in the Zero, only relatively small numbers were still involved, even with an existing combat scene and the expectation of a larger war in the Pacific on the near horizon. Only 328 fully operational Zero fighters were in service, even as late as the time of Pearl Harbor.

The manufacture of radio equipment was still mainly in the hands of civilian industry, and lacked impetus. The IJN was readying itself for much greater demands, however, and in 1940 a special naval communications equipment manufacturing establishment was set up with the founding of the NUMASU Ordnance Depot. The following year saw the further expansion of radio equipment for the increased numbers of fighting planes called for under the Fourth Naval Replenishment Plan which finally embodied the 'air strength first' lobby's demands. Despite this, even with adequate budgets secured for the planes themselves, the

1. The Japanese used the imported English word 'Zero' quite freely, often more so than their own *Rei*.
2. *Ku = Koukuu* = Aviation.
3. Technical Air Intelligence Center, Japanese Aircraft –Performance and Characteristics – TAIC Manual No. 1, TAIC, NAS Anacostia, Maryland, December 1944. The Japanese Kulshee (*Kruesi*) design RDF was basically a direct copy of the American Fairchild Aero Compass, imported into Japan and copied with an approved licence, and which used low to medium frequency (M/F) bands from 160 kilohertz to 385 kilohertz (KHz). Geoffrey Kruesi of Dayton, Ohio, was the original designer. The frequency range was 170–460 KHz, 450–1,200 KHz, with loop and fixed-wire type antenna.
4. Takashi Doi, Yokohama WW-2 Japanese Military Radio Museum, Yokohama, to the author, 13 February 2006.
5. *Ibid.*

production of their equipment still lagged behind in 1941.

The equipment, as fitted on the starboard side of the pilot's cockpit in the Zero, comprised a receiver/transmitter unit[6] with a top-mounted control board.[7] Shock-absorption was suspension by simple bungee cords to the mounting, itself a perforated former, situated on top the rear wing spar. The receiver was cooled by the adjacent air intake. In front, and at a slightly higher level, was slung the Kulshee radio homing equipment control board, with its control lever on a separate, small board, just abaft the radio control board. The power supply for this equipment was via the dynamotor[8] situated at the pilot's port elbow. There was a fixed-wire aircraft antenna located inside the transparent cover behind the pilot's head, with a wooden forward-raked radio mast positioned at the after end of the cockpit cover supporting the aerial, which was affixed atop the main-plane. The pilots had throat-type microphones, but later these were replaced with microphones integral with the oxygen masks.

The *96-Ku-1* short-wave radio, was of the high frequency (H/F) type, with the frequencies controlled by quartz crystal oscillators, in a two-tube configuration. It worked at the lower end of the band, covering from 3,800 to 5,800 KHz. The power output was 7 watts. The radio had a maximum voice broadcast range of approximately 50 miles at an altitude of 10,000 feet, under the best atmospheric conditions, which was more than ample for air protection over the fleet. A single control was used for tuning. Special units were equipped with special code keys for operating the set in telegraphic mode and this had a longer reach, but was not particularly pertinent for CAP

work. Reception was through a superheterodyne circuit.[9] This was also crystal controlled, with five tubes.[10] There were two controls for receiver tuning. All up the radio fixtures and fitting weighed in at 38 pounds. These short-wave radios were allegedly unreliable[11]. Throughout the war voice radio communication remained indifferent.[12] Nonetheless, the Americans had concluded by 1944 that 'the majority of Japanese airborne sets have been well constructed and of orthodox design, although they have lagged behind the Allies in technique'.[13]

Japanese pilots (in common with those of most other air forces) therefore often tended to communicate with each other through a series of aerial manoeuvres, waggling the wings and hand gestures. This meant that co-ordination with regard to group fighter tactics was lacking, this situation being exacerbated by the Japanese pilot's natural inclination for individual skill in one-to-one combats.

Land-based zero Wings, like Saburo Sakai's *Tainan*, even considered these radios to be so unreliable as to be a burden[14] and many pilots ripped their radio equipment out and cut off the radio masts as weight-reducing measures. Land-based units in forward combat areas also tended to suffer from poor maintenance and lack of spare parts. Nor was the problem confined to navy aircraft, Major Yohei Hinoki of the 64th *Sentai* (squadron) also ordered his almost useless radio equipment to be removed from his Ki-43-1c Oscar fighter. However, he was reprimanded by his air group commander, the famous Tateo Kato, himself a firm believer in radio communication as a way of co-ordinating aerial combat, who ordered the radio be reinstated.

The British described the Zero's radio equipment as a

---

6. Shigern Nohara, *Mitsubishi A6M Zero Fighter*.
7. Starting only with the A6M3, only the control panel was mounted to the pilots starboard hand, with, in this and later marks, the set itself shifted to the after end of the cockpit, behind the pilot's seat, but still on the starboard side.
8. Dynamotor is a rotating electric machine with two armatures, used to convert alternating current to direct current. The separate power supply avoided the current fluctuations that normally occur in an aircraft's principal electrical system.
9. Originally invented by Edwin H. Armstrong of Manhattan, this was a highly selective means of receiving and amplifying weak, high-frequency electromagnetic waves.
10. The total tubes used were UX47Z (two), UX134 (two), UY133A (one), UZ135 (one) and UX109 (one). (TAIC Manual No. 1).
11. Japan was not alone in having airborne radio difficulties. Other naval air forces soon came up against unforeseen problems. The Royal Navy equipped their aircraft with short-wave radios, while the RAF used the wider band radios. This meant that, on combined operations like the attack on the German battle-cruiser *Scharnhorst* at Trondheim, Norway, in June 1940, the naval Skua Dive-

bombers were unable to communication with their RAF escorting fighters, with catastrophic consequences. See Peter C. Smith, *Skua*.
12. Based on information provided by Japanese officers for General Douglas Macarthur's Military History Section, Headquarters, Army Forces Far East, March 1945. *Operational History of Japanese Naval Communication, December 1941–August 1945*. Reprinted 1995 by Aegeon Park Press, California.
13. TAIC Manual, No. 1.
14. Sakai Saburo, *Samurai*. Sakai later amplified this in an interview with Michael Ahn of Microsoft in 2000, just before he died on 22 September. He declared that the radio was useless and that the pilots of his unit knew a week before the outbreak of war it was useless. Reception was just 'a bunch of noise'. Sakai was adamant that, 'it was the worst piece of equipment in the Japanese Navy' and he maintained that nothing could be heard. As for hand-signal communications in lieu during combat, 'there was nothing to communicate.' Microsoft Combat Flight Simulator 2, Microsoft game studios. Tainan was the home airbase of the unit, in Southern Taiwan (Formosa).

transmitter and separate receiver working in the band 3.8 to 5.8 Mc/s (Megacycles) one-spot frequency with crystal control being provided on both, and with carrier wavelength (cw) working possible in addition to radio-telephony. The transmitter 'used two tetrode valves of a type similar to the American 807', operating as crystal oscillator-amplifier and anode modulator, obtaining power from the separate rotary transformer. The output power was in 'the order of 8 watts'. The receiver was a simple superheterodyne employing five valves of low-consumption 1.5 volt filament series. The intermediate frequency was 500 kc/s (Kilocycles), and for CW reception, the detector was made to oscillate. An additional small rotary transformer was provided for the receiver. The chassis and cover assemblies are both described as 'being fabricated from duralumin sheet', of light weight, and simplicity in design appeared to be a major consideration in this respect. This was in stark contrast to the German and Italian designs which, by comparison to the Japanese, appeared 'elaborate, expensive and wasteful of production man-power'. A homing receiver installation was 'usually installed in the Zero, with a fixed loop mounted within the cockpit cover.'[15]

In discussion, the radio mechanic Mr H. Horwood said that he 'wished to stress the need for simplicity and reliability in the design of electrical equipment on aircraft', which he felt more necessary in wartime than in peace, since many aircrews did not have the advantage of long flying experience. He went on to assert that the electrical designer 'should therefore make a drastic change in his safety and reliability factors'. His next point seemed particularly relevant to the Zero experience. 'It is not always possible make a machine failure-proof, especially when weight and space have to be taken into account'. His argument was that while efficiency was important, 'reliability must loom larger in the mind of the designer. Similarly, simplicity of operation is imperative to permit rapid action in an emergency'.

In essence, however, it would seem that the dictates of simplicity and light weight overrode the factor of reliability in the radio equipment of the Zero to the extent that the sets were regarded as useless encumbrances rather than vital

tools. With regard to the problems caused by insufficient and inadequate screening of static discharge, Mr C. P. Edwards commented that unscreened intercommunications wiring was acceptable when the output level of carbon microphones was comparatively high, when all DC (Direct Current) motors on the aircraft were thoroughly suppressed, including the supply side of the rotary transformer, and when the wiring was run in troughs of sheet aluminium with detachable covers.

The removable of the radio equipment was not universal, despite some contrary and uninformed views recently expressed. It certainly did *not* apply, as suggested, to carrier-based aircraft of course, who essentially had to retain their wireless sets for control and homing purposes[16], although the extent to which they were actually used, and their effectiveness, is disputed. In the manufacture, installation and maintenance of airborne radio there was a glaring deficiency. The attitude of the Zero pilots to their usage, it ranged from indifference to contempt. One authority comes squarely to the view that this lack of reliability resulted in an 'every man for himself' approach to fighter aircraft defence in the IJN; or at least that that was a principal factor.[17]

The IJN's aerial radios were initially well made[18], but suffered from interference from unshielded ignition wiring and static discharges from unbonded airframe components[19], which reduced their performance considerably. Later, mass-production by subcontractors with relatively unskilled labour coupled with a growing lack of raw materials for essential components reduced manufacturing quality also, but this was all *after* Midway. These handicaps were further compounded by a certain lack of co-operation by, or misunderstandings between, the aircraft manufacturers themselves (including Mitsubishi and Nakajima) and the companies building the radio equipment.[20] However, in the case of the Zero, the radio was from the outset part and parcel of the basic requirement kit, and one which was duly incorporated by Chief Designer Jiro Horikoshi.

However, one aspect of the inbuilt radio communications package that appears to have suffered in the case of the

15. C. P. Edwards, *Enemy Airborne Radio Equipment*.
16. David L. Woods, *Signalling and Communicating at Sea*, Vol. 2.
17. Eric M. Bergerud, *Fire in the Sky: The Air War in the South Pacific*.
18. *Operational History of Japanese Naval Communications December 1941–August 1945*.
19. Takashi Doi, Yokohama WWII Japanese Military Radio Museum, Yokohama, Japan.
20. The American intelligence view of Japanese communications equipment in general was that it 'comprises a complex, modern system highly flexible and efficient. Older equipment is obsolete by American standards, but ruggedly built'. Specifically, Japanese radio equipment 'has varied from poor to excellent. All the early equipment captured has shown both poor design and construction and appeared to be several years behind American standards.' They are in general extraordinarily difficult to service . . . a by-product of the haste with which Japanese engineers have copied . . . from foreign-built radios. SRH211. *Japanese Radio Communication and Radio Intelligence. CICPAC/CINCPAC Bulletin 5-45. 1 January 1945*. Box 21. SRH211. The Layton Papers, Box 21, Item 17, Piece 1).

Zero, indeed seems almost to have been unforeseen or ignored in the overriding desire to reduce weight to the bare minimum, was interference. The proper installation of the correct wiring, the shielding and 'earthing' (grounding or bonding) of the equipment, the subsequent testing, all lacked focus. The aircraft's ignition system, left largely unshielded, led to enormous disruption of reception and transmission of signals. The static electricity that was generated by the very passing of the aircraft itself through the sky was a well-known hazard, but was little catered for, and this could make 'atmospherics' a major factor in the ability of the pilot to decipher transmissions. It has been alleged that it was not until captured American aircraft were dissected and examined in detail and their anti-static measures revealed that the true extent of the cause of much of their problems became apparent to the Japanese, who then took appropriate steps, but this was long after Midway was fought and lost.

With the expansion of demand, the traditional manufacturers found themselves under enormous pressure to meet demand and deadlines. The supplying of sufficient radio sets and the rush to install them on the production lines overrode the necessity of correct procedures being adhered to and inspected. It may be indicative of this attitude that the foremost aircraft designer of the day, Dr Jiro Horikoshi, designer of the Zero, makes absolutely no reference whatsoever to the radio equipment installed in his masterpiece, (other than to mention briefly the original Navy specification), while going into great detail on all other aspects of the build.[21] No great study had been made of the optimal methods of ensuring that the radios, once in place, were fully screened and thus working at their best, because neither sets of manufacturers, aircraft and radio, had any specialist teams looking at the problem as a whole. Inspection checks were supposed to be made, but were often perfunctory in the haste to get the radios off the production line, or the aircraft themselves out of the factory gate. This was deep-rooted. It was not just ironic mockery when the Chief Navy Inspector of the Nagoya District, whose job was to liase between Mitsubishi Heavy Industries and the Aeronautical Establishment, had chided the latter in the mid-thirties, 'Don't ever mention words such as inspection and leadership.'[22]

Servicing of the equipment using silk (non-conductive) gloves was one elementary precaution that was not always taken. But here again, the support teams who both maintained and serviced the Zero's radio equipment aboard the carriers, were far more able (both because of their own technical abilities, being still mainly professionals at this stage of the war, and the sophistication of the equipment to which they had immediate access) to minimize these problems than their colleagues ashore on some remote atoll at the end of a problematic supply line, in the years that followed.

Thus even two or three years after Midway had been fought, the Zero's radio equipment remained inferior to that of the enemy. The 261 *Kokutai,* land-based at Saipan some eighteen months later, and flying the A6M2, reported that radios used for long-range transmission had 'low performance'.

In contrast to the Japanese, the US Navy flyers changed their radio communication frequencies every other day, and on occasions the two wavelengths were coincidently exactly the same. At such times only the American aviators could be heard, which seemed graphically to illustrate the differences in the effectiveness of the two aerial radio systems. Local atmospherics could also affect transmissions of course but this was common to both sides and not a built-fault.

Despite this all the Zero fighters in action at Midway were fitted with radios with which their air officers could, in theory at least, communicate with them. A persistent and virulent attack was made on me for daring to state this simple truth in an earlier study. Therefore I took the opportunity to ask surviving Zero pilots who fought at the battle what the facts were. All repeated that, they did have radios, and, on rare occasions, even used them, even if they could not always rely on them. Lieutenant-Commander Iyōzō Fujita, ace Zero pilot credited with at least twenty kills (who probably achieved more), working from the carrier *Soryū,* and who flew in the CAP over the 1st *Kidō Butai* at Midway, (and was shot down by 'friendly fire' for his pains but rescued by the destroyer *Nowaki*) was typical. In an interview conducted at his home on 5 November 2005, I asked him specifically whether the allegation, made publicly for many years, that 'the IJN did not have any such persons because their aircraft mostly had no radios'[23], was true. The response was immediate.

---

21. Horikoshi, Dr Jiro, *Eagles of Mitsubishi: The Story of the Zero Fighter.*
22. *Ibid.* However, it must be borne in mind that neither Horikoshi, nor his American translators and editors at the Washington University Press seem to have been *au fait* with some factual aspects of World War II. For example, he claims that the Zero both fought against and outfought, the Supermarine Spitfire over Ceylon in 1942, shooting down seventeen of them – no mean feat considering there was not one single Spitfire within 1,000 miles of Ceylon at the time, only Hawker Hurricanes and Fairey Fulmars!
23. J. P. Redman.

Q: 'There is a man who maintains that the Zero fighters at Midway were mostly not equipped with radios. What is your opinion of this claim?'

A: 'He is totally incorrect. I can confirm that *all* the Zero fighters on my unit, and, as far as I know, in the whole force at Midway, were fitted with radio. They were contacted by each ship's *Hickōchō* on a single common radio frequency'.[24]

Other questions and answers included the following: -

Q: 'Were all Zero fighters at Midway equipped with the Type 3 radio?'

A: 'Yes, all were so fitted with R/T.'

Q: 'Could the aircraft carriers communicate by radio with the Zeros?'

A: 'Yes, via long-range R/T.'

Q: 'At what distance could this be done?'

A: '50 miles plus.'

Q: 'Whose job was it?'

A: '*Hickōchō*.'

Q: 'Could the Zeros at Midway communicate with each other by radio?'

A: 'Yes, by throat microphones when in formation. But mainly there was too much interference.'

Q: 'Was the CAP mounted by the Zero at Midway stacked at predetermined levels?'

A: 'Yes, initially we took direction from the carriers to altitudes and sectors.'

Q: 'How many Zeros were maintained at each altitude level?'

A: 'It varied all the time, and was depending on the time and conditions.'

Q: 'Do you know why there was no high CAP over the force when the American dive-bombers arrived overhead?'

A: 'The need to land and rearm after each interception. Each of our 20 mm cannon only had sixty rounds per gun.'

Q: 'What type of aircraft were on the carrier decks at the time the SBD bombs hit?'

A: 'As far as I could tell only fighters were on deck when the bombs hit.'

Q: 'Does that mean, as far as you could see, all the Vals and Kates remained below in the hangars at the time the bombs hit?'

A: 'Yes.'[25]

In an interview, Takeshi Maeda, who was aboard the *Kaga* during the battle, and witnessed the SBD attack from the flight deck, expressed similar opinions. In Maeda's view, 'The Zero radios were practically useless due to interference noise. The carriers just could not effectively convey orders to the defending fighters'. He did not say on what he based this opinion, other than general knowledge presumably by conversations with Zero pilots of his own group.

The Assistant Communications Officer aboard the flagship *Akagi*, Taemi Ichikawa, told me: 'We could certainly talk directly to the Zeros, but the radios by which they talked to the pilots were very noisy and unclear'.[26] This was confirmed by the late Lieutenant-Commander Zenji Abe, who stated: 'The Zeke was equipped with wireless telephone but the noise on the phone was heavy and made it on occasions, almost useless'. Abe also commented that, aside from communication with the airborne aircraft, additional duties of the *Hickōchō* included 'advising his commanding officer about course and speed of his ship when planes were taking off and landing, as well as personnel management of air officers and airmen aboard'.[27]

Commander Noritaka Kitazawa of the Military History Department at the National Institute for Defense Studies in Tokyo, along with others, stated:

The trouble for the Zekes was their wireless telephone was earthed to the body of the fuselage. As a result, the noise of the telephone made it almost useless. Finally, most of this static was removed from the radios toward the end of the Pacific War, but it was by then too late. Some Zeke pilots said they would rather have had an extra 20 kg of avgas instead of the useless radio.[28]

Therefore, while the Zero fighters that provided the fighter protection for Vice-Admiral Chūichi Nagumo's carrier force, the 1st *Kidō Butai* were all fitted with the best radios available in 1942, this still did not make airborne communication easy.[29] The navy itself was clear that radio telegraphy was essential if the Zero was to be effective in

---

24. Recorded interview with Lieutenant-Commander Iyōzō Fujita, at his home in Daizawa, Setagaya-ku, Tokyo, on 5 November 2005. Pressed subsequently, Fujuta could not recall who was in overall control of the CAP at the crucial time at Midway because he had taken off earlier from *Soryū*. (Telephone conversation, 11 March 2006.)

25. *Ibid.*

26. Interview with Rear-Admiral Taemi Ichikawa at his home in Matsudo City, 3 November 2005.

27. Zenji Abe, letter dated 10 March 2006.

28. Commander Kitazawa to Commander Sadao Seno, 12 March 2006.

29. Nor should we forget that the American radios were hardly reliable pieces of apparatus. For example, during the

39. The radiomen/gunners of Scouting Squadron Six aboard USS *Enterprise* (CV-6) on 12 May 1942. Radioman Third Class John W. Snowden is in centre of the front row. Many of the other radio-gunners have signed their names. (*Norman J. 'Dusty' Kleiss*).

40. The officers of Scouting Squadron Six aboard USS *Enterprise* (CV-6) on 12 May 1942. (*Norman J. 'Dusty' Kleiss*).

41. Scouting Squadron Six aboard USS *Enterprise*, 24 January 1942. (*Norman J. 'Dusty' Kleiss*).

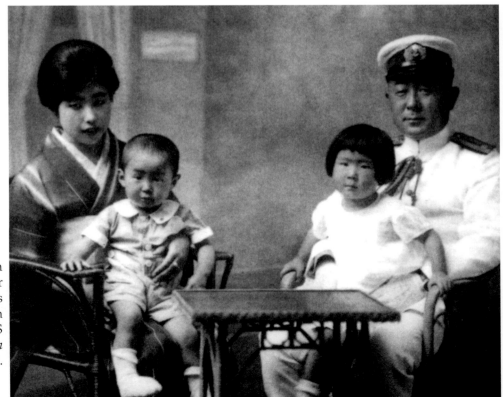

42. Rear Admiral Tamon Yamaguchi, Commander Carrier Division 2 with his family. He fought back with the *Hiryū* against three US carriers. (*Courtesy of his son Mr. Soukei Yamaguchi*).

43. Lieutenant (junior grade) Norman J. 'Dusty' Kleiss of Scouting Squadron Six aboard USS *Enterprise* 24 January 1942. (*Norman J. 'Dusty' Kleiss*).

44. Dauntless *en masse*. Deck part of SBDs aboard the USS *Enterprise* (CV-6) on 4 March 1942, *en route* to raid Marcus Island. Note the individual aircraft numbers on both wings and old-style 'red meatball' in the centre of the white star national markings on the wing, still carried at this date. (*National Archives, College Park, Maryland*).

45. The pilot's 'Ready Room' aboard an American aircraft carrier. This photograph was taken aboard the *Essex* Class carrier *Lexington* (CV-16) later in the war but all were generally smiliar. Here the squadron aircrew assemble prior to a combat sortie to be briefed fully on the nature of the target, its bearing, course and speed, and prevailing weather conditions, and on aircraft allocation prior to take-off. Note that they have their individual chart-boards to plot the information relayed by teletype and verbally. (*US Navy Official*).

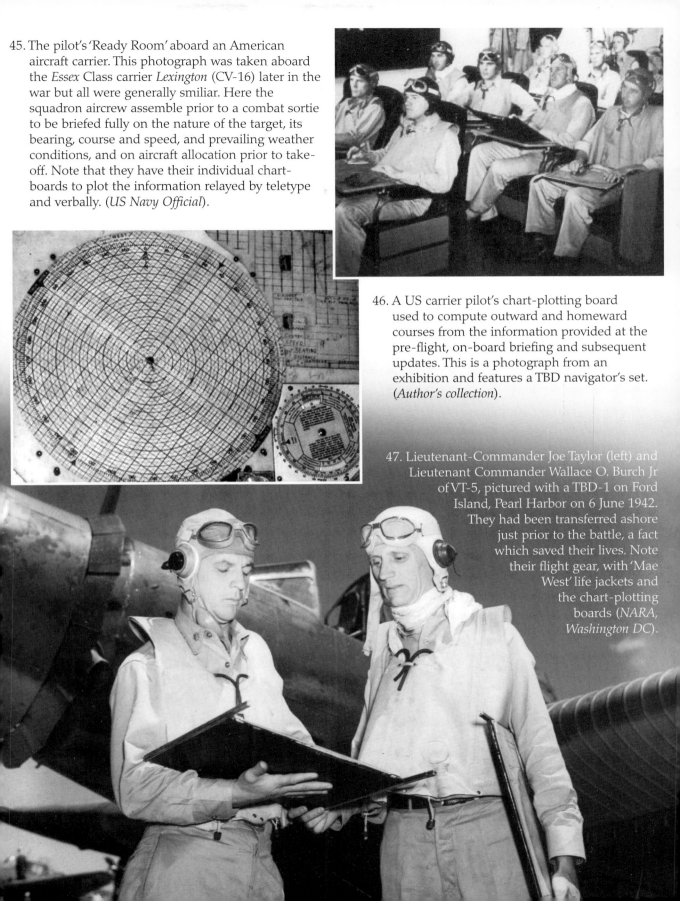

46. A US carrier pilot's chart-plotting board used to compute outward and homeward courses from the information provided at the pre-flight, on-board briefing and subsequent updates. This is a photograph from an exhibition and features a TBD navigator's set. (*Author's collection*).

47. Lieutenant-Commander Joe Taylor (left) and Lieutenant Commander Wallace O. Burch Jr of VT-5, pictured with a TBD-1 on Ford Island, Pearl Harbor on 6 June 1942. They had been transferred ashore just prior to the battle, a fact which saved their lives. Note their flight gear, with 'Mae West' life jackets and the chart-plotting boards (*NARA, Washington DC*).

48. Douglas SBD-3 Dauntless dive-bombers 'warming up' aboard the carrier *Yorktown* (CV-5) prior to take-off for a strike on the morning of 4 June, 1942. (*Naval institute Photo Collection via Naval Historical Foundation, Washington DC*).

50. Manhandling the SBD. Aircraft 11 of Bombing-8 aboard the *Hornet* is hand-manoeuvred across the carrier's flight-deck. Note the mixture of old-style and new-style helmets at this stage of the war, and the freshly painted white star on the Dauntless, now with no trace at all or any hint of the 'red meatball', illustrating the dominance of the rising sun marking in the spring of 1942. (*Clayton Fisher*).

49. Commander Stanhope C. Ring, 'Sea-Hag' of *Hornet*'s Air Group. (*US Navy Official, via Clayton Fisher*).

51. 'Bombing up' an SBD on the deck of an American carrier during the Battle of Midway. The bomb is resting on its loading trolley and the three-man ordnance team are preparing to affix it to the swinging crutch beneath the aircraft. (*US Navy Official*).

52. After the Ready Room information and briefing and the agreed flight details to the target had been decided upon, the SBD pilots were fed last-minute updates and information on the flight-deck right up to the moment of departure via the flight-deck information boards. This is *Hornet*'s despatch team with on such piece of interesting data. (*Clayton Fisher*).

53. Ready to go! This is the first launch of *Hornet*'s Air Group 8 on the morning of 4 June 1942. Immediately astern of the ten F4F Grumman Wildcat fighters of VF-8, are the SBD-3s of VS-8, with aircraft 9 (centre), the mount of Ensign Clayton Fisher, who had been assigned, much to his dismay, as one of two wingmen for 'Sea-Hag' (*CHAG or Commander, Hornet Air Group*).

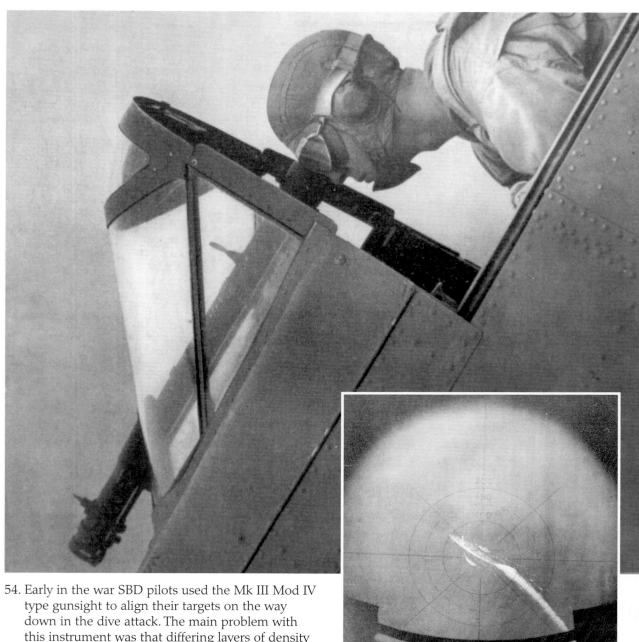

54. Early in the war SBD pilots used the Mk III Mod IV type gunsight to align their targets on the way down in the dive attack. The main problem with this instrument was that differing layers of density tended to make the sight 'mist over' during the descent. This rather old-fashioned method and sight was later replaced by the Mk VIII adjustable sight from the SBD-5 onward. (*US Navy Official via Clayton Fisher*).

55. Target nicely centred! Pilot's-eye view of a turning warship through the gunsight. Allowance for wind speed and drift, speed and course of the target vessel, correct altitude for release of type of bomb carried, and so on, all had to be calculated by the SBD pilot on the way down. (*US Navy Official via Clayton Fisher*).

56. There was only one hero at Midway (Admiral Raymond Spruance, Commander Task Force 16). Commander Clarence Wade McClusky Jr, c.1943, a former fighter pilot who led the SBDs to fame and glory. (*Courtesy of Mrs C. Wade McClusky Jr, via Naval Historical Foundation, Washington DC*).

57. The incomparable *Sugar Baker Dog*. Despite the plethora of books and conflicting theories that continued to surround the Battle of Midway, the cardinal fact is that it was by dive-bombing, as conducted so efficiently by the SBD Dauntless aircraft, and dive-bombing alone, that the battle was won. (*Ray Wagner courtesy of N. Paul Whittier Historical Aviation Library at the San Diego Aerospace Museum*).

58. The Bel-Geddes diorama depicting the attack by the VB-6 and VS-6 from USS *Enterprise* upon the Japanese aircraft carriers *Kaga* and *Akagi* on the morning of 4 June 1942. (*National Archive, College Park, Maryland*).

59. Admiral William I. Martin, seen here when he was commander of the US Sixth Fleet in the Mediterranean, 1967-9, one of the many former SBD pilots who fought at Midway and went on to achieve flag rank in the navy. (*Admiral William I. Martin*).

60. 'Dusty' Kleiss and John Snowden making their exit aboard S-7 after hitting the *Kaga* with one 500lb and two 100lb incendiary bombs. Snowden added to that tally by managing to shoot down a Zero fighter, which tried to attack them. (*Original painting reproduced by permission of Dave Grey*).

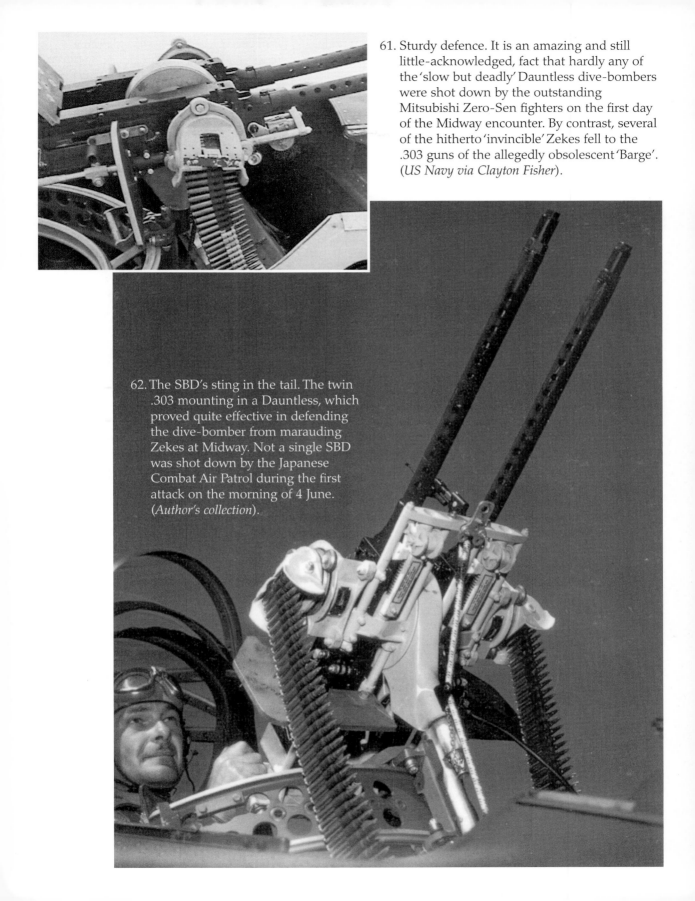

61. Sturdy defence. It is an amazing and still little-acknowledged, fact that hardly any of the 'slow but deadly' Dauntless dive-bombers were shot down by the outstanding Mitsubishi Zero-Sen fighters on the first day of the Midway encounter. By contrast, several of the hitherto 'invincible' Zekes fell to the .303 guns of the allegedly obsolescent 'Barge'. (*US Navy via Clayton Fisher*).

62. The SBD's sting in the tail. The twin .303 mounting in a Dauntless, which proved quite effective in defending the dive-bomber from marauding Zekes at Midway. Not a single SBD was shot down by the Japanese Combat Air Patrol during the first attack on the morning of 4 June. (*Author's collection*).

63. A Douglas SBD-3 Dauntless dive-bomber (Bu No 4542), coded B-15, of Bombing Squadron Six (VB-6), is manhandled across the flight-deck after landing back aboard the carrier *Enterprise* (CV-6) with damage taken durning her attack on a Japanese target during the morning of 4 June 1942. (*Naval Institute Photo Collection via Naval Historical Foundation, Washingto DC*).

64. Welcome back! A hive of activity as SBDs crowd the deck part forward aboard the USS *Hornet* following the return of a strike. Watched by Admiral Mitscher (forward in peaked cap) and other observers from the bridge, the deck crew wheel away a 500lb bomb that had been brought back undelivered; aircraft 10 bears the scars of the Japanese reception committee on her starboard aileron; an armourer removes the ammunition belt from the starboard wing of 15; while a pair of jeeps manouevre an aircraft across the flight-deck. A photo taken later in the war. (*Clayton Fisher*).

65. A fire-fighting station aboard the USS *Yorktown* (CV-5). Although rather primitive and limited these facilities, especially the Foamite foam generator with the funnel-shaped delivery, enabled the damage-control parties to contain the damage caused by the three dive-bomber hits on 4 June. (*Naval Historical Foundation, Washington DC*).

66. The scene inside the hangar deck of a US carrier earlier in the war. Artisans are shown working on a Grumman F4-F Wildcat (3-F-14) fighter under the watchful eye of a petty officer. Across the hangar roof run the mass of pipes, including the all-important sprinkler system. To create maximum space for working and arming aircraft, the planes could be hung from the hangar roof itself, and both TBD Devastator torpedo bombers (3-T-3) left and SBD Dauntless dive-bombers (2-S-3) can be seen so stacked. The calm, measured, pristine world of the pre-war US Navy hangar deck bears little resemblance to the chaos, hell and frenzy of the Japanese carrier's combat rearming and rearming again on the morning of 4 June 1942, but it conveys the claustrophobic working conditions. (*NARA, Washington*).

67. A Japanese Val dive-bomber home's in on the *Yorktown*. A dramatic still from a movie film shot by William G. Roy Photographer's Mate Second Class with a 35mm Bell & Howell motion picture camera, which was later recovered by Otis Kight (VF-42). (*Copyright William G. Roy, Naples, FL*).

68. On the receiving end. The flight deck of the USS *Yorktown* (CV-5) after the Japanese dive-bomber assault. Corpsmen can be seen treating casualties around one of the quadruple 1.1in anti-aircraft mountings near the carrier's bridge structure. (*National Archives via Naval Historical Foundation, Washington DC*).

69. A Japanese Kate torpedo-bomber from *Hiryū*'s second attack wave. Having dropped her torpedo at the *Yorktown* she receives flak hits and trails smoke as she makes a low-level turn to try and escape across the screen. Another still from a movie film by William G. Roy, with a 35mm Bell & Howell motion picture camera, which was later recovered by Otis Kight (VF-42). (*William G. Roy, Naples, FL*).

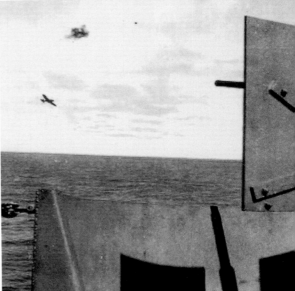

70. William G. Roy, with the hand-held camera with which he shot some of the most memorable photographs of the battle from on board the carrier *Yorktown*. (*Copyright William G. Roy, Naples, FL*).

71. Japanese Kate torpedo-bombers brave the barrage at low level to deliver a pincer attack against the carrier *Yorktown*. (*William G. Roy, via NARA, Washington DC*).

72. The *Yorktown* listing after heavy damage. She was hit by three bombs and four torpedoes and abandoned twice before she finally gave up the fight. (*William G. Roy, via NARA, Washington DC*).

73. The *Yorktown* settling after heavy damage. She was hit by three bombs and four torpedoes and abandoned twice before she finally gave up the fight. (*William G. Roy, via NARA, Washington DC*).

74. The final plunge of the USS *Yorktown*, as recorded by naval photographer William G. Roy. A massive hole caused by torpedoes hits can be seen in her hull (left) and her LSO platform can be discerned on the right. On arrival back at Pearl Harbor, Roy was forbidden to look at the very photographs that he had taken! (*Naval Historical Foundation*).

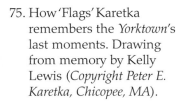

75. How 'Flags' Karetka remembers the *Yorktown*'s last moments. Drawing from memory by Kelly Lewis (*Copyright Peter E. Karetka, Chicopee, MA*).

76. The destroyer USS *Hughes* (DD-410) was sent to stand by the abandoned *Yorktown* overnight on 4/5 June. (*Naval Historical Foundation, Washington DC*).

battle as an organized group, but hardly any fighter pilots were so enamoured of it as to study its effect on tactics. Morse code was still being taught to student pilots undertaking their basic training at Tsuchiura two years or more after Midway, but many found it difficult. A rear-seat man in a bomber tapping signals out on a Morse key if all else failed appears reasonable, but doing the same in a single-seater interceptor is hardly feasible in the midst of high-speed aerial combat.

This is not to confuse communication in the air with the actual tactics of aerial fighting. John B. Lundstrom[30] has used Air Intelligence reports[31] to refute allegations by Thomas G. Miller Jr[32] and others that Japanese pilots had not evolved tactics beyond World War I 'dog-fighting'. But faced with radio equipment that continually malfunctioned or underperformed, the natural temperament of the young fighter pilots, imbued with the spirit of attack, led many to revert to the old methods of contacting each as being simpler but, more vitally, faster and more effective.[33] But it did involve a considerable risk. IJN fighter pilots were imbued with slogans, one of which was 'Team work first and avoid being separated from the fleet', in other words, follow the established doctrine as laid down and proven. This stricture to conform does not sit easily with a young fighter pilot's natural flair and improvization.

However, that did not preclude their use, uneducated and opinionated claims to the contrary. For example Table 13 is a translation of a captured Japanese document taken from a Japanese flyer shot down off Torokina, Bougainville on 5 November 1943.[34]

However, in relation to the Midway encounter, the total dependence on individual look-outs on the screening warships or the Zero pilots aloft themselves for making visual sighting of the incoming enemy, and then somehow communicating that information to whoever could best deal with it, proved terminal. It was not so much that the airborne flight leaders had to resort to gestures and 'follow-me' type physical examples, as that incoming enemy strike forces might not be spotted at all!

The *Hickōchō*

For the Japanese in particular, the speed with which aircraft could be refuelled and rearmed were to be crucial factors. So, also, was the rate at which these re-readied aircraft, be they A6M2s to reinforce the CAP, or D3As and B5Ns for a strike force, could be brought up on deck and spotted. The average aircraft complement of a Japanese carrier in 1941–2 would be seventy-two aircraft, stowed in twin hangars, with a ratio of fighters/dive-bombers/torpedo-bombers of 27/27/18. Usual stowage arrangements had the fighters in the mid-to-forward of the upper hangar, the dive-bombers in the after end of the upper and the forward end of the lower hangar and the torpedo/attack-bombers in the after end of the lower. A further twelve aircraft could be partly assembled on the hangar walls with special fittings. It was a tight fit for all types, most being stowed slant-wise to a constricted matrix. While at sea these aircraft were lashed to rings welded to the hangar decks, with further securing done by chains and screw strainers for wheels, and rope lashing for the stern and wing tips. Getting these gridlocked machines fully fuelled and armed up on deck called for some complex choreography at the best of times. It requires little imagination to picture the scene after the orders and counter-orders on the morning of 4 June!

The double hangar arrangement of Japanese carriers[35],

Midway battle, Lieutenant (jg) James S. Gray, Jr, commanding the *Enterprise*'s VF-6 supplying top cover to the torpedo-bombers, had communicated a sighting report back to his carrier, but had not heard the prearranged plea from Lindsay begging him to 'Come on down, Jim' as VT-6 was being chopped to bits 20,000 feet below him. On the contrary, he claimed in his report that 'a prearranged call for help from Torpedo Squadron Six was not given.' Of course he was not over Lindsay, but the fact remains that he heard nothing. Gray had similar radio problems on 6 June, and he was far from alone in this.

30. John B. Lundstrom, *The First Team, Pacific Naval Air Combat from Pearl Harbor to Midway*.

31. US Army Headquarters Far East Command, Military History Section, Japanese Research Division, *Japanese Monograph, No 113, Task Force Operations – November 1941–April 1942)*, Washington, DC.

32. Thomas G. Miller, Jr, *The Cactus Air Force*. Although this viewpoint has its origins in the opinions of the American F4F pilots themselves.

33. Lest it be thought this was exclusively a Japanese problem, it should be pointed out that American and British fighter radio equipment, although marginally better than that of the Japanese at this date, was nothing much to write home about either. John B. Lundstrom, for example, applies the words 'primitive', 'bum' and 'not very reliable even under ideal conditions.' See *The First Team: Pacific Naval Air Combat from Pearl Harbor to Midway*.

34. Confidential – Combat Intelligence Center, South Pacific Force, Item #862 (S-3508), IN Box No.5 Numbered translations of Japanese Documents, 23, Item #862. Naval Historical Centre, Washington Navy Yard, DC.

35. The Japanese had, in fact, already tried and tested the open hangar system favoured by the US Navy, but had subsequently rejected it. Two reasons were given for it being discarded; the first related to the weather damage and flooding which could be sustained, and the second to the difficulty of keeping them light-proof during night-flying operations. The penalty was that aircraft engines could not be run, and therefore warmed up, below.

Table 13: Call Signs and Voice Communication Numbers for the use of Fighter Unit (fc TAI) Control

UNIT NAME	VOICE COMMUNICATION NUMBER	CALL SIGNS
21ST AIRFLOT (sf)		
1st *BUTAI* (TN:? 1B)	#101	YO
2ND *BUTAI* (2B)	#202	TA
3rd *BUTAI* (3B)	#303	RE
1st RESERVE	#707	O
2nd RESERVE	#808	KU
All Fighter Planes	#00	00
-? – TN: See Note*		
1st *BUTAI* Fighters (1B fc)	#100	YO 0
2nd *BUTAI* Fighters	#200	TA 0
3rd *BUTAI* Fighters	#300	RE 0
DIRECT AIR COVERAGE		
(JOKU CHOKUEI)		
(YH) Altitude 2000 or less	#2	2
Altitude 2000 to 4000	#4	4
Altitude 4000 to 6000	#6	6
Altitude 6000 t0 8000	#8	8
Altitude 800 to 900	#9	9
PLANE FLIGHT (fY)		
1st *BUTAI* (1B)		
All Plane Flights (fY)	#20	KA 0
Plane Flight 1	#21	KA 1
Plane Flight 2	#22	KA 2
Plane Flight 3	#23	KA 3
2nd *BUTAI* (2B)		
All Planes (fY)	#25	KA 5
Plane Flight 1	#36	KA 6
Plane Flight 2	#37	KA 7
Plane Flight 3	#38	KA8

SHOTAI	11	12	13	14	15	16	17	18	19
	SHOTAI	SHOTAI	SHOTAI	SHOTAI	SHOTAI	SHOTAI	SHOTAI	SHOTAI	SHOTAI
AI	(11D)								
KANA	I	RO	HA	NI	HO	HE	TO	CHI	RI

* Translator's note –Characters not clear

coupled with the fact that the majority of their aircraft did not have fully folding wings, just folding wing-tips, in order to expedite aircraft handling, complicated this procedure. The elevators used to move the aircraft up and down from the flight deck, were themselves unarmoured and had to be large in order to accommodate these non-wing-folding aircraft. This in turn meant larger apertures and a weakening of the structures of both flight deck and upper hangar.

One solution was the adoption of a three-elevator layout, as was done with the *Soryū* and *Hiryū*, but this introduced such unacceptable stresses in the centre of ship's hull that it was abandoned almost immediately.[36] But whether two or three elevators were employed, the time taken to raise or lower each from the lower hangar to the flight deck level was just fifteen seconds.[37] On the optimistic assumption that everything went smoothly every time (unlikely!) one can do

36. US Naval Technical Mission, *Aircraft Arrangements and Handling.*
37. *Ibid.* Also NavTechJap Report, *Characteristics of Japanese Naval Vessels, Article 3* – Surface Warship Hull Design, Index No. S-01-3.

one's own calculations on launching strikes and recovering same. In practice, with damaged aircraft, flight and hangar deck accidents and congestion, any figures produced in the calm of one's home are likely to be purely academic. What is certain, based on fact rather than theory, is that the Japanese could get far more aircraft into the air, organized and on their way to the target than the Americans could, for all the latters later claims to 'superior doctrine'; and Midway proved that conclusively! Much of this was down to the *hickōchō*.

The responsibility that rested on the shoulders of the four *hickōchō* (flight operations officers) belonging to the 1st *Kidō Butai* was heavy. These men were Commander Shogo Masuda, the senior *hickōchō* aboard the flagship *Akagi*; Commander Takahisa Amaya of the *Kaga;* Commander Ikuto Kusumoto of the *Soryū* and Lieutenant-Commander Susumu Kawaguchi of the *Hiryū*.[38] They oversaw the basic mechanics of all the carriers' flying operations that ensured they would fit seamlessly into the battle plan with the maximum effectiveness and the minimum hitches[39].

The 'command centre' (or the closest to it the Japanese possessed) for the *hickōchō* was the air control station, an extension jutting out inboard of the rear of the carrier's small island structure, overlooking the flight deck. In this cramped spot they had radio transmission equipment to communicate with airborne aircraft[40], poled *seibiki* (control flags) to control deck movements, signal lamps to communicate with the sister carriers and the rest of the fleet and voice-tube communication from the ship's captain at the forward end of the command bridge and down to the hangar decks. They could thus oversee the flight-deck operatives, who manually manoeuvred the crowded deck parks of aircraft in readiness for launching, overseen by their on-deck *shō-hickōchō* (deck launching officer).

The duties of the *hickōchō* in the midst of a fast-moving air-sea encounter were onerous and comprehensive, but he did have two junior officers as his assistants, plus a flight deck officer (*seibiin*). As originally defined, each *hickōchō* was responsible for the control of his own carrier's aircraft, and this was no sinecure. The job entailed overseeing the correct arming, and refuelling, a quick turn-around, and ordering the best sequential grouping ready for launching.[41] The launch itself was initiated by the simple process of the *hickōchō* standing in the bridge wing, holding up a white flag. The aircraft then flew off in sequence at twenty-second intervals, without any further signals at all until the white flag was lowered. The airborne placement to the best advantage (numbers, height, direction) of the protecting Zero fighter protection was predetermined, but the ship talked to the airborne aircraft as best they could. The recovery of all the carriers' aircraft was according to the dictates of the captain of each individual vessel. Within that limitation, the usual routine was for the aircraft to fly down-wind some 500 yards away from the flight deck. When all was ready to receive them the *seibiin* used a signal lamp to indicate that everything was clear to land. The aircraft made a turn abreast the bridge structure and placed itself at a height of about 600 feet, some 800 yards astern of the ship. There were again no further signals or bats necessary (as with the LSO in Western carriers), the pilot used his own skill to follow the light landing-aids and the steam jet wind-across-deck indicators to get himself down. Thus it was the pilot's responsibility to estimate the wind speed, varying his approach according to how he read the steam jet at the front of the flight deck, or as indicated by the alignment of the various deck lights. The *seibiin* would only give a pilot a 'wave off' in an extreme emergency. Sometimes, indeed, in a tight emergency situation, incoming aircraft would land in so close a sequence, that if one missed or 'bounced' the

---

38. Commander Shōgo Masuda, 50th Class, died 8 September 1980. Commander Takahisa Amaya, 51st Class, died 1 December 1983. Lieutenant-Commander Susumu Kawaguchi, 52nd Class, died 26 February 2001. Lieutenant-Commander Ikuto Kusumoto, 52nd Class, killed in action over Guam Island 10 August 1944.

39. There has been much made of the 'revelations' in some recent studies of Japanese carrier doctrine, and claims that this has only come about since westerners troubled to examine original Japanese material. This certainly has some validity, but in truth the basic facts have been available since early 1946, and are written in clear and basic English for anyone to study. The US Naval Technical Mission to Japan in the immediate post-war months, included, among its many reports, full details of carrier operational details. As the Chief of the Mission, Captain C. G. Grimes, informed the CNO on 4 February 1946, these reports were, in fact, the results of Allied, and not just American, research and the one

relevant to these pages was compiled by Commander N. Hancock, Royal Canadian Navy, assisted by Lieutenant-Commander (A) S. Edgecumbe, Royal Navy, with Lieutenant (jg) G. R. Clauson, USNR, acting as interpreter and translator. US Naval Technical Mission to Japan, *Aircraft Arrangements and Handling.*

40. A typical carrier of the period, the *Shōkaku* for example, was equipped with two long-wave transmitters, one long/short wave transmitter and nine short-wave transmitters, three long-wave receivers, twenty-one short-wave receivers and four very-short-wave receivers, two long/short-wave wireless radiophones, one short-wave wireless radiophone and four very-short-wave wireless radiophones, four direction finding sets and one all-band-receiver/scanner.

41. A 'spotted' Japanese striking force would be parked at the rear of the flight deck to give the maximum take-off run (their carriers were not equipped with catapults/accelerators at this stage of the war).

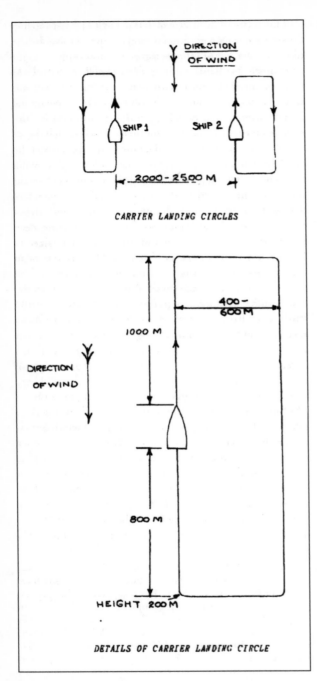

DIRECTION OF WIND

SHIP 1   SHIP 2

|← 2000 - 2500 M →|

CARRIER LANDING CIRCLES

400 - 600 M

1000 M

DIRECTION OF WIND

800 M

HEIGHT 200 M

DETAILS OF CARRIER LANDING CIRCLE

Diagram 2.   Japanese Carrier operations – Details of Carrier Landing Circle. (US Naval Technical Mission)

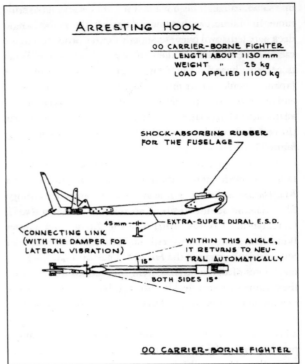

ARRESTING HOOK

OO CARRIER-BORNE FIGHTER
LENGTH ABOUT 1130 mm
WEIGHT "   25 kg
LOAD APPLIED 11100 kg

SHOCK-ABSORBING RUBBER FOR THE FUSELAGE

45mm   EXTRA-SUPER DURAL E.S.D.

CONNECTING LINK (WITH THE DAMPER FOR LATERAL VIBRATION)

WITHIN THIS ANGLE, IT RETURNS TO NEUTRAL AUTOMATICALLY

15°   BOTH SIDES 15°

OO CARRIER-BORNE FIGHTER

Diagram 3.   Japanese carrier operation – Navy Type OO Carrier-borne Fighter Arresting Hook. (US Naval Technical Mission)

arrestor wire, it could ram the aircraft ahead before the barrier had time to come up.[42]

Once on the flight deck the aircraft's taxiing was controlled by the *seibiin,* but the resetting of the wires and the barrier was controlled by the *hickōchō.* With a smooth-running team the Japanese aimed at landing intervals of twenty-five to thirty seconds for their fighter aircraft, with forty to forty-five seconds for torpedo-and dive-bombers. Even so, a landing crash was a rarity, averaging about 3 per cent.

To aid them in this manoeuvre, the A6M2s were equipped with a specially designed arrestor hook, which enabled the pilot himself to disengage it from the arrestor wire.[43] The procedure varied slightly according to the capability of the carrier concerned but generally each had eight or more arresting wires stretched across the flight deck, located between the forward side of the rearmost elevator

---

42. The Japanese only employed such barriers when they were maintaining a deck park forward. On war operations only the after barrier was employed; the forward barrier was kept for training and as a spare.

43. The deteriorating manufacturing situation in Japan as the war progressed forced the IJN to abandon construction of this superior type of arrestor hook after the spring of 1944.

up to the bridge. These wires were held at a height of 6¼ inches by lifting bars set at the extreme edges of the deck, each wire led down over guide pulleys to an arresting engine compartment located under the lower hangar-deck. As each pilot was given the signal by the *seibiin*, he let down his arresting hook and made a shallow glide approach. As soon as the aircraft's hook engaged a wire, a pulley system activated a ram in a hydraulic cylinder, which forced oil through a set of restrictors and into an air-loaded accumulator. The shape of these restrictors, plus the extra pressure of the air in the accumulator as it was activated, gave a constant deceleration to the aircraft and brought it to a halt. In 1942 the arresting engine employed on carriers was the *Kure* type, which could stop a 4 ton aircraft at a speed of 30 yards per second within a distance of 35 yards. The wire was reset electrically under this system and could be done within twelve seconds.[44] The key to a fast and safe recovery lay, of course, in a combination of good equipment and well-trained air and deck personnel. In 1942 the Japanese were high on both these attributes, but within a very short time both qualities were become more and more a rarity.

As if the dizzying combination of all these responsibilities were not sufficient, because the Japanese organized their carrier air groups in two-carrier *Kōkū sentai* (carrier divisions) as unified wings, utilizing a mix of the three main types (fighter, dive-and torpedo-bomber) as a single unit, the *hikōkitai*, in a double-wave series of strikes, the *hickōchō* could find himself responsible for the divisional mate's aircraft also. But with the formation in April 1941 of the revolutionary new six-carrier *Dai-ich Kōkū Kantai* (First Air Fleet), a new, higher-density attack was both possible, and, indeed, considered most desirable, to crush any opposition by sheer weight of numbers. This was, of course, a natural extension of the existent Japanese policy of attack over all else. First and foremost Japanese naval air power was a strike rather than a defensive weapon, in exactly the same way that the Zero fighter, the heavily armed heavy cruisers, the new destroyers and the new *Yamato* class battleships were. They all had one thing in common, they projected power. But it could add even more to the complexity of the *hickōchō*'s responsibilities, especially defensively. Commander Sadao Seno told me: 'I cannot find any record that control of the CAP over a carrier formation was the responsibility of the flag carrier's *hickōchō* for as I long as have been checking the battle reports'.[45]

Here the Japanese method of fighter defence control was suspect. Although the *hickōchō* were not the *exact* equivalents of fighter direction officers (FDO's), the advantages of a centralized control, as recently introduced by the Americans with the Combat Information Centre (CIC)[46], as a sort of 'evaluation and clearing house' for all the disparate sighting reports coming in from the screen and outlying ships of the fleet, were not lost on the Japanese. They might not have a dedicated centre built into their carriers, but some form of centralized direction of a finite and highly valuable resource was obviously desirable. After all, despite some retrospective American musings[47], the Japanese were leaders, not novices, in carrier air operations. It was evident that for the control and allocation of the *Kido Buntai*'s Zero CAP as a whole, central direction was desirable, if attainable. After all, four separate officers transmitting instructions to each of their own of four separate three-plane *shōtai* was an obvious recipe for confusion.

Barde was scathing: -

> The security of the Mobile Force rested on the Combat Air Patrol from the four carriers. In terms of numbers the CAP appears to have been adequate but the control of the fighter aircraft does not indicate any degree of centralization. The records of the Mobile Force do not reflect whether the Zeros were controlled in a fighter director central or by each carrier. Regardless of *how* it was done, the security was sufficiently weak to allow all planes to become engaged at low altitudes.[48]

Intriguingly, there is some indication that, at Midway, a form of centralized fighter direction might perhaps have been in place, with the senior officer of the *hickōchō* quartet, Commander Shogo Masuda aboard *Akagi*, having overall control of the placement of all four of the carrier fighter patrols.[49] With a quartet of contributing flight decks, this initially entailed covering the four points of the compass out

---

44. Later in the war this system was replaced by a hydraulic system more suitable for the heavier weights of the new-type carrier aircraft coming into service. This could reset a wire within five to seven seconds.
45. Commander Sadao Seno to the author, 17 March 2006.
46. The USS *Hornet* (CV-8) had been completed with a prototype of this type of information hub just a few weeks before Pearl Harbor.
47. For example, Parshall, and Tully, in, *Shattered Sword: The*

Untold Story of the Battle of Midway, say 'The Japanese would never manage to make this leap'.
48. Robert E Barde, *The Battle of Midway: A Study in Command*.
49. Commander Yoshida Akihiko to Mark R. Peattie, 5 May 1993. See Peattie, Mark R. *Sunburst: The Rise of Japanese Naval Air Power, 1909–1941*. However Mark Peattie confirmed to me that Yoshida Akihiko quoted no sources or references for this statement in the letter. (Peattie to the author, 7 March 2005.) The opposite view is taken by

to a depth of about 15 miles, with a *shōtai* of Zeros responsible for each, stacked at height placements that were paired at 6,500 feet and 13,000 feet respectively, to cover any eventuality. Standing instructions stressed the need for the standing air patrols to protect their carrier from all incomings and not to over-concentrate on any one threat to the exclusion of all others; however, this was easier to say than do.

If the skies were clear these four groups would have a good chance of spotting any incoming hostile aircraft in good time to make a reasonably distant intercept. However, in conditions of, heavy or even patchy cloud, the chance of being surprised was increasingly heightened. The screening destroyers were moved out to the horizon to provide maximum eye warning. This had the effect of weakening the protective anti-aircraft screen they could give the carriers themselves of course. The Japanese tended to rely on much smaller destroyer screens than the Americans, probably, as in the case of the Royal Navy, simply due to lack of sufficient ships of that type to mount a double screen. It is worth noting that the British experience of dive-bombing (both the *Illustrious* and the *Formidable* had been dive-bombed by the Junkers Ju87's Stukas in the Mediterranean in January and May 1941, and suffered severe damage) had led to the allocation of one, and later two, destroyers with the major task of providing a close-range barrage directly over their assigned carrier. This was later extended by the addition of a specialist anti-aircraft cruiser tasked solely with the additional defence of an assigned carrier. Even then, under heavy attack, this dedicated protection proved insufficient.[50]

Japanese practice at Midway was very different. The majority of their destroyers, other than the usual plane guards, were stationed as far out toward the horizon as possible in order to act as anti-submarine deterrents as well

as additional air-raid-warning stations. Thus their own anti-aircraft firepower did not supplement the aircraft carriers' own gun defences to any great degree other than as an additional barrier to incoming low-flying torpedo aircraft. There has been some criticism of Japanese destroyers' anti-aircraft potential, claiming that their main armament was 'low-angled' and 'practically useless' against aircraft. This is incorrect; the eleven destroyers escorting the four Japanese carriers at Midway were of the *Kaguro* and *Yugumo* classes, practically brand-new vessels and much more powerful than most contemporary British and American destroyers. Far from being impotent against aircraft, their main armament of six 5 inch 50 calibre guns were *specifically designed* as dual-purpose weapons. Thus, although it is claimed they were unable to elevate high enough to fire on aircraft, the guns of these destroyers had an elevation of up to 75 degrees to do this very job. In addition, each ship also had *two* pairs of twin 25 mm lighter anti-aircraft weapons, not one as claimed.

Any ship, destroyer on the screen or battleship and heavy cruisers on the escort, which sighted incoming hostiles would open fire with a splash barrage to draw attention to the location of the enemy, or lay smoke as another visual indicator, but this still relied very much on the Zeros overhead, who might have their attention focused elsewhere, both noticing and reacting with sufficient alacrity and numbers in the time remaining. This meant that, even at optimum performance, interceptions of enemy aircraft were often made close in, with the resultant scrimmage and vulnerability to losses from 'friendly' anti-aircraft fire while in hot pursuit across the fleet.

However, by far the greatest handicap for the *hickōchō*, escorting cruisers and defending *chutai* alike was the lack of ship-or air-borne air defence radar.[51] Without this significant apparatus Japanese defenders' warning about inward

---

Jonathan Parshall who kindly elaborated the summary of his own extensive research to me in this way; 'I have to say that my understanding of the matter is different than Yoshida's – everything I have seen seems to indicate that each carrier's *hickōchō* was essentially controlling his own carrier's CAP elements.' He adds, very pertinently that 'the level of control they exercised . . . was pretty minimal'. (Parshall to the author, 8 March 2005.) The picture presented of the Japanese CAP at Midway is that it acted amorphously; reactively flowing naturally toward the latest perceived threat, almost like quicksilver on a sheet of glass or a flock of starlings wheeling in the sky. Incidentally, like so many documents relating to Midway, this letter appears to have disappeared. Mark Peattie told me he no longer had it and had loaned it to Jonathan Parshall who told me that he definitely does not have it!

50. On Russian convoy PQ18 mounted in September 1942, the escort carrier *Avenger* was provided with two dedicated

Hunt class destroyers, *Wilton* and *Wheatland*, with a predominantly anti-aircraft oriented main armament. On the famous *Pedestal* convoy to Malta, mounted the month before, each of the three fleet carriers was allocated her own *Dido* class anti-aircraft cruiser: *Eagle/Charybdis*, *Victorious/Phoebe* and *Indomitable/Sirius*. Even so the Ju87s, attacking at the same time as the Italian SM79 torpedo bombers in much the same pattern as at Midway, but better co-ordinated, split the defensive fire sufficiently to get through to *Indomitable*, which the dive-bombers hit several times and put out of action at a crucial time. (See Peter C. Smith, *Pedestal: The convoy that saved Malta* and *Arctic Victory: The story of Convoy PQ18*.

51. Development of radar was well underway in the IJN, with Kure Naval Arsenal being the centre of that research (Yasuzo Nakagawa, *Japanese Radar and Related Weapons*). Just prior to Midway, in May, the battleships *Ise* and *Hyuga* were dry-docked at Kure Navy Yard, and fitted with experimental

attack forces was handicapped beyond hope. Whereas any British or American battle fleet by this stage of the war would have some long-range data on such an attack, with direction of approach, height, speed and numbers perhaps the most essential, and thus be able to vector defenders out to meet it, the Japanese at Midway were denied this essential. Visual warning alone remained to them, be it airborne, from the defending CAP aloft at 10,000 feet, or from the outer destroyer screen pushed out toward the horizon or other screening vessels. Against high-flying aircraft coming out of the sun, this was often insufficient.

Then again, if faced with a choice of targets, such a policy left the choice of which to go after to the individual pilots, or more likely to the *shōtai* leaders, the *buntaichō*. It was perceived wisdom in all the three major navies that hits by torpedo-bombers were by far the most serious threat to surface ships, be they heavily protected battleships (with the fate of the Pearl Harbor battle line and *Prince of Wales* and *Repulse* examples fresh, stunning and irrefutable proof) or aircraft carriers. A hit below the water line was still more likely to sink a ship than a bomb from above. On the other hand, once a dive-bomber had committed to its attack dive, it had to be knocked down to stop it, and carriers were especially vulnerable to such attacks; after all they did not have to be sunk to be put out of the battle, any hit that prevented the flight deck being utilized instantly transformed a major aircraft carrier from a powerful offensive asset to a bulky liability. A dilemma indeed, and a weighty decision for a young naval aviator, probably a mere lieutenant having to make a snap decision in the heat of battle.

Only a limited number of fighter aircraft could be maintained aloft at any one time. The decision that had to be made all the time a fleet was in range of enemy air power was 'How many?' Equally pertinent, especially with regard to protection against dive-bombers, was 'How high?' A carrier fleet with unlimited resources might maintain many fighters overhead, landing them to refuel and rearm at two-hour intervals, and sending aloft replacements. Also, such an ideally situated fleet would be able to stack its fighters at various altitudes to deal with the multiplicity of threats – low-level torpedo-bombing, high level approachs by dive-bombers, high-altitude bombing and so on. Two years on,

with twelve to fourteen aircraft carriers rather than just four, US task forces could do this, and even have the luxury of an exclusive night-fighter carrier as well, but this was hardly practical for the Nagumo force in 1942. Not even the 1st *Kidō Butai*, which, it must be recalled, was only at two-thirds its maximum strength, could dream of such resources, especially when fighters also had to be allocated to escort outgoing strikes at the same time. The Japanese disposed four carriers, with a nominal eighteen Zeros embarked in each, and that was it.

In the 1930s, following studies to find the best ways to operate its growing carrier fleet, the general consensus reached by the Japanese air specialists was similar to that reached in the US Navy, that no incoming air threat could ever be totally stopped by the fleet's defences.[52] The answer was always to get in the first blow and make it decisive. This concept appealed, and tended to obscure the next obvious question: what if the enemy got in first ?

The Japanese answer was to maintain a small standing air patrol, a *shōtai*, but to have another warmed up and spotted on the deck ready to be scrambled away at the first sign of attack, with a third in reserve. This meant that the enemy, already dangerously close, would have more time to approach, even though the Zero could climb at 4,000 feet a minute, and interceptions were therefore made close in, often when the enemy aircraft was already under gunfire from the screening warships.

Indeed, gunfire from the outer screening destroyers, was sometimes the first indications of approaching enemy aircraft; certain warships, closer in (at Midway, notably the heavy cruiser *Chikuma*) were good at spotting such attacks and laid down a 'splash barrage' with their main 8 inch battery to alert defending pilots to the danger. The Japanese *hickōchō* had an awesome responsibility for, with very finite resources, they had to be ready to vector Zeros out to any point of the compass at very short notice. Moreover, they had to do the directing, for such it was, with unreliable radio equipment and to recipients who had little or no faith in its reliability. Also, it should be noted, at the Midway battle at least, every fighter aircraft used the *same* wavelength, regardless of which carrier it flew from, or which *hickōchō* it belonged to.[53]

radar sets, both *Ise* and *Hyuga* with the Type 21 (Type 2 Model 1) 1.5 m air scanning set, and *Hyuga* additionally with the Model 103 prototype surface scanning set, atop their bridges. Neither was a resounding success; the former was adopted 'with reluctance', while the latter proved to be too unwieldy. Eric Lacroix and Linton Wells *Japanese Cruisers of the Pacific War*. They stated it was 'hard to operate, and the antenna was quite cumbersome'. The set installed on *Hyuga* was removed prior to the battle. Even had the sets

worked perfectly, it would have made no difference as neither of these battleships was allocated to the Nagumo force.

52. See Bōeichō Bōeikenshūjo Senshishitsu, *Kaigun kōkū gaishi* (historical overview of Japanese naval aviation), Senshi Sōsho, Asagumo Shimbunsha, Japan, 1976.

53. Battle Report of the *Kaga*, contained in *The Midway Operation*, DOC Translation Extracts, DOC No. 160985B – MC 397.901.

However, having radios and using them were very much two different things. One of the *Soryū* pilots who flew CAP on 4 June, Kaname Harada, gave this information to Mike Wenger, whose deep research and knowledge of Japanese carrier operations is unrivalled among current historians. Harada stated that the CAP stacking and compositions were all decided aboard each carrier individually, prior to the launching of each day's strike. Fighter pilots naturally preferred to accompany the strike forces, rather than 'waste' their time circling above the fleet at assigned altitudes; this was all part of the Japanese offensive psyche. Each *shotai* was assigned designated sectors and altitude parameters to observe, although Kaname stated that they were not rigidly adhered to. This zoning was also 'flexible' with regard to distance out from the fleet, with about 40 miles being the furthest the chain was let out; although Kaname stated that, in reality, few pilots ventured out much more than a third of this distance from their home carrier in case they could not find their way home again (navigational skills were not among fighter pilot's premier attributes!).

Kaname also informed Mike Wenger that, once the *shotai* was airborne, they were, in essence if not in theory, virtually on their own; in fact they received no instructions whatsoever. Should enemy aircraft be encountered and engaged, the theory was for the engaging pilot to transmit '*To, To, To*' on his transmitting key; but they rarely had time to do this in practice. Even communication between different *shotai* was problematical and relied more on hand signals and facial expressions than radio.[54]

That was the scenario when incoming hostiles were detected, by whatever method. But what if they were not spotted? That risk had been acceptable at first. In the first heady flush of victory and with the overwhelming weight of five or six large carriers working in harmony with a combined force of many hundred aircraft, each successive opponent had been simply overwhelmed, not only qualitatively, in aircraft performance, but also quantitatively. Even

so, a warning had been sounded during the Indian Ocean sortie of April 1942. On the 9th of that month, a striking force of nine RAF Bristol Blenheim Mk. IV twin-engined light bombers, from No. 11 Squadron, based at Colombo, Ceylon, and led by Squadron Leader K. Ault, had been the first enemy force actually to catch a glimpse of the feared 1st *Kido Butai* and make an attack against it.[55]

Incredibly, these relatively slow aircraft had achieved some surprise and had penetrated the fleet's defensive full overhead fighter patrols undetected! The eruption of 500 pound SAP bombs off the flagship *Akagi*'s starboard bow at 1025 was a measure of just how flat-footed the Japanese force had been caught. Fortunately, for them the RAF's methods of attack, with Blenheim's bombing from 11,000 feet, was never to be an accurate method of bomb delivery, and every single bomb missed the target. The Zeros recovered and quickly pursued the retiring enemy, shooting down five of the nine[56], and so damaging all the remaining four that they had to be written off. But it could have been very different had the attackers been dive-bombers.[57]

The fact that the Zero was a fast and highly manoeuvrable fighter[58] has led some to state that their actual location over the fleet mattered little as they could quickly recover and adapt, both horizontally and vertically (they had a fantastic rate of climb for the period). But that would not, and in fact, did not, help in the event of total surprise by an enemy force, especially if that force was dive-bombers which, once committed to their final attack dive, had to be totally taken out to be stopped from delivery. There was simply not time to do this in practice.

Everyone, without exception, seems convinced that there was a total breakdown in the discipline of the CAP at the time the SBDs arrived overhead, with all the Zeros either down on the deck 'swatting' Devastators or being taught a severe lesson in marksmanship by Thach's F4Fs. However, there is an intriguing comment in the Battle Report of VS-6. 'Although several Japanese fighters were

---

54. Harada Kaname to Mike Wenger, via Jon Parshall to the author, 10 March 2006. I am indebted to all three for kindly sharing this information with me.

55. Michael Tomlinson, '*The Most Dangerous Moment*', gives a very one-sided account of this episode. Eleven aircraft had taken off from the Racecourse airstrip in two flights, but two aborted the mission. The aircraft also carried two naval observers to make sure the ships they found were enemy ones! They had already made two unproductive sorties and failed to locate the Japanese. It was a case of third time lucky.

56. The aircraft shot down over the fleet were those piloted by Squadron Leader K. Ault, Flying Officer E. Adcock, Pilot Officer R. Knight. Sergeant Stevenson and Sergeant McClennan, with their crews, both naval observers were also lost.

57. A fact that even so anti-dive-bombing an organisation as the RAF finally admitted, forming a force of four squadrons of such aircraft composed of the new American-built Vultee V-72 Vengeance aircraft, and practising anti-shipping tactics continually for a return visit from Nagumo, which never materialized of course. See Peter C Smith, *Vengeance! The Vultee Vengeance Dive Bomber*.

58. Iyōzō Fujita told me that the Zero, 'was a pleasure to fly.' He said that in the role of 'a short-range interceptor, she was far more manoeuvrable than a Wildcat, with a much tighter turning circle', but that 'height advantage was the most desirable scenario, enabling us to dive to attack.' If it came to a slugging match, then things changed: 'the Wildcat was stronger, while the Zero caught fire more easily', so this was best avoided.

observed overhead in position to attack, no attacks were pressed home against 6-S-1 and 6-S-2. A Messerschmitt type fighter was seen to attack 6-S-8 and the fighter was seen to crash into the water in flames.'[59]

The Zero fighters which were alleged to have been in position to attack the SBDs but failed to do so may have been out of ammunition. The incomprehensible account of an SBD being attacked by a Bf109 has been repeated in accounts of other battles; it is as if some American's still could not believe that the Japanese were building and flying fighters as good as the Zero but just had to have had German assistance.[60]

In the final analysis the SBDs had to be intercepted *before* they went into their attack dives. This was a common problem when opposed to dive-bombing. There was much talk of Stuka massacres by the RAF in 1940 and later, when, it was claimed, once the Ju87 pulled out of its dive the Hurricanes and Spitfires, impotent to stop them on the way down, could easily 'swat' them before they re-formed to give mutual defence. But, in the event, the SBDs lost not a single aircraft to protecting Zero fighters.[61] More pertinent, even if every single Dauntless had been shot out into the sea upon recovery from their dives, the damage they inflicted would have already been done! Shutting the door after the horse had bolted in this instance would have meant revenge, but it would not have altered the outcome, the carriers would still have been ravaged. As was the case on 22 October 1926 when VF-2 dived down on the totally surprised US fleet off San Pedro, once committed, dive-bombers proved that there was no defence.

Whatever the theories of whether the carriers could influence the way their fighters protected them, once the first bombs hit in that catastrophic four minutes on 4 June, three of the four *hickōchō*, regardless of their previous capabilities in this respect, immediately ceased to have any bearing on the matter whatsoever. None was killed,

strangely enough, but any communication that might have existed, abruptly ceased. Nor, save for *Hiryū*, did it matter any more; the *Akagi, Kaga and Soryū* were instantly erased, at least as far as having any combat battle value was concerned.

Black Shoe, Brown Shoe

A great deal of bitterness and argument is generated by the old dispute over which type of senior officer was best fitted to command carrier task forces as they developed during World War II. The arguments are by no means confined to the US Navy; both the Royal Navy and the IJN experienced the same schism in thought and opinion, both at the time and ever since. This battle has continued long after the actual events that originated it and has, to a large degree, over-shadowed it. Like the mythical Operation Orient red herring, a plan that never existed, the blue sea versus blue sky debate is now fought less by the dwindling numbers of veterans, or even by historians, but more and more, on the Internet, with discussion groups contributing a heady mix of both intelligent and well-informed opinion, watered down by a great deal of uninformed, naïve or opinionated input.

Probably Admiral Marc Mitscher's remarks made almost twenty years before the Battle of Midway, are as good a definition of the 'brown shoe' argument as one is likely to see. He stated that, with regard to aviation in the general scheme of naval warfare, the naval aviation officer:

> . . . feels that it is important enough to be commanded by personnel who know, and will appreciate, and can advance the viewpoint of the flying man. He feels that experienced aviation men should have administration of the training of aviation personnel and detail of aviation personnel. He feels that aviation development of the Navy presents a career, and that once he

59. Confidential Report of Action, June 4–6, 1942, from Commander, Scouting Squadron Six to Commanding Officer, U.S.S. *Enterprise*/Commander, *Enterprise* Air Group, dated 20 June, 1942.

60. In this strange impression the Americans were not alone. In the April attacks in the Indian Ocean, the British C-in-C afloat, Admiral Sir James Somerville, reported that the dive-bombers, which sank many of his ships, might have been German Stukas (Junkers Ju87s). Navalized versions of both the Bf109 fighter and the Ju87 dive-bomber *were* the intended air complement of the built, but never commissioned, German aircraft carrier *Graf Zeppelin* but, as far as is known, never flew from any Japanese carrier deck, and were most certainly *not* at Midway. The Bf109, moreover, was not a radial-engined aircraft and so had a totally different profile to the Zero, but the aircraft reported might very well have been

the 13 Shi prototype Yokosuka D4Y *Suisei* (Comet) which the Allies codenamed Judy, piloted by Lieutenant Takemori Kondō. She had an in-line engine, which could account for the mistaken identification. This aircraft was used in a high-speed reconnaissance role during the battle.

61. The figures are illuminating. The Japanese 'Great CAP' had thirty-six Zeros in the air and got off a further seven re-inforcements before the carriers were hit. Of these forty-three defending fighters, thirteen were lost – six to F4Fs, one to the Devastators, one to friendly anti-aircraft fire, two ditched and three were lost to the SBDs' defensive fire. Of the thirty left aloft, ten *Kaga* machines, seven from *Akagi*, and six each from *Hiryū* and *Soryū*, all save one managed to land aboard *Hiryū*; the remaining one from *Akagi* maintained a lone sad patrol over her mother ship, almost as a mark of respectful mourning, until lack of fuel forced her to ditch.

takes up aviation he should be permitted to follow the general aviation line throughout his life. He feels that Navy aviation presents a new problem not quite similar to any of the past problems of naval experience.[62]

Another US naval officer, much later, made the opposing case. Admiral Sir James Somerville recorded a dinner he hosted on 7 November 1944, when he was in Washington DC. As well as Commodore Clarke, present was Captain Adolphus Dayton Clark, who had been the United States Navy Liaison Officer aboard the aircraft carrier *Ark Royal* when she was fighting the Italian *Regia Aeronautica* almost single-handed in the western Mediterranean in the dark days of 1940–1.[63] Somerville, himself a 'black shoe' man, but one of the few who took the trouble to fly with his aircrew and find out their problems by listening to them, understood the argument perfectly. He wrote:

Clark was critical of the American practice of putting their air Admirals in command of Task Forces. He considered that not only had this been overdone, but that it was easier for a surface force commander to have good tactical appreciation of the possibilities of use of air, rather than vice versa; he considered that the lack of 'follow up'[64] by American surface forces in the previous encounters with the Japanese was due to the air Admirals not knowing how to handle surface forces.[65]

Whatever the validity of Clark's later opinion, at Midway the argument generated controversy on the conduct of operations by both the Japanese and American commanders. One of the most controversial incidents on the Japanese side was the decision to hold back the Val dive-bomber groups of Takashige Egusa aboard the *Hiryū* and *Soryū*. This, it has been alleged, was the last chance for the Japanese to mount a telling blow against the American task forces. They were held back because Nagumo was fixated on delivering a combined, concentrated blow by all his force. If he had unleashed the Vals with whatever fighter cover was available while he yet had the chance, at least some retaliation would have been achieved. Coupled with this charge, which amounted to an accusation of inflexibility because such a piecemeal attack was against the then current Japanese carrier operations orthodoxy and doctrine, was another argument; just *who* was running the airborne side of the 1st *Kidō Butai*, Vice-Admiral Chūichi Nagumo or Commander Minoru Genda?

How long was it necessary to hold back the Vals while the Kates were rearmed from bombs for a second strike against Midway Island, to the torpedoes essential to take on the American Task Forces?

Takeshi Maeda told me that his Kate torpedo-bomber was below in the hangar having a torpedo loaded. He was part of the second attack unit and had already had his torpedo replaced by a bomb – which was now being replaced by a torpedo. 'The order was for all seventeen or eighteen *Kaga* and *Akagi* torpedo-bombers to take off at once with what they had, and that a fighter escort of eighteen Zeros from *Hiryū* and *Soryū* would escort us'.[66] However, changing from torpedo to bomb was one thing, changing from bomb to torpedo another. 'The torpedo was much more complicated and required specialist handling. The torpedo was retained by many more bolts, the depth settings required fine adjustment and special technicians had to be used for this, restricting the number and lengthening the time taken, of which there were relatively few for eighteen aircraft.' Maeda estimated three hours was the time such a switch would take for the whole Kate force.

Taemi Ichikawa, who was aboard the *Akagi*, gave me a slightly different figure of two and a half hours for the changeover.[67] Ichikawa said that the sea was calm but that the carriers were continually heeling over as they changed course while under attack, which slowed things down. A 250 kg bomb was less of a handling problem than an 850 kg

62. Statement of Commander Marc A. Mitscher before the Morrow Board, Washington DC on 6 October 1925, contained in Aviation Hearings, General Board, 2 Vols, Washington, Navy Department, 1925. Navy Historical Center.

63. Captain Clark was later in command of the American part of the Mulberry harbour at the Normandy landings that was wrecked by a gale.

64. Presumably this criticism would include not just Midway, but the Coral Sea, Santa Cruz and Philippine Sea battles also at this date. However, only at the latter was there any sizeable American battleship force strong enough to 'follow up' if allowed to. In the latter case, the battleship admiral Lee, had been asked if he wanted a night surface action, and had replied he considered his heavy ships were just not yet ready for such an encounter.

65. The *Somerville Papers*, Churchill College Archive, Cambridge. SMVL 2/3. Entry for 8 November 1944.

66. Interview with Takeshi Maeda at Annex Dai-Ichi Hotel, Tokyo, Friday 4 November 2005.

67. Interview with Rear-Admiral Taemi Ichikawa at his home in Matsudo City, 3 November 2005.

torpedo, not only because of the weight difference, but also because of the bulk and complexity of the latter. This meant that the rearmed Kates 'were never on deck' before the first bomb struck the ship 'just abaft the lift'. This bomb strike gave Ichikawa the superficial appearance of inflicting 'only a scratch', but in fact its effect was to be terminal. Exploding among the massed ranks of the Kates and their torpedo warheads the bombs caused them to cook off spreading the fire and flames. It destroyed the hanger fire curtain, instantly hampering all subsequent efforts to curtail of the blaze. Ichikawa told me, 'They tried to put out the fires but they could not – it was impossible to get at the seat of the fire as the carrier just circled.'

There was no gainsaying the pedigree of the 1st *Kidō Butai*'s Air Officer, Commander Minoru Genda. He had proven himself a highly able fighter pilot aboard the *Akagi* early on in his meteoric career, with a penchant for exhibitionism that found its expression in the naval air acrobatic formation team, which was a popular draw at air fairs all over the Empire. His natural flair and feel for flying could be duplicated throughout the pre-war elite of the IJN's aviators of course, but he had broadened its dimension by a stint as a flying instructor at Yokosuka Naval Air Station in 1932, where he proved articulate enough to convey his skill to his pupils. The station's own fighter unit, which Genda headed, was also charged with testing new aircraft and, was known as the 'Genda Circus'. A further deepening of his overall insight came with a tour of duty aboard the *Ryūjō* during combat missions off China, followed by a shore-based assignment as an air staff officer, where organization under pressure was added to his portfolio of abilities. Diplomacy was a desirable facet to add to this dazzling rainbow of talent and this he attained as Assistant Air Attaché in London, where he was when war broke out, not returning to Japan until 1940. He was able to witness how the Royal Navy's Fleet Air Arm, with their far inferior

aircraft, were able to influence events at sea. The attack on the Italian main fleet base at Taranto during which three battleships were torpedoed, must have given him a great deal of food for thought![68]

However, to aspire to the highest commands, a naval officer needed more than these attributes; the final piece of the jigsaw was influential patronage, and this Genda achieved in spades, being backed by the top man. He had caught the eye of no less than Admiral Isoroku Yamamoto himself, who seemed to see a kindred spirit in the confident and aggressively self-assured young air ace. He personally selected him for this key role in the First Air Fleet.

Genda had long made known his total conviction of the ascendancy of air power over conventional sea power, which came to be identified with his opposition to the construction of new battleships, of which Japan only ever built two, *Yamato* and *Musashi*.[69] While still a lieutenant-commander at the Naval Staff College, in 1935–7, Genda had written a contentious paper on what armament he thought was vital to conduct an effective war against the USA, in which he consigned the battleship fleet to the role of jetty hulks, to the predictable fury of most of his peers on the Naval Staff.[70] But Yamamoto, who had long propagated similar revolutionary views was naturally delighted! Genda's future was assured and he was duly assigned as Nagumo's Senior Air Officer in April 1941. He could not have been in a stronger contrast with his boss, Vice-Admiral Chūichi Nagumo.[71]

On the American side the 'black shoe versus brown shoe' debate was, if anything, more heated, and has continued so down the many decades that followed Midway. Marc Andrew Mitscher, was an out-and-out 'brown shoe' admiral, yet many would say his command's air group hardly shone as examples of how it should be done on that fateful 4 June.

---

68. Genda seemingly failed to learn the biggest lesson of all about the Royal Navy's backwardness in matters of air power at sea; the bitter lesson of having its aircraft designed, built and controlled by another service, the RAF, which had no concept of or sympathy for its potential or application, and indeed was disdainful of it. Despite this obvious disaster, Genda, perhaps influenced by his army friends, was later enthusiastic about combining Japan's army and naval air forces into one combined service. See Atsushi Oi's 1951 document '*The Japanese Navy in 1941*', contained in Donald M. Goldstein and Katherine V. Dillon, (eds), *The Pacific War Papers: Japanese Documents of World War II*, Potomac Books, Dulles, Virginia, 2004. Oi concluded that lack of air-mindedness on the part of the Army 'resulted in one advantage to naval aviation. The Navy could develop her land-based aviation as she wanted.'

He could also have quite legitimately added, *her carrier-based aircraft also*!

69. Plus a third, *Shinano*, which was completed as an aircraft carrier. By contrast the Royal Navy completed six new battleships between 1940 and 1946; both the German and French Navies completed two battleships and two battle-cruisers each; the Italian Navy built three battleships; while all other powers were out-built by the 'air-minded' the United States Navy which completed no less than ten battleships and two battle-cruisers between 1941 and 1945.

70. Genda, Minoru, *Kaigun kōkūtai shimatsuki* (A record of the particulars of the Japanese naval air service), 2 volumes, Bungei Shunjū, Tokyo, 1961-62.

71. To be fair to Nagumo, by the time Midway was fought, he had far more experience of actual wartime carrier operations than any of his American opposite numbers.

Table 14: SBD Losses in 1st Attack at Midway 4 June 1942

Unit	No in attack	Shot down	Damaged	Ditched	Returned
VB-3	17	0	0	0	17
VS-6	17	1 (by Flak)	2	7	8
VB-6	14	0	2	7	7
VB-8	19	0	3	3	16
VS-8	19	0	0	2	14
TOTAL	83	1	7	19	62

Mitscher was either lucky or unlucky with his biographer, according to one's viewpoint. Certainly the title 'Magnificent' has stuck, and was a deserved epitaph for the man and his accomplishments. Theodore Taylor emphatically displayed his newspaper reporter and press agent credentials to their fullest extent in its writing, but the seeker after facts will come away rather bruised. Among the statements made with regard to Midway alone, what are we to make of the claim that on 4 June VB-8 scored hits 'on a battleship and a heavy cruiser' when no Japanese battleship was hit in the entire battle; or that the reason Spruance avoided a night encounter with possibly superior enemy forces was because he thought 'another enemy carrier might be lurking nearby' when it was being caught by the Japanese battleship's force in a night surface action that influenced the move, or 'At 1150, *Hornet* planes attacked two cruisers and a destroyer. The cruisers *Mogami* and *Mikuma* were sunk by dive bombing' when only the *Mikuma* was sunk.[72]

Who Invented Dive-bombing?

It has become a self-perpetuating myth that the US Navy invented dive-bombing. Listen to one typical account: 'From all indications, it seems logical to conclude that Wagner was the first to demonstrate the feasibility of attacking in the near-vertical mode, that is, in dives of 70 degrees or greater.[73]

To what does the following passage refer to?

We found her with all aircraft lined up on deck just about to turn into the wind, so that they could take off, and therefore presenting a most vulnerable target to our bombs and machine-guns. We made an initial

dive on our target in formation, then split up for individual dives in a converging bomb attack, after which we would zoom up away from the ship in all directions, rejoining in formation when well out of range of the anti-aircraft defences.

The Battle of Midway? No, nor to *Lexington* versus *Saratoga* in 1937. No. In fact it is from a memoir written by a British navy flyer of an exercise held by the Royal Navy's Mediterranean Fleet on 27 July 1928. What it describes is the airborne striking force from the carrier *Courageous* surprising the carrier *Eagle* in a dawn dive-bombing attack.[74] Another decade before that, there is the following:

'At Bernot I found four barges. The fog lifted slightly . . . I dove straight for the barge. As I pulled up and looked back I could feel the effect of the explosion. I had hit the middle barge square amidships". Second Lieutenant Harry Brown, RFC, carrying out his dive-bombing mission on 14 March 1918 in an SE5a aircraft on the Western Front.'[75]

SBD Immunity at Midway

As we have seen among the many epithets applied to the Douglas SBD Dauntless dive-bomber were 'the Barge', 'the Clunk' and such, which indicated a sort of fond resignation, implying that she was an obsolescent and inadequate aircraft, but loveable. This is to do the SBD a disservice; and her long-awaited replacement in service, the Curtiss SB2C Helldiver, seemed to generate ever great derision, deserved or not, the kindest of which was 'Son of a Bitch, Second Class', due more to her slow development and unforgiving

72. Theodore Taylor, *The Magnificent Mitscher*, Naval Institute Press, Annapolis, 1991.
73. Thomas Wildenberg, *Destined for Glory: Dive Bombing, Midway, and the Evolution of Carrier Airpower,* describing the attack made by VF-2 under Lieutenant-Commander

Frank D. Wagner on the US Fleet in the San Pedro Roads on 22 October 1922.
74. Owen Cathcart-Jones, *Aviation Memoirs*.
75. W. H. Brown, Memoirs.

flight characteristics than anything else. But among the many derogatory names applied to the Dauntless, one was more representative than the others 'Slow But Deadly'. Slow, yes, but she was a bomber and should not be compared with fighters in performance, a common misconception about all World War II dive-bombers.[76] The 'Deadly' part was well-deserved, having been hard-earned in a hundred or more dive-bombing attacks, from Midway in the central Pacific to the northern coast of France, and from the jungles of the Solomon Islands and the Philippines to the bleak coast of Norway.[77] But she could also be deadly in defence. Like her Japanese contemporary, the Val[78], she showed surprising resilience and was often pressed into service to supplement the fighter defences of the fleet in the early days of the Pacific War.

The breakdown of the SBD attacks was as in Table 14.

76. Dive-bombers did not have to be slow aircraft, witness the North American A-36 *Apache* and the Soviet Petlyakov Pe-2 *Peshka*, which were as fast or faster than many contemporary fighter aircraft. See Peter C. Smith, *Straight Down! The North American A-36 dive-bomber in action*.
77. Peter C. Smith, *The Douglas SBD Dauntless*.
78. When British Fairey Fulmar fighters briefly tangled with the Aichi Vals off Trincomalee in April 1942, the former came off worse, losing two of their number without loss to the Vals. This led the British admiral, Somerville, to describe the Vals to his superiors in London as fighter dive-bombers, and claim this was a 'novel' aspect of attack! Michael Simpson, *The Somerville Papers*.

Part Three

Duel to the Death

Chapter Eight

One Against Three

With three-quarters of the proud Japanese carrier fleet blasted and burning before their eyes, the fate of the battle suddenly depended on just one carrier and the fearless fighter who commanded her. Could he reverse the terrible situation they found themselves in? Could the best air group in the *Kidō Butai* pull off a miracle? Should he even try?

That the carrier battle was not all over after the one devastating SBD strike was due to one man, Rear-Admiral Tamon Yamaguchi.[1] He was deified by the Japanese for that decision, but recently has been vilified by modern American historians. In judging his actions and motivations one must keep in mind the man's beliefs and conditioning, and above all his mindset. We know that he was deeply imbued with the code of *Bushido* [The Way of the Warrior,

a code of honour and conduct similar to European Chivalry], and that, ultimately he was to follow that dignified way to immortality. We can respect that and even honour it. But could he have saved *Hiryū* to fight another day? *Should* he have done so from a strictly military sense? The arguments rage and no doubt will always do so. While it is certainly legitimate to question his judgement and expertise[2], nobody ought to doubt his courage and fighting spirit. Yamaguchi might have been many things, but he was no quitter!

Kobayashi's Attack

Launching of the *Hiryū*'s first counter-punch commenced at 1045. The time gap between the American SBDs' assault

---

1. Vice-Admiral Tamon Yamaguchi (1892–1942). b. Shimane Prefecture on 17 August 1892. 1912 at Etajima Naval Academy, 40th Class. Midshipman aboard old ex-Russian cruiser *Soya* from July.1913 served aboard battleship *Settsu*. Sub-Lieutenant from December. 1914 served on light cruiser *Chikuma* from May. 1915 served on battleship *Aki* from February to December. As lieutenant (jg) attended Gunnery School and 1916 Torpedo School, basic courses.1916 3 Special Battle Group as Navigation Officer. 1918, joined staff of 2nd Special Task Fleet, serving on destroyer *Kashi* from July, promoted to lieutenant in December. Escorted former German U-boats home as part of repatriation agreements.1919, Yokosuka naval dockyard, and aboard the repair ship *Kanto*, then at Kure and advanced course at Torpedo School. 1921–3 attended Princeton University, New Jersey. Served aboard battleship *Nagato*, then Instructor as Submarine School. 1924, lieutenant-commander, Naval College 'A' course, graduating with honour.1926 staff 1st Submarine Squadron. 1927 Navy General Staff, promoted to commander December 1928 and again visited the USA.1929 in delegation to London Naval Conference to 1930, Attendant to Plenipotentiary. 1930 XO on light cruiser *Yura*, then on staff 1st Flotilla. 1932 Instructor at Naval and Military Colleges. Promoted to captain in December and appointed as Naval Attaché in

Washington, DC until August 1936. Appointed in command light cruiser *Isuzu* then in command battleship *Ise* from December 1937. 1938, promoted to rear-admiral in November, Naval General Staff. December became first Assistant and then CoS Japanese 5th Fleet to November 1939. 1940, appointed in command 1st Carrier Fleet and then commander 2nd Air Division, *Soryū* and *Hiryū*, November 1940, which he led from Pearl Harbor to Midway. Generally recognized as Yamamoto's heir apparent, but elected to go down with his ship on 4 June 1942, posthumously promoted to vice-admiral.

2. This quality is hardly mentioned in the arguments and counter-arguments, but Yamaguchi came late to naval air power, having spent most of his sea service in battleships, cruisers and destroyers, and anyway was more noted for his academic and diplomatic skills. Looking at it clinically, it could be claimed that he was no more attuned to carrier warfare when he took command of CarDiv 2 in 1940, than Fletcher or Spruance were when they were pitched into it two years later, but he was highly intelligence, had the natural aggressiveness that was attuned to the aviators' temperament (just like Halsey and Browning) and, best of all, he learned fast. Yamaguchi in those two years in command also had real experts like Egusa at his elbow and the combination made *Hiryū* and *Soryū* the two more proficient carriers in the IJN by Midway.

Table 15 – *Hiryu*'s first (Dive-Bomber) attack on Yorktown 4 June 1942

Buntai	Shōtai	Pilot	Radio/Gunner	Result Bomb
1	1	Lt Michio Kobayashi (*buntaichō*)	WO Yoshinori Ono	Lost
		Kihichiro Yamada, PO1c	Yoshiteru Fukunaga PO1c	Lost
		Hideo Sakai PO3c	Buichi Yamaguchi PO3c	Lost
	2	Lt Takemori Kondō (*buntaichō*)	WO Takashi Maeda	Lost
		Nobumichi Nakao PO2c	Hidemitsu Okamura PO1c	Lost
		Masao Seki, Sea1c	Kunio Tanaka, PO1c	Lost
	3	Tamotsu Imaizumi, PO1c	Rihei Kazuma, PO1c	Lost. Miss, unknown type
		Takayashi Tsuchiya, PO2c	Hayata Egami, PO2c	Miss, SAP
		Naoshi Koizumi PO3c	Yoshiaki Hagiwara, PO2c	Lost. Hit HE
2	1	WO Toshikatsu Nishihara	Lt Michiji Yamashita (B)	Lost
		Sadao Matsumoto, PO1c	Nobuhiko Yasuda, PO1c	Miss, HE
		Junichi Kuroki, PO3c	Yasuhiko Mizuno, Sea1c	Lost
	2	WO Iwao Nakazawa	Ens. Shimematsu Nakayama	Hit, SAP
		Tetsuo Seo, PO1c	Chikayoshi Murakami, PO3c	Miss, unknown type
		Sumio Kondō, PO1c	Yoshiaki Iwabuchi, PO3c	Lost
	3	WO Shizuo Nakagawa	Ryuji Ōtomo, PO1c	Hit, SAP
		Kōzō Ikeda, PO2c	Takumi Shimizu, PO3c	Lost
		Issei Fuchigami, Sea1c	Yoshinaru Nakaoka, Sea1c	Lost

and the *Hiryū*'s launch, has been held up as verification of the fact that the Japanese carriers had been nowhere near ready to launch when nemesis overtook them. Another view could well be put forward that, as the only flight deck now left, *Hiryū* had little choice but to postpone her attack in order to land every Japanese aircraft still airborne and clear them out of the way, which naturally slowed down her response.

A full force of eighteen D3A1 *kanbaku* (dive-bombers) was launched under the command of Lieutenant Michio Kobayashi[3], flying aircraft BII-201. One-third of this force had not yet been rearmed with the anti-ship 250 kg SAP (Semi-Armour-Piercing) bomb and six were sent away still toting the 24 kg HE (High-Explosive) land-attack bomb meant for Midway's defences but also suited to taking out flak defences on an enemy carrier.

Like their American counterparts that fateful day, Michio's Type 99s were given an exiguous fighter escort, a mere half-dozen A6M2s being all that could be spared. As we have already seen, these soon became embroiled in expensive attacks on straggling groups of returning SBDs and so the Aichis initially had to go into the battle against a fully prepared enemy defence alone and unprotected. After the assumed 'easy kills' had actually so damaged the Japanese opportunists as to reduce the *kansen*'s numbers by a third, the undamaged quartet hastened after the D3A1s but, by the time they finally arrived over the battle scene,

they were too late to offer much help. They became embroiled with the superior numbers of F4Fs of the American CAP and lost three of their number, Noboru, Suekichi and Yutaka, in the resulting scrap. Only the solitary Zero of Shigematsu survived to return to *Hiryū*.

Announcing the departure of this force Yamaguchi informed the C-in-C at 1054, 'All our [available] planes are taking off now for the purpose of destroying the enemy carriers', but lest that be misinterpreted as an all-out strike by his full air group, he added the fact that a second force, comprising nine torpedo-bombers with three Zeros, would be sent within the hour, this being the time still required for the switch-over from bombs to torpedoes then still taking place. Meanwhile, he stated, he was continuing to close the enemy rather than put his tail between his legs and flee. Had he known that *Hiryū* was facing odds of three to one, he might have acted differently, but it is doubtful. No son of the *Teikoku Kaigun* (IJN) would simply throw in the towel, no matter how the dice were loaded.

The experienced Yamaguchi was not prepared to be caught again with aircraft ready to go, so he sent what he had and prepared the others. Only then did he inform Nagumo of what he had done. While he might have preferred a stronger strike there was nothing Nagumo could now do to influence the matter. Indeed, many historians have speculated that Nagumo's woes might have been less had he allowed the same common sense to prevail some hours

---

3. Lieutenant Michio Kobayashi (1914-42). b. 28 October 1914 in Sizuoka Prefecture. 1932 entered Etajima 1 April. 1936, graduated 19 March. 1942 Midway KIA 4 June.

earlier, the argument being that it might not have stopped the attacks on his carriers but there would have been fewer casualties, less fire and bomb risk and the American carriers would have suffered far greater retaliation had he just got aircraft into the air and onto the enemy, no matter how armed. Many CAP fighters would certainly have had to ditch because of this, but their pilots could have been rescued and they were all ultimately to be lost anyway, plus their carriers and over 3,000 of his officers and men[4], because of the dithering.

At least part of Yamaguchi's resolution and defiance in the face of catastrophe seems to have rubbed off on his dour commander, for Nagumo radioed Yamamoto at 1230 that he had resumed operational control from the bridge of the *Nagara*. He added that 'after attacking the enemy' he intended to head north.

The closest American group, Fletcher's TF-17, was less than 100 miles distant, with Spruance's TF-16 some 30 miles or so to the north-west. During the fighting Spruance and Mitscher could observe from the flak bursts that *Yorktown* was in a scrap, but the gap was sufficient for the attacking Japanese to glean no inkling of the presence of two further US carriers. The D3A1s headed towards the enemy at their best speed.[5]

The Americans Marshal Their Defences

The small Japanese force had already materially assisted the American defence by the unnecessary and irrelevant diversion of half its slender fighter screen against returning SBDs, which were mistaken for torpedo-bombers. A relief CAP of six F4F-4s had been put into the air by *Yorktown* and they had barely clawed their way into the sky above the

ship when, as the Japanese climbed higher, the first radar contact was made. The report was of unidentified planes, on a bearing of 255 degrees, at a distance of 32 miles. This was close indeed and the acting FDO aboard *Yorktown*, Lieutenant-Commander Oscar Pederson, CYAG, immediately alerted the nearest of the twelve Wildcats, (six of the original CAP orbiting and six of the relief still climbing), to intercept. This was the four-plane division led by Lieutenant (jg) Richard G. Crommelin. The broadcast '50 bogeys at Angels 10, bearing 255 degrees', reached them but not all were able to comply immediately.

Further reinforcements were on hand for TF-16 had its own CAP and on hearing the various signals, the FDO of the *Enterprise*, Lieutenant-Commander Leonard J. Dow, vectored eight of *Hornet*'s F4Fs to lend a hand. Only two fighters of this force heard and understood, and moved off to comply. Even so, the eighteen D3A1s now faced fourteen fully alert American interceptors, while their own fighter escort, just four *kansen*, were not yet in the frame. It is therefore not surprising that so many of the *kanbaku* were destroyed before reaching attack dive positions; rather, it is a wonder that any reached that position at all. But seven did!

Kobayashi Strikes

The Vals, homed in to the target by *Chikuma*'s No. 5 float-plane[6], had got their initial visual sighting of TF-17 at 1155, with the American ships spread out in their fighting formation some 25 miles distant. Previously, *Yorktown* was at the centre of an arc of warships, with the heavy cruisers *Portland* (CA-33) and *Astoria* (CA-34) placed ahead off her port and starboard bows respectively. Further out and ahead of these three ships the slender screen of just five

---

4. The total Japanese casualties at the Battle of Midway were recorded in exact detail by Hisae Sawachi in *Midowei Kaisen: Kiroku* as 3,057, including one civilian technician aboard the carrier *Soryū*. The latter was presumably assigned to tend to the still not fully operational Yokasuka D4Ys in her care. US casualties from all the engaged services, were about a tenth of the Japanese figure.

5. The (estimated) American wartime figures given for the Val 11 (also known as the Val Mk I, or Type 99 Mk I) are as follows:
    a) Maximum speed 241 mph (at 7,700 feet)
    b) Maximum speed 219 mph (sea level)
    c) Cruising speed, 75% power, 178 mph (at 6,500 feet)
    d) Speed and altitude to give maximum range, with full bomb load of 1,050 lb (1 x 550 lb and 2 x 250 lb) at 75% power with fuel capacity of 265 US gall 178 mph at 6,500ft.
    e) Speed and altitude for maximum range with full bomb load of 1,050 lb at best power settings with fuel capacity of 265 US gal, 135 mph at 6,500 feet.
    For these purposes the D3A1's *Kinsei* 44 engine was rated

1,000 hp for take off at sea level, and 1,060 hp military power at 6,500 feet. The fuel octane rating was 92. See Technical Analysis Division of Office of Chief Naval operations, *Recognition Manual*, ATD #T-1, Section 132, Sheet 132a, dated October 1943, Washington, DC.

6. This aircraft, piloted by PO3c, Hisashi Hara, had performed superlatively and his reports had been the best of any scouting aircraft on either side of the battle. He was to die for his devotion to duty, being subsequently shot down by two F4Fs from VF-6, flown by Lieutenant (jg) Rhonald Jackson 'Buster' Hoyle (FO) and Machinist William Howard Warden. The 13-Shi prototype Yokosuka D4Y1 Type 2 carrier bomber (the Comet or Judy) originally from *Soryū*, and crewed by PO1c, Masatada Iida, and Petty Officer Isamu Kondo, had also homed in on TF-17 and sent back sighting-signals, but due to her radio malfunction, these were distorted and Yamaguchi was unable to read them. *Hiryū* also retransmitted to Kobayashi the *Chikuma* floatplane's original sighting signal reporting the enemy 070 degrees 90 miles distant from *Kidō Butai*.

destroyers, *Anderson, Hammann, Morris, Hughes* and *Russell*, were extended in an arc from 295 to 065 degrees.

It can be seen that this disposition gave maximum anti-aircraft protection against an attack from ahead, but left the flanks and rear wide open. To plug this gap the *Astoria* moved in directly astern of the carrier while *Portland* moved ahead of her, so their heavy anti-aircraft batteries now fully covered the fore-and-aft approaches of the *kanbaku*. This situation the very experienced Kobayashi quickly summed up. Had his Vals been able to attack at full strength in two nine-plane divisions, it is doubtful whether *Yorktown* would had survived. As it was each leading *buntai* was in turn chewed up by the Wildcats and each Japanese pilot more or less had to use his own split-second judgement of where the weakest spot in the American defence was, and how he was able to take advantage of it. But they were not amateurs at this sort of thing, and even at less than half strength, they still had the ability to punish.

At midday, with his still intact force climbing to attack altitude, Kobayashi radioed *Hiryū* the exciting news. 'We are attacking the enemy carrier. 0900.'[7]

Soon after this the Wildcats slammed into the Japanese formation at the point-blank interception range of just 15 miles. A whirling dogfight commenced, and, while the Val was no fighter, she was manoeuvrable and had forward-firing guns. Even Kobayashi apparently jettisoned his bomb and joined in the *melee,* hoping to act as a kind of temporary substitute Zero, thus deflecting the American interceptors long enough to allow others of his dive-bombers to get through and make their attacks. When last intercepted thus, off the west coast of Ceylon in April a few weeks before, the D3A1s had actually won the dogfight with the Royal Navy's Fulmar fighters, destroying two without loss to themselves. They found the F4Fs rather more of a handful, and one pilot, Lieutenant (jg) Arthur J. Brassfield, claimed to have destroyed three *kanbaku* single-handed. Others followed.[8]

Undeterred as their companions fell to the Wildcats, seven of Kobayashi's dive-bombers managed to break through the fighter screen and face the equally prepared flak defences. From 1210 these seven dive-bombers attacked in the sequence: 1 unknown, 2 unknown[9], 3 Tsuchiya, 4 Matsumoto, 5 Nakayama, 6 Nakagawa and 7 Seo. The *Hiryū* received the following signal confirming this. 'Number One. Am bombing enemy carrier. 0910.'

Meanwhile the 2nd *Buntai* had found the open gap in the screen of warships and made their attack runs from the south, approaching from the starboard quarter. The *Yorktown* reported:

At about 1359 [local] while fuelling the fighters which had returned on board, Radar detected an enemy attack group coming in from a bearing about 250 degrees true, distance 46 miles. These planes had apparently come in at a low altitude and when first detected by Radar where observed to be climbing. Radio Electrician V. M. Bennett, USN, Radar Operator, estimated that there were between thirty and forty planes in the attack group.

As soon as the enemy attack group was detected by Radar, the fuelling of planes was discontinued and the sixteen VSB planes of *Yorktown* Attack Group, which were then in the landing circle, were directed

---

7.   Throughout the Japanese used Tokyo time for their communications. It was 0900 in Japan.

8.   Brassfield described the D3A1s as 'ash gray' in colour; others stated that they were 'muddy brown' on top surfaces and silver underneath. Currently the 'expert' consensus is that they were painted dark green on upper surfaces and sky gray underneath with black engine cowlings. From the deck of *Yorktown* at the time, they did not look like any of those images. Andy Mikus commented, 'to me they appeared to be black and orange. For many years I couldn't look at a checkerboard without a sense of dread. Even billboards having those colors invoked fear.' *A Clear Day.*

9.   My own researches at the Military History Center in Tokyo, and examining the various combat reports of the CAP and TF-17 warships during my visits to the various Washington DC archives, both during research for this book and my earlier volume *Aichi D3A1/2 Val* failed to turn up any definitive clues with which I could positively identify these two aircraft. Consequently in my detailed account, I chose not to speculate on the identities of these two dive-bombers. However, Hugh Bicheno (an intelligence officer in Argentina during the 1970s, and later a freelance security consultant elsewhere in Latin America, who has written books on various campaigns, including the Gulf Wars) in his book *Midway*, flatly stated that these D3A1s were those of Imaizumi and Koizumi. I asked him whether he had found a source which had escaped me, and if so whether he would kindly share this with me, and he courteously replied immediately: 'My Map and Appendix D ('Killing Strokes') were reconstructions based on John Lundstrom's *The First team* (Annapolis 1984) and Robert Cressman (ed) *A Glorious Page in Our History* (Missoula 1990). If memory serves, Koizumi and Imaizumi seemed the most likely other survivors, along with Tsuchiya, of the first Wildcats' interception of the first *chutai*'. (E-mail, Bicheno to the author, 30 October 2006). Lundstrom himself scrupulously states that the identities of the brave aviators, 'remain forever unknown'; while of the second he wrote, that its crew also 'remain anonymous.' (*The First Team*). Cressman, while closely following Lundstrom, makes no comment whatsoever on the identities of either aircraft, (*A Glorious Page*). In other words, the Bicheno identification is merely a 'best guess', based entirely on secondary sources, and has no real factual validity.

---

to form a combat air patrol in order to clear the landing circle and the general area of own anti-aircraft gun fire. An auxiliary gasoline tank on the stern, containing about 800 gallons of clear aviation gasoline, was dropped over the side. Fuel lines were drained and filled with CO_2 and all compartments were closed down and secured.

Yorktown cranked up her speed in excess of 30 knots, despite the earlier advice from the engineering experts back at Pearl who had stated she would never be good for much over 25, and her consorts tried to keep pace with her.

The incoming D3A1s were simply identified as 'a large group of planes' without any reference to type, 'approaching from 250 degrees distance 46 miles'. At first, the low-level approach puzzled the Americans, for the aircraft could well have been torpedo-bombers . This was deliberate policy on the part of Kobayashi, a lesson learned from earlier battles. The Americans recorded that the D3A1s, 'came in at a low altitude presumably to avoid Radar detection, until they were within 40–50 miles, and then commenced climbing; as a result, they were not picked up on the Radar Screen until they were well within 50 miles of the fleet. This is quite different from the Coral Sea Battle when the Japanese Attack Group came in as a unit at high altitude and were picked up 68 miles out.'

But, when the Japanese aircraft began to gain altitude, TF-17 realized that they were, in fact, Vals.

The CAP were vectored out in two waves and intercepted a large group of enemy dive-bombers about 15–20 miles from the task group at an altitude of 8,000–10,000 feet. The enemy formations were broken up by our fighters and many of the dive-bombers shot down before they arrived at the attack position. The Radar Operator stated he believed there were at least five groups of enemy planes and estimated that there were a total of at least thirty to forty planes in the attack group. The pilots that took part in the action reported that they counted at least eighteen dive-bombers and about eighteen fighters. Only seven bombers were able to get through and make an attack, obtaining three direct hits and several close misses. The Combat Air patrol shot down a total of thirteen VB ('Vals') and two VF (Zeros) and damaged seven VB and three VF.

In the air the Wildcat pilots piled into the dive-bombers with enthusiasm but, as always, wildly exaggerated their prowess.

All our fighters in the air were vectored out to intercept the enemy and did intercept at from 15 to 20 miles. The enemy attacking planes were reported as being a squadron of eighteen bombers supported by eighteen fighters. They were attacked vigorously. As the attacking planes approached the ship they could be seen clearly through binoculars, and it appeared that the organized attack had been broken up. Planes were seen flying in every direction, and many were falling in flames. Of the entire group seven got through the combat patrol and these made thee hits on *Yorktown*, having released their bombs at about 500 feet. It is believed that none of the enemy planes escaped.

They added, 'Many of our fighters ran out of ammunition even before the Japanese dive bombers arrived over our forces.' But of course, there were only four Zero's, not the eighteen claimed by the Wildcats; the Vals were not completely wiped out by fighters and anti-aircraft fire; five survived from the seven that attacked. There were not up to forty Japanese aircraft, just two-dozen.

Although the CAP was reporting great slaughter, Fletcher's ships knew that, ultimately, they would have to defend themselves. *Yorktown*'s after-action report stated:

Just before the attack began, the ships of Task Force-Seventeen were in anti-aircraft screening formation, radius of screen one mile, speed 25 knots. As the attack approached, speed was increased to the maximum (about 30.5 knots, 284 rpm) with the main steam line cross connection valves closed in the superheated fire-rooms, and radical turns were made to avoid bombs. The enemy bombers were under intense anti-aircraft fire from automatic guns as they approached their release points.

The ploy of putting the *Yorktown*'s own returning SBDs into a waiting circle to clear the field of fire, although well-intentioned, on occasion tended to cause more confusion. The destroyer *Hughes* (DD-410) reported of the Dauntless formation:

Some of these planes with wheels down were flying in the vicinity of [enemy] formations during the dive bombing attack which came a few minutes later, thus making it somewhat difficult to distinguish between enemy bombers and our own.

The enemy aircraft, totalling at least eighteen dive bombers, were seen to be engaged about 0002 by our fighters, bearing about 260 degrees (True) from the

Hughes. At this time two large splashes under the planes indicated that two enemy planes had jettisoned their bombs. At least five enemy planes were observed to burst into flames while others were seen to hit the water.

Because of visibility conditions, enemy planes were only seen when their silver painted [*sic*] underbodies reflected light. At 0006 Enemy planes appeared over *Astoria* (CA-34) at which time the *Astoria* was observed to shoot down two planes. At 0100 enemy dive-bombers appeared over *Yorktown*, *Hughes* opened fire with 5 in battery firing a total of twenty-four rounds at these bombers while diving. Four enemy dive-bombers were observed diving and each dropped a bomb. One of these planes burst into flames after releasing a bomb; and the second disintegrated after releasing bomb. The remaining two pulled out the dive, circling to the right; one paralleling the course of the *Yorktown* in a southerly and westerly direction; the other circled around the stern of the *Hughes* then paralleled her course in a south-westerly direction, keeping out of range of 20 mm guns. One 5 in gun fired at the first of these two planes until it was in line with the *Yorktown*, and two 5 in guns fired at the second plane as it passed ahead and to starboard. Neither of the planes appeared to be damaged. At the time enemy dive bombers were identified at Type 99 Dive Bombers.

The first Val started on down on the *Yorktown* at 1420, while the fleet was at 30° 51'N, 176° 52' W, about 160 miles north-east of Midway island, which bore about 190. The weather was recorded as 'excellent', with a light Force 2 wind blowing form the south-east and just 3/10 cloud, with about 20 miles clear visibility.

An eyewitness account from the Gunnery Officer (CGO)[10] of the *Yorktown*, describing just how the D3A1s went about their business, makes interesting reading. Lieutenant-Commander Davis was an inspirational figure, directing the ship's anti-aircraft batteries through the flight deck loud-speaking system, with his pronounced and laid-back southern accent, from a highly-exposed vantage point atop the pilot house. His 'calm, clear voice, no different from his normal manner of speaking during gunnery drills, was not only an inspiration to the guns' crews and to all who heard him, but was a great aid to the Captain in manoeuvring the ship to avoid bombs and torpedoes.'[11] Davis himself wrote:

One at a time, seven planes were seen to break away and approach the ship, altitude about 12,000 ft, slant range about 8,000 to 10,000 yd. The forward director took control of the starboard 5 in battery and opened fire on these planes. This fire was ineffective since the planes circled or approached their diving points by a curved path. On two occasions, when bursts appeared close to a plane, he was seen to circle away for another approach. These planes were not in formation so it was necessary to shift target continuously as planes circled to turn away. On reaching a point sufficiently low, individual planes were seen to go into shallow glide until they had reached a position angle of about 60 degrees at an altitude of 6,000 to 8,000 ft, then go into a steep glide or dive toward the ship. As the first plane dove, Group III shifted to local control using 1 second fuse (800 yard).

Immediately after the first dive Group III shifted back to director control for the rest of the action. The director followed three planes in on their approach and preliminary glide, then shifted to planes reported by lookouts as making a torpedo attack on the starboard bow.

Three planes approached at an altitude of about 100 ft as for a torpedo attack from the starboard bow. When bursts appeared near them at a range of about 8,000 yd, they turned away. At from 12,000 to 15,000 yd, they turned again for another approach. This was reported about three times after which two of these flew away and the third took a position on our starboard beam, and circled between 15,000 and 20,000 yd at an altitude of about 2,000 ft. This plane remained here for about 30 minutes then disappeared. About the same tactics were employed by three planes, which approached once on the starboard quarter and twice on the port quarter. These planes were fired on by the port 5 in battery in control

---

10. Lieutenant-Commander Ernest J. Davis. He was recommended for the Navy Cross for his work that day, the recommendation praised his 'clear thinking, sound judgement, thorough understanding of the problems of anti-aircraft gunnery, and his knowledge of his men and his extraordinary ability to instil into them an aggressive, fighting spirit'.

11. Captain E. Buckmaster to Admiral Chester A. Nimitz, Action Report: USS *Yorktown* (CV-5), dated May 25 1942 (CVS/A16-S/(CCR-10-hps), contained in CincPac Report, Serial 01849, dated 28 June 1942, held in WWII Action Reports, Modern Military Branch, NARA, College Park, Maryland. Cited hereafter as Buckmaster to Nimitz.

of the after director and all disappeared upon the completion of the bombing attack. None of these planes on either side pressed home an attack nor was any seen to drop torpedoes. These were probably SBDs trying to avoid being shot down by their own ship's fire. The Japanese who survived the CAP interception adopted a very different profile – they meant business!

As the first bomber started his dive, fire was opened with all automatic guns on the starboard side (ten 20 mm, four 1.1 in mounts, twelve .50 calibre and two .30 calibre). This plane was cut into at least three large pieces before he reached the bombing point. The bomb was released, however, and was seen to tumble as it fell. It struck the flight deck about 15 ft inboard and about 20 ft aft of 1.1 in gun mount number 4, killing twelve men in mount 4 and five men in mount 3 instantly and wounding four men on mount 4 and fourteen on mount 3. The uninjured and some wounded men immediately replaced the others and continued fire on their mounts through the remainder of the action. This fire of course was a much-reduced rate. The pieces of this plane fell close aboard on the starboard quarter.

Lieutenant John D. Lorenz was the Battery Officer on Mount 3, just abaft the *Yorktown*'s island and right of the heart of that hit. He later related his memory of those terrible moments.

The sky was turning black from anti-aircraft fire but on they came. I glanced over my crews. It was to be our last fight together but none of us realized it. I saw those faces, which I had seen so many times behind the battery. They were grim and determined.

Moments passed, then I heard the word, 'Diving attack starboard beam.' Yes, they were coming straight for us right out of the cloud. From then on it was smoke, flame and tracer bullets. The explosive bullets were blowing our enemy apart. The Japanese bomb came loose from the plane, it fell towards us! The plane that dropped the bomb was gone so we merely shifted our fire to the next plane. We continued firing. Then that bomb hit.

I don't remember much for the next few seconds. I was stunned, dazed and knocked down. I found myself back up against the splinter shield, my legs tangled beneath me, my helmet and pistol knocked off and my clothes torn open. It seemed that fire was all around me and the smoke made things worse. Finally I was able to regain my senses and stood up. The gun had ceased firing but I heard others faintly. My ears were ringing. The sight that met my eyes was appalling. The complete gun crew was down. It seemed strange and unbelievable to see them in a heap like this. I had never expected to see them that way. One sailor was lying on top of the rest, badly hit. I didn't want to know who he was.

I climbed back up to the mount. The guns were firing again. I saw two men behind the four guns, standing over the fallen crew. Smith was firing one of the guns by himself. His back and legs were bleeding; from the amount of blood I knew he was badly wounded.

Chief Gunner's Mate Noland[12] had been hit in the left wrist and both legs. Still, he was feeding ammunition and was firing the other two guns with his good hand, and even correcting damages to the gun itself. The other gun was out of commission.[13]

The skipper of the destroyer *Morris* (DD-417), Commander Harry B. Jarrett[14], was open in his admiration for the way the Japanese dive-bomber pilots went about their business. 'The enemy attacked with resolution in the face of heavy and effective fire. The dive-bombers, in particular, did not appear to be deterred in the slightest by the fact that few of them were reaching their objectives. Dive-bombing attacks were made at a steep angle and pressed home to a low altitude.'

He admitted:

12. Robert Noland. Mount Soledad Memorial.
13. Lieutenant John D. Lorenz, interview printed in *Sea Power*, May 1943. Lorenz was awarded the Navy Cross for this action.
14. Vice-Admiral Harry B. Jarrett (1898–1974). A famous destroyer skipper in World War II. As well as commanding the *Morris* in the North Atlantic and in the battles of Coral Sea and Midway, he commanded the destroyer screen of the fast carrier force during the Palau campaign, (for which he received the Silver Star) and the Philippines, and commanded the bombarding force at the Marshall and Marianas campaigns, for which he was awarded the Legion of Honor. He was Commander Scouting Line on the 1945 Okinawa, Formosa and Tokyo raids. He ended the war commanding the light cruiser *Astoria* (CL-90). After the war he was a staff member of Training Command, US Atlantic Fleet and served as Plans and Policy Officer (Naval Reserve) of CNO. Became Senior Military Attaché, Taiwan. He then returned to sea duty, commanding the 4th Destroyer Squadron and 4th Cruiser Squadron. 1953 Deputy Inspector General, Navy Department. 1954, November, retired from navy. The frigate *Jarrett* (FFG-33) was named in his honour.

It was very difficult to see the planes until they were almost at the bomb release point, due to the fact that there were high clouds and the planes came in from the sun. About six enemy planes were seen to fall in flames by fighter attack, when still out of range of guns. Only one plane came within range of this ship, and it was well forward on the bow when firing commenced. The first plane that dropped a bomb scoring a hit on *Yorktown* on flight deck aft of island, came in from well astern of this ship. The plane made a suicide dive [*sic*] with no attempt to pull out. The plane fell into the water just astern of *Yorktown* after release of its bomb. From the after conning station, the total number of enemy bombing planes observed to come in and deliver attack was not over six. It is doubtful if any of these escaped to return to their ship.

The captain of another destroyer, the *Anderson* (DD-411), Lt. Com. John K. B. Ginder, USN, more accurately counted seven Vals making attack dives against the carrier. The destroyer, along with her companions, was attempting to follow, as best she could, the frantic gyrations of Fletcher's flagship as she was swung around at high speed, attempting to maintain station with 10 degrees of bearing at between 1,500 and 2,000 yards distance.

Three bombs were seen to fall astern of the *Yorktown* and one near miss on the starboard side amidships. Several splashes were seen around the *Yorktown*. A large flash was seen aft of the stack on the carrier. A bomb was seen to hit the *Yorktown*. *Yorktown* began to make heavy black smoke. *Yorktown* hit three of the dive-bombers with AA fire. A wing was shot off of one plane. All three dive bombers crashed into the water astern of the *Yorktown*.

The *Anderson* engaged one D3A1 flying at about 10,000 feet, some 5 miles off her starboard quarter, bearing 220 degrees true, with her whole main battery.

This plane, starting a dive-bombing attack on the *Yorktown*, was seen to pass behind bursts of this ship's AA fire but was not seen coming out from the bursts. Results of this firing are not known. Both starboard and 20 mm guns opened fire on an enemy dive-bomber, on parallel course, distant 1,000 yd, altitude about 200 ft, on the starboard quarter, and continued to fire at this plane until it bore on the star-

board bow. This firing appeared to be accurate. Tracers were observed to be passing all around the plane. This plane then passed out of range and few seconds later crashed into the sea. Lookouts above the bridge and bridge personnel reported that the plane had been hit by the fire of the starboard 20 mm guns.

The *Yorktown*'s own report confirmed that she nailed three of the Vals as they made their dives.

Of the three which made hits, two were shot down just after releasing their bombs and the other went out of control just as his bomb was released. The bomb from this plane tumbled in flight and hit just abaft No. 2 elevator on the starboard side, exploding on contact, and making a hole in the flight deck about 10 x 10 ft. This hole was repaired within about 25 minutes. The bomb killed five and wounded fourteen men of 1.1" mounts 3 and 4, on machine guns in the vicinity, in the after end of the island structure, and below in the Hangar. Fragments pierced the Hangar Deck. Fires were started in three planes on the Hangar Deck, the two damaged planes from *Enterprise* and one *Yorktown* plane fuelled and armed with a 1,000 lb bomb. Lieutenant A. C. Emerson, USN[15], Hangar Deck Officer, released the sprinkler system and water curtains in the two after bays and quickly extinguished this fire which otherwise would have undoubtedly developed into a serious conflagration.

Lieutenant-Commander Davis, the Gunnery Officer, recorded in the same official report:

The second plane to dive was cut to pieces as he reached the bomb release point. His bomb was released, tumbled down to miss close astern and exploded on contact. The pieces of the plane fell in the wake of the ship. Splinters from this bomb killed two and wounded four of the crews of the 50 calibre machine-guns by the after port corner of the flight deck and on the port side of the first superstructure deck aft, wounded some men on the fantail guns and started several small fires on the fantail. These fires were quickly extinguished by the remaining men under the direction of the Battery Officer.

This first bomb was described as a 'delayed-action, projectile type bomb, weighing approximately 800 lb and

---

15. Lieutenant Alberto C. 'Ace' Emerson.

measuring approximately 12 in in diameter' and was of the 'dive release' type. The dive-bomber experts watching the Aichis attacking estimated that the angle of dive for this attack was approximately 70 degrees, with a low release altitude of about 500 feet. The actual impact point was at ship's frame 36, to starboard, about 17 feet to starboard of the ships centreline. The bomb pierced No. 1 elevator, travelled forward to port, piercing the elevator pit at around frame 32, some 7 feet from the centre line, and exploded on the third deck, at centre line frame No. 32, in compartment A-305, which happened to be the rug and cleaner stowage space. This missile had travelled through No. 1 elevator and the second deck, a distance of some 50 feet from its initial impact point.

The actual detonation 'was of high order'. The splinters averaged 1 inch in diameter. The explosion ripped open a hole about 14 inches in diameter, and the resulting blast effect ruptured the bulkheads in A-305 and blew a 4 foot hole in the deck above. More splinters travelled vertically and pierced the second deck in No. 1 elevator pit in numerous places. Yet more splinters scythed their way aft, penetrating armoured bulkheads from No. 38 onward and opened the forward bulkhead of A410-A, others continuing on down to penetrate the overheads of A-506-M and A-510-M.

One of the ship's medical officers[16], Lieutenant Joseph Pollard[17], described the carnage that followed this explosion. His eyewitness account conveys exactly what war involves, and it is far from the clean, academic world of the Internet war-gamer or Hollywood movie producer.

I was overwhelmed with work. Wounded were everywhere. Some men had one foot or leg off, others had both off; some were dying – some dead. Everywhere there was need for morphine, tourniquets, blankets and first aid. Battle Dressing Station #1 rapidly overflowed into the passageway, into the parachute loft and into all other available spaces. I called for stretcher-bearers to get the more seriously wounded to the sick bay where they could receive plasma, etc., but the passageways had been blocked off due to the bomb hits. So we gave more morphine, covered the patients with blankets, and did the best we could. Many patients went rapidly into shock. All topside lights were out and I never realized that flash-

lights gave such miserably poor light. There was no smoke in Battle Dressing Station #1, which was fortunate. Water hoses were dragged into the passageway in an attempt to control a fire somewhere forward in the island – the hose had been perforated by shrapnel and sprayed water all over the deck and on some of my wounded who were lying in the passageway. Our water tank was very useful to us as there was a great need for drinking water and none was otherwise obtainable.

I went up to the flight deck. The first thing that I noticed was Mount #4. A pair of legs attached to the hips sat in the trainer's seat. A stub of spinal column was hanging over backwards – there was nothing else remaining of the trainer. The steel splinter shield was full of men – or rather portions of men, many of whom were not identifiable. Blood was everywhere. I turned forward and saw great billows of smoke rising from our stack region. We were dead in the water and it suddenly dawned on me how helpless we were lying there. A repair party was rebuilding a portion of the flight deck. Then I was called aft where there were several casualties from shrapnel, which came from a near miss of the fantail. There were wounded also along the catwalk along the starboard side.[18]

The attack continued. The CGO wrote:

Three planes dove from the port beam, only one of which dropped a bomb. This bomb exploded in the stack and heavy black smoke soon covered the after director, the after starboard automatic gun batteries and Group III 5 in guns. This plane crashed in the water close aboard on the port side.

The next bomb hit came from the port side, piercing the flight deck and exploded in the stack, starting fires as follows: (a) on the stack where paint caught fire and flaked off in patches, starting other fires wherever this burning paint fell. (b) in the Photographic Laboratory where photographic film caught fire, in the XO's Office and First Lieutenant's Office.

Aside from personnel casualties, the most serious effect of this bomb hit was that it ruptured the uptakes from boilers 1, 2 and 3, completely disabled boilers

---

16. Beside Pollard, the *Yorktown*'s medical team, led by the Medical Officer, Captain W. D. Davis, comprised Lieutenant (jg) Edward A. Kearney, Dr A. M. French, Dr N. E. Dobos (Flight Surgeon).

17. Commander Joseph P. Pollard, who later was to serve as

Senior Medical Officer of the carrier *Coral Sea* (CVB-43) in 1953–4.

18. Pollard, *Oral History*, Bureau of Medicine and Surgery, Washington DC.

2 and 3 and extinguished fires in boilers 2, 3, 4, 5 and 6. The fire-rooms containing all saturated boilers (1, 2, 3, 4, 5 and 6) were filled with smoke and gases from the bomb hit and from the boilers themselves. In spite of the difficult situation, personnel of No. 1 boiler remained at their station and kept this boiler steaming with two burners. By closing the throttle, steam pressure was able to be maintained at 180 lb and No. 1 boiler was thus able to keep steam auxiliaries going. Speed immediately dropped to about six knots, and at 1440, about 20 minutes after the bomb had hit, all engines were stopped.

This second bomb was also described as a heavy, delayed-action bomb, which pierced the flight deck and frame 95, some 10 feet inboard of the carrier's island. It continued to travel outward and to starboard, piercing the port side of the uptakes in the hangar at frame 95. This weapon struck the second deck in the vicinity of the passage at frame 95 inboard of the XO's officer and the communications and radio office (C and R). The resulting detonation punched a 15 foot aperture through the second deck, totally wrecking the XO's office, the C and R office, the oil and water test laboratories and intakes and uptakes to fire-rooms 2, 3, 4, 5 and 6. On the third deck the laundry was totally destroyed.

This explosion, again described as of 'high order', started a large fire and many smaller ones, the latter being quickly stifled by prompt damage-control action. However the smoke from the main fire, the bomb explosion and the damaged uptake bellowed up, filling the wardroom spaces and the messes forward on the third deck, and made all six fire rooms untenable. Fragments of the bomb pierced and bulged the forward area of the stack and the burning paint added to the picture with smoke filtering into the vital spaces in the carrier's island structure itself. It looked bad from a distance, both to concerned eyes on the escorting warships and to the eager eyes of the surviving dive-bomber aircrew, but it looked worse than it really was.

It certainly looked good to Kobayashi, who had survived the combat so far.[19] Circling at 500 feet and bombless, he was keenly observing his men at work. As the smoke billowed up from the *Yorktown* he, or one of his subordinates, was able to transmit one last message of hope: 'Number Two. Fires break out on carrier. 0901.'[20]

This was the final transmission, and, if it was Kobayashi who actually sent it, at the moment of his triumph a pair of Wildcats hacked him down.[21]

This was by no means the end of *Yorktown*'s ordeal by fire. Another dive-bomber bored her way down.

A sixth plane circled forward and dove from ahead under considerably lessened fire. His bomb struck number one elevator and exploded above the fourth deck, starting fires in the sail locker and rag stowage. Water used in fighting this fire leaked into the forward 5 in handling room through the reach rod stuffing boxes. Heat from the fire made it necessary later to evacuate and flood the forward 5 in magazine.

Another description of this third bomb hit reads thus:

The third bomb hit came from starboard, pierced the starboard side of No. 1 elevator and exploded on the fourth deck, starting a persistent fire in a rag stowage space, adjacent to the forward gasoline stowage and the magazines. The magazines were flooded, it is believed that the surrounding of the gasoline tanks by CO_2 as has been previously described, prevented the igniting of gasoline.

This bomb was fitted with an instantaneous fuse and struck the flight deck about 10 feet starboard of the centre line, at frame 132. A 12 foot hole was punched through the flight deck and the resulting splinter storm swept along the flight deck itself, scything down gun crews at the mountings, and also penetrated down into the upper hangar area. Slithers of metal went through bulkheads like paper into the aircraft engine overhaul shop, the sheet-metal shop and the torpedo shop, and even continued on down into the lower deck area to D-201-L, D020-L and D301-L. Three loaded and armed aircraft parked abaft No. 2 elevator caught fire. A disaster was averted by the quick reaction of the damage-control team, with all the hangar sprinklers and water curtains activated by remote push-button control and doing their job efficiently even though the water main in the sheet metal shop had been ruptured.

The bomb from the seventh plane missed on the starboard beam. Of these seven planes which dove on the

---

19. Kobayashi was a very brave man, alone in the sky and surrounded by enemy fighter aircraft (one of whom Lieutenant (jg) Elbert S. McCuskey, VF-3, had already attacked him but had run out of ammunition at the crucial moment), who probably knew that he was doomed but continued to send back reports to the very end.

20. This time is obviously incorrect, a mistake for 0911 (Tokyo time), but whether it was Kobayashi or some other Val pilot, who transmitted it, a one-digit error was understandable given their dire situation.

21. Lieutenant (jg) Thomas Clinton Provost III, and Ensign James Alex Halford, Jr, of VF-6.

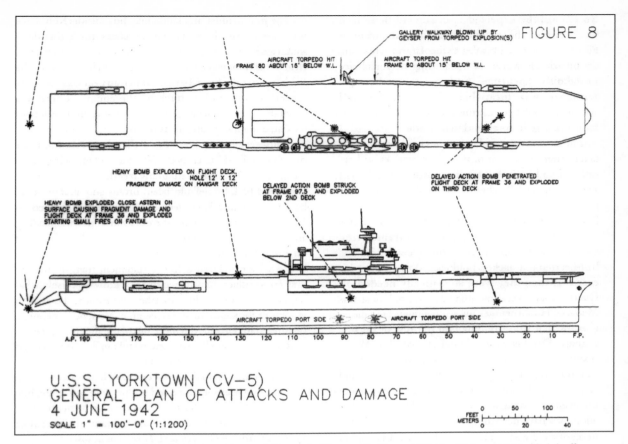

Diagram 11. General Plan of Dive-bombing and Torpedo Hits on *Yorktown* (CV-5) of 4 June 1942. (Originally presented at FAST 1999, Seattle, August 99. Reprinted with the permission of the Society of Naval Architects and Marine Engineers, New Jersey)

ship, three were definitely shot down by automatic guns; a fourth plane was damaged by gunfire and it is believed to have fallen less than a mile from the ship.

Two of the bombs that hit, one by 1.1 in machine-gun mount 4, the other close aboard off the port quarter, exploded on or near contact. Both of these dropped from planes badly damaged in the air, and both were seen to tumble in their fall. Examination of some fragments of one of these indicated that they were of about the same construction as those with delayed action. It is believed possible that these may have detonated in the air.

At the time of the dive bombing attack, torpedoes were being placed on the hangar deck for rearming. Some splinters from the bomb that struck near the 1.1 in machine gun mount pierced the flight deck and caused several fires among planes being rearmed on the hangar deck in the near vicinity of these torpedoes.

Watching the whole thing from the 'gas shack' was Andy Mikus, who recalled the eerie silence that followed the tumult and hellish din of the action itself, when *Yorktown* slid to a standstill.

Being on a ship dead in the water gives one a strange feeling. A ship is a vibrant, dynamic, living thing. With her great power plant knocked out and her throbbing heartbeat stopped, the *Yorktown*, in motionless silence, sprawled listlessly in the sea. There was no power to work the big guns or ammunition hoists; no power to lift or lower elevators; no power to work the radio or radar.

Command Decisions

Mikus also commented on the strange hiatus that overtook the American forces at this time.

No one can be expected to command three task forces under these conditions, and so Admiral Fletcher transferred his flag to the *Astoria*. He made the mistake, however, of transferring responsibility to Admiral Spruance. And this is not because Spruance was incapable of handling overall command, but because there was no real need for such a change in command to be made.

The *Astoria* or one of her planes could easily have taken Fletcher to one of the other carriers and re-established him in full dignity.[22] Admiral King had already accused Fletcher of leaving the 'scene' in the presence of the enemy. This was a reference to our first stop at Tongatabu to replace gas tank linings and was certainly undeserved. By transferring command as he now did, a feeling grew that he was half-hearted and lacked boldness. Withdrawing his carriers when they were so critically needed off Guadalcanal several months later not only lost this Medal of Honor winner his sea command but cast a shadow that would follow him the rest of his life. Perhaps Fletcher deserved better than this. When Spruance was hesitant, he was said to be rightfully cautious. When Halsey carelessly lost both lives and ships in a typhoon, he was not relieved of command but even went on to five star rank. Political consideration may have determined in Halsey's case and the necessities of war in Fletcher's. I leave it to a higher jury; perhaps to the Admirals assembled in Davey Jones' Locker.[23]

Fletcher's idea at this stage appears to be for Spruance to continue the fight with TF-16, while he concerned himself exclusively with the salvaging of the *Yorktown*. Whether this was a unilateral abrogation of his responsibilities as the man in charge, as some still hold, or a common-sense decision resulting from existing circumstances, as Lundstrom and many others maintain, will always be debateable. Transferring himself and his staff, along with communications and intelligence personnel, from the stationary, blind and deaf *Yorktown* to the *Astoria* was quite clearly logical; suddenly removing himself from decision-making in the midst of a battle may be considered to have been less obviously so. However, having made that decision, rightly or wrongly, Fletcher's first duty was to make it clear to his nominated successor that the ball was soon to be in his court; until he did so the American fleet was, in effect, leaderless and under attack by the enemy. There was inevitably a period of dangerous uncertainty, and the longer it existed the more dangerous it was.

While we can agree that 'Fletcher intended for Spruance's TF-16 to carry the fight for the time being'[24], the latter actually remained unaware that the mantle of command had, by default, fallen on his shoulders from at least the time that *Yorktown*'s communications faltered, to 1238, when Fletcher made the decision to transfer his flag, and even after his superior officer had established himself on Poco Smith's flag plot aboard the *Astoria* at 1323. Indeed, we can agree with the statement that, during the first *Hiryū* attack, 'Spruance did not know precisely what happened'[25], but further, that he *continued* to be kept in ignorance for some considerable time. Mitscher, of course, continued to remain even more out of the picture, receiving nothing much from Browning and still totally unable to read the coded transmissions from Nimitz.

Once settled in on *Astoria*, Fletcher's first order from his new flagship was not addressed to Spruance informing him that he was thinking of letting him take over tactical control of the battle, but instead, to the captain of the cruiser *Portland* ordering him to take *Yorktown* in tow.

Nobody on any American warship knew the location of the enemy carrier (or carriers) busy doling out death and destruction to the *Yorktown*, so they all had to sit and 'take it' until the mystery assailant was found. TF-16 was busy flying off and landing fighter aircraft, and this necessitated steering courses that widened the physical gap between the two forces[26], so Fletcher instructed Spruance via 'talk between ships' (TBS) to 'join this unit' as soon as possible and he also composed a message for Nimitz advising him of his decision, which was to be flown ashore to Midway for transmission from there in an effort to maintain secrecy, although the Japanese would seem to have been pretty much aware of *Yorktown*'s position anyway.[27]

---

22. In fairness to Fletcher, he *did* consider this option but decided against it as he deemed it might cause too much confusion.
23. Andy Mikus, *A Clear Day*.
24. Lundstrom, *Black Shoe Carrier Admiral*.
25. *Ibid.*
26. This separation of the two US task forces had both advantages and disadvantages, in that it kept TF-16 immune from the attentions of *Hiryū*'s strikes (although it has to be admitted these strikes were so weak that to have further dispersed them against all *three* US carriers would have rendered them all pretty ineffectual). The separation tended to delay somewhat the assistance that Spruance and Mitscher's Wildcats could give TF-17, however.
27. Indeed, John Lundstrom states, 'The Japanese obviously had the *Yorktown*'s exact location'. (*Black Shoe Carrier Admiral*).

Atrocities

That the Japanese had a good idea of the composition of the American fleet late on 4 June, was not just down to good scouting work on the part of their cruiser floatplanes, or even of the high-speed D4Y from *Soryū*. Another, shameful, factor was involved.

Ensign Wesley F. Osmus[28] managed to scramble clear of his rapidly sinking TBD, which sank immediately, taking the body of his rear gunner[29] to the bottom with her.

Unfortunately for him, Osmus was sighted by look-outs aboard the destroyer *Arashi*, the command ship of Commander Kosaku Ariga[30] of DesDiv 4, which had just completed her fruitless hunt for the submarine *Nautilus*. The captain of *Arashi*, Commander Yasumasa Watanabe[31], instructed that the swimmer be picked up. The ship hove-to, lowered her whaler and hauled Osmus from the drink. If he was glad to be saved from a watery fate, then he was doomed to an early and awful disillusionment.

He was forced to sit on the deck of the destroyer as she got underway once more. His injuries from the crash were examined by the destroyer's Surgeon-Lieutenant Katsukich Ishizaka, who reported only minor burns on hands, arms and face. Only one officer had even a smattering of English by which to interrogate the prisoner, and this was the ship's Torpedo Officer, Lieutenant Kiyusumi Tanikowa. He instructed that Osmus be moved to a position adjacent to the bridge so the senior officers could hear the translated responses and then he got to work.[32]

Both Ariga and Watanabe remained out of sight, inside the ships chart-house. They framed the questions and Tanikowa laboriously wrote them out on paper and gave them to Osmus who replied in kind. Tanikowa then conveyed the answers to his superiors who then came back with the next question. It was a slow, laborious process, not aided by the fact that Tanikowa frequently threatened Osmus with his sword during the questioning. Having obtained the young pilot's rank, name, age, and place of origin the interrogation produced the name of the aircraft carrier his squadron had flown from, the *Yorktown*. Later he gave more important details, most importantly that the *Yorktown* was operating with *two* other carriers, although separately. This was duly passed over by *Arashi*'s skipper to the *Nagara,* which in turn relayed it on to Yamaguchi at 1300, who now knew just was he was facing[33]. Ten minutes after receiving this shattering news, Nagumo ordered the

28. Ensign Wesley Frank Osmus, USNR (1918–42). b. Chicago, Ill 2 September 1918. Educated at University of Illinois, Liberal Arts and Sciences. Enlisted in USNR at Naval Reserve Aviation Base Glenview on 26 March 1940 as seaman 2c. Volunteered for elimination flight training on 14 April. After one month's instruction he was released from active duty on 14 May and received a discharge on 3 September on appointment as aviation cadet, USNR on the 4th. Trained at NAS Pensacola from 9 September 1940 and then at NAS Miami from 12 March 1941. Designated as naval aviator 25 March. 12 April reported to NAS San Diego for further flight training, and appointed ensign 22 April.15 August 1941 reported to VT-3 of Air Group 3, aboard carrier *Saratoga* (CV-3). Commenced familiarization with TBD from 20 October. December 1941 involved in the abortive relief of Wake Island. 11 January 1942 *Saratoga* damaged by submarine *I-6* AG-3 ashore at Pearl as pool for operational carriers. Joined *Yorktown* 30 May 1942. Murdered by captors on night of 4/5 June 1942. Post-humously awarded Purple Heart and Navy Cross. The destroyer escort USS *Osmus* (DE-7010) was named in his honour

29. Benjamin R. Dobson, Jr, ARM3c.

30. Vice-Admiral Kosaku Mikoto Ariga, IJN (1897–1945). b. Nagano Prefecture 1897. Ariga went on the command the battleship *Yamato* at the Battle of Leyte Gulf, and, was killed aboard her, aged 47, during her final sortie on 7 April 1945 when she was sunk, appropriately enough, by US Navy torpedo-and dive-bombers off the Nansei Islands. He was credited with saying, 'What a glorious way to die', but his treatment of Osmus was anything but glorious. His last testament letter is displayed at the Yasakuni *Jinja* and reads: 'My heart's desire is the building of the new order of Greater East Asia Co-Prosperity with the spirit of universal brotherhood. As the commander I lead the newest and most efficient destroyer flotilla of the Imperial Navy. The destruction of the foreign invaders is truly my greatest long-cherished desire. From the first I do not hope to return alive'. He finally got his wish and Osmus was most aptly avenged.

31. Rear-Admiral Yasumasa Watanabe (1900–43). Etajima 49th Class. Specialised in torpedo warfare. 1927–29, 2nd Lieutenant, Torpedo Officer aboard destroyer *Shiokaze*. 27 January 1941 appointed in command destroyer *Arashi*. Midway. 28 December 1942, transferred to command of destroyer *Hatsukaze*. 1 July 1943, appointed ComDesDiv 1 aboard the old destroyer *Numakaze,* which he selected as his flagship on 20 August. The division was engaged in local convoy escort duties and, while returning to Japan after escorting a convoy from Moji to Formosa, was sunk with all hands by a four torpedo salvo from the American submarine *Grayback* (SS-208) south of Okinawa on 18 December 1943.

32. A more detailed account of this case is given by Wrynn V. Dennis in the article *Missing at Midway* in *American History Illustrated*, Vol 27, No 3, Harrisburg, PA, dated July 1992, pps 34–34 and 62. See also Robert E .Barde, of Manchester Community College, as *Midway; Tarnished Victory*, an article in *Military Affairs* magazine, Vol. 47, No 4 (December 1983), Washington, DC, pps 188–192.

33. No reflection on the honour of any of the three young Americans should be implied by the fact that they gave such information to their enemies. The US Navy had conspicuously failed to brief any of them against the possibility of such interrogations and they had been given absolutely no instructions at all on how to react.

battleship *Haruna* and heavy cruiser *Tone* to send out more search planes to hunt along an arc from 0 to 090 degrees true to try and locate TF-16.

Having extracted all they could from Osmus, Watanabe ordered his execution and Chief Sato was given the grisly task. They took the young man to the stern of the destroyer and threw him overboard. In desperation Osmus managed to get a hold on the stern rail and stopped himself from falling further, but a fire-axe was brought and he was killed with a blow to the back of the head, his lifeless body falling in the ships' wake.

A similar fate befell VS-6 Ensign Frank O'Flaherty[34] and his radioman, Bruno Gaido, AMM1c.[35] They were part of the SBD stragglers that took station on Lieutenant Charles R. Ware after the attack of 4 June, as already related. They had been forced to ditch through lack of fuel very early on, but were witnessed by Ensign John McCarthy's[36] radio man, Earl Howell[37] to have survived and were last seen inflating their life raft and clambering aboard it, seemingly safe and sound. No American eye saw them again.[38]

Instead, the duo were plucked from the ocean some time later by the destroyer *Makigumo*. They were interrogated and revealed similar information. For six days they were incarcerated and fed by their captors and must have felt they were destined to live, if only as prisoners of war (POWs). As they became familiar with their jailors, especially Ensign Koju Kanechiku, who daily asked them what they wanted to eat and treated them reasonably, the young ensign even relaxed enough to show his captors pictures of his wife in a gesture of friendship, but this failed to soften their hearts.

Eventually, after about six days, *Makigumo* was ordered north the Aleutians. A direct order was given by Fleet Command for the destroyer to get rid of her prisoners, as they had outlived their value. Her commanding officer,

Commander Isamu Fujita, was squeamish enough to regard cold-blooded killing aboard his ship as being 'unlucky' but he had no compunction with carrying out his instructions in a less bloody but equally inhumane manner. A request went round the ship for volunteers to carry out the deed, but, to their lasting credit there proved to be no takers. Even the offered bribe of the unfortunate O'Flaherty's cigarette lighter, inscribed 'To my matchless husband', failed to elicit any responses. He ordered both men bound with ropes. They were then tied to weighted 5-gallon kerosene cans filled with seawater to make them heavy and callously thrown overboard to drown. The *Makigumo*'s Navigation Officer, Captain Shigeo Hirayama, later testified that both men went to their deaths, 'quietly, with no sign of fear.'[39]

These pitiless war crimes only came to light after the war. In late 1946 the ONI team investigating Japanese action records for Midway found in one of the many boxes held at the Federal Records Office at Alexandria, Virginia a document relating to three American airmen plucked from the sea by two destroyers, who had given vital information. Cross-checking revealed that none of these three men had been registered as POWs in Japan subsequent to the battle. The Navy Department asked Supreme Command Allied Powers (SCAP) in Tokyo to investigate further, which, with full Japanese co-operation, they did.

No retribution was meted out to the criminals who ordered and carried out these acts, but fate had already dealt with some of them. The *Makigumo* was mined off Guadalcanal in 1943 while trying to avoid a PT-boat attack, sinking but with little loss of life.[40] The majority of her crew, including regrettably Fujita himself, survived and were rescued by the destroyer *Yugumo*. The *Arashi* was also sunk in action, at the Battle of Vella Gulf on 6 August 1943, with

34. Ensign Frank Woodrow O'Flaherty, USNR (1918–42). b. Tonopah, Nevada, 26 February 1918. Resided Kansas Cit, Missouri. 1940 on 25 September, entered the USNR. 27 January 1941, after initial flight training was appointed as aviation cadet. On completion of flight training was commissioned as ensign on 12 September and joined VS-6 as part of AG6 aboard the carrier *Enterprise* (CV-6). Murdered by his captors at Midway. He was awarded the Navy Cross. The destroyer escort *O'Flaherty* (DE-340) was named in his honour.

35. Bruno Peter Gaido, AMM1c (1920–42). b. Beloit, Wisconsin 1920. 1938 Enlisted in navy. As aviation machinist's mate (AMM2c) assigned to VS-6 aboard carrier *Enterprise* (CV-6). Took part in Marshall Island raid, firing on enemy aircraft from an SBD parked on the carrier deck until its tail was sheared off. Admiral Halsey promoted him to AMM1c on the spot. At Midway was shot down, interrogated and ultimately murdered. Posthumously awarded

DFC and Purple Heart for Midway. Despite his bravery, no warship was ever named after Gaido, but, thanks to the work of Rear-Admiral James D. 'Jig Dog' Ramage, he was honoured in 1996 as the first inductee into the Enlisted Aircraft Roll of Honor; his proclamation read 'His courage in combat and when facing death were exemplary'. Dusty Kleiss wrote 'Peter Gaido was the bravest man I ever met'.

36. Ensign John Reginald McCarthy.

37. Earl Edward Howell, ARM2c.

38. The wartime publication by Howard Mingos, *American Heroes of the War in the Air*, (Lanciar Publishers, New York, 1943), of course concludes that both men died on their raft, as indeed did the navy itself until after the war.

39. Gordon W. Prange, with Donald Goldstein and Katherine Dillon, *Miracle at Midway*.

40. The *Makigumo* sank on 1 February 1943, in position 09°15' S, 159°47' E, south of Savo Island, with the loss of five dead. There were 237 survivors.

the loss of 173 of her crew.[41] Sadly, Watanabe had moved on, having become captain of the destroyer *Hatsukaze* on 28 December, but the 'Osmus jinx' followed him, the *Hatsukaze* herself being lost with all hands at the Battle of Empress Augusta Bay on 2 November.[42] Watanabe again escaped, for he had been appointed in command of DesDiv 1 on 1 July. Here, on 18 December 1943, he finally got his just deserts when his flagship, the destroyer *Numakaze*, was sunk with all hands by submarine attack off Okinawa. Despite the fact that thirty surviving members of Watanabe's original *Arashi* crew were located and interrogated post-war, not a single person was ever brought to trial.[43]

Resurrection

While the *Yorktown* had been hard hit, she had, thanks to her preparations, avoided, if only by the narrowest of margins, the catastrophic conflagration that had overtaken her three Japanese opposite numbers. Her speed was reduced to just 6 knots, and finally, at around 1440, engines were stopped. Meanwhile the damage-control teams had swung into action quickly and effectively. Down in fire room 1, Chief Charles Kleinsmith[44] and his six-man team

worked liked Trojans. Although the casings here were red hot and ruptured, and the fire brick was loose and broken, this boiler continued to operate on two burners. They were thus able to maintain auxiliary steam pressure on hand at 180 pounds per square inch, enough to run the auxiliary power circuit. Soon this power produced sufficient current for fans to restart, which cleared the stack smoke and noxious gases from other fire rooms and eventually the carrier began to get underway once more, albeit at slow speed. Crews with gas masks, found to be more efficient than rescue breathing gear, went into No. 4 fire room and lit fires beneath that boiler, which was cut in at 1520. Twenty minutes later all engines were put ahead, and she gradually worked up to 15 knots speed, with another 5 knots being added ten minutes later. As a morale-booster, Captain Buckmaster ordered the hoisting of a new battle ensign at the truck as a sign of defiance, which evoked spontaneous cheering from some of the watching escorts.

As well as fighter reinforcements and the landing aboard the *Enterprise* and *Hornet* of airborne *Yorktown* aircraft, all Spruance and Mitscher could do was keep their powder dry and pray the Japanese would continue to leave them alone.[45] Casualties from their own strikes had been devastatingly

41. The *Arashi* was sunk by gunfire and torpedoes from the destroyers *Craven* (DD-382), *Dunlap* (DD-384) and *Maury* (DD-401), between Kolombangara and Vella Lavella, sinking in position 07° 50' S, 156° 55' E.

42. More irony, *Hatsukaze* collided with the heavy cruiser *Mogami,* and was badly damaged, being easily finished off by US destroyers in position 26° 01' S, 153° 58' E.

43. Nothing at all can excuse such treatment, and there were other cases that took place, but it should be noted that such terrible inhumanity was by no means widespread in the IJN. We must also keep in mind the words of Major Edward F. Hoover, Assistant Operations Officer of 5th Bomber Command at the Battle of the Bismarck Sea on 4 March 1943: 'We sent out A-20s and Beaufighters to strafe lifeboats. It was rather a sloppy job, and some of the boys got sick. But that is something you have to learn. The enemy is out to kill you and you are out to kill the enemy. You can't be sporting in a war'. Alas, as recent events in Iraq have exposed, no nation on earth is totally immune from ignorance and abuse among the ranks of its armed services. While, most certainly, *some* individuals in the IJN interpreted the *Bushido* code as treating a surrendering enemy with contempt, it was more usual to regard an opponent who had fought well and bravely with respect. For a totally opposite experience one can refer to the sinking of the *Prince of Wales* and *Repulse* on 10 December 1941, when the three escorting destroyers were left completely unmolested to rescue survivors; or of Takashige Egusa directing the hospital ship *Vita* toward the survivors of the Indian Ocean sortie in April 1942, and also of the treatment afforded the survivors of the British destroyer *Encounter*, sunk in the north Java Sea on 1 March 1942, by the rescuing Japanese destroyer *Ikazuchi*, on the

express orders of Commander Shinsaku Kudo, who told the survivors, 'You have fought bravely. I respect the Royal Navy for that. You are now honourable guests of the Imperial Japanese Navy'. See Sir Samuel Falle, 'Chivalry', article in USNI *Proceedings*, Vol 113, January 1987. This theme has been further expanded by my friend Ryunosuke Valentine Megumi, of Okinawa, in his book *Tekihei wo Kyuzyoseyo!* ('*To Save Mine Enemy'*), Soshisha, Tokyo, 2006.

44. Charles Kleinsmith, PO1c (1904–42). b. 28 September 1904, Zionville, Pennsylvania. Enlisted in US Navy on 26 October 1922 as apprentice seaman. Became a fireman 2c and served aboard the battleships *Wyoming* (BB-32) and *Maryland* (BB-46). 5 October 1926, honourably discharged from service. 20 December 1928, re-enlisted and served successively on light cruisers *Milwaukee* (CL-5) and *Cincinnati* (CL-6), heavy cruiser *Portland* (CA-33) and light cruiser *Honolulu* (CL-48). Married Mary Agnes, and set up home at Long Beach, California 27 December 1939 assigned to carrier *Saratoga* (CV-3) as Chief Watertender. 31 October 1940, transferred to carrier *Yorktown* (CV-5). At Midway, despite dangerous heat and smoke problems, organized boiler room No. 1 and regained power on the vessel, enabling her to get underway for the second Japanese air attack. Failed to survive her sinking and posthumously awarded the Navy Cross. The high-speed destroyer transport USS *Kleinsmith* (APD-134) was named in his honour.

45. Strangely, the Japanese scouting planes seem never to have reported Spruance's force during the course of these *Hiryū* strike missions, although the latter were close enough to *Yorktown* to see the flak bursts of the action. Admiral E. P. Sauer's report to Admiral Fletcher noted: 'Heavy smoke (oil fire) and AA bursts, bearing 315° (T), distance about 12

heavy, and it must also be remembered that not all the aircraft that had found temporary succour at Midway had reported the fact, so losses appeared even worse than they actually were – and that was catastrophic enough. Ring was later blamed for the ditching of his fighter escorts, but the *Enterprise* group had also suffered heavily in that respect, and many, McClusky among them, placed the blame for that squarely on Browning's absurdly optimistic Point Option, which TF-16 did not get within 40 miles of, and he compounded the error by failing to update the hapless pilots on the true state of affairs.

Spruance therefore contented himself, at 1434, with reinforcing Fletcher's screen with the heavy cruisers *Pensacola* (CA-24) and *Vincennes* (CA-44) and the destroyers *Balch* (DD-363) and *Benham* (DD-397). This denuding of his own (intact) carrier's screen with four valuable ships to aid the already (perhaps mortally) damaged *Yorktown* was both altruistic and risky. As Lundstrom correctly states Spruance had no idea of the whereabouts (or the number) of the intact Japanese carriers;[46] he only knew that at least one was extremely active and busy reducing the odds and that, for all he knew, he might be next on the menu. Concentrating on preserving what he had might have been a wiser option[47], but fortunately it was never put to the test.[48]

Fletcher meanwhile rapidly transferred his flag from the *Yorktown* to the *Astoria*, in exactly the same way as his opponent, Nagumo, had been forced to abandon the *Akagi* for the light cruiser *Nagara*. Both commanders were destined to spend the rest of the battle thus displaced. But whereas Nagumo was planning an all-out night assault with his two battleships and his fearsome Type 93 torpedo-equipped destroyers to avenge the day's air disasters, Fletcher abdicated responsibility to his subordinate.

At about 1540, one hour and ten minutes after the bomb explosion in the uptakes, sufficient repairs had

been effected to the uptakes to enable boilers 1, 4, 5 and 6 to be cut in. After boilers 4, 5 and 6 were put back on the line, number 1 was secured in order to eliminate discharge of gases from that boiler into other fire-rooms. At 1550 the engine room reported ready to make 20 knots or slightly better.

It was only just in time for, at 1426, the radar on Fletcher's new flagship picked up a plot at 33 miles range; *Hiryū* was not done yet, she was hitting them again.

Hiryū's Second Strike

Unable to operate her own fighter aircraft for a time, and with many of her anti-aircraft guns out of action, *Yorktown* seemed a comparatively helpless target, but in fact, safely out of sight of the Vals, Spruance's TF-16 was just over the horizon, and was able to lend a hand.

> As soon as the bomb explosion had so slowed the ship as to prevent landing and flying off planes, the attack group planes in the air were directed to land on one of the other carriers. As the planes of the combat patrol required fuelling, they, too, were directed to land on one of the other carriers. All of the previous combat patrol had to land for fuel or ammunition, and a relief patrol of four fighters had been sent by *Hornet*, then about forty miles away. These four planes had been relieved in turn by six *Yorktown* planes which had been rearmed and refuelled on board *Enterprise*.

The *Hiryū* had, by dint of great effort, managed to get her second strike group away at 1330, and it was led by Lieutenant Jōichi Tomonaga.[49]

The torpedo-bombers were given a fighter escort of six A6M2s, again all that could be scraped together. Because of

---

miles' and should therefore have been perfectly visible to the Japanese observers above the battle scene. The first sighting of TF-16 was not made by a *Tone* floatplane until 1550.

46. Lundstrom, *Black Shoe Carrier Admiral*.

47. Fletcher presumably thought so too, for he later sent the cruisers back.

48. In fact, Admiral Edward P. Sauer 'assumed temporary command of Task Group 17.4 (*Balch*, *Benham*, *Morris*, *Anderson*, *Hammann*, *Hughes* and *Russel*), while *Yorktown* steered various courses at speeds of five knots, smoking heavily from forward section of stack'. Action Report: Commander Destroyer Squadron Six, Pacific Fleet, Admiral E. P. Sauer to Admiral Frank Jack Fletcher, A-16-3, Serial 094, dated 12 June 1942.

49. Captain Joichi Tomonaga (1911–42). b. 9 January 1911 at

Ooita. 1928 entered Etajima on 7 April. Graduated 17 November 1931, 59th Class. April 1933 ensign served aboard the heavy cruiser *Atago*. July 1934, qualified as pilot at Aviation School, promoted to lieutenant (jg). Assigned to Omura Naval Air Group, Nagasaki prefecture. November 1934, assigned to carrier *Akagi*. 1935 at Kasumigaura Air Flying Corps as instructor pilot. 1937, promoted to lieutenant, *buntaicho* at Tateyama Air Base, then as Chief Air Squadron at Usa Air Base despatched to China with his dive-bomber unit for active combat duties. December 1937 lieutenant, assigned to carrier *Kaga*. 1939–42 *buntaicho*. 1941, September, Instructor Pilot at Kasumigaura Air Base. April 1942, appointed air unit commander, carrier *Hiryū*. June 1942, KIA Midway. Promoted to captain posthumously.

Table 16: – Hiryū's Second (Torpedo-bomber) Attack on Yorktown, 4 June 1942

Chutai	Shōtai	Pilot	Observer	Radioman/Gunner	Result
1	1	Lt Jōichi Tomonaga	Ens. (Special Service) Saku Akamatsu	Sadamu Murai, PO1c	Lost
		Yashikichi Ishii, PO1c	Masamatsu Kobayashi, PO1c	Kiyokasu Shimada PO3c	Lost
		Hachirō Sugimoto, PO1c	Sadayoshi Hijikuro, PO1c	Kazunari Yaguchi, PO3c	Lost
	2	WO Yukio Obayashi	Hiroyuki Kudō, PO1c	Mitsuru Tamura PO1c	Lost
		Takeshi Suzuki, Sea1c	Kiyoaki Saitō, PO1c	Mutsuo Suzuki, PO2c	Lost
2	1	Toshio Takahashi, PO1c	Lt Toshio Hashimoto	Tomio Koyama, PO3c	
		Takurō Yanagimoto, PO2c	Chikashi Etō, PO1c	Kiyoshi Kasai, PO2c	
		Yoshimitsu Nagayama, PO3c	Toyohiro Nakamura, PO1c	Haruo Obama, Sea1c	
	2	WO Shigero Suzuki	WO Susumu Nishimori	Takayuki Horii, PO1c	Ex-Akagi
		Harumi Nakao, Sea1c	Taisuke Maruyama, PO1c	Giichi Hamada, Sea1c	

earlier casualties over Midway, which included both *buntaichō*,[50] Lieutenant Jōichi Tomonaga, the *hikōtaichō*, was flying BII-310.[51] Its port wing tank was damaged over Midway, and, although patched up, it still leaked. With *Yorktown* but 90 miles distant, Tomonaga was confident he could reach her, attack and return on just the starboard fuel tank.

All was set for a 1245 launch, but Yamaguchi held them back a little longer while he and his staff analysed, as best they could, the three brief incoming radio signals from Kobayashi. The eight *Hiryū kanko* plus the air group leader's machine, were joined by a stray Nakajima, which had been launched earlier from *Akagi* on a scouting mission.[52] Finding their recent home and sanctuary had been turned into a flaming charnel house in their absence, this aircrew, Warrant Officer Shigero Suzuki, Warrant Officer Susumu Nishimori and PO1c Takayuki Horii, had gratefully put down on *Hiryū* and had been 'volunteered' for the revenge attack, something they were all more than eager to partake in. This enabled the attack to be split into two five-plane *chutai*[53], so that if enough aircraft survived,

Table 17 – Fighter Escorts for Hiryū's Tomonaga Strike

1	Lt Shigeru Mori	Lost
	Tōru Yamamoto, PO2c	Lost
2	WO Yoshijirō Minegishi	
	Kenji Kotaka, Sea1c	
3	Akira Yamamoto, PO1c	Lost
	Masahi Bandō, PO3c	

a classic split (or 'scissor') torpedo-bomber assault was a theoretical, even if not a likely, possibility.

Minimal fighter pilots were available, and thus the escort of A6M2s was again just one *buntai* of three divisions of two plane *shotais* led by Lieutenant Shigeru Mori. Only four of these were from *Hiryū*, Mori having with him PO2c Toru Yamamoto, Warrant Officer Yoshijiro Minegishi and Sea1c Kenji Kotaka. The numbers were made up with two more 'refugees', this time from the *Kaga* holocaust, PO1c Akira Yamamoto[54] senior *shotai* leader aboard *Kaga* and a Pearl Harbor veteran[55], and PO3c Masahi Band Bandō.[56]

---

50. Lieutenant Rokurō KIA and Lieutenant Hiroharu Kadano severely wounded.
51. The ID codes of the IJN aircraft are a matter of considerable dispute. However, Captain Noritaka Kitazawa, informed Mr Allan Alsleben that a 1936 Navy Ministry regulation, amended on 15 November 1936, was that these codes were allocated to the *carrier*, rather than the unit embarked, and these could only be altered by the ministry itself. Kitazawa to Alsleben 1 November 1999.
52. *Senshi Sosho*, Vol, 43.
53. *Chutai* was never official terminology, but was an informal word for a small group of aircraft (of no specific number but usually less than six). *Shotai* covered a force of three aircraft;

while *buntai* indicated two or three *shotai*, but *chutai* was unofficially used when the number was smaller than this. *Chutai* has now become acceptable parlance due to its widespread usage by post-war Western researchers, historians and gamesters.
54. *Senshi Sosho*, Vol. 43.
55. Yamamoto survived this mission, returning safely but being forced to ditch at 1730. He was rescued by the destroyer *Hagikaze*. He was later KIA over Yachimata 24 November 1944 with flying with Yokosuka Air Group.
56. Bandō also returned safely at 1640, and subsequently survived *Hiryū*'s sinking and the war.

The second strike was finally let off the leash at 1331. By that time both the brutal interrogations of captured American airmen and the verbal report of the returning Comet had revealed that, even after Kobayashi's stalwart effort, at least two enemy carriers still remained intact a mere 80–90 miles out to the south-east. Climbing to 13,500 feet the two torpedo *chutai* and their fighter cover bored on. After an hour the hard-driving Tomonaga was rewarded with the sight of one of these vital enemy targets off to port, some 30 miles distant. At 1432 Tomonaga deployed his unit to the attack.[57]

Meanwhile his target, unknown to him the reinvigorated *Yorktown*, was so much back in business that she had been able to start refuelling ten of her own F4F-4s up on her flight deck. This activity was brought to an abrupt end with the radar plots warning at 1450 of an incoming hostile formation, 33 miles distant on a bearing of 340 degrees. Yet again the avgas was drained and secured with CO_2 while four of six airborne Wildcats were vectored out to intercept. Rather than sit on deck and wait for whatever was coming their way, those fighters with fuel (eight had as much as 23 gallons), were rapidly despatched to join in the fight and many were still launching as the Japanese attack broke over them.

On arrival in sight of the enemy, Tomonaga and his men must have been convinced that they had found the second, and hitherto untouched, American carrier. Their eyes had recently been filled with the vision of three of their own carriers turned into blazing funeral pyres after being hit by dive-bombing attack; their ears had been filled with Kobayashi's last message that his target was on fire. The two impressions merged and they thought they knew what to expect. What they saw in front of them bore no resemblance to either image; the American carrier was moving fairly fast,

there was no smoke and flames, as they might have expected, nor indeed, any really obvious signs of damage.[58] To their minds, as she loomed up in their sights, she could only be a new, fresh target and, if they could sink or neutralize her, *Hiryū* would then face a one-against-one carrier duel with the last remaining US carrier on the field of battle. The traditional *kansen* attack method, *nikuhaku-hitchū*[59], was never more relevant, provided they could achieve it. Given the close back-up readily available to the Japanese, which included Nagumo's two battleships and accompanying destroyer flotilla, plus Kurita's fast-approaching heavy cruiser division, that battle was still a winnable one and not the hopeless, egoistic gamble some recent American portrayals have painted it[60], even leaving aside the more distant and even more powerful Japanese forces.

The American CAP hastened to intercept and made contact at about 10–14 miles out from the ships, at which time the incomings were definitely identified as torpedo-carrying aircraft rather than yet more dive-bombers. The American ships were steaming away from the enemy planes to put them at a disadvantage and give the interceptors more time, but the Kate boring in at almost 200 knots was no easy shot like the Devastator and, splitting into two halves, they began to let down, with Toshio Hashimoto's *chutai* executing a swerving approach to pincer the *Yorktown* between two combs of missiles in the classic manner.

The approach of the *kankō* was assisted by a mistake by the leading group of American Wildcats, which somehow misinterpreted the FDO's instructions and missed their target in light cloud.[61] The fighters were recalled promptly from their overshoot while others, following on, headed for higher altitudes assuming the enemy were dive-bombers

---

57. Ikuhiko Hata, '*Kaeri Zaru Tomonaga Raigekitai*'.
58. So efficient were *Yorktown*'s damage-control teams under Commander Clarence E. Aldrich, that even the 10 foot hole in her flight deck had been repaired in less than half an hour.
59. The Japanese roughly equates to 'Get close, hit hard.' It applied to aerial torpedo delivery, but was also appropriate to the decisive effect of the surface fleet, if they could just get under the guard of the American carriers under cover of darkness.
60. Over-obsessive hindsight and concentration on the attributes of the fast-waning on-hand US air power tend to blank-out the tremendous potential of the available surface firepower of the Japanese force in a night action to many recent historians. The one-sided outcome of the Battle of Savo Island should give them pause for reflection. Fortunately, at the time, Fletcher and Spruance certainly did not share such cosy and naive confidence in their invulnerability. To those who aver that Yamaguchi would have done

better to 'cut and run' while he had the chance, one asks whether, in America's own proud naval history, it would have been better to have said, 'Better hold off because of the torpedoes' or 'I think I may have to give up the ship because things look bad' or even 'I think I have ceased to fight!' rather than to prevail, no matter what the odds, as they did off the coast of Samar. If such thoughts are deemed 'unthinkable' for American naval officers, why should they not be equally unpalatable to a Japanese naval officer?
61. According to John Lundstrom's analysis in *The First Team*, Oscar Pederson's 1429 instruction to Lieutenant Scott McCuskey to convert the magnetic heading from the cruiser *Pensacola*'s radar plot, (which the FDO relayed out to the CAP) into a true heading, termed 'arrow', was not understood by the VF-3 pilot who adopted a vector or literal approach, which could have resulted in a 10 degree interception course error or more. Alternatively, of course, it might have just been a straightforward sight/height mix-up in the heat of the moment.

again. But there were plenty of Wildcats to go around and some at least were soon in among the Nakajimas. It was thought at the time that at least three Japanese bombers were destroyed before they could deploy to the attack. Some of these interceptions cut it very fine and at least two Wildcats[62] were destroyed by the escorting A6M2s in short order.

Instant Action

Andy Mikus gave a rather colourful account of events as he recalled them.[63] He wrote of how *Yorktown*'s own fighters:

> . . . thundered down the flight deck and roared away with only 25 gallons of gas in their tanks. In these desperate straits, our pilots had no choice but to engage the enemy under the hail of our own bullets. One of them, John Adams[64], had no sooner become airborne, rolled up his wheels, charged his guns and banked to port, when a torpedo bomber crossed his sights. The Japanese torpedo-bombers always seem to attack in pairs. Adams shot down the plane in his sights and hit the wingman too, but not before the 'Long Lance'[65] was dropped. Both Japanese planes as well as the pursuing Adams were racing within a torrent of destroyer fire. But even with the two Nakajimas out of the action the destroyer continued to fire at Adams! He survived but was livid with anger for a long time afterward and almost came to blows with the destroyer's gunnery officer whom he later encountered ashore in Pearl[66]. Ensign Tootle[67] also

took off from a deck, which must have seemed like the bottom of a canyon the sides of which were red-hot tracers rising from 20 mm guns along both catwalks. Needing three hands, as never before, he was banking and firing even before the wheels were retracted. His flight lasted only 36 seconds but time enough to riddle an incoming plane so close to a destroyer that his ejected casings littered its deck below him.

The *Yorktown* had actually worked up to a speed of 19 knots[68] by 1600, which in itself was an excellent achievement, but this was clearly insufficient to save her and ahead emergency full speed on all engine's was ordered. The main steam line cross-connection valves in the superheater fire rooms were closed, as the carrier cracked on to 23 knots steering a course 090 degrees to maintain a wind over the bow to aid further launchings.

Obeying Tomonaga's urgent 1440 radio command, 'All go in' those Kates that evaded the Wildcats' attentions now faced the heavy barrage from the screening ships, which took a further toll of their numbers. The biggest barrage was laid down by the cruiser *Pensacola* which was firing her main armament, as well as every anti-aircraft weapon able to bear. The four surviving Kates of the 1st *chutai*, now almost down to 200 feet and ready to launch, had to pass that ship to get at the carrier and suffered accordingly. Tomonaga himself appears to have fallen victim to a late F4F intervention, and is usually credited to Thach, the VF-3 commander. He certainly shot up the port wing of one B5N2 with garishly coloured *shikikan-hyoshiki* markings[69], and saw it splash just astern of the *Yorktown*, but not before

---

62. These two F4's from VF-3 were F-2 piloted by Lieutenant (jg) William Stone Woollen, A-V (N) and Ensign Harry Bonaparte Gibbs, A-V (N).

63. Andy Mikus, *A Clear Day*.

64. Captain John Paul Adams, A-V (N). b. 20 February 1944, Horton, Kansas. Retired as a captain 1972.

65. Photographer's Mate Bill Roy related a similar story, 'These were Long Lance Type 97 [sic] torpedoes. They had 2,200 pound warheads coming at a speed of 40 miles per hour. I was tracking the torpedo plane with my telephoto lens and saw the plane disappear, but the white wake was coming directly port side, towards me. I knew we would be hit.' But of course the 24 inch, 30 foot long Type 93, the so-termed 'Long Lance', torpedo, with its 1,080 pound warhead, actually weighed 5,952 pounds, which was *heavier* than the 5,024 pound B5N2 herself! The Long Lance was definitely *not* capable of being hauled by a Kate, or any aeroplane, or fired from any submarine for that matter, it was strictly a surface-launched weapon. In reality, Tomonaga's Nakajimas toted the standard 18 inch 1,764 pound IJN aerial torpedo. It had the advantage of being rugged and reliable, and, unlike

its US counterpart, usually ran true! Also, it did not leave *any* wake, white or otherwise!

66. However, John Lundstrom attributes Adams's problems not to friendly fire but to having to fly right through the blast of his *kankō* target when it blew up in mid air, (*The First Team*.)

67. Ensign Milton Tootle, Jr, A-V (N).

68. Buckmaster to Nimitz.

69. *Shikikan-hyoshiki* translates as 'leader insignia' and these vertical stripes were usually in the same colour as the air squadron colour, although 1st Air Squadron used yellow instead of red. For *shotaicho* (three aircraft inclusive of leader and the smallest tactical unit) Vals and Kates used one stripe beneath the code letters; for *buntaicho* (informally *chutaicho*), leading two or three *shotais*, two stripes; for *hikotaicho* (the most senior officer of a whole carrier air group, not necessarily a pilot because if an aircraft carried more than one man as crew, then the *hikotaicho* would be an observer) one stripe *above* and two stripes *below* the code letter. When Tomonaga took over as *Hikotaicho* aboard *Hiryū* he painted up his three *yellow* stripes, even though the Flying Dragon's normal stripes were blue.

launching its torpedo, which appeared to be running straight and true.[70]

While the 1st *Chutai* was getting chewed up, the Zeros duelled with other Wildcats, losing most of their number, but flaming one F4F just as it cleared the deck[71], between them they occupied the majority of the defending fighters, although not all. In any event Hashimoto's second group found gaps in the defences and four launched their torpedoes from a height of around 100 feet and at ranges down to 650 yards.[72] Violent evasive action by *Yorktown* was attributed by some to avoiding at least two of the torpedoes launched at her, but two others could not be dodged.

The first torpedo struck at around 1620. The impact point was on her port side at frame 90 and the detonation shook the ship up considerably. Captain Buckmaster later listed the effects of this hit: 'A heavy jar felt throughout machinery spaces, lost lighting when main circuit breakers went out on after board, steam dropping rapidly. Ship took decided list to port. Emergency diesel generators cut in, but circuit breakers failed to hold, evidently due to short circuits'.[73] The ship's rudder was jammed solid at 15 degrees to port.

PhoM2c Bill Roy[74], was a very busy man that day. From vantage points on both the signal bridge and flight-deck of *Yorktown* he took a memorable series of motion and still pictures that are both graphic and poignant; indeed they are classics of their age. He recalled:

> The torpedo went deep into the *Yorktown*. The explosion caused a rumble throughout the ship and the deck rose up under me, trembled, and fell away shaking. I was knocked down. *Yorktown* rolled to port.
>
> The second torpedo quickly followed. I had just started filming again when it hit. There was a great sheet of red flame and smoke and water going skyward with a loud shattering explosion in front of me. The 20 mm guns and crews on the flight deck catwalk above the explosion were gone. Once more the *Yorktown* shuddered violently, stem to stern, and rolled over hard to port with the hangar deck in the water.[75]

Again Captain Buckmaster recorded the incident. 'Approximately 30 seconds later second torpedo hit about frame 75 port. Main and auxiliary steam pressure had now

70. Thach interview with John Lundstrom, October 1974, cited in *The First Team*.
71. This was flown by Ensign George A. Hopper, Jr of VF-3, who did not survive.
72. Warrant Officer Susumu Nishimori's torpedo-release mechanism failed at this critical juncture and his missile 'hung-up' on him, preventing an attack.
73. Buckmaster to Nimitz.
74. Commander William Glenn Roy. b. (1919) b. 27 December 1919 at Coaling, Alabama. Moved to Florida in 1920. Educated Columbia High School and excelled at track, football and basketball. Lake City National Guard. Enlisted USN September 1939. Obtained a private pilot's licence 1940 at Glen Rock Airport, Virginia Beach, Virginia. Served in engineering department of battleship *Arkansas* (BB-33) in Atlantic Fleet, working from Norfolk, Virginia. Became ship's photographer as additional duties. Naval School of Photography, NAS Pensacola, for four months, qualifying in basic, advanced aerial and oblique photography and aerial mapping, and motion picture camera operation, film processing, editing and production. Graduated in 1942 and joined carrier *Yorktown* (CV-5) at Norfolk as PhoM2c. Present at Marshal raids, Coral Sea and Midway battles, awarded Citation by CincPac for Midway. CASU 5 [Cooperative Administrative Support Unit] at NAS San Diego. NAS Pensacola at Instructor Motion Picture and Aerial classes. 1943, 1 May promoted to chief petty officer, aerial camera reconnaissance classes. Promoted to chief master at arms at Pensacola. After the war, USNR at NAS Jacksonville, Chief Photo Laboratory, Air Wing Staff 741. Lieutenant-commander. 1953 direct commission as Photo Officer and Navy Intelligence Officer

with VP-741 flying P23V-2s to Bermuda, Azores, London, Gibraltar and North Africa. NAS Anacostia, Head of Photographic Department. 1960, Retired from navy as regular commander. 1951–70 missile, space and range work, with Dr Werner von Braun. Contract Manager, Missile and Rocket Programs for Martin Aerospace on *Matador* programme. Contract Manager on Gemini space vehicle programme, and Martin-*Titan III* programmes. City Commissioner Lake City twice. 1960 Manager, Advanced Programmes Cape Canaveral Test Division, Martin. 1964 University Professor MBA Florida Institute of Technology, Melbourne, and Master of Business Administration programme. Qualified to practice law various bars and had private practice at Altamonte Springs and Naples, Florida. 1966 formed Missile, Space and Range Pioneers, Inc.1968 Contract Manager Dow Chemical Company for NASA Apollo-Saturn moon programme, etc. International lawyer for Dow. 1973 Presidential Commission on Federal Government Procurement. 1981 retired with rank of Lieutenant-Commander. Currently resides at Naples, Florida. with his wife Barbara.
75. Lieutenant-Commander William G. Roy, *I Filmed the Battle of Midway from USS Yorktown (CV-5)*. When *Yorktown* was abandoned Bill taped up three cans of exposed film and stuffed them under his dungaree shirt and life jacket before jumping overboard. After several hours in the water he was rescued by the destroyer *Hammann*, whose own demise he also filmed from back aboard the *Yorktown* once more as a volunteer member of the salvage party! He generously loaned me an enormous number of his photographs and graciously granted me his permission both to quote from his memoirs and to use his photographs in this book.

been lost, ship continued to list heavily to port. With list fast approaching 30°, word was received to standby to abandon ship'.[76]

The irrepressible Mikus, who seems to have seen everything that day, also recalled the incident.

One of these daring pilots now banked to the left off our port bow, close enough it seemed to be hit by a thrown ball and his second seat man rose up and vigorously shook his fist at us. He had good cause to be angry; three of their carriers were doomed and his own would soon suffer the same fate. And yet at the time, I wondered why he was taking it so personally.[77]

Deep Damage

The two torpedo hits occurred so close in time that the subsequent report confessed that the 'damage caused by each torpedo individually is almost impossible to reconstruct.'[78]. The combined effect was disastrous. 'Both torpedoes hit the port side at the same depth, estimated to be about 11 ft above the keel or about 15 feet below the water line. The first torpedo is reported . . . to have hit at frame 92; however, fuel tanks as far aft as frame 105 were reported damaged with flooding extending to frame 107'.[79]

In contrast to the battleships *California* (BB-44) and *Nevada* (BB-36), damaged by Japanese aircraft torpedoes at Pearl Habor, which both cases suffered no damage at a distance of more than 36 feet from the point of impact, the damage area on *Yorktown* extended to about 52 feet, and appeared 'unusually extensive for an aircraft torpedo.'[80] The port gallery walkway from about frame 84 to frame 100 was carried away by the geyser from this explosion with the centre of the damage about frame 92. The second torpedo reportedly hit at frame 80, which was consistent with the flooding of the ship. Although the *Yorktown* shook from the heavy dull explosions, '*no* general flexural vibration of the ship was noted. No flash or flame was noted from the explosion, nor were any fires started.'[81]

The three American carriers had torpedo defence systems that varied from four layers over the engine-room spaces to three layers elsewhere. In *Yorktown*'s case the extreme inboard layer of tanks was empty and offered no protection at all, but the two outboard layers were completely full of fuel oil, in line with the then current liquid loading practice. The Bureau of Ships later estimated that the ship's skin was destroyed for about 20 feet vertically and 20–30 feet horizontally; that No. 1 bulkhead was destroyed, that No. 2 bulkhead was ruptured and pushed inboard, and that No. 3, which was the holding bulkhead, was deflected inboard and its connections severed at both top and bottom, which permitted rapid flooding of the port firerooms and forward generator room.

That much was estimated, but what was known for certain was that the force of the two torpedoes in conjunction blew the fourth deck up into compartments A-432-L, B-402-L, B-414-L and C-404-L, completely flooding these fourth-deck living spaces. The blasts also warped the quick-acting doors in bulkheads 82.90, 106, 112 and 130 on the third deck, port side, rendering them non-watertight. The result was predictable; with *Yorktown*'s port fuel tanks from frame 69 to frame 107 stove-in or warped, the sea flooded into fire rooms 2, 6 and 8 and the forward generator room. Buckmaster reported the third deck flooded to a depth of 8 feet and the forward and after engines likewise under water as far as the first platform deck. This flooding was aided by the water already entering via the bomb-fragmented uptakes from No. 2 boiler, 'and was added to by the improper closure of the quick-acting watertight doors as the crew abandoned these spaces.'[82]

The loss of power which Captain Buckmaster ascribed to the after switchboard being 'destroyed' was questioned. The Bureau experts questioned a survivor from that area and also took into account the report of the engineering officer, and both indicated that the after switchboard was, in fact, intact but short-circuited. The report concluded:

Men on watch in the forward switchboard room were apparently killed before they could isolate the board. After all steam was lost the after emergency generator cut in automatically and tried to energize the after board. Since this board was shorted through damaged leads forward, the breakers repeatedly kicked out. It is not clear why the breakers on the after board connected to the damaged leads were not

---

76. Buckmaster to Nimitz.
77. Mikus, *A Clear Day*.
78. War Damage Report, USS *Yorktown* – Loss in Action June 4–7, 1942. Midway. With references – (a) CO *Yorktown* ltr. CV5/A16-3 (CCR-10-per) dated 18 June 1942 (War Damage Report); (b) CO *Yorktown* ltr, CV5/A16-3 (CCR-10-oah), dated 18 June, 1942 (War Action Report) and (c) CO *Yorktown* ltr, of 17 June, 1942 endorsed by CincPac ltr.

A16/Midway, Serial 01982, dated 7 July 1942 (Loss of *Yorktown*). Cited hereafter as *Yorktown* Damage Report.
79. *Ibid.*
80. *Ibid.*
81. *Ibid.* My italics. Contrast this sober assessment with some historical accounts.
82. *Ibid.*

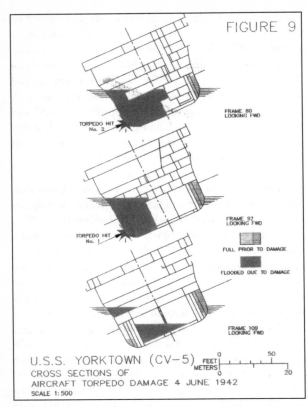

FIGURE 9

FRAME 80
LOOKING FWD

TORPEDO HIT
No. 2

FRAME 92
LOOKING FWD

FULL PRIOR TO DAMAGE

FLOODED DUE TO DAMAGE

TORPEDO HIT
No. 1

FRAME 109
LOOKING FWD

U.S.S. YORKTOWN (CV-5)
CROSS SECTIONS OF
AIRCRAFT TORPEDO DAMAGE 4 JUNE 1942
SCALE 1:500

FEET | 0 ... 50
METERS | 0 ... 20

Diagram 12. Cross-sections of Aircraft Torpedo Damage to *Yorktown* (CV-5) on 4 June 1942. (Originally presented at FAST 99, Seattle, August 1999. Reprinted with the permission of the Society of Naval Architects and Marine Engineers, New Jersey)

opened to permit the use of the board for intact circuits.[83]

Turning his head as his *kankō* made a high-speed withdrawal, Hashimito had the great satisfaction of seeing two enormous upheavals of dirty-white water and smoke erupting from the port side of the American carrier and he knew he had been successful. Jubilantly his radio operator transmitted news of this achievement to the waiting Nagumo. 'I carried out a torpedo attack against an enemy carrier and saw two certain hits.'[84]

On receipt of this news Yamaguchi must have felt vindicated. Two down, one to go! (The Japanese were still under the impression that *Yorktown* was one of the hitherto undamaged carriers.)

Abandonment

These two torpedo strikes appeared to be mortal blows, both to those aboard the *Yorktown* and those, like Fletcher, observing her from a distance. The carrier was dead in the water once more and heeled over to port. The Chief Engineer, Lieutenant-Commander J. F. Delaney, reported that all the fires had been extinguished. All the lights were out and the heel of the ship made movement very difficult. The aftermost auxiliary diesel motor was operational but the switchboards had been knocked out so there was absolutely no chance of resuming power, and Aldrich informed Buckmaster that he could not correct the list without it. The list increased remorselessly, reaching 26 degrees, and with the carrier's great flight deck canted over alarmingly, both men thought she was going to continuing tipping – and indeed might roll over at any time.[85]

Buckmaster decided to get the crew off the ship while there was still time. He signalled his decision to Fletcher and the escorting ships closed in to lend assistance.

Meanwhile the able men went down lines over the ship's side into rafts and ship's boats sent across from the destroyers. Captain Buckmaster then made a final tour of his command, which he described.

The Commanding Officer then inspected the starboard side from the catwalk and 5-inch gun platforms, and then returned to the flight deck opposite No. 1 crane. He then proceeded down through Dressing Station No. 1 and forward through the 'Flag Country' and the Captain's Cabin to the port side and down the ladder to the Hangar Deck. On this inspection no live personnel were found. By this time the port side of the Hangar Deck was in the water.[86]

The wounded took priority, and the Battle Dressing Station and Sick Bay were cleared with some difficulty. Lieutenant Joseph Pollard, gave a vivid description of what this entailed in the moments just after the torpedoes struck home.

I knew we were completely helpless but did not want to admit it. Just then word came over the speaker, 'Prepare to abandon ship.' I was dumbfounded. It was incomprehensible. A man lying beside me with one foot shot away and a severe chest wound turned his head towards me and asked, 'What does this mean for us?' and turned his head away. He knew

---

83. *Ibid.*
84. Message file, *Japanese story.*

85. Buckmaster to Nimitz.
86. *Ibid.*

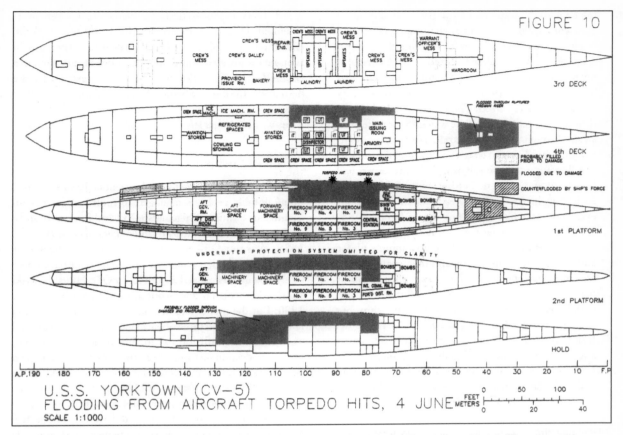

Diagram 13. Flooding from Aircraft Torpedo Hits on *Yorktown* (CV-5) on 4 June 1942. (Originally presented at FAST 99, Seattle, August 1999. Reprinted with the permission of the Society of Naval Architects and Marine Engineers, New Jersey)

that he would have no chance in the water. The man was later seen in the Naval Hospital in Pearl Harbor on the way to recovery. We listed more and more to port until it was almost impossible to stand on the slick deck. We searched frantically for life preservers for the wounded, taking some from the dead. Our stretchers had gone below to the sick bay and we had difficulty finding enough for our wounded. All who could possible walk did so. I went up on the flight deck and walked along the starboard edge being very careful not to slip and slide the width of the ship and off the port side. The ship rolled slowly with the swells but the water was not rough and after each roll she returned to her former position. I thought a big wave might possibly capsize her. A bulkhead giving way below might also let her go over. Our list was about 30 degrees [*sic*]. The speakers were now dead and when word was passed to abandon ship, it did not get to me. Several life rafts were in the water but

the lines over the side were not long enough to reach the water. Lieutenant Wilson and I tied some lines together and lowered some wounded. Meanwhile the sick bay wounded were being lowered from the hangar deck.

Captain Buckmaster came up to me as I was on the verge of going over the side at a place we had lowered some wounded on the starboard side aft of the island structure. There were several life rafts of wounded floating below me. He asked what I waiting for. I told him I was waiting to get off all the wounded and that we had searched the topside structure and the catwalks and I was sure that we had every man that was alive from this area on the life rafts. He said something to the effect that 'They said the Captain should be the last to leave the ship. I'm ready to go now. Would you leave?'

I chose a big line and went over the side. I stopped at the armor belt for a rest. It was at least 75 feet from the deck to the water and I still had some 20 feet to go. I worked along the armor belt to a spot, which was immediately above a life raft. The line there was a small one and soon after I started down a corner of my life jacket got inside my grip and I began slipping. The fingers of both my hands were rather badly burned before I realized. Then I released the line and dropped the remainder of the way into the water and swam through the oil to the raft. We took on board several wounded who were close by until the raft was overflowing and the few of us with life preservers had to get out and swim or hold on with one hand. As each wave broke over our heads the oil burned our eyes and noses like liquid fire. It was impossible to keep from swallowing some of it. Someone would swim alongside and say hold me up a minute please and proceed to vomit the oil and then swim on. We had nine stretcher cases and about 25 men on or hanging on to our raft. We tried to flutter kick and paddle our raft away from the side of the ship, but each wave seemed to bring us back against her side. If she capsized we would be carried down by suction and not have a chance. Finally, someone got the bright idea of paddling aft along the side of the ship and we began to make some headway. By doing this we finally got free of her stern.[87]

Evacuating almost 2,300 men was no easy operation. The evacuees slid down rope lines and clambered down cargo nets, slipping and dropping into the ocean, then tried to reach one of the numerous life rafts the various ships had thrown overboard to assist. The destroyers also lowered their boats, although some ships found that their boats had been damaged by the air action earlier. The destroyers were faced with many dilemmas in carrying out this work. In the midst of hundreds of men in the water, it was impossible to turn the ships' screws to manoeuvre when an air attack warning sounded. The mounting pile of oil-soaked rags around the gun decks made it impossible to use these weapons for defence until the rags had been dumped over-

board. The very limited destroyer medical teams were overwhelmed. One small destroyer, the 1,500 ton *Benham*, embarked a total of 725 *Yorktown* survivors, and her captain later gave a detailed and graphic account of just what this entailed.[88] In all, 2,270 survivors were rescued by the destroyers, the last one being taken aboard *Balch* at 1846.[89]

Thus was *Yorktown* left.

Japanese Survivors

The attack had been costly to the slender Japanese force. Some notable veterans managed to return, among them Lieutenant Yasuhiro Shigematsu, XO 2nd *Buntaicho* and a veteran of Pearl Harbor, who landed back aboard *Hiryū* at 1338. Warrant Officer Yoshijiro Minegishi, the senior *shotai* leader, flying a damaged aircraft, got her back down safely aboard *Hiryū* at 1230, while PO1c Hitoshi Sasaki managed to return to *Hiryū* but was forced to ditch, also at 1230. But the incomparable and inspirational Tomonaga failed to turn up and three of the five *kankō* were so damaged as likely to be unfit for any further immediate combat. However, despite very high claims of 'kills' by the American fighter pilots, the total Japanese loss from this second strike was four B5N2s and just two A6M2s. In reply the F4Fs lost four aircraft, although only one pilot was killed.

By 1600, following a verbal debriefing of the few survivors, Yamaguchi's staff were convinced in their minds that heavy damage had been inflicted on a second American carrier, and duly signalled this conclusion to Nagumo, who received the cheering news on the bridge of new flagship *Nagara* at 1635.[90] By this time Nagumo himself had received more recent information from the battlefield zone that seemed to pour cold water on Yamaguchi's optimistic analysis. One of the scouting floatplanes from the cruiser *Tone* had reported (at 1550), that she had sighted *two* American carriers, along with a pair of escorting ships.[91] The signal did not specify whether either, or both, these carriers were damaged in any way, but it was still a douche of cold water on the hopes emanating from *Hiryū* where the

87. Pollard, Oral History.
88. Rear-Admiral Joseph M. Worthington, 'A Destroyer at Midway', article in *Shipmate*, March 2006. The editor of the magazine claims that 'never before or since as far as *Shipmate* knows has any destroyer rescued more survivors', and also added that 'history probably offers no statistically comparable rescue operations'. However, running her close would be the old British destroyer *Sabre* (950 tons), which at Dunkirk lifted 1,700 men in two trips, an average of 850 men. The three destroyers *Electra*, *Express* and *Vampire* between them rescued a total of 2,081 survivors from the *Prince of*

Wales and *Repulse* off Malaya on 10 December 1941.
89. The individual figures given in Admiral Sauer's Action Report were: *Benham* 721, *Balch* 544, *Russel* 499, *Anderson* 204, *Morris* 193 (including Commander Laing, RN), *Hammann* 85 (including Captain Buckmaster) and *Hughes* 24.
90. Nagumo Report.
91. It would seem that *Tone*'s aircraft had finally homed onto Spruance's TF-16, but another of her team fell to the Wildcats' guns before she could enlarge on her sister's information. The *Chikuma* was preparing some of her own scouts to take over the watch.

indefatigable Yamaguchi was organizing a third strike, to be made at dusk, from the scrapings of every flyable aircraft he could muster. The plan was to utilize four D3A1s and the experimental D4Y as dive-bombers for a combined assault with the five remaining B5N2 torpedo-bombers along with fighter cover assembled from the hotch-potch of seventeen available A6M2s from the various carrier air groups which had now all made *Hiryū* their home.

The dog-tired Hashimoto was informed that he would be leading the third strike, which Yamaguchi originally scheduled for 1630. This proved beyond the endurance even of *Hiryū*'s exemplary survivors and so it was reluctantly postponed to 1800 to give the aircrews time to eat and rest. This delay was perfectly understandable: these brave men were gallant and willing, but they were not robots. This final, last-chance attack was destined never to be mounted, however for the Americans counter-attacked and arrived before they could be launched. The ten-plane Japanese strike force was armed and fuelled and made ready to be brought up from the hangar deck later, meanwhile the flight-deck was kept free for the operation of the CAP,

which the *hikocho,* Kawaguchi, had stacked over the reunited *Kidō Butai* at various levels from 1627 onward.

Fletcher Bows Out

'Dusty' Kleiss's diary reflected the puzzlement that many American aviators felt about what they saw as these premature abandonment of the *Yorktown*. 'She was abandoned while we were on the attack above and seemed strangely alone without any protection. At this later date I still can't understand it.'[92] Fletcher appeared, on the face of it, to have washed his hands of her.[93]

Commander Michael B. Laing, RN[94], the Naval Liaison Officer aboard the *Yorktown*, considered that Buckmaster's decision to abandon ship was premature, and that he should have confined himself to getting away the useless mouths but retain key personnel aboard and continue to fight to save the vessel. American opinion might bridle at this suggestion (Lundstrom alleges that: 'Laing's report to the Admiralty was so critical of how the US Navy fought at Midway it remains classified in Britain today'[95]). Laing had

---

92. Lieutenant N. J. Kleiss, *Dairy of the War.*

93. Fletcher's reputation for apparently 'ducking-out' when things got bad earned him the wartime nickname of 'Haul-Arse Jack' from the US Marines. Perhaps very unfairly, they blamed him for the failure to reinforce Wake Island in December 1941, and were later to become embittered at being 'abandoned' by him when he pulled the carriers out at Guadalcanal later in 1942. The hard criteria of 'three strikes and you're out', certainly applied to the judgements of the men on the spot and, with Wake, Midway and Guadalcanal as seeming justification, they never forgave him. Their verdict was, predictably, later reinforced by post-war Marine Corps historians, and, more damningly, by naval analysts like Bates and Morison as well. Even Nimitz turned against him. Most recently, respected historian John B. Lundstrom has sought to re-establish the Fletcher reputation by dint of some good, solid research, although some feel that, in his eagerness to 'do right' by his man, he may have gone too far the other way. Anyway, the rightness or wrongness of things do not count a jot when it comes to legends and reputations, for, once a label is applied, it tends to stick, and fairness and justice rarely remove the stains. The Commander-in-Chief of the Royal Navy's Home Fleet during the first year of the war, Admiral Sir Charles Forbes suffered the same fate. Due to very poor intelligence reports, and execrable RAF air reconnaissance during the winter of 1939–40, he repeatedly failed to intercept various sorties by German battle-cruisers and pocket battleships. This earned him the cruel epithet of 'Wrong-Way Charlie' from the lower deck. This jibe stuck, despite the fact that Forbes, alone among senior servicemen and British politicians, got it absolutely right about assessing the possibility of a German invasion of England in 1940, while Winston Churchill and the rest, got it totally wrong.

94. Captain Michael Bryan Laing, (1901–78). b. Sunderland, Co. Durham, December 1901, son of Bryan Laing, shipbuilder and Eleanor *née* Leather. 1917–19 service in World War I. 1918 acting sub-lieutenant. From 15 September 1921, sub-lieutenant. 15 April 1923, serving aboard destroyer *Wolfhound*. Acting lieutenant. 3 October 1923, lieutenant. January 1925, serving aboard destroyer *Whitshed* in Mediterranean. July 1927 at HMS *Excellent,* Whale Island, Portsmouth, qualified for gunnery duties, and at RN College, Greenwich. April 1940 Assistant Gunnery Officer aboard battle-cruiser *Repulse*, Atlantic Fleet. 15 April 1931 lieutenant-commander. January 1932 Flotilla Gunnery Officer, 2nd Destroyer Flotilla, aboard flotilla leader *Stuart*, Mediterranean. January 1934 HMS *Excellent*, Gunnery School. February 1936 Gunnery Officer of heavy cruiser *Norfolk*, and Fleet Gunnery Officer, East Indies. 30 June 1936 commander. August 1938 HMS *Excellent*. July 1939 staff course, RN College Greenwich. September 1939 Staff Officer Operations, Vice-Admiral Reserve Fleet, aboard light cruiser *Effingham*, Portsmouth. April 1940 Staff Northern Patrol, *Pyramus* at Kirkwall. February 1941, XO carrier *Furious*. 1 January 1942, OBE. April 1942 British Naval Mission, Washington, DC, then RN Liaison Officer aboard *Yorktown* for Midway. 30 June 1943 captain. December 1943 Deputy CoS to C-in-C Mediterranean. Planning officer for amphibious landings in Sicily (1943) and south of France (1944). August 1944 remained Deputy CoS to C-in-C, Mediterranean. 23 January 1945 Mentioned in Despatches and Legion of Honour. 11 December 1945 CBE. After the war appointed in command of aircraft maintenance carrier *Unicorn* from 13 September 1948. 8 July 1952 retired. Resided at Therfield, Royston, Herts. Died 3 January 1978 at home.

95. Lundstrom, *Black Shoe Carrier Admiral.*

previously served in the western Mediterranean and he may have been influenced in his opinion by the loss of the carrier *Ark Royal* in November 1941. In that case a detailed Board of Inquiry was convened.[96] The *Ark*, steaming at 22 knots, was hit by a single torpedo, fired by the German submarine *U-81*, the point of impact being between the keel and the starboard side of the ship, abreast of her island structure. As in the case of *Yorktown*, the damage inflicted by this hit was much greater than had been previously predicted, a hole 130 feet long by 30 feet wide being blown in her side. Flooding took place in the starboard boiler room, air spaces, oil tanks, main switchboard room and lower steering position. But, again as in the case of *Yorktown*, it was the alarming canting over of the huge flight deck that brought about the most concern. An initial list of 10 degrees had, within twenty minutes, increased to 18 degrees[97], and her apparent imminent capsizing caused her commanding officer, Captain L. E. H. Maund,[98] who, just like Buckmaster, was concerned for the safety of his crew, to order the ship be abandoned. By the time it was realized she was not going all the way over, just under fifty minutes from the time of the detonation, many personnel essential to the damage-control teams, had already been taken off by destroyers. Again, in a similar manner, on abandonment several watertight doors and covers had been left open and although counter-flooding was implemented, the inrush of water continued. Over a period of twelve and three quarter hours, the list increased steadily, to 20 degrees, then 27

degrees, then to 35 degrees and the *Ark Royal* finally capsized and went down after holding briefly at 45 degrees from vertical. The official British naval historian was later to state: 'The general conclusions were that the list taken by a damaged ship may appear more dangerous than it is.'[99] but this is a decision easier taken in the cold academic calm of a post-war office than standing on the tilting deck of a stricken aircraft-carrier in the midst of battle with thousands of lives in the balance.

The decision of Captain Buckmaster to get everyone off the *Yorktown* was fully backed up by Fletcher, who again, himself was profoundly influenced by 'the appearance of the *Yorktown* at the time the order was issued'[100]; indeed at one point Fletcher wondered whether Buckmaster might have left things too late. Nimitz also gave Buckmaster his backing.[101]

Despite the constant fear of further Japanese air attacks, the destroyers *Anderson, Balch, Benham, Morris* and *Russell* between them rescued the bulk of the *Yorktown*'s 1,700 survivors. Yet the carrier herself remained very much afloat. Fletcher had signalled Nimitz at 1615 that *Yorktown* was listing badly but not settling, and requested tugs in the hope of salvaging her. In addition to the destroyers there were by now four heavy cruisers standing by and one of these could have been told to commence the process of getting her moving, handing over to the tugs from Pearl in due course.[102] After reflection, Fletcher opted against this option, causing further puzzlement, then and since.

---

96. See *Loss of Ark Royal*, Classified BoE, File ADM234/508, held at National Archives, Kew, London.

97. The then British counter-flooding instructions were only considered practicable for a list of up to 8 degrees.

98. Rear-Admiral Loben Edward Harold Maund (1892–1957). b. Hemel Hempstead, Herts, son of Edward Arthur Maund and Constance Alice Macartney Iredell. Acting sub-lieutenant. 30 July 1913 sub-lieutenant. 1914–18 World War I war service with Dover Patrol, Grand Fleet (including Jutland 1916) and Atlantic convoys. 30 December 1914, lieutenant. Appointed captain of destroyer *Scorpion*. 30 December 1922, lieutenant-commander. 23 July 1923 wireless signal duties. Director of Training and Staff, Admiralty, then Staff Officer, Operations, to C-in-C, East Indies aboard light cruiser *Chatham*. February 1926 light cruiser *Caradoc* in Mediterranean Fleet, then XO light cruiser *Curlew*. 31 December 1927 commander. 31 January 1928 Naval Assistant Secretary, Committee of Imperial Defence. 15 September 1931 XO carrier *Furious*. October 1933 Senior Officers' War Course, RN College, Greenwich. 30 June 1934 captain. 30 June 1935 Assistant Director Plans Division, Admiralty. 17 August, captain of light cruiser *Danae*, China Station. March 1938 Seniors Officers' War Course, RN College Greenwich. 1 July 1938 Commandant, Inter-Service Training and Development Centre, Portsmouth. April 1940 Naval CoS, to Flag Officer, Narvik,

Norway. February 1941, Operations Division, Admiralty. 19 April 1941–13 November 1941, captain of carrier *Ark Royal*, including *Bismarck* operation and three Malta convoys. Appointed CBE for *Bismarck* action. 17 May 1943, Director Combined Operations, Middle East, Alexandria. 12 January 1943, Naval ADC to HM King George VI. 8 July 1943 retired. 17 May 1942, recalled to service as acting rear-admiral. 25 August 1943 Director of Combined Operations, India, at Bombay. 1 October 1944, Rear-Admiral Landing Ships and Craft. 1 March 1946, retired again as rear-admiral. Became director of A Kershaw and Sons, Ltd. Author of the excellent book on combined operations, *Assault from the Sea*, Methuen, London, 1949. Died at Frittleworth, Sussex on 18 June 1957.

99. Captain S. W. Roskill, *The War at Sea, Volume 1 The Defensive*, HMSO, London, 1954.

100. Fletcher's *First Endorsement* CTF-17 to Secnav, dated July 1942, to CO USS *Yorktown* to Secnav, *Loss of Ship*, dated 17 June 1942.

101. Nimitz's *Second Endorsement* CTF-17 to Secnav, dated 7 July 1942, to CO USS *Yorktown* to Secnav, *Loss of Ship*, dated 23 June 1942.

102. In the event the 950 ton ocean tug *Vireo* (AT-144), a former *Lapwing* class minesweeper, anchored at Hermes Reef some 160 miles from *Yorktown*'s location, was the nearest to hand, but, at 10 knots maximum speed it would take her some time

If *Yorktown* was not to be towed then, with night coming on and the possibility of the Japanese finding her and taking her as a propaganda 'prize', Fletcher would have been fully justified in sending his erstwhile flagship to the bottom of the Pacific Ocean. But he did not favour that choice either; instead he chose to steer east to seek out TF-16. So the *Yorktown*'s former close companions all steamed away, but after a while Fletcher had second thoughts. At 1800, when some 12 miles distant he signalled to the Commander of DesRon 6[103] to detach a suitable destroyer. The *Hughes,* which was considered to be the most combat-ready of the escorts, was therefore ordered to reverse course and go back to the vicinity of *Yorktown* again. Her new role was specified as standing watch on the drifting hulk throughout the night. Her commanding officer[104] was informed by his commander that he had the discretion to put her down with torpedoes if a serious fire broke out again, or an enemy force put in an appearance. However, should *Yorktown* remain afloat and viable by morning, Fletcher planned to send ships back with a fully effective selected salvage crew aided by volunteers mustered from the various rescue ships. This was done and TF-17, minus the two orphans, vanished over the horizon.

Meanwhile, although Fletcher, who still remained the Officer in Tactical Command (OTC) of the combined American force, was involved with these matters, Spruance's and Mitscher's airmen had been carrying on the with the battle itself. For the *Hiryū* had been spotted at last, her luck had finally run out and retribution had been meted out. As dusk fast approached and no word of any night-time dispositions or intentions had reached him from *Astoria*, Spruance decided to force the issue as tactfully as he could, hoping to elicit some response from his superior officer who was fast vanishing over the eastern horizon. Accordingly, at 1811, he sent a TBS message to Fletcher, '*Hornet* and *Enterprise* groups now attacking fourth carrier reported by your search planes. *Hornet* about 20 miles east of me. Have you any instructions for further operations?'

Fletcher signalled back briefly: 'Negative. Will conform to your movements.' As TF-16 was, Spruance informed Fletcher, on a westerly course in order to recover her strike aircraft after dealing with the *Hiryū*, and Fletcher's force, already 30 miles distant, was continuing to hasten *eastward*, there was, of course, absolutely no 'conforming to movements' whatsoever; in fact the two groups were rapidly steaming away from each other! No matter; at least Spruance could read into Fletcher's signal that he now really had the ball and could plan accordingly. From this point, and *only* from this point[105], the final outcome of the Battle of Midway officially became Spruance's responsibility.

---

to reach the scene. The 1,270 ton ocean tug *Navajo (AT-65),* then *en route* to French Frigate Shoals from Pearl, though capable of 16 knots, was even further distant. Finally, a third tug, the *Seminole* (AT-64), a sister ship, was instructed to sail from Hawaii as a back-up. Captain John V. Noel related how the *Seminole*'s skipper heard news during a poker game that *Yorktown* had been damaged and correctly anticipated he would be ordered to her assistance. He also alleged that the destroyer minelayer *Sicard* (DM-21) received news of the battle from her coding machine. USNI Oral History.

103. Captain Edward P. Sauer.

104. Lieutenant-Commander Donald J. Ramsey.

105. It is important to note the time of the precise point of transition; some historians (Captain Edward L. Beach, *Salt and Steel, Reflections of a Submariner,* and Bates in his Report) have tried to write Fletcher out of the scenario much earlier, while others (notably the journalist Fletcher Pratt, 'The Mysteries of Midway', and 'The Knockout at Midway', which were later given some official credence by the navy's own Bureau of Personnel and repeated in his post-war book, *Fleet Against Japan,* to which Nimitz himself, perhaps unwisely, contributed a Foreword) do not even acknowledge his overall position in command whatsoever!

Chapter Nine

The Fog of War

There was turmoil across the battlefield. From the bedlam of blazing sinking carriers, Nagumo and his staff had to rearrange their plans and, far astern, Yamamoto, with griping stomach pains working up to something worse, was beginning to see his complex web unravelling at frightening speed. The Americans were elated, but were far from sure that they had done the whole job. Were there yet more Japanese carriers lurking over their shoulders? Would the Japanese press on and land on Midway anyway? Strangely, far from clarifying matters, the death and destruction of 4 June only seemed to make things much less clear.

Nautilus Tries Again

As the Japanese carriers slowly and agonizingly went through their death throes, American submarines sniffed around, scenting easy pickings. However, they went unrewarded. During the early hours of the afternoon, the *Grouper* (SS-214) a brand new boat only launched the previous October and commanded by Lieutenant-Commander Claren E. Duke, sighted two burning carriers some way off and proceeded to make a cautious approach. Alert defenders picked her up and several depth-charges and bombs were dropped by destroyers and seaplanes in her vicinity, without causing any damage. At 1314 two very heavy explosions were heard and Duke assumed that he had underestimated the distance to the targets. Not wanting a

sinking Japanese aircraft carrier to 'blow up and sink on top of us', Duke moved off without making a periscope search. His aim was to get between the two crippled ships and perhaps sink both with one attack. However, when he did finally venture to periscope depth at 1420, a vigilant destroyer immediately pounced and subjected him to a series of persistent attacks, some 170 explosions being recorded in total, effectively driving him[1] from the field of battle having achieved nothing.

The ball then passed to a much more resolute player, none other than Brockman, whose dogged determination once more placed the *Nautilus* in an ideal position to make an attack. At 1029, soon after the SBDs had been about their deadly business, Brockman's persistence paid off, and he sighted three masts on the horizon, bearing 005 degree true. He raised the vertical antenna and intercepted a radio message stating that a carrier had been damaged. He took a good look around. 'Large clouds of gray smoke were seen at four places over the horizon. The nearest cloud of smoke had not previously been sighted, so continued to close it at the best speed that the condition of the battery and probably future operations for the day would allow'.[2]

Three aircraft were also observed, approaching his position so the periscope was lowered and the cautious approach resumed. At 1145 Brockman noted: 'Identified the source of smoke as a burning carrier. The carrier was still about 8 miles away and was in latitude 30° 13' N, longitude 179° 17' W. Decided to overtake if possible and to attack'.[3]

---

1. Commander Claren E. Duke's luck continued to be bad even after Midway. On the *Grouper*'s second patrol from Pearl Harbor she sank the merchant ship *Tone Maru* off the China coast on 21 September. On 1 October he sighted another 7,000 ton freighter off the Sing Pan Islands, and sank her at 0704 with several deliberate attacks, firing a total of six torpedoes. Unfortunately, his victim turned out to be the *Lisbon Maru* (Captain Kyoda Shigaru) which had left Hong Kong on 27 September 1942 with 1,816 British POWs aboard,

guarded by twenty soldiers under Lieutenant Hideo Wada, while a further 778 Japanese soldiers were also being transported. Around 900 of the British POWs were lost when their guards battened down the hatches after the attack, thus confining them below decks.

2. Brockman, Confidential Narrative, USS *Nautilus, Report of First War Patrol*.

3. *Ibid*.

Three-quarters of an hour passed and the range had not decreased appreciably, so Brockman increased his speed to two-thirds ahead on both motors. This did the trick and, at 1253, another snap look revealed two cruisers escorting the carrier, which was 'tentatively identified' as of the *Soryū* class. She was on an even keel and the hull appeared to be undamaged; there were now no flames and she seemed to be under control. By 1300, however, it was seen that the target, which had been making 2–3 knots headway, had now stopped. As they closed with her Brockman could see that boats near her bow were making efforts to pass a towing hawser into her and 'many men were seen working on her forecastle (*sic*)'. He held a discussion with his officers and they decided to make the carrier the sole object of their attack, hoping to get five torpedoes into her 'on the starboard or island side'. Constant checks were made on the silhouettes of American and Japanese carriers to be quite sure of the identity of their intended victim, and they were all quite sure she was a *Soryū* class ship. But she was, of course, the much larger *Kaga*.

By 1359 *Nautilus* was in a perfect position and Brockman attacked.

Fired three torpedoes at the carrier from periscope depth. Attempts to fire the 4th torpedo were unsuccessful. Immediately prior to firing each torpedo, the Torpedo Data Computer generated bearing was checked by a periscope bearing. Mean run of torpedoes was 2700 yards. The wakes of the torpedoes were observed through periscope until the torpedoes struck the target. Red flames appeared along the length of the ship from the bow to amidships. The fire which had first attracted us to the attack had been underneath the demolished after flight deck and was nearly extinguished by the time the *Nautilus* reached the firing point. The fire again broke out. Boats drew away from the bow and many men were seen going over the side. All 5 officers in the conning tower observed the results of the torpedoing.[4]

Brockman and his team can certainly be said to have earned the cataclysmic result that was described in the report, but nothing of the kind occurred. In fact, two of the torpedoes missed completely, one ahead and one astern of the huge target, while the third, although it certainly struck the *Kaga* full on, failed to explode at all! Even more humiliatingly, it

simply broke up, the warhead sinking away to the depths; the stern section remained afloat and even afforded some of the Japanese survivors unexpected salvation as a means of keeping afloat.

Brockman was not left long to absorb the results of his work (or rather lack of them), for the destroyer *Hagikaze* quickly followed up the tell-tale tracks to deliver depth-charge attacks and was quickly joined by her companion, the *Maikaze*. These attacks were accurately delivered and Brockman had once more to concentrate on survival. It was not until 1610 that he was again able to come to periscope depth. He duly reported that his target 'was afire along the entire length' , and that 'heavy black smoke enveloped the carrier and formed a cloud over the ship to a height of a thousand feet". He compared this cloud in height to the funeral pall of the *Arizona* at Pearl Harbor for, like SBD pilot Gallaher, he too had witnessed that ghastly event.

Removing the Emperor's Portrait

One by one the three great carriers succumbed to their fate.[5] First of the luckless trio to give up the ghost was the *Soryū*. Fifteen minutes after the first bomb hit, her engines stopped and, with her steering gone, she wallowed around in the ocean swell. At 1045 'abandon ship' was ordered, but even so the hulk remained afloat for many hours. She finally sank in position 32° 42' 5" N; 178 37' 5" W at 1913. As she went down there was a huge underwater explosion, presumably from her boilers.

Kaga, least hard hit it seemed, was the next to sink. The fires continued gaining and at 1325, the symbolic removal of the Emperor's portrait took place, signifying that her end was predictable. Gallant efforts nonetheless persisted to keep her afloat, but, by 1640, the situation was declared hopeless. At 1925 there were two enormous explosions, presumably from the main fuel tanks, and the huge ship disintegrated, going down in reported position 30° 20.3' N, 179° 17.2' W.

Akagi had been hit at 1026, and, after being rocked by a series of explosions that gutted her innards, Nagumo had left the ship at 1046. Within less than three-quarters of an hour the great ship had stopped and the surviving aviators began transferring to the destroyers. Although the flagship's engines somehow restarted at 1203, she could only loop around to starboard. Nothing could be done and, at 1338, once more the Emperor's portrait was removed. The *Akagi*

---

4. *Ibid.*
5. Highly detailed accounts of how these carriers' crews met their fates are contained in several books, notably Parshall

and Tully's *Shattered Sword*, Fuchida's *Midway* and Cressman/Ewing's *Glorious Page,* in addition to the official account in *Senshi Sōsho*, Vol 43.

came to a halt again at 1350 and ten minutes later the survivors began to abandon ship. She was finally scuttled at 0200 on the morning of 5 June, in position 30° 30'N, 178° 40'W.

It was the end of an era.

Death of the *Flying Dragon*

Clay Fisher has complained:

Very little has been written about the attack on the *Hiryū*, We all have read about how the Battle of Midway was won in approximately ten minutes the morning of June 4th. But it was the *Hiryū*'s dive-bombers and torpedo planes that caused the sinking of the *Yorktown*. In the afternoon the *Hiryū* was still operating and the *Hiryū* had to be destroyed for closure of Battle of Midway.[6]

We can only agree, and once again ask why she was was allowed several hours total freedom to organize and mount her gallant fight back against the odds.[7]

The fact that some enemy carriers had survived that slashing first SBD flight caused grave concern aboard Spruance's flagship. In fact, Spruance, 'obviously believed'[8] that only two enemy carriers had been hit, signalling to Fletcher that he should search the north-west squadron for possible third carrier.[9] Fletcher apparently shared that belief as it conformed to his steadfast (but erroneous) belief that another pair of Japanese carriers

lurked north-west of him somewhere. Returning aviators from the morning strikes, with their eyewitness accounts of three enemy carriers on fire, ought surely to have disabused both admirals and narrowed down the number of enemy carrier survivors to just one, along with her recent location.[10] However, the rapidity with which the first *Hiryū* counter-strike developed prevented many from doing so. For example two VB-6 'visitors'[11], both at the end of the fuel supply and desperate to get down anywhere, slapped down aboard *Yorktown* just before the Japanese strike broke. Both men had vital information to impart, but were bustled out of the way and, although they were still on board the *Yorktown* when she was first abandoned, neither was asked what they knew of the enemy.

Spruance appears to have been better served. For example, Commander William H. Buracker[12], the *Enterprise*'s Operations Officer, was already busy taking notes from the returning flyers, McClusky being the first, followed by Best and Gallaher as each came back on board, with a view to a second strike in order to finish the job.[13]

McClusky was the first to return. Taking his plotting board with him he climbed the ladder to flag plot. He briefed both Spruance and his staff on his actions and what he had seen. All listened attentively, the Admiral thinking and measuring reports and resources, Browning asking questions on conditions over the target, distance, location and enemy opposition.[14]

---

6.   E-mail, Fisher to Vickrey, 6 September 2004.
7.   I have seen opinions expressed by some researchers, that the best thing Yamaguchi could have done after the destruction of *Akagi*, *Kaga* and *Soryū* was to turn and run, putting as much distance between himself and the Americans as he could in the hope of evading destruction. Such a suggestion indicates an incredible lack of understanding of the Japanese mindset and conceptions of warfare and honour of that time.
8.   Lundstrom, *Black Shoe Carrier Admiral*.
9.   CTF-17 to CincPac, Message 050001 June 1942. TF-16, Communications Log, CincPac Secret and Confidential Message File (CSCMF) 1940–42, on film roll 14, Record Group 38, held at National Archives II, College Park, Maryland. Thomas B. Buell claimed that Spruance 'had not thought about Fletcher during the morning', but this is patently untrue. (Buell, *Quiet Warrior*).
10. Lundstrom agrees, but states that due to the 'hectic' events aboard *Yorktown*, 'no one had the opportunity to brief Fletcher.' (Lundstrom, *Black Shoe Carrier Admiral*). Quite why the commander of TF-17 was kept in the dark by all about him on such a crucial piece of information, knowing, as everyone around him must have done, his obsession with the 'missing' enemy carrier division, is baffling, indeed

almost defies belief. Thach, whose negative views on Fletcher are clear enough, nonetheless cleared the admiral regarding Thach as being one source, for he was adamant that Morison's allegation that Thach *did* brief Fletcher, made in Volume 4 of *Naval Operations*) were totally fallacious; indeed he was moved to confirm this was not the case in writing to Morison on 11 April 1949. That nobody else told Fletcher, however, is remarkable.
11. Lieutenant (jg) Wilbur Edison Roberts, A-V(N), with William Burr Steinmann AMM1c and Ensign George Hale Goldsmith with the wounded James William Patterson, Jr, ARM3c.
12. Captain William Houck Buracker, a naval aviator himself, busy noting details of the fire and death aboard the three Japanese carriers at this time, was to experience the same inferno when, as captain of the light carrier *Princeton* (CVL-23) at Leyte Gulf, his command was hit by a kamikaze on 24 October 1944 and destroyed with heavy loss of life. He survived this to go on to become Professor of Naval Science at the US Naval Institute after the war.
13. Buracker to Barde, letter dated 28 October 1966.
14. Robert E. Barde, *The Battle of Midway: A Study in Command*.

At the end of his debriefing, McClusky, many of whose air group, just like Ring's, never made it back, running out of fuel and ditching never to be seen again because they bravely followed CEAG's search pattern[15], was seen to be bleeding. He was taken down to sickbay, were it was found he had been hit in the upper arm, and he was hospitalized for the rest of the battle.[16]

The surviving dive-bomber crews tucked into a light lunch ('coffee and sandwiches in the ready rooms') while their aircraft, those that were flyable, were refuelled and rearmed and, most importantly, had their suspect oxygen bottles replaced.

If Fletcher *was* indeed kept in such ignorance of the true situation with regard the number of enemy carriers already attacked, no such lack of awareness seemingly applied to Spruance and Browning for, at 1404, the former was signalling to Nimitz at Pearl details of the attack as gleaned from their own returning aircrew, stating boldly that 'all four CV believed badly damaged.'[17] For good measure Spruance threw in the damaged enemy's position, which was totally incorrect, being based on the 1015 transmission of James S. Gray, which had placed the enemy 38 miles north-east of the actual attack location. Yet many SBD pilots, Richard H. Best among them, had reported only three carriers burning and one unmolested.[18] Lieutenant Penland's debriefing diagram indeed specifically indicated the fact that one CV 'was not attacked.'

Fletcher's report makes no mention of the Spruance signal that all four enemy carriers had been damaged, only noting that *Yorktown*'s returning aviators had 'probably destroyed one enemy carrier.'[19] He added that radio intelligence indi-

cated that the enemy had sighted his carriers, while a radar contact picked up an apparent snooper, bearing 320 degrees, 25 miles out, which evaded fighter interception.

Buell and others state that some sort of heated debate ensued between the admiral and the tempestuous Miles Browning, with the latter urging an immediate all-out strike on these damaged carriers to finish them off. In the end, Browning was again over-ruled, much to his impatient disgust and growing frustration. Spruance determined to hold back his force until the new location of the enemy was confirmed, assuming that they had moved on since the morning attack. Certainly an undamaged *Hiryū* might well have done so, but (at least according to Spruance's 1404 signal), she was also assumed by him to have been among those crippled! How, then, could four badly damaged carriers have proceeded off the scene of their mortal wounding at a nifty 25 knots as Buell has it? Even the distant sight of the *Yorktown* under attack did not produce any reaction, other than to detach two cruisers and two destroyers from his own screen to assist[20], although by then it must have been perfectly obvious that at least one undamaged Japanese carrier was operating. Not until Adams's 1430 fortuitous sighting report was received did Spruance finally grant permission for a strike to be mounted.

There was, of course, no question of fighter protection. Losses had been too heavy and any that were available would clearly be required to defend the ships from further enemy strikes. The inertia of the morning had handed the initiative back to the enemy and Admiral Tamon Yamaguchi and his depleted team were making the most of it. But in any case, if Spruance believed only one of the

---

15. Out of a total SBD launch of thirty-two aircraft, half failed to return. Eleven of the dive-bombers just disappeared for ever, but, unlike *Hornet*'s lost sons, nobody blamed the air group commander for this inevitable combat attrition. McClusky himself had reached the designated Point Option and found it barren of ships. He was forced to break radio silence and speak to Lieutenant Leonard 'Ham' Dow, Staff Communications Officer, asking if Point Option had been changed; only then did he learn that indeed it had! Moreover, the amazed air group commander was informed, it was now 60 miles further along! McClusky made the additional miles and got down with just 5 gallons of fuel left after first approaching *Yorktown* by mistake. He landed despite a 'wave-off' by the LSO because he had no choice, others were less fortunate. Dickinson was forced to ditch and was rescued by the destroyer *Phelps*, the very same ship he had spent his two years' sea time aboard before commencing flight training!
16. The *Enterprise*'s XO designate, Commander Walter F. Boone, had first noticed the blood. 'My God, Mac, you've been shot,' he blurted out.
17. CTF-16 to CincPac, repeated CTF-17, Message 0502041

June 1942. TF-16, Communications Log, CincPac Secret and Confidential Message File (CSCMF) 1940–1942, on film roll 14, Record Group 38, held at National Archives II, College Park, Maryland.
18. Best told Lundstrom that he stated this fact 'in earshot' of Spruance on the bridge, but that nobody questioned him, nor apparently any other returning pilot, any further on the matter! Best to Lundstrom, dated 15 May 2000, cited in *Black Shoe Admiral*.
19. Frank Jack Fletcher, Action Report, *Battle of Midway*, dated 14 June 1942, A41273, contained in Box 105 (1–40 Series) at National Archives II, College Park, Maryland.
20. Naval aviators still cite this as a classic example of 'Black Shoe' caution; see Jimmy Thach's unforgiving dismissal of Spruance's and Fletcher's abilities to command carrier task forces. Much more senior officers than Thach certainly agreed with that judgement. The pre-war struggle to get aviators in command billets by such advocates as Admiral Jack Towers, (see Clark G. Reynolds, *Admiral John H. Towers: The Struggle for Naval Air Supremacy*) was seemingly vindicated during World War II and brought about a complete change of policy after the war.

Japanese carriers remained, then he might also have believed that there would be very few Zero fighters left aloft to defend their base anyway by the time the SBDs arrived. Some of the Dauntless pilots certainly thought so. They were in for a shock!

In the event *Enterprise* scraped up a makeshift force of twenty-five SBDs to attack the Japanese force, which had been very accurately reported by VS-5's Lieutenant Samuel Adams as comprising a single carrier, two battleships, two heavy cruisers and four or more destroyers in position 31° 15' N, 179° 05' W[21] on course 000 degrees, speed 20 knots. These two reports (one by voice the other by morse key) placed *Hiryū* on a bearing of 265 degrees from TF-17 and at 110 miles range.

The force consisted of fifteen aircraft from acting VB-3[22], seven from VS-6 (two other damaged SBDs could not be made combat-worthy in time) and four from VB-6. Of these eleven were armed with 1000 pound bombs and thirteen with 500 pound bombs. Because McClusky remained incapacitated, Gallaher of VS-6 took over as air group leader. These aircraft began flying off at 1530. One was forced to abort[23] but the remaining two dozen dive-bombers droned off into the distance, alone.

Why was this? *Hornet* had suffered appalling losses herself that morning, but with the return of the SBDs from Midway Island she had a respectable number on hand. Indeed, since 1456, they had been sitting ready for launch, just awaiting the 'go' signal from Spruance, but this had not arrived. Stanhope Ring wrote:

About one hour after my landing the remaining aircraft of the Group were ordered launched for the next attack. Both Rodee and I were spotted on the hangar deck so, when launchings were suddenly terminated after the aircraft on the flight deck had taken off, the 'Group' command devolved upon Lieutenant Stebbins[24] of VS-8. He did a magnificent

job of locating and attacking the enemy forces and is wholly deserving of all the credit for the success of the operation as far as *Hornet* Group was concerned.[25]

Ring declined to state the reason for this, 'sudden termination' and the strange scratching of his own launch along with his fourteen SBD companions, but that came out later.

At 1310, Mitscher had figuratively tapped Spruance on the shoulder, advising him that *Hornet* had a twenty-strong dive-bomber force sitting poised and ready to go. It made no impression. At 1515 *Hornet* took in a signal from Spruance's flagship advising her that the staff did not know the position of the enemy carrier whose aircraft were currently pummelling the *Yorktown* just over the horizon.[26] At 1518 another signal came in, giving the details of Adams's contact signal, received on *Enterprise* half an hour earlier! But there was still no instruction for *Hornet* to attack. Not until 1539, just as the last SBD of the *Enterprise* was taking off was *Hornet* instructed to launch her own attack group, minus fighter aircraft, against the same target.

What was going on? Buell was in no doubt where the failure lay, Miles Browning had fouled up yet again. 'The staff had collapsed.' He is worth quoting in full, if only as some sort of balance against the eulogies and the 'canonising' of Browning subsequent to the battle, and since.[27]

They were a free-wheeling staff, accustomed to impulsive decisions and hasty plans. Before Midway they had muddled through without any major mistakes. The staff officers were capable and willing, but erratic Browning provided neither leadership nor cohesion. Thus the staff became progressively more confused and disoriented as the battle progressed, unable to cope with the need for

---

21. Adams and Dickson had completed their own sector searches and, like all their companions, had sighted nothing. It was only Adams's conscientious additional sweep south, undertaken on his own initiative, (and surely a decision to rank in intelligence with McClusky's decision to turn north earlier that day), that came up trumps, the *Hiryū* having advanced at a more modest 15 knots towards the Americans instead of the estimated 25.

22. Lieutenant Gallaher led this composite squadron in the afternoon attack. Leslie of course was the senior squadron CO, but was drying out aboard the *Astoria*. Lieutenant DeWitt Shumway was his XO and Best was CO of VB-6, but Gallaher was senior to these, so Gallaher it was who led the strike. Ensign Robert M. Elder's aircraft could not be made operational in time to join the strike.

23. S-16 from VS-6, piloted by Lieutenant (jg) John Norman West.

24. Captain Edgar Erwin Stebbins, (1916–91). b.16 September 1916, Houston, Texas. Entered the US Navy 12 July 1935. Graduated from US Naval Academy, Annapolis, as ensign 30 June 1937. 1939, 1 October, lieutenant (jg). 1942 temporary lieutenant as from 2 January, confirmed 1 June. At Midway was the XO of VS-8. 1943 1 May lieutenant-commander. 1943 September acting commander (P), CO of the carrier *Boxer* (CV-21). After the war 1955, from 1 July, captain (T) 1966 Commander, Fleet Air at NAS Alameda. 1967, retired from navy on 1 July. Died 14 December 1991 at Oakwood and interred Travis County cemetery.

25. Stanhope Ring, *Lost Letter*.

26. Buell, *Quiet Warrior*.

27. See, for example the current *Wikipedia* adulation.

Table 18: Composition of the Afternoon Strikes Against *Hiryū* 4 June

Despatched from USS Enterprise – *"VB-63"*					
1st Div	VS-6	Lt. Wilmer Earl Gallaher	Thomas Edward Merritt, ACRM(AA)	S1	
		Ens. Reid Wentworth Stone	William Hart Bergin, RM1c	S2	
		Ens. Richard Alonzo Jaccard	Porter William Pixley, RM3c	S11	
		Lt. (jg) Norman Jack Kleiss	John Warren Snowden, ARM3c	S7	
		Ens. Vernon Larsen Micheel	John Dewey Dance, RM3c	S17	
		Ens. James Campbell Dexter	Donald L Hoff, RM3c	S18	
		Lt. Frank Anthony Patriarca	Jack Richard Badgley, ACRM(AA)	S13	Hangar deck – not launched
		Lt. (jg) John Norman West	Albert R. Stitzlelberger, ARM2c	S13	Hangar deck – not launched
2nd Div	VB-6	Lt. Richard Halsey Best	James Francis Murray, ACRM(PA)	B1	
		Lt. (jg) Edwin John Kroeger	Gail Wayne Halterman, RM3c	B2	
		Ens. Frederick Thomas Weber	Ernest Lenard Hilbert, AOM3c	B3	
		Ens. Stephen Clement Hogan, Jr	Eugene K. Braun, Sea1c	B12*	*Flew with VB-3.
	VB-3	Lt. DeWitt Wood Shumway	Ray Edgar Coons, ARM1c	B13	
		Ens. Bunyon Randolph Cooner	Clifton R Bassett, AOM2c	B15	
		Ensign Paul Wahl Schlegel	Jack Alvan Shropshire, ARM3c	B-3	
		Lt. (jg) Osborne Beeman Wiseman	Grant Ulysses Dawn, ARM3c	B16	
		Ens. Milford Austin Merrill	Dallas Joseph Bergeron, ARM3c	B17	
		Ens. Stephen Clement Hogan, Jr (VB6)	Eugene K Braun, Sea1c	B-12	
		Lt. (jg) Gordon Alvin Sherwood	Harman Donald Bennett, ARM2c	B17	
		Ens. Roy Maurice Isaman	Sidney Kay Weaver, ARM3c	B8	
		Ens. Phillip Walker Cobb	Clarence E. Zimmershead, ARM2c	B9	
		Lt. Harold Sydney Bottomley, Jr	David Frederick Johnson, AMM2c	B10	
		Ens. Charles S. Lane	Jack Charles Henning, ARM2c	B11	
		Ens. John Clarence Butler	David Donald Berg, ARM3c	B12	
		Ens. Robert Keith Campbell	Horace Henry Craig, AMM1c	B4	
		Ens. Aldon W. Hanson	Joseph Vernon Godfrey, ARM3c	B5	
		Ens. Robert Haines Benson	Frederick Paul Bergeron, ARM3c	B6	
Despatched from USS Hornet					
	VS-8	Lt. Edgar Erwin Stebbins	Ervin R. Hillhouse, ARM2c		Strike and VS-8 Leader
		Lt. Ben Moore, Jr. (PO)	Richard C. McEwen, ARM2c		
		Lt. Orman Griffith G. Sexton III (GO)	William L. Payne, ARM2c		Aborted and recovered

	Pilot	Gunner	Notes
	Lt. (jg) Albert Harold Wood	Richard T. Woodson, ARM2c	Woodson volunteered to replace John Lewis Tereskerz, ARM3c who was unavailable to fly.
	Lt. (jg) Ivan L. Swope	Harmon L. Brendle, ARM2c	
	Ens. Phil J. Rusk	John H. Honeycutt, ARM2c	Aborted and recovered
	Ens. Hellmuth E. Hoerner	David T. Manus, ARM3c	
	Ens. Harold H. White	John S. Urban, ARM3c	
	Ens. William E. Woodman	Gerald A. McAffe, ARM2c	
VB-8	Lt (jg) Fred Leeson Bates	Clyde S. Montensen, ARM1c	
	Ens. Henry John Nickerson	Elmer Edwin Jackson, ARM1c	
	Ens. Roy Philip Gee	Donald L. Canfield, ARM1c	
	Ens. Kenneth B. White	Leroy Quillen, ARM3c	
	Ens. Robert P. Friez	Clarence C. Kiley, ARM1c	
	Ens. James Clark Barrett	William H. Berthold, ARM3c	
	Ens. Clayton Evan Fisher	George E. Ferguson, ARM3c	

disciplined planning and the coordination of complex task force operations.[28]

Eventually, however, *Hornet* got her initial deck strike airborne between 1604 and 1613, and they circled the ship, waiting for CHAG and their squadron leaders to join them. There were nine SBDs from VS-9 toting 1,000 pound bombs and seven from VB-8, which still had aboard the 500 pound bombs they had embarked on Midway Island. By rights Ring's fifteen further dive-bombers should have been brought up on deck and launched in their turn to add yet further punch to the attack, but, as we have seen, this did not happen. It seemed that Spruance and his staff somehow 'forgot' about the extra SBDs warming up below and, seeing only an empty deck, turned the ship west to follow up on the new Point Option for the first strike. The enemy were assumed to bear 278 degrees at a range estimated at 162 miles. With the carrier heading west there was no question of launching any more aircraft, for the wind still blew from the south-east. By the time this schoolboy howler had been rectified Mitscher flip-flopped once more and decided it

would now take far too long. At 1624 Stebbins was instructed to proceed with what he had.

The VS-8 SBDs were all armed with 1,000 pound bombs for this strike, while VB-8 carried the 500-pounders they had loaded up with during the stop-over on Midway Island, except for Clay Fisher, who still retained his 500 pound bomb from the aborted morning mission.

As in the morning Kroeger and Weber were flying as Best's wingmen. Best got a hit on *Hiryū* with his 1,000 pound bomb, just as he had one in the morning. Thus VB-6 sank *Akagi* single-handed in the morning and Best was again largely responsible for taking out the *Hiryū* that same afternoon.

The official report of the *Enterprise* flyers reflects the very different scenario of this second attack. As they approached the enemy force the American aviators could clearly see 'to the south . . . three large columns of smoke'[29] which marked their earlier success. They began their assault from up-sun, from 19,000 feet. At this time 'enemy O fighters appeared, estimated between 6 to 12, and attacked during the push-over, followed down and attacked

---

28. Buell, *Quiet Warrior*. Lundstrom totally disagrees with Buell, apparently dismissing the contradictory signals between *Enterprise* and *Hornet*, as well late instruction. Instead, he places the blame squarely on Mitscher, asserting: 'The egregious handling of the *Hornet* was solely his respon-

sibility'. (Lundstrom, *Black Shoe Carrier* Admiral).

29. Confidential *Battle of Midway Island, June 4 – 6, 1942*; *Second Attack, June 4, 1942*, contained in report of USS *Enterprise* (CV6) Sea, June 8, 1942, held at National Archives II, College Park, Maryland.

after pull-out'. The attack group split the attack between the carrier ('*Soryū* class') and the accompanying battleship. The *Hiryū* was making a tight turn to port in an attempt to escape her fate and Gallaher recalled that he just did not believe a carrier could turn so fast. It was sufficiently radical a manoeuvre that it caused Gallaher to miss well astern[30] and it threw Stone's aim off as well. Luckily the following aircraft were able to adjust their attacks to compensate and soon the *Hiryū* became totally smothered in bombs. 'Six direct hits were observed on the carrier', although the report had to confess: 'An accurate count of hits is again impossible due to flames and resulting smoke', but they left her, 'aflame from bow to stern'. This number was confirmed by the target's Air Officer, Captain Susumu Kawaguichi.[31] However, the post-battle analysis by the ONI reduced this to four certain strikes. It was sufficient.

The protecting CAP fought hard to save their ship; they only had her one deck to return to and were determined to save it if they could. It was to prove the toughest of all four attacks for the SBDs. The *Hiryū* had in place a high-altitude CAP with some very experienced A6M pilots on the alert and they caught the SBDs just as they began rolling into their dives.[32] The Japanese pilots were only too well aware that they had to take out the SBDs and pushed home their attacks most aggressively, most firing their 20 mm cannon whose explosive shells had no trouble punching into and ripping apart a Dauntless like a can-opener opening a tin of beans. Weber (who had hit *Akagi* in the morning) was the first to go, then Butler and Wiseman, who were flying as the 'tail-enders' in the formation, the most vulnerable position. Bud Merrill recalled that these two crashed into the sea almost simultaneously.

In Merrill's opinion, such was the deadliness of this attack that, if the SBDs had been intercepted slightly earlier, many more dive-bombers would have been lost and, indeed, *Hiryū* might have survived to fight on. Clayton Fisher flew in a tail-end position in the *Hornet*'s SBD formation that arrived over the target zone a few minutes after the initial composite squadrons attack, having been delayed in their launch by the recovery of those VB-8 aircraft which returned from Midway island. Fisher recorded: 'The *Hornet*'s SBDs were never attacked by the Zero fighters. The only Japanese aircraft I observed was a cruiser's scout biplane flying near a destroyer. This was when we knew we had complete control of the air at the Battle of Midway'. Fisher admitted that he had always known that the *Hornet*'s SBD pilots were extremely lucky not to have had to contend with the Zekes. 'I didn't realize, until I talked to Bud Merrill, just how deadly those Zero's were that afternoon'.[33]

Richard Best gave this account of his significant contribution.

Of the original 18 dive-bombers in VB-6, only four remained operational. Our first section came aboard intact. The sixth section leader was too shot up from AA fire over the *Kaga* to fly in the afternoon, but a wingman from the fifth section did come aboard undamaged. Two VB-6 planes running low on gasoline landed on the *Yorktown*, which was twenty miles west of *Enterprise*. Unfortunately, these planes were lost on the *Yorktown*. Of the remaining SBDs, only three crews were found in their rubber boats after they had to ditch for lack of fuel.

We were held on board until late afternoon when twenty-four remaining serviceable SBDs were launched: six from Scouting Six, four from Bombing Six and fourteen from Bombing Three, who, upon their return from attacking the *Soryū*, were diverted to *Enterprise* when the *Yorktown* came under attack. The commander of Scouting Six led the attack as he was the senior aviator. I followed with my few planes, and the fourteen SBDs of VB-3 brought up the rear.

This time we went straight to the target, the *Hiryū*. She had six or more Zeros aloft who came straight for us as soon as they sighted us. Simultaneously, the *Hiryū* put up what appeared to be a stationary barrage at 20,000 feet. Neither defense was any deterrent. We came in over the port and starboard bows and left the carrier aflame and out of control. My right wingman was shot down in the dive, probably by the Zero that was following him down.

---

30. Gallaher attempted to 'throw' his bomb and the radical action required to do this badly wrenched his back, so much so that he was barely able to land back aboard the carrier as he could not bend down sufficiently to reach the tailhook lowering handle on the cockpit floor. He had to be lifted from his aircraft and suffered with the problem for the rest of his life. The stresses on dive-bomber pilots were immense; another Midway veteran eventually lost an eye due to the strain put on the blood vessels in his diving attack that day. Dick Best's oxygen bottle had malfunctioned during the morning attack and he had inhaled soda fumes, damaging his lungs. After his second mission he started to cough up blood next day and ended up in Fitzsimmons Hospital, Denver, Colorado and retired from the service two years later.

31. Kawaguichi, Interrogation No. 11, USSBS.

32. *Ibid.* Also, among the published accounts Hugh Bicheno gives one of the best descriptions, (and it has the added bonus of also contains some refreshingly good maps) (Hugh Bicheno, *Midway*).

33. E-mail, Fisher to Vickrey, 6 September 2004.

The afternoon attack was quite unlike the morning one. Everyone and his brother was firing at us. Both sides of the *Hiryū* from the bow to the stern were laced with muzzle blasts of innumerable AA guns (maybe even small arms fire).

I had never seen such a continuous curtain of muzzle blasts. Even a battleship on her starboard quarter was firing at us. This time, I didn't risk observing the bomb fall. I jinked furiously until I was out of AA range, due west of the Japanese force. I was turned south to give them wide berth with due respect for the Zero capabilities. I was well south of them before I turned back to the east. When I saw smoke columns off to the south, I flew south to identify them and, at a reasonable distance, I saw three carriers were the victims of our morning attack, dead in the water and burning.

I returned easily to the *Enterprise* and, for the first and only time, I came in from a right-hand circle because the specified approach was from the starboard beam. I felt like the lord of creation and my own master. It probably shocked the LSO but he gave me an 'R' all the way aboard.[34]

Dusty Kleiss of VS-6 described how they had sighted the Japanese force and initially concentrated on the carrier, which:

. . . made a sharp 180 degree turn at beginning of attack. 1st and 2nd bombs were misses. 3rd was a hit. I don't know where mine (the 4th bomb, a 500# job) landed because of the flames from the bomb hit ahead of me. Two direct and several indirect hits were made.

Nice fire started but not anything in comparison with the fire started in morning attack.[35] Some planes of the combined attack group left carrier after seeing it on fire and dropped bombs instead on one of the battle-wagons, which received at least two direct hits [*sic*]. Two fighters had attacked us (particularly

Gallaher, the skipper, just at push-over point), but had not particularly bothered anyone. A biplane attacked me after pull-out. Snowden set his engine to smoking and he left us. A seaplane then got on our tail, but couldn't – or didn't – gain on me (with wide open throttle). I joined up with 2 B6 planes, one of the pilots of which had been hit by a cannon but could still fly. The four of us rushed back to the ship. A fighter trailed us, but the 6B6 pilot was intent on reaching the ship. (I didn't know he had been wounded.)[36]

The A6Ms *did* however, bother some people, rather a lot! Weber was flying with the composite flight that afternoon, having been one of Dick Best's wing in the morning attack on *Akagi*. Ironically, after this tremendous dual achievement, Bill Vickrey recalled: 'Best had activated latent tuberculosis and never touched a stick nor a throttle again but he went out like the champion I always found him to be. He started bleeding through his mouth and nostrils shortly after he landed after the strike on *Hiryū*.'[37]

Weber's loss was, perhaps, predictable given the toughness of this opposition. Although the official report stated that he made his dive and never came out of it, Dick Best's long-time rear-seat man, Commander Jim Murray, was to give Bill Vickrey a more plausible version of events. In what was described as 'a pretty solid description', Murray stated that facing rearward of course and thus having a very clear view of events, he was sure that a Zero got to Weber pretty early on in the sequence. Murray confided that Weber 'was a very poor pilot and nearly always lagged behind. Best kept warning him, 'You will get burned one day if you continue to lag,' and Murray thought that was what happened that afternoon.[38]

Another veteran of VB-3, who did not make it home that afternoon, was Lieutenant (jg) Osborne Wiseman.[39] Flying as leader of the second division of the so-called 'Bombing 63', he seems to have carried out his dive but to have been one of the first victims as the A6M2s swarmed in on them after the pull-out. Nobody saw him go and he was only

34. Lieutenant-Commander Richard H. Best, Personal Narrative, 2001, courtesy of The International Midway Memorial Foundation, 5530 Wisconsin Avenue, Suite 1147. Chevy Chase, Maryland 20815, USA.
35. Probably because, at this stage, *Hiryū* had very few aircraft left to explode and burn.
36. N. J. Kleiss, *Logbook of the War*.
37. E-mail Vickrey to Fisher, 9 September 2004.
38. *Ibid.*
39. Lieutenant (jg) Osborne Beeman 'OB' Wiseman (1915–42). b. Zanesville, Ohio 20 February 1915, son of a carpenter,

grandson of a doctor. Educated at Sheridan School and then Theodore Roosevelt Jr. High School, then Lash High School, graduating in 1932. Entered US Naval Academy Annapolis 22 June 1934, graduating as midshipman on 2 June 1938. Early sea duty was spent aboard the carrier *Saratoga* (CA-3) and the destroyer *Roe* (DD-418). Applied for flight training and entered NAS Pensacola, gaining his wings on 17 March 1941. Assigned to VB-3, joined *Saratoga* again and served with her until she was torpedoed by Japanese submarine *I-25* off Oahu on 11 January 1942. NAS Ford Island then Doolittle raid aboard *Enterprise* (CV-6).

missed when he failed to re-form at the rendezvous. Neither he nor his rear-seat man's[40] bodies were ever recovered.

Gallaher was convinced that his and Best's ten aircraft were sufficient to erase the *Hiryū* on their own, and therefore directed the other fifteen, which included one attached from VB-6, to attack one of the Japanese battleships instead. For this Gallaher was much criticized; typical is Barde's comment: 'There was no positive assurance that they would be able to deliver their bombs on the target, particularly with fighters already claiming their attention. The value of the carrier was of such transcending importance that every conceivable resource at his command should have been employed to insure its complete destruction.'[41] He does not mention the other fact, which is that a 500 pound bomb could really hurt a carrier, but would hardly make a dent on a battleship. In the event, only two pilots[42] attacked the *Haruna* and no hits were scored on any Japanese battleship.

Watching *Hiryū* die

The Air Officer aboard *Hiryū* was Captain Susumu Kawaguchi.[43] He was also interrogated by the USSB [United States Strategic Bombing Survey] team[44] and gave these answers which reveal just a little of the death of his ship.

Q. How and when was the *Hiryū* hit?
A. The *Hiryū* was hit six times during the fourth attack by dive-bombers. One on forward elevator. Two just aft of forward elevator. Three just forward of after elevator. Lifts damaged. Fire. Many engineering personnel killed. The floor of the lift flopped against the bridge. We were unable to navigate.

Q. When the *Hiryū* was hit were any planes on board?

A. Very few, about 20 planes had come back. They had been launched to attack American carriers after they returned from Midway.

Q. 'Will you confirm the position of the island in relation to bow of ship?

A. *Akagi* – port, *Soryū* – Starboard, *Kaga* – Starboard.

Q. Were you attacked by horizontal bombers later that day?

A. It was about sunset the same day after the dive-bombers gave us six hits that we got about ten misses from Boeings. I think it was B-17s or something else. It was medium altitude horizontal-bombing. I didn't think they were very high and was astonished at the distance away from the ships when they released bombs.

Q. How many bombs dropped?

A. About ten bunches.

Q. Where did they hit?

A. They didn't hit – bombs landed about 500 metres away.

Q. Were any of the battleships hit at that time?

While flying scouting mission ahead of fleet sighted by Japanese patrol ships and dropped weighted message warning of this in order not to break radio silence. This caused early launch of B-24s. With VB-3 assigned to *Yorktown* (CV-5) for Midway operation. Attacked battleship *Haruna* in morning sorties and flew with composite force from *Yorktown* against carrier *Hiryū* in afternoon attack where he was lost. Posthumously awarded the Purple Heart, Navy Cross. His own motto was 'None but himself can be his parallel.' The destroyer escort *Wiseman* (DE-667) was named in his honour in 1943.

40. Grant Ulysses Dawn, ARM3c.
41. Barde, *The Battle of Midway: A Study in Command.*
42. Ensign Robert Keith Campbell and Ensign Robert Haines Benson.
43. Captain Susumu Kawaguchi. (1895–2001) b. Nagasaki, 27 September 1902. 1921, entered Etajima 26 August. 1924

graduated 24 July as midshipman. Became a pilot and later specialized in aircraft gunnery. 1941 Chief Air Office aboard carrier *Ryūjō* and in early 1942 took part in attack on Davao, Philippines, and in Java Sea area. 1942, April–June Air Officer *Hiryū*. June, after Midway segregated at Kanoya NAS. September 1942, XO, then October 1942–November 1944, Commanding Officer, Kanoya Naval Air Station with additional duties in Ordnance Test Flight Department, Naval Technical Air Arsenal. Ordnance Officer, Staff, Air High Command HQ, Navy Department, Tokyo, November 1944–July 1945. 1945 retired from navy. Died 5 February 2001.

44. USSB Nav No 2, USSBS No. 11, dated 10 October 1945. Interrogating officer was Captain C. Shands, USN. Also present were Brigadier-General G. Gardner, USA and Lieutenant Paine Paul, USNR.

A. I think that something touched the *Kirishima* or *Haruna* in the stern, didn't do much, no difficulty in navigation as a result.

Q. Was that a result of the horizontal-bombers?

A. No, this was the dive-bombing attack. One of them dived and dropped a bomb on the *Kirishima* but horizontal bombs didn't hit the *Kirishima*.

Q. How were the other carriers hit?

A. All got hit from the dive-bombers.

Q. How was your ship finally sunk?

A. The fire got to the engine rooms by the next morning and stopped the ship, whereupon a Japanese destroyer was called on to sink it with torpedoes.

Q. How many men and pilots were lost on the *Hiryū*?

A. About 60 pilots and a total of 500 men of crew of 1500.

Q. Did the *Hiryū* of any of the other carriers or ships have radar?

A. No, not any. As soon as we got back they put them on the carriers. July 1942 both battleships and carriers received them.

Q. How did you control your fighters in the air?

A. 'At first at Midway we set the[ir] course on the ships and turned them loose on the first attack. No radio.

Q. Which type of attack did you most fear, dive-bombing, torpedo, or horizontal-bombing?

A. The worst is dive-bombing.

Q. Why?

A. You can't avoid it, but you can avoid torpedoes dropped at long range.

The famous story of how Yamaguchi gathered the surviving crew members around the bridge and led them in a rousing thrice repeated *banzai* ['Ten Thousand Years' – the traditional salute to the Emperor.] in the direction of the Emperor, followed by the singing of the National Anthem, is the stuff of legends. Likewise the dignified way he and the ship's captain, Tomeo Kaku, prepared to accept their fate as true *samurai*, might arouse derision and scorn in many modern Western eyes, but it represented a belief in something greater than self.

The destroyer *Makigumo* fired two torpedoes, one of which passed under the carrier, as the *coup de grace* to the blazing hulk, and then departed, but *Hiryū* was to remain as stubbornly reluctant finally to bow out as her opposite number, *Yorktown*, was to do!

Hornet's First Sting

Arriving later, the *Hornet* strike's experience was very different from what had gone earlier. Now the high sky was clear of defending fighters and the main target, the carrier, was heavily on fire and obviously doomed. Stebbins accordingly allocated his two squadrons suitable alternative targets; the heavy cruisers *Tone* and *Chikuma* were attacked at 1330 and 1340 by VB-8 and VS-8 respectively. The latter attacked out of the sun from 15,000 feet, the hazard of heavy anti-aircraft fire from the enemy ships being supplemented by high-flying B-17s callously dropping their full bomb loads right through the attack dive-bomber formation! Inevitably, the B-17 salvoes totally missed both friend and foe alike!

The VS-8 attack was pressed home, with Bates leading, but missing with his bomb by some 50 feet off his target's starboard bow. Nickerson was next but his bomb detonated in the sea at least twice that distance astern of the twisting and turning cruiser. Gee was third down, and claimed a direct hit on the ship's stern. Then came the Second Division led by White, who missed, then Friez whose bomb fell even further off target. The last pair in were Barrett, who claimed a hit on the cruiser's starboard quarter and last in was Clayton Fisher, whose bomb just failed to release at all. Alas for all their claims, VS-8 scored no hits whatsoever.[45]

Clay Fisher later decribed his attack.

---

45. Individual Aircraft Action Reports, VS-8, contained in CO Bombing Squadron Eight, Enclosure (A) to VB8 War Diary June 1942, pp 14, held at National Archives II, College Park, Maryland.

By the time the *Hornet* SBDs arrived over the *Hiryū* the *Enterprise* and *Yorktown* SBDs had fatally damaged her. Our flight leader led us over a heavy cruiser, which was firing a lot of heavy AA stuff at our altitude. I was the last SBD to dive and observed a bomb hit amidships of the cruiser. About half way down in my dive a stick of bombs exploded about 50 yards off the port side of the cruiser. B-17s above were dropping their bombs through our dive paths.

Evidently my dive brakes had not stayed fully extended and I realized my airspeed was too high. I hit the electrical bomb release switch and did not feel the small jolt when the 'wishbone'[46] releasing the bomb would hit its stop. I had a hung bomb. The wishbone keeps the bomb from hitting the propeller in a dive. I collapsed my speed brakes, completely blacked out as I pulled back hard on the control stick. I could feel the tremendous acceleration of the plane as I was recovering from the dive.

I finally levelled out [at a height of] just over 300 feet and was passing over the stern of a destroyer I had not seen hidden under a patch of clouds. Shrapnel from the destroyer's guns was falling in the water below me. Their gunners were not leading my plane enough. My airspeed indication was still pegged and it finally started moving slowly back to 145 knots, our cruising speed.

I never knew what my maximum speed was, but that SBD gave me a real wild ride and didn't shed anything. I finally was able to shake the bomb loose

with the manual release and by jerking the control stick back hard a couple of times.[47]

'Put me someplace tonight where I can attend to them in the morning,' was Spruance's request to his staff that night, but Robert J. Oliver, Spruance's Flag Lieutenant, commented, 'Browning and Buckmaster were of no help [to Spruance] on the night 4 June'. He also revealed that relations with Fletcher were 'touchy' and this, Oliver believed, was because Nimitz 'did not really want Spruance subservient to Fletcher.'[48]

If the first day of battle had ended in triumph for the American's, with the promise of yet more victories to follow, the second day turned out to be a day of frustration and missed opportunities. At 0045 Task Force Sugar, as Spruance's carriers had been dubbed, changed course to avoid possible contact. It was not until 0420 that it altered course to close Midway once more.

The *Mikuma*'s Ordeal

While Spruance was shying away from Midway in fear of a night contact with powerful Japanese surface forces, one such force was speeding toward the island. This was the CruDiv7, four heavy cruisers commanded by Rear-Admiral Takeo Kurita[49], which had been detailed off by Nagumo at 0300 on 4 June, as the main bombarding force for the Midway invasion. It comprised the heavy cruisers *Kumano* (Flag), *Suzuya* (1st Division); *Mikuma* and, bringing up the rear, *Mogami* (2nd Division). These were 12,400 ton ships,

---

46. The fork that held the bomb and carried it out clear of the propeller arc when diving. Clayton told me, 'None of the other *Hornet* pilots had trouble releasing their bombs.' He never found out what caused his problem. Fisher to author, 4 October 2006.

47. Fisher to author, 29 September 2006.

48. Oliver to Buell, 5 October 1971. Oliver's relations with Browning were not good. He related how when he was asked to stand watch on one occasion, Browning sneeringly remarked to Spruance, 'Is Oliver competent to stand a watch?' Spruance is alleged to have 'blown up' at this remark. According to Oliver, Spruance quickly 'lost confidence in Browning.' Handwritten notes from tape dated 5 October 1971. Oliver Papers, Box 3, Folder 12, Naval Historical Center, Newport, Rhode Island.

49. Vice-Admiral Takeo Kurita (1889–1977). b. 28 April 1889. Graduated Naval Academy Etajima 1910. Specialized in torpedo warfare. 1910 midshipman, served on the protected cruiser *Kasagi*, 1911 on protected cruiser *Niitaka*. 1911 sub-lieutenant, served on *Tatsuta*. 1912 Torpedo School, 1913 lieutenant (jg), Gunnery School, then aboard the battleship *Satsuma*. 1915, served on destroyer *Sakaki* and then armoured cruiser *Iwate*. 1916 lieutenant, Sasebo naval

dockyard, then the old light cruiser *Tone*. 1917 destroyer *Kaba*, then Naval College. 1918 Torpedo School advanced course. 1918–19 XO destroyer *Minekaze*. 1920 destroyers *Yakaze* and *Hakaze*, then destroyer *Shigure*. 1921 commanded destroyer *Oite*. 1922 lieutenant-commander, Instructor at Torpedo School. 1924 stood by to command destroyer No.2 of *Kamikaze* class while building.1925 commanded destroyer *Hagi*. 1926 commanded destroyer *Hamakaze*. 1927 commanded destroyer *Urakaze*. 1928 Torpedo School, Kure naval yard. 1930 CO 25th destroyer flotilla. 1932, CO 10th destroyer flotilla. 1932 captain and CO 12th destroyer flotilla. 1934 commanded light cruiser *Abukuma*. 1935 Chief Instructor, Torpedo School. December 1937 commanded battleship *Kongo*. 1938 rear-admiral. September 1940 commanded CruDiv7. 1942 commanded Western Attack Group at Dutch East Indies invasion. Indian Ocean sortie. Midway. July 1942 to July 1943 Vice-Admiral, Commander BatDiv3. Guadalcanal, bombarding Henderson Field. Central Solomons. July 1943 replaced Kondo as C-in-C 2nd Fleet. 1944 Battles of Philippine Sea and Leyte Gulf. December 1944 Commander Etajima. October 1945 to reserve, had served total of 38 years in IJN. Died 19 December 1977, aged 88.

originally built as light cruisers but modified by Kure Navy Yard to carry a main battery of ten 8 inch guns in five twin turrets and reclassified[50]. They were fast ships, credited with a top speed of 37 knots, which, if true, was faster than most destroyers. It may have been for this reason that they were selected to make the fast final run into Midway in order to deluge its defences from its forty heavy guns prior to the troops disembarking; and also the reason why, for the final dash, Kurita, even though he was an old destroyer man, decided to leave their destroyer escorts of DesDiv8 behind. If so, the latter move was soon regretted. These big ships also had good protection, with an armoured belt of 3.9 inch thickness, with increased to 4.9 inches over the main magazines. Their deck armour, however, was much less, just 2.4 inches maximum and that was to prove insufficient against determined dive-bombing.

A softening-up bombardment by naval artillery was considered essential to the Japanese landing. The principal defences, once all American air power had been eliminated, were the USMC artillery batteries emplaced around both islands. The heaviest weapons the marines could bring to bear were the 7 inch former naval guns. There were two two-gun batteries of these available to the Seacoast Artillery Group[51], the Sand Island Battery and the Eastern Island Battery.[52] The actual Japanese landing plans were very basic, at least as they described them. The initial assault was to be made on Sand Island by two battalions (totalling some 1,500 officers and men) of the Special Naval Landing Force.

> We were going to approach the south side, sending out landing boats as far as the reef. We had many different kinds of landing boats but did not think that many would be able to pass over the reefs. If they got stuck the personnel were supposed to transfer to rubber landing boats. We had plenty of equipment for a three month occupation without help, but were not sure of our boats.[53]

The army's 1,000-strong Ikki Detachment[54] would land on Eastern Island. Once established these units were to be reinforced by the 11th and 12th Construction Battalions and sundry administration units. The experience of Wake Island earlier in the war had shown the Japanese that the marines would be no walk-over, so a heavy and annihilating bombardment was an obvious requirement to clear the way. That the Japanese would attempt an assault with only a makeshift or *ad hoc* bombardment 'on the hoof' seems very unlikely at this stage of the war.

The marines were indeed ready. As long ago as 1921 a brilliant USMC officer Major Earl H Ellis[55], had laid down

---

50. It has recently become 'fashionable' to maintain that these four ships could not have inflicted much damage on the USM defences at Midway, even if they had delivered their bombardment. Wake Island is cited as 'proof'. It is a view I do not subscribe to, and Kurita's subsequent bombardments of Henderson Field on Guadalcanal in October proved quite effective. The new 20.32 cm bore, 50 calbre, twin 8 inch gun, (known as the Type 3 (Model 1914) *2 GO,* to distinguish them from the old Type 3 which they replaced) had been specially developed by the IJN during 1930–1 specifically to achieve the best possible weaponry under the terms of the various naval treaties still being complied with by Japan at that time (but soon to be abandoned). They had a maximum range of 21,100 yards, which outranged the biggest USMC artillery ashore. Much effort had been put into concentrating dispersion patterns, and in 1938 the Type 98 (Model 1938) gunfiring delay installation had been introduced as a further aide. This device incorporated a 'trigger time limiting' feature, which reduced the time of firing to under 0.2 seconds between the firing of each gun in the twin turret. It had the effect of ensuring that each shell left the gun barrel at a different time, which reduced mutual interference in flight and reduced dispersion by between 10 and 15 per cent. This resulted in tight salvo delivery in battle. These cruisers carried 120–126 rounds per gun and so could have delivered a total of between 4,800 and 5,040 shells into the Midway defences. These weapons had a rate of fire of 4–5 rpm and the muzzle velocity was 2,756 feet per second. Doubt has also been cast on whether the four cruisers were equipped with any special shells suitable for shore bombardment work, although again at Guadalcanal just a few months later there seemed to be no shortage of such ordnance! In any case AP might well be suitable in some cases. Whether fragmentation or high-capacity (HC) shells were more suited for bombarding shore targets is a moot point, especially if what they wanted to do was penetrate concrete emplacements. The Japanese had a common type 0 HE shell weighing 277.4 lb as well as their normal ship-to-ship AP Type 91. See US Naval Technical Mission to Japan, report 0–19, *Japanese Projectiles General Type* and USA Naval Technical Mission to Japan report 0–47(N)-1, *Japanese Naval Guns and Mount–article 1, Mounts Under 18',* Washington DC.

51. Commanded by Lieutenant-Colonel Lewis A. Hohn, USMC.

52. Sand Island battery commanded by Captain Ralph A. Collins, Jr, USMC, and Eastern Island battery commanded by Captain Harold R. Warner, Jr, USMC.

53. Captain Yasumi Toyama, IJN, during USSBS Interrogation No. 60, on 1 October 1945. See also Japanese (JICPOA) translation *Japanese Land Forces No. 2,* original dated 20 October 1942. JICPOA had been established in September 1943, and post-war conducted widespread translations of Japanese documents.

54. Commanded by Lieutenant-Colonel Kiyonao Ikki.

55. Lieutenant-Colonel Earl 'Pete' Hancock Ellis, USMC (1880–1923). b. Iuka, Kansas, 19 December 1880. 1900 enlisted as private in USMC. December 1901 second lieutenant. 1902 based at Cavite, Philippines, from April. 1903 first lieutenant. Later served in West Indies and at NS Guam. 1908 captain in Philippines again. 1911–13 Naval War

the basic principles for Pacific atoll warfare, whether attacking or defending, his main contention being: 'The landing will entirely succeed or fail practically on the beach'.[56] Kurita's force had an important function to fulfil but he needed to time his arrival off Midway to coincide with the elimination of US air power there and the arrival of the occupation convoy. He pushed his four ships on hard at high speed throughout the early morning blackness and on through the hours of daylight and into the following night.

The disastrous outcome of the carrier battles of 4 June finally brought an abrupt cessation to Kurita's onward rush toward Midway. His squadron was now dangerously exposed and could expect no support from the air, whereas the Americans, who should have been crushed, had aviation potential both on Midway and at sea with one, or possibly, two intact carriers operating. Kurita had come within about 60 miles of his goal, but to press on any further was clearly suicidal. At 2245 that night Nagumo finally remembered his subordinate and signalled to Kurita that the bombardment was, for the moment at any rate, cancelled. Unfortunately the signal was mistakenly sent to the CruDiv8 and had to be retransmitted when the error was finally discovered. As a result it did not finally reach its intended destination until 0230 next morning. Aboard the *Kumano*, at the head of the hastening line, Kurita took in the bad news and signalled his racing column to slow and turn back to the north.

In the meantime, however, hostile eyes had already sighted the scurrying squadron. At 0215 the submarine *Tambor* (SS–198), proceeding on the surface during the hours of darkness as ordered, sighted 'four large ships' on a course of 50 degrees some way to the south of her, bearing 279 degrees true. The captain of the submarine[57] was in a dilemma because he had already been warned of the presence in his area of friendly forces. He was therefore unable to make a snap attack on sight, and instead turned south to attempt to identify the swiftly moving force.[58] He almost immediately lost contact and that would have been the end of the brief encounter, had not Nagumo's belated order, by yet another of the strange coincidences with which this battle was studded, not arrived on the *Kumano*'s bridge shortly afterward.

Kurita's turn, by cruel chance, steered his division straight for the *Tambor*, then still blindly casting about for them. Although the cruisers had slowed down to about 28 knots, they were still closing rapidly, and it is doubtful whether any head-on snap shot by the submarine, given the vagaries of the American torpedoes, would have done any harm before they swept by. Fate was not to be cheated, however. A keen-eyed watcher aboard the flagship sighted the tiny silhouette of the *Tambor*'s conning tower away in the murk ahead on the port bow and bellowed a warning. The *Kumano* immediately turned hard to port in an evasive manoeuvre, signalling back down the line for her consorts to conform.

The immaculate formation immediately disintegrated into a wildly weaving but still fast-moving mêlée. The reactions of each ship varied in progressively staggered reactions as the red alert reached them in sequence. The next astern, *Suzuya*, made a half-hearted turn, saw her leader looming up dead ahead and hastily had to turn to starboard to avoid cutting her in half, a very close call. The third ship in line, *Mikuma*, tried to conform with the violent reaction of her next ahead as best she could, but opted for a starboard turn to avoid *Kumano*. This was all well and good, but, unfortunately, this placed her directly crossing the 'T' of the rearmost vessel, the *Mogami*, which had safely

College, and origins of War Plan Orange, the Navy's plan for a naval war with Japan. 1916 Major and served as Aide-de-Camp to Major-General Commandant George Barnett. March 1917 on US entry to World War I assigned to Quantico, Virginia. Arrived in France November. January 1918 returned to United States. February Office of Naval Operations, Washington DC. June 1918 returned to France on staff of General John A. Lejeune. June–July 35th Division, Wesserling then Adjutant 64th Brigade. August Brigade Adjutant 4th Marine Brigade Pcount-a-Mousson, Nancy. August temporary Lieutenant-Colonel. Served in the Sainte Mihiel salient operation September 1918 and again in Meuse-Argonne offensive October–November 1918, including taking of Blanc Mont. December crossed Rhine and reached Koblenz, Germany at time of Armistice. Awarded Croix de Guerre with Gold Star and Chevalier of Legion of Honour. Returned US August 1919, Quantico, then Santo Domingo, Brigade Intelligence Officer, 2nd Marine Brigade. 1920 Navy

Cross. Convinced of inevitability of war with Japan, requested assignment to South America and Japan to complete his earlier work in that region. Given 'leave of absence' from HQ Quantico and returned to Pacific on secret work. 1921 travelled around Pacific area, Australia, Japan and Philippines. Started to prepare a detailed war plan for amphibious operations from his findings and accurately predicted the course of the Pacific War as it developed twenty years later. While still engaged in his probing he died mysteriously at Palau, in the Japanese mandated Caroline Islands on 12 May 1923, aged 43. Body returned to United States and interred at Arlington National Cemetery.

56. See Major Earl H. Ellis *War Portfolio – U.S. Marine Corps, Advanced Base Operations in Micronesia 1921*.

57. Lieutenant-Commander John Williams Murphy, Jr.

58. An early (and noncommittal) account of Murphy's reactions is contained in Theodore Roscoe, *United States Submarine Operations in World War II*.

turned to port and then, seeing the rest of her squadron vanishing ahead, had turned sharply back to starboard again to catch up. The *Mikuma,* with all eyes seemingly on avoiding the First Division to starboard, failed to see her sister thundering up from the south and only a last-minute veering off to port again by that ship prevented a right-angled collision. This could not avoid a crash completely, however, and the *Mogami* slammed into the *Mikuma* almost abreast her bridge.

The *Mikuma*'s side armour was, as we have seen, quite substantial, and stood up pretty well to the blow, but a port fuel tank was ruptured by a 65 foot tear above the protective belt, and the leaking contents left a clear trail on her wake. The *Mogami*'s fragile and unprotected bow was crumpled up for 40 feet or more by the impact. The shearing metal was compressed and forced out from the ship and acted like a huge uncontrollable rudder, leaving her truncated hull terminated just in front of her foremost twin 8 inch gun turret. She rapidly lost way and slid to a halt. Both cruisers' engine rooms and boilers remained operational, which gave some faint hope.

The threat of the *Tambor* still remained, and so Kurita was unable to stop to aid the cripples for fear of putting his remaining two ships at risk. He sped on, but signalled *Mikuma* to stand by her sister, and also ordered his two distant destroyers to close them and render what assistance they could. He could have been under few illusions that either vessel would survive; daylight was fast approaching and the two damaged ships were in easy range of everything the enemy cared to send their way.

Eventually *Mogami* managed, by means of superlative damage limitation, which included jettisoning her full torpedo armament, to get underway once more and even worked up to 12 knots. Fear of submarine attack at such a snail's pace, was uppermost, but they need not have worried. *Tambor* was totally in the dark about the havoc she had brought about, and had lost touch again. There was still some doubt about whether the ships sighted had been friend or foe and maybe there was relief that they had not had to make a decision to attack when still in doubt.[59] At all events, only the most obscure of sighting reports was sent and that not until 0437, when a second signal revealed that

they were enemy and that one had her bow damaged. Finally, at 0602 the *Tambor* sent a detailed report to both Midway and Honolulu of two *Mogami* type cruisers, bearing 272 degrees some 115 miles from Midway, on course of 270 degrees. After that she lost touch, although she did pass through *Mikuma*'s oil slick about ninety minutes later.

Nocturnal Activities

Others had been astir during the dark hours, which had seen much activity for no result. A series of sighting reports had been sent in by one of the Catalina patrols[60] the previous afternoon. The first sighting, made at 1558, was merely of three burning ships about 170 miles north-west of Midway, and this was supplemented by a further report of two cruisers on the same bearing made at 1609. These were clearly *Akagi, Kaga* and *Soryū,* but it was not until 1745 that it was confirmed by the VP that these blazing hulks *were,* in fact, Japanese carriers and the SBDs' claims were finally confirmed. An airborne Zero looking for revenge drove the PBY away before she could make any further amplification, but that last sighting was sufficient to initiate some late action back at Midway.

On receipt of the news, the marine commander, Captain C. Simard, ordered Lieutenant-Colonel Ira Kimes, commanding MAG-22, to conduct a strike with all available aircraft. Kimes consulted with the senior surviving pilot, Major Benjamin Norris, who had been through the mill on the 4th and knew his men would stand no chance in a daylight mission should any Japanese carrier remain intact enough to despatch A6Ms to their defence. Norris therefore opted to mount a night sortie, hoping to achieve the vital surprise so necessary to a successful attack. This was agreed, and arming commenced as soon as the congested state of Midway's crowded runways permitted.

In total the marines mustered twelve serviceable dive-bombers, which Norris again split into two attack units.[61] The six SBD-2s were placed under the command of Captain Marshall A. Tyler, USMC[62], the squadron XO, while Norris himself took command of the six flyable SB2U-3s, all aircraft being armed with a single 500 pound

---

59. The fact that Spruance's son, Lieutenant Edward Dean Spruance, a submariner against his father's best advice, was one of her officers failed to raise her game any.

60. Piloted by Ensign Theodore S. Thueson.

61. Report of CO, VMSB-241.

62. Major Marshall Alvin 'Zack' Tyler (1910–71) b. Kingston, Rhode Island, 6 September 1910. US Naval Academy, Annapolis, commissioned as second lieutenant, USMC 3 June 1933, Marine Base Philadelphia. 1934–35 service

aboard the battleship *Pennsylvania* (BB-38) 1935–36 NAS Pensacola, flight training. Promoted to First Lieutenant June 1936. 1936–39 Marine Base, Quantico, Virginia. Sea service 1938. Promoted captain. July 1939–January 1941, MAG-2, San Diego. January 1941–November 1942, MAG Pearl Habor. Awarded Navy Cross for his work at Midway. Promoted to major August 1942, to US Air Station, Cherry Point, North Carolina. Promoted to temperoray colonel January 1951, full colonel September 1953. Adjusted by

bomb. The whole force departed from 1915, climbing off into the night sky. The enemy was reported on a bearing of 338 degrees some 200 miles out, but, although the two groups kept together and searched diligently, no sign whatsoever was found of any burning ships.[63]

The hunt was finally abandoned and the two groups of dive-bombers were now faced with the task of returning safely to Midway. This was easier said than done, for the night had grown tempestuous, with squalls and lowering clouds extending from 500 up to 6,500 feet, to add to the usual navigation hazards of night flying. One SB2U-3, piloted by Second Lieutenant Sumner H. Whitten[64], became separated from the group but after some anxious hours finally managed to make landfall at 0145 from the light of the burning oil tanks on Sand Island. The abortive mission was not without loss, however. During the return, and while still about 40 miles from base, at an altitude of about 10,000 feet, for no accountable reason the Vindicator flown by Norris suddenly banked sharply over to starboard. Thinking he was taking avoiding action or in trouble, his companions tried to follow him as he dived steeply toward the sea, but were forced to break away at 500 feet.[65] Nothing was ever heard again of Norris or his radio-gunner.[66]

While the marine dive-bombers had scoured the area in vain for the enemy, another group was engaged on the same mission. These were the eight Elco-built patrol torpedo (PT) boats of Motor Torpedo Boat Squadron (MTBRON)

1[67], commanded by Lieutenant Clinton McKellar, Jr. Seventy-seven footers, with a displacement of just 54 tons, and a crew of seventeen, these little craft were driven by petrol engines and had a top speed of 39 knots in good conditions. Their range was limited, about 500 nautical miles, and their punch was four 21 inch torpedoes carried externally plus a couple of .50 calibre machine guns.[68] These little craft loaded an extra 200 gallons in deck-stored drums, risking the obvious hazard these presented, and set off at 2115 at their best speed. This had to be reduced, for in the heavy swell the boats were 'bumping' alarmingly, and waves were coming aboard and swirling below decks.

PT-29 and *PT-30*, having been based at Kure Island, had a head start and reached the reported position of the enemy earlier than the others, at 2315, but, like their Marine aviator colleagues, saw no sign of the enemy. The remaining boats joined up and a box-search was commenced, with the little flotilla quartering the area methodically as the night lightened. They stood as little chance as the aircraft of succeeding in a full daylight assault, so, at around 0430 on the 5th, they independently turned back for base. Frustratingly, on their way back, two of the boats, *PT-20* and *PT-21*, caught a glimpse of a column of black smoke, which they estimated was 40 miles west of their position. They turned toward it but lost sight of what must have been the final marker of one of the Japanese carriers, and found nothing but sundry wreckage, which they identified as

Watson Board. Retired 1 September 1955 with rank of brigadier-general for combat and more than twenty years' active service. Died Valley Forge General Hospital, Phoenixville, Pennsylvania, 8 November 1971.

63. It was strange that not one of the Japanese carriers were sighted, for, while both *Kaga* and *Soryū* had been sunk by their escorting destroyers around 1925 and 1915 respectively, long before the marines dive-bombers got near. The *Akagi* lingered until 0520 before being similarly despatched, and *Hiryū* still remained defiantly afloat at dawn.

64. Lieutenant-Colonel Sumner H. Whitten, USMCR. b. (1917). b. Waltham, Mass. on 17 August 1917. Lived at Waban, and educated at Newton High School and Amherst College, during which he flew light aircraft, graduating in 1940. February 1940, enlisted in Marine Corps as a private. June 1940 active duty Boston navy yard, then NAS Squantum for elimination flight training. October 1940 NAS Pensacola as private first class. At Saufley Field with Squadron 1, in Squadron 2 for section tactics, and for preliminary dive-bombing. Squadron 3 for instrument training. Radio Navigation at Mobile, Alabama and Crestview, Florida. Made marine cadet. NAS Opa Locka, carrier training April 1941. Graduated and assigned MAW-2 NAS North Island from May with Advanced Carrier Training Group. December 1941 Marine Corps Air Station (MCAS) Ewa, Hawaii, assigned to VMSB-231. Transported to Midway by destroyer January 1942. Awarded the Navy Cross for

Midway. Returned to Pearl in B-17 operations officer VMB-234, to Guadalcanal February 1943, operations against Tokyo Express, Munda and Kahili, Bougainville. April 1943 dive-bomber instructor NAS Vero Beach. NAS Deland Gunnery Officer. Major, on Admiral's staff NAS Jacksonville. West Coast SB2C-4s and Grumman TBMs, then Forward Air Control Program with General James C. Magee, 4th Marines. Marine Corps liaison to USAAF 1st Air Support Control Squadron for Japanese invasion. At sea when war ended. MCAS Cherry Point, with MAG-14 preparing foreign deliveries of surplus aircraft, SB2C-4s to Greece, TBMs to UK and F4Us to France. Korean War as CO VMF-312 with F4U-4B Corsairs. NAS El Toro. Converted to jet aircraft. Flew from carrier *Oriskany* (CV-34). 1 Marine Air/Ground Brigade. Atomic weapon training Albuquerque, New Mexico then Amphibious Warfare Training Command. Resigned December 1954 as lieutenant-colonel. Joined Convair, flight-testing F-102 and F-106 and Atlas missile programme. Joined Lockheed and Skunk Works projects, followed by Northrop. 1979 retired a second time.

65. MAG-22 Report.

66. PFC Arthur B. Whittington.

67. *PTs-20, -21,-22, -24, -25,-26, -27, -28, -29* and *-30*. PT-23 had broken down earlier while *en route* from Hawaii and had to turn back.

68. For further information see Victor Chan, *American PT Boats in WWII* and *Devil Boats: PT War Against Japan*.

belonging to the enemy. All the boats thus returned empty-handed.

One more war vessel was astir that night, and she was Japanese. The submarine *I-168* (Lieutenant-Commander Yudachi Tanabe) had not been privy to the invasion cancellation order and was dutifully carrying out her part of the operation as scheduled. Tanabe brought his 1,400 ton boat to the surface south-east of Sand Island and, at 0120, commenced firing with his single 4.7 inch 45 calibre gun. This puny weapon was not going to cause much damage to the US defences, and nor did it, most of the eight rounds loosed off landing in the lagoon before Tanabe submerged again at 0128 and sloped off to the north. Searchlights probed the dark waters and the marines loosed off 42 futile rounds of 3 inch and 5 inch of their own[69], and that was that. The little spat did, however, do what it was designed to do, upset the defenders and keep them jittery about what was coming next.[70]

Uninspired as the *Tambor*'s reactions had been, merely by her presence she had converted two of the Emperor's fastest warships into struggling stragglers, thus delivering two easy targets into the hands of the assembled US airmen, who would surely be far more eager to take advantage of this unexpected situation. Aircraft from Midway itself were, of course, early astir and they did not have to search very far or very hard; that oil trail on their doorstep practically guaranteed a day of discomfort for the IJN.

The *Tambor*'s sighting report received early verification when a VP also reported two battleships (*sic*), damaged and streaming oil, bearing 264 degrees, distance 125 miles, course 268 degrees speed 15. The VP-23 Catalina[71] followed up with a confirmed sighting of a pair of 'large capital ships', both damaged, one leaking oil. One crew member recalled poignantly their isolated part in great events, echoing the refrain of most PBY crews. 'I spotted an oil slick and we tracked it until we spotted what looked like two large enemy ships. We radio contacted the base and followed them for about three hours; then returned to Midway. We never found out what happened to the ships we had spotted.'[72]

It was to be a common theme from the attacking aircraft over the next two days that *Mikuma* and *Mogami* were reported as battleships, battle-cruisers or capital ships. The inability of even navy pilots to identify targets correctly was commonplace. In the case of these two ships, the one having her bows curled back reduced her overall length in comparison with her sister ships, and, on casual examination gave the ratio expected between a large cruiser and a battleship. Thus were they often reported. At over 616 feet in length ships of the *Mogami* class were actually only about 20–30 feet longer than American heavy cruisers of the various classes then currently accompanying TF-16 and TF-17, but this made no difference. Similarly, when the destroyers *Arashio* and *Asashio* joined up, they were scaled up as 'cruisers'.

Reports were continuous during the morning, but were confusing. At 0719 a patrol plane reported five ships bearing 325 degrees, distance 200 miles, course 338 degrees. At 0800 a patrol plane reported two battleships, one carrier on fire, three heavy cruisers bearing 324°, distance 240 miles, course 310 degrees. At 0820 a patrol plane reported a carrier, bearing 335 degrees, distance 250 miles, course 245 degrees. This resulted in Midway and Hawaii directing their respective air components against the two crippled cruisers, while the two surviving American carriers, in effect, did nothing at all until very late in the day, and then concentrated their resources against a 'fifth' Japanese carrier which did not exist.

The Marine Aviators' Last Sortie

Despite their night-time wanderings, the marines were first off; and at 0700 twelve dive-bombers of VMSB-241 began taking off again, each armed with a single 500 pound bomb. Once more they were divided into two sections, with the SBD-2s being led by Captain 'Zack' Tyler, their third commander in twenty-four hours, and the Vindicators by Captain Richard E. Fleming.[73] Their target was assigned as the occupation force, which was west of Midway and being trailed by two damaged 'battleships', bearing 269 degrees about 130–150 miles out.

---

69. Battery C fired a 5 inch star-shell and Batteries B (5 inch), D and E (3 inch) contributed the rest. Despite the almost point-blank range, and the fact that E battery was credited with three direct hits, no shell hit *I-168* whatsoever. (Lieutenant-Colonel R. D. Heinl, Jr, *Marines at Midway*).

70. Lieutenant-Colonel Robert L. McGlashan, in his response to the second of two post-war questionnaires, also brought out the very pertinent fact that the marines' response to Tanabe's brief bombardment might have done more harm than good, in that 'it was feared that firing on this submarine might

disclose active battery positions to a subsequent pre-landing bombardment.' Lt Col R. L. McGlashan II, response to Marine Corps Historical Section Questionnaire, dated 12 August 1947).

71. Piloted by Lieutenant (jg) Norman K. Brady.

72. Bill Forbes, 'Pearl Harbor Story, World War II Encounters and Accomplishments by VP-23 December 7, 1941 through January 1943'.

73. Captain Richard Eugene Fleming, (1917–42). b. St Paul, Minnesota, on 2 November 1917. Educated at St Thomas

It took both groups of marine dive-bombers about three-quarters of an hour to locate the wide oil-slick, 'evidently the wake of a wounded ship'[74], and follow it to its source. The two limping cruisers, now joined by the two destroyers, came into view about twenty minutes later and, at 0805, Captain Tyler ordered his prearranged battle plan into motion. The aim was a combined attack, with the SBDs making a conventional dive attack, approaching the enemy from astern and out of the sun, plummeting down from 10,000 feet, while the SB2U-3s again made a glide run in from 4,000 feet. Tyler's force was met with heavy anti-aircraft fire but claimed very near misses by all six aircraft, without loss.

Fleming's glide approach, it was subsequently claimed[75],

caught his target, the *Mikuma*, by surprise, but their defensive fire was equally heavy and precise. Leading the charge, Fleming's aircraft was soon hit heavily forward and began emitting dense smoke from the engine. Notwithstanding this damage, he held his aircraft on course and managed to release his ordnance before, just as he began the pull-out sequence, the entire aircraft burst into flames and plunged into the sea.

The captain of the *Mogami*, was later alleged to have watched this attack and to have observed: 'I saw the dive bomber dive into the *last turret*[76] and start fires. He was very brave'.[77] The last part of this much-quoted statement was perfectly true, Fleming's bravery and courage is undisputed, but the first part is utter nonsense. Despite the fact that the

---

Military Academy, graduating with Class of 1935 as top student officer. Further education at University of Minnesota, president of the Delta Kappa Epsilon fraternity, Bachelor of Arts degree 1939. Enlisted in Marine Corps Reserve and volunteered for flight training January 1940. Trained at NAS Pensacola, finishing top of class. April 1942 promoted first lieutenant. May 1942 promoted to captain. Assigned NAS San Diego. Flight officer VMSB-241 on flight from Hawaii to Midway. President Franklin D Roosevelt presented Congressional Medal of Honor to Fleming's mother, Mrs Mechael E Fleming on 24 November 1942. The destroyer-escort USS *Fleming* (DE-32) was named in his honour and so is Fleming Field, South St Paul. Cadet colonel promotion ceremony and presentation of the Fleming Sabre commemorates his name.

74. Lieutenant-Colonel R. D. Heinl, *Marines at Midway*.
75. *Ibid*.
76. My italics. The wreckage continually and incorrectly said to be that of Fleming's SB2U was atop 'X' turret, which was not, her last turret, which was 'Y' turret astern and below it, on the ship's quarterdeck (or fantail in American parlance).
77. Lieutetant-Colonel R. D. Heinl, *Marines at Midway*. It would appear that Captain (later Rear-Admiral) Akira Soji, whose was interviewed by the USSBS, only made this statement some time after the war, and he later denied it, reaffirming that *Mikuma* suffered no damage whatsoever in that attack, a fact also attested to by *Mogami*'s damage control officer, Captain Saruwatari. It would appear that his memory mixed up this attack with a similar incident, which he witnessed at a later period of the war. This took place when the heavy cruisers *Maya* and *Myoko* of the 5th Cruiser Squadron under Rear-Admiral Omori were part of Vice-Admiral Kondo's 2nd Fleet during operations off Guadalcanal. On the night of 15/16 October, these two heavy cruisers carried out a bombardment of Henderson Field, firing 989 8 inch shells into the area. Next morning, during their subsequent withdrawal toward Shortlands, the force was discovered by two SBDs from VB-10 on routine patrol. Both aircraft made steep 70 degrees plus dive-bombing attacks from an altitude of 17,000 feet. One aircraft, piloted by ensign R. A. Hoogerwerf, dived on the *Myoko*, but missed astern. The other SBD, piloted by Ensign P. M. Halloran A-V (N), with E. Gallagher, ARM2c, as the rear-

seat man, selected the *Maya* as their target, but also only scored a near miss astern of that ship. However, during the pull-out phase of the attack dive, the starboard wingtip of Halloran's Dauntless brushed the mainmast of the *Maya* and the dive-bomber tipped over, crashing full-tilt into the port side of the cruiser's quarterdeck. Both aircrew were killed instantly, as were thirty-seven of the ship's crew, while the flaming avgas from the pulverized SBD in turn ignited the ready-use 4.7 inch ammunition in lockers. As a precaution *Maya* jettisoned her torpedoes but the fire was brought under control and she was able to return to port under her own power. This is the incident confused with Fleming's attack and used in Heinl's misleading account. The Fleming 'suicide attack' yarn was given credence by inaccurate analysis of later photographs of the damaged vessel after real bomb hits, incurred on the following day, had detonated the powerful explosives contained in her starboard Type 93 torpedoes and blown debris from her upperworks aft onto her elevated 'X' turret. However Soji should not be blamed entirely, because the story that Fleming had deliberately crashed his doomed aircraft into *Mikuma*'s after gun turret was given widespread current coverage at the time. This myth much more probably owed its origins to a typical piece of yellow newspaper journalism. Robert J. Casey, a reporter for the *Chicago Daily News*, was 'imbedded' aboard the heavy cruiser *Salt Lake City* (CA-25) during the battle. He later interviewed Fleming's widow and included the story in his wartime book *Torpedo Junction: With the Pacific Fleet from Pearl Harbor to Midway*, Bobbs Merril, Annapolis, 1942. The story is still regularly being trotted out however, a recent example being the Sumner Whitten interview with Jon Guttman in the July 2002 edition of *World War II* magazine, in which he states that Dick Fleming 'flew his plane into the ship, killing himself and his gunner.' It should be pointed out that as long ago as November 1942, the citation on Fleming's Congressional Medal of Honor, accurately stated: 'Undeterred by a fateful approach glide, during which his ship was stuck and set afire, he grimly pressed home his attack to an altitude of five hundred feet, released his bomb to score a near-miss on the stern of his target, *then crashed* [in] *to the sea in flames* [my italics].' Even before Heinl's account appeared the myth had been demolished. Walter Karig, a journalist and writer of children's fiction, had been story is entirely untrue, it has become one of great 'untouchable' legends of Midway, and still presented all over the Internet as 'fact'. The VMSB-241 eyewitness stated Fleming's blazing machine crashed into the sea and neither crew member[78] made any attempt to get free. Indeed this was how it was officially reported by MAG-22. On the Japanese side *Mikuma* soon after broadcast a combat report that she had suffered *no* damage at all from either of these attacks.

The marine flyers claimed one hit forward on an already damaged heavy ship, and one close miss astern. When they left at 0830 the target vessel was 'listing and turning in circles to starboard', but in truth no hits were registered.

The Air Corps Try Once More

The dive-bombers were reinforced by a force of twelve B-17s, PatWingTwo [Patrol Wing Two] at Oahu despatching three different squadrons contributing six bombers apiece to Midway that day. The Fortress formations were sent against the same objective, but only eight of them actually attacked. Five of the big bombers carried eight 500 pound demolition bombs apiece, and three had just four 500 pound bombs.

The first group of four B17s made contact with two 'battleships' at 0830, bearing 270 degrees 130 miles from Midway. These army aircraft attacked from an altitude of 20,000 feet, and observers claimed two 'probable' hits and three near misses from the nineteen bombs dropped. They received heavy anti-aircraft fire from the ships but escaped damage. This first element, led by Colonel Brooke E. Allen, was followed by a second flying at the same height, which dropped twenty bombs against a second 'battleship' of the same enemy force. They reported scoring one direct hit on the stern of this ship and four near misses.

Captain Ernest R. Manierre[79], flying the lead aircraft (a/c 2660) of the second element from 23rd Bombing Squadron, left a detailed account of the mission.[80] He was better qualified at ship spotting than most of his contemporaries, having spent a thirty-month spell in the US Naval Reserve between 1935 and 1937. His unit took off at 0430 Midway time with three other B-17s in company.[81] The bombers made rendezvous at a point some 50 miles west of Midway at 1500 feet and then climbed on a course of 270 degrees to an altitude of 10,000 feet, which they attained when some 100 miles out. At this point they received their mission instructions which read: 'Attack two enemy battleships: Bearing 270 degrees distance 130 miles.'

On receipt of this signal the whole force of eight bombers climbed up to 20,000 feet and continued on their existing course. Manierre recorded:

---

made a USNR captain by Navy Secretary Frank Knox in order to record the war 'as it happened'. His version of the Fleming attack was published as part of the *Battle Report* series, Volume Three, *Pacific War: Middle Phase*, Rhinehart and Company, New York, 1947. His version has Fleming pulling away after delivering his bomb, and only then bursting into flames and disintegrating. That should have been clear enough but Heinl chose to ignore both it and the citation, and instead appropriated Halloran's true gallant last action to make a better story; and everyone has followed his version ever since. N.B. American naval and marine World War II flyers usually referred to their aircraft as 'ships' a fact which often puzzles land-based flyers (as well as many modern historians!).

78. Fleming's rear-seat man was PFC George A. Toms.
79. Colonel Ernest Roderic Manierre, (b. 1917) b. Hartford, Connecticutt 1935 US Naval Reserve 20 March–10 October 1937. 1937 enlisted US Army as aviation cadet at Springfield, Massachusetts. On 12 October flying cadet to 5 October 1938. 1937 Randolph Field and Kelly Field. 1938 officer service from 6 October to 31 December. 1938 primary, basic and advance flying training as second lieutenant (P), then 9th Bomb Group, Mitchell Field, to February 1941. 1941, October first lieutenant. 1941 to January 1943 Pacific service with 5th and 11th Bomb Groups, 1942 Hawaii, including Midway operations, 1942–3 Guadalcanal and Papua, New Guinea, 52 combat missions in B-17. 1942, April captain. June promoted to major. 1943 Hendricks Filed, as student flying instructor, B-17s, four-engined flight training, then

Deputy Director of Training. 1943 November promoted to lieutenant-colonel. June 1944–July 1945, Director of Training, Combat Gunnery Officers' School, Laredo. 1945 2126th Army Air Force (AAF) as Director of Research and Liaison then Air Base Commander, with B-25s, AT-11s and A-26s). December–June 1946, 610th AAF Elgin Field, Squadrons X and A. 1946, June–September, 612th AAF, Elgin. 1946 September–October 4020th AAF, Wright Field. 1946 October, 41st AAF, Air University, Maxwell Field. 1950 July, promoted to colonel, served in Alaska. 1955 DCS/O (Deputy Chief of Staff) HQ ATMTC (Operations Air Transport Movement Control), Patrick AFB. 1959 July IG (Inspector General), HQ. 314th Air Division, Osan AB, South Korea. 1960 August, guided missile opmm. (Office Personnel Management) course, Jupiter Liaison Officer, Redstone Arsenal, Huntsville, Alabama. 1961 space systems orientation course. Ch, SM78 (Jupiter) Weapons Supply Division, MOAMA (Mobile Air Material Area), Brookley AFB. 1963, October, Dep. for Foreign Technology, Patrick AFB. 1968 Nuclear Weapons Orientation Course. 1968 31st December, retired after 30 years service at Patrick AFB. Awards include Silver Star, DFC, Air Medal, Asiatic-Pacific Campaign Medal.

80. Ernest Manierre, Special Mission Report, 23rd Bomb Sq (H) dated 9 June 1942, contained in ADM199/1302, held at National Archives, Kew, London.
81. No. 2 was a/c 9211 piloted by Major George Blakey, No. 3 a/c 9011 piloted by Captain Seeburger and No. 4 a/c 2403 piloted by Captain Whitaker.

218

At approximately 0830 Midway time, we observed the two battleships below us about four or five miles apart. The first element took the battleship on the right using a collision [*sic*] course of about 370° from the sun. Our element took the battleship on the left, our collision course being about 220° and out of the sun.

Anti-aircraft fire was observed but was very ineffective, mostly being below our altitude. No planes attacked us. We attacked from 20,000 feet true at a speed of 165 miles per hour indicated using Plan B [element formation bombing] on a collision course of approximately 220° . We were to drop all eight bombs.

In the event, he was only able to release four of his bombs, his No. 2 dropped eight, No. 3 four and No. 4 four. Their inability to release their full bomb loads was recorded as 'due to mechanical failure of the equipment'. Manierre continued, 'Turned to course of 90 and returned to base, landing at 1030 Midway time'. He claimed, 'one hit on battleship'. It was not so. In fact, far from damaging the Japanese ships any further, within a short while *Mogami* was able to increase her speed from 12 to 14 knots.

A Brief Respite

Having been subjected to three determined attacks – dive-, glide-and altitude-bombing – all before breakfast, the Japanese crews of the crippled cruisers probably felt that, although they had survived so far, once the American carriers got their teeth into them, there would be little hope. That would also have been the expectation of the American dive-bomber pilots, but for the rest of the day, the little group of Japanese ships struggled on, continuing their tortuous route to safety totally unmolested.

These ships owed their immunity for the rest of the 5th not to a lack of further sightings by the patrol planes from Midway, which consistently saw them crawling away from Midway, but to the vague communications of the *Tambor*, and vitally, the interpretations placed upon those sightings by Fletcher, Spruance and others. But it was not just the wretched performance of Lieutenant-Commander Murphy, sub-standard though it was (and which so annoyed an angry and deeply disappointed Nimitz[82]) but deeper failings on the American side. Commander Thomas Hunnicutt, in his dispassionate but surgical analysis[83], summed up the misdirected floundering on 5 June thus:

After the devastating US air attack on the four Japanese carriers an opportunity to converge on the scene of battle by at least half of the arc submarines presented itself. The CINC and COMSUBPAC [Commander Submarine Pacific] knew of the large number of surface forces, including the possibility of other carriers, in the area. It would be expected that these would converge on Vice-Admiral Nagumo and his remaining forces to render aid. Warships converging and slowing to render aid make fat, overlapping targets for submarines. However, instead of taking advantage of the situation the CINC and COMSUBPAC withdrew *all* submarines to a 100 miles radius arc (station time no later than dawn, 5 June) then to a five mile radius arc (directed at 0609, 5 June) of Midway because it was concluded the invasion would still occur. An irony of Midway is that it is remembered as a triumph of intelligence. It was a triumph of *strategic* intelligence through the partial breaking of the Japanese code and the brilliant analysis by the Codebreakers. It was not a triumph of *operation* intelligence.

The CINC and COMSUBPAC failed to recognize this general retreat. This, coupled with six to twelve hour delays in turning around intelligence and directives to submarines, took the submarines out of the battle area again on 5 June as it had on 4 June.

This failure of operational intelligence and communication also resulted in one submarine report causing Rear-Admiral Spruance to detour to Midway early on the morning of 5 June vice continuing west to engage the Japanese.

It appears that *Tambor*'s contact signal of 0215 was not receipted by Midway until 0306 and not by Rear-Admiral English at Pearl until 0400. Hunnicutt states, 'Rear-Admiral Spruance, on receiving the report, turned his carriers toward Midway at 0420 and steamed in that direction until about 0930'. He concludes:

While the *Tambor*'s vague report triggered the redeployment of submarines and a carrier task force to a spot barren of combat, the CINC and COMSUBPAC C3I system failed to prevent it. The system was unable to integrate and analyze the report in terms of the sighted ships' identity or to other data, especially the search planes' reports. The operational

---

82. See Willmott, *The Barrier and Javelin*. Lieutenant-Commander Murphy was replaced by Lieutenant-Commander Stephen H. Ambruster as *Tambor*'s CO

before her next patrol took place.

83. Commander Thomas G. Hunnicutt *Operational Failure of US Submarines at the Battle of Midway*.

failure of the US submarines at Midway took the CINC, a submariner, as well as the submarine force by surprise.

Having relinquished control of the battle to Spruance and decamped to the heavy cruiser *Astoria*, Fletcher had taken TF-17 away to the east during the night, only later detaching the destroyer *Hughes* (DD-410) to stand by the abandoned *Yorktown*. He told the destroyer's skipper, Lieutenant-Commander Donald J. Ramsay, to prevent anyone from boarding the ships. If there was any danger of her being seized by the enemy, or if a serious fire reignited, *Hughes* was to sink her at once.[84] And that was that as far as Fletcher was concerned on 5 June.

Spruance had moved *Enterprise* and *Hornet* off to the east out of harm's way once they had recovered all their aircraft, and he maintained this course until midnight, then altered its to 000 degrees. For three-quarters of an hour he held to this course but a suspicious radar contact caused considerable alarm, course being altered first to the east again, and then south for a while. Mitscher's biographer records that he did not agree with this caution and felt they ought to have steamed west in pursuit of the enemy.[85] By 0200 Spruance had brought his force onto a course of 270 degrees. The Americans were still fretting over the 'fifth' Japanese carrier (how Nagumo must have wished that she had really existed outside the minds of his foes!) and Spruance was rightly shy of running his carriers into Japanese battleships or heavy cruisers in the night, which would have made mincemeat of his force. On the other hand, he did not want to be too far from Midway at dawn in case the Japanese still intended to carry out their invasion, no matter what. He later recorded:

I did not feel justified in risking a night encounter with possibly superior enemy forces, but on the other hand, I did not want to be too far away from Midway in the morning. I wished to have a position from which either to follow up retreating enemy forces or to break up a landing attack on Midway. At this time the possibility of the enemy having a fifth CV somewhere in the area, possibly with his occupation force or else to the northwestward still existed.[86]

Adding to his hesitation was the previous evening's notification from the B-17s that had attacked a burning carrier at 1830. They reported interception by enemy fighter aircraft still operating even though the *Hiryū*'s flight deck had been chewed up more than an hour before. This might signify that another enemy carrier was, after all, still potent and working in the area. Decreasing visibility to the north did not help clarify the matter. Spruance was reluctant to take that chance, even though he later maintained he had not believed that the Japanese, 'after losing four carriers and all their planes, would remain in an offensive frame of mind'. He therefore notified Nimitz, 'Plan now to close Midway to attack enemy force believed 50 miles west of there'. By 0600 the two American carriers were in position 29° 50' N, 175° 44' W, steering south-west some 130 miles north-east of Midway.

There was no shortage of information from the PBY patrols; their sighting reports streamed in all day. The problem was that their content was so concise and the locations given varied so much, that, on the bridge of the *Enterprise,* they *added* to the confusion rather than clarifying it.[87] The most worrying was from 8V55[88] of VP-24 at 0820, which merely stated one carrier bearing 335 degrees, distance 250 miles, course 245 degrees, with no indication at all that it was showing any signs of damage. This would place a potentially fully operational Japanese carrier within 220 miles of Spruance's force, and well within the reach of an enemy strike. Strangely, Spruance shrugged this potential threat off. Another PBY pilot, Lieutenant Donald G. Gumz of VP-44[89], having sent in the 0800 report of the 'burning carrier' modified his original sighting when he

---

84. CO USS *Hughes* to CincPac, *Operations in Conjunction with USS*. Yorktown *from time of abandonment until sinking,* dated 16 June 1942, held National Archive II, College Park, Maryland.

85. Theodore Taylor, *Magnificient Mitscher*.

86. CO USS *Enterprise* to CincPac, *Battle of Midway Island, June 4-6, 1942,* dated 13 June 1942.

87. Buell berated the VP squadron's work this day, stating that 'their performance as inept as it had been the day before'. (*Quiet Warrior*).

88. Piloted by Ensign David Silver.

89. Captain Donald George Gumz (1914–87). Graduated US Naval Academy, Annapolis 1936. Lieutenant (jg) at NAS San Diego October 1941. VP-44, at Midway flew with ACRM Joel C. Stovall as his radioman. Commanded VB-116 on its establishment at NAAS Camp Kearney, under Fleet Air Wing (FAW) 14, until 2 February 1945. March 1944 squadron began receiving PB4Y-1 Liberator aircraft. Advance training at Holtville, California completed by May. Advanced echelon embarked for Pearl Harbor aboard escort carrier *Breton Woods* (CVE-23). June 1944 NAS Kaneohe, Hawaii. July 1944 deployed to Eniwetok, flew missions against Truk, Ponape and Wake Island. August 1944 North Field, Tinian under FAW-1, flying missions at Iwo Jima. After the war saw service in Korea and Vietnam before retirement. Died 1987 and interred at Maple Leaf Cemetery, Oak Harbor, Washington.

landed back at Midway by stating that at 0930 he had seen a second carrier, 'not burning'. This startling news only slowly found its way to Spruance by a circuitous route via CincPac. Exercising his 'tactful' rather than 'tactical' control, Nimitz only 'recommended' to Spruance that this group be hit, 'particularly carriers'. Spruance was in no hurry to comply and TF-16 continued to steer a westerly course north of Midway throughout the morning, while the Commander and the air staff chewed things over.

Spruance Finally Decides to Attack

The final decision was that the enemy group reported to the north-west, contained the most promising targets (which had originally been given as one burning carrier and two battleships, one of them damaged). They seemed to be heading for the protection of a weather front which would hide them from retaliatory strikes and were already a good way toward it. The attack plan therefore involved a considerable stern chase, which consumed the best part of the rest of the day. At 1100 TF-16 had set a course of 300 degrees at a brisk 25 knots in order to close the range between them and the enemy remnants to the north-west. While the American carriers and their accompanying warships pounded on, and what was left of their air groups prepared for battle, there was nothing much more to be done. *Mogami* and *Mikuma* were left to Midway to deal with as they continued their westward crawl. Meanwhile the lure of the mythical carrier just beyond the horizon beckoned like the Lorelie[90]; as irresistible a lure to Spruance that June afternoon as it was to be to Halsey at Leyte Gulf many months later, but which were to prove illusory.

As midday came and went there were disquieting signs that this chase just might end in disappointment. A returning PT boat was met, which gave the bad news that she had seen nothing at all that way. Later, intercepted radio talk from B-17s also returning empty-handed from a similar futile search did not bode well either. Spruance declined to launch air searches of his own from either carrier, presumably because this would hinder the speed of advance of his force, nor were the various idle float-planes sitting on their catapults on the various escorting cruisers utilized. Absolutely no aerial activity at all disturbed the onward progress of the task force. Admiral Nimitz, still exercising his 'tactical control' from distant Pearl, chipped in with the news that two enemy carriers, one burning and one

smoking, had been sighted at 0800, in company with two battleships, three cruisers and between five and ten destroyers in position 32° N, 179° 32' E. This group was on a course of 310 degrees at a speed of 12 knots.

However, it was not until 1400, when the enemy was estimated to be some 240 miles away, that Spruance deemed them to be within extreme striking distance and the American carriers prepared for launching. Mustering the most battle-worthy dive-bombers remaining to VB-6 and VB-3 (a combination christened 'Bombing 63' by the aircrews) the *Enterprise* could despatch thirty-two aircraft, and *Hornet*, it was hoped, would be able to launch a similar number. However, even this basic decision was not reached without further bizarre tantrums and disharmony aboard the *Enterprise*.

The attack plan, as conceived by the mercurial Miles Browning (who, eager as ever to hit first, had been continually urging the launching of an attack throughout the day), envisaged the Dauntless squadrons operating at their maximum range. After the heavy losses of the day before, this seemed to be risking fate once too often. Moreover, Browning insisted that the SBDs be armed with the most potent weapon for this strike, the 1,000 pound bomb. It might well have looked good on paper, with the keen and brilliant brain of Browning computing the maximum damage to the enemy at the earliest possible opportunity, but what looked impeccable in theory caused some consternation in the squadron briefing rooms when it was revealed. Nobody had ever before argued with Browning, and no ensign or lieutenant (jg) was going to attempt to outface the irritable and irrational CoS now. However, the stern test of combat had brought greater maturity and confidence in themselves and their own judgement, to the young aircrew. Those that had bravely outfaced almost certain death at the hands of a ferocious enemy the day before, were rather less inclined to kowtow to the home-grown bully now. Many felt the plan was flawed, that it once again put them at needless risk, or was just plain 'gut-feeling' wrong.

The Air Group Commander, Wade McClusky, was in his sick-bed, but he, if anyone, was felt to have the courage to stand up to Browning. The leader of the *Enterprise* strike, Lieutenant DeWitt Wood Shumway, after conferring with Lieutenant Wally Short, took his men's concerns to him. Sick or not, the details had McClusky up on his feet and out of the sickbay in short order. During their passage they gathered in Lieutenant Wilmer Earl Gallaher

---

90. The Lorelei is a 430-foot high rock opposite St Goar, Germany, on the right bank of the Rhine. It was the legendary home of a siren, whose call enticed passing sailors, so entrancing them that they wrecked their boats and died. The legend has had an enduring fascination, as well as the epic poem by Heinrich Heine (1797–1856), Max Bruch (1838–1920) based his opera, *Die Lorelei* upon it, while there was also an unfinished opus by Felix Mendelssohn (1809–47).

to swell McClusky's indignant entourage. These three may naively hoped that more senior officers would be approachable and hear them out on their viewpoint. In the event a few, Captain George Murray among them, agreed and, adding him to the group they made their way up to the carrier's flag deck.

Browning was in conference with the air staff, but this made no difference to McClusky; he barged right in. If the group had hoped they would get a calm hearing they were soon disillusioned; nobody was going to tell Browning how to run an air strike, as he quickly made clear. In vain it was pointed out that, turning to the wind to fly off the strike would add further precious miles to an already tight round trip, that the extra weight of the bigger bomb would add to the problem, that the enemy, far from steaming toward them and thus reducing the distance, were actually still steaming away and therefore, with only about 10 knots speed difference, the selected Point Option was even more unlikely to be achieved than it had been the previous day.

Rearm with 500-pounders, urged McClusky, delay the launch for an hour at least to give the aircraft a chance of getting back. Browning refused to concede any of these points. 'Have you ever flown an SBD?' McClusky demanded. Browning, a renowned pioneering dive-bomber pilot, was not taking that as an argument from a man who only a few weeks ago had flown nothing but fighter planes. He came back emphatically, that, yes he had! McClusky countered immediately, asking Browning whether he had ever flown an SBD with self-sealing fuel tanks (which had a smaller capacity than the old type they had recently replaced), with armoured seats (more weight), carrying a 1,000 pound bomb and full tanks. Browning was forced to concede he had not, but was not on the back foot for long and the conversation, never conducted calmly on either side, soon degenerated into a out-and-out shouting match.

For a time, the sanctified flag shelter of the *Enterprise*'s bridge in the midst of a decisive battle resembled more a knock-down-drag-out scrap in a Bronx bar room! Spruance could not allow this to go on for very long, and he intervened. Before their admiral both sides calmed down and each stated their case. One of the group made the point that, if they were ordered to go then they would, but if Browning's plan were followed, they would be unlikely to return!

To the incredulous amazement of Browning, Spruance came down on the side of the aviators. According to Buell he told McClusky, 'I'll do whatever the pilots want.' Browning could not comprehend how Spruance, this aviation-know-nothing cruiser sailor that he felt he was saddled with instead of the understanding aviator and kindred-spirit Halsey, could reject his vast knowledge and expertise.[91] The humiliation was too much to take and Browning turned on his heel, fuming, and strode away from the shelter to ship's bridge. While the replanning of the strike went ahead without any input from the Air Officer, he 'wept and raged and screamed' before retiring to his personal quarters with the door locked, where he remained sulking. It took some time for a friend, Marine Colonel Julian P Brown[92], who was the Staff Intelligence Officer, to coax him out again to resume his duties in the face of the enemy.[93]

The *Enterprise* SBDs were duly rearmed with 500 pound bombs, an exercise which, after all, caused only a slight delay to the revised schedule, and they began launching at 1512. The attack bearing was 324 degrees, range 265 miles. The new Point Option was made on 315 degrees allowing for a high-speed run at 25 knots. The task force commander's preoccupied air staff continued their cavalier attitude toward Mitscher's staff and did not bother to inform 'Sockem' Soucek of the change of ordnance, so half of *Hornet*'s air group launched without changing over. Spruance later viewed this as an act of insubordination on the part of Mitscher[94], Mitscher, not surprisingly and with far greater justice, saw it as yet another act of incompetence on the part of Spruance's team. Mitscher's men looked for the enemy on a bearing of 325 degrees True, at 240 miles range[95], and nobody could blame Ring for the difference this time! In the end, it did not matter. No TF-16 aircraft found that imaginary Japanese carrier, but they *did* attack the enemy!

---

91. Thomas B. Buell, *The Quiet Warrior.*
92. Colonel Julian Brown, from Belmont, Massachusetts. who, as a young marine captain had won a Navy Cross with the 2nd Marine Brigade in Nicaragua in 1927, was not one to condone such hysteria from a friend and colleague. They had served together on Halsey's staff from the beginning of the Pacific War. Brown told Barde that, although Browning was 'a brilliant officer with a great command of the English language and how to use it', he was, nonetheless, 'a very difficult person. Temperamental. Halsey was the only one who could handle him.'
93. Major F. G. Sandford, Jr, later wrote how such a 'frenzied approach to fanatical obsessions destroy the cohesion and teamwork essential to the accomplishment of his own goals'. Such a person, Sandford observed, 'eventually destroys himself', and that is what, ultimately, Browning did. (Major F. G. Sandford, Jr, letter '*Death of a Captain*' in *Proceedings*, March/April 1986, US Naval Institute, Annapolis.
94. The 1,000 pound bomb loads actually came to Spruance's attention when, at the end of the mission, a pair of *Hornet*'s SBDs made emergency landings aboard *Enterprise*.
95. USS *Hornet*, Secret *Report of Action – 4–6 June 1942*, dated 13 June, 1942. CV8/A16-3, Serial 0018, OF10/Ld.

The One That Got Away!

Just how elusive fast-moving warships could prove to be, if well handled, was demonstrated that day by the Japanese destroyer *Tanikaze*.[96] She was a 2,003-ton ship of the powerful new *Kagero* class, the ultimate expression of the *tokugata* or 'special type' that had begun with the *Fubuki* class ships. *Tanikaze* was the latest refinement of the type and had been constructed by the Fujinagata shipbuilding yard at Osaka. She had been launched on 1 November 1940, and when completed was 364 feet, carrying six of the dual-purpose 50 calibre guns in three twin mounts, one forward and two aft, capable of elevating to 75 degrees to engage aircraft targets, along with four dedicated 25 mm anti-aircraft guns and eight torpedo tubes in two twin mountings for the feared 24 inch torpedoes. When built she was considered the 'last word' in destroyer design and her 52,000 shp engines could drive her lean hull through the water at 35 knots. They were to prove themselves that day. She had a crew of 239 officers and men and was under the command of Commander Motoi Katsumi.[97]

When she had run her trials she had been allocated to DesDiv 17, part of DesRon 1, belonging to the 1st Fleet. Hitherto the *Tanikaze* had had a very busy war, having been part of the escort for the *Kidō Butai*'s opening attack on Pearl Harbor on 7 December 1941, the attacks by *Hiryū* and *Soryū* on Wake island between 21 and 23 December; the strike on Rabaul on 20 January 1942 and the subsequent landings at Kavieng, the attack on Port Darwin on 19 February, and the strike on Tjilatjap on 5 March. On 7 March she had formed part of the covering force when the battleships *Kongo* and *Haruna* conduced a powerful bombardment of Christmas Island. After a pause she had been part of the screen for the Nagumo force that had routed the Royal Navy in the Indian Ocean in April.

Following this intense period of high-speed steaming *Tanikaze* had been docked for an overhaul at Kure navy yard from 27 April in readiness for the Midway operation. Refitted as new, she again formed part of the carriers' escort and sailed with the 1st *Kidō Butai* from Hiroshima on 27 May. Aboard her was a 20-year-old signalman, Masashi Shibata[98], who had joined the navy at the tender age of sixteen and, after studying signals at Kure and seamanship at Yokosuka naval schools, and training service aboard a battleship of the fleet, had been assigned to the *Tanikaze* in May 1942.

Shibata's duties aboard the destroyer included standing watches, keeping the ship's log and acting as signalman for semaphore flag and lamp signals, with the added duty of ship's bugler, during which he blew the various sound commands via the tannoy system. His battle station was on the starboard side of the ship's bridge, at the 12 cm telescope. He was later to describe conditions aboard the *Tanikaze* as close-knit, 'like a family,' with the crew completely united with her captain. Shibata later made a record of his experiences, which Clayton Fisher kindly made available to me, and from it we can experience just what it was like to be on the receiving end of a dive-bombing attack at Midway.[99]

Around noon on the 5 June, the second day of the battle, our forces had lost most of their aircraft, so we rejoined the Main Force under Admiral Yamamoto, the C-in-C. For the time being we thought that now we were safe. Then we received a semaphore message from the flagship, the battleship *Yamato*, ordering the *Tanikaze* to return to the *Hiryū* and rescue any survivors and then to sink the *Hiryū* if she was still afloat.[100] Only the *Tanikaze* was sent on this mission, which we considered suicidal. However, we

---

96. *Tanikaze* poetically translates as 'Wind from the mountain to the Valley'.

97. Commander Moto Katsumi (1899–1944). Entered Etajima 1917. Specialized in torpedo warfare. 1941, appointed in command *Tanikaze*. 1944 KIA.

98. Masashi Shibata (1922-2002) b. Chiba Province 1922. Enlisted in IJN 1938 and served aboard *Tanikaze* during most of the battles of the Pacific War, including Midway and Santa Cruz. When *Tanikaze* was sunk in the Sibutu Passage, near Tawi Tawi, 90 miles south-west of Basilan by the US submarine *Harder* (SS-257) on 9 June 1944, 114 of her crew were killed. There were 126 survivors rescued by her sister ship, the destroyer *Urakaze*, including her captain, Lieutenant-Commander Ikeda (who died of his wounds two days later) and Shibata, who was also badly wounded. After the war Shibata established his own very successful company in Osaka, which provided specialized services in soil erosion using small trees, plants and other methods, like netting. The

company leased land in Oregon to grow these trees and plants for their seeds, which were shipped back to Japan, as land there was too expensive for the purpose. In 1991 Shibata and his wife visited California and met up with three of his former enemies from Bombing Squadron 8, Captain Roy Gee, Commander Clayton Fisher and Commander Don Adams, and their wives at the Hotel del Coronado. Shibata presented his hosts with a small-scale model of the *Tanikaze*; they in turn presented him with a small pair of naval aviators Gold Wings. Shibata donated money for World War II memorials for both Japanese and Americans on some of the battle areas in the Pacific. He died of cancer aged eighty.

99. Masashi Shibata, *The Destroyer Tanikaze Returns From 'The Sea of Death'*. I have slightly amended the original text, but only edited it in order to make more correct sense in the English language; no facts have been tampered with.

100. The signal actually read: 'According to reconnaissance by *Hōshō* plane at 0720, the *Hiryū* was burning in position FU

223

were unable to locate *Hiryū*. The Captain decided that *Hiryū* must have already sunk[101] and so we reversed course to rejoin the Main Force.

Suddenly a lookout shouted, 'Enemy Aircraft, 130 degrees!' I quickly took my binoculars and saw about thirty aircraft. The General Quarters alarm was sounded for the crew to take their anti-aircraft battle stations. Captain Katsumi addressed the crew over the ship's PA system saying: 'We have fought well up to now, but this time we should be prepared to die with dignity.' We hastened to our battle stations.

In fact, both *Enterprise* and *Hornet* had finally launched some fifty-eight SBDs, thirty-two and twenty-six respectively, but two *Hornet* aircraft aborted the mission. The first mixed group, totalling thirty-two, dive-bombers from VB-3, VB-5, VB-6 and VS-6, set off in staggered sections from between 1512 to 1543, to attack a force of two battleships, one carrier, two heavy cruisers and five destroyers in response to the misleading series of PBY reports received that morning. Half the group formed a scouting line at low altitude while the remainer climbed to an altitude of 18,000 feet. Lieutenant DeWitt Shumway was acting CEAG and Lieutenant-Commander Stanhope Ring was finally back in the air as CHAG for this mission, with Ensign Benjamin Tappan[102] as his wingman, heading eleven VS-8 dive-bombers, with five more VS-8 aircraft along with three more from VS-8, due to follow.[103] Lieutenant-Commander Rodee was also due to follow on behind, leading *Hornet*'s second phalanx of ten VS-8 aircraft and five of VB-8. The *Hornet*'s action report states that these were armed with 500 pound bombs (according to Spruance's wishes) but Rodee was to claim many years later that they carried 1,000-pounders.[104]

The *Enterprise* group recorded that they continued on course 324 degrees true for 265 miles without making contact. The ceiling was 13,000 feet, with heavy overcast and general hazy visibility. Course was then changed to 230 degrees true and then to 150 degrees true and a '*Katori* class cruiser' was seen on course 310 degrees upon which the SBDs climbed to 11,000 feet to gain attack altitude.[105]

Both carrier's aircraft searched diligently for the non-existent enemy carrier, Ring's force, up at 18,000 feet, passing over *Tanikaze* at 1715, but dismissing her as 'A lone cruiser on course 210'[106], and not worthy of their attentions. Ring was to note how they had received notification that an enemy carrier was 'disappearing to the westward into a front'. He continued:

We searched to the extreme range of 325 miles from *Hornet* but discovered nothing except one light cruiser. On the way out on the search we flew over the scene of the 4 June attack on Japanese CVs and observed many survivors in the water. Since the search for the carrier proved negative we returned to attack the CL, which was about 275 miles from our task force. Although AA fire was neither excessive nor uncomfortably accurate, the dive-bombing attack was a fizzle. I never saw a ship go through such radical maneuvers at such high speed as did that Jap.[107]

However, after casting about in vain, Ring, not surprisingly, was loathe to return empty-handed yet again, and decided to attack this 'cruiser' for want of anything more worthwhile. He was later joined by Shumway's force, nine SBDs from VS-6 and seven more from VS-5, flying some 5,000 feet lower than Ring. In position 33° 00N, 177° 00E, they commenced their dives.

In the words of *Hornet*'s official report, at 1810 'Blue aircraft ordered to attack by the *Hornet* Air Group Commander. *Hornet* group attacked, followed by *Enterprise* group. Target increased speed to 25 knots, fired

---

RO RI 43. A number of survivors were on deck. Investigate condition and take off survivors'. Decrypted Japanese ('Orange') intercept, indexed under ship's name *Hōshō*, Record Group 38, Records of the Chief of Naval Operations, Translations of Intercepted Enemy Radio Traffic and Miscellaneous World War II Documentation, 1940–45, Entry 344, Box 1299, held at National Archives at College Park, Maryland.

101. The *Hiryū* finally went down some time between 0907 and 0915, having been torpedoed by the destroyer *Makigumo* four hours earlier, unknowingly leaving thirty-nine survivors aboard her.

102. Captain Benjamin Tappan, Jr.

103. In the event this second group of *Hornet* SBDs (five of VB-8 from the hangar deck and three of VS-8 still toting 1,000

pound bombs), failed to make contact by 1720 and returned to the carrier with their bombs, landing back aboard her at 1830.

104. Robert Elmer Barde, *The Battle of Midway: A Study in Command.*

105. USS *Enterprise – Air Battle of the Pacific, June 4–6, 1942,* dated 13 June 1942, pp 6. NARA declassified NND968133, held at National Archives, College Park, Maryland.

106. Confidential *War Diary, Bombing Squadron Eight,* from: 1 June, 1942 to 30 June, 1942 to Chief of Naval Operations (Office of Naval Records and Library). (SC)AIV-1/FVB8, Doc No 62849, 384, held at National Archives, College Park, Maryland.

107. Stanhope Ring, *Lost Letter.*

Table 19: VB-8's SBD Attack on *Tanikaze*, 5 June 1942

Sequence	Pilot	Crew	Estimate
1	Lt-Cdr Robin Ruffin Johnson	Joseph G. McCoy, ACRM	Miss wide
	Ens. Phillip F. Grant	Robert H. Rider, ARM2c	Miss wide
	Ens. William Douglas Carter	Oral L. Moore, ARM2c	Miss wide
2	Lt. James Everett Vose, Jr.	Joseph Yewonishon, ARM2c	Miss wide
	Lt. John Joseph Lynch (MO)	Wilbur L. Woods, ARM1c	Port side astern – 100 ft.
	Ens. Roy Phillip Gee	Donald L. Canfield, ARM1c	100 ft astern
3	Lt (jg) Fred Leeson Bates (EO)	Clyde S. Montensen, ARM1c	Not recorded
	Ens. James Austin Riner, Jr	Floyd A. Kilmer, ARM2c	Not recorded
	Ens. Arthur Caldwell Cason, Jr	Alfred D. Wells, ARM3c	Not recorded
4	Lt Alfred Bland Tucker III (XO)	Champ T. Stuart, ARM1c	25 ft directly ahead
	Ens. Gus G. Bebas	Alfred W. Ringressy, Jr, RM3c	Port Quarter – 100 ft
	Ens. Don Dee Adams	John B. Broughton, Jr, ARM2c	Close astern – 50 ft
5	Ens. Frank E. Christofferson (NO)	Barkley V. Poorman, ARM2c	Not recorded
	Ens. Joe Wiley King	Thomas M. Walsh, ARM3c	Not recorded
CHAG	Lt-Cdr Stanhope Cotton Ring	Arthur M. Parker, ARM2c	No drop
Section	Ens. Clayton Evan Fisher	George E. Ferguson, ARM3c	100 ft astern
	Ens. Benjamin Tappen, Jr	James H. Black, Jr ARM2c	50 ft astern

Table 20: VS-6's and VB-6's SBD Attack on *Tanikaze*, 5 June 1942

Sequence	Pilot	Crew	Aircraft
VS-6. 1	Lt Frank Antony Patriarca (EO)	Jack Richard Badgley, ACRM (AA)	6-S-13
	Ens. William Robinson Pittman	Floyd Delbert Adkins, AMM2c	6-S-16
	Ens. Richard Alonzo Jaccard	Porter William Pixley, RM3c	6-S-11
2	Lt (jg) Norman Jack Kleiss	John Warren Snowden, RM3c	6-S-7
	Ens. Eldor E. Rodenburg	Thomas James Bruce, Sea2c	6-S-9
	Ens. James Campbell Dexter	Donald L. Hoff, RM3c	6-S-18
3	Ens. Ried Wentworth Stone	William Hart Bergin, RM1c	6-S-2
	Ens. Vernon Larson Micheel	John Dewey Dance, RM3c	6-S-17
	Ens. Clarence Earl Vammen, Jr.	Milton Wayne W. Clark, AMM2c	6-S-1
VB-6. 1	Lt Lloyd Addison Smith (XO)	Hermann Hull Caruthers, AMM2c	6-B-4
	Lt (jg) Edwin John Kroeger	Gail Wayne Halterman, RM3c	6-B-2
	Ens. Lewis Alexander Hopkins	Edward Rutledge Anderson, RM3c	6-B-12
2	Lt Harvey Peter Lanham	Edward Joseph Garaudy, ARM1c	6-B-10
	Lt (jg) Edward Lee Anderson	Walter George Chochalousek, ARM1c	6-B-1
	Ens. Arthur Leo Rausch	Harold Lewellen Jones, AOM3c	N/A

anti-aircraft batteries continuously and manoeuvred radically and skilfully. No direct hits were made but there were many near misses'.[108] It was also recorded that 'it is estimated that 5 500-lb bombs landed within 100 feet of the target'.[109] Lieutenant-Commander Johnson reported that during the dive, 'windshields fogged badly. Sights fogged completely and it was impossible to use them.' The end result was 'many near misses, one paint scraper astern'. Ring's own attack was again a frustrating one, as he overran the target and had to go round again, attacking last, and even

---

108. *Ibid.*
109. USS *Hornet* – Secret, *Report of Action – 4–6 June 1942*, dated 13 June, 1942. CV8/A16-3, Serial 0018, OF10/Ld, pp 5. Lieutenant Penland of VB6 was critical of both the mission and the accuracy of his unit. With regard the former, he wrote 'An attack on enemy forces by SBD dive bombers is not feasible when their position is not known accurately and when the enemy is more than 200 miles distant. This group departed at 1730 and searched for the enemy until 2030, at which time the attack was made. The last confirmed position of the enemy force was 1000'. With regard the embarrassing lack of success he stated it demonstrated that

then accidentally pressed the pilot's microphone on the throttle handle (a device installed to aid formation flying), rather than the bomb-release button, which was mounted forward of the throttle handle, during his dive. Nor did Ring utilize the alternative emergency bomb release handle to do the job.

While Ring remained as an impotent observer of this target, the rest of the group made attacks in succession, but all missed. Tappen left his leader and made a belated dive into the deepening dusk. He clearly recalled the flash of the destroyer's main guns in the gathering gloom. Because he was some way behind the others, the *Tanikaze*'s two after-most turrets could devote themselves to him alone and a near miss sent shrapnel through his cowling, shutting his engine air intakes, which quickly shut down the engine itself. Tappen hastily switched to low blower but, distracted, his bomb missed astern. After the *Hornet* team had made their attacks it was the turn of VS-6 and VB-6 from *Enterprise*.

'Dusty' Kleiss' recorded, 'The little devil fired everything he had at us, put on full speed (about 40 kts.), zigzagging nicely, and was most difficult to hit. I saw several close misses, but no hits. One of the pilots said he saw a direct hit. Anyhow, some of the plates may have been sprung.'[110]

What was it like on the receiving end?

A starboard lookout shouted, 'Many dive bombers approaching from the starboard quarter'. The captain ordered, 'Port helm, maximum speed,' and then, 'Open fire!' and all *Tanikaze*'s guns began to roar. One-by-one, more than thirty dive-bombers attacked the *Tanikaze,* dropping their bombs. Huge columns of water, higher than our masthead, surrounded the *Tanikaze,* although no bombs hit her directly.

We needed someone to watch the bombers and tell the Captain when to change course and make evasive turns. I volunteered to be that lookout. I climbed out of a window hatch on the ship's bridge and leaned my body backward so I could see the sky and prepare for the next wave of dive bombers.[111]

As each dive bomber approached, I shouted, 'Enemy bomber, Right, or enemy bomber, Left.' Captain Katsumi stood in front of the compass and gave commands to turn each time I shouted the aircraft positions. From my elevated position above the bridge I could see the pilots in their cockpits as some of them pulled out of the dives at quite low height. I can recall that some had goggles and white mufflers. I was struck by the appearance of those American pilots with their red faces and large noses, but I could also see the fighting spirit of the 'Yankees'.

No sooner had we again felt safe after the dive-bombers had departed, than the B-17s from Midway began an attack on us in two waves. Thanks again to the superb ship handling of our captain, we again survived unscathed. We were then attacked again by dive-bombers from either the *Hornet* or the *Enterprise*. I had no time to count the aircraft, but again there seemed to be more than thirty.

One of the bombs damaged the stern of our ship, close to the waterline and the after starboard side of the hull began to leak and had to be patched from the inside. Some bomb fragments came inboard and penetrated the #2 gun mount, igniting the magazine. All the six gun-crew were burnt to death. In compensation the gunnery team of #3 mount scored a direct hit on one dive-bomber and it fell into the sea astern.[112]

We had fired off almost all of our ammunition and our guns so overheated from the constant firing that, for a time, they were unable to shoot. Later, all the crew assisted with moving about ninety shells from the damaged gun mount. Our faces were blackened by gun smoke and our hands and clothes were soaked with sweat and covered with smoke dust.[113]

The sun was beginning to set. I never felt a sunset

---

pilots required much more practice in the art, and he recommended that each pilot drop at least five bombs per week to maintain proficiency. (J. R. Penland, Lieutenant, U.S. Navy, Commander Bombing Squadron Six, Report, Action with Enemy. Declassified NND968133, NARA 4/22, held at National Archives, College Park, Maryland.)

110. N. J. Kleiss, VS-6 *Log of the War*. Actually the *Tanikaze* was fast, but not *that* fast, and she could not make 40 knots; there was no direct hit and no plates were sprung.

111. The newer classes of Japanese destroyers of the 'special type', all had fully enclosed bridges, unlike British destroyers of this period, which had open-top bridges. This meant less weather and injury protection for the Royal Navy bridge personnel,

but the trade-off was that they enjoyed unlimited visibility by day and night, which other nations' destroyers lacked.

112. This was a confirmed 'kill', the aircraft concerned being the mount of Lieutenant Samuel Adams and 27-year-old ARM1c Joseph James Karrol of VB-5. Although 'Dusty' Kleiss noted in his log at the time that, 'Lieutenant Adams landed in water, was recovered', this was later proved to be incorrect and both aircrew were killed. (N. J. Kleiss VS-6 *Log of the War*).

113. In fact Shibata's memory played him false after almost half a century and he got the order of attack rather mixed up. Actually the *Tanikaze* was first attacked at 1636 by five B-17s, which achieved nothing but misses on either bow; then,

could be such a blessing. The Captain offered us all cider and dry bread. I will never forget how tasty that bread was. We worked all through the night to repair the damage and tend to the wounded. In the morning, around 0600, we buried the bodies of our six dead shipmates at sea. I played the bugle as a tribute to their memories. I could not stop my tears. I felt fortunate to be one of the of the crew of this honourable ship, *Tanikaze*, and to have assisted Captain Katsumi at his side on the bridge during her historic fight.

Meanwhile a disconsolate VB-8 made their way back to base unrewarded yet again. Ring recorded:

Group doctrine had called for individual return rather than complete rendezvous. This was a mistake, perhaps, in the absence of air opposition, but under the circumstances was essential since diminishing fuel supply precluded wasting time and fuel to get the group together, Ens. White of VS-8 joined me on the return trip. *Hornet* Group had never qualified in night landings aboard, which fact would be expected to cause some concern under the circumstances. Actually, the night landings were themselves made without incident or difficulty. One plane, of VS-8, Lt. Davis pilot, ran out of gasoline in the groove and made a water landing, but personnel were picked up by plane guard destroyer.

It proved fortunate for me that Ens. White had joined company because when I lowered my wheels preparatory to landing, he, by frantic signalling to me got across the idea that only one wheel was extended. My first thought was that a fragment of shell from the AA fire of the cruiser had damaged an hydraulic line

but after a bit of violent maneuvering both wheels extended properly.

The official report said '2030 attack was completed and return started. 2101 sunset. Due to change in *Enterprise* YE setup *which was not promulgated*[114] and the fact that the range of the *Enterprise* YE is greater than that of the *Hornet*, five airplanes had difficulty in locating the *Hornet*'[115] In the end most pilots landed between 1930 and 2030, but three[116] were forced to put down on the *Enterprise* at 1945.

Behind that bald statement lies some trauma. Clayton Fisher explained:

We did not have enough fuel to waste trying to form a formation so we returned to the carrier strung out in a long column. We were running out of daylight and knew we would have to make night carrier landings. The *Hornet* pilots had only made one night carrier landing on our shake down cruise.

Some of the *Hornet* pilots became lost because they could not pick up the weak *Hornet* radio homing device. We had been briefed that the coded signal from both carriers would be the same but they were different. Some of the *Hornet* pilots could only hear the *Enterprise* stronger homing signals and used the wrong course to the task force. The *Hornet* turned on a powerful searchlight and pointed it to a vertical position to provide a homing beacon. A couple of planes ran out of gas in their landing approaches and were rescued by a destroyer.

Commander Don Adams from Bombing Squadron Eight was preparing to ditch his plane while he still had engine power. His radioman spotted a light and Don was finally able see the

---

at 1808 by eleven SBDs of VB-8, led by CHAG, who identified her as a 'light cruiser.' The second dive-bombing attack was by thirty-two SBDs against 'a *Katori* class light cruiser', in the attack sequence first the *Hornet* group and then the *Enterprise* group. Finally, from 1845 onward, thirteen further B-17s from Midway dropped a total of fifty-six 500 pound bombs on a, 'large cruiser', inevitably claiming to have scored three direct hits and four near misses, which again was a total fabrication. However, the *Tanikaze*'s remaining two 5 inch turrets excelled themselves and the flyers reported 'heavy' defensive fire. Also lost in this attack was one of the Flying Fortresses. This machine, *City of San Francisco*, had accidentally dropped her bomb-bay mounted fuel tank along with her bombs during the attack. Her pilot, Captain Robert S Porter, left the formation and was followed by the squadron commander, who last saw it heading for Midway. At 2330 Porter radioed, 'out of gas and

landing' but no trace of the bomber or her crew was ever found. Recent accounts which credit *Tanikaze* directly with her destruction are incorrect. Another B-17 ran out of fuel and ditched 50 miles out from Midway, the impact killing the radio operator, Sergeant F. E. Durrett, but the rest of the crew were rescued. Nor was this all: one of the returning SBDs, crewed by Lieutenant Ray Davis and ARM1c Ralph Phillips, was also forced to ditch in the subsequent night landing, both aircrew being fished out of the sea by the destroyer *Aylwin* (DD-355). Therefore, by both directly and indirectly bringing about the destruction of two American dive-bombers and two heavy bombers, this one small Japanese warship amply avenged the loss of six of her crew that day.

114. My italics. Another Browning omission?
115. *Hornet* War Diary.
116. 8-B-2, 8-B-4 and 8-B-8.

Hornet. He was astern of her, made a straight-in landing approach and ran out of gas when his tail-hook engaged the arresting gear wire.[117]

Rodee's force had failed to make an attack at all, and VS-8 under Johnson became separated. For six of the VS-6 pilots[118], this was their first night landing; moreover these pilots had no previous experience whatever of night flying in the Dauntless and had no night field carrier landing instruction. Nonetheless they all got down safely, although Ensign Ammen did so aboard the *Hornet*. Kleiss summed up all their feelings about this mission. 'This flight not worth the gas, bombs, and loss of a plane'.[119] Rodee later expressed the opinion that his sortie was 'futile'.

What Size Pickle-barrel?

Flush with the headlines like those in the *New York Times*, proclaiming their omnipotence[120], the USAAC publicly radiated the supreme confidence of having been proven right all along.[121] The heavy bomber had prevailed, just as Billy Mitchell[122] had proved it would twenty years earlier. Underneath the ballyhoo and razzmatazz however, there was considerable doubt and honest reflection that perhaps not everything had gone quite as the Army publicity machine[123] and their ever-willing acolytes, the newspaper reporters, were saying it had. The new commander of the 7th Air Force, Willis Hale, was to do nothing to correct these totally false

---

117. Clayton Fisher in an address to the Victory at Midway Celebration aboard the nuclear-powered aircraft carrier *John B. Stennis* (CVN-74) secured alongside Naval Air Station North Island, 29 June 2001, and given to the author for reproduction.

118. Dexter, Jaccard, Micheel, Pittman, Rodenburg and Vammen.

119. N. J. Kleiss, VS-6, *Log of the War.*

120. The lead story in the 12 June edition of the *New York Times* was by Robert Trumbull, who thundered out headlines like 'Big Bombers Won' and 'Carriers Targets' over a story consisting entirely of fictitious USAAC achievements. It was parroted by similar headlines in the local Honolulu newspapers, which claimed the B17s had smashed the Japanese carriers, and these fables greeted the returning navy flyers on their return to Pearl.

121. Mitchell's allegations, although they benefited by the originality of their method, and the predictable media adulation of the 'new' apparently triumphing over the 'old' in the bomber-versus-battleship debate that raged between the wars, were built on sand. The heavy bomber was *never* to sink a moving battleship, nor a carrier either, at sea during the entire war. More, the whole foundation of Mitchell's argument was based upon a series of trials during which he circumvented the rules and treated it merely as a publicity stunt rather than a serious experiment. The whole farce was exposed many years ago see Gene T. Zimmerman, '*More Fiction than Fact – The Sinking of the Ostfriesland'.*

122. Major-General William 'Billy' Mitchell (1879–1936). b. 29 December 1879 at Nice, France, son of the wealthiest man in Wisconsin, Senator John L. Mitchell. Raised at West Allis, Milwaukee, Wisconsin. Educated Columbian College. 1898 enlisted as an 18-year old private for Spanish-American War, seeing service in Cuba. Commissioned in US Army Signal Corps along Mexican border. 1906 instructor at Army Signal School, Fort Leavenworth. Duty in Philippines and Alaska. 1910 joined General Staff aged 32. 1915 joined Aeronautical Division, US Signal Corps which predated Army Air Service. 1916, paid for private flying lessons in Virginia as the army thought him too old at 38 to train. Promoted to lieutenant-colonel. 1917 World War I to France under General Pershing, on liaison duties with British and French. 1918, September, planned and commanded Allied air forces during battle for Santi-Mihiel salient. Promoted to brigadier-general. Awarded DSC, DSM and other medals. 1919 Deputy Director Air Service. Army Corps of Engineers after the war. Increasingly in dispute with superiors and made vehement attacks on War and Navy Departments. 1921 series of bombing tests against captured German warships, starting with submarines and destroyers working up to battleship *Ostfriesland*, which was attacked while moored and stationary and in a non-secured condition until sunk, contrary to the agreed rules. Also sank the old 1898 battleship *Alabama* (BB-8) under similar conditions. 1922 in Europe met with Italian advocate of strategic bombing Giulio Douhet author of *The Command of the Air*, and promulgated that doctrine relentlessly. 1924 duty in Hawaii, followed by tour in Far East. Predicted war with Japan and attack on Pearl Harbor. Harangued Lampert Committee and 1925, in his reverted rank of colonel under peacetime cutbacks, Air Officer at San Antonio Garrison, Texas. Publicly attacked navy and army senior officers over loss of airship *Shenandoah* in September 1925 with charges of 'criminal negligence'. Was brought before court martial on orders of President Calvin Coolidge. Found guilty of insubordination and suspended from duty for five years without pay. Resigned commission on 1 February 1926 and retired to Virginia. Spent the rest of his life campaigning for an independent air service, writing included *Winged Defense* (1925) and *Skyways* (1930). Died of influenza and heart condition in New York hospital on 19 February 1936. Interred at Forest Home Cemetery, Milwaukee. The North American B-24 medium bomber (a half-hearted type he despised); and the General Mitchell International Airport at Milwaukee were both named in his honour. 1946 posthumously awarded Congressional Gold Medal of Honor, 2004 posthumously commissioned as major-general. Biographies include Alfred H. Hurley, *Billy Mitchell: Crusader for Air Power* and Burke Davis, *The Billy Mitchell Affair.*

123. Most of these headlines resulted from press releases to Associated Press and from a KGU radio interview, networked in the United States via NBC. The originator of most of this fiction was most probably Major-General Howard C. Davidson. This worthy claimed nine B-17s scored five hits, one probable hit and four near misses and left two enemy ships aflame – but only nine of 36 bombs

228

stories; indeed, under his reign relations with the Navy further deteriorated.[124]

The summary of operations by Brigadier General Howard Davidson[125], Commander, Hawaii, covered a wide spectrum. On attacking ships he wrote:

No great difficulty was experienced in hitting surface ships at altitudes of 4,000 to 25,000 feet.[126] The Japanese apparently have the reverse of a bombsight mounted on their surface craft and can estimate the time at which the bombardier making his run will have to release his bombs.[127] At this point the ship begins to maneuver, adding to the difficulty of hitting it by precision bombing. In order to aid in this computation enemy fighter airplanes appeared to be stationed above the fleet for the purpose of giving the exact altitude of our bombers to the ships of the fleet. This aided them in calculating the time of bomb release and also was a great aid in antiaircraft fire. The antiaircraft gunfire of the Japanese fleet was heavy but

---

landed anywhere near the ships and no hits were scored. Unabashed Davidson then claimed a dozen hits and an enemy cruiser (the US submarine *Graph*) sunk on 4 June, while stating the four B-26s scored two hits – which, as we have seen was quite untrue. All this misinformation was given official backing well after the war by the Office of Information Services, which in their *Brief History of Seventh Air Force, 1940–45*, OIS, Washington, DC, 1947, repeated the claims that the B-17s had made, '22 direct hits and six probables' on ships of the Japanese fleet. The 1979 history by Kenneth C. Rust, *Seventh Air Force Story . . . in World War II,* finally came clean but still insisted that the heavy bombers made 'a significant contribution' to the battle.

124. Brigadier-General Willis Henry Hale (1893–1961). b. 7 January 1893 Pittsburg, Kansas. 1912 graduated from Kansas State College. Became instructor at Culver Military Academy, then Instructor at New York Military Academy. 1913, third lieutenant Philippine Constabulary during Oto Campaign and at Panay Island, awarded campaign ribbon. 1917, commissioned into US Army, 15th Infantry, China. 1918 to France with American Expeditionary Force (AEF), aide to Major-General Harry C. Hale, CO 84th Division (his uncle). 1923, attended Advanced Flying Training School, Kelly Field, and earned his wings. Spent most of his subsequent career with heavy or medium bombers. 1924, November, transferred to Air Service. 1928, June, graduated ACTS (Air Corps Training School), Langley Field. 1934, June, graduated from Command and General Staff School, Fort Leavenworth. 1937, June, graduated from Army War College, Washington, DC. 1938–40, General HQ, Air Force, Washington, DC. 1941, CoS 3rd Air Force, MacDill Field. 1942, January, appointed to VII Bomber Command. 1942, 20 June, appointed i/c 7th Air Force to April 1944. 1943, quarrelled with his superior, an experienced naval aviator, the dour Vice-Admiral John H. 'Genial John' Hoover. 1944, March, after death of Lieutenant-General Millard F. Harmon, became Deputy Commander 20th Air Force. Task Force-59 (COMAIRFORWARD) at Saipan, Isley Field, then Iwo Jima. 1949, October, as major-general commanded 9th Air Force, Langley Field until August 1950. 1950, July, CO 1st Air Force, Atlantic, until February 1951. Died at San Francisco 25 March 1961. See Major S. H. E. Peter, *Hale's Handful . . . Up from the Ashes: The Forging of the Seventh Air Force from the Ashes of Pearl Harbor to the Triumph of VJ-day,* Air University Press, Maxwell AFB, 2000.

125. Major-General Howard Calhoun Davidson (1890–1984) b. Wharton, Texas 1890. Graduated from US Military Academy West Point, and appointed second lieutenant of infantry on 12 June 1913. 22nd Infantry at Texas City until November 1914, then Naco, Arizona, to February 1915 and Douglas, Arizona, to July 1915. Transferred to 24th Infantry in Philippines to 1915, transferred to 27th Infantry. July 1916 first lieutenant. Aviation Section, Signal Corps, attended Aviation School, San Diego, graduating as junior military aviator, an 'Early Bird'. 1st Aero Squadron, Columbus, New Mexico on Mexican border patrol and punitive expedition 1916–17. Captain, May 1917 with 3rd Aero Squadron. Commandant, School of Military Aeronautics, Cornell University. World War 1 service in France, Personnel Officer Air Service HQ Paris and Tours. 2nd Aviation Instruction Center to August 1918 and major (temporary) June 1918. Corps Air Service Commander, VII Army Corps 1918 to April 1919. Student, Sorbonne, Paris April – July 1919. Reverted to captain October 1919. McCook Field, Dayton various administrative posts. Promoted major July 1920. September 1921 to Army Air Service. Assistant Military Attaché London, July 1922 to 1926. Commanded Bolling Field, January 1928 – August 1932, then Air Corps Tactical School, Maxwell Field, to 1933. Instruction course Fort Leavenworth. Graduated 1935. Promoted lieutenant-colonel August 1935. CO 19th Bombardment Group at Rockwell and March Fields. Office of Air Corps, DC 1936. Promoted colonel (temporary) August 1939. Army War College 1940–41. Commanded 14th Pursuit Wing, Wheeler Field, Hawaii. Promoted brigadier-general (temporary) April 1941. Commanding General Hawaiian Interceptor Command to December 1941. Commanding General 7th Air Force to November 1942. CO USAAF Technical Training Command, Gulfport. August 1943 assumed command 10th Air Force after Generalissimo Chiang Kai-shek objected to Major-General Bissell. In command of Eastern Air Command, Strategic Air Force, at New Delhi, India, to August 1945. Promoted major-general (temporary) January 1944. Retired 30 June 1946. Died 7 November 1984.

126. They dropped a total of 346 bombs, claimed to have sunk one carrier (*Soryū*) and one destroyer, and to have damaged another carrier (*Akagi,* one battleship, (*Haruna*), no less than five heavy cruisers and two troopships. In fact, they hit nothing at all.

127. The 'reverse bomb sight' was in fact just common sense observation. In that sense Japanese warships did have such equipment. They *all* did, their captain's brains!

ineffective. The only serious hit obtained by the guns was on the wing of a B-17. On the other hand, the fire of automatic weapons was quite accurate and caused some losses.[128]

A rather more sober (and accurate) assessment was given at a lower level included in the same report.

It is apparent to everyone that an alert skipper can maneuver out from under any single level bombardier's salvo dropped from medium or high altitude unless pure luck is on the bombardier's side and a wild bomb hits.[129] On the other hand it is equally practical and mathematically correct that given sufficient high-level bombers dropping in pattern, no surface craft can maneuver from under and at least one hit will be assured. To determine this pattern and to be able to provide one readily, requires a large amount of training by units operating against a maneuvering target. It is recommended that the service of a target towed by a naval vessel maneuvering violently be provided this command for training purposes along these lines.[130] Identification of Japanese carriers is facilitated by recognition of the 'rising sun' painted on the flight deck.

"That's what you say."

One distressing feature of USAAC's way of operating was their total failure to admit the slightest criticism. Admiral Layton found this in some of the post-battle analysis. During one such session the question of the sinking of one of the heavy cruisers of the Japanese CruDiv 7 came up.

Layton recounted one bruising encounter with an USAAC representative in full cry:

The Air Corps was very belligerent about the sinking of one of the ships of CruDiv 7 and insisted they had sunk the ship – which I told them was not borne out by the facts, because we had information at that time that the ship was still afloat and was *en route* to Japan. He said, 'I thought you'd say that' and at that point, he produced a picture [photograph]. I said, 'Well, in the first place, this is not a battleship, this is a submarine which is making a crash-dive,'[131] 'That's what you say', and things like this, you see.'

It so happened that their photo intelligence was perhaps not as good as the Navy's. It so happened through no fault of their own, they had received some minimal – approximately nil – training in flying over water or of identifying ships from 20,000 feet, and they were not particularly trained for this.[132]

The air force finally admitted this particular mistake in this manner: 'About 1140 on 6 June six B17s made contact with a large submarine that was mistaken for a cruiser, 20 1000 pound demolition bombs were dropped from an altitude of 9500 feet, and photographs of the pattern showed several near misses. The submarine was friendly and not damaged.'[133]

One thing that puzzled the returning navy flyers in the aftermath of the battle was that their own C-in-C, Nimitz, refused to stand up for them in public and expose the USAAC's bragging yarns for the sham that they knew they were. When Rear-Admiral Eller[134] was working on the after-action report, he also came up against this point, but

---

128. Davidson, confidential report, contained in CincPac File A16, *Battle of Midway*. (ADM199/1302, held at National Archives, Kew, London).

129. Although of course, Billy Mitchell had once famously declared that it was easier to hit a ship under way than stationary one!

130. These results only reflected a similar lack of results from the Italian *Regia Aeronautica* against the Royal Navy in the Mediterranean two years earlier, when they were strictly following Douhet's similar principles and conducting mass formation high-level bombing. On 9 July 1940, in the aftermath of the Battle of Calabria, Savoia Marchetti Sm79 and Sm 81 tri-motor bombers from the 11, 34, 35, 36,37, 40, 41 *Stormo* made seventeen deliberate attacks between 1643 and 2110 against the British Mediterranean Fleet. They dropped a total of 514 bombs and failed to score a single hit. See Peter C. Smith, *Action Imminent: Three Studies of the Naval War in the Mediterranean Theatre During 1940*.

131. The photograph was, of course, of the submarine *Grayling*, crash-diving to avoid the bombing on 6 June. This did not

stop the army aviators boasting on the radio, 'We returned to the cruiser and landed a direct hit on him'.

132. Layton interview by Kitchen.

133. Davidson, Confidential report, contained in CincPac File A16, *Battle of Midway*, (ADM199/1302, held at National Archives, Kew, London).

134. Admiral Ernest McNeill 'Judge' Eller (1903–92). b. Marion, Virginia on 23 January 1903. Educated North Wilkesboro High School, and North Carolina State College, Raleigh. 1921, entered US Naval Academy, Annapolis North Carolina. Editor of *Trident* magazine. 4 June 1925, graduated as ensign. 1925–6 served aboard battleship *Utah*, (BB-31) June 1926, Naval Torpedo Station, Newport, Rhode Island. January 1927, service aboard the battleship *Texas* (BB-35) to May 1927. 1927 submariners course at New London, Connecticutt. Feb 1928 served aboard submarines S-33 (ex-*Cachalot*) and then *Utah*, now a demilitarized gunnery ship. April 1932 to 1935 Naval Academy, Department of English and History. 1934 Master of Arts in Psychology from George Washington University. 1935,

revealed that Nimitz's defence was that, to debunk the air force would risk jeopardizing the breaking of the Japanese codes, and that he was just not prepared to do.[135]

Even after Midway had been fought and won, some high-ranking personnel in the USAAC remained hesitant about committing their forces further. Brigadier-General Tinker's brave showing against Wake Island was inspirational, and the B-17s, although total failures as anti-ship weapons, were crewed and flown gallantly enough. But there was still, despite the fact that they were basking in the totally misplaced glory of 'winning' the battle unaided, a reluctance to further commit. Rochefort much later revealed an instance of this, and of how Nimitz, his exhortations failing, resorted to guile to get them to co-operate further. Although Nimitz was perfectly content to let them grab all the head-lines and, much to the irritation of his young SBD aircrews, pointedly refrained from revealing the truth lest the enemy learn from it, he did manage *one* quiet piece of duplicity, which must have given him some measure of quiet satisfaction.

During Rochefort's interview with Commander Kitchen, she asked him whether he could quote any specific incident to illustrate how Nimitz compromised. Rochefort replied with a story about a combined-services meeting after the battle. The question of possible Japanese intentions came up. What were they doing now and had they actually retired or were they regrouping to have another shot? It was suggested that the best thing to do was send out more long-range aircraft to keep up the watch that had proved so successful prior the actual battle. Nimitz spoke to Tinker, asking him just what was available. Tinker told him what he had, including four long-range Consolidated B-24 Liberators. However, if he sent these aircraft out then there would be nothing much left in reserve to defend Hawaii, other than damaged B-17s under repair. Nimitz was convinced the Japanese were not coming back, let alone eyeing Pearl Harbor again after the drubbing they had just had, but he nonetheless wanted every available aircraft out at Midway, just in case. Rochefort recalled how, Nimitz promised Tinker, that, if he sent the heavy bombers back to Midway, he (Nimitz) would turn over the full operational control of all the aircraft aboard the carrier *Saratoga* (which was due to arrive at Pearl from the West Coast, and which would fly off her aircraft to Ewa while the carrier entered harbour), during the entire period of her sojourn at Pearl Harbor. To this Tinker readily agreed.

Admiral Nimitz asked him to get the order under way then. I noticed at the time that the Navy Air man, who I think was Admiral Bellinger, I thought he looked a little bit surprised at the moment, but he said nothing and the conversation went on. They discussed other things. Only well after the request had been given the OK, by which time the heavy bombers were already on their way to Midway, did Nimitz reveal that the *Saratoga* would only be in Pearl for a few brief hours before moving on, after re-embarking her full air group again![136]

Fleet Machine Gun School aboard *Utah* to 1938. Naval Academy again until 1940, September 1940–May 1941, Assistant Naval Attaché, London, and Observer in Royal Navy on radar, anti-aircraft and related information, which he took back to BuOrd, Washington DC. May 1942 to carrier *Saratoga* (CV-3) as Gunnery Officer. 1942–45 Staff of CincPac as Assistant Gunnery and A/S Training Officer, with additional work writing war reports. Awarded Legion of Merit. May 1945 commanded attack transport *Clay* (APA-39) in China and Japan. Awarded Legion of Merit, China Service Medal. December 1945–March 1946, 12th Naval District, Office of Public Information then similar duties at Navy Department from April to July 1946. 1946 Director Public Information with rank of Commodore. August 1948 National War College, then Staff Planning at Joint Chiefs of Staff from June 1949. 1950 Commander, Middle East Force, Persian Gulf-Indian Ocean. May 1951 in command of heavy cruiser *Albany* (CA-123). April 1952 Office of CNO, International Affairs. 1953 hospitalized. April 1954 Retired List. Between 1930 and 1956 authored many article for the USNI *Proceedings* magazine. September 1956 recalled as Director Naval History and Curator Navy Department, DC. Retired on 23 January 1970. Died at his home in Annapolis, of a heart condition on 30 July 1992, aged 89. The Naval Historical Center has the annual Ernest M. Eller Prize in Naval History in his honour.

135. Eller, Oral History, Vol. II, USNI, Annapolis.
136. Rochefort Interview by Kitchen for Oral History, 1969.

Chapter Ten

The Final Blows

Now that the Japanese had lost the last carrier of their fighting quartet, and had finally faced the grim fact that the Americans still apparently had at least two untouched carriers of their own it was time to cut their losses. If they could have closed and grappled with their enemy at close range, there was still ample fight in them, enhanced also by a burning desire for revenge. But too late it was realized that their forces were still too dispersed, too far away to marshal even a token force for air cover. The Americans too, cast off the uncertainties of the previous day and decided that, after all, there were still some easy pickings to be had.

Mikuma's Nemesis

Dawn rose on the morning of the third day of the battle. PBYs were early astir once more from the Midway runway and lagoon. Fresh contact reports came in early and continued; again they were not always accurate. Spruance sent off no less than eighteen SBDs, including six from VS-6, armed with 500 pound bombs, at 0502 to scour a wide arc between 180 and 360 degrees out to 200 miles from him. The first result was a report at 0640 of two heavy cruisers and two destroyers steering south-west at 15 knots, bearing 275 degrees some 400 miles from Midway. A second report five minutes later had them bearing 280 degrees, 435 miles from Midway at 10 knots.

During the forenoon an enemy force was seen retiring to the westward by Ensign William D. Carter, flying Dauntless 8-B-2 from the deck of the *Enterprise,* at about 150 miles range. 'Slim' Moore, his radio operator, called in '1CA, 1CV [instead of CB for battle-cruiser, a verbal phonetic mistake, B sounding like V from his pilot], Lat 29°, 33'N, Long 174° 30'E, course 270°. This caused quite a stir – a carrier said to be part of this force, and although this was considered unlikely, it could not be ignored. Nor was there any mention of damage to the carrier. The *Hornet* launched her air group, at 0730, and employed the 'deferred departure' method of despatching. The group comprised eleven SBD-3s of VB-8 under Lieutenant-Commander Robert R. Johnson and twelve SBDs of VS-8, plus two *Enterprise* dive-bombers, one of VS-5[1] and one of VS-6, both of which had 'parked' aboard *Hornet* overnight, led by Lieutenant-Commander Walter F. Rodee. The whole phalanx was organized by Ring, as CHAG, to search and attack this force. Eight of the SBDs carried 500 pound bombs, the remainder 1,000-pounders. As Japanese carriers were on the menu this force was provided with a fighter escort of eight Wildcat F4F-4s of VF-8[2].

En route to the enemy, Ring recorded, 'I received a CW message from *Hornet*[3] stating that enemy force might consist of cruisers rather than carriers as first reported. In as much as we believed that all enemy carriers had been sunk on 4 June this made sense'.[4] The knowledge that they

---

1. VS-5 aircraft piloted by Lieutenant (jg) William Francis Christie with Alvin A. Sobel, ARM1c; VS-6 aircraft piloted by Ensign Clarence Earl Vammen, Jr, with Milton Wayne Clark, AMM2c.
2. Fighter commander for this sortie was Lieutenant Warren Woodrow Ford, with the Second Division led by Lieutenant (jg) J. F. Sutherland, A-V (N),
3. Strictly speaking from the *Hornet* via the *Enterprise*. Ensign William D. Carter, who had flown the search mission from *Enterprise*, had corrected his 'false' radioed sighting report,

both by message drop and also on his return to the *Hornet*. He told Mitscher that he had radioed 'CV' but had meant to radio 'CB'. This information Mitscher immediately passed over to Spruance's staff for analysis. Browning duly radioed CHAG at 0850 telling him that the target 'may' be a battleship rather than a carrier, but, of course, it was really the *Mikuma*. This further confused Ring when, arriving over the target, **no** battleship was seen, and no carrier, only the heavy cruisers!

4. Ring, *Lost Letter*.

Table 21: First VB-8 Attack on Cruisers, 6 June 1942

Sequence	Pilot	Crew	Estimate
1	Lt. Alfred Bland 'Abbie' Tucker III (XO)	Champ T. Stuart, ARM1c	25–50 ft starboard bow
	Ens. Frank E. Christofferson (NO)	Barkley V. Poorman, ARM2c	Miss
	Ens. Don Dee Adams	John B. Broughton, Jr, ARM2c	Dropped on DD – possible hit
2	Lt. John Joseph Lynch (MO)	Wilbur L. Woods, ARM1c	Portside off bow 50–75 ft
	Ens. Henry John Nickerson	Elmer Edwin Jackson, ARM1c	Miss
	Ens. Clayton Evan Fisher	George E. Ferguson, ARM3c	Port Quarter – 100 ft
3	Lt. (jg) Fred Leeson Bates	Clyde S. Montensen, ARM1c	Paint scraper 25 ft port beam
	Ens. Joe Wiley King	Thomas M. Walsh, ARM3c	Miss
4	Lt-Cdr. Robert Ruffin Johnson (CO)	Joseph G. McCoy, ACRM	25–50 ft directly astern BB
5	Ens. Philip F Grant	Robert H. Rider, ARM2c	Dropped accidentally prior to dive
	Ens. James Austin Riner, Jr.	Floyd A. Kilmer, ARM2c	Starboard bow 50–75 ft

could expect no aerial opposition naturally made the mission simpler and the group was able to cruise at medium altitude rather than the usual high altitude (14,000 feet). Meanwhile contact had been established, and maintained, by a pair of Curtiss SOC Seagull float planes from the heavy cruiser *New Orleans* (CA-32)[5], and their reports guided the attack force in toward the target. Eventually Lieutenant-Commander Johnson, who was with VB-8 on the left flank of the scouting line, espied the Japanese ships for himself and, at 0930, duly radioed the good news to CHAG: 'Stanhope from Robert, enemy below on port bow'.[6] Ring, however, seeing no battleship among the ships below, pushed on for a while, then deciding these must really be the targets, turned back out of the sun to attack and radioed back this fact. Back aboard *Enterprise,* the keyed-up

Browning at once responded; 'This is Red Base. Blue attack group, report position and results your attack. Go ahead.'

Hornet's team then made a concentrated attack on the two cruisers, commencing at 0950. Ring recorded, 'Everyone did much better than he had the day before, when buck fever probably had us. Hits were registered on each of the two large cruisers (*Mogami* class) and the escorting destroyers were bombed and strafed.'[7]

Two hits were made in this attack, one bomb penetrating into the warrant officers mess[8], the other penetrating the *Mogami*'s No. 5 mounting, ripping off the top of the turret and killing the entire gun crew. In return anti-aircraft fire claimed two VS-8 victims[9], and other aircraft were slightly damaged.

It is interesting to note that in Mitscher's report on this

---

5. 6-CS-12 piloted by Lieutenant Samuel R. Brown, Jr, and 6 CS-11 piloted Lieutenant (jg) Wilfred H. Genest, A-V(N).

6. *Hornet*'s air group used first name calls for the radio traffic throughout the Midway battle, as this was felt to be safer. However, Ring wryly recorded that the Japanese were sharp, and within a few minutes a second message, 'in a very oriental tone', came in over his headphones: 'Stanhope from Roberts, Return to base!'

7. Ring, *Lost Letter*. The eight Wildcats made low-level machine-gun attacks in two lines of four aircraft each against a cruiser and a destroyer respectively.

8. Statement of Fireman 3c Kenichi Ishikawa see *Interrogation of Japanese Prisoners taken after Midway Action 9 June*

1942, dated 21 June 1942, CincPac File A8/(37) JAP/(26), Serial 01753, from Commander-in-Chief, United States Pacific Fleet to Chief of Naval Operations (Director of Naval Intelligence) via Commander-in-Chief, United States Fleet, held NARA College Park, Maryland. He ascribes this hit as taking place two days prior to the sinking, but was understandably confused on times having been adrift on a raft for two days and three nights.

9. The two casualties were 8-S-12 crewed by Ensign Don 'T' Griswold, A-V (N) and Kenneth Cecil Bunch, ARM1c, which was hit, smoked and crashed into the sea, and 6-S-1 crewed by Ensign Clarence E. Vammen, Jr, and Milton W. Clark, AMM1c, which disintegrated in mid-air after a direct hit by a heavy-calibre shell.

Table 22: First VS-8 Attack on Cruisers, 6 June 1942[10]

N.B.   All VS-8 Records appear to have gone down with *Hornet* when she was sunk at the Battle of Santa Cruz Islands. VB-8's logs were rescued but not VS-8's. Walter Rodee's son and heir, John, has tried to locate the relevant log books that Walter told Weisheit about, but can find nothing at all. (Clayton Fisher and George Walsh assisted in this vain search). Barry L. Zerby of Modern Military Records (NWCTM) confirmed what I found through my own searches at College Park, that:- "We examined the US Navy war diaries for aviation squadrons but found that there were none for this squadron. We know of no other body of records that would contain this kind of information." Zerby to the Author, 21 February 2007. Therefore Table 22 and Table 28 must, perforce, remain incomplete for now.

Sequence	Pilot Crew Aircraft		
1	Lt.-Cdr. Walter F Rodee	John L. Clanton, ACRM (PA)	
2	Lt. William J. 'Gus' Widhelm (XO)	George D. Stokely, ARM1c	
	Ens. Clarence Earl Vammen, Jr. (from VS-6)	Milton Wayne Clark, AMM1c	6-S-1*
	Lt. (jg) William Francis Christie (from VS-5)	Alvin A. Sobel, ARM1c	
3			
4			
5			
6	Ens. Don 'T' Griswold, A-V (N)	Kenneth Cecil Bunch, ARM1c	8-S-12*
7			
8			
CHAG	Commander Stanhope Cotton Ring	Arthur M. Parker, ARM2c	

*Destroyed.

sortie, it was emphasized that all pilots of this attack insist that the principal target was definitely a BB (probably *Kirishima* class) and not a CA'.[11] Which does not say much for the *Hornet* air groups target identification either, as the battleships had two turrets forward and two aft, and upright funnels, as well as the usual 'pagoda' style bridges; while the much smaller *Mogami* had a distinctive forward raking funnel and a totally different gun layout with three turrets forward.

After delivering their ordnance, CHAG led the *Hornet* group back to the carrier, making a 25 mile detour to the south to see if there were any other Japanese forces in the area, but they saw nothing. On returning to the carrier after the three-hour mission, CHAG discovered that, due a faulty

radio, none of his signals reporting the sighting and the attack had been received by Mitscher, nor had Ring received a request from *Hornet* for the latitude and longitude of the enemy.[12] Captain Mitscher therefore ordered Ring not to take part in the second strike[13], which was quickly being organized.

Meanwhile the *Enterprise* strike had gone in against the same unfortunate vessels. 'Dusty' Kleiss recorded: 'I made 200 mile leg. Scouting hop to NW. Bad weather at 170 miles. One plane made contact with Battle Cruiser (or CB), CA and 3 DDs. *Hornet* attacked force and claimed several hits on CAs. We made rendezvous at 1300 [1100] (31 VSB and fighter escort) and proceeded to attack.'[14]

---

10. The compositions of the VS-8 strikes are unclear, because Walt Rodee failed to file any after-action reports on the two strikes he led that day. The conspiracy theorists hold that this omission was at the direction of Ring and/or Mitscher, but the squadron diary should have been able to clear it up. One clue provided by Clayton Fisher of VB-8 indicates an alternate reason for this gap in history. 'Art Cason, a pilot in VB-8, saved most of our pilots flight log books from our squadron office before he abandoned the *Hornet* when she was sunk a few months later. Art was able to abandon the *Hornet* without getting himself or the log books wet. A destroyer had pulled alongside the *Hornet* and its bridge extended over the steeply sloped flight deck. All Art had to do was step onto the destroyer's bridge. Art and I had a

chance meeting in November of 1942 at NAS North Island, and he told me he had my log book. I'm sure the VB-8 log books were the *only* air group flight logs that did not go down with the *Hornet*.' Fisher to the Author, 5 January 2007.

11. *Report of Action – 4–6 June 1942*, CV8/A16-3, Serial 0018, OF10/Ld, dated 13 June, 1942.

12. Ring's1946 memory is at variance with Robert Cressman, et al, *A Glorious Page in our History: The Battle of Midway 4–6 June 1942*.

13. Gordon W. Prange, in his account, incorrectly has Ring leading the second *Hornet* strike, but this was just not so. (*Miracle at Midway*.) Lundstrom followed suit (*The First Team*.)

14. N. J. Kleiss, *VS-6 Log of the War*.

The attack group was led by Lieutenant Short of VS-5 and was made up of thirty-one dive-bombers from VB-3, VS-5, VB-6 and VS-6, all armed with 1000 pound bombs. These bombers were also provided with liberal fighter protection for this mission against the four surface ships, (three of them reportedly badly damaged) – indeed far more liberal than when attacking through the fully activated *Kido Butai* CAP on 4 June! Twelve Wildcats, in two sections from VF-6[15] escorted them in. The TBDs also flew this mission, making their macabre swan-song. Three of VT-6's Devastator's were fit to fly and they accompanied the force, as it was felt that their torpedoes would be suitable for delivering the *coup de grâce* to any big cruiser that the dive-bombers had knocked all resistance out of. But their commanding officer[16] was given very strict instructions, by Spruance personally, not to risk an attack if any anti-aircraft fire was forthcoming ('if there is one single gun firing'). The Japanese were as prickly as ever and so, in the event, the torpedo-bombers obeyed instructions and did not attempt an attack. As before, therefore it was all down to the SBDs!

The *Enterprise* air group took their departure at 1045. The dive-bombers proceeded independently, with the lead group ultimately climbing up to an altitude of 22,500 feet. At 1057 Browning radioed to Short, confirming that the 'battleship' was his target, and she may have moved along from the last reported position which, if true, would appear to indicate she was in good fighting as well as steaming condition.

At noon the leading SBDs reported sighting one heavy cruiser, one light cruiser and two destroyers. Like Ring before him, Short could not see the reported battleship with this group of enemy vessels, so continued onward for another 30 miles, before turning back to attack. VB-6 was the rear dive-bomber section aloft, leaving at 1115, while the three TBDs trailed well behind them, but they never joined up of course.[17]

In the perfect weather conditions, recorded as, 'unlimited visibility, unlimited ceiling' they again found the ships in position 29° 28N, 173° 11E at 1240. VB-6 made their approach at the lower altitude of 19,000 feet, and encountered heavy defensive fire as they did so. A split attack, with a high-speed run-in was adopted at 1215 for the dive, with bomb release at 2,000 feet. The majority of the SBDs went for the heavy cruisers, which they claimed to have heavily damaged. A few attacked the light cruiser, hitting her at least once, while when the Wildcats arrived, they strafed the destroyers. In all, VB-6 claimed six hits on a heavy cruiser and one on a light cruiser, with 1 destroyer afire from hits from planes of other squadrons. They also recorded an explosion on the heavy cruiser.

The destroyer that was hit was the *Arashio* (Commander Hideo Kuboki) and the SBD that hit her was flown by Clay Fisher. He gave me this account of that action.

The *Hornet* and *Enterprise* launched about twenty dive-bombers to try and finish off the cruiser and the two destroyers that had been bombed that morning. We found the cruiser *Mikuma* dead in the water and a lot of men in the water. The destroyers near the cruiser were picking up survivors out of the water. The VS-8 flight just ahead of us hit the cruiser with two 1000-pound bombs and triggered a huge explosion. The debris must have reached over 1,500 feet. The destroyers started pulling away from the cruiser. The CO of VB-8, Ruff Johnston, diverted our flight division to target the destroyers. I selected a destroyer that was in a shallow turn and increasing its speed. The destroyer did not put up any AA probably because of survivors exposed on the open deck. It was easy to line up for a dive-bombing run. I dropped my bomb from about 1,500 feet and my gunner told me we got a direct hit near the stern. The destroyer went dead in the water. Ruff Johnson confirmed the hit. I later found out the destroyer was the *Arashio,* and due to superb damage control efforts by the crew, the ship did not sink and was able to reach Wake Island. There was terrible suffering among the wounded survivors while *en-route* to Wake Island.[18]

The *Arashio* and *Asashio* were 2,370 ton (fully laden) sister ships, built in 1937, and were the first of the *tokugata* or 'new' destroyers to be designed and completed after Japan had withdrawn from the various naval treaty restrictions. They carried six 5 inch 50 calibre dual purpose guns in

15. The F4F-4s were led by Lieutenant James S. Gray and Lieutenant (jg) Rhonald J. 'Buster' Hoyle.
16. Lieutenant (jg) Robert E. Laub and William Colquitt Humphrey, Jr, ARM1c flying 6-T-4; Ensign Jamie S. Morris and David R. Butler, ARM2c flying 6-T-3; and Warrant Machinist Harry August Mueller and Ronald Walter Graetz ARM3c flying 6-T-5.
17. The ONI recorded: 'After failing to make contact with our bombing planes, they found an enemy ship independently

and circled an hour awaiting our bombers which did not appear. Finally, lack of fuel forced them to return to the *Enterprise*. This clearly indicates the presence of two enemy groups'. However, Ronald W. Graetz later recalled things differently, stating that, although they circled the cruisers and occasionally turned toward them to draw their fire, the reason they did not attack was because the dive-bombers were getting the job done anyway!
18. Clayton Fisher to the author, January 2006.

Table 23: VS-6 Attack on Cruisers, 6 June 1942

Sequence	Pilot	Crew	Aircraft
1	Lt. (jg) John Norman West	Jack Richard Badgley, ACRM (AA)	6-S-16
	Ens. Ried Wentworth Stone	William Hart Bergin, RM1c	6-S-2
	Ens. Richard Alonzo Jaccard	Porter William Pixley, RM3c	6-S-11
2	Lt. (JG) Norman Jack Kleiss	John Warren Snowden, ARM3c	6-S-7
	Ens. Vernon Larsen Micheel	John Dewey Dance, RM3c	6-S-17
	Ens. James Campbell Dexter	Donald L. Hoff, RM3c	6-S-18

Table 24: VB-6 Attack on Cruisers, 6 June 1942

Sequence	Pilot	Crew	Aircraft
1	Lt. Lloyd Addiston Smith	Herman Hull Caruthers, AMM2c	6-B-1
	Lt (jg) Edward Lee Anderson	Walter George Chochalousek, ARM1c	6-B-16
	Ens. Don Lelo Ely	George H. Arnold, Sea2c	6-B-2
2	Lt. Harvey Peter Lanham	Edward Joseph Garaudy, ARM1c	6-B-10
	Ens. Harry Warren Liffner	Miles L. Kimberlin, AMM3c	6-B-17

three twin turrets, and eight 24 inch torpedoes in two quadruple torpedo tubes, with reloads. This was coupled with engines developing 50,000 shp that gave a maximum speed of 35 knots, making them formidable destroyers. They had operated together since the start of the Pacific War in DesDiv 8, which had been assigned to DesRon 4 for Midway.

Clay Fisher's direct hit had indeed caused suffering aboard, especially among the survivors from the *Mikuma*, many of who had been huddled together on the upper deck astern. The bomb apparently failed to penetrate (had it done so, or had it ignited the depth charges astern, she would have lost her stern and almost certainly have been sunk), but instead detonated immediately on impact, close to her rearmost 5 inch turret. The blast was outwardly

deadly, killing thirty-seven[19] men instantly with scores more horribly injured, including Commander Nobuki Ogawa[20], the commander of DesDiv 8, but was not lethal. Even so a fire broke out below and *Arashio* failed to respond to her helm. By incredible dedication, her small damage control party, reinforced by volunteers from the able-bodied *Mikuma* men, fought the flames vigorously enough eventually to bring them under control and finally put them out. Hand-steering was rigged up, with orders being passed down a human chain. Fortunately, her engines and boilers remained intact and flooding was minimal. The *Arashio* was scarred and hurt, but she managed to maintain steerage and dragged herself along in the wake of *Mogami* and *Asashio*[21] toward safety.[22]

After the attack, Lieutenant Penland wrote:

---

19. Not 'scores' as Lord would have it (*Incredible Victory*).
20. Rear-Admiral Nobuki Ogawa (1895–1944). b.12 November 1895 in Kouchi prefecture. A torpedo specialist. 1918, 21st November, graduated from Etajima as midshipman, posted aboard the training vessel *Hitachi* for sea training, voyage to Australia. 1919, 1 August, promoted to ensign assigned to battleship *Hyuga*. 1919, 1 December posted to Gunnery School, elementary course. 1920, May–September, Torpedo School, elementary course. 1 December to destroyer *Kaede*. 1923, 1 November, appointed to Kure Naval Intake School as instructor. 1924, promoted to lieutenant. 1925, to destroyers as Navigation Officer, then Torpedo School advanced course. 1927, appointed as torpedo officer aboard destroyer *Nadakaze*. 1928, 10 December, appointed torpedo officer aboard light cruiser *Kitakami*. 1929, torpedo officer aboard light cruiser *Isuzu*. 1920 promoted to lieutenant-commander. 1932, 20 February, Torpedo Officer heavy cruiser *Takao*. 1933 Torpedo Officer battleship *Kirishima*. 1934, 1 April,

appointed in command of new destroyer *Minazuki*. 1936, became captain of destroyer *Yugiri* until 20 May, then to Reserve. 1937, 1 February, appointed in command of destroyer *Shirayuki* then on 1 December, promoted to commander. 1940, became XO of heavy cruiser *Chikuma*. 1941, 10 April, became commander DesRon5, until 20 October when appointed commander DesRon12. 1942, 14 March, appointed commander DesRon8 and promoted to captain on 1 November. 1943, 5 December, appointed in command of gunboat *Tatara*. 1944, 24 February, KIA, west of the Mariana Islands and posthumously promoted to rear-admiral.

21. The *Asashio* ('Morning High Tide') was not hit, other than by machine-gun fire when strafed by the Wildcats. Even so, her thin hull plating and upperworks proved no protection and twenty-two of her crew were killed.

22. The *Arashio* ('Rough Sea Flood') recovered sufficiently to escort *Mogami* on to Truk, which they reached on 14 June. She was repaired and back in action within a short time.

236

Table 25: VB-3 Attack on Cruisers, 6 June 1942

Sequence	Pilot	Crew	Aircraft
1	Lt. DeWitt Wood W. Shumway (XO)	Ray Edgar Coons, ARM1c	3-B-3
	Ens. Robert Martin Elder	Leslie Alan Till, ARM3c	3-B-14
	Ens. Milford Austin Merrill	Jack Alvan Shropshire, ARM3c	3-B-6
	Ens. Robert Keith Campbell (GO)	Dallas Joseph Bergeron, ARM3c	3-B-4
	Ens. Aldon W. Hanson	Joseph Vernon Godfrey, ARM3c	3-B-5
2	Lt. (jg) Gordon Alvin Sherwood (EO)	Harmon Donald Bennett, ARM2c	3-B-7
	Ens. Roy Maurice Isaman	Sidney Kay Weaver, ARM3c	3-B-8
	Ens. Bunyon Randolph Cooner	Clarence E. Zimmershead, AMM3c	3-B-9
	Lt. Harold Sydney Bottomley (FO)	David Frederick Johnson, AMM2c	3-B-10
	Ens. Charles S. Lane	Jack Charles Henning, ARM3c	6-B-10

Table 26: VS-5 (VB-5) Attack on Cruisers, 6 June 1942

Sequence	Pilot	Crew	Aircraft
1	Lt. Wallace Clark Short, Jr (CO)	John W. Trott, ACRM (PA)	6-S-7
	Lt. Harlan Rockey Dickson	Joseph Michael Lynch, Jr ARM2c	6-S-8
	Ens. Carl Herman Horenburger	Lyn Raymond Forsee, ARM3c	6-S-9
2	Lt. John Ludwig Nielsen	Walter Dean Straub, ACRM (PA)	6-S-10
	Lt. (jg) Nels Luther A. Berger	Otis Albert Phelps, ACRM (PA)	6-S-11
	Lt. (jg) David Render Berry	Earnest A. Clegg, ARM2c	6-S-12
3	Ens. Benjamin Gifford Preston	Harold R. Cowden, ARM1c	6-S-15

All scouts and Flight leaders should carry binoculars in order to identify enemy ships. The largest ship of this enemy formation was positively identified by various pilots as a battle cruiser, battleship and heavy cruiser [he could have well added a light cruiser to the list as this was a frequent report]. It proved to be a cruiser of the *Mogami* class (Identified from close-range photographs).[23]

'Dusty' Kleiss recorded his part in this attack thus:

We believed this to be same force *Hornet* attacked earlier (they reported several hits on each CA and the sinking of one DD) and that they exaggerated greatly the damage done. The Battle Cruiser was of *Mogami* class, only larger, and was supposed to contain Commander of Second Orange Fleet.[24']

Speed of enemy 25 kts. course 240° T. No BB of other force within 50 mi. radius. Attack made from 20,000 feet. I was 4th in dive, believe I got a hit near stack which was blown to pieces. Of our 5 planes, 3 made direct hit and 3 hit within 50 feet. (One plane did not dive and returned to ship because oxygen supply failed.) Fighters strafed DDs, setting one afire and damaging the other. Other CA had direct hit on stern, but could make 15 knots.

Our target a complete mass of wreckage dead in the water and burning from stem to stern.[25]

VB-3's action report recorded that visibility was excellent, with unlimited ceiling and a 12 knot south-westerly surface wind. The ten SBD-3s and 3As found the enemy in

---

However, it was only a short respite for, during the air-sea battle in the Bismarck Sea the following spring, she took three bomb hits on 3 March 1943 and collided with the *Nojima*, which proved fatal. After 176 survivors were taken off she was abandoned and sunk by further attacks the following day in the Dampier Strait, going down about 55 miles south-east of Finschhafen. Among those killed was Commander Kuboki

23. Penland, *Action With Enemy Report.*

24. Signals from the *Mikuma* requesting aid were picked up by

Lieutenant Gilven M Slonim's *Enterprise* onboard RI team and interpreted as originating from Kondo himself aboard the 'battleship'. This hasty assumption was immediately disseminated to the SBDs by Spruance at 0950 without further analysis. Thus we have the strange spectacle of the senior American commander on the spot informing his men on their way to attack a Japanese force, that a Japanese admiral who was not with that force was aboard a battleship which did not exist!

25. N. J. Kleiss, VS-6 *Log of the War.*

Table 27: Second VB-8 Attack on Cruisers, 6 June 1942

Sequence	Pilot	Crew	Estimate
1	Lt. Alfred Bland Tucker II (XO)	Champ T. Stuart, ARM1c	Miss astern, very close
	Ens. Don Dee Adams	John B. Broughton, Jr, ARM2c	Miss
	Ens. Joe Wiley King	Thomas M. Walsh, ARM3c	Hit on starboard bow, just inside waterline
2	Lt. John Joseph Lynch (MO)	Wilbur L. Woods, ARM1c	Hit on stern of cruiser
	Ens. Clayton Evan Fisher	George G. Ferguson, ARM3c	Hit on stern of destroyer
	Ens. Henry John Nickerson	Elmer Edwin Jackson, ARM1c	Hit on stern of "light cruiser"
3	Lt. (jg) Fred Leeson Bates (EO)	Clyde S. Montensen, ARM1c	Miss
	Ens. James Clark Barrett	William H. Berthold, ARM3c	50 ft astern of "light cruiser"
	Ens. Gus G. Bebas	Alfred W. Ringressy, Jr, RM3c	Paint scraper on "light cruiser"
4	Ens. Frank E. Christofferson	Barkley V. Poorman, ARM2c	Miss
	Ens. Robert P. Friesz	Clarence C. Kiley, ARM1c	Hits on forecastle, near side near waterline
5	Ens. James Austin Riner, Jr	Billy Rex Cottrell, ARM2c	50 ft from destroyer

29° 28'N, 1750 35'E at 1455 (Zone +10) and their prey manoeuvred in circles during the attack. The dive-bombers made their approach from the south-west at high speed at an altitude of 15,000 feet, dived and released at 2,000 feet, retiring to the east. The ordnance employed was Mk 13 1,000 pound bombs, with Mk 21 nose and Mk 23 tail fuses with 1/100 settings. The attacks by divisions and sections were made from all around the compass on a *Mogami* class cruiser, and, splitting the defence, met with little anti-aircraft fire. Ensign Isaman made a lone attack against an undamaged cruiser, thought to be of the *Atago* class, scoring a direct hit aft, and this was followed by a second, upon which heavy fires broke out. In total, Lieutenant Shumway estimated that they had scored eight direct hits on one target and two on another, with no misses. He reported that they witnessed the largest ship burning furiously, with one internal explosion, and that she was, 'shattered and abandoned'.[26] The SBDs suffered no damage whatsoever in return and all ten returned safely to *Enterprise*.

Similar results were claimed by VS-5, whose seven SBD-3s attacked at 1445. They recorded: 'No battleship encountered so attack was made on Japanese CA'. This force approached at an altitude of 21,000 feet from up-sun and down wind, noting that the target turned down-wind. Most released at about 3,000 feet, and claimed five direct hits and two close misses. The target 'emitted heavy black smoke and stopped'. No dive-bomber was inconvenienced and they effected their rendezvous by section down-wind of the cruiser, which they left 'severely damaged and rendered out of action'.[27]

Hornet's second strike was led by Lieutenant Walt Rodee, and Ring graciously acknowledged it as being 'even more successful than the first. And the group had the satisfaction of witnessing a terrific explosion aboard one of the cruisers. Later intelligence indicated that *Mikuma* was sunk as a result of this attack.'[28]

One 'battleship' could clearly be seen burning fiercely from 50 miles away with two destroyers in attendance, and a 'light cruiser' stopped 2 miles to the westward as, approaching in two six-plane divisions at an altitude of 13,000 feet, VB-8 found the target in 29° 30'N, 172° 30' E under low, broken cloud at 1,500 feet. As VB-8 passed around to the up-sun sector VS-8 was heard announcing their attack, and they were seen to commence it. As they did

26. Lieutenant D. W. Shumway, Acting Commander Bombing Squadron Three, Action Report, *US Aircraft – Action with Enemy*, dated 10 June 1942.

27. Lieutenant W. C. Short, Jr, Scouting Squadron Five, Action Report, *Report of Participation in the Major Battle with Japanese Forces in the Midway Island Area*, dated 7 June 1942.

28. Ring, *Lost Letter*.

Table 28: Second VS-8 Attack on Cruisers, 6 June 1942
(Incomplete – see note for Table 22.)

Sequence	Pilot	Crew	Estimate
1	Lt-Cdr Walter Fred Rodee (CO)	Arthur M. Parker, ARM2c	
2			
3			
4			
5			

so they could see the 'light cruiser' and destroyers get underway and scatter. They watched as VS-8 made their attack on the 'battleship' and 'light cruiser' and 'three heavy after explosions' were noted on the former, and either several hits or very close misses were made on the latter.

Ruff Johnson's report stated that, during the approach of the squadrons, the Japanese anti-aircraft fire was heavy and effective out to a surprisingly long range. 'I believe that the battleship fired its main battery at a low section that was rendezvousing outside normal AA gun range. The reason for this belief is that I was positive we were at least 18,000 yards from the battleship where the splashes occurred'. After watching VS-8's attack, the 'battleship' was seen emerging from under a cloud and, 'as it started to fade out I noted the stern kick to port indicating to me a turn to starboard. Allowing for this change of course, it was possible for me to use the sun and cloud to obscure the squadron from the objective, and to dive straight down the axis of the target. For this reason the first half of the squadron had no AA fire from the Battleship with which to contend.'[29]

VB-8 then attacked out of the sun and down-wind, most releasing their 1,000 pound bombs with 1/100 second delay fuses at a height of 1,500 feet and withdrawing westward at heights that varied from 50 to 500 feet. They claimed four hits and many near misses. One of the pilots attacked the southern destroyer and made a 'very probable hit' on her stern. As they were withdrawing fifteen minutes later, the 'battleship' was seen on fire, the 'light cruiser' hauling off to northward, smoking with both destroyers approaching the 'battleship'.[30]

Although the Cressman account makes the excited boasting of one young pilot 'as easy as shooting ducks in a rain barrel'[31] a chapter heading for recording this action, in reality the amount of punishment taken by these big Japanese cruisers was an eye-opener to the Americans, and especially to an old cruiser man like Frank Jack Fletcher. He later wrote:

Experience gained at Tulagi, the Coral Sea and Midway has shown clearly that an excessive number of direct hits with 1000 pound bomb fused with Mk 21 and 23 fuses (1/100 second delay) is required to destroy or severely damage a large enemy ship. It is believed that the fuse setting is too short to permit the bomb to penetrate sufficiently to obtain the maximum destructive force. It is suggested therefore that a 1/25 of a second delay action fuse be supplied for use with the present type 1000 pound bomb. For use against armoured ships such as battleships and heavy cruisers, it is essential that an armor piercing bomb, capable of being carried by our present type dive bombers, be procured immediately.[32]

A run by VB-6 photographic aircraft at 1915 obtained several now classic shots, both up-sun and across-sun, of the pulverized *Mikuma* being abandoned in 29° 28'N, 173° 11' E. She was burning heavily amidships, 'with explosions occurring on average once very five minutes.' The survivors were leaving the doomed ship via the extreme bow and stern. At least five boats and one dark red rubber raft were seen, with other crew members clinging to lumber and floating debris. The other three ships had left her and were plodding doggedly along in 29° 24'N, 172° 20' E. They still had fight left in them, *Mogami* engaging the aircraft with anti-aircraft fire from her main 8 inch battery.

In fact hits were registered on both the *Mikuma* and the

29. R. R. Johnson, Lt-Cdr, U.S. Navy, Confidential Report, *Attack Report of 6 June 1942*, dated 7 June 1942. Declassified NND968133 4/22 NARA. Held National Archives, College Park, Maryland.
30. Throughout the narratives of this attack, the 'battleship' was of course the *Mikuma* and the 'light cruiser' the bowless *Mogami*.

31. Robert Cressman, et al, *A Glorious Page in Our History*.
32. Frank Jack Fletcher to Commander-in-Chief, US Pacific Fleet, Battle of Midway – Forwarding of Reports, dated 26 June, 1942. Declassified NND968133 4/22 held at National Archives, College Park, Maryland.

destroyer *Arashio*. The *Mikuma* took at least five direct hits[33]; one, on the roof of 'C' turret, just before her bridge, peeled off the turret roof and sent splinters into the crowded bridge and put all the forward turrets out of action. The splinters and resulting debris from this hit, as well as devastating the bridge area, also ignited some anti-aircraft shells stacked in the ready-use-racks[34], causing heavy damage to her command positions and severely wounding her commanding officer, Captain Shakao Sakiyama.[35] He was taken aboard the *Asashio* and was later transferred to the *Suzuya* for urgent medical treatment. Two further hits meanwhile smashed into the stricken vessel on the starboard side forward, and penetrated into her engine room and boiler spaces. Before she could begin to recover from this deadly strike at least one, and probably two, bombs struck the aircraft deck, and one penetrated the armour and detonated in the port after engine room. The resulting fire quickly caused the evacuation of the other two, intact, engine rooms. Now powerless *Mikuma* slid to a halt, a broken wreck and a sitting duck. Worse yet, the impact of so many explosions deep inside the cruiser in effect broke her spine. She began to heel over to port and take in water from multiple fractures in her stricken hull. She was clearly doomed even at this stage, and the *Mogami* duly signalled as much to the C-in-C.[36] The already mortal damage inflicted was now further compounded and the decision not to jettison her torpedoes, as *Mogami* rather more wisely had done, proved to have been a grave mistake. These further two bombs set off a raging fire in the near vicinity of her tubes amidships. The 24 inch (torpe-

does) each had warheads containing 1,874 pounds of explosives.[37] Despite the crew's best efforts under the inspirational leadership of her XO[38], this inferno proved unquenchable, spreading aft. Eventually, just before 1400, it reached and detonated several of the torpedo warheads and started a chain reaction.

It is not clear how much this colossal detonation contributed to *Mikuma*'s loss; as she was obviously doomed before it occurred. Superficially, the blast effect was dramatic; her mainmast was brought down; the upper rear part of her funnel was blown away; and other parts of the 'midships superstructure was torn apart by the blast, with much of the blackened debris thrown up and scattered aft, including chunks that landed on the after turret roof and lent a certain fallacious credence to the press story of Captain Fleming's so-called 'suicide attack'. It took more than two hours from the time of the bomb hits themselves to the time that the torpedo warheads finally 'cooked off' with such intensity. Half the twenty-four stowed warheads were on that side of the vessel but, as could be seen from the photographs, much of the venting of the blast was, upward and outward, as the source of the detonation was on an upper-deck. We have seen how deadly confined explosions could be, with no ability to disperse their force vertically or laterally, in the destruction of the Japanese carriers, but with *Mikuma*, much of this power was outwardly dissipated. Even so, such an enormous explosion could only further weaken the already over-strained keel structure of the ship and confirmed the inevitable.

At 1750 the *Enterprise* despatched a pair of SBDs on a

33. Captain Hiroaki Tsuda, Chief Navigator of the battleship *Hyuga*, stated that *Mogami* was hit four or five times by bombs and that he thought *Mikuma* was hit about ten times, but as he was at least 50 miles away from the scene of the action, this could only have been hearsay. Lieutenant-Commander Tei Nishikawa (Etajima 51st Class) the *Mogami*'s Gunnery Officer stated that *Mogami* received four bomb hits killing about 100 men. (*Interrogation of Japanese Prisoners taken after Midway Action 9 June 1942*), dated 21 June 1942, CincPac File A8/(37) JAP/(26), Serial 01753, from Commander-in-Chief, United States Pacific Fleet to Chief of Naval Operations (Director of Naval Intelligence) via Commander-in-Chief, United States Fleet, held NARA College Park, Maryland.

34. Ishikawa, *Interrogation*.

35. Captain Shakao Sakiyama (1892–1942). b. 28 August 1892 in Kagoshima prefecture. 1914, 19 December, graduated from Etajima 42nd Class as midshipman, joined battleship *Aso* for sea training. 1915 transferred to the battleship *Suwo* 27 August and on 13 November promoted to ensign. Joined the protected cruiser *Niitaka*. 1917, 1 December, became lieutenant (jg). 1918 served aboard the battle-cruiser *Kirishima*. 1919, 1 November transferred to the armoured cruiser *Nisshin* and then on 2 December to the battleship

Satuma. 1920 promoted to lieutenant. 1921 joined destroyer *Take*. 1922 transferred to destroyer *Akikaze*. 1924, promoted to captain, assigned to minesweepers. 1925, moved back to destroyers and promoted to flotilla staff. 1938, 20 November, 1 December 1931, commanded various coastal destroyers. 1932, February, appointed to staff of port fortress of Oominato. 30 September, resumed sea duties as captain of 1st class 'Special Type' destroyer *Asakaze*. 1933, 15 September, promoted to commander. *1935,* 15 November, appointed in command of new destroyer *Ayanami*. 1936, became XO of training cruiser *Iwate*. 1937, 1 December, as captain, placed in command of DesRon15. 1938, appointed in command of light cruiser *Abukuma*. 1940, became commanding officer of the heavy cruiser *Mikuma*. 1942, died of wounds, 7 June, on board heavy cruiser *Suzuya*, and was posthumously promoted to rear-admiral.

36. Matome Ugaki et al, *Fading Victory: The Diary of Matome Ugaki, 1941–1945*.

37. This was more than double the equivalent warhead on torpedoes carried by American heavy cruisers (727.5 pounds) and that, coupled with their range and lack of bubble trail, was what made these weapons so deadly in surface actions.

38. Commander Hideo Takashima.

Table 29: Comparison of IJN/USN Dive-bombing Attacks on Heavy Cruisers

	Dorsetshire/Cornwall – by D3A1s, 5 April 1942	Mikuma/Mogami by SBDs, 6 June 1942
Air Cover	Nil	Nil
Total number of dive-bombers that actually attacked	80	80
Ship's radar	1	0
Tonnage of targets	9,900 tons	13,000 tons
Speed during attacks	25–26 knots	14 knots (max), down to stopped
Maximum deck armour protection	4 inch	1.4 inch
Percentage of hits achieved*	88 per cent	27.5 per cent
Percentage of target ships sunk*	100	50

* If the direct hits on the two escorting destroyers *Arashio* and *Asashio* are included then the number of direct hits scored by the SBDs increases by two; conversely, however, the percentage of targets sunk when attacked reduces to 25 per cent. This compares with the US Navy's pre-war dive-bombing percentages which were around 20 per cent. The improvement in combat is explained by the fact that at Midway the Japanese carriers were obligingly turning into the wind to launch their own aircraft, thus enabling the SBDs, in the main, to dive from sunward right along the lateral axis of the steady-direction target without requiring cross-wind allowance or drift.

photographic mission[39] to try and verify whether or not the ship attacked was a battleship or a heavy cruiser. After considerable argument, Colonel Julian Brown's common-sense recommendation to obtain a solution of the mystery was finally followed. The photographs taken of *Mogami*'s dying later went round the world and showed her still being abandoned, with men in the water, sliding down ropes and clustered astern, an unforgettable epitaph.

It is a remarkable testimony to *Mikuma*'s stout construction that, even after all these blows, she remained defiantly afloat for some time afterwards. But her demise could not be delayed for ever and, at around 1930 she eventually rolled over onto her port side and sank, along with at least 650[40] of her crew, in position 29° 28'N, 173° 1' E. Although 240 of her complement were subsequently rescued[41] some of these died in subsequent attacks on the destroyers.[42] However, a far larger number of these unfortunates died over the course of the following days from exhaustion and

drowning. One of the very few who did survive recounted that: 'he found himself on a raft with nineteen other men, after having jumped over the side. He estimated there were several hundred men in the water, but the majority of the crew had not been able to get off the ship, before she turned over'. He told how the twenty men on his raft had no food or water and that one by one they either died or fell off the raft while asleep at night until there were just two left alive.[43] This must have been the fate of scores if not hundreds of his former shipmates.

Mogami, her port hull and upperworks riddled like a colander with over 800 splinter perforations[44], managed to steam away at speeds of up to 20 knots.[45] At 0900 on the morning of 7 June the *Kumano* and *Suzuya*, which had joined the main body just three hours earlier, were detached again and sent back south along with the *Atago* and *Chokai* of CruDiv 4 to escort *Mogami* home. They rendezvoused with her and the two destroyers at 0600 on 8 June and

---

39. The SBDs were 6-S-18 of VS-6 piloted by Lieutenant (jg) Cleo John Dobson, USNR, the assistant LSO, with CP (PA) (Communication Personnel) (Photographer Assistant) J. S. Mihalovitch behind the camera. She was accompanied by 3-B-10 of VB-6 piloted by Lieutenant (jg) Edwin John Kroeger, with *Fox Movietone News* cameraman Al D. Brick in the rear seat.

40. As with everything to do with Midway, there is hot debate on the exact war complement of the *Mikuma* on her last sortie. The peacetime complement of 850 officers and men can safely be said to have been increased by at least a hundred or more, as with warships of all nations.

41. *Senshi Sōshō.*

42. Lieutenant-Commander Otokichi Shibata, the *Suzuya*'s

Navigation Officer, stated later: 'We received a message saying that about half of the survivors from the *Mikuma* were killed when the second destroyer was hit'. Interrogation Navy No. 66 USSBS No. 295 dated 7 November 1945.

43. Ishikawa, *Interrogation*.

44. Interestingly, a British light cruiser, HMS *Penelope*, underwent a similar ordeal while working from Malta in the spring of 1942. She had so many bomb splinter holes in her upper-works and funnels that her crew christened her HMS *Pepperpot*. Nonetheless this was equally superficial damage and her watertight integrity was not compromised. Like *Mogami*'s escape to Truk, *Penelope* was able to escape under her own power to Gibraltar.

45. Matome Ugaki et al, *Fading Victory*.

steered directly for Truk. Here, the local repair facilities patched up the *Mogami* sufficiently to enable her to reach her home port of Kure, where she was substantially rebuilt, her after turrets being replaced by a seaplane deck a la *Tone*. Thus transformed, she returned to full combat action. Despite her horrendous condition and long ordeal, the *Mogami* had suffered less than two hundred casualties, of which only ninety proved to be fatal.[46]

The *Asashio* had been sent back after dark on the 6th by Kondo to see if she could locate further *Mikuma* survivors and also to scuttle the wreck to prevent her falling into enemy hands, but, of course, no trace of the cruiser was found other than a mass of oil. However, on 9 June, two *Mikuma* survivors[47] were recovered from a raft, where they had survived three nights, by the submarine *Trout* and taken to Pearl Harbor.

It is interesting to compare the different results achieved by the D3A1 dive-bombers of the IJN and the SBDs of the USN in attacking a pair of heavy cruisers.

The 'Fifteen second Sinking'!

The USAAC made the only other 'contribution' to the final day's combat. Damaged B17s were being recycled back to Hawaii by this time, but additions were being sent out and there were still twenty-six of the heavy bombers operational, sufficient to mount a final strike – and it was a sensational one. A force of eleven B17s was despatched at 1145 with the retiring transport force as its principal target. After searching for a time, the bombers were unable to find these plump juicy transports and, at 1640, they finally called off the search, turning back in two separate sections.

One section, consisting of six bombers, was finally rewarded with a sighting at 1640, on a bearing of around

262 degrees, some 400 miles out from Midway. The first element of three bombers made a precision attack from an altitude of 9,500 feet, putting down a pattern of sixteen 1,000 pound and four 1,100 pound demolition bombs[48] on a heavy cruiser, and reported scoring two direct hits. They took photographs to confirm their success, which later revealed no hits but several near misses. This attack swiftly vindicated all Billy Mitchell's predictions, for the target vessel, 'sank in fifteen seconds'.

Only later did it transpire that the 'heavy cruiser' was, in reality, the American submarine *Grayling* (SS-209), and her 'sinking' was a crash-dive in an understandable attempt to avoid 'friendly fire'. She received no damage from the attack, although her skipper later reported that the first bombs, 'fell near her bow'.[49] Thankfully, she was able to continue her patrol unaffected. The *Tambor* (SS–198) was later to be similarly attacked from the air, and she came off rather worse than her sister, having to cease her patrol and return to Pearl for repairs.[50]

It is easy to laugh, as Walter Lord, does at what he called these 'ex-salesmen and truck drivers' who claimed to have won the battle single-handed, yet never scored a single hit, and at their total inability to distinguish between friend and foe, or between a 1,400 ton submarine and a 14,000 ton heavy cruiser, or a direct hit and a wide miss. But, in their defence, most of them had never been given any training in ship recognition. Moreover, the navy flyers, who ought to have known much better, often proved equally as dismal in ship and aircraft identification.[51] Mistaking a radial-engined IJN A6M for an in-line-engined German land-based Me109 in the middle of the Pacific Ocean speaks volumes. The excuse is that the young flyers, even after six months of war, had no idea what a Zeke, their principal and most feared opponent, looked like.[52] But there were deeper errors at a

---

46. The figures quoted in *Sensho Sōshō*, are nine officers and eighty-one other ranks killed, 101 men wounded.

47. Chief Radioman Katsuichi Yoshida, suffering from crushed ribs, and 21-year-old Fireman 3c Kenichi Ishikawa.

48. The second element of the following three B-17s received no signal to attack, but the two wingman dropped by mistake anyway, their bombs falling well wide. Only the leader of second element held his fire.

49. Report of Lieutenant-Commander E. Olsen to Rear-Admiral English, quoted in ONI, *The Battle of Midway June 3-6, 1942, Combat Narrative*, held at NARA, College Park, Maryland.

50. The *Tambor* was straddled and the explosion damaged both her periscopes and every one of her four battery lower motors, leaving her unable to dive.

51. For example it did not arouse comment by, or appear incongruous to, the USAAC, that Captain Colin Purdie Kelly, Jr, flying a B-17, had been credited with having already sunk the battleship *Haruna* off Luzon on 10 December 1941. He, in

fact, had attacked the cruiser *Ashigara* or a transport ship, and completely missed his target. No matter, Governor Spessard Holland of Florida sent a condolence telegram to his parents stating he had sunk the Japanese battleship, for which he was awarded the Medal of Honor and was widely lauded in the American press, just as Fleming was to be, for diving his plane (a four-engined heavy bomber!) into the *Haruna*'s smokestack and sending her to the bottom. Kelly was indeed really a hero, and so was Fleming, and both men fully earned their honours, but *not* for doing that. Yet, when the *Haruna* appeared at Midway untouched and unharmed, the USAAC undaunted by this apparent miracle, duly claimed (again incorrectly) to have sunk her once more!

52. And before hackles are aroused, I am not questioning the *courage* of these young men, which on both sides, was outstanding. They all belonged to a generation that put country before self, something that is now but rarely seen, and their bravery was undisputed. What *is to be* questioned is the fact that they were sent to war lacking such basic knowl-

much higher level. For example, not until the photographs had been developed and showed the *Mikuma* for what she was, a heavy cruiser, were Spruance and his staff finally convinced that they had not really been attacking a battleship after all. Spruance was to write:

> All through the day there had been no question in our minds that a BB was involved. That evening when questioning the pilots of the two photographic planes, I found one of them quite certain that a CA of the *Mogami* class, and not a BB, was involved. The photographs bore him out. The ship is the same as the one appearing in the 1940 *Jane*.[53] Everyone who saw this ship says she appeared to be much larger than a CA. From this fact and from her toughness, I suspect that her displacement may be considerably in excess of 10,000 tons.[54] She was reported as definitely larger than the other cruiser accompanying her, which may have been a CL or DL. I believe the larger ship sank during the night.[55]

Many back at Washington were convinced that the *Hornet* and *Enterprise* attacks that day had been directed at two different groups of Japanese ships, not the only error made by that team.

The *Yorktown* Finally Succumbs

When the *Yorktown* had been abandoned on 4 June, the cruisers of Spruance's force rejoined TF-16 (Sugar), while Fletcher sent part of TF-17 to refuel eastward well clear of her with the rest. Only a solitary destroyer, *Hughes,* was left to stand by the crippled carrier during the night. Signalman Peter E. Karetka recalled how they spent that night 'alone with the *Yorktown*. We stood close in for protection. Some lights were showing aboard and we could hear items sliding off the carrier, hitting the water.'[56]

All hopes of getting her back to Pearl again were finally dashed with the arrival on the scene of the submarine *I-168*. Veteran submarine officer Commander Yahachi Tanabe[57] was destined to bring down the curtain on the final act of the Battle of Midway in spectacular fashion.

---

edge. The blame for that lies firstly with the lack of resources; for which we can blame short-term thinking by politicians who scorned expenditure on defence between the wars to gain votes; but ultimately with the attitudes and mindsets of the populations themselves, whose collective will it was in those years that this expenditure was not forthcoming until too late.

53. This is a reference to the well-known standard warship recognition book of that era, *Jane's Fighting Ships*, at that date edited by Francis E. McMurtie. This annual publication (known colloquially as *Jane's*) had been originated many decades earlier by Fred T. Jane and was the layman's bible to seapower; however, one would have expected Spruance and his Intelligence team to have far superior sources to hand than that, often very inaccurate, work for their reference.

54. He was quite correct; the *Mogami* had an official deep displacement of 13,668 tons after her pre-war rearming. But Captain Murray, taking passage aboard *Enterprise* in readiness to relieve Spruance on his promotion, was still not satisfied. He stated: 'A close scrutiny of the excellent photographs, the observations of an experienced photographer, and a direct comparison with our 8 inch cruisers, leads to the firm belief that this *Mogami* class heavy cruiser is in reality a battle-cruiser of at least 20,000 tons'.

55. Spruance report, quoted in ONI, *The Battle of Midway June 3–6, 1942, Combat Narrative*, held at NARA II College Park, Maryland.

56. Peter E. Karetka, contemporary hand-written notes 4–6 June, 1942, developed into *"Flags" at Midway*, 'My Memories of Midway'.

57. Commander Yahachi Tanabe (1907–90). 1925 entered Etajima as cadet. March 1928, graduated 56th Class. November 1929 sub-lieutenant, second class. December 1931 sub-lieutenant, first class. November 1934, volunteered for submarines. Lieutenant. December 1938, underwent the *Otsu* course for submarine officers at the Submarine School. March 1939, qualified and appointed to submarine *RO-58*. June 1939, Communications Officer aboard submarine *I-8*. November 1939, appointed Staff Officer (Communications), SubRon2. November 1940, lieutenant-commander. July 1941, underwent the *Kō* course for submarine command. 15 October 1941, appointed in command submarine *RO-59* training new intakes in Inland Sea.1942, 31 January appointed in command submarine *I-168*, (undergoing repairs at Kure in April, renumbered from *I-68* in May) until 29 June 1942. 7 June sank carrier *Yorktown* (CV-5) and destroyer *Hammann* (DD-412) at Midway. 4 August 1942 appointed in command submarine *I-176*, operations patrols Rabaul, Solomon Islands, San Cristobal, Indispensable Reef and supply missions to Guadalcanal and Buna. At Battle of Rennel Island, 19 October 1942, torpedoed and damaged heavy cruiser *Chester* (CA-27). 19 March 1943, wounded by American aircraft machine-gun fire during a B-25 attack on Lae harbour. March 1943, attached to Yokosuka Naval Station. July 1943, became instructor at Submarine School. 1 May 1944, commander. June 1945, joined Special Ordnance Section. August, 1945, attached to Naval General Staff as IJN representative at Atsugi, and made preparations for arrival of General McArthur. November 1945, retired to Reserve. After the war co-authored article with Joseph D Harrington, 'I Sank the Yorktown at Midway'. Died at home in Oomiya City, Saitama Prefecture on 29 April 1990.

Left to Die

For some American's, the evacuation of the *Yorktown* was not quite complete. When she was abandoned, two inmates of her sick bay had been given up for dead: seaman from the Third Division, Norman Pichette and a Fourth Division Leading Seaman, George K. Weise. Pichette had a bad stomach wound and was written off as a non-recoverable case. Weise had been manning an anti-aircraft gun near the stack and, when the second bomb hit, the concussion had thrown him forward in his seat fracturing his skull against the gunsight, before being blown out onto the flight deck, with his whole right-hand side paralysed. Weise recalled lying in the sick bay under the blue battle lights and hearing the 'abandon ship' horn sounding. 'The Third Class pharmacist's mate had his arm behind me, holding me up while asking the First Class Mate, 'What about him?' The First Class said, 'Leave him. He's gonna die anyway.' The Third Class was crying during the entire ordeal. He didn't want to leave me'.[58]

After they had been abandoned Pichette called over to Weise asking what they should do. Weise, unable to move himself, suggested Pichette wrap a sheet round his waist and belly and try to make it up on deck and attract some attention. Incredibly this is what Pichette managed to do, firing a machine-gun into the water alongside, before losing consciousness from the effort. The destroyer *Hughes* saw the bursts on the water, and, at 0951, sent across her motor launch and took him aboard to her sick bay. Here, Pichette regained consciousness long enough to inform *Hughes*'s medical officer that there was still at least one other live man left in *Yorktown*'s sick bay, then he relapsed and died shortly afterward, being buried at sea from the destroyer later.[59]

Hughes sent her motor boat back to *Yorktown* and extracted Weise. He recalled lying on the mess table and having a blood transfusion using the doctor's own blood.[60]

The *Hughes* boarding party also discovered secret ciphers and code books which had been left aboard, unsecured, from the previous day.

The Tanabe Attack

At 0735 (Tokyo time) Commander Tanabe, recorded in his submarine's logbook that the Commander of SubRon 3 gave a direct order to *I-168* to make an attack on the carrier *Yorktown*.[61] That same evening Tanabe received a second order to advance to the assigned position of his target.

Dawn on the 7th found *I-168* surfaced and scanning the horizon, and at 0410 Tanabe sighted off the starboard bow 'several black points [dots] on the eastern horizon'[62] at an estimated distance of 21,000 yards, and commenced a cautious approach. At 0600 two American destroyers were in view, forcing him to submerge. He continued his approach at an agonizing 3 knots. As he got closer the number of escorts he could count increased to seven.[63]

The salvage effort had been resumed at first light, with the hand-picked teams and the volunteers totalling twenty-nine officers and 141 men[64], all assigned predetermined and specific duties: fire-extinguishing, weight distribution, including the dumping overboard of aircraft, a 5 inch gun mounting, five 20 mm gun mounts and the port anchor and other heavy items to lessen the heel. The *Hammann* was sent back alongside the carrier's port side to assist with these objectives by playing her hoses where required and serving as a base for those aboard. The fire in the rag store, which was the most persistent blaze was finally put out and the pumping of water via three submersible pumps from the port third deck at frame 125 to the starboard fourth deck through frames 130–150 proceeded apace[65] and, with other measures, started to bring the list down from 26 to 22 degrees.

---

58. George K. Weise to Peter E. Karetka, cited Thomas B. Allen, 'Return to the Battle of Midway'.
59. Norman Pichette hailed from Athol, Massachusetts. about one-and-a-half hours drive from eyewitness Peter Karetka. Many years later, his brother visited Karetka with his family from Florida. Peter told me, 'After much talk, he thanked me for bringing closure on Norman for the family. This was the *first* info they had ever received on him, other than the fact he had died from injuries'. Karetka to the author, 15 November 2006. Karetka, now eighty-five, enlisted in the USN in November 1940 receiving an honourable discharge in December 1940.
60. *Ibid.*
61. Translation of *I-168* log via Military History Department, National Institute for Defense Studies, Tokyo. Cited hereafter as '*I-168*, Log'.
62. *I-168* Log.
63. There were just six destroyers on the screen: *Balch* (DD-363), *Benham* (DD-397), *Gwin* (DD-433), *Hammann* (DD-412), *Hughes* (DD-410) and *Monaghan* (DD-354), plus the *Vireo*, which was towing the *Yorktown*, but the latter looked from a distance just like a seventh escort. Through his scope Tanabe also mistook the towing movement for the carrier 'drifting', although he was unable to determine how fast and in what direction the movement was. What it did mean was that he had to abandon his initial attack plan and make an alternative approach, which further complicated matters.
64. Buckmaster to Nimitz, contained in CincPac report, Serial 01849, dated 28 June 1942. NARA, College Park, Maryland.
65. Buckmaster to Nimitz, *War Damage Reports*.

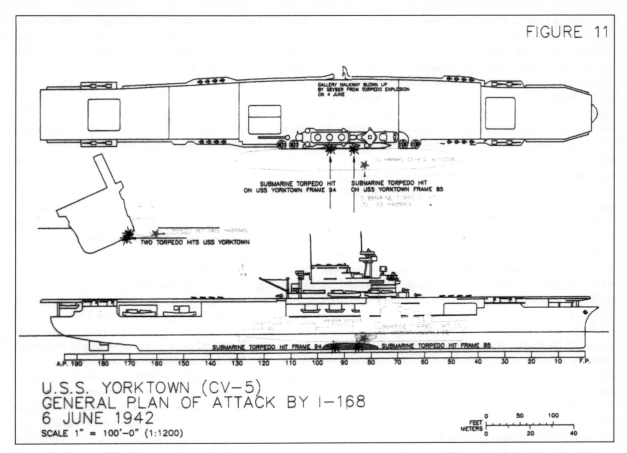

Diagram 14. General Plan of Attack by *I-168* on *Yorktown* (CV-5) on 6 June 1942. (Originally presented at FAST 99, Seattle, August 1999. Reprinted with the permission of the Society of Naval Architects and Marine Engineers, New Jersey)

Tanabe crept closer, raising his periscope at about 16,000 yards range. He estimated there was a high chance of detection and so he also rigged for depth-charging. In this he was unduly alarmed; no sonar detection was made by any of the escorts. The proliferation of escorts made this a risky move, so he decided to continue his approach blind, by sound and calculation. As a result he overshot.

By 0937 (Tokyo time) the Japanese submarine had eased her way to within about 500 yards of the 'big carrier'.[66] Tanabe judged that, although he was now well within the screen, this was too close for the torpedoes to operate effectively and that they would run beneath the carrier. He therefore made a 360 degrees turn to open up the distance to the correct range. After a heart-stopping twenty-eight minutes of careful manoeuvring, *I-168* was in position and, at 1330 (local time) Tanabe made a careful precision attack.

He fired two torpedoes initially, and then, within three seconds, two more, all at a range of about 1,300 yards. He was rewarded after just forty second, with four 'big sounds'.[67] These were the explosions of all four of his salvo striking home.

In fact alert lookouts aboard the destroyer *Monaghan* sighted the tracks of the torpedoes and made a TBS broadcast warning of incomings. The *Hammann* also sighted them but, at less than 1,000 yards off her starboard beam, there was barely time to signal full astern on her engines and order her 20 mm guns to try and detonate the warheads in the water, before they struck home. She had her back broken by the first torpedo and sank in two halves alongside the carrier. The next two passed below her and slammed into the *Yorktown*, the first at about starboard frame 85, and the second at around frame 94, while the last missile

---

66. *I-168* Log.

67. *I-168* Log.

apparently passed astern of her. These flooded three starboard fire rooms, the interior communication room, the switchboard room and central stations.

The *Hammann*'s skipper, Lieutenant-Commander Arnold E. True[68], had one rib broken and was incapacitated, but her XO[69], ordered 'abandon ship'. In truth the ship abandoned them, going down in less than three minutes, and compounding her demise and the damage to *Yorktown* when her depth-charges exploded as she sank[70], killing many of her crew in the water. One eyewitness from the salvage party compared their passing as the way that ' a windshield wiper erases the droplets from a windshield.' As one of *I-168*'s torpedoes had missed, the detonations of these charges must have been the fourth 'big noise' logged by Tanabe. Water immediately began pouring back into the carrier, and, although this inrush initially further rectified the list to just 17 degrees, the ship now seemed doomed. Aboard the *Vireo*, indeed, it was thought she might go straight to the bottom, and the tow was hastily cut.

The counter-attacks by the American destroyers were immediate and fierce, and the depth-charges often well placed. The *Balch* and the *Benham* assisted the tug in rescuing the *Hammann* survivors from the sea and once more evacuating the salvage team from the carrier, but *Gwin, Hughes* and *Monaghan* were looking for retribution. From 1335 onward their attacks were intense. Tanabe recorded in his ships log that '*I-168* took big damage, that #2 battery was unusable, the forward torpedo room was flooded, as a result *I-168* was unsubmergable [*sic*].'

What it meant within the close confines of the shaken submarine was a lessening of power and of oxygen supply. Seepage of chlorine was more serious, so much so that at one point the boat began rising and threatened to break the surface. Tanabe considered he had no option but to open the hatch, prepare his single gun and fight a hopeless fight on the surface against his assembled foes. At 1640 *I-168*

broke cover in full view of the three hunting destroyers, which were estimated to be about 11,000 yards distant. They soon began to close in, firing as they came. Tanabe sent what he expected to be his final signal to *Rengo Kantai* (the main battle fleet), stating simply, 'We sank *Yorktown*.'[71]

The Japanese skipper was wrong on both counts. The *Yorktown* still remained stubbornly afloat, having taken damage far in excess of what her designers and constructors would have considered possible. She was not nicknamed 'the Fighting Lady' for nothing! And *I-168*, incredibly, was not doomed yet either, for her engineers reported that they had 175 pounds of air in the submarines tanks and that their electric motor was again functioning. With the hounds at his very heels, Tanabe bundled his gun crew back inside and closed the conning tower hatch as *I-168* crash dived once more. The depth-charges continued to detonate, but at increasing distances from the slow-moving vessel.

Commander Tanabe, thanks to skilled seamanship and a well-trained crew that kept its head, eventually managed to creep away to safety and by 1850 (local time) had cleared the area and surfaced once more, recording to command ashore that they had not only escaped being sunk but had, in addition to the *Yorktown*, sunk an enemy destroyer. A long dangerous and exposed journey followed, made more difficult by the fact that the original plan for *I-168* to refuel at Midway had, perforce, to be abandoned! Tanabe once again proved equal to the challenge and eked out his fuel by using just two engines. Thus it was not until 19 June that they finally limped into Kure, with just 1,750 pounds of fuel oil left. She immediately went into dry dock for repairs.[72] By his dogged perseverance and audacious and skilled attack, Commander Tanabe had achieved more than the entire *Kidō Butai* and main battle fleet combined had done, and brought to the Battle of Midway Japan's only success.[73] It was but limited consolation, true, but it contrasted starkly

---

68. Rear-Admiral Arnold Ellsworth True (1901–79). b. Owenton, Kentucky, 23 January 1901. Graduated US Naval Academy, Annapolis 1920. Served in surface ships, cruisers, destroyers and miscellaneous. 1929 studied aerology and meteorology. 1931 awarded MSc degree from Massachusetts Institute of Technology. 1936, Aerological Officer, Fleet Air Base, Pearl Harbor. 1938–9 Naval War College. Appointed in command destroyer *Hammann* (DD-412) August 1939 until her loss on 6 June 1942. 1942–3, commanded DesDiv 4. Awarded Navy Cross and DSM for Coral Sea and Midway. 1944–5, Navy Weather and Aerology duties. December 1946, retired as rear-admiral. Died at his home in Palo Alto, California on 11 December 1979.
69. Lieutenant Ralph W. Elden.
70. *Hammann*'s casualty toll was high; nine officers and seventy-two men were killed and many injured.

71. *I-168* Log.
72. The *I-168* herself, repaired and renewed, was only to survive another year for, on 27 July 1943, under a new captain, she was sunk with all hands by four torpedoes from the American submarine *Scamp* (SS-277) in the Steffen Strait between New Ireland and New Hanover in 02° 50'S, 149° 01'E.
73. The *Sensuikan* (Japanese submarine arm) has been highly criticized after the war for its concentration on attacking American warships instead of adopting a German-style *guerre de course* against merchant ships and convoys. This criticism started with the Mochitsura Hashimoto book *Sunk! the Story of the Japanese Submarine Fleet 1942-5*. Itself a defeatist and largely self-flagellant study, it set a trend that has largely continued. However, this chorus of criticism ignores the fact that this was what they had been trained for and had practised for twenty years. The IJN submarine fleet had been specifi-

246

with the repeated failure of the American submarines, with the notable exception of the *Nautilus*.

Still the American carrier refused to accept her demise. All night she lay afloat, while the seven little ships resumed their guardianship. Captain Buckmaster was upbeat, signalling that he hoped to reboard with his teams at first light next day. But it was not to be. At 0501 on 7 June, the gallant ship finally gave up the struggle.

Captain Buckmaster later reported to Nimitz that *Yorktown* had 'turned over' onto her port side, as she sank 'in about 3,000 fathoms of water'.[74] Her resting place was officially recorded as 30° 46'N, 167° 24' W. According to most of the watchers aboard the assembled warships, she rolled over on her port beam ends at 0443, wallowed for a while in that undignified pose, then slid away into the depths, stern first.

The loss of the *Yorktown* has created many myths; even the actual manner of her sinking still arouses controversy. Why was she abandoned, not once, but twice? How well were the evacuations carried out, considering that some men were definitely left behind? Did she sink 'with all battle flags flying' as Buckmaster maintains, or with just a solitary battle flag at her truck? Finally, did she turn turtle as she went down, as was attested to by hundreds of eyewitnesses and from photographs taken at the time, since released by the navy, which certainly purport to show her so?

A highly detailed marine forensics analysis was conducted on the sinking by the Society of Naval Architects and Marine Engineers (SNAME), a team of six specialists examining all aspects of her damage and loss, including the underwater reports on her wreck by Dr Robert Ballard's remotely operated vehicle (ROV) cameras in 1998.[75] Their conclusive description of the *Yorktown*'s last moments says:

> Slightly after sunrise the flight deck on the port side was reported to be in contact with the water surface. At 0701 on 7 June *with a loud cracking noise and great billows of foam*[76], the *Yorktown* capsized to port. A large gaping hole could be seen on her star-

board side as she disappeared below the water and sank in 16, 650 feet of water.

Although War Damage Report No. 25, already cited, estimated that the two submarine torpedoes struck the ship at frames 85 and 94 respectively, photographs of the ship's turn of the bilge, taken before she sank, showed that they probably hit much closer together than at first thought, and that the resultant overlapping damage 'combined to produce one large hole'. The team concluded that as most of the released energy from these two explosions vented into the ship, wreaking havoc in the outer fire rooms on her starboard side and the central station, just forward of the foremost boiler room, all of which were flooded. 'Based on visual evidence, there appeared to be a single hole in the bottom plating of the ship, just inboard of the turn of the bilge'. The team concluded that: 'Once there was a large amount of flooding water in the *Yorktown*, its free surface effect negated the vessel's transverse stability, causing her to capsize and sink.'[77]

One respected member of the society, Jacques B. Hadler, who commented on the team's findings, had been a member of the War Damage Analysis Group in the Preliminary Design of the Bureau of Ships (BuShips) from November 1942. That group was headed by Commander (later Admiral) Ernie Holtzworth, Mac Nicholson from the same US Naval Academy class and Jerry Strope, a graduate from the Webb Institute of Naval Architecture. Halder recalled:

> I do remember we spent a large amount of effort in trying to determine the location of the two torpedo hits launched by the *I-168*, which resulted in the capsizing of the *Yorktown*. Apparently they were closer together than we estimated. The major design lesson that I learned from this loss was the poor arrangement of the boiler and engine rooms. I understood from Captain Kniskern, then head of Preliminary Design, that the liabilities of the

---

cally built as another factor in whittling down the superior American battle fleet prior to the main surface battle. In 1942, the Japanese submarines were actually the most successful of the IJN's arms at doing this. Japanese submarines in that year sank the carriers *Yorktown* (CV-5) and *Wasp* (CV-7) and damaged the carrier *Saratoga* (CV-3), the new battleship *North Carolina* (BB-55) and the heavy cruiser *Chester* (CA-27) among others. Nor should it be forgotten that exactly the same role had been envisaged for the Royal Navy's big O, P and R class submarines, built in the late 1920s and early 1930s, whose main mission had been to defend the approaches to Singapore and Malaya against the Japanese fleet. Had they not all been withdrawn to the Mediterranean

in 1940–1, where their large size made them vulnerable, they might have offered a better defence than the *Prince of Wales* and *Repulse* were able to do when the time came. As it was they were just squandered wholesale in unsuitable waters. Just how highly trained and prepared for this role the Royal Navy submarines were before the war, and how very much they mirrored IJN attitudes, is explained in Alastair Mars's book, *British Submarines at War 1939–1945*.

74. Buckmaster to Nimitz.
75. Robert O, Dulin, Jr, et al. '*The Loss of the* USS *Yorktown*'. (CV-5) – A Marine Forensics Analysis.
76. My italics.
77. Robert O, Dulin, Jr, et al. '*The Loss of the* USS *Yorktown*'.

Yorktown-Enterprise machinery arrangement were recognized when they were designing the *Hornet*. However, President Roosevelt, who followed the details of major ship designs, insisted that the *Hornet* machinery spaces should be a duplicate of those of the *Yorktown-Enterprise* class.[78]

Bill Roy, who took so many of the memorable photographs of the great old ship's last battle, recalled:

Next day, early dawn, at 5.30 a.m. June 7, 1942, *Yorktown* seemed to be on an even keel. We had hopes to salvage the ship and save her. The list of *Yorktown* was then noticed to be increasing rapidly to port and, at 7.01 a.m., *Yorktown* turned over to her port side and sank stern first in about 3000 fathoms of water . . . I was on the bridge of the destroyer with Captain Buckmaster taking pictures with a K-20 aerial camera. It was the only camera that had film. Buckmaster told the destroyer captain, 'take me through the debris where *Yorktown* sank.' We cut through the flotsam. Buckmaster said, 'Come about and go through again.' We did. Then Captain Buckmaster said, 'Go through again.' The destroyer skipper said, I am taking her back to Pearl.[79]

Others have very different memories of her final appearance. One, Peter Karetka, a signalman on one of the destroyers, still positively asserts, all photographic evidence to the contrary, that she sank right way up. 'She slid gracefully, like a lady, beneath the waves, no dive, no gurgle, no foamy froth, no plume of water or screws showing – a sad but proud moment for me.'[80] The reasoning behind this memory he was to later explained this way:

The *Yorktown* went under with a slight list to the port and bow angle. The open hangar deck was being flooded to a point where it would have neutral buoyancy. This is keeping the carrier level by equal pressure on the hangar deck. The flight deck is taken over by the sea creating equal pressure on the top side of the flight deck as well as the underside of the flight deck. This now acts as a horizontal stabilizer.

As the carrier keeps sinking in a glide fashion the island starts disappearing. This now acts as a vertical rudder, if you will, in steerage and helps keep the carrier in an upright position, plus the carrier's deep draft. Put all of this together it allows for a nice glide path to the ocean floor, keeping the *Yorktown* upright during her descent to the ocean floor.

If the carrier had rolled over, the pressure of the water against the guns would have either ripped the guns off or at least changed their positions.[81]

So strongly did Karetka feel about this that when he met a *Yorktown* survivor[82] in 2000 who confirmed his own memory, he took him before a notary public to swear an affidavit to that effect. However, despite a stubborn and

---

78. *Ibid.*
79. William Roy, 'I filmed the Battle of Midway from USS *Yorktown.*' Bill also told me recently that, when they returned to Pearl Harbor despite the fact that he had taken all those stirring and memorable photographs personally, was strictly forbidden to enter the photographic laboratory where they were being developed, and this was despite the fact that he had secret clearance. He never saw any of his pictures until the navy released some of them later. Bureaucracy gone mad! The 35 mm cine camera film just vanished and was only later fortunately retrieved by Lieutenant-Commander Otis G. Kight, who was at that time a flight-deck seaman with VF-42. Bill told me: 'Cathy Marsh Munro went to the National Archives, Washington DC and located the 35 mm movie film of the battle that I had taped up the 3 cans, placed under my shirt and life jacket, when I abandoned *Yorktown* on 5 June and passed over to a photographer aboard the heavy cruiser *Astoria*. That had been the last I saw of the 35 mm movie film until, about 2–3 months later, San Francisco, California, Market Street, and the Telenews Theater one-hour newsreels of war footage, there it was!' William G. Roy to the author, 8 November 2006.
80. Peter E. Karetka "Flags" at Midway'. How Peter recalls the event in his sketch from memory, and the earlier appearance of *Yorktown* on the 4, when she was first abandoned, from photographs, are very, similar, and this might well be the reason. Peter Karetka is still sticking to his 65-year old memory, undaunted, and recently convinced *The Republication*'s journalist Cynthia Simson. See article *Seaman Makes Truth his Lifelong Mission*, 6 June 2007 edition, Springfield, MA.
81. Peter E. Karetka, *Reflections*. Also the photographic evidence of Robert Ballard's 1998 underwater expedition to the *Yorktown* wreck site shows the ship resting upright on the seabed, with accumulated debris on her flight deck. See Robert Ballard, *Return to Midway*. The photographs of *Yorktown* upside down are genuine, however, and Parshall and Tully are among many who refute Karetka's theories as taking no account of hydrodynamic forces acting on a body falling through a liquid medium, which generally reasserts the original centre of gravity. Both the liner *Titanic* and the battleship *Bismarck*, battered and holed, were both found upright on the bed of the Atlantic.
82. The late Alvin L. Evasius, a *Yorktown* survivor who lived at Brimfield, Massachusetts. See his public notary office document, sworn at Chicopee, Massachusetts and dated 26 November 2000.

continuing campaign against the Naval Historical Center for publishing the seemingly irrefutable photographic evidence of the carrier upside down before she took the final plunge, this veteran's specific memories will, no doubt, accompany him to his grave unproven.

Karetka totally and sincerely remembers it that way, no matter what, just as Best refused ever to change his opinion on which carrier he had sunk in the first attack, Gay insisted that he had witnessed the whole battle from under his life raft, Penland sketched out his plan of the enemy fleet while still 'fresh' in his mind on his return to his carrier and so many pilots remembered seeing Japanese strike aircraft parked all over their carriers after decks, ready to take off just before they were hit. It can be 'proved' to them over and over again that their memories are just not possible; but they were there and they had their own fixed perception. Who are we to deny them that memory, misguided or not?

The SNAME Forensics team concluded that the huge torpedo hole on *Yorktown*'s port side, extending as it did from Frame 74 to Frame 90, some 45 feet, was. 'much larger that one would expect from a 450-pound TNT equivalent explosive charge of the standard Japanese aerial torpedo in use in mid–1942 (Type 91, Modification 2)'. They therefore believed 'that this torpedo hole is the result of two torpedo hits that were so close together as to make one large opening'. They found that the torpedo which struck further aft appeared to be much higher than the forward one, which indicated that the two had different depth settings. 'In any event, the closeness of these two torpedo hits is compelling testimony to the skill of the Japanese aviators piloting the torpedo planes'.[83]

The team also explained how the *Yorktown* could turn turtle on the surface just prior to sinking but still end in an upright position on the seabed.

It is characteristic of slender bodies like ships to turn sideways when dropped, that is to take up a position that maximizes drag and minimizes vertical velocity. This is easily observed if one drops a folded piece of paper from ceiling height. Generally, end-on stability requires that the center of pressure be well aft of the center of gravity: this is the main reason that we add tail fins to bombs, arrows, and airplanes. The *Yorktown*'s center of gravity and center of pressure were like nearly co-incident. In the absence of other information, it would thus appear reasonable to assume that the *Yorktown* most likely descended to the bottom in a 'falling leaf' motion and impacted in a nearly horizontal position'.[84]

Structural distortion to the bow section of the vessel, revealed by the ROV probe, seemed to confirm this theory.

The fact that the *Yorktown* was lost at all, was in itself a bitter pill for many naval aviators to swallow. 'Dusty' Kleiss recorded: 'The handling of the whole affair looks extremely stupid to me'.[85]

Barde was cutting: 'The responsibily of this indecision rests squarely with the Task Force Commander, Frank Jack Fletcher. Throughout 4 June he had performed magnificently as the officer in tactical command. When the *Yorktown* was left behind, the alert mind of Admiral Fletcher seemed to have remained on the scene as well.'[86]

Yamamoto Throws in the Towel

Yamamoto's signal of 1040 had still sought to pull the cat out of the bag despite the appalling and totally unexpected devastation of the *Kidō Butai*. His intentions were certainly clear enough at that time. 'Main Force of Invasion Force (less BatDiv 3) plus DesRon2 and CruDiv 8, by attacking and destroying the enemy carrier force, will rescue the *Mogami* and *Mikuma*.'

As Layton was to note, although Spruance did not know it, during his attacks on the two cruisers they had acted as 'live bait' by Yamamoto to draw the American force into a position where land-based aircraft from Wake Island could attack them. It was something of a last resort to inflict some damage on the enemy. It could all be summed up, Layton considered, in the Japanese symbol *kakugo*, could be variously interpreted according to context as perception, resolution, expectation, readiness or, most likely by the 6th, resignation.[87] By ordering the Main Force, which was under his direct command (and about which the Americans still knew nothing), to proceed to a position about 330 miles north-west of Midway (even though it was not far from the enemy carriers) the Japanese C-in-C hoped to facilitate the safe extraction of most of the occupation forces. He relied on withdrawing to the cover of an area forecast to have bad weather and reduced visibility, which would hamper what remained of the American carrier-based air power.

Again, although his opposition to battleships was

---

83. Robert O. Dulin, Jr, et al. 'The Loss of the USS *Yorktown* (CV-5)'.

84. *Ibid.*

85. N. J. Kleiss, *VS-6 Log of the War*.

86. Robert Barde, *The Battle of Midway: A Study in Command.*

87. Layton records held at Naval War College, Box 38, folder 42, card notes, *Cover and Deception.*

deep-rooted, he was forced by circumstance to rely totally upon their inherent strength; both in offence for a decisive night action against, at best, heavy cruiser opposition, and in defence, because of their ability to absorb far greater punishment than had crushed his elite, but oh-so-brittle, carrier vanguard.[88] Admiral Yamamoto was therefore to count on the ability of his battleships to absorb any air attacks on his force, believing, almost one feels despite himself, that his battle line could easily do so without taking serious damage. It must be remembered that dive-bombers might be able hit battleships, but such hits were never fatal; it always took torpedoes to put them under the water, sometimes dozens of torpedoes. But the Americans had already expended almost every one of their torpedo-bombers, Spruance had just one single section of TBDs left fit for service and, even if they all got through, three torpedo hits was not going to cripple, or even deter, the Japanese battle line. We have already seen that Spruance was reluctant to commit them, holding them back from attacking the already heavily damaged heavy cruisers for fear of further loss. Unfortunately for Yamamoto, the collision between those two heavy cruisers, which so reduced their speed of withdrawal, negated his plan.

Thus, all the earlier fire and dash with which the Japanese hoped to reverse the stunning events of 4 June had finally stuttered to a halt by the 6th, and the concentration of every one of Yamamoto's wide-ranging squadrons, although achieved in limited form, only resulted in a humiliating withdrawal, not the fire-and-fury of a pitched night surface battle which might redeem the outcome.

The American verdict on Yamamoto's plan and performance were almost universally scathing.[89] The Naval War College Report summary was typical of many similar analyses that followed the same line of argument.

The Japanese planning for the Midway operation was not sound. Japanese forces were not adequately coordinated. This was because their initial positions were so widely separated that the American forces were able to strike certain groups, notably the Mobile Force and Crudiv 7, before the latter forces were able to concentrate with stronger forces. The factors of mutual support and concentration appear to have been disregarded for purposes of possible envelopment of American forces.[90]

Admiral Kondo expressed similar views.

Even in the Midway operation alone, the covering force for the invasion was too separated from the carrier group force to cooperate with it. In fact, when our carrier group was reported as having received severe damage from enemy carrier-borne [air]craft, the covering force for the invasion hurried with increased speed to the engagement area, ordering the convoy to withdraw, but our fleet failed to launch a night action upon the enemy.[91]

Again, the assumption that the disastrous situation could still be retrieved by a night action, which they were bound to win, encapsulated the basic flaw in Japanese thinking: that the Americans would duly oblige them by steering west in the night. Broadcasting alluring messages of damaged battleships was just one ploy used in a futile attempt to get

---

88. Another weak point in Yamamoto's overall plan, which is never discussed in analysis of Midway, was his seeming reliance on the Mobile Force carriers both to take out the Midway Island defences and then also to assist in the annihilation of the American fleet, should it tardily 'turn up' in defence. But in committing his finely honed air groups to the first task, Yamamoto must have taken into account on the balance sheet of probability, that they would suffer, at least *some* casualties. For even if the Japanese aircraft only lost a percentage of their total strength, that would nevertheless automatically make them that much weaker by the time they had to take on the Americans. In any carrier-to-carrier duel, in order to win it, it was accepted that you had to be at your maximum strength. So, Yamamoto's plan would always have as its core a weakened *Kidō Butai* for the main battle (and keep in mind it was supposed to be luring and annihilating the American fleet which was his principal aim in fighting the battle at all). Midway itself was supposed to be just the bait. Like Verdun, where the Germans attacked merely to make the French feed in troops to be pulverized, the lure somehow became the obsession once battle was

joined! Unless, all along, the battleship-hating Yamamoto was always going to rely on the battleships to finish off the enemy (after all, why else bring them along?). If *that* was what was in his mind, then it must follow that his plan was no more radical than all the other plans that the despised Japanese surface-ship admirals had been practising for the previous two decades.

89. But not totally so. 'Any graduate of the Japanese staff system of war college of the 1930s, and probably their American counterparts as well, would have been thoroughly at home with the existing plan. Yamamoto's dispositions were designed to engage the American fleet no matter from which direction it came'. (Ronald H. Spector, *Eagle Against the Sun: The American War With Japan*.) Also, 'With 20/20 hindsight, many historians have portrayed the Japanese plan of attack on Midway as overly complex, but perhaps 'sophisticated' describes the plan more appropriately.' (Captain Robert S. Burrell, 'Miracle at Midway'.

90. Bates Report.

91. Kondo interview with Prange, 28 February 1947, reproduced in Goldstein and Dillon, *The Pacific War Papers*.

the Americans to take the bait. As in the very root of Yamamoto's original grand design, this assumed that the enemy would always do as the Japanese hoped they might do. The Japanese so-called 'victory fever' itself, did not so much exude over confidence in their own abilities and potential – these were well-founded – as attribute their enemy with stupidity, and that was what proved fatal. Fortunately for the Americans, it assumed too much! Spruance and Fletcher were far from stupid; they refused to offer themselves up on a plate for the 18.1 inch guns of *Yamato* and very sensibly kept as much space as possible between those questing muzzles and their own slender hulls. Consequently the Japanese found themselves flailing at thin air!

As Layton put it:

It was not until 0300, after Yamamoto had concluded that our surviving carriers were not going to be suckered into a night action[92], that he finally swallowed the bitter pill of defeat. 'Midway Operation Cancelled' was the signal that caused the transports to head back for Saipan. The covering force was ordered to join up with the remnants of Nagumo's Striking Force and rendezvous with the main force northwest of Midway. Only the Aleutian Islands was to go ahead as scheduled.[93]

The same scenario continued to be played out, but by the 7th the penny had finally dropped. Yamamoto and his staff had gone from a state of confidence to a 'state of growing unease'[94], on the evening of 6 June, at which time the battleships *Yamato, Nagato* and *Mutsu* of the Main Body were steering south to cover Kondo and Nagumo and yet still remotely hoped to take apart the American forces in a night battle. However, Yamamoto, suffering severe stomach cramps and in much pain, had not pushed ahead at maximum speed, maintaining a moderate 18 knots, possibly to help conserve fuel, which was becoming as much a problem for the Japanese as it was for the Americans.[95] Finally, the combined Japanese force turned back for home.

And so the two forces steadily drew apart. *Saratoga* might be hustled to sea from Hawaii, but it was already too late for her intervention.[96] The Japanese bombers on Wake Island might be on standby to strike hard blows at the US carriers, but they were never destined to get the chance. The Japanese steamed homeward, licking their wounded pride, harbouring anger and promising revenge to come, but they knew they had been outthought and outfought. Consolation, such as it was, came from the conquest of two cold, bleak islands in the Aleutians, plus exaggerated claims of having sunk two US carriers among other ships and shot down 120 enemy aircraft. In return they admitted the loss of just one carrier, with a second and a cruiser damaged and the loss of just thirty-five aircraft![97]

Yamamoto's reputation never fully recovered.[98] The war moved south to the sweltering Solomon Islands in 1942 and Midway was never seriously threatened again. That they had been reprieved seemed to some beyond belief. The victors headed for Pearl once more, mourning those empty

---

92. Suppose the Americans had their battleships with them, would it have made any difference? They might not have had reservations about meeting Yamamoto's heavyweights. The closest the seven veteran battleships (*Colorado, Idaho, Maryland, Mississippi, New Mexico, Pennsylvania* and *Tennessee*) of Rear-Admiral Walter S. Anderson and Vice-Admiral William Satterlee Pye's TF-1 got to the battle was 1,200 miles out from San Francisco, where they paraded up and down from 31 May to 17 June, along with the escort carrier *Long Island* (AVG-1) with twelve F4F-4s and eight Curtiss SOCs embarked, and then returned to harbour. The speed of the old battleships, if nothing else, precluded them taking any meaningful part in Midway. Not until the new, fast battleships appeared could American commanders find useful employment for the suddenly redundant 'capital ships'. For further debate on the matter see David C. Fuquea, 'Task Force One: The Wasted Assets of the United States Pacific Battleship Fleet, 1942', in *Journal of Military History*, Vol, 61, No 4, October 1997.
93. Layton, *And I Was There.*
94. Parshall and Tully, *Shattered Sword.*
95. The planned rendezvous with their tanker force, already postponed once, was put off yet again and the battleships

refuelled their destroyer escorts on the 6th, slowing their advance to the intended battle area yet further.
96. 'Dusty' Kleiss recorded in his diary, 'Considerable hard feeling between *Enterprise* and *Sara* crews. Seems like the *Sara* tried to sell themselves as the Galloping Ghost. *Sara* rushed to our support . . . .just in time to clear Pearl channel and go back.'
97. Reuters press release, London, 10 June 1942.
98. His next big idea was the *I-Go* Operation, a massive series of air attacks using much of the laboriously reassembled naval air power, working from shore bases instead of their carriers, in a three-day series of strikes against Allied positions in the Solomons. Between 7 and 12 April 1943, attacks were made all down 'the Slot' in the Solomons, then against Buna and Port Moresby in New Guinea. The Japanese claimed to have sunk two cruisers and seven transports, with numerous other ships damaged, as well as installations and airfields destroyed. In truth, just one destroyer, two small escort ships and a solitary tanker were sunk, while Japanese losses were heavy. The death of Yamamoto a few days after this fiasco set the seal on his fate, and, although much mourned, militarily he was little missed.

messes[99], but confident and proud of what they had achieved.

Home is the Sailor, Home from the Sea.[100]

And so the Battle of Midway came to an end. It did not end in one final climactic clash, as Hollywood would have it, but just fizzled out, as battles usually do, with both sides tired and weary. For the Japanese the exhaustion was compounded by defeat, the first real taste of it they had experienced in nine months of war. Their squadrons slunk home; their wounded were moved ashore and into hospitals by night, almost like criminals. It was a sour and bitter homecoming. It was as if the hierarchy wished to shut the very thought of the battle out of their minds, or wish it away. No public post-mortem was held, only a furtive secret inquiry behind closed doors. As one historian was to summarize, the effects of the battle:

> American morale soared: in Tokyo the profound significance of the defeat was overlooked. On June 10 the navy conveyed to the liaison conference an incomplete picture of the results of the battle, on the ground that the real extent of damage was a military secret not to be entrusted to all members. Only the Emperor was accurately informed of the carrier and pilot losses, and he chose not to inform the army immediately. Army planners, inaccurately briefed on

the real significance of the Coral Sea and Midway defeats, continued for a short time to believe that the Combined Fleet was healthy and secure.[101]

When asked on the homeward voyage how the news would be broken to the Living God at the Imperial Palace in Tokyo, Yamamoto had courageously replied, 'I will tell the Emperor', and he was as good as his word. What is not clear is whether the Emperor himself really took on board the true significance of Midway. The Marquis Koichi Kido[102], as Lord Keeper of the Privy Seal, had the Emperor's ear at all times. He discussed Midway with his ruler on 8 June and later confided to his diary:

> I had presumed the news of the terrible losses sustained by the naval air force would have caused him untold anxiety, yet when I saw him he was as calm as usual and his countenance showed not the least change. He said he told the navy chief of staff that the loss was regrettable but to take care that the navy not lose its fighting spirit. He ordered him to ensure that future operations continue bold and aggressive. When I witness the courage and wisdom of the emperor, I am very thankful that our imperial country Japan is blessed with such a sovereign.[103]

Be that as it may, the true measure of the Japanese defeat was in their silence on the subject. As a secret US intelligent

---

99. Clayton Fisher recalled: 'In the *Hornet* officers' dining area each squadron was assigned their own dining table. The torpedo squadron's table was empty of pilots. I visited the torpedo squadron's ready room. Nothing had been removed. Also the pilots' uniforms were still hanging on hooks, left there after the pilots changed into flight suits. Later another pilot and I inventoried the personal effects of two of the torpedo pilots. It was a very emotional and depressing experience'. Commander Clayton Fisher, narration to the Victory at Midway celebration aboard the USS *John B. Stennis* (CV-74), NAS North Island, 29 June 2001.

100. Requiem:

> Under the wide and starry sky
> Dig the grave and let me lie:
> Glad did I live and gladly die,
> And I laid me down with a will.
>
> This be the verse you 'grave for me:
> Here he lies where he long'd to be;
> Home is the sailor, home from the sea,
> And the hunter home from the hill.

Robert Louis Stevenson, 1850–94.

101. Herbert P. Bix, *Hirohito and the Making of Modern Japan*.

102. Marquis Koichi Kido (1889–1977). b. 18 July 1889, grandson of Kido Takayoshi, one of movers behind the Meiji Restoration. Attended Kyoto University. From 22 October 1937 to 26 May 1938, Minister of Education, and 11 January 1938–5 January 1939 Minister of Welfare in the Prince Konoye Government. 5 January 1939–30 August 1939, Minister of Home Affairs in the Hiranuma Kiichiro Government. 1940–45 served as Lord Keeper of the Privy Seal. Closest confidant and chief advisor to Emperor Hirohito, whom he knew since childhood, he had free and unrivalled access to the throne. Advised acceptance of Hideki Tojo as Prime Minister in 1941, but advised against invasion of Dutch East Indies lest it bring in the United States into war against Japan. 1945 advised the Emperor to deliver a personal speech to stop the fighting. 1945, adviser to General MacArthur and AOF (American Occupation Forces) during occupation. Despite this, was charged as Class A war criminal by the International Military Tribunal and his diary was used as evidence in camera. Found guilty on five counts and given life imprisonment in the Sugamo Prison, Tokyo. In 1948 and in 1951, he advised the Emperor to abdicate but recommended the future punishment of war criminals be done under Japanese law at the end of the occupation. 1953 released from jail due to health problems. Lived at Oiso, and had an apartment at Aoyama, Tokyo. Died 6 April 1977, aged 88. Interred at Tama Cemetery, Tokyo.

103. Marquis Koichi Kido, *The Diary of Marquis Kido, 1931–45*.

report for the Pacific Ocean Area noted wryly on 24 June, 'There has been no mention of Midway in the radio traffic since the middle of June.'[104] They had little enough to celebrate about Midway; all they did have was the success of Commander Yahachi Tanabe, and he was duly granted the honour of a personal audience with the Emperor.

Secretly the navy held an inquest into what had gone so terribly wrong. Their doctrine, never fully developed, had been revealed to have glaring holes in it, mainly defensive. The CAP had been adequate for a long time, but was finally worn down by attack after attack. The direction, such as it was, proved ineffective at maintaining discipline against such a succession of threats. Lack of radar was being addressed, but to shield the carriers from dive-bombing attacks they needed more than that.

They finally came up with a new concept for carrier operations, which was applied to the 3rd Fleet.[105] The main thrust here was that each the carrier divisions were to be increased from two to three ships, with two heavy 'attack' carriers as before, supplemented by a light carrier (CVL), the latter having the primary task of providing each division's CAP requirement, leaving her two larger sisters free to go for the enemy unhindered by the chore of maintaining a fighter umbrella over the force.[106] This concept demanded many more carriers of course, as well as additional air groups. The conversion of merchant ships and seaplane carriers was expedited to provide the new light carriers, although these tended to be slower than the custom-built carriers. By 1944 the IJN had assembled three such divisions of three carriers each, and these were utilized in battle for the first (and last) time at the Battle of the Philippine Sea. The question of effective control of the CAP, however, which relied on a combination of effective radar, much more efficient radios and a centralized control, does not seem to have been fully addressed; indeed it could not be until the basic components had been manufactured.

By the time the IJN had assembled its nine carriers, it had not once but twice squandered its fighter pilot strength to a far higher degree than at Midway. Thus, even if the doctrine had improved by 1944, the human material had deteriorated from the first class quality of 1942, to a very third-rate substitute and there was no balance. In addition the power of their enemy had waxed enormously in all fields and not only did nine carriers now face twelve, but those twelve

were backed by a large number of brand-new fast battleships so a surface action was no longer feared by the Americans.

The once proud Japanese carrier force ended its days at Leyte Gulf, reduced to the humiliating role of 'live bait' while the outcome of the last great battle descended once more upon the battle line, now much reduced and short of fuel. The wheel had come full circle in a few short years.

The American carriers returned to Pearl. *Hornet* launched her planes on 13 June and they landed at Ford Island. Clayton Fisher recalled: 'My log book shows a three hour flight. I have no ideas why we were launched so far out. All I remember is how emotional it was to again see Diamond Head.'[107]

The carriers followed their aircraft into Pearl some time later. Lundstrom records that, 'the carrier task forces entered Pearl to cheers and triumphal celebrations'.[108] These celebration's were well-merited and might indeed have been held when they arrived at their berths, but there are many who remember that prior to that their reception from the soldiers as the ships proceeded through the fairly narrow entrance to the channel to the harbour, with their proud crews at attention and lining the decks in the traditional manner, was a sour one. Army personnel from the two fortresses flanking the entrance, jeered and mocked the ships and their crews. James F. Murray, an ACRM (PA) who flew as rear-seat man with Best in VB-6, recalled this bitter 'welcome'.

On 13 June TF-16, with the remainder of TF-17, entered Pearl Harbor. The planes left the carriers outside, and flew into the Naval Air Station Kaneohe to receive an aircrew reception and celebration. I remained aboard and rode her into the harbor. (As one enters the navigation channel one passes close by an Army Fort and Hickam Field, the Army Air Corps base.) The Army had gun emplacements bordering the channel, which were manned. The task force ships flying their huge battle flags were led into Pearl Harbor by *Enterprise*. As our ship came up the channel the Army gun crews and other spectators were yelling, 'Where was the Navy at Midway', and 'Tell us where you were hiding' and many more derogatory remarks.[109]

---

104. Secret Information Bulletin, dated June 14, 1942: Subject: Japanese Naval Ops; Estimate of. 1. General, in collection at Naval Historical Center, Washington Navy Yard, DC.
105. *Senshi Sōsho*, Vol. 83.
106. See *Research on Mobile Force Tactics*, Yokosuka Kokutai, dated 1943, on this proposed set-up, and *Mobile Force Doctrine*, Yokosuka Kokutai, dated 1944, for arrangements

as used at Battle of Leyte Gulf. Military History Department, National Institute for Defense Studies, Tokyo.
107. Fisher to the author, 16 November 2006.
108. Lundstrom, *Black Shoe Carrier Admiral*.
109. James Francis Murray, former aviation chief radioman, 'Narrative of the Battle of Midway' in Reese, *Looking Back*.

There was no response from the sailors – discipline would not allow it – but it was hardly the 'conquering hero' reception they felt they had earned. Once the crews got ashore and read the USAAC massive claims propagated by Hale in the local newspapers, it became very obvious what had been going on. Even so, there was little reaction. A kind of numb resignation took over. Lieutenant Harold S. Bottomley[110] of VB-3 recalled: 'On arriving in Honolulu, we found out that the Army Air Force had won a great battle at Midway, and had turned back the invading fleet!'[111]

Clayton Fisher said:

I don't remember hearing about any trouble with the crews when they went ashore. When we all heard about the newspaper articles about how the B-17s had sunk all the carriers and won the Battle of Midway it seemed unbelievable.

On 23 July I flew an OS2U, a monoplane cruiser scout plane (the float had been removed and a landing gear attached) from Ford Island to Hickham Field to pick up some gun sights. A young green-ass Second Lieutenant B-17 pilot that had just arrived from California approached me and asked, 'What is that funny looking plane you are flying?' Then he told me about the big four-engine B-17 he was going to fly and how the B-17s had won the Battle of Midway. I was burning inside, but I just walked away from him.[112]

The US Army comes out of this with little lustre. Claiming the total credit and full publicity for a victory in which their contribution and achievements had been nil was contemptible enough; jeering at the true victors as cowards was beneath contempt.

The claim on *Timeline: Battle of Midway* is that 'Midway was the largest of naval battles of World War II, both in terms of forces involved and the area those forces covered'. Both statements are untrue. Midway was most certainly not the largest naval battle – that was Leyte Gulf in 1944, larger by far in number of ships engaged and lost. Midway was not even the largest *carrier* battle; that place belongs to Philippine Sea, when twelve American carriers took on nine Japanese carriers. Then what, in history, was Midway? It was the turning point[113], the line in the sand when the Japanese overreached themselves and the Americans stood and fought them to a standstill. There were plenty of Japanese victories still to come, and, much more killing, but no more simple victories. The tsunami had met the cliff and, surge though it might, could advance no more.

That was the true significance of Midway.

---

110. Rear-Admiral Harold Sydney 'Syd' Bottomley, Jr, (1915–90). b. Merchantville, New Jersey on 13 October 1915. 1942 Lieutenant VB-6. Awarded Navy Cross for Midway. 1960, February, appointed in command of carrier *Bon Homme Richard* (CV-31) at Yokosuka. March amphibious operation *Bluestar*, visited Bombay, May Alameda, Refit Puget Sound. Left ship in December.

111. Harold S. Bottomley, 'Narrative of the Battle of Midway', in Reese, *Looking Back*.

112. Fisher to the author, 16 November 2006.

113. Rear-Admiral Ernest M. Eller certainly viewed it thus. See *Oral History*, Volume II, USNI, Annapolis, Maryland.

Part Four

The Midway Legacy

Chapter Eleven

Conclusions and Consequences

In the immediate aftermath of Midway, one lesson stood out clear and sharp. It was crystallized by 'Sockem' Soucek, the Air Operations Officer of the carrier *Hornet*, in his report to Marc Mitscher, a few days after the battle, and he linked it with a prophetic warning against too much euphoria. 'Through superb intelligence work we were given the advantage; we cannot expect such advantages on every occasion in the future'.[1]

The success of COMINT at Midway was a two-way street, as Henry F. Schorreck pointed out thirty-three years later.

> Comint's contribution to victory in the Battle of Midway had a dramatic effect on those who used Comint and on the Comint Profession itself.

> For Admirals King and Nimitz and other senior military commanders, Midway clearly demonstrated the value of Comint and the ability of Cryptologic professionals to function successfully under wartime conditions. It would take some time, perhaps, for this conviction to spread throughout the lower echelons of command, but for those at the top, who knew what had happened and had seen it work, there was no longer any doubt. Later in the Pacific war, it became an offence punishable by court-martial for a tactical commander who had been provided ComInt to disregard it.

> The success at Midway established the Comint profession and gave it the recognition and respectability it needed-when it needed them most.[2]

Although the other post-battle lessons that were absorbed influenced the way the future carrier battles in the Pacific theatre were conducted, they were, strangely, far less dominant than would at first appear. Although the Pacific War was undoubtedly a carrier-dominated war, there were, in reality, very few carrier-to-carrier battles after Coral Sea and Midway; only the smaller Santa Cruz and Eastern Solomons in 1942 and finally the ultimate clash at the Philippine Sea in 1944, really fitted the bill. In total, there were just five carrier-to-carrier battles ever fought over a period of twenty-five months.[3] Night surface actions predominated in the Solomons, while at Leyte Gulf the Japanese carrier force had been reduced to 'live bait' which the impetuous Halsey eagerly, and predictably, duly swallowed. Later, a more detailed analysis was done, with some equally surprising results, but, by that time the war was over and a different scenario, that of the Cold War, was in play, which made most of the lessons irrelevant. Just as important to the first post-war studies, was the fact that although many of the intercepted Japanese radio messages were finally decoded and could be studied in retrospect, others were still to remain highly classified for decades into the future and a true picture was still not fully revealed.

The Immediate Post-battle Analysis

CincPac was quick to examine the most obvious lessons from the Midway encounter and to apply them practically to the Pacific War as it was then developing. In his report[4] Nimitz stated, 'This action brings out some new lessons and drives home other definite ones previously learned'.

---

1. Air Operations Officer to CO *Hornet*, CV8/A16, OF29-AS, dated 12 June, 1942.
2. Henry F. Schorreck, 'The Role of Comint in the Battle of Midway', SRH-230, article in National Security Agency's, *Cryptologic Spectrum*, Summer 1975 (declassified per Part 3, E.O. 12356, 4 February 1983).
3. James P. Levy, *Race for the Decisive Weapon: British, American and Japanese Carrier Fleets, 1942-1943.*
4. CincPac File No. A16. *Battle of Midway* (ADM 199/1302, National Archives, Kew, London).

(i) Nimitz held that the concept of a 'mobile air force', with aircraft despatched freely from a central base, was impracticable in the mid-Pacific. There were inadequate facilities and servicing facilities at the scattered and small island bases. The huge intake of fresh pilots did not have the training or skill to operate effectively in remote and unfamiliar localities and the distances involved were too great – 'We could not get fighter reinforcements to Midway on 4 June after virtually all the fighters there had been put out of action combating the one short Japanese raid.'

(ii) There was a mismatch of available land-based aircraft. Whereas the navy PBY Catalina's had excellent range they were rendered impotent by any enemy air opposition. The army's B-17s and B-24s were better in this respect and should be made available to the navy. High-altitude bombing was dismissed as useless, as we have seen, whereas torpedo and dive-bombers were 'the only truly effective weapon'. The Marines had been equipped with inferior aircraft and in future 'ought to be furnished with the very best fighting planes available.' Shore-based aircraft strength, 'was not adequate in number or in types and could not alone have stopped or even checked the Japanese advance.'

(iii) There was the urgent need for the introduction of a grid system capable of easy application, universally acceptable to both navy and air force instead of separate ones. 'Both were available during the Battle of Midway. Neither was used. Instead, recourse was had to designating positions either by bearing and distance from a prearranged reference point or in latitude – longitude coordinate.' Nimitz wrote 'The present British lettered coordinate system, SP 02274, provides for designating positions by either bearing and distance from any even degree latitude–longitude intersection or in encoded latitude–longitude coordinates. This system has worldwide application, distribution to Allied naval forces, is already complete, and security is good. We should adopt it'.

(iv) The Commander-in-Chief Navy (CINCH) complained that the 'excellent coordination of dive bombing and torpedo plane attacks, so successful in the Coral Sea, was missing in the Battle of Midway'. He put this down to the Japanese concentrating their fighters against the Devastators, but he also recorded that the TBDs, 'are fatally inadequate' and that the TBF, though 'much improved' still needed fighter support and that long range carrier fighters were essential.

(v) Tribute was paid to the Japanese CAP; the enemy 'apparently had fighter protection over their carriers from about 20,000 feet on down to the torpedo plane attack level'. The fact that Gee reported no CAP at 20,000 feet on the 4th is ignored. Nimitz concluded, 'We shall have to establish at least 2 levels of fighter combat patrol.' One other conclusion was made in respect of air combat, and that was that the F4F-4 'is markedly inferior to the Japanese Zero in speed, maneuverability, and climb'. However, he paid tribute to the present overall superiority that in the Battle of Midway enabled American carrier fighter squadrons 'to shoot down about 3 Zero fighters for each of our own lost'. He attributed this partly 'to our splendid pilots' and partly to armour, armament and leak-proof tanks. An increase in the number of fighters in each carrier from eighteen to twenty-seven was still not sufficient and he called for an even higher percentage of VF types. Another recommendation was that replacement carrier air groups should be formed as complete, highly trained units and held ready ashore.

(vi) Nimitz called for greater emphasis on training for both anti-aircraft gunners and aircraft personnel.

(vii) There was an overriding need for the launching of attack groups and the conducting of their attacks 'with the absolute minimum loss of time'. He acknowledged that once the attack had been joined the pilots had shown resolution (unfortunately some had not, but this was not acknowledged in Nimitz's report), but he felt their losses would have been smaller and their success greater with closer co-ordination.

(viii) One of the biggest disappointments had been the aircraft tracking of enemy formations, which CINCH described uncompromisingly as 'unsatisfactory'. He put the blame on inadequate types and numbers of planes, but a neutral observer cannot help thinking that lack of reports on the enemy, even when sighted, were as great a contribution to the failure of this arm, which is surely down to the aircrews themselves. The Japanese method of using scouts from tenders he felt warranted examination, but he added an important rider: 'No matter how efficient this search and tracking, carriers should still maintain an alert search with their own planes, accepting reduction in offensive power for greater security. The Japanese have been very successful with non-carrier searching, but in the Coral Sea and at Midway they were caught *with planes on deck*.'[5]

(ix)   CINCH considered that American fighter direction in defence of the fleet had improved over the Coral Sea experience, adding, 'Development of tactics in stationing fighters at various altitudes and distances from the carrier, along with the Fighter Direction School now being established in Oahu, should produce further improvement'. He also called for 'superfrequency voice sets for fighter direction'. Nimitz also praised the success of placing all Midway aircraft, both army and navy, and all submarines, on a common radio frequency, which meant that 'communications were swift and efficient'. No comment was made of the lack of communication between the TBD squadrons and their fighter escorts or their group commanders.

(x)   Nimitz recommended the fitting of all carriers with two search radar sets, one of which, and preferably both, should be at least equal in performance to CXAM [Built by RCA], as the SC [Built by General Electric] did not meet this requirement.

(xi)   The draining of the fuel from *Yorktown* prevented her from sharing the grisly fate of the four Japanese carriers when dive-bombed, coupled with the use of carbon dioxide in the system.

(xii)   Anti-aircraft gunnery, Nimitz felt, was improving with every action. However, a larger number of automatic weapons was required, while the greatest need was for these to be fitted with directors and lead computing sights.

(xiii) Similarly, CINCH called for a larger torpedo warhead as an urgent requirement, along with a design that enabled 'much higher speed drops'. Likewise, the dive-bombers would have required fewer direct hits, and fewer of the enemy ships would have escaped, had the 1,000 pound AP bomb been available.

(xiv)   Nimitz commented on the value of a close screen to protect the carriers from torpedo attack, with a minimum of four cruisers and a squadron of destroyers operating in close proximity to the carrier for this task.

(xv)   Strangely, in view of their total failure to achieve anything whatsoever, Nimitz praises the 'superior operations' of the B-17s of the 431st Bombardment Squadron which, he felt, benefited from prolonged experience with naval forces during coordinated patrol operations.

(xvi)   Nimitz's final lesson was universally recognized by friend and foe alike, both then and now. He concluded: 'Correct information is still one of the hardest things for a commander to get in action. It is especially difficult in such a battle of many battles as this one was, spread over a vast sea area'. Despite the difficulties, Nimitz considered that all the American commanders had performed well. He considered that commanders of TF-16 and TF-17 and NAS Midway 'showed sound judgement and decision in correctly interpreting the many confused situations that came up during the action'.

Intelligence

Among the first assessments to have a marked effect on participants of the battle concerned the Intelligence

---

5.   *My italics.* Nimitz, at least, apparently believed the reports of some of the SBD pilots that the Japanese had their air groups spotted at the time of the attacks on them, rather than still down in the hangars.

community. Almost as soon as the battle was over the bitter feuding between Hawaii and Washington DC came to a head. With the departure of Rochefort and Layton's mentor, Captain Laurence F. Safford, and the establishment of the Redman brothers in positions of power, they swiftly moved to have those that they found irritating removed and also, if some accounts are to be believed, to instantly rewrite history!

The epic battle was but three weeks in the past when both Redman brothers took steps that belittled the work, results and whole ethos of both Rochefort and Layton.[6] The US Navy's Advanced Intelligence Centers was the excuse and a seemingly innocuous handwritten memo from the senior brother in OP-20-G to Vice-Admiral F. J. Horne, was the leading salvo. In it, Joseph merely informed Admiral Horne that 'the endorsement is addressed to Vice CNO (DNI). Copy to Office of the Chief of Naval Operations OPVAN (DNC). I am preparing some material on it and will discuss with you'.[7] This was in reference to a 'secret letter 0116 W' from Admiral Nimitz dated 28 May, in which the CincPac had mentioned 'the inadequacy of the present intelligence section of the staff,' and also COMINCH's[8] reference dated 12 June.[9]

This was followed up by another memo, dated 20 June, on the subject of RI organization.[10] Redman started off by giving a potted version of the history of RI, 'through the piping times of peace extending over a period of some twenty odd years'. He said that RI had 'struggled and was never allowed out of the closet'. However, now that war was upon them that had all changed, in fact, 'many activities are desirous of having a finger in the pie'. He did not flinch from indicating pretty well just whose fingers he was anxious to remove. 'You are familiar with those outside the Navy proper. The following will be confined to organization within the Naval Service'.

Redman asserted:

Intelligence, as such, properly belongs under the jurisdiction of ONI. Whether Radio Intelligence should be directly under ONI is a moot question. Basically such seems to be sound, i.e. all Intelligence activities be consolidated and headed up under a single director. On the other hand, practically, there are many objections. Simply one might say they just don't speak our language. The intercept material must be obtained by operators trained in the *Kana* code.[11] The source of the operators is Naval Communications. Never has this service been up to allowance, and any operators so diverted and trained have been at a sacrifice. Again the intercept equipment belongs to Communications, which is responsible for its technical characteristics, procurement and upkeep. Also, the question of traffic analysis involves personnel and only those familiar with radio communications can properly administer this work'.

Correlated with this work is the DF [Direction Finding] organization, which is entirely a matter of radio communications. And in the background of all this is the communication network and cryptographic aids involved in the worldwide exchange of intercept information. He also listed three other 'recent developments' – TINA, identifying enemy radio operators by their inherent characteristics of hand-sending; radio fingerprinting (RFP), by which individual ship radio transmitters could be identified by their emission characteristics; and distance measuring to enemy transmitters via use of ionospheric data. In Redman's opinion RI could not 'thrive and function efficiently except under direct control of Naval Communications'.

6. One of the ironies of this tragedy was that Rochefort had hung a notice over his desk, which encapsulated his motivation, 'We can accomplish anything provided no one cares who gets the credit.' Unfortunately there were those in Washington DC who were not so adverse as Rochefort about basking in glory.

7. Memo, *Advanced Intelligence Centers*, Redman/20G to Adm. Horne, dated 17 June 1942. Record Group (RG) 457, National Archives, College Park, Maryland, formerly held at the Naval Security Group (NSG) Repository, Crane, Indiana.

8. COMINCH = Commander-in-Chief, US Fleet. Selected by King, so legend has it, as CINCUS was too much like 'Sink Us'.

9. Admiral Nimitz had endorsed the setting up at Pearl Harbor of the Intelligence Center, Pacific Ocean Area (ICPOA) as early as May 1942. One of the chief instigators, Captain Arthur McCollum had gone to Washington DC and obtained the sanction of Admiral King on 12 June. ICPOA later was to become JICPOA (Joint Intelligence Center, Pacific Ocean Area) just over a year later and had grown to a staff of two thousand by the end of the war. See John Prados, *Combined Fleet Decoded*.

10. *Memo*, Radio Intelligence Organization, Redman to Horne, dated 20 June 1942.

11. Properly, the *Kata Kana*, (nicknamed 'hen tracks') a simple method of phoneticizing the spoken Japanese tongue into forty-eight characters. The Japanese used this as their unique telegraphic code, and the alphabet or syllabary, contains almost double the combinations of dot-and-dash as Morse. The US had obtained the Japanese Navy Code Book for 1918 and over two decades some operators had managed to learn how to translate it. It was read then transcribed into Romanized (*Romaji*) characters by way of a special typewriter, the RIP-5.

But what was the current situation? Chaotic, or so he implied. Cheltenham intercept station was under the DNC; Bainbridge under Com 13, Honolulu under Com 14 while Bellconnen at Melbourne was under Comsowestpacfor [Commander, South West Pacific Force]. As for the army, 'what control is exercised . . . by virtue of unity of command, is unknown'.

Having made his case in a detailed lead-up, Redman now concentrated on what was really vexing him.

> Under Com 14 direct control of the Radio Intelligence Unit has been, by virtue of seniority, in the hands of an ex-Japanese languages student (a Commander). On CincPac's Staff the intelligence received from the Com 14 Radio Intelligence Unit is handled by an ex-Japanese language student (a Lt. Comdr.). [You could almost see the scorn as he wrote the words!] They are not technically trained in Naval Communications, and my feeling is that Radio Traffic Analysis, Deception, and Tracking, etc. are suffering because the importance and possibilities of the phases of Radio Intelligence are not fully realized. The unit in Melbourne is in charge of an officer who was trained in the Radio Intelligence Section here, and I am advised the co-ordination, standardization and realization of combined radio intelligence unit objectives worked out more smoothly in the Melbourne Unit than in the Com 14 Unit.[12]

He totally ignored the fact that the 'ex-Japanese language students' actually forecast the Japanese plans far more accurately than either Melbourne or Washington DC. What he appeared to imply was the importance of the 'smoothness' of the operation rather than its accuracy.

He concluded:

> Strong people should be in strong places, and I do not believe the Pacific organization is strong because the administration is weak in so far as Radio Intelligence is concerned. I believe that a senior officer trained in Radio Intelligence should head up these units rather than one whose background is

Japanese language. They should confine their activities to Intelligence as such, i.e. the product of Radio Intelligence.

He finished by saying that he was attaching additional background material prepared by OP-20-G, 'which he was preparing for you, and which he now requests be relayed to you along with my memorandum'. Finally, in the interest of 'immediately improving this situation', he suggested that 20-G visited Honolulu to get first-hand information, 'on which to base recommendation for remedial action'.

Meanwhile, on the same day, his brother, Commander John Redman, put his signature to a letter prepared by Wenger which included that fateful reference to 'inadequacy', but making it appear in the context that the men themselves were inadequate, not their numbers, powers or facilities, as Nimitz had surely implied.

Among the many recommendations was the following, which marked down both Layton and Rochefort for early replacement: 'Assign a *properly qualified* [13] officer in charge of the intelligence center in Hawaii who will have additional duties on the staff of the CinC Pacific in order that proper relations between the intelligence activities and the operational staff may be maintained'.

John Redman added, for the CNO's digestion, the incredible assertion that 'experience has indicated that units in combat areas cannot be relied upon to accomplish more than the business of merely reading enemy messages.' King swallowed all this, hook, line and sinker. Rather than endorsing Nimitz's recommendation of Rochefort for a medal for the invaluable contribution he had made to the US Navy's first victory of World War II, King turned him down flat under the blanket assertion that 20-G deserved 'equal credit' for the 'correct evaluation of enemy intentions'. This was not just untrue, but, as Stephen Budiansky wrote, 'was a whopper'.[14]

His detractors were not content with humiliating and removing their rival[15], who had been proved so correct, they also appeared to be trying to rewrite history. Budiansky again revealed the barefaced affrontry of it all:

> A year later, Commander John S. Holtwick[16], who had run the IBM machines at Station Hypo called on

---

12. Of course, as Frederick D. Parker pointed out, this totally ignored the fact that both Rochefort and Layton *had* been trained in OP-20G! (Frederick D. Parker, 'How OP-20-G Got Rid of Joe Rochefort.')
13. My italics.
14. Stephen Budiansky, *Battle of Wits: The Complete Story of Codebreaking in World War II*.
15. Joseph Redman had served in the Asiatic Fleet in the mid-

1930s, as had Rochefort, but it is not known whether the former's seeming animosity towards the latter had its roots there or not. Redman, being a former submariner, had rather more in common with Nimitz; indeed both men had commanded the same submarine, the *C-5*, at different periods of her life, which perhaps provided some affinity.
16. Captain Jack Sebastian Holtwick, Jr, (1907–87). Born Indian Territory (later Oklahoma), February 1907. Family

Joseph Redman, by that time a Rear-Admiral. In the course of conversation Redman remarked that Station Hypo had 'missed the boat at the Battle of Midway', but Washington had saved the day. The lie took Holtwick's breath away – especially since Redman knew that Holtwick *knew* the opposite was true.[17] That was the first real inkling they had of how completely Washington had stolen credit for the victory at Midway. Shortly before his death in 1985, Dyer[18] wrote: 'I have given a great deal of thought to the Rochefort case and I have been unwillingly forced to the conclusion that Rochefort committed one unforgivable sin. To certain individuals of small mind and overweening ambition, there is no greater insult that to be proved wrong.'[19]

Washington now went in for the kill, with concentration as their principal weapon. In October Rochefort was called back to the Navy Department for 'temporary additional duties'. Nimitz protested, but was blandly told that the recall was just to obtain some first-hand advice. Rochefort himself knew what was coming to him, and told his friends, 'I won't be coming back'. Of course, he was often his own worst enemy, and his subsequent actions, as he later readily admitted, made his expulsion from future Intelligence work almost self-imposed. Nonetheless many certainly agree with Budiansky's summary of this period:'The denouement of the Battle of Midway was not one of the US Navy's finest hours!'[20]

Redman, by an ironic twist of fate, had meantime become Communications Officer to CincPac. As Nimitz's intelligence chief in the midst of a desperate war, he could hardly be ignored, and reports that Nimitz, angered by Redman's treatment of Rochefort, 'refused to speak' to him should perhaps, be taken with a pinch of salt! However, very soon Redman had ingratiated himself fully with Nimitz, so much so that, after the war, that worthy was making speeches praising Redman to the heavens. He was to state:

Upon assuming command of the US Pacific Fleet on 31 December 1941, I found a well-functioning communication system capable of great expansion. Could it expand rapidly enough to handle the far-reaching demands suddenly thrown upon it? It could and did, to my great satisfaction. Large quantities of electronic equipment and increasing numbers of installation and maintenance personnel began to flow to Pearl Harbor from the Electronics Division, Bureau of Ships, directed by Commodore Jennings B. Dow. At the same time the Communications Division of the Officer of the Chief of Naval Operations, under Rear-Admiral Joseph R. Redman, supplied trained operators. Thus, the Pacific Fleet Communications Officer, Captain, later Rear-Admiral John R. Redman, could expand Pacific Ocean area communications to meet all operating, logistic, intelligence, and other command require-

---

later moved to San Pedro, California, where he worked with his father as a photographer. Entered US Naval Academy, Annapolis, aged seventeen (lied about his age) and graduated 1927. 1935–9 with OP-20-G at Pearl, including breaking of JN-25 and building the Purple Machine to decipher it. Commanding officer of the fleet oiler *Platte* (AO-24) April–December 1947. Commanded amphibious warfare command ship *Estes* (AGC-12), lead ship of Operation Ivy, the hydrogen bomb tests at Eniwetok, November 1952. After retirement from navy served as CoS, National Security Agency at Laurel, Maryland. Chief Engineer Haller, Ramond & Brown (HRB Singer) at State College, Pennsylvania. Retired to Kaneohe, Hawaii. Died January 1987, buried at the Punchbowl, Honolulu. Author of several unpublished MSS, including *Naval Security Group History to World War II*, SRH 355, RG 457, National Archives, College Park, Maryland.

17. Anonymous typed secret memorandum, *The Inside Story of the Battle of Midway and the Ousting of Commander Rochefort*, (The so-called 'A' Memorandum), with marginal comments by Rochefort, ONI, Washington, *circa* 1943. Edward T. Layton Collection, Naval War College, Newport, Rhode Island. Rear-Admiral 'Mac' Showers, who brought this to light, recently informed me: 'So far as I'm aware, there

has been no identification of the author of this paper. It's still an occasional point of discussion among the decreasing number of persons who might have a legitimate guess. I doubt we'll ever know,' Showers to the author, 20 December 2006.

18. Captain Thomas H. 'Tommie' Dyer (1902–85). Born Osawatomie, Kansas, May 1902. Graduated from US Naval Academy, Annapolis 1924. Served tours as radio and communications officer. In May 1931 was transferred to Department of Naval Communications cryptanalytic organisztion OP-20-G, trained by Agnes Driscoll. Originated methods of using IBM tabulators to speed up automatically the decryption of codes and ciphers. July 1936 transferred to what became the Communications Intelligence Unit (CIU) at Hawaii. 1938 formed with intercept and D/F stations at Heiia and Wahiawa. 1941 was Assistant OIC *Hypo* and chief cryptanalyst under Rochefort. 1946–9 Naval Security Station, Communications Support Activity, Washington, DC. June 1949, with Safford joined Armed Forces Security Agency (AFSA). 1952–4 Chief National Security Agency (NSA), Tokyo. 1954–5 Historian NSA. Retired from navy in 1955.

19. Stephen Budiansky, *Battle of Wits: The Complete Story of Codebreaking in World War II*.

20. *Ibid*.

ments. This gigantic task was accomplished so efficiently that the Pearl Harbor headquarters was able to exercise complete and effective control of the operations of the far-ranging forces on, under and above the sea. The radio silence usually imposed upon the forces afloat made absolute confidence in the integrity of our communications system a matter of paramount importance. This confidence was earned and well merited.[21]

The British Viewpoint

Of course the only other nation which was operating aircraft carriers in battle was Great Britain, and, although two decades of RAF control over their aircraft had crippled their early lead in naval aviation and reduced them to a very poor third place in the rankings behind the United States and Japan, the Royal Navy was still a major player. Therefore the viewpoints of Royal Navy officials who examined the immediate reports of the Midway battle in 1942, were relevant, offering as they did a more objective viewpoint than those of the two protagonists themselves. The British views make for a uniquely objective take on the conduct and lessons of the battle, as far as it was then known, and this, being professional, was not tainted with the propaganda of the media of the day.

The report of the Midway battle[22] went the rounds of the Admiralty between August and October 1942 and the range of opinions was wide, as a note from the DACD confirmed:

Two personal signals to 1st Sea Lord from BAD were circulated inside the Admiralty by instructions of the 1st Sea Lord. Both [BAD's 2145Z/31 1915Z/28] dealt with Midway Island Battle lessons, and contained information of interest to the Air Ministry regarding torpedo attacks and operations by shore based aircraft. Submitted for approval to send copies to Air Ministry. It is desirable that this information should be studied by the Inter-Service Torpedo Attack Committee.[23]

BAD in Washington, in a 'Most Secret' cable signal, timed 1915Z/28 July to the First Sea Lord, had submitted a preliminary report giving their viewpoint of the lessons learned. Their findings were mixed. On intelligence available to the Americans they were unequivocal: 'US Intelligence was brilliant and enabled Task Forces to be operated with great tactical advantages at outset of battle'. They qualified this, in much the way that Mitscher himself had done in his own report, by recording: 'Delays were experienced due to C-in-C Pacific Fleet signalling appreciations to Task Force Admirals in high grade ciphers not held by 'private' carriers. This entailed long visual signalling messages being passed to private carriers before they could send off attack groups'. They pointed out that the various task forces did not maintain continuous watch on all shore-based reconnaissance frequencies. 'Enemy reports rebroadcast from shore station(s) were received in some cases more than 2 hours after original report'. Nor was the American reporting of the ongoing situation very efficient.

Tracking (shadowing) on whole was unsatisfactory, in that it was not continuous, it also did not include any comprehensive account of enemy loss. This resulted in Task Force-Commanders not knowing which part of enemy fleet were being attacked by other units, this was particularly so in the case of attack carrying shore based Marine Corps and Army Air Corps aircraft.

They concluded that some of these problems might have been overcome 'if US had an organization similar to our Duty Q', although it was admitted that 'is doubtful if our present organisation would have allowed for comprehensive report of 2 widely separated enemy forces, reaching all necessary authorities'. They added the warning that 'our present and future operational type carrier borne aircraft with possible exception of Fireflies[24] are unlikely to be allowed to remain in the vicinity of enemy fleet while his carriers can still operate fighters'. A suggestion was that

---

21. Fleet Admiral W. Chester Nimitz, in his Introduction to Linwood S. Howarth, *History of Communications-Electronics in the United States Navy.*
22. Admiralty, Information on Midway Island Battle, dated 11 August 1942. From DACD to various departments. A.C.D.18/42. Contained in ADM 199/1302, National Archives, Kew, London. Main report contained in *Admiralty Weekly Intelligence Report No. 126*, dated 7 August 1942.
23. Admiralty, *Information on Midway Island Battle.*
24. Fairey Firefly. Designed, as were all Royal Navy aircraft, to

fulfil a multi-rôle function, this was a two-seater with the emphasis on fighter qualities at a time when single-seater naval aircraft had already become the accepted norm in the Japanese and US navies. It first flew in December 1941 but did not join operational service until two years later and did not see combat until 1944. It had a maximum speed of only 316 miles per hour, but was heavily armed with four 20 mm Hispano cannon and could carry two 1,000 pound bombs or eight 60 pound rockets, which made very versatile. Developed through various marques, it was still flying combat missions as late as the Korean War.

heavily protected, long-range, shore-based aircraft 'such as the B 17' could be made available and supplied with proper naval observers, 'for duties similar to our duty Q'. This option could also be considered for any Royal Navy fleet that would in future operate in the Pacific or Indian Oceans.

One thing the British commented on was the fact that many of the American naval aircraft were not fitted with IFF.[25] This was a common problem encountered by British warships when trying to distinguish the rare sight of RAF aircraft among the incoming enemy bombers, the RAF pilots being notoriously reluctant to switch on and use this device, even when it was fitted. In the case of Midway the report considered the lack was a contributory factor in the loss of the *Yorktown*.

It appears probable the Japanese did not know position of US carriers until US aircraft carrier *Yorktown* broke R/T silence on power to vector fighters on to aircraft which subsequently proved to be friendly. The attacks on *Yorktown* developed subsequently at a time commensurate with them having been organized on D/F bearings of these transmissions. The danger of unauthenticated R/T was shown when Japanese asked by R/T using correct calls, for position of US carriers.

Other lessons flagged up included 'the necessity for a fighter escort in daylight', which was emphasized by the 'total loss of Torpedo Squadron 8 whose escort inadvertently joined up with striking force from another carrier'. No comment was made on the fact that, under Japanese organization, fighter aircraft from any of their carriers routinely provided escort for each other's strike aircraft, with no apparent problems. But they did flag up 'the necessity for fighters to have the same range as other attack aircraft', citing the fact that 'several fighter forces landed in the sea owing to lack of fuel'. They considered that the 'most hopeful' solution to the problem of fighter escort range was to fit all naval fighters with a drop tank for use on the outward leg.

With regard to fighting qualities, they commented:

Zero fighters again out-performed and out-manoeuvred F4F-4s but were much more vulnerable and again there are reports of Zero[s] being reluctant to attack aircraft in formation. Even as few as 2 would

cause them to open fire ineffectually at long range. It is obvious in every report that come[s] in that the superior courage of skill of US aircraft crews more than made up for deficiency of their equipment.

However, in the enclosed 'Sequence of Events' the verdict on the American fighter tactics and aircraft in defence of Midway Island itself, were far more severe.

The superiority of the Japanese Zero fighters over the American fighters in climb and manoeuvrability is very evident, but this superiority was aided by the faulty tactics of the American fighters. The latter apparently made no attempt to hold off the Japanese fighters with a portion of their fighter force while the remainder dealt with the bombers. They appear to have gone 'bald-headed' for the Japanese bombers in small un-coordinated detachments, with the result that the escorting Zero fighters, in spite of their inferior armament and lack of armour, shot them to ribbons. In fact, the Zero fighters were presented with the one form of combat in which their lack of armour did not matter.[26]

John B. Lundstrom is just one American historian who would not agree with that analysis[27]; nor would he think much of the next comment made by BAD: 'When it was obvious that Japanese carriers were out of action C-in-C Pacific Fleet made signal suggesting that time was propitious for night surface attack, it is not quite clear why this was not done'. The effect, however, was that 'results of battle have strengthened US Naval opinion that Commanders of Task Forces containing carriers must be aviators'. Again, what skills and knowledge expert aviators could have brought to a night battle with nothing more powerful than a few heavy cruisers against an enemy force containing battleships fully trained for night fighting, is not made clear!

Of one thing there was no doubt: 'US dive-bombing was most successful and opinion is expressed that very high Japanese aircraft losses were due to carriers being on fire from stem to stem [stern] thus rendering it quite impossible for any aircraft to get back aboard them.'[28]

The follow-up telegram from BAD, dated 1 August 1942, commented briefly on the fact that the six Grumman TBF-1 torpedo-bombers ('all that were available') although

---

25. IFF = identification, friend or foe.
26. 'Sequence of Events' – contained in ADM 199/1302, National Archives, Kew, London.
27. See John B. Lundstrom *The First Team: Pacific Naval*

Air Combat from Pearl Harbor to Midway.
28. BAD to 1st Sea Lord, 1915Z/28, in Admiralty, *Information on the Midway Island Battle.*

'a well-armed plane, cannot go through fighter opposition without fighter protection'. This was a lesson that the British had only just relearned when obsolete Fairey Swordfish torpedo-bombers of No. 825 Squadron, based ashore, had attacked the German fleet steaming up the English Channel in February 1942 and most of their RAF escort failed to appear. All six had been shot down in short order in much the same way as the more modern Avengers and the Devastators had been slaughtered at Midway, and equally to no avail[29].

Among other points, BAD noted that *Yorktown* had drained her petrol system and filled in with carbon dioxide prior to being attacked and that this had ensured that there was no petrol fire despite heavy bomb damage; also, that Admiral Nimitz had recommended the 'immediate adoption by the US Army and Navy of British system of lettered co-ordinate SP 02274'. Nimitz also reported that the fire screen was again very effective against torpedo aircraft. 'We are endeavouring to ascertain what screening diagram was in use at time', and, 'he again asked for VHF for fighters.'[30]

At the end of August a more detailed report[31], was circulated round the Admiralty and to the Air Ministry, and led to many pertinent comments, although the originator pointed out that they 'had purposely consulted summaries only and not the detailed reports. No doubt many additional lessons on air tactics, principles of fighter direction etc can also be learned. It is hoped, however, that the memorandum does cover all the main issues'.

It was noted that it was only late in the battle that it had been learned that the US aerial attacks had caused the enemy to change course, but that this complete change of course was not observed by the shore-based planes. Also, the Americans stated: 'Even our active participants in the numerous attacks, were unable to give confidently any accurate account of the damage inflicted.' This lack of on-the-spot reporting was inhibiting for the American commanders and the British observed:

It is important for the Senior Officers to know the results of an attack and its effect on enemy's move-

ments that at least one high performance observation plane should accompany the main striking force and remain to observe results. If there is a shadowing aircraft in addition so much the better, but the shadower may have been driven off and continuous shadowing should not be relied upon.[32]

While the American reports showed that the escorting US fighters were operating at too high an altitude, so that they missed the Japanese fighters which concentrated on the torpedo planes and that most hits were obtained by bombs as the torpedo planes were shot down, the enemy regarded the latter as the greater danger and concentrated on torpedo planes, leaving dive bombers a free hand.

By this time the Royal Navy had undergone a rather similar ordeal, with the crippling of the carriers *Illustrious*, *Formidable* and *Indomitable*, the latter being the most recent victim during the August convoy for the relief of Malta, The Royal Navy had operated three aircraft carriers together as part of the protecting fleet, but lost one to submarine attack, and the other two were damaged, one severely, by air attack.[33]

The Director Airfield and Carrier Division noted :

The results of air attacks on carriers in this action show that the dive bomber is the best neutralizing agent. To finish off damaged ships the torpedo is probably the better weapon. In the first wave therefore the dive-bomber should be regarded as the primary weapon, the torpedo plane providing the diversion. Since the diversion may come off as the greater success, and as it must be a sufficient menace to attract a great part of the enemy's attention, it must not be so weak as to be ineffective. The first three waves of the US striking forces had dive bombers, torpedo aircraft and fighters in the following proportions respectively, 7:3:2; 7:3:2 and 3:2:1.

On the whole the proportion 3:2:1 in the initial striking force launched against enemy carriers seems to be about right. At least an equal number of fighters

29. Winston Churchill is said to have wept when he heard of the Devastator massacre; it is not on record whether he, a former Chancellor of Exchequer who had advocated cutting back the Royal Navy's budget when he was in office, was equally upset by the loss of 825 Squadron's antiques!

30. BAD to 1st Sea Lord, 2145Z/31, in Admiralty, *Information on the Midway Island Battle.*

31. Deputy, Air Co-operation Division, Admiralty dated 24 August 1942, Memorandum on *Broad Tactical Lessons of Midway Island Battle.* A.C.D. 24/42, in *op. cit.*

32. In passing, it is of interest to note that it was common practice, from the very early days of the war, for the German *Luftwaffe* to send such an aircraft with their striking forces. In particular the Junkers Ju.87 Stuka dive-bombers, short-range aircraft, were often accompanied by a twin-engined Junkers Ju. 88 bomber fitted out with cameras to record actual results. Here, as in many things, the Luftwaffe were ahead of the game in 1942.

33. See Peter C. Smith, *Pedestal: the Convoy that saved Malta.*

as are sent as escorts should be retained for the defence of the carriers.

There has been in a tendency in some quarters as a result of the heavy losses of torpedo aircraft to call for a larger proportion of fighters. This temptation to increase fighters at the expense of striking force aircraft must be resisted for general oceanic operations. The best method of defending our own fleet is by attacking the enemy's carriers *not* the enemy's aircraft. A point to be noted is that in these attacks the losses of torpedo aircraft are likely to be proportionately higher than the losses of dive bombers.

Although the casualties in some of the attacks by both sides were very high, the overall casualties of the victors were not great. Also, when considering probable losses in a major fleet action it must be remembered that very high aircraft casualties can be accepted provided the tactical object is achieved. Such actions will only occur two or three times in a long war and aircraft casualties in them cannot be compared with losses sustained in routine operations either over land or sea. The victory was a result of the US Fleet having information, which the Japanese lacked, and of their possessing sufficient striking force aircraft to neutralize the enemy's carriers quickly. Since one cannot guarantee having the benefit of superior intelligence, a reasonable proportion of fighters must be carried, but their number should never exceed those required to give the carrier force a reasonably good umbrella.

The conclusion arrived at therefore is that for general operations the carrier should carry approximately equal numbers of torpedo aircraft, dive bombers and fighters, with a bias in favour of dive bombers at the expense of torpedo aircraft.

It was stated that the results of the torpedo attacks proved that 'attacks on warships with fighter escort by small forces of torpedo aircraft, even when the latter are themselves escorted, are likely to result in heavy losses, but that such attacks pressed home by well trained and determined crews should score hits'. Exactly how this conclusion was reached is hard to gauge, as no torpedo-bomber attacks could have been more determined that those mounted at Midway, but they scored not a single hit (although one was, totally falsely, claimed by the sole survivor). The British summary was that better co-ordination between all arms – torpedo-bomber, dive-bomber and fighters – would have reduced the losses. While the US dive-bombers flew at 2,000–11,000 feet and torpedo planes at 1,500 feet under cloud, the Japanese

dive-bombers flew at about 9,000 feet and torpedo planes at 5,000 feet. The Japanese formations all flew low in order to avoid radar detection and then climbed before delivering their attacks. The US fighters flew too high and missed the Japanese fighters, which concentrated on the torpedo planes; the Zeros were described in a typical British understatement as 'very troublesome'. They remarked that in the first attack the American torpedo aircraft became separated from the dive-bombers. 'The reason is not known but the different heights at which the two formations were flying must have made it extremely difficult for the formations to keep together, especially if there was much cloud about'. The British concluded that, taken all round, it seemed best for the dive-bombers and torpedo aircraft to aim at releasing their missiles simultaneously, as this would provide the defences, both aerial and gunnery, with the most difficult scenario to counter. This had been done by the Germans and Italians during *Pedestal* and had resulted in heavy damage to the *Indomitable*. It was noted that while the Americans used radar constantly, there was 'no evidence' that the Japanese used it.

Dive-bombing was something else, and the conclusion on the British side was that 'with fresh well-trained crews, even in the face of heavy opposition the number of direct hits should equal about 15% and 20% of the number of aircraft taking part'.

In essence, for the Royal Navy, the Midway results only confirmed what had already been worked out before the war from multi-carrier exercises in the Mediterranean. They summarized:

In an ocean battle of today, where the main forces taking part are carrier borne aircraft, the first objective is to neutralize the enemy's carriers. Though a carrier may be made extremely difficulty to sink, its fighting efficiency, i.e. its ability to operate aircraft, is fairly easily impaired. Hence, the first object is to damage as many of the enemy's carriers as possible. Once all the enemy's carriers are neutralized it is comparatively easy to finish them off with the second striking force. The enemy is deprived of his reconnaissance and his fighter umbrella. This is exactly what happened in Midway Island battle.

Again, part of that conclusion was false. Because the Japanese relied almost exclusively on scouting aircraft carried by its escorting battleships and cruisers, with a few exceptions this left the carriers free to concentrate on the dual roles of strike and defence, to the exclusion of reconnaissance. The Americans, who relied on land-based aircraft, were badly served and even their carrier aircrew rarely kept their commanders informed of what was taking place, or even of the results of strikes.

Admiral Sir James Somerville, as commander of the British East Indies Fleet, was the most likely British officer to encounter the Japanese enemy once more. He was also the man who had the most knowledge of their tactics, of course, having been defeated by them only two months earlier. Despite this, he raised thirteen questions, which the Admiralty passed on to Nimitz. The C-in-C of the US Fleet could only offer four answers from the reports available to him. He stated that the lessons learnt were that:

1   The Japanese fear torpedo plane attack and concentrate fighters as defence against them.
2   Torpedo planes are also the most effective Japanese weapon.
3   Japanese torpedo aircraft press their attacks well home and must be met by fighters 'well outside screen'.
4   The screen itself was most effective when close in and between attacking torpedo aircraft and their target.

The Director of Naval Air Division(DNAD) gave the following view: That the fighter directing officer of a carrier, 'shoulders great responsibily and must be a first class officer'. That both internal and external communications 'must be 100% efficient', and that reliable long-range radar warning 'at all heights', was vital. 'Not only does it result in more efficient fighter direction, but it economizes in standing fighter patrols'. He added a point with which both Nimitz and Nagumo would probably have concurred. 'We shall *never* have enough fighters.'[34]

He also concluded that 'the Midway battle confirms the importance of the dive-bomber. We must develop the use of dive-bomber aircraft without delay'. These were brave words, but, with the Royal Navy's only true dive-bomber, the Blackburn Skua, relegated to the role of target tug more than eighteen months earlier because it could not act effectively as a *fighter* aircraft. The Vought SB2U Vindicator rejected because it could not act effectively as an anti-submarine aircraft (roles for which these aircraft were not primarily designed,) and the American SBD Dauntless totally rejected by Britain as 'obsolete', the Royal Navy had

not a single dive-bomber on its books. They hoped to get numbers of the new American dive-bomber, the Curtiss SB2C Helldiver[35] under Lend-Lease some time in the distant future, but had no home-grown types even remotely ready for embarkation.[36]

The DNAD's conclusions in October 1942 were therefore pretty much the same as those reached by Admiral Somerville in April the same year: that the Royal Navy, with the retarded and outmoded aircraft if had, could only rely on the cover of darkness to attack the enemy. 'We must exploit to the full our present lead in equipment for night air attack. In order to do this we must concentrate on training in night torpedo attack and night flying generally'.

When the Admiralty conclusions were circulated, not everyone agreed with these findings. The Deputy Director, Naval Air Division at the Admiralty, wrote on 20 October:

There is fairly general agreement now on the need for a very strong carrier borne air striking force to hit fast and hard. The effort of this initial blow may be all that the squadrons of the first line carriers can do. To follow up after the opponent is groggy and to deal the KO one of two following are required:

(i)   Strong surface forces, or

(ii)   Aircraft from support carriers.

Of these only surface forces which can be expected to be immediately available are those in support of the carriers [with which Yamamoto must have by then be in rueful agreement!]. If these are to be used they must be slipped from the carriers as soon as it is evident the enemy has been hit hard, leaving only the bare minimum for the carriers.

The Director of Gunner and Anti-aircraft Warfare wrote on 14 November 1942:

The American ships at the time of Midway Battle were under armed in close range automatic weapons by our standards, and the high morale of the Japanese airmen resulted in the aircraft attacks being pressed home to well within the effective range of close range

---

34.   Emphasis in original.
35.   A totally false hope, as it turned out, as this move was blocked by Admiral Ernie King. See Peter C. Smith, *Curtiss SB2C Helldiver*.
36.   DNAD's sad list included: using the two-seater Fairey Fulmar fighter 'a proportion' of which 'can dive-bomb up to 60° with a 500 pound bomb' (but which never did), using the

still untried Fairey Barracuda which 'promises to be a good dive-bomber'; using the obsolescent Fairey Albacore TSR, a biplane; still using the even more ancient Fairey Swordfish, another biplane relic of a bygone age but still being used in the front line by the Royal Navy; and the future hope of using the Fairey Firefly and Fairey Firebrand, building as fighters but which, he hoped, 'will be developed as dive-bombers'.

weapons. (This has seldom been the case with German aircraft and practically never the case with Italian; since our warships have been equipped with tracer firing weapons).

With regard to the deterrent effect of the screen, he was of the opinion that 'the value of a close screen of destroyers backed up by cruisers was emphasized when the carriers were attacked by torpedo aircraft. Against Japanese airmen the Americans prefer the screen at about 2000 yards'. However, British destroyers remained almost as woefully equipped with anti-aircraft guns as they had been on outbreak of war. By contrast both American and Japanese destroyers shipped powerful dual-purpose armaments, something the Royal Navy was unable to achieve until the war was almost over.

The Director of Signal Department observed, on 27 November, that:

Admiral Nimitz's report points out need for VH/F to fighters for other limited range R/T communication. This is also our view. VH/F to Fighters is already under consideration but there are certain technical difficulties to be overcome. VH/F intercommunication between FDOs is already being fitted . . . Approval has now been given to fit two aircraft warning RDF sets in large carriers . . . It is remarked that either of our main warning sets (Types 279 and 281) is considerably superior to the American counterpart.

The Director of Training and Staff Duties noted:

On the night of 4/5 June, after the destruction of the Japanese carriers, the US carrier force, instead of closing the enemy, withdrew Eastward. Com-mander TF-16 'did not feel justified in risking a night encounter with possibly superior enemy forces'. On the night of 5/6 June the US carrier force was steaming West in pursuit of the Japanese Occupation and Support forces. Speed was reduced to 15 knots, and one of the reasons given was the 'undesirability of running down any Battleships in the dark'. The successful offensive use of carrier borne aircraft should not obscure the fact that, in this action, a fundamentally defensive role was imposed on the US force by Japanese superiority in surface ships; and that this superiority was largely responsible for the safe withdrawal of most of the Japanese ships after having suffered complete defeat in the air.

The final summary by DNAD was made on 9 October. He listed the key elements to be noted of by the Royal Navy:

1: The weapons carried by aircraft have become the arbiters of the war at sea.
2: Enemy aircraft carriers must be the first and principal object of attack.
3: Carrier groups must be organized and trained as a whole for both fighter escort and concerted attack.
4: Standardization of methods should be employed by all carriers.
5: There was a firm requirement for reserve carrier groups.
6: Fighter direction was crucial for defence.

In other words, Midway marked the watershed in air-sea warfare and the aircraft carrier was confirmed as now holding the mantle of 'capital ship' in the major fleets of the world.

77. The forward twin 5in gun mount of a *Fubuki* class destroyer. This photograph show the guns at low depression for surface action, but this mounting was designed specifically for a dual-purpose capability and, as can be seen by the gun-barrel slots in the foward mounts face and roof, the guns could elevate to 75 degrees to engage aircraft. (*Courtesy* Ships of the World).

78. A division of the Imperial Japanese Navy's *Kagero* class destroyers. When these ships joined the fleet they were regarded as the finest destroyers in any navy in the world. They carried six 5in guns in twin mountings capable of elevating 75 degrees to engage aircraft as well as two sets of torpedo tubes carrying the most powerful underwater punch then known. One of the ships of this class, the *Tanikaze*, showed just what they were capable of by surviving attacks by both B-17s and serveral dozen SBDs and managed to shoot down at least one of her attackers in return. (*Courtesy Jim Culberson, Sea Bird Publishing Inc., Melbourne, FL*).

79. The one that got away! On 5 June 1942, the solitary Japanese destroyer *Tanikaze* ('Wind from the Mountain to the Valley') of the *Kagero* Class, commanded by Captain Katsumi Motoi, was subjected to almost non-stop attack by eight Boeing B-17 heavy bombers and no fewer than thirty-eight SBDs from both *Enterprise* and *Hornet*, and survived them all. This was largely due to Signalman Masashi Shibata, who lay on his back half in and half out of the ships bridge window, watching each aircraft as it attacked and calling down to the helmsman just as the bomb was released. Many years later, in 1991, Shibata, now a successful businessman, met some of his former tormentors at a reunion at the Hotel del Coronado, San Diego; from left to right; Don Adams, Mr Masashi Shibata, Clayton Fisher and Roy Gee. (*Copyright Clayton Fisher*).

80. Colonel Ernest Roderic Manierre. As a captain pilot in the USAAC with Patrol Wing Two, based at Oahu, Hawaii in June 1942, Manierre led one of the many small formations of Boeing B-17 Flying Fortress four-engined bombers against Japanese naval targets during the battle. (*USAAF Official*).

81. Another one that got away! The submarine USS *Grayling* (SS 202), running at 12.9 knots on the surface. It was in this configuration that she was attacked by B-17s during the battle and forced to crash dive. The USAAC claimed that they had 'sunk a Japanese heavy cruiser in record time' and refused to believe Layton when he explained that, actually, they had not! (*Naval Historical Foundation, Washington DC*).

82. And one that didn't get away! The Japanese Heavy cruiser *Mikuma* after heavy attacks by *Enterprise* and *Hornet* SBDs on 6 June. This photograph was taken from the *Hornet*'s combat file (serial 0018) and shows smoke from three different bomb hits pouring away from her. This photograph has never been published before and is also the only one that shows the two destroyers, *Arashio* and *Asashio*, in position upwind of the crippled ship in her last hours. (*NARA, Washington DC*).

83. Another view of the Japanese heavy cruiser *Mikuma* on fire after attacks by SBDs from *Enterprise* and *Hornet* on 6 June 1942. (*Naval Historical Foundation, Washington DC*).

84. Flying log book of an SBD at Midway. This is the battle record of Clayton Fisher of the *Hornet*'s Scouting Squadron. Note the first mission on 4 June, with a four-and-a-half-hour flight duration marking up. (*Clayton Fisher*)

June, 1942

Date	Type of Machine	Number of Machine	Duration of Flight	Character of Flight	Pilot	Passengers	Remarks
1	SBD³	4636	3.3	S	Self	Ferguson	Search 54 cL
4	SBD³	4579	4.5	B	"	Ferguson	Sent to attack Jap carriers Bomb NO CONTACT 55 cL
4	SBD³	4579	2.8	B	"	Ferguson	Dive Bombed Jap Battleship FIRST TIME UNDER FIRE 56 cL
5	SBD3	4579	4.0	B	"	Ferguson	Dive Bombed Jap light cruiser near miss, astern NIGHT LANDING AFTER ATTACK 57 cL
6	SBD³	4575	2.2		"	Ferguson	Dive Bombed Jap Heavy Cruiser 500# Bomb - near miss Port Quarter 28 cL
6	SBD³	4599	1.8		"	Ferguson	Dive Bombed Jap Destroyer 1000# Bomb - hit Fantail 29 cL
13	SBD³	4579	3.0	F	"	Ranson	Hornet to Pearl Harbor
19	SBD³	4520	2.0	K	"	Ringressy	Tactics
19	SBD³	4520	1.0	K	"	Ringressy	"
23	SBD³	4520	1.3	G	"	Hickman	Bombing
25	SBD³	03316	1.5	G	"	Ferguson	"
26	SBD³	03316	1.0	G	"	French	"
27	SBD³	4565	1.4	G	"	F.O.N.	"
27	SBD³	63256	0.7	G	"	Ukrine	"
30	SBD³	03241	0.7	G	"	French	Bombing

Total time to date | 31.5

85. Japanese prisoners of war on board the USS *Ballard* (AVD-10), after being found in a lifeboat after the Battle of Midway. They are engine-room survivors from the aircraft carrier *Hiryū*, left behind when the ship was abandoned and sunk. They are on their way to Midway Island, the only members of the Japanese Fleet to set foot there, *en route* to Pearl Harbor for internment. (*National Archives, via Naval Historical Foundation, Washington DC*).

86. The Texas Hero! Ensign George Gay, the only survivor from Waldron's doomed TBDs of VT-8 is pictured recovering at Pearl Harbor Naval Hospital in June 1942. He was to become a celebrity back in the USA, while other survivors from the Avenger section of his squadron were ignored. After the war his story of what he witnessed, like Topsy, 'just keep growing'. Historians and colleagues alike have largely down-played his memoirs, written shortly before his death. (*US Navy, via Naval Historical Foundation, Washington DC*).

87. Ensign Clayton E. Fisher of the *Hornet*'s VS-8, relaxing at Pearl Harbor immediately after the battle. (*Clayton Fisher*).

88. Veteran. The author in discussion with dive-bomber exponent Lieutenant-Commander Zenji Abe at the Yasukuni Shrine, central Tokyo, 21 April 1998. (*Copyright Peter C. Smith*).

89. Veterans. Signed photograph showing, from right to left: B5N2 Pilot Taisuke Maruyama from the *Hiryu*, who torpedoed the carrier *Yorktown* on 4 June, W. G. Roy, who filmed the battle from the deck of the *Yorktown* and who was part of the salvage party; Lieutenant Commander Richard H. Best, SBD-3 pilot of VB-6, who helped to sink two Japanese carriers at Midway. (*Copyright William G. Roy, Naples FL*).

90. Veterans. Takeshi Maeda. Honorary President of Unabarakai, the veteran IJN pilot's association, at an interview with the author in the Dai-Ichi Hotel, Shinbashi, Central Tokyo on 4 November 2005. As a young Lieutenant he flew a Kate torpedo-bomber from the aircraft carrier *Kaga* and was aboard her at the Battle of Midway. (*Copyright Peter C. Smith*).

91. Historian Ray Wagner, seated in the Boardroom of the San Diego Aerospace Museum, during a meeting with the author and Clayton Fisher to discuss the influence of Ed Heinemann and the SBD on the outcome of Midway, 28 March 2006. (*Copyright Peter C. Smith*).

92. Veterans. Lieutenant-Commander Iyozo Fujita, during an interview with the author at his home on 5 November 2005. Fujita was an ace Zero pilot from the carrier *Soryū*, who flew with the CAP over the 1st *Kido Butai* at Midway, and was shot down by 'friendly fire' during that battle, being rescued by the destroyer *Nowaki*. A leading IJN ace, he later wrote of his exploits in the book *Zero Fighter*. (*Copyright Peter C. Smith*).

93. Veterans. Commander Clayton E. Fisher, outside the San Diego Aerospace Museum during one of his interviews with the author on 28 March 2006. (*Copyright Peter C. Smith*).

94. Veterans. Captain N. Jack 'Dusty' Kleiss Sr, at his home in San Antonio, Texas, during an interview with the author on 1 April 2006. (*Copyright Peter C. Smith*).

95. Veterans. Commander Mitsuo Fuchida. Fêted as the hero of Pearl Harbor and other battles, Fuchida was reduced to an observer's role at Midway due to illness. However, he subsequently became far more famous for his eyewitness account of the battle, which for many decades was taken as the only true and worthwhile Japanese viewpoint. His acccount had been increasingly criticized in recent years and he, just like the American Professor Samuel Eliot Morison, is now vilified by some American historians and researchers. (*Author's collection*).

96. George J. Walsh, with his SB2C Air Group Eighty aboard the carrier *Ticonderoga* (CV-14) in the Pacific. This former dive-bomber pilot has been a tireless campaigner for what he preceives as lack of recognition for the dive-bomber's role at Midway. (*George J. Walsh*).

97. The Victor of Midway! An SBD releases a bomb from the swinging crutch, with the perforated dive flaps extended and her twin 303s watching the skies astern. The true victor of the Battle of Midway. (*Copyright US Navy via Clayton Fisher*).

Chapter Twelve

Post-War Conclusions

The 'Bates' Report

The most detailed analysis of the Midway battle conducted in the immediate aftermath of World War II was the strategical and tactical analysis conducted by the US Naval War College, which appeared in 1948 (the so-called 'Bates Report').[1] Yet even this made clear in its Foreword that, although it was based on information from both Allied and Japanese sources that was wider, more complete and more up-to-date than that available to previous writers, it was still not the final word.

> Complete information from all sources was not available to the Naval War College. This is especially true concerning Japanese information. Orders appear to have been issued after the abortive Midway operation that all references to the defeat at Midway were to be deleted from war diaries and similar papers. Fortunately, however, all commands did not comply with this directive in its entirety, so that certain key information which should have been deleted was available for this analysis. For the above reasons new facts and circumstances may come to light from time to time which may change some of the analyses produced herein.[2]

What the authors of the report did not state, was that not all available *American* documentation and data was made available either! The most important omissions were obviously the intelligence reports, but there were also many eyewitness testimonies which were readily available, or could have been obtained, just five years after the events, from the many survivors who were still alive and in full mental health. This makes the report less than complete, but it is still worthy of consideration even now, to view just what conclusions were reached. Also, like almost everything connected with Midway, the analysis, and the way it was conducted were not free of controversy.

At the time it was set-up, it was between two of the principal participants of the battle itself, one of whom held the President's Chair at the Naval War College – Admiral Raymond A. Spruance himself. Thus it was Spruance who, early in 1946, had received the directive from the CNO, none other than Fleet Admiral Chester W. Nimitz[3], requiring the Naval War College 'to study and evaluate the battles of World War II in which the Naval Service participated'. The War College was left to decide on the title, method of presentation and form of such evaluations. Spruance regarded this directive as 'a new and important responsibility' for the War College and set about establishing a research department to carry out the task. Initially this group was to comprise four 'especially selected officers'. To head this team Spruance selected Commodore Richard W. Bates[4], who was at that time in the US Naval Hospital, Oakland, California. Spruance wrote to Bates on 19 June 1946:

---

1. *The Battle of Midway including The Aleutian Phase; June 3 to June 14, 1942. Strategical and Tactical Analysis*, US Naval War College, 1948 (NAVPERS 91067). Command File World War II for OP-29-B.
2. *Ibid.*
3. Nimitz was CNO between 15 December 1945 and 15 December 1946.
4. Admiral Richard W. 'Rafe' Bates (1892–1973). b. San Francisco. Graduated from US Naval Academy, Annapolis,

1915. Ensign aboard battleship *Ohio* (BB-12) and cruiser *Maryland* (ACR-8) then the gunboat *Yorktown* (GBT-1) in Central American waters. Then became XO of the cruiser *Cincinnati* (C-7) off South America to 1918 and gunnery instructor aboard the Cuban gunboat *Cuba* to 1919. Became XO of the *Sprouston* (DD-173) 1919–20. Post-graduate Annapolis 1920, then Columbia University. MSc 1922, study and practical experience with GEC Schenectady, New York and Westinghouse, East Pittsburg, Pennsylvania became

I have recently, through a visit to Washington by Commodore Carroll (now attached to the War College), inquired into your availability to take charge of this work. BuPers has informed me that you could be assigned to this duty provided your physical condition will permit, and that if assigned you would be ordered on a temporary duty basis to allow you to retain your rank.[5]

The offer was accepted and Bates assembled his initial team. By 1949 the group comprised Commander David C. Richardson[6], Captain W. H. Ashford[7] and Captain R. S. Smith[8], plus one civilian.[9] Midway was not the first project and the smallness of the team and the amount of exploration required for verification meant that work was, in Bates's own words, 'a painfully slow process'[10]. People that were still alive and in high places stood to have their reputations called into question so everything had to be proceed with the utmost circumspection. However, by February 1948, Bates was able to reassure Captain R. C. Parker[11] that he was 'ready now' to send him the first draft of the Midway analysis, 'which has been finished but not entirely so, as the lessons will be drawn later'.[12] Bates also revealed some of his thinking as well.

Electrical Officer (EO) of battleship *Maryland* (BB-46) 1922–25. Post-Graduate School 1925–27 and EO aboard light cruiser *Richmond* (CL-9) 1927–30. Service with Hydrographic Office, Honolulu, followed by command of the destroyer *Buchanan* (DD-1), oiler *Ramapo* (AO-12) and destroyers *Long* (DD-209) and *Clark* (DD-361), with DesRon 3. At Naval War College as student, then staff, then command of heavy cruiser *Minneapolis* (CA-36) at Wake Island, Gilbert Islands and sinking of light cruiser *Katori* off Truk in 1944. On staff of CinC Pacific Feet May–August 1944, then CruDiv 4 as CofS Bombardment Fire Support in 7th Fleet, Philippines. CofS BatDiv 2 at Lingayen-Luzon landings and at Okinawa in 1945. May 1945 appointed Commander of Motor Torpedo Boat Squadron, Pacific Fleet and by December CofS Philippine Frontier where his health suffered requiring hospitalization. 1946 to Naval War College as Head of Research and Analysis, before retiring in 1949 with rank of rear-admiral. Continued work at War College with World War II Battle Evaluation Group until termination 1958. Vice President Naval War College Foundation, in 1969, President in 1972 until his death 27 December 1973. Personal papers 1915–73 acquired by Naval War College in 1974 and held and arranged in three series. Referred to hereafter as Bates Papers.

5. Spruance to Bates, dated 19 June 1946. Bates Papers, Enclosure 0004.

6. Vice-Admiral David Charles Richardson (b. 1914). b. Meridian, Mississippi, 8 April 1914. Attended Meridian High School and prepped for the Naval Academy at Marion Military Institute, entering US Naval Academy, Annapolis, on 27 June 1932 and graduating as ensign on 4 June 1936, 119th in his class and with a Bachelor of Science degree. Served two years aboard battleship *Tennessee* (BB-43), and when detached was Communications Officer of the destroyer *Downes* (DD-375) until February 1939. Flight training at NAS Pensacola, to April 1940, joining VF-5. Saw service aboard *Saratoga* (CV-3), *Ranger* (CV-4), *Yorktown* (CV-5) and *Wasp* (CV-7) flying F3Fs and F4Fs including combat over Guadalcanal in 1942 with four confirmed 'kills'. Earned the Purple Heart, three Distinguished Service Medals and the Distinguished Flying Cross. Tactics training in Florida at the Fighter Training Units at Jacksonville and Sanford followed by command of FTUs at Vero Beach and Daytona Beach. 1945, January, joined staff of Commander Air Force, Pacific Fleet and Carrier Group Readiness training at Hawaii followed. Awarded Bronze Star. After the war attended Royal Navy Staff College, Greenwich, London, January–June 1946, before joining the team at Naval War College. 1948, September, appointed Commander Carrier Air Group 13 aboard *Princeton* (CV-37), from August 1948, with NATO planning role. 1949 October, Joint Chiefs of Staff, Washington DC for Joint Strategic Plans Group. 1952, XO of carrier *Badoeng Strait* (CVE-116) from April and during Korean War. Staff C-in-C South at Naples, as War Plans Officer from August 1953. 1954–7 Officer of CNO (Air Weapons Analysis). Operations and Intelligence Officer Southern Europe, and then in 1959 commanded oiler *Cimarron* (AO-22) followed by carrier *Hornet-II* (CVS-12) in the Mediterranean. 1961–4 OP-06 and OpNav, then Commander Fleet Air at Norfolk. 1966, Commander TF-77 as Commander Attack Carrier Striking Force during the Vietnam War, for which he earned the Distinguished Service Medal. Assistant DCNO (Air), then as vice-admiral (dated 14 August 1968) was C-in-C 6th Fleet in Mediterranean once more, 1968–7 for which he was awarded the Gold Star. Championed Ocean Surveillance Information System (pre-World-wide Military Command Control System) in order to monitor Soviet naval operations. Deputy C-in-C Pacific Fleet, to retirement on 1 July 1972. From his home in southern California where he lived with his wife, *née* Jeannne McHugh Simonds, by whom he had six children, David W. Suzanne, Robert, Ruthanne, Schamber and Samuel, he worked as an advisor and consultant with continued interest in Intelligence work and in 1997 he published a critical analysis of the Dorn Report on Pearl Harbor and strove to clear Admiral Kimmel's name.

7. Captain W. H. Ashford was later to command the carrier *Midway* (CVB-41) in 1954.

8. Captain R. S. Smith.

9. Evelyn M. Cherpak, Head, Naval Historical Collection at the Naval War College told the author, 'I have no idea who the civilian was'. (Cherpak to author, dated 9 May 2006.)

10. Bates to CoS, dated 9 December 1947. Bates Papers, Enclosure 0818.

11. Captain R. C. Parker had commanded the Alaskan Sector of the 13th Naval District from 1940, with the old gunboat *Charlestown* (PG-51) as his flagship, and later commanded the big floating dock, *AFDB-1* between August 1944 and January 1946. She had been sent to the Philippines Sea Frontier in 1945 where Bates was serving at the time.

12. Bates to Captain R. C. Parker, dated 2 February 1948. Bates Papers. Enclosure 0015.

I am getting it ready to deliver to Admiral Spruance for his general comments, so that any points that he disagrees with I may have a chance to discuss with him, and, if he desires, delete it. Also, I have refrained from saying many things that I should have liked to say, but I think that your advice in this matter was correct and therefore I have only hit the key successes and mistakes. You may not remember this, but you advised me that my work was fine because I did not hang on little things but tried to hang on to big things.[13]

In contrast to these fine sentiments, another member of the team later remembered Bates's approach rather differently. In an interview conducted at Coronado with Paul Stillwell[14] in 1992, the then respected Vice-Admiral David C. Richardson, gave this account.

During my second year at the Naval War College I was in the analytical section on the staff, making analyses of actions of World War II. This was part of the post-war work done by Rafe Bates. I did all of the original work on researching the latter part of the Battle of Midway and all of the Savo Island battle. Thanks to Samuel Eliot Morison[15] and his translator, Roger Pineau[16], we had Japanese combat diaries.

It was interesting to me that when we finished the analysis of the Battle of Midway, with its criticisms of the functioning of command, Rafe Bates had taken it upon himself to rewrite some of the history in order to extol Spruance all the more. Spruance rejected it. The three of us who were working there – two captains and myself, a commander – were very upset and objected strenuously to the final version.

Bates took it up to Spruance. Spruance went

13. *Ibid.*
14. Commander Paul Stillwell, USNR, a Vietnam War veteran served in the reserve from 1962 to 1988, with a period of active service from 1966 to 1969 aboard the tank landing ship *Washoe County* and the battleship *New Jersey*. He did not officially retire until 1992 after service in the First Gulf War in 1988. 1966 graduated from Drury University, Springfield, Missouri, with a BA in History, and in 1979 with a masters degree from University of Missouri. 1972 after graduate school work in PR for St Louis Cardinals. 1974–81 was progressively Departments, Managing and then Senior Editor. 1981–7 Editor of Naval Institute *Proceedings*, Annapolis, MD, and a respected author of many naval histories, including *Carrier War: Aviation Art of World War II, Air Raid: Pearl Harbor!* and books on the battleships *Arizona, New Jersey* and *Missouri*. 1987–92 Editor-in-Chief *Naval History*. More recently Director of History at the United States Naval Institute, and also television work for NBC, CNN, ABC, CBS as well as the Discovery and History Channels, including the *Battleship* documentary of 1997. Awarded the Alfred Thayer Mahan Award. He lives in Arnold, Maryland. With wife Karen and three sons.
15. Rear-Admiral Samuel Eliot Morison (1887–1976). b. Boston, Massachusetts on 9 July 1887. Educated at Noble's School, at St Paul's, Concord, New Hampshire, and then Harvard University, graduating with a Bachelor of Arts degree in 1908. Studied at Ecole Libre des Sciences Politiques, Paris 1908–09, and was post-graduate at Harvard resulting in a Doctorate of Philosophy in 1912. Married Elizabeth S. Greene in 1910 (d. 1945) by whom he had four children. Instructor at University of California, Berkeley, and later at Harvard in 1915, becoming a professor in 1925 and appointed to Jonathan Trumbaull Chair in 1940, until he retired in 1955. War service as a private in US Army during World War I. Attached to the Russian Division of American Commission and on Baltic Commission until June 1919. Was Harmsworth Professor of American History at Oxford University 1922–5.

1939–40 Harvard Columbus Expedition, winning Pulitzer Prize for his account, *Admiral of the Ocean Sea*, in 1942. 1941–2 American History teacher at Johns Hopkins University. On 5 May this noted civilian historian was given a Naval Reserve commission by the President for the specific purpose of assembling the material for the fifteen-volume *History of United States Naval Operations in World War II*, which for many years was the standard reference work, first as a lieutenant-commander then a captain. He served afloat in the Atlantic on the destroyer *Buck* (DD-420); at the North African landings aboard the light cruiser *Brooklyn* (CL-40), and in the South Pacific aboard the battleship *Washington* (BB-56), PT-boats and the light cruiser *Honolulu* (CL-48), being present at the Battle of Kolombangara. Later, aboard the heavy cruiser *Baltimore* (CA-68), then *Honolulu* again at the Marianas in 1944. 1944–5 was aboard the coastguard cutter *Campbell* (W-32) in the Mediterranean and aboard the battleship *Tennessee* (BB-43) at Okinawa and Iwo Jima. 1945 Promoted to rear-admiral on Naval Reserve in 1951. Among many awards were Legion of Merit, Victory Medal, Commander of the Order of White Rose of Finland, Vuelvo Panamericano Medal of Cuba and Commander of the Spanish Order of Isabella the Catholic. Remarried in December 1949, Mrs Priscilla B. Shakelford. Was editor of *The American Neptune* and *The New England Quarterly* and awarded many international literary prizes and equally as many honorary degrees from schools and universities in England and the USA. Died at Boston on 15 May 1976, following a stroke. His ashes are interred at Northeast Harbor, Maine. Despite being a highly honoured academic with a stirling record of war participation in the face of the enemy, much of his work on World War II naval operations has been attacked and derided by a new generation of Internet revisionists and some serious American naval historians alike in more recent years.
16. Lieutenant Roger Pineau, a Japanese language specialist during World War II, who took part in the post-war interrogations of Japanese naval officers.

through it and sent it back, saying. 'If there's any one real hero in this battle, his name is Wade McClusky.' He made Rafe Bates revise the work by removing fancied thinking and explanations.[17]

Another former Naval War College staff member to which Bates sent the draft manuscript around this time, was Admiral Henry K. Hewitt[18], who was the US Naval Representative on the United Nations Military Staff Committee in New York. Bates advised Hewitt that he was sending a draft of the Battle of Midway under a separate cover and that he was 'now working on the lessons of Midway, and if you happen to see any in there that you think worthy of publication, a short comment or recommendation thereon would be appreciated'. He added: 'I think you will find from this study that the Japanese pretty well understood carrier warfare but would have done better had they considered American capabilities more than intentions.'

Stillwell pressed Richardson on this point, asking, 'In what way was Bates writing the report?' Richardson replied:

He was being very critical of all sorts of actions by people in command other than Spruance – unwarranted criticisms. He was inclined to be critical anyway; it was an ego thing. If he could find a little bit of a reason for criticism, and in almost anything that anybody does there's room for some criticism, then he would condemn. But he extolled Spruance enormously, and he ran down other people. It was very unfair. It wasn't based on good evidence. There was often nothing to support his criticisms.

He also accused Bates of trying 'to browbeat all the time', adding, 'If he could get anything on you, he'd just drive you nuts'.

Stilwell asked, 'What do you mean 'if he could get anything on you?' Like what?'

Richardson replied, 'If he could succeed in putting a squeeze on you, he would exploit that'.

On 10 May, Bates was able to advise Spruance that the analysis of Midway was complete. He added: 'All the matters discussed by you on your sheet have been included as modified by the conferences'.[19] He went on to list some of the bones of contention.

(a) The item concerning the contact report discussed on page 325 is not quite clear yet. What is included in the article is as reported by Captain Mitcher [sic].

(b) The discussion of the *Hornet* VB Group is still in the book. No change whatsoever has been made on it for the reason that Admiral Brown said that he felt that Commander Air Group 8 did not handle himself well and that the book should properly include a comment concerning his actions. Admiral Brown reread what is in the book and considers [it to be] correct.[20]

(c) You will find in the battle lesson one in particular with which you may disagree. In this connection I should like to invite your attention to Battle Lesson No. 6. I have tried to rewrite this to accord with what I think your views are. I feel that you concur that it is much better to control naval forces from a base as near to the

17. Vice-Admiral David C. Richardson, Interview of Sunday, 29 March 1992 at Coronado, California, conducted by Paul Stillwell. Referred to hereafter as Richardson, Stillwell interview.

18. Admiral Henry Kent Hewitt (1887–1972). b. Hackensack, New Jersey. Graduated from US Naval Academy. Served aboard the battleship *Missouri* (BB-11) during the Great White Fleet's circumnavigation of the world 1907–09. As ensign served aboard battleship Connecticut and destroyer *Flusser* (DD-20). Lieutenant jg. As lieutenant taught mathematics at Naval Academy then commanded the survey and patrol yacht *Eagle*. During World War I commanded the destroyer *Cummings* (DD-44). After the war Gunnery Officer aboard battleship *Pennsylvania* (BB-38). Commander of the heavy cruiser *Indianapolis* (CA-35), took President Roosevelt to Buenos Aires 1936. Rear-admiral 1939. From 1941 commanded Atlantic Fleet Task Groups on Neutrality Patrols, then was appointed Commander Amphibious Forces, Atlantic, from April 1942 to 1945, which included major landings from Operation Torch

onward (Morocco, Sicily, Salerno, Anzio, South France). Chairman of Pearl Harbor inquiry. After the war commanded US Naval Forces Europe, and acted as advisor at the Naval War College and then at United Nations. Retired from the navy in 1949. Died Middlebury, Vermont 15 September 1972. Personal papers 1903–1972 (2,000 items, 10 containers) held at Naval Historical Foundation Collection in the Library of Congress. MSS61740.

19. Bates to Spruance, dated 10 May 1948. Bates Papers, Enclosure 0828.

20. At this date, the man concerned, Captain Stanhope C. Ring, was the commanding officer of the carrier *Boxer* (CV-21) (from July 1947 to July 1948), and she made two cruises from San Diego to Pearl Harbor as well as making history by flying off the first jet aircraft from an *Essex* class carrier. He was hardly beyond all human reach and contact, but nobody concerned with the analysis apparently thought it relevant to ask him, a key eyewitness who was being severely criticized, what his views on the matter were or include him in the list of pre-publication readers!

scene of combat as possible than from one far away. Such a condition would have obtained Midway had facilities been available ashore. You have stated that such facilities did not exist. However, the conduct of the action indicates plainly in my mind the truth of the basic lesson, 'Keep your command post as near to the scene of action as possible.'

Spruance was not the only pre-publication reader who found himself at issue with Bates version of events. Samuel Morison wrote from Sea Cove, Maine on 27 August, thanking him for the analysis 'I have had your "Midway" at my elbow here, and have constantly referred to it. A grand job, and it has saved me from countless errors and omissions.' (But, of course, relying so heavily on Bates may also have led Morison to commit some other 'errors and omissions' for which, seven decades later, he is being vilified). Despite the adulation, however, he went on to refer to matters on which he differed from Bates, in particular, 'the identity of *Nautilus*'s victim'. He went into detail of why he though the submarine sank *Kaga* and not *Soryū* He also asked, 'Did you ever find out why *Enterprise* was so slow in launching VT on 4 June?'[21]

The Midway analysis as rewritten by Bates, and then further amended, was duly adopted, but the original draft vanished, like so much documentation on Midway, into the blue!

In the summer of 1948 Bates wrote to Richardson, now with CarDiv 2 at San Diego, asking the whereabouts of the 'original' copy of the Midway analysis. Richardson's replied of 13 August, read:

I regret that you were inconvenienced through not being able to locate the needed copy of Midway. That copy I retained in my custody until just a day or two before I left at which time I turned it into the archives, and indicated its special importance. As I recollect I specified that it should not be kept with the other Midway material. I did not anticipate that our section had further need of it, and I did not think casual investigators of Midway should see it.[22]

However, in the interview with Paul Stilwell on 29 March 1992, Richardson revealed what had actually occurred. Bates, he told his interviewer,

. . . was missing a document. It was a copy of the Midway analysis before Bates reworked it. He rewrote it, but the original submission still existed. I was in charge of the archives. One of the two captains – I don't remember which one – told me to put that book away where Rafe Bates wouldn't get it. It would be our defense, because when this version by Rafe Bates got published, there would be a lot of damn sore people, and properly so.

So I gave it to the head civilian in the archives and said, 'Commander Bates is going to want this. [They all knew him very well.] It's to be put away and kept there. Don't give it to him!

Months later, I was out on the *Princeton* in Tsingtao.[23] I got a very commendatory letter from Bates, saying ' How we miss you.' He could lay it on. Then, ' By the way, would you please let me know where the draft Midway battle analysis is. Did you by any chance take it with you?' [Laughter]

I wrote him back and said, 'No, sir. Sorry, but I did not take it. Thank you very much for your very kind remarks. I did not take this book with me.

Stilwell: 'And you didn't tell him where it was?'

Richardson: 'I didn't tell him where it was, no. So then I got another letter, and now it was threatening. "This is a very serious matter. Will you tell me where that book is?"' I wrote back and I said. 'What I told you is absolutely true. I don't have it.' He said. 'I'm sure if you look, you will find it somewhere' I said, "I do not have it. I did not take it." Well, that was the end of it. The final version was the one Bates had redone and which then had numerous additional changes directed by Spruance'.

Despite this spat, Richardson told Stillwell, 'But I liked Bates. I admired him, parts of him. Sometimes he was fabulous, and sometimes he was just an egotistical ass. The next time I went to see him, I was a rear-admiral [Laughter]'.[24]

21. Morison to Bates, dated 27 August 1948.
22. Richardson to Bates, 13 August 1948, Bates Papers, Enclosure 0066.
23. Richardson had left the Naval War College by this time, and, after a six-week modified syllabus at Jacksonville, Florida, had joined CarDiv, *Princeton* (CV-37) and *Tarawa* (CV-40), under Rear-Admiral Ginder, in command of the former's air group. He actually received Bates's first letter while still at US Naval Air Station San

Diego, prior to the carriers sailing east.
24. Richardson, Stillwell interview. Evelyn M. Cherpak, Head, Naval Historical Collection at the Naval War College told the author: 'Unfortunately, we don't have a copy of the original Midway analysis, although I've heard that it existed once upon a time'. As Bates later became Vice President of the Naval War College Foundation, he would have had ample time and opportunity to finally locate and deal with it had he so wished.

When Admiral Shafroth[25] wrote to the Naval War College in November, requesting a further four copies of the Midway analysis for the General Board, Bates replied and added: 'I am extremely interested, naturally, in your reactions to the Battle of Midway, as my objective in preparing these evaluations is to endeavour to present the true facts and, wherever possible, the problems which confronted the principal commanders on both sides at all times'.

He revealed that the Battle of Midway analysis had followed the precedent of the Coral Sea study and had not been published 'until the principal commanders concerned had had an opportunity to read them and comment; then if the comment seemed suitable, the book would be changed to suit the comment. The Admiral [Spruance] approved'. He continued: 'The Battle of Midway has been studied by both Admirals Spruance and Theobald, to say nothing of others such as Admiral Smith[26], who was CoS for Vice-Admiral Pye with TF-1, and by Admiral Brown, Captain Sylvester, and by certain students of the War College in committee'.

One may think that this was rather a selected list, with 'principal commanders' like Fletcher and Mitscher not mentioned, whereas Pye was very remote from the scene of battle.[27]

---

25. Vice-Admiral John ('Jack') Franklin Shafroth, Jr (1887–1967). b. Denver, Colorado, 31 March 1887, son of 'Honest John', the US Senator and Governor of Colorado. Graduated from the US Naval Academy, Annapolis, 1908. Served in the Mexican campaign 1914. During War War I served aboard the battleships *Arkansas* (BB-33) as navigator and *West Virginia* (BB-48) as XO. 1938–40 commanded the heavy cruiser *Indianapolis*. 1942 as rear-admiral in command South-East Pacific Area. March 1944-March 1945, Inspector General, US Fleet Vice-admiral. In 1945 appointed in command of BatDiv 2 and conducted the first bombardments of Japanese home islands by Task Unit 34.8.1. with the battleships *South Dakota* (BB-57), *Indiana* (BB-58) and *Massachusetts* (BB-59), two heavy cruisers and nine destroyers, on 11 July 1945. After the war on the General Board. Died after a stroke at his home in Westerly, Rhode Island on 1 September 1967, buried at Arlington National Cemetery.

26. Vice-Admiral William Ward 'Poco' Smith (1888–1966). b. Newark, New Jersey, 8 February 1888. Educated at Springfield High School, New Jersey 1905 entered US Naval Academy, Annapolis, as midshipman. Graduated on 4 June and awarded Class of 1871 Sword for excellence and commissioned as Ensign. 1909-1911, served successively aboard the battleships *Ohio* (BB-12), *Michigan* (BB-27) and *North Dakota* (BB-29) and with Navy Rifle Team at Wakefield, Masseuchusetts. 1911, October, until August 1914, served aboard the monitor *Monterey* (BM-6) on Asiatic Station, with landing parties at Amoy, Foochow and Swatow during Chinese Revolution of 1912, then in command of the dry dock *Dewey* and the Hull Division at Naval Station, Olongapo, Philippines, then aboard gunboat *Wilmington* (PG-8) in Chinese waters. Married Elizabeth Virginia Purdy, 2 September 1913, by whom he had a son, William, who became a West Point graduate. 1914, October, to July 1915 served aboard the battleship *North Dakota* (BB-29) again, and *Utah* (BB-31). 1915 Office of Naval Communications, Washington, DC. 1918, commanded destroyers *Downes* (DD-45) and *Allen* (DD-66), and was on the staff of the Commander, Naval Forces, European Waters based at Queenstown, Ireland, during World War I. Between the wars served successively in the Atlantic in command of the destroyers *Fairfax* (DD-93) from March, and *Herbert* (DD-160) from January 1920, then at the Bureau of Engineering (BuEng), Washington, DC. 1923, September, to February 1925 commanded the destroyer *Williamson* (DD-244) in the Pacific then Flag Secretary to Commander, Scouting Fleet and Manufacturing Officer, Naval Torpedo Station, Newport. 1929–30, commanded the gunboat *Sacramento* (AG–19) as part of Special Service Squadron. Served with Chinese Expeditionary Force and Asiatic Fleets and in Central and South America in second Nicaraguan Campaign, for which he received the Order of Merit for salvaging the steamer *Heilo* from Corinto harbour entrance. 1931-4, XO, Bancroft Hall Naval Academy, then XO aboard heavy cruiser *Salt Lake City* (CA-25). 1936-9 Head of Mathematics, Naval Academy, commanded the light cruiser *Brooklyn* (CL-40). On 1 February was CoS to Admiral Kimmel at Pearl Harbor, then Administrative CoS to CincPac. 1942, January, promoted to rear-admiral. Commanded the heavy cruisers of Task Forces 11, 17 and 8 early in the Pacific War from the *Astoria* (CA-34) at Coral Sea and escorted the carrier *Yorktown* (CV-5) of Fletchers task force at Midway. He commanded the cruiser force in Aleutians with CTG 8.1 and CTG.8.6 and later CTF 11, including bombardment of Kiska in 1942, being awarded the Distinguished Service Medal, before becoming Commander, Naval Transport Service Force, Pacific Fleet from January 1943 to February 1945, as a vice-admiral from 6 March 1945. He hoisted his flag aboard the battleship *West Virginia* (BB-48) for the voyage home to San Francisco in November 1945. Decorations included DSM for Coral Sea and Midway. 1946, Member of the General Board, Navy Department. Retired from the navy on 1 October, but appointed by President Truman in May 1946 as Chairman of US Maritime Commission 1946-9, including the 'Magic Carpet' return of troops home. Worked for the reinvigorating US mercantile fleet after the war and was a member of SNAME. 1950-6, Vice-President of Fruehauf Trailer Company, Detroit. Michigan, until 1950. 1957 President of US Naval Academy Alumni Association. Author of *Midway: Turning Point of the Pacific*. Died 30 May 1966 at the US Naval Hospital, Bethesda, and is interred at the Naval Academy Cemetery, Annapolis.

27. Vice-Admiral William Satterlee Pye, had commanded the battle fleet at Pearl Harbor, was appointed to command TF-1 formed around the surviving battleships of his old battle line, *Pennsylvania, Colorado, Maryland, Tennessee, Idaho, Mississippi* and *New Mexico,* which formed at San Francisco with ten destroyers on 15 June 1942. But this force, with a screen of ten destroyers, did not return to Pearl Harbor until 1 August, almost two months *after* the Battle of Midway. b.

Bates's Battle Lessons

The most significant part of the Bates Report was the battle lessons. We can summarize most of them, but some are worthy of detailed examination. Bates first credited the Doolittle Raid with being instrumental in bringing the Japanese to battle. He also cites Japanese over-confidence at the results of the Coral Sea battle as another major factor. The two incidents combined, it was concluded, resulted in the Japanese overreaction, and the fact that they 'now activated the Midway operation well ahead of its original schedule'.

Therefore, although the Doolittle mission was 'too weak to accomplish much material damage, yet it engendered such fear in the Japanese as to cause them to expedite action in other theaters'.

In trying to fathom the mental process followed by the Commander, Mobile Force, the War College analysis drew a blank. They concluded that 'he may have followed the method of intentions rather than the method of capabilities in his estimation of the enemy'. Evidence that this was so included an assumption that the Americans did not have the will to fight, but might be provoked into a counter-attack if Midway was invested. There was, they felt, also the assumption that the enemy would not have surface forces with carriers as a nucleus at the time of the planned initial attack. It was felt that the Japanese commander *should* have known that the Americans were still capable of moving carriers into the area to defend the island. They also felt that, although Nagumo flew air searches in case American forces were present, and held back an air group to strike at them if they materialized, he did not give the search sufficiently serious consideration. They felt that the number of search aircraft was inadequate, and those that were sent were despatched 'in a haphazard and staggered fashion'. They summed up Nagumo's perceived failings succinctly: 'He disregarded the search before it was completed, broke the spot of his standby air group, and ordered it rearmed for land objectives.'

The War College team concluded, from Nagumo's errors, that a commander 'should list the enemy course of action in order of priority.' However, the biggest lesson to be drawn from Nagumo's catastrophic defeat was that in case of doubt, he should give the higher priority to those enemy courses which he considers more dangerous to himself'. In other words, a second strike against Midway could have waited; the island was not going anywhere and could have been attacked again at any time. Its sting had already been drawn, all the attacks mounted from there had been dismal failures and had taken casualties, it was no big threat, and even if it had been, the Japanese ships could move out of range if they chose, with the troopships turned back and held for a day or two. What was hideously dangerous to the 1st *Kidō Butai* was the possibility that American carriers were on their flank and just awaiting their chance.

Surprise was a big factor in the planning of both sides. Here Rochefort and the Hypo team gave the Americans the edge, but they were aided by the fact that the Japanese 'appeared to believe that they could conduct an operation of such vast scope as the Midway operation with complete secrecy'. The Americans did not escape censure, however, for, despite the ace Intelligence had put in their hand, the actual surprise achieved at the start of the battle was 'purely a fortuitous circumstance, as their carrier task forces would probably have been discovered much earlier had the Japanese commander conducted a more timely and better coordinated search'.

Therefore although surprise was always to be desired as 'a most potent factor', indeed 'the soul of every operation', Bates concluded that it must not be counted upon too strongly when planning. Most importantly: 'In considering surprise, the enemy's intelligence potentialities should not be overlooked.'

The attacks by the shore-based air forces of all types, as well as being ineffectual in themselves, failed the American task force commanders by not delivering a regular and continuous stream of sighting reports. This failure to keep the sea-going commands in the picture about enemy movements 'seriously handicapped' them at the crucial times,

---

Minneapolis, Minnesota 9 June 1880. Spanish Campaign 1898. Graduated US Naval Academy, Annapolis, 1901. Ensign 1903. 1901–05 served aboard five battleships and an armoured cruiser and on staff of Naval Academy and Naval War College. 1915–17 commissioned and commanded destroyer *Jacob Jones* (DD-61). Staff Atlantic Fleet C-in-C during World War I, awarded Navy Cross. 1919–21 staff of CNO. 1922–3 XO battleship *Pennsylvania* (BB-38): Commanded DesRon then ashore at Navy Department, DC until 1927. Commanded minelayer *Oglala* (CM-4) and headed US Navy Mission, Peru. Commanded battleship *Nevada* (BB-36) 1932–3. Rear-admiral, CoS to Commander, Scouting Force, Naval War College and commanded destroyers. Vice-admiral Commander, Battleships, Battle Force, at Pearl Harbor Commander, Battle Force 1941. 1941 acting Commander US Pacific Fleet for two weeks in December, cancelled Fletcher's Wake Island relief mission. Led surviving battleship force; until October 1942. President of Naval War College and commander Naval Operating Base, Newport 1942–4. Issued an interim report on the Battle of Midway strongly critical of Spruance, which the latter refuted. Retired July 1944, but remained as War College President until December 1945. Died at Bethesda, Maryland, 4 May 1959.

especially on the 4 and 5 June. The conclusion was obvious: the supply of 'complete and accurate tactical intelligence' from such units was essential. They concluded that continuous training was the only way to ensure 'a thorough understanding' of this need. In fact, the problem was never overcome, and merely reflected the experience of the Royal Navy in trying to get meaningful information from the RAF in the first three years of the war, when the two did not even use the same wavelengths in their radios and could not talk to each other.

Bates's team considered, somewhat inconsistently in view of their earlier findings, that the Japanese 'thoroughly understood the value of air reconnaissance', and by the use of battleship-and cruiser-mounted aircraft for this function, freed up their carrier aircraft for battle, whereas the Americans had to rely for a large part on their scouting squadrons to carry out this role; and such a reliance had tied down the *Yorktown*, for example, for a time on the first day. 'Continuous accurate information concerning the enemy's movements and composition' was regarded, quite rightly, as essential, but future American task force commanders were advised: 'Whenever such Commanders feel that the shore based searches are inadequate and that additional searches were necessary, they should if practicable, employ their ship based aircraft for such searches', which did not move things along at all from 1942. Throughout the war the Japanese consistently outreached the Americans in both searching and striking, so the problem was never resolved. Even at the Battle of the Philippine Sea over two years after Midway, the enemy always found the US task groups long before they themselves were sighted.

Another seemingly incurable problem commented upon was the poor recognition and identification shown by Japanese and American aviators of all types. Both ships and aircraft were continually misidentified, while hits and claims on ships and planes alike were enormously exaggerated. Again, although they recommended that personnel be trained in both recognition and identification, it is a problem that has never been resolved. Admiral Nimitz had immediately requested the fitting of IFF on all American aircraft but, as the British had already found, it was one thing to fit this device, and quite another to persuade the aircrews to turn them on! Another requirement was for the

navy to have its own long-range reconnaissance aircraft manned by specialist crews rather than rely on a sister service with little knowledge of naval matters to do it for them.

Although the task forces of the two combatants used very different screening diagrams to provide anti-aircraft defence to their core carriers[28], neither proved very effective as 'gunfire did not appear to be as effective as had been anticipated.' More ships and more guns per ship seemed to be the solution, and the American, Japanese and British Navies had all followed this route already to the best of their ability. While the Japanese fighters were extremely effective against all types of American torpedo-bombers (Devastators, Avengers and Marauders alike, regardless of speed or defence, were all chopped down with ruthless efficiency), the Americans proved far less able to cope with the Japanese Kates, due, the War College thought, to the superior quality (of both aircraft and aircrew) of the 1st *Kidō Butai* at that date.

However, the most important lesson, and it was the same one as had been noted in the 1920s war games, was that: 'neither the American nor the Japanese anti-aircraft formations were particularly successful in defeating enemy dive-bomber attacks once the attacking planes had succeeded in evading the combat air patrol'. In other words in 1942, as in 1926, there was still, 'no defense against it'.

The question of interrogation of captured American pilots, and the useful information the enemy received from it was discussed, but as 'unscrupulous enemies' always had the 'means of forcing information out of all but the hardiest', the only solution was to keep aircrew, and indeed all naval personnel, ignorant, as far as humanly possible, of important data.

Like intelligence, the widespread use of radar gave the Americans a further edge, in that they could avoid being surprised by incoming enemy air attacks and could intercept further out, theoretically, giving a better chance of defeating attacks. It had to be admitted that, despite this, the Japanese aircrews still managed a high level of penetration through to the target, though with heavy losses. This had already been taken to its ultimate parameters later in the war with the *kamikaze*, and defenders either had to knock the attacker down or punch it to pieces before it hit, or take

---

28. The American task forces operated well apart from each other, each with the carrier double-ringed by a circular screen, cruisers on the inner circle (2,000 yards) destroyers in the outer (3,000 yards). The screening ships adjusted their course and speed to comply with the movement of their carrier charges. Conversely, the Japanese operated all their carriers as a single unit, and although they placed their protecting battleships, cruisers and destroyers in a ring

formation, it was at a much greater distance from the carrier core (up to 10 miles at times) and all their ships manoeuvred independently save for certain destroyers assigned to each carrier. The Japanese air defences were co-ordinated from all four carriers and assigned according to need; each American carrier looked after herself with regard the CAP, and sometimes supplemented these with dive-bomber patrols at low level to deter enemy attacks.

almost unacceptable casualties. More fighters at the expense of attack aircraft, more anti-aircraft guns (and heavier ones, the 20 mm was considered useless by 1945 and a 3 inch weapon was under development) and picket ships had already been pressed into service. Radar was another ace, but it was not a panacea, as Savo Island and similar battles had already shown. Certainly, had the Japanese possessed even a rudimentary set or two at Midway, the crucial SBD attack would have been predicted and probably intercepted, which would have made the attacks 'considerably less effective' with who knows what effects on the final outcome.

The lesson was clear,

Other technological devices may in future wars give unusual and, in some cases, almost unsurmountable advantages to those who have them. It is therefore of extreme importance that every effort is made to insure that own forces are equipped with the most advanced technological devices and that Commanders are not forced into action against an enemy better equipped in similar devices. It is of equal importance that Commanders understand the utility of these devices and know something of their capabilities and *limitations*[29].

The former point is one that American and British navies did take on board, but the latter was more difficult to ensure, as American losses in the Gulf and British losses in the Falklands War were to demonstrate.

The desirability of all the different aircraft comprising a carrier air group (CAG) having similar capabilities with regard to range was considered. Fighters would always have different characteristics from bombers, of whatever type; it was inevitable and unavoidable. Only the use of all-purpose fighter-bomber types could partially overcome that, but at a cost to their fighting qualities. The British experience with the Blackburn Skua early in the war was a clear lesson that an aircraft designed as a dive-bomber just could not act as an effective fighter aircraft. Even so, some level of 'evening out' of performance was thought desirable by the War College. 'The necessity for gaining air superiority at the point of contact may be so vital to success as to demand a concentrated attack of all planes. In such case it may be desirable to sacrifice individual plane performance towards the success of the whole'.

The question of whether, in carrier-to-carrier combat, it was the better option to sink some enemy carriers outright or just to put as many flight-decks out of action as quickly as possible was considered. The fact that the *Hiryū* escaped the first attack and was able to counter-attack, not once but twice, was considered salutary. The report admitted that: 'in any action involving aircraft carriers on both sides, the priority of targets will vary depending upon the tactical situation', but nonetheless they concluded that 'it is generally preferable to destroy the flight decks of as many of the enemy carriers as possible, even if only for a short period, in preference to attempting to sink a few number of carriers'. That, they considered, was the way to gain air superiority during the decisive phase of the action.

This was true, but in the post-war world, it was academic. Only two navies initially had sufficient numbers of aircraft carriers to operate anything like a World War II task force: the US Navy and the Royal Navy, and the former far outnumbered the latter, besides being allies. The likelihood of any future carrier-to-carrier battles was remote and became more so after the Healey cut-backs, following a successful RAF campaign, almost totally eradicated the Royal Navy's carrier fleet.[30]

The War College team moved on to consider fighter strength, but only in so far as it affected the American carriers. They concluded that, despite having their strength increased from 'an authorized eighteen to a temporary twenty-seven', the numbers were still insufficient. 'They were unable to provide adequate fighter protection for the different elements of the air attack groups and for the defense of the task forces'. The problem identified was a difficult one, and had already reappeared at the time of the *kamikaze* threat. They could only recommend that the composition of carrier air groups be continuously reviewed

29. My italics.
30. Interestingly, there was one occasion when an American versus British carrier battle was briefly, 'on the cards'. This was during the Suez crisis of 1956. The British carriers *Eagle, Albion, Bulwark, Ocean* and *Theseus*, along with the French carriers *Arromanches* and *Lafayette* were among the Allied warships deployed against the Egyptian forces. The US Sixth Fleet, commanded by Charles R. 'Cat' Brown, with the carriers *Coral Sea* (CV-43) and *Randolph* (CVA-15), later reinforced by the *Forrestal* (CVA-59) and *Franklin D. Roosevelt* (CVA-42), was operating independently in the area south of Crete. President Dwight Eisenhower was angered

by the Anglo-French action, and the CNO in Washington DC, Admiral Arleigh Burke, signalled Brown, 'Situation tense; prepare for imminent hostilities'. Brown signalled back; 'Am prepared for imminent hostilities, whose side are we on?' This certainly put the so-called 'special relationship' into *very* clear perspective! Another carrier-to-carrier scenario was an equally brief possibility during the Falklands War of 1982, but before the British carriers *Invincible* and *Hermes* could get within range of her, the Argentinian navy carrier *Independencia*, steamed back to the safety of her base at her top speed and never ventured out to sea again until the fighting was all over!

and 'timely adjustments' be made according to the situation as to the type and numbers of each type assigned. However it was not that simple because 'both procurement and training problems are involved in addition to the purely military considerations'. They admitted that it was 'likely that only minor readjustments can be made immediately before or during an operation'.

The team then returned to the Japanese, or more especially Nagumo, whom, they considered to be most emphatically to blame for his own catastrophe. By his decision to break the spot of his standby attack group, which was armed to attack any surface craft encountered, without having completed his air search for such craft, Nagumo 'placed his carriers in a state of non-readiness for instant action. He was hit in this unsatisfactory condition of readiness' and duly paid the price. Bates was unable to give a clear answer to this constant dilemma, while accepting as inevitable that 'momentous deviations from decisions made during the planning phase of a military problem' were unavoidable and should be made 'without hesitancy', it had to be accepted that 'should the Commander make an undesirable departure from the plan' like Nagumo, the chances of failure were increased.

Also on the Japanese side Yamamoto was criticized on two major counts. 'The Japanese planning for the Midway operation was not sound. Japanese forces were not adequately co-ordinated'. The report spelt it out: 'The factors of mutual support and concentration appear to have been disregarded for the purpose of possible envelopment of American forces'. The conclusion was that the close co-ordination of diverse task forces and groups operating under the same command be thoroughly considered.

Not surprisingly, the report came down hard on the USAAC's used of high-level horizontal bombing. Including five small sorties flown against an American submarine, the B-17s flew fifty-five sorties and dropped twenty 1,000 pound, eighty-three 600 pound, 223 500 pound and eight 300 pound bombs, delivering a total weight of 183,700 pounds of ordnance or 91.85 tons. They failed to score a single hit. The contrast with the SBDs was stark, for they dropped 108.6 tons of bombs and torpedoes and scored thirty-four hits; if the torpedoes dropped are omitted the difference would be even greater. It was not difficult for the report to conclude that 'the horizontal bomber was entirely ineffective against maneuvering surface ships'. The SBDs, however, 'were highly effective against the same targets and proved themselves vastly superior to horizontal bombers for warfare on the sea'.

John B. Lundstrom wrote that Bates was biased against Fletcher, but there is little evidence of it in the final report. Moreover it was not Fletcher but Spruance, into whose hands Fletcher had handed over control some time previously, who made the final decision for TF-16 to withdraw to the eastward to avoid being ambushed in the darkness by Japanese battleships, rather than rushing into the night to deliver further heavy air attacks on them the following morning. Mitscher, his biographer was to record, was against this decision and 'felt that the task force should have steamed westward in pursuit of the Japanese'.[31]

Bates then turned his searchlight on Spruance, Fletcher, Gray and Ring. According to Lundstrom, the report's criticism was very biased in favour of the former.

At 0615 on the 4th, with his force heading toward the now located enemy and closing at 25 knots on course 240 degrees true), and with his carrier air groups 'on deck and ready for take-off', it was acknowledged that Spruance faced a 'vitally important decision': whether to launch his attack immediately, without waiting for further information about the enemy course and composition, and at the extreme range of the torpedo-bombers , or delay. Bates stated that Spruance's mental processes in making this decision were 'not fully explained', but he acknowledged that, due to errors in reporting, the enemy were actually 202 miles distant and not the 176 Spruance thought they were, and some 40 miles north-west of where they had been reported. What was known was that the Japanese outreached the Americans and delay might prove fatal. There were other factors to consider, but Bates concluded that it was the range of the Devastators that was the controlling factor. Spruance's decision to hold on for another hour, far from being castigated, was, in fact, praised. 'This was a courageous decision, and one which paid off handsomely. It was an excellent demonstration of the will of the Commander; that quality which, in conjunction with the mental ability to understand what is required, enables the Commander to ensure for his command every possible advantage which can be obtained.'

Launch commenced at 0705 with the enemy on an estimated bearing of 239 degrees true, and an estimated distance to target of 155 miles, the *Enterprise* and *Hornet* components of TF-16 having separated into two units with their own screen, as was then their custom. This separation varied considerably during the day from between a few thousand yards to 25 miles. Although Bates noted that 'it took more than one hour to launch the attack groups', no adverse comment was made on this other than to comment that Spruance's instruction to CEAG to proceed without wasting further time waiting for their torpedo aircraft to get

31. Theodore Taylor, *The Magnificent Mitscher*. Taylor credits George R. Henderson, *Hornet*'s XO, with this opinion.

off the flight deck 'was open to question, as the plan for the attack called for each carrier attack group to make a co-ordinated bombing and torpedo attack'. So there was a fourteen-minute gap between CEAG's departure at 0752 and the Devastators at 0806. Spruance's subsequent course of 240 degrees true at 25 knots as Point Option, was tacitly approved with the words, 'This would reduce the distance the air groups would have to fly in returning to their parent carriers and would, at the same time, increase the effectiveness of subsequent air operations owing to the decreased flying time'. So Spruance, according to Bates's assessment, was pretty much all right.[32]

There was, however, one sting in the tail, and that concerned the despatch of the carrier air groups. Bates commented, 'Although CTF 16 had initially directed both the attack groups of his command to take deferred departure, he subsequently modified this directive for the *Enterprise* group.' The combining of both the dive-bombers in one massive group and the torpedo-bombers in another from both the Spruance carriers, 'with a reasonably powerful fighter escort available for each group', would have permitted a co-ordinated attack by two powerful attack groups on one bearing, instead of five different units. But although the Japanese could achieve this, it seemed beyond the Americans at this period of the war.

What of Fletcher? In truth the criticism was fairly muted, despite what is alleged. His decision to make a dawn search was conditioned by a fear of being outflanked from the north-east, rather than doing the outflanking. It was cautious, certainly, but wise? Bates only comments that Fletcher 'appears to have realized also that should the Japanese approach Midway from the north or eastward, the Striking Force would no longer be on the flank of the Japanese Mobile Force, but would instead be between that force and Midway. In this case the Japanese might discover his force and attack it before attacking Midway'. Bates acknowledged that 'this was a distinct Japanese capability, and Commander Striking Force recognized its danger to himself'.

Fletcher's 0607 signal, releasing the *Hornet* and the *Enterprise* to make their own separate attacks on the enemy, pass without comment or criticism, other than to emphasize that the reasons for including the words 'when definitely located' in the order indicated his inert caution and that

Fletcher still 'did not trust the air report'. On recovering his search planes at 0630, Fletcher conformed TF-17's course and speed to that of Spruance's ships. It was thought that this was in order to maintain a strong CAP of twenty-eight fighters over the combined force, but that proved impossible. No criticism was made.

Bates then emphasized Fletcher's caution. Having received intelligence which led him to believe that there were four or five enemy carriers, he only had certain confirmation on the location of two of them, and decided to hold off CYAG's attack. The War College considered that Fletcher was thus more influenced by his experience at the Coral Sea, 'wherein the Japanese nearly surprised him', than the 'often repeated' fact that 'it is generally best to throw all of your available strength into action against enemy surface or aircraft in a co-ordinated attack than to launch them piecemeal in uncoordinated attacks'. In his defence, it was admitted that; to leave the flight decks of two or three enemy carriers undamaged would invite the destruction of his own force. In the end, Fletcher finally launched a partial attack, and kept a reserve force back just in case any further enemy turned up. 'By doing this he acted similarly to Commander Mobile Force' – an unspoken criticism of Fletcher perhaps?

The mistakes of Gray and VF 6 were catalogued: mistaking VT 8 for VT 6; holding himself aloof at 20,000 feet despite losing visual contact with the torpedo-bombers when about 10 miles out from the target; failure to notify his carrier of the composition and location of the enemy force while he circled aimlessly above it until the time of his departure from the battlefield; and continuing 'circling at a high altitude while the torpedo planes were being attacked'. Bates raised some questions on this impotence. 'Presumably, Fighting Squadron 6 was guarding a common frequency with Torpedo Squadron 6, which appears to have been other than the frequency assigned and being used by Torpedo Squadron 8. He could not then know when these planes required his help. He could not see them for the intervening cloud layer'. If his help was to be effective, it had to be available immediately. It required, therefore, both the maintenance of sight contact with the torpedo planes and a positioning of the protective fighters in close or intermediate covering position. Bates concluded: 'The failure of VF Squadron 6 to contribute to the success of this

---

32. It is instructive to compare Bates's assessment of Spruance with a more recent judgement. Darrell L. Herriges wrote in 1994:'Spruance demonstrated the following cognitive characteristics without conflicting evidence: judgement, an ability to work outside the rules, *coup d'oeil* [comprehensive grasp], objectivity, knowledge of the capabilities of one's people [Miles Browning excepted, one assumes!] and

material resources, superior intelligence and deliberate modesty'. Moreover, he also demonstrated, 'without conflicting evidence: moral courage, determination, firmness, energy and staunchness'. See Darrell L. Herriges, *Operational Level Air Commanders: A Search for the Elements of Genius.*

attack may be attributed partially to the dual objective assigned, i.e., protection of both dive-bombers and torpedo planes which had different flight characteristics; partially to the weather which prevented sight contact with the torpedo planes at vital times; and partially to his justified belief that fighters would be found at a high altitude'. Gee was therefore pretty much exonerated. As to why he *stayed* high when there were obviously no enemy to engage up there, no questions were raised.

What of Ring? With regard to CHAG's failure to make any contact with the enemy, Bates commented:

> When the dive bombing groups departed from the *Enterprise* and from the *Hornet* to attack the Mobile Force, it is possible that the flight leaders may not have been adequately instructed regarding the salient features of the problem. For it must be noted that the flight leader of the *Yorktown*, was so instructed. As a result of this the *Hornet* flight leader turned south through an incorrect analysis of his problem and failed to find the Mobile Force. The *Enterprise* flight leader, on the other hand, turned north through a correct analysis of his problem, as did the *Yorktown* flight leader [who had been *directed* to turn north]. Both found the Mobile Force. Had the *Enterprise* and *Yorktown* flight leaders decided to turn south or been ordered to do so, the result of the action might well have been disastrous.

Ring was thus placed squarely in the dock. 'The responsibility for decisions made by the flight leaders while airborne, rest squarely upon the flight leaders themselves'. And Ring had guessed wrong. However, Bate's criticism was tempered with a caveat that seemed to switch at least, some of the blame on Mitscher, or at least his staff. The War College team noted that, 'as a flight leader in his plane is alone, without the facilities of a flag plot or staff, he should be looked out for to a far greater extent than would be normal with surface ship commanders. Carrier Commanding Officers should insure that the flight leaders are fully briefed prior to launching, and, as feasible, advised in the air whenever necessary.'

There seems little evidence to back up the first point; Ring, along with all his commanders, was briefed very well before departure. The evidence, muddled and vague though it is, would seem to clearly indicate that there certainly was a discussion, and not a very harmonious one, during which options were discussed. The subordinate commanders, in the main, tended to disagree, especially on the course to adopt to the target, but, in the end, CHAG, as was to be expected, had the final say. Once in the air, Waldron at least rebelled and, certain of his own feelings, broke ranks and steered his squadron according to his hunch. His hunch was right and he found his enemy, but at the cost of losing the protection and company of the rest of the *Hornet* air group and the ultimate almost total sacrifice of his squadron.

However, there is no record of Ring being given *direction* from above to steer north or south at the end of his outward leg should the enemy not appear. It would appear, unless evidence subsequently comes to light, that in making the fatal decision, like CEAG, but unlike CYAG, Ring was left to his own devices on that. Mitscher's biographer was later to write, in 1953[33], that. 'Ring, Rodee, Johnson[34], Mitchell, and Waldron ran up to the bridge for *final instructions*'[35], which would indicate that he *was* directed, but other fragmentary records do not back this claim up. Rather, it was a full briefing, not an instruction, a fact which was attested to by Ring himself, with the final decision left to the airmen themselves.

It is certain that in the case of the second part of the argument, there was absolutely no question of CHAG being 'advised in the air' *en route* to the target, or at any other time. In fact Ring himself was to make much of this in his own defence, as we shall see. Mitscher and Ring were friends and the former had full trust in his CHAG. Moreover, as Taylor

---

33. Theodore Taylor, *The Magnificent Mitscher*.
34. Rear-Admiral Robert Ruffin 'Ruff' Johnson (1902–70). Graduated from the Naval Academy, Annapolis 1926. After sea service he attended Flight School in 1930 and became an aviator. Spent his early days in aviation at the Naval Academy Flight Tactical Department, with extra duties in VN-8 flying midshipmen around Chesapeake Bay on induction flights. Appointed in September 1941 to form, work up and command VB 8 for the *Hornet,* and led that unit at Midway. Following the battle, served ashore on the staff of Admiral Mitscher. Joined the Air Support Control Unit of the Pacific Fleet's Amphibious Force, before becoming CoS CarDiv 4. Returned ashore with the Office of the Joints Chiefs of Staff, before becoming the CO of NAS Norman, where the navy had leased and enlarged the Max Westheimer Flying Field and set up a primary flight training unit and enlisted boot camp. Later CoS to Commander, Fleet Air, at Ault Field, NAS Whidbey Island, at Oak Harbor, Puget Sound, Washington. Continued his training connections in 1944-5 when he commanded the former British escort carrier *Charger* (CVE-30) back at Chesapeake Bay training pilots for Atlantic operations. After the war, on retirement from the navy, joined the ConVair Aeronautics Corporation at Coco Beach, Florida, as Lead Flight Test Engineer and later became part of the MX-1593/B-65 Atlas Missile Programme team. He died at Bethseda Navy Hospital, Maryland, on 8 July 1970, aged 68.
35. My italics.

admits a few lines later, 'Radio silence was maintained. Squadron commanders were in charge, with Stanhope Ring, as senior, over them. Mitscher could not contact, advise, or assist. He would have to wait until they got back to find out what happened.'[36]

Bates, while admitting that the Commander of VT 8 totally failed to report enemy contact to CHAG, thus leaving him in the dark and continuing to fly to the southwest, was adamant that Ring 'must have been well aware of the fact that he had reached the estimated point of contact with the Japanese Mobile Force'! Therefore CHAG's subsequent actions, in particular his decision to turn south at the end of his outward leg, rather than north, 'require analysis'.

Bates presented the following points:

(a) Ring headed for the enemy rendezvous, 'on the assumption that the enemy reported position, its speed – 25 knots, and its course – 140° were all correct'.

(b) Ring felt that the 1st *Kidō Butai* had been attacked by aircraft from Midway, 'but did not necessarily know that this was so'.

(c) Thus, when the enemy were not found where they were expected, Ring had to find them.

To do so he had to consider three points:

(i) Ring's navigation was off course, 'due to the effect of drift which was difficult to determine because of overcast sky at the time of launching'.

(ii) The enemy's reported position was incorrect.

(iii) The estimated course and speed made good by the enemy were incorrect. i.e. the Japanese had not continued toward Midway but had turned toward the American carriers.

Bates considered that Ring should have judged that, with 25 mile visibility at the position of expected contact, the errors must have been very large and the chances of finding the enemy slim indeed. 'However, if the course and speed were not seriously incorrect, or the drift was slight, he should be able to locate them by the employment of the expanding square, as embodied in the Current Tactical Orders, which would have given a good chance of finding the target if the errors were small. This he failed to do and Bates regarded this failure as 'questionable', for he considered that Ring, as an experienced naval aviator, knew well enough that aircraft sighting reports were usually inaccurate and should have allowed for that accepted fact. 'Also he knew that the estimated speed of advance along the enemy course from its reported position was 25 knots and that this speed of advance was about all that could be sustained.'

But there was more. The report considered that Ring failed to realize that if, due to launching of aircraft, or avoiding incoming attacks, or to attack their enemy, the 1st *Kidō Butai* had turned north, they would best be found by employing the expanding square search northward, whereas using it to the south, 'would probably bring failure'. Quite why Bates should consider that Ring should so reason is not clear; what if Nagumo had, in fact, continued on toward Midway?

Interestingly, in view of the subsequent furore decades later, Bates raised no questions regarding the actual heading of CHAG from form-up to rendezvous[37], despite the failure to have it officially recorded. As to Waldron's break-away and change of course, Bates recorded that 'at 0920' the Commander VT Squadron 8 'sighted the Japanese carrier force to *the northwestward*, and commenced his approach', but failed to report this to anyone else, even though he was talking to his unit as they all went to their deaths.

The Japanese Conclusions

With regard to intelligence, the Japanese were beaten hands down before a shot was fired. A recent study noted that:

Adm. Isoroku Yamamoto did not even have a full-time intelligence officer on his staff until after the Battle of Midway. Instead, Imperial Navy leaders relied only upon on-the-spot estimates by operational commanders – supplemented by inputs from a radio intelligence system that consisted of a series of listening posts running from the Kurile Islands south to Formosa [Taiwan] and east across the Mandates [the Marianas].'[38]

---

36. Theodore Taylor, *The Magnificent Mitscher*.
37. It is interesting that, on the accompanying map to the report, the *outward* tracks of the *Hornet* and *Enterprise* attack groups are not shown, only some return tracks. Moreover the 'expected position of interception' is shown as a *combined* one for the whole of TF-16, not two separate ones for CHAG

and CEAG, even though the official COMINCH report had stressed; 'These two groups proceeded independently to attack.'
38. Christopher A. Ford, *The Admirals' Advantage: U.S. Navy Operational Intelligence in World War II and the Cold War.*

Admiral Nobutake Kondo, C-in-C 2nd Fleet from December 1941 to August 1943, was one of most prominent of IJN commanders to survive the war. His views on Midway are included in papers, based on written notes he had kept during the war, that he made available to Commander Masataka Chihaya[39] in 1947.[40] He maintained that up until Midway Japan had always been successful because she only attempted operations under adequate air cover or with 'at least approximate information' of enemy intentions. Midway, he stated, 'was utterly different. We met with fiasco because we did not get any sign of the existence of any American task force near Midway Island'. He blamed both lack of long-range reconnaissance aircraft and establishing the submarine screen for this failure. He stated ruefully, 'It seemed that our intention of that operation had been revealed to the enemy.' With regard to Japanese security lapses, he felt that using Saipan (which he stated, 'was not adequate from the viewpoint of keeping secrecy') rather than Truk was a factor. Not only did he consider the latter more suitable for the Japanese to 'disguise our next intentions as either for east or south', but would have given a better approach to Midway, utilizing Wake Island air cover.

Kondo also criticised Yamamoto's distribution of forces, as 'too widespread'. Even without the Aleutian complication, he thought that the covering force for the invasion 'was too separated from the carrier group force' to enable the two to co-operate. He also seemed to regret that Nagumo had called him back while he 'hurried with increased speed to the engagement area', as the Japanese thereby failed to launch a night action upon the enemy. Interestingly enough, there are strong echoes of all these sentiments contained in the *Senshi Sōsho*, which arrived on the scene much later.

The War History Room of the Japan Defense Agency examined the battle in detail in the Midway volume, part of its huge series on World War II.[41] In Chapter 14, 'Examination of the Failure of Our Operations', they devoted a whole section to the key element of the defeat; America 'deciphered our code'. They lamented the fact that, due to their inability to distribute the new Code Book D-1 and Table #9 to replace the old issues of both in the time available, this Navy Code was, 'most certainly broken'. They continued:

Breaking our code, even partially, undoubtedly increased the reliability of America's strategic estimates and gave them some definitive intelligence on our concepts of operations and furnished them with a substantial outline of our plans for operations in the future. There is no doubt that from early May onward a great many of our radio messages dealt with operational matters. As there is very little of that material now available, it is not possible to speculate as to which of these messages were broken, but subordinate forces undoubtedly communicated their intended movements to other forces concerned, based on the overall plan. There is no doubt that there were many radio messages concerning the 'MI' operation during the early days of May, but we have no reference material containing the geographic designators 'AF', 'AO' or 'AOB'[42]; undoubtedly, there were radio messages concerning future reconnaissance operations by the *Kimikawa Maru*[43] and Submarine Squadron 1 that contained the geographic designators 'AO' and 'AOB'. We have no radio files to show how the enemy confirmed 'AF' to be Midway, but the diary of Commander Sanagi[44] of

---

39. Commander Masataka Chihaya. (1910–97). b. 1910, entered Etajima Naval Academy, 58th Class. Graduated 1930. Wanted to become naval aviator but because his brother Takehiko (Lieutenant, KIA Midway) had become a pilot he could not due to policy of the time. Became a gunnery specialist and served mainly in capital ships before the war. December 1941–September 1942 AA Gunnery Officer, Staff, aboard battleship *Musashi*. September–November 1942, Staff 11th Squadron 1942, at Truk and in Solomon Islands. August 1943–February 1944, Naval War College, Tokyo. March 1944–February 1945, Operations Staff Officer, 4th Advanced Southern Fleet, Ambon Island. February–September 1945, Staff, Combined Naval Fleet, Tokyo. 1945, Personnel Bureau, Navy Department, Tokyo. Retired after eighteen years service. Interrogation NAV No 49, USSBS No. 201. After the war worked as freelance researcher and translator (and considerable contributor) for Professor Gordon Prange on staff of General Douglas MacArthur and on many of his works. Also worked for *Reader's Digest* in Japan, in the same roles, and for Goldstein and Dillon. In his own right, author of many books including *Fading Victory: The Diary of Admiral Matome Ugaki, 1941–45*, *IJN* Yamato *and* Musashi: Battleships, *IJN* Yukikaze, *destroyer, 1939–70*, *IJN* Kongo: Battleship, *1912–44*. Died 1997.

40. These became part of the Gordon W. Prange archive and were later edited and published by Goldstein and Dillon in *The Pacific War Papers*.

41. Defense Headquarters History Office, *Senshi Sōsho*, Vol 43.

42. 'AF' = Midway, 'AO' = Aleutians, 'AOB' = Kiska.

43. *Kimikawa Maru* was a converted auxiliary seaplane tender which sailed from Akkeshi Bay on 6 May 1942 with the *Kiso* to reconnoitre the Aleutians, returning to Ominato, from which she later sailed as part of Rear-Admiral Kakuta Kakuji's 2nd Strike Force.

44. Commander (later Captain) Sadamu Sanagi, Staff Officer Operations Section, First Bureau, Naval General Staff, 1942. His wartime diary was obtained by Gordon W. Prange after the war, and utilised by the students who wrote up his notes in the book on Pearl Harbor, *At Dawn We Slept*.

the Naval General Staff contains the entry 'Midway is short of fresh water', and a radio message to that effect was indeed transmitted.

But it was not just the ability of the enemy to read their messages that concerned the anonymous authors at the ministry thirty years after the event; they extended their comments to include the lamentable failure of their own intelligence services to crack the American codes in the same way, which left Yamamoto and his subordinate commanders in the dark regarding their opponent's strengths, intentions and, most importantly, locations.

Our Navy was not able to break the American military's code; our intelligence appreciations and strategic estimates were primarily based on communications intelligence which was derived from enemy traffic analysis, call sign identification, direction-finder bearings, and the interception of plain language transmissions.[45] As an example, we could estimate when a strong American force sortied from port or was operating, because their air patrols in that area became intensified and expanded and many patrol planes' messages then came up on the air; we could also ascertain the general area of the enemy's intended attack because of their custom of stationing submarines in that general area, in advance of the planned attack.[46]

All these clues and pointers would seem to have been available to the Japanese prior to Midway. How then did they fail to communicate them to Nagumo in sufficient detail to alert him to his precarious position on the morning of the 4th, with half his force returning from Midway and the other half frantically rearming for a second strike at the same target, and three American air striking forces about to descend upon him from his flank? The Japanese historians give a clue that it might have been because such information was not taken as seriously as it might have been. 'However, it is said that since the beginning of the war, only a few of our many intelligence estimates based on communications intelligence really 'hit the mark', and *our navy's confidence in them was, therefore, relatively low.'*[47]

Did the Japanese recognize that the game was up after Midway? It is unlikely; only Fuchida and Genda stated that they thought the war was lost after Midway, but that was in post-war reminiscences. Fuchida, as we have seen, appeared to have an agenda for survival in defeat by telling it as the victors wanted to hear it; while Genda, who became a general and the CoS of the Japanese Air Defence Force after the war, was similarly in hock to the Americans.[48] The average Japanese was told little or nothing of how the war was going, the Emperor seems to have been in self-denial most of the time, but even among those who could see the whole picture Midway did not mark the decisive turning point; most point to Guadalcanal with its high attrition rate of trained men and aircraft, while others, both naval men 'in the know' and industrialists, point to the fall of Saipan as the warning bell that indicated the game was up.[49]

Two Post-war British Viewpoints

Another perspective on the battle from a thoughtful and perceptive British naval historian, Captain Russell Grenfell[50], deserves inclusion.[51] Although written, like Kondo's essays, only a few years after the end of the World War his views are thought-provoking.

---

45. Layton was later to emphasize that this meant the frequent and unrestrained chatter of US Navy and USAAC aviators while airborne on combat missions. See Rear-Admiral E. T. Layton, US Naval Institute *Proceedings*, Annapolis, June 1979.
46. *Senshi Sōsho*, Vol 43.
47. *Ibid*. My italics.
48. During talks with veterans in Japan recently, I was very surprised to feel the general contempt, even derision, for the opinions, actions (or inaction) and decisions of Genda, both at the battle (where they felt he influenced Nagumo in holding back the strike), and since.
49. See USAAF, *Mission accomplished; interrogations of Japanese industrial, military, and civil leaders of World War II*, US Government Printing Office, Washington DC, 1946.
50. Captain Russell Grenfell, RN (1892–1954). Born 10 April 1892, into an old Cornish naval family around St Just. Joined the Royal Navy. 1914 lieutenant served on battleship *Revenge* at Jutland 1916. On teaching staff of Royal Naval College, Greenwich. Retired from navy in 1944. Important

books include *The Bismarck Episode*, and *Main Fleet to Singapore*, both of which contain more common sense than all the subsequent books on these subjects combined; equally impressive was his *Sea Power*, written under the pseudonym of 'T124' a masterly eye-opener on British defence policy up to 1940. Other publications included *A Cruiser Commander's Orders, The Art of the Admiral; The Men Who Defend Us, Sea Power in the Next War, Service Pay,* and *Nelson the Sailor*. His final work was his best, the brilliant and uncompromisingly revisionist study, *Unconditional Hatred: German War Guilt and the Future of Europe*. Died 4 July 1954, while preparing a book on the Norwegian Campaign of 1940. Survived by his wife, Helen *née* Sheppard and children Julia, Kate and Frank. Various papers covering the period 1940–54 are held at the Churchill Archives Centre, Cambridge (GBR/14/GREN) and the Liddell Hart Centre for Military Archives, Kings College, London. (GB 0099 KCLMA Grenfell).
51. Captain Russell Grenfell, *Main Fleet to Singapore*.

He started with the premise that the desire of Admiral Yamamoto for a naval action to bring what remained of the American fleet to battle was both sound and sensible. What Grenfell thought strange was the way Yamamoto went about it. The French military genius Napoleon Bonaparte had stated: 'When contemplating battle it is the rule to concentrate all your forces and neglect none. One battalion often decides the day'. This tried and tested truism was totally abandoned by the Japanese planners and, thought Grenfell, they thus squandered their temporary advantage of overwhelming superiority. Coral Sea cost them three carriers, one sunk, one damaged and one with her air group destroyed. Those three could have tipped the scales at Midway, and the Port Moresby operation could well have been delayed – and would have been much more likely to succeed with the American fleet, and especially its carriers, eliminated. Likewise the Aleutian operation, which though perhaps desirable was not an urgent requirement, could have been dispensed with, and thus added two more carriers to the Midway fight. Thus two heavy carriers and three light carriers were absent when they were most needed, in the really crucial Battle of Midway. In Napoleonic terms not one battalion, but five regiments!

This dispersal of forces was compounded by the dispersal of the battleships in various 'penny packets', very few of which could provide the powerful support of their main armaments, nor their very heavy anti-aircraft batteries, for the defence of the carriers. This failure to concentrate all available forces compounded the lack of Japanese intelligence. Of course, as Grenfell noted, 'It would be difficult to exaggerate the value to the latter of the Japanese backwardness in cypher technique'. With regard to the decision Nagumo had to make early on the 4th, on whether to retain his striking force in case American carriers arrived or to hit Midway a second time, Grenfell admitted that it was 'a tricky decision'. An hour after making the decision to rearm his deck park came the sighting of at least one American carrier, but now the first strike was returning and needed to be landed. Grenfell described Nagumo's dilemma perfectly.

For him it must have been a period of almost insupportable anxiety. He could not range up and fly off an attacking force against the American carrier or carriers and recover his Midway aircraft at the same time. Nor could he complete this recovery without being chained to his previous course and thus making

it easier for enemy aircraft to find him; and soon he had the ugly news from his search planes that American carrier aircraft in large numbers were coming in his direction. Leaden minutes dragged by while his own returning aircraft continued to come down on their carriers' decks.[52]

Once the recovery was completed, Nagumo changed course 90 degrees to port, 'but *before he could bring up a striking force on deck*[53], a group of enemy torpedo planes came in sight'.

Grenfell also contrasted the two American admiral decisions that morning. TF-16 despatched every available aircraft from its two carriers, 'Admiral Spruance believing in the principle of the concentrated blow'. In contrast, TF-17 acted very differently. 'Admiral Fletcher kept *Yorktown*'s aircraft on board for nearly two hours longer and then sent off only half of them. Apparently, he did not believe in concentration'.

Grenfell blames Yamamoto's battle plan of 'pursuing two conflicting objects simultaneously. The use of the Japanese carrier aircraft to bombard Midway Island clashed with the requirement of the naval battle that he was anxious to bring about'. Nagumo's agitated vacillations on the morning of the 4th 'vividly illustrates the essential antagonism between the two duties his Commander-in-Chief had imposed on him'. It was, Grenfell considered, an error of strategy that went a long way towards losing the Japanese the battle'.[54]

Had those extra aircraft carriers been present, there would have been sufficient aircraft to do both jobs: soften up Midway and tackle the American carriers. If the argument was that the Japanese expected to have time to do one job before turning to the other, then 'the disastrous outcome stands as a solemn warning that comfortable assumptions of the enemy's absence, always hazardous, are particularly so in the air age'.

Of course the Japanese could have sent a strong battleship force ahead to conduct a bombardment that would have delivered thirty or forty times the weight of explosive that any air attack could deliver onto the Midway defences in a night bombardment, as they did at Henderson Field in Guadalcanal later in the war. Even if the Japanese battleships had been retained until daylight to complete the job, the American carriers would have had to decide whether to attack them or the Japanese carriers; splitting their forces would have left them open to pulverizing counter-attack. Nor would the battleships have been completely helpless; air cover could have been provided by some of the smaller

---

52. *Ibid.*
53. My italics.

54. *Ibid.*

carriers. The difference is capabilities in types is often forgotten, Grenfell reminded us.

A battleship or cruiser which has been bombarding one target can switch its guns round to another in a matter of seconds, and can go on firing with hardly a break till its ammunition runs out. But the carrier, as at present constituted, suffers embarrassing lacunae when its aircraft are coming down, going up, or refuelling and rearming, during which it is peculiarly vulnerable to attack. Even with skilfully planned and directed operations, these 'dead' periods introduce an inevitably high degree of chance into carrier warfare, which tends to make an encounter between two carrier fleets unusually speculative.

For the British, of course, the fate of the carrier *Glorious*, destroyed by the German battle-cruisers *Scharnhorst* and *Gneisenau* off Norway because she had no aircraft ready for her own defence, was a terrible warning of just how a potent weapon of war could be transformed into a mere large, unprotected target.

This led to Grenfell's final thought on Midway. For its time it was quite radical. Rather than embarking larger numbers of attack aircraft, as was customary, to knock out the enemy flight decks, why not just carry extra fighter aircraft? This did away with the need to search for the enemy at long range; let him come to you and then destroy his aircraft. Without aircraft, carriers were impotent. In fact this is precisely what had been done at the Battle of the

Philippine Sea in 1944, but the American Commander, on that occasion, exercised the same caution in following up as some had criticized Fletcher for at Midway. At all events, by the time of the Battle of Leyte Gulf, targets – more especially decoys – were what the once-proud and feared Japanese carrier fleet had been reduced to.

Grenfell wrote:

> Suppose that Admiral Yamamoto had filled his four large and two small carriers up with fighters. He could then have had – allowing for the smaller size of the fighter – about 400 Zero fighters against 104 Wildcat and Buffalo fighters and 240 mixed carrier-borne and land-based torpedo planes, dive-bombers, Flying Fortresses, Catalinas and Marauders. So armed, it is to be regarded as unlikely that Admiral Yamamoto could have captured Midway Island without overmuch loss to himself.[55]

Of course what Grenfell overlooked was the fact that Yamamoto did not have that many experienced Zero pilots on hand to pursue such a policy, even if it had occurred to anyone to adopt it, and even if there had been that number of Zero's on hand. Indeed shortage of aircrews was the reason why the undamaged *Zuikaku* could not take part in the Midway battle, something Grenfell did not appear to realize.

Five years after Grenfell's thoughts on the subject, another British perspective appeared. This was the 'official' historian, Captain Stephen W. Roskill[56], with his

---

55. *Ibid.*
56. Captain Stephen Wentworth Roskill (1903–82). b. London 1 August 1903. Educated at Mr Egerton's School, London, and Horris Hill, Newbury 1911–16. 1917–20 the Royal Navy Colleges Osborne and Dartmouth. 1921–20 Midshipman aboard light cruiser *Durban*, China. Research assistant to Lieutenant-Commander Stephen King-Hall which gave him his literary and research appetite. Sub-lieutenant, then lieutenant first with the sloop *Wisteria*, North American and West Indies Station, 1925–6, then the battleship *Ramillies* 1927. German Language Officer at Freiburg-in-Breisgau 1926–7. Then specialized in gunnery at Greenwich and HMS *Excellent* 1929–30. Married Elizabeth Van den Bergh in 1930, and they had four sons and three daughters. Gunnery Officer battleship *Royal Sovereign*: 1933–5 aboard the aircraft carrier *Eagle* before becoming Gunnery Instructor *Excellent* 1935–6, and then, as commander, Gunner Officer of the battleship *Warspite* 1936–9. 1939–41 Admiralty staff. 1942–3 back at sea with the New Zealand-manned light cruiser *Leander* in the South Pacific, becoming her captain in 1944. 1944–5 BAD in Washington. Awarded DSC in 1944. After the war was senior British observer of the atomic bomb tests at Bikini

Atoll in 1946, before becoming Deputy Director of Naval Intelligence 1947–8, but was forced to retire due to deafness brought about by heavy gun firings in earlier appointments. Became the naval contributor to the Military History Series at the Cabinet Office Historical Section in 1949, and between 1954 and 1961, produced the strangely formatted three-volumes-in-four-books series, *The War at Sea 1939–1945*; Other important historical works include *Hankey: Man of Secrets; Naval Policy Between the Wars, Documents Relating to the Naval Air Service 1908–1918; A Merchant Fleet at War; HMS Warspite; the story of a Famous Battleship; The Strategy of Sea Power; Its Development and Applications; The Secret Capture; Churchill and the Admirals.*Was Senior Research Fellow and then Pensioner Fellow of Churchill College, Cambridge between 1961 and 1982, CBE in 1971, and First Archivist of the Archive Centre until his death in on 4 November 1982. His name and work is commemorated by the establishment of the biannual Stephen Roskill Memorial Lectures held at the Wolfson Lecture Hall. For brief biography see John Ehrman, *Stephen Roskill, 1903–1982 – Member of Fellows of British Academy*, British Academy, London, 1985.

belated second volume of *The War at Sea*.[57] Roskill was a highly respected scholar and historian and anything he wrote at that time was considered definitive. However, he noted in his section on Midway that he was 'deeply indebted to the fully and brilliantly told story in Volume IV of Professor S. E. Morison's *History of United States Naval Operations*, and, as Morison himself had written to Bates that his volume had in the first place relied heavily on the War College Report, there was little that had not already been covered ten years earlier! Morison, of course, at that time enjoyed a similar reputation for infallibility to Roskill, but, like Fuchida[58] on the Japanese side, much of what he wrote, and what Roskill relied on, has been challenged and some of his allegations discredited. Not much can be learned therefore, save perhaps on one of two particular aspects.

On Internet message boards (and indeed elsewhere) there is much uninformed comment about the fact that 'the British refused to loan the Americans a carrier in their hour of need'. Roskill attempted to refute that particular slur as long ago as 1957, but, his efforts do not appear to have had any effect. He pointed out the hard fact that both the British carriers of the Eastern Fleet, *Formidable* and *Illustrious*, having carried out the Madagascar operation, were undergoing essential repairs at Kilindini. This just left *Indomitable*, but Admiral Somerville's reaction to this request, recorded in his pocket diary on 20 May, was 'Quite useless'.[59] When the Admiralty asked Somerville whether, instead, he could attack Sumatra or the Andaman Islands as King had requested, the best he could offer was to sail Force A towards Ceylon, a somewhat nebulous threat.

Roskill's recording of this was ambiguous to say the least. He stated that no British carrier 'could have steamed the 11,000 miles from Kilindini to Pearl Harbor by the south of Australian in time to take part in the Battle of Midway'. But this is *not* what King had asked for, indeed the last thing King wanted was the Royal Navy with their antiquated aircraft, getting in the way of Fletcher's force. What he had actually asked for was for a carrier to go to the South Pacific as a diversion, and that *could* have been achieved, though admittedly to little purpose.

Roskill was surely also on dubious ground when he also wrote that: -

It is clear from the Admiralty's records that neither the nature nor the quality of the American Navy's intelligence regarding Japanese movements and intentions reached London until the 19 or 20 May. On the former date Admiral E. J. King, the American Chief of Naval Operations, signalled an 'appreciation' to Admiral Pound and asked either for a British aircraft carrier to be moved from the Indian Ocean to the south-west Pacific, or for air attacks to be made on Rangoon and the Andaman Islands, or for action to be taken to interrupt Japanese communications between Singapore and Rangoon'.

He also asserted that it was not until late on the 22 May when the head of BAD[60] in Washington DC had talked with King, that the British were first aware that an attack on Midway Island was a really strong possibility'. Yet we know that British Intelligence was deciphering Japanese signals

---

57. S. W. Roskill, *The War at Sea 1939–1945*, Volume II: *The Period of Balance*.
58. Captain Mitsuo Fuchida (1902–76). b. Nara prefecture, on 3 December 1902. 1921 Etajima, 52nd Class, contemporary of Minoru Genda. 1930s fought in China and eventually notched up 3,000 flight hours before the war. Specialized in precision altitude bombing. Lieutenant-commander at Naval Staff College. 1939 Flight Commander aboard carrier *Akagi*. August 1941 – July 1942, including Pearl Harbor, Commander Car Div 1 Air Groups. February 1942 Port Darwin attack. Midway, broke both ankles fire fighting when *Akagi* hit. Hospital for one year. June 1943, appointed Senior Staff Officer, 1st Air Fleet, Kanoya, then at Tinian in Marianas. April 1944 Staff Officer (Air Operations) Combined Fleet at Oyodo and from September 1944 at Hiyoshi until the end of the war. After the war became a farmer and testified at War Crimes Tribunals.1949 met Jacob DeShazer, former Doolittle aircrew corporal, then a Free Methodist Missionary. 14 April 1950 converted to Christianity. 1950s published his books *The Truth of the Pearl Harbor Operation* and *Midway: The Battle That Doomed Japan*, initially to wide acclaim but more recently largely discredited by many. 1952 became Christian missionary and toured US with Worldwide Christian Missionary Army of Sky Pilots. Died, of diabetes, in Kashiwara, near Osaka, 30 May 1976, aged 73. Biography by Gordon W. Prange, Donald M. Goldstein and Katherine V. Dillon, *God's Samurai: Lead Pilot at Pearl Harbor*. See also Rev. Paul A. Hughes, *'Hero of Pearl Harbor'*, on *Believe His Word. com.*
59. Simpson, *The Somerville Papers*.
60. Admiral Sir Andrew Browne Cunningham, who had just succeeded Admiral Sir Charles Little. Cunningham himself was a tough customer, so he could handle King's legendary cantankerousness better than most. He recorded that King, 'always had a rooted antipathy to placing United States naval forces under British command, though he raised no objection to British forces and units being under United States command whenever he thought it fit and proper.' (Admiral of the Fleet Viscount Cunningham of Hyndhope, KT, GCB, OM, DSO, *A Sailor's Odyssey*, Hutchinson, London, 1951.)

and passing them to Hawaii, predicting just that![61] So to say, as Roskill does: 'If any misunderstanding arose on this occasion, it seems that it was brought about partly by American slowness in giving the Admiralty the full intelligence of which they were possessed by the middle of May'[62], seems rather disingenuous.

Roskill's other conclusions followed almost exactly those of Grenfell and Morison. Nagumo's decisions, first to commit half his striking power before he knew that American carriers were in the vicinity, and secondly, ordering the ninety-three aircraft which he had kept in hand to deal with enemy warships to change their armaments from shipping to land targets, Roskill considered 'a fatal mistake'. He made no comment on the positioning of the American task forces prior the battle and stated unequivocally, 'Spruance had done brilliantly', adding that he totally shared Morison's view that 'he had been wise not to commit his two surviving carriers and their depleted aircrews to a headlong pursuit. Had he continued westwards instead of withdrawing east with the *Enterprise* and *Hornet*, he might well have run right into the powerful surface forces which were seeking action with him during the night of the 4th–5th.'

Roskill's conclusions were unarguable, in that tactically, 'the victory of Midway was revolutionary', while strategically 'the consequences were far reaching'. He felt the situation had been 'transformed overnight' by the American carriers, adding: 'Rarely can such rich benefits have been derived from so few ships'. On the Japanese side his view was that their plans were 'radically altered as a result of this defeat, though the change was not at once accepted'.

Many Voices

Down the decades there have been many more books on Midway, of varying accuracy and value. Some writers enjoyed many years of unchallenged 'authenticity', in particular Fuchida on the Japanese side and Morison on the American, but these accounts have become tarnished and devalued almost to the point of ridicule in recent years. Another doyen of 'Midway authors' was Walter Lord[63], and his version of events[64] was also accepted, almost without question for many decades.[65] Then came the 1977 film[66], and with it, the 'book of the film'. This latter was considered so inaccurate that, in the UK I was hastily commissioned to present a factual account of the battle to offset it.[67] Although this book never claimed to be 'definitive' it did at least set the record straight in time for the film's London premier at the Empire, Leicester Square, and even the film's producer, Jack Smight[68], was moved later to acknowledge that he regarded this, rather than the account based on the film script itself, as his preferred version of the history of the battle.

I stand by my summaries of the brave men on both sides. One charge that has been levelled at me over this book was contained in Ronald W. Russell's recent summary of Battle of Midway round-table participants.[69] He was only the

61. See section 1, *Intelligence.*
62. S. W. Roskill, *The War at Sea,* Vol II.
63. Walter Lord (1917–2002). Born Baltimore, Maryland, son of a lawyer. Attended Gilman School and then Princeton University as History student. Graduated 1939, then studied Law at Yale. Joined Office of Strategic Services (OSS) as code clerk, then Agency Secretariat based in London 1942–5. Achieved fame with his book on the sinking of the RMS *Titanic, Titanic: A Night to Remember,* Holt Reinhart, New York, 1955, which was filmed in 1958. Followed this up with a stream of similar books on Pearl Harbor (*Day of Infamy,* Holt, Reinhart, New York, 1957); Midway (*Incredible Victory*); the war of 1812 (*Dawn's Early Light,* W. W. Norton, Baltimore, 1972); the Alamo (*A Time to Stand, the Epic of the Alamo,* University of Nebraska, 1978) and the *Titanic* yet again (*The Night Lives On, the Untold Stories and Secrets behind the 'Unsinkable' Ship – Titanic,* Harper Collins, 1969). A bachelor, he developed Parkinson's disease and died at his Manhattan home aged 84 on 19 May 2002.
64. Walter Lord, *Incredible Victory,* Harper & Row, New York, 1967.
65. Although, I never totally did so. I much admire the *extent* of Lord's research, but not the *depth.* Talk of the dropping of concrete blocks and cans of beans on Midway, presumably by the professional Japanese aviators from the *Kidō Butai,*

as if these were factual truths, plus the far too numerous examples of 25-year-old casual conversations, uttered in the heat of battle, as authentic historical narration, were just too rich a mix of journalistic hyperbole for me to swallow uncritically.
66. *Midway,* starring Charlton Heston, Henry Fonda and Glen Ford.
67. Peter C. Smith, *The Battle of Midway* New English Library, London, 1976.
68. Jack Smight (1925–2003). b. Minneapolis, Minnesota, son of an Irish emigrant family. Attended High School with the future actor Pete Arness and both played in the junior band. Joined the US Army Air Corps and trained as a flight navigator. Served in the Pacific during the war. On leaving the Air Force, enrolled as a drama student in the University of Minnesota and there met up with Arness once more, who was to achieve fame under the name Peter Grave. Smight and Arness went to Hollywood in 1949 to be met by Arness's elder brother, James, destined to become the star of the series *Gunsmoke.* Smight worked his way up to become a successful, if patchy, film director. His work included *Harper, Airport 1975, Damnation Alley* and *Eddie,* the latter winning an EMMY award. He died from cancer in Los Angeles, on 1 September 2003 age 78.
69. Ronald W. Russell, *No Right to Win: A Continuing Dialogue with Veterans of the Battle of Midway.*

messenger of course, but he stated: 'Some readers on the round table have criticized his book for what they view as anti-American undertones'. It would seem that, in attempting to present an objective account of this battle from a neutral viewpoint, I had stumbled into what can perhaps be viewed as the parochial (or even paranoid) view, very prevalent in America recently. This mindset assumes that there is only one point of view on this battle, as with everything, the American one. While one can agree (as I do) with President Bush's assertion on the war on terror for example that 'one is either for us or against us', that should not extend to stifling all debate or presentation of alternative views on such an historic event as the Midway battle.[70]

For those who have not read my first account, here is a taste of what I wrote: 'In this battle proof was amply provided, had it ever been needed, that the American fighting man was the equal of any in the world'.[71] I also still stand by my conclusion that Midway was neither the last nor the largest of carrier-to-carrier battles, but was the most important because:

What Midway *did* decide was that the seemingly irresistible tide of Japanese victory could be halted. The Japanese were beaten at their own game, and resoundingly beaten. Henceforth it was America, rather than Japan, who held the moral ascendancy, and, although Japan retained some initiative for a little longer, she was forced more and more to adopt a defensive posture. Such a course was entirely alien to her. And of course the development of the Pacific War more and more into a war of attrition could end one way, as Yamamoto had foreseen.

Nor do I recede from my final conclusion of thirty years ago.

In the history of sea warfare Midway was therefore a major milestone. For the United States Navy it was a coming of age, the real cornerstone of a fleet that hitherto had seen little major fighting. It was in fact the sound base on which the assumption of the mantle of the greatest sea-power on the globe was finally built. The trident passed across the Atlantic from great Britain to the United States in 1942, and that position of awesome responsibility the Americans still hold, albeit falteringly now, to this day [1976].[72]

A much more important milestone than my little paperback history, was achieved with the publication of John B. Lundstrom's *The First Team*[73]; although this dealt pretty much exclusively with fighter tactics, nor did it concentrate exclusively on Midway. As such, many important issues relating to this battle did not arise, or were not touched upon, although the research and thought that went into the book were obviously a huge leap forward from anything that had gone before. Lundstrom devoted a whole chapter to 'the F4F-4 controversy', quoting, Jimmy Thach's VF-3 man bitter tirade to the effect that it was 'surprising that any of our pilots returned alive', and that the Wildcat was 'pitifully inferior in climb, manoeuvrability, and speed' to the Zero. In these allegations he was fully backed up by Jim Gray of VF-6. Lundstrom, however, pointed out that the ratio of kills in air combat up to the end of the battle were three to one in favour of the F4F; and that between February and June 1942 fourteen Zeros were destroyed against the loss of just ten Wildcats. The skill of the pilots might have been equal but the US Navy's application of deflection shooting, and the ability of the Wildcat to take punishment, proved paramount. In contrast, the speedier, longer-legged and more manoeuvrable Zero proved terribly fragile when cornered.

The next book to tap into newly released sources with both knowledge and insight was a combined effort paperback, with Robert J. Cressman, then the Head of the Ships' History Branch of the Naval Historical Center, and Steve Ewing fronting a veritable host of contributors, some given high acknowledgement, other less so. This book, perhaps

---

70. Interestingly, having been accused by some members of the Battle of Midway Round Table (BOMRT) of anti-Americanism, I have also been accused by critics of being pro-Nazi by writing about the Junkers Ju.87; of being pro-Japanese by writing on the Aichi D3A1/2, and also the biography of Captain Egusa; and of being unfair to the Soviets in describing their lack of contribution to Russian convoy PQ18. But just how these descriptions fit with my writing the only detailed books on the American Curtiss SB2C Helldiver and North American A-36 aircraft, which American historians have scorned to write about, is unclear. I have been praised by Americans for being fair to the Italians in my book *Action Imminent*, but damned by some of their fellow countrymen for exposing their machinations in my

work on the sinking of the *Helle*! Likewise, I am probably accused by somebody, somewhere, of being pro-Soviet or Communist, for writing about the Petlyakov Pe-2 and have certainly been publicly taken to task for apparently knowing nothing about Japanese aircraft despite my research in Japan, by a self-appointed expert in England! Somewhere along the line I must have got my impartiality just about right to have engendered all these very diverse and opposing reactions.

71. If this sentence is taken as containing, 'anti-American undertones' then one wonders just what level of uncritical one-sided adulation would satisfy such critics.

72. Peter C. Smith, *The Battle of Midway*.

73. John B. Lundstrom, *The First Team: Pacific Naval Air Combat from Pearl Harbor to Midway*.

the last of the 'Pre-Internet generation' books, many of which can barely conceal their withering contempt for older, more sedate and methodical research, first appeared in 1990.[74] With such a star-studded showcase of newer 'authorities' the book was widely acclaimed, although it did not appear as authoritive to me as Lundstrom's solo work. As its publisher's details indicate, its chief claim to uniqueness was that it featured just about every known photograph remotely connected with Midway and the battle, with particular attention being paid to captioning. This was refreshing enough, but many of the fascinating details 'behind the scenes' were well researched and presented for the first time in book form.

The conclusions reached by this volume are credited exclusively to Steve Ewing.[75] He is charitable to both Yamamoto and Nagumo. The C-in-C's biggest mistake, according to Ewing, was in commanding the widely dispersed elements of his fleet from afloat, with the crippling limitation of enforced radio silence, rather than from back in Japan, and it is interesting to compare this conclusion as to the best way to command with that of the Naval War College in 1947. Ewing suggests that it was 'doubtful that any Japanese commander would have made decisions much different than Yamamoto in the spring of 1942'. Timing was all, the need to strike before the Americans could rebuild their strength, the phases of the moon for the actual landings, that the landings were necessary to get the Americans to react and so on.

Ewing gave prominence to the fact that one of the biggest criticisms of Nagumo was the Japanese variant of the 'brown shoe, black shoe' controversy, in that the commander of the 1st *Kidō Butai* was not an aviator. Ewing demolished this by quoting Commander Izuyo Fujita, who thought a different commander would not have made much difference. The main thing was that Nagumo was 'surrounded by competent staff'. We know, of course, that Nagumo did listen to his air advisors including Minoru Genda, whose writ ran large during the battle. It was largely due to his advice, and that of Rear-Admiral Ryunosuke Kusaka[76], his CoS, that the repeated requests for an immediate strike at the American carriers with what was available by Rear-Admiral Tamon Yamaguchi was ignored. Genda was later to hint that this might have been mistaken, but Nagumo, 'black shoe' or not, went with that advice for good or ill.

On the American side Ewing's two main conclusions were that the Americans won the battle due to breaking the Japanese code, and what he describes as the 'fortuitous arrival' of the SBDs, which may be less than fair to McClusky and Leslie's leadership and reasoning qualities. There is no criticism of Nimitz's strategy, even if he had almost as little control over events as Yamamoto despite being land-based. Fletcher's decision to launch at long range on the morning of 4 May is not even mentioned, while Spruance is given credit for sharing Nagumo's ability to take advice from his advisors, especially the unpredictable (and occasionally hysterical) Commander Miles Browning. Stanhope Ring's ability to control his air group, despite Ewing labelling him 'the epitome of the naval officer in

---

74. Robert J. Cressman, et al. *A Glorious Page in our History; The Battle of Midway 4-6 June 1942*. Among the other contributors whose names do not appear on the title page are John Lundstrom, Mike Wenger, Bob Lawson and Dr. Robert E. Barde, the latter's contribution in particular, being especially deserving acclaim, according to Lundstrom.

75. See Appendix One of Robert J. Cressman et al. *A Glorious Page in Our History*.

76. Vice-Admiral Ryunosuke Kusaka (1893-1971). b. 25 September 1892 in Ishikawa prefecture, into an upper-class business family. Entered 41st Class Etajima Naval Academy 1913, midshipman 19 December 1913. Served aboard the armoured cruiser *Adzuma* 1914 and then the protected cruiser *Otowa*. Sub-lieutenant 1915 and served aboard the battleship *Kawachi,* then the armoured cruiser *Yakumo* 1916. As lieutenant (jg) served from 1917 aboard battle-cruiser *Kongo*, before attending Gunnery School base course 1918. Torpedo School basic course the same year and joined the Light Cruiser *Kuma* 1919. 1920 attended Naval Gunnery School advanced course Gunnery Specialist aboard battleship *Mutsu*. This was followed by sea service aboard the destroyer *Susuki* 1921, the submarine depot ship *Kanto* 1922 and the battleship *Yamashiro* 1922. 1924 appointed to Yokosuka Naval Department. 1925 attended Naval Staff College A course 1925, and on graduation, although not himself an aviator, re-specialized in naval aviation. 1926 lieutenant-commander. Became Instructor at Kasumigaura Air Group. 1928-9 Naval Staff College. 1930 promoted to commander and joined 1st Carrier Division. 1934 promoted to captain and served in Naval Aviation Department. Between desk assignments in Tokyo and with 24th Air Flotilla enjoyed periods at sea including XO Iwate 1934, in command of the carrier, *Hosho* in 1937 and *Akagi* in 1940. 1941 promoted to rear-admiral. Became CoS 1st Air Fleet in April 1941 and helped plan operation at Pearl Harbor. Continued in that role 1941-2 although he shared Nagumo's opposition to Operation MI originally, but he even retained his position post-Midway. In November 1942 became CoS Southeast Area Fleet for the period 1943-4. November 1944, CoS Combined Fleet as vice-admiral. Ended war in command 5th Air Fleet, Kyūshū which was in near mutiny after suicide flight of former commander, Vice-Admiral Ugaki. Although accused by Western historians of lacking boldness, he acted courageously enough at that time, putting his life at risk in insisting at a mass meeting of rebellious officers that the Emperor's edict to surrender was, to be obeyed. After the war he was author of the now largely discredited history, *Rengō Kantai ('Combined Fleet')* in 1952. Died 23 November 1971 aged 79.

intelligence, industry, bearing, and ability,' was questioned as was the choice of course ('the wrong route') despite the fact that McClusky also missed the enemy on the way out and that it was the 'turn north' or 'turn south' decision that was the main difference between success and failure.

On the individual points raised by the Battle of Midway symposium of May 1988, Ewing reached no conclusion on whether or not Midway would have served any useful purpose to the Japanese had it been taken; he was also one of the first to realize that the exaggerated claims by Walter Lord and others of the huge loss of front-line naval pilots at Midway were nowhere near the disaster claimed, although it was left for a later book to confirm just how small a percentage had been killed – fewer than 25 per cent overall (the massacre of their support teams was another matter). On whether Midway was a turning point, Ewing was ambiguous, favouring Guadalcanal in some respects. As well as some hardly related issues, the summary concluded that the Aleutian operation was in no way diversionary, and that the decision to abandon *Yorktown* was correct. On who sank the *Hiryū*, another once very acrimonious debate, Ewing concluded that it was 'at the very least a shared "kill"'.

Understanding of Japanese doctrine, especially with regard to their maritime aviation, still remained a specialist area in the West and was little understood. Most people relied on the translation of Masatake Okumiya and Jiro Horikoshi's, interesting but rather patchy and chaotic 1956 study[77] for their basic knowledge. Thankfully, the publication of Mark R. Peattie's welcome appraisal in 2001[78], finally set out the basics intelligently but, great step forward that it was, it was a general history and did not include Midway.

One important consideration that finally found its champion as a major cause of the Japanese defeat was lack of radar. The Americans had it, and were able to intercept Japanese attacks in time, even if with patchy effectiveness. The Japanese lack of the same early warning proved fatal to all four carriers in both the 4 June American strikes. What became known as the IJA Type A aircraft interference detection system, which operated at 7.5–3.75 metres/40–80 MHz, and which picked up aircraft penetrating a beam established by a transmitter and receiver separated by some hundreds of miles, was first worked in the period 1938–9. More pertinently the IJN Mk 1 Model 1 pulse-radar set, operating at 4.2 metres/71.4 MHz with a 3 metre/100MHz fixed-site warning radar did not appear until 1941. Pulsed radar had been late in development, and gained little or no impetus by the visit to their German ally by a team of technical experts in 1941, as neither side saw any percentage for them in exchanging information. Some eighty Mark 1/1[79] sets were built, with 10–30 microsecond pulse width, and it had a maximum range at 5Kw of 90 miles. The Mk II, Model I, set which followed was specifically designed for warship use, with the same pulse width etc., but operating at 1.5 metres/200 MHz and this enabled a ship to pick up incoming aircraft at the same range of 90 miles. What flexibility Nagumo could have had with these sets fitted to his four carriers and two battleships at Midway! Unfortunately, they proved too fragile for most seaborne conditions and failed to impress. So it was not lack of inventiveness on the Japanese side that led to lack of radar coverage, but lack of will or conviction. This attitude was reflected throughout the whole range of radar research in the 1920s and 1930s. Ironically, the work of Dr Hidetsugu Yagi[80] on directional antennae actually enjoyed far greater applications outside Japan than back in his homeland.

Commander LeCompte succinctly summed the situation up thus:

Without an adequate early warning or command-and-control system, they were unable to ensure air superiority over their own fleet. But the Japanese did not lose the Battle of Midway during the ten minutes that followed the slaughter of the US torpedo-bombers . They lost it in their laboratories in the ten years before the attack.[81]

Then there were smaller books written with specific agendas in mind, notably former Marine Major Weisheit's revisionist work for the Ensign C. Markland Kelly, Jr,

77. Masatake Okumiya and Jiro Horikoshi, with Martin Caidin, *Zero! The Story of the Japanese Navy Air Force 1937–1945*.
78. Mark R. Peattie, *Sunburst: The Rise of Japanese Naval Air Power, 1909–1941*, Naval Institute Press, Annapolis, 2001.
79. Mark I = land-based class set; Mark II = ship-based class set.
80. Dr Hidetsugu Yagi (1886–1976). b. 28 January 1886 at Osaka. 1919 awarded Doctorate of Engineering at Tohoku University. Worked on a simple-structured ultra- or extremely short-wave directional antenna, along with assistant Dr Shintaro Uda. 1925, published the basic theory of the Yagi-Uda Directional Antenna. 1926 patented the antenna.

Ignored in Japan was put into production in Europe and United States. (Most US Navy dive-bombers, for example, employed this type of antenna for their onboard radar sets from 1943 onward.) 1943–5 worked on dielectric sealed encasement antenna for submarine radar technology. Also on VHF on 2 metre bandwidth.1946 President of Osaka University and Japanese Amateur Radio League. 1952 became President of Yagi Antenna Inc. Died 1976.
81. Commander Malcolm A. LeCompte, *US Naval Reserve*, 'Radar and the Air Battles of Midway'.

Foundation in Baltimore.[82] Weisheit painstakingly tracked down five of the surviving pilots from *Hornet*'s ill-fated flight of 4 June and over the phone got from Admiral W. F. Rodee the information that the departure bearing was, '260–265 degrees. It was almost due west'. This finding revolutionized thinking on this controversial subject, but although it received wide acceptance, it was not universally agreed to.

Clayton Fisher told me:

I have read, and reread, Weisheit's book and felt he worked hard to establish his premises. He spent a lot of effort to make a case for the VF-8 pilots being confused with their YE/ZB. If you could hear a code letter you were no longer lost! June 5th the *Enterprise* and *Hornet* were supposed to be transmitting the same YE/ZB codes but they were not. That day the *Hornet* signal was very weak and the *Enterprise* signal was stronger. *Hornet*'s SBDs that tried to use the *Enterprise* signal became lost but the vertical search light finally turned on saved them. I'm not sure that the VF-8 pilots could even tune in the *Enterprise* YE/ZB signal so I don't think they tried to use the *Enterprise* YE/ZB on June 4th.[83]

Just as Weisheit's volume paid tribute to the fighter pilots who did not make it back, Kernan's[84] paid a tribute to all the torpedo bomber crews lost on 4 June. As an enlisted teenage ordnance rating aboard the *Enterprise* Kernan, who in later life became a professor of English Literature and a highly respected academic at both Yale and Princeton, was able to combine first-hand knowledge of the way the navy of 1942 worked in practice with a clear and uncluttered presentation of facts as he saw them. The result was a biting and acid criticism of wholesale blunder, failure and self-sacrifice that extended from the Naval Torpedo Works at Rhode Island, via the BuAer in Washington DC to what he perceived as basic failures of command on the spot.

Kernan's memories of those days are those of an air mechanic rather than a sailor, by which I mean there was none of the sentimentality of a professional seaman involved – facts were facts. Thus, ships and planes were 'it' not 'she', ships were 'tied up' not 'secured', officers in his squadron were 'Indians' or 'Ringknockers', revealing a rigid and non-socializing hierarchy of class, as in Great Britain at its worst, rather than in the world's greatest democracy!

Calling a spade a spade certainly cleared the air and Professor Kernan's conclusions were far from flattering to the US Navy, but they ring true.[85] However his account attracted widespread condemnation from some who resented such straight talking. One such outraged critic (anonymous, as they so often are) stated that the 1st *Kidō Butai* took longer to launch a strike than the Americans, and that this made the Japanese 'inflexible' – incredible reasoning. However, others pointed out that, that outside Hollywood, not everyone engaged in a battle is a Superman.

There things lay until Jonathan Parshall and Antony Tully combined their long interest in Japanese naval aviation and their connection with dedicated web sites with consummate marketing skills to launch the most detailed study yet in the English language on the Japanese side of the Midway story.[86] They did not just upset the applecart with their radical approach and irreverent conclusions; they lifted it by all its corners and threw it into the ditch! Their research was breathtakingly comprehensive and detailed and they clinically demolished any hint of opposition to their conclusions even before their book was published, as with Dallas W. Isom's reasonings.[87] Critical acclaim for their findings has been unanimous and their book has instantly acquired iconoclastic status. Fortunately, they still appear to remain totally nice people, ready to consider, that other viewpoints might exist (if not concede them) and the almost total adulation their work has received does not appear to have nullified their objectivity. Considering the reverence earlier historians like Samuel Eliot Morison, Mitsuo Fuchida and Walter Lord once enjoyed, and the quite bitter reviling of those studies now currently

82. Major Bowen P. Weisheit, *The Last Flight of Ensign Markland Kelly, Junior, USNR with a New, Corrected Charting of the Flight of VF-8 from USS* Hornet *During the Battle of Midway*.
83. Clayton Fisher to the author, 29 June 2006.
84. Alvin Kernan, *The Unknown Battle of Midway; The Destruction of the American Torpedo Squadrons*.
85. Kernan's style reminded me very much of a Captain Roger Hill's war memoir, *Destroyer Captain*, (William Kimber, London, 1975), which I recommended for publication and subsequently edited. Here too was a straight-talking man and a frank and uncluttered account of some of the biggest British naval blunders (the scattering of Russian convoy PQ17 and

the loss of the cruiser *Charybdis* in the English Channel) from a first-hand and brutally honest source. Here too, honesty was met with both incredulity and dismay by reviewers, and also by the publisher. I was roundly taken to task for standing up for several obviously correct statements, which they considered were controversial and differed from the 'accepted' establishment line. I managed to preserve some of Hill's descriptions of events fairly intact.
86. Jonathan Parshall and Anthony Tully, *Shattered Sword; The Untold Story of the Battle of Midway*.
87. Dallas W. Isom, 'The Battle of Midway: Why the Japanese Lost', and 'They Would Have Found a Way'.

displayed on some internet sites, Parshall and Tully's level-headedness is probably wise, as well as genuine.

There is a feast of conclusions; take your pick by turning to Chapter 24 of the book.[88] A few of these revelations were already familiar to those who studied the battle in recent years, or who read the *Midowei Kaisen* volume of the *Boeicho Boeikenshujo Senshibu* when it appeared in 1971; but many will be startled at their findings. Their main contention, that because all four Japanese carrier decks were continually in operation flying off or landing on Zero fighters to reinforce the CAP that fended off attack after attack on the morning of 4 June, all the claims and even the eyewitness reports of some American dive-bomber pilots about massed air striking forces revving up in readiness for take-off at the moment of the SBD attack, are false. But that had already been well established by the *Senhi Sōhō*. That Fuchida described this as fact, thereby misleading all Western historians ever since, is but one of many 'misstatements' that condemn his book to the indictment by Parshall and Tully as being 'irretrievably flawed'. And not on their word alone; they cited other Japanese sources, some named, some anonymous, who told them that both Fuchida's *Midway* and Ryunosuke Kusaka's *Rengō Kantai*[89] were, 'nonsense books, which were meant to conceal failure and incompetencies . . . and to protect each other'.

Other sacred cows were duly lined up and slaughtered with equal effect and impartiality. The self-inflicted mass-destruction of his beloved VT-8 by Waldron by attacking alone and without fighter cover not only failed to score a single hit, but did not even aid the SBD attacks because they did not take place until an hour after the last VT-8 Devastator had been chopped into the sea; even that posthumous satisfaction was therefore denied to them, despite Alvin Kernan's passionate eulogy. Brave they were, but *effective* – not one jot! Did Yamamoto withhold vital intelligence information received from Tokyo from Nagumo? He certainly did not relay it on, but he did not have to as Nagumo was perfectly capable of receiving it directly himself. Did the hold-up in launching the No. 4 scouting floatplane from the heavy cruiser *Tone* doom the 1st *Kidō Butai*? No Parshall and Tully claim that by launching late the American forces were detected earlier than if she had gone on time!

Other accounts received equally short shrift. Lord's *Incredible* and Prange's *Miracle*[90] titles are both dismissed, and quite correctly in my view, as mythmaking exaggerations, because the battle came down to four flight-decks against three flight-decks and an unsinkable runway, with the odds actually in favour of the Americans. Here, though, as an author of long-standing, I am prepared to give both men, journalistic backgrounds notwithstanding, at least some sympathetic benefit of the doubt; for knowing how publishers arbitrarily change titles, jackets (and even facts) to help sell books, even in the face of the strongest protest, and, having been served that way myself on occasions, it is just possible that, Lord and Prange were innocent parties to publisher sales hype.

Shattered Sword is certainly a *tour de force* and things will never be the same when discussing the Battle of Midway. Will it be the last word? Even Parshall and Tully doubted that and almost immediately old embers have been blown on and old passions reignited by the publication of John Lundstrom's *Black Shoe Admiral*[91], which is a highly-detailed, spirited but, many respected critics and some veterans claim, highly biased and one-sided view of Fletcher's conduct at Midway.[92] Lundstrom's defence of Fletcher is certainly total, and his disparaging of his critics vehement. He wrote:

Expected to surmount steep odds if necessary to thwart the enemy, Fletcher was also strictly enjoined to preserve his force, for the nation could not afford to lose it. Just surviving a close engagement with Japanese carriers was a signal achievement, let alone the seizing of and retaining the strategic advantage in every battle. Wise in hindsight and severely discounting the friction of warfare, Fletcher's detractors held unreasonably high expectations of just what could be achieved under those circumstances.

He contrasted the 'remarkably effective performance' of *Yorktown* on the morning of the 4th with the 'dramatic failure' of Mitscher's *Hornet*, and concludes that the 'fundamental reason' for this difference was that 'Fletcher did not already think he knew it all', whereas Mitscher and Miles Browning 'epitomized the know-it-all attitude'. He ended his study by describing Fletcher as 'truly a fighting admiral who never lost a battle.'[93]

---

88. 'The Myths and Mythmakers of Midway'.
89. Ryūnosuke Kusaka, *Rengō Kantai*.
90. Gordon W. Prange, *Miracle at Midway*.
91. John B. Lundstrom, *Black Shoe Admiral: Frank Jack Fletcher at Coral Sea, Midway and Guadalcanal*.
92. For instance George Walsh wrote on 9 July 2006: 'Lundstrom assigns base motives to everyone who dared to criticize Fletcher'.
93. *Ibid*.

However, that should not prevent further searching questions being asked on his conduct. One particularly vexing puzzle for many former carrier aviators with regard to Midway was posed by George Walsh. 'Why did Admiral Fletcher select so distant a launch position on the morning of June 4th?' His contention was that under the original plan the US fleet was to take a dawn position 200 miles north of Midway, but, in practice, both task forces were 260 miles north-east of Midway. Once the enemy carriers were located Spruance had to turn further away from the enemy into a light south-east wind to launch his strikes. Fletcher, additionally, had to run north-west, again *away* from the Japanese, to recover his northerly search SBDs.

'With days to prepare and knowledge that the Japanese fleet would be attacking from the north-west into the prevailing wind,' reasoned Walsh, 'why did Admiral Fletcher take up such a poor opening position?' He added that while much has been written about the argument between Spruance and Browning over the 0700 launch from TF-16, nobody has raised the question of why they were so far out of position three hours after sunrise. After all, under cover of darkness the Americans could easily have moved 50 or more miles closer to Midway and the anticipated track of the Japanese, at least to the planned 200-mile position. Walsh listed the advantages this would have given the American flyers.

This would have resulted in properly coordinated attacks by our Air Groups, shorter range to the targets and an increase of their impact. Earlier arrivals would have allowed time for searches. Losses that occurred in combat and from ditching after fuel exhaustion would have been minimized. If Nimitz's admonition 'Don't lose my carriers' dictated Admiral Fletcher's position he was also in error. The extra 50 or 75 miles meant nothing to the Japanese with their longer ranging aircraft.[94] His best defence for his carriers was an early knockout of the Japanese carriers and their offensive power. This had been demonstrated in the war games of the 1930s.

Walsh says: 'I would suggest that much of the confusion and misfortunes that plagued our carriers' attacking squadrons at the Battle of Midway evolved from this first error of taking a position too far northeast at the birth of day of 4 June, 1942'.[95]

He found some backing from other naval officers who had studied the battle[96], but little or none from the various 'authorities', official and semi-official. Others who have studied the battle minutely reach different conclusions on the original placing of American forces.

Lundstrom for example, states: 'After sundown Fletcher swung southwest intending to be two hundred miles north of Midway at dawn on 4 June. . .' and later, 'Early on 4 June Fletcher steered TF-17 and TF-16 southwest at 13.5 knots to be two hundred miles north of Midway at dawn.'[97]

Bates's report confirmed that both US task force, 'continued on base course 210° (T) speed 13.5 knots, zigzagging towards an 0430 position in Lat. 31° 30' N, Long. 176° 30' W, which position bore 013° (T), distant 202 miles from Midway'.[98] The initial American launch was actually not made until 0700. The one-hour delay by Spruance was praised by Bates but he was diligently trying to make up some of the faulty long-range position he had been placed in.

This was a courageous decision, and one which paid off handsomely. It was an excellent demonstration of the will of the Commander; that quality which, in conjunction with the mental ability to understand what is required, enables the Commander to ensure for his command every possible advantage which can be obtained.[99]

It will be recalled that Bate's praise was the 'watered-down' version of the 'critical analysis'. Lundstrom's verdict on this is withering: 'Given how flattering even the final product was, Spruance must have rejected a virtual hagiography of himself'.

However, Robert J. Oliver was equally flattering to Spruance when he gave this pen portrait of the man he had served so loyally to Thomas B. Buell.

---

94. Indeed the initial *Kidō Butai* launch against Midway Island was at 240 miles range.
95. George Walsh to the author, 2 August 2006.
96. Captain Grant C. Young, commented on 'the flaws in the strategic planning by the fleet commanders which led them to divide their carrier assets beyond mutual support range' as well as 'failures in carrier operational and air group training and lack of air discipline'. Most importantly, he stated that, 'although proper recognition was paid by the Navy authorities for the heroic actions by the participating SBD squadron leaders and crewmen which led to victory in the Battle of Midway, little cognisance has been taken by the various media, for the benefit of the greater American public, of their thrilling achievement'. Captain Grant C. Young to George J. Walsh, 15 October 2004. Reproduced by permission of George Walsh.
97. Lundstrom *Black Shoe Admiral*.
98. Bates, Report.
99. *Ibid*.

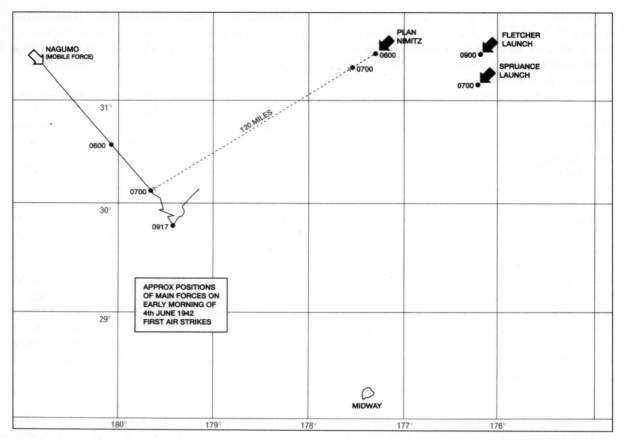

NAGUMO
(MOBILE FORCE)

PLAN
NIMITZ

FLETCHER
LAUNCH

SPRUANCE
LAUNCH

0600

0900

0700

0600

0700

120 MILES

0700

0917

31°

30°

29°

APPROX POSITIONS
OF MAIN FORCES ON
EARLY MORNING OF
4th JUNE 1942
FIRST AIR STRIKES

MIDWAY

180°   179°   178°   177°   176°

Map 2: A possible Nimitz attack plan for US task forces on the morning of 4 June 1942. This would have resulted in a combined earlier attack, and at shorter range, by all three US carriers than the attacks ultimately conducted by Task Force Sixteen and Task Force Seventeen. (Copyright George Walsh 2007)

Spruance had the most logical and disciplined mind of any man I have known. He appeared to have thought out every possible situation in advance so that he already knew what he wanted to do when the time for action came. He spent many hours thinking about how to deal with the enemy, but he did not let his mind become cluttered. He cleared out the fog by taking strenuous walks and by extensive reading of non-professional subjects.

Spurance's brand of leadership was simple, direct, effective, and utterly without frills. He set high standards. He was quick to recognize a job well done and equally quick to indicate dissatisfaction with less than standard performance. He was always positive and never showed any sign of hesitancy in any of his actions. He always had a deep appreciation of his mission and a firm determination to attain the objec-

tive. His instructions were explicit and his orders crystal clear. In battle, he was quiet, calm, and fearless, totally disregarding his own personal safety. Above all he set an example by his impeccable personal conduct.[100]

Further revelations will no doubt follow for others are lining up to have their turn to dispute even Parshall's and Tully's account, as outlined in Ronald Russell's opus[101], so their general acceptance might not last very long. Those including Elliott Carlson's forthcoming biography of Joe Rochefort, a third novel based on the battle by Larry Schweikart, and no doubt many more. Truly Midway is a battle whose distant rumblings seem destined to echo on and on into the far distant future, even though any practical lessons in sea-air warfare that it imparted were already obsolete as early as 1945!

---

100. Oliver to Buell, dated 5 August, 1971.

101. Ronald W. Russell, *No Right to Win.*

The Russian perspective

To the Russians, both under the Soviets during the Cold War and since, Midway has remained of little or no interest, even to naval historians.

Historian Alexander Bolnykh[102] stated unequivocally:

For the USSR during the period 1941–1945, the Pacific was not a secondary, but a *negligible* theatre of war. I remember an exhibition of military posters taking place about twenty years ago. For me the poster impacted from two sides for 1942, the landings in Tunisia and the battle of Stalingrad, but there was nothing connected to the Pacific Ocean. Absolutely nothing.

In chronological order, the Supreme Command of the USSR from some time in November 1941, clearly understood that an attack from the Japanese would not occur. Therefore it was at liberty to throw its highly trained forces from the Far East into the Moscow battle. Later, their armies went to Stalingrad, Kursk and any place where they were needed.

Before the termination of the war with Germany, the USSR could not even think of striking into northern China, therefore the situation in the Pacific was not even considered. The first hints of a change of interest occurred in the winter of 1944–45. After taking Konigsberg, a proportion of the Soviet armies that had been involved were taken from the front and transported to the Far East. I know this for a fact for my grandfather (a major) fought at Konigsberg but finished the war in Port Arthur.

In post-war histories the Battle of Midway is considered in Russia as a large defeat for the Japanese, but not a *decisive* one. It rates approximately in importance to the battle for Moscow in the winter of 1941, which stopped the Germans as Midway stopped the Japanese, but did not end their ambitions or ability. A good parameter of the total lack of importance that Russia places on Midway, and indeed the whole Pacific theatre, is that, up to now there is no book by a Soviet or Russian naval historian devoted to it.[103] I do not speak of any closed works of the Naval Academy. And that for over sixty years since the end of the war!

So I repeat, Midway was COMPLETELY[104] unnoticed in the USSR. There is not ANY word about Midway in the memoirs of the C-in-C of the Soviet Navy, Admiral Kuznetsov.[105] He talks only about Northern convoys and Normandy, and nothing else!

Finally, to bring Russian views right up to date Bolnykh added:

I have received a copy of *Shattered Sword*, and don't understand the noise around this book. It gives some interesting details but not any serious changes. We have had detailed discussions earlier, where it was estimated, in Russian analysis, that the odds in this battle, due to the intelligence information and so on, were about 60 to 40 in favour of the Americans. So there was not any 'miracle' or anything like it.[106]

A British naval officer writing in 2005, came to a similar conclusion, stating that 'the probability of success resided with the Americans even before the first wave of aircraft had left the decks of the carriers of Vice-Admiral Chuichi Nagumo'.[107]

If Only?

There are an increasing number of books and articles with an 'alternative history' theme to them, ranging from the absurd to the ridiculous.[108] I tend to share the view of former Hypo cryptanalyst Admiral Donald Showers, who once remarked that they 'cause me to use my delete key

---

102. Alexander Bolnykh to the author, 29 June 2006.
103. He added, 'We talked to Yauza [a Moscow publisher] about it and if we can agree I shall write the FIRST!'
104. Capitals in original.
105. Nikolai Gerasimovich Kuznetsov, with Vladimir Krivoshchevkov (trans), *Memoirs of Wartime Minister of the Navy of the Soviet Union.*
106. Bolynykh to the author. This is true only up to a point, because actually there *is* a chapter in the memoir devoted to the Pacific War but it is only concerned with the period July–August 1945, and even then is merely the usual bombastic Communist nonsense churned out by the propaganda houses, and of little or no value as an historic document.

107. Commander J. J. Short, *Was Japanese Defeat at Midway Inevitable?* student paper, Ministry of Defence, London, 2005.
108. The list seems to grow almost daily among one of the originals in the field: is David Downing, *The Moscow Option: An Alternative Second World War;* Greenhill Books, London, 2006, which, despite its title, spends more time on Pacific and Indian Ocean speculation than the Eastern Front; the publishers describe the book as 'provocative', but I find 'preposterous' a more apt description, especially as to a Japanese naval attack Panama – throughout, any pretence at meaningful logistics just goes out of the window. Richard E. Osborne's *If Hitler Had Won . . . ,* Riebel-Roque Publishing

more than anything else' and I am at one with him that such books are 'a pointless cause'.[109] One exception to the inanity of such speculative postulating, which contains much of merit, was produced by Drs Frank J. Stech and Christopher Elsässer of the Mitre Corporation for presentation at the 72nd MORS Symposium, Naval Postgraduate School, Monterey, California, 22–24 June 2004.[110] It is not so much 'What if?' as 'If Only?' in that it concentrates on the pre-battle intelligence aspect of the battle, applies a psychological instead of a cultural perspective to it from the Japanese viewpoint and then applies the analysis of competing hypotheses (ACH). At its simplest, their basic argument is that although the Japanese had more than enough hints, clues and downright direct information to conclude that the US Fleet would be at sea and waiting to ambush them, because each of these pieces of data was considered in isolation from the others, the 'obvious' conclusion was not reached. In the author's words, 'People often dismiss important evidence, prematurely prune alternative hypotheses, and jump to conclusions.'[111]

They point out that, although today's sophisticated approach, via the Bayesian belief network, was obviously not available to the Japanese of May 1942, they could have come to the same conclusions during the war plan reviews, table-top presentations and naval exercise prior the battle, had not 'the Japanese planners ultimately dismissed the identified problems, or met them with inadequate half-measures or inappropriate ripostes'.

Three possible outcomes of Operation MI were clearly available to Yamamoto, his planners and staff.

1   That, as Yamamoto planned for, the Americans would be totally surprised, Midway would be occupied and only then would the Pacific Fleet come out, because it could not afford not to, and thus be destroyed by the Japanese fleet, which by that time would have had all its units in place for the task. If all the clues were analysed, then the probability of this desirable outcome were rated as 69 percent likely in April, but only 29 per cent likely in May and this shrank to minus 2 per cent the day before the battle.

2   That the Americans would be taken completly by surprise by the occupation of Midway, but would accept the *status quo* as beyond dispute and seemingly would not respond[112], the likelihood of this occurring was only rate at 20 per cent in April, and this fell to just 1 per cent in May and minus 1 per cent on 3 June.

3   That the Americans, far from being surprised, would be aware and would be waiting in ambush themselves for the 1st *Kidō Butai* to commit themselves, and this was, in fact what happened. In April this possibility only rated as a 10 per cent possibility, but by May this had risen to 70 per cent and on the eve of comabt all known factors had made it almost the only option at 98 percent certain.

The Japanese would not, for various reasons, accept the latter possibility as feasible and duly paid the price. But the authors of this remarkable paper, painstakingly detailed in Appendix 1 of this work (*Events and Evidence*), facts that could, and should, have given the Japanese almost all the evidence they required to be aware that option 3 was a very real possibility on 4 May.

The fact that the 1st *Kidō Butai* was surprised by the British Blenheims in the Indian Ocean, that the Japanese invasion convoy had been surprised by the US carrier strikes at Lae and that the *Shōkaku* had been surprised by the SBDs at Coral Sea were all discounted[113]. Similarly that

Co. Inc, Indianapolis, 2004, has America invading the Congo among other flights of fancy, but events in the Pacific are not much changed.

109. Admiral Showers, 2003, as quoted in Russell, *No Right to Win*.

110. Frank J. Stech and Christopher Elsässer; *Midway Revisited: Detecting Deception by Analysis of Competing Hypothesis*; MITRE Corporation, McLean, VA, 2004.

111. *Ibid.*

112. Not in the paper but to be considered is that if option 2 came about, the Americans could still retrieve the situation by merely waiting for a time and date of their own choosing, because obviously the Japanese could not maintain their huge fleet in a waiting position in mid-Pacific forever. That way the Japanese would have got their advance base cheaply and could use it as a jumping-off place for further advance,

or a sentry-box to prevent any more 'Doolittles' occurring while they proceeded to cut Australia off from all contact with the USA at their leisure.

113. However, in my opinion Stech and Elsässer make a grave error when they state in the same appendix that the *Kidō Butai* was 'surprised by the British cruisers *Dorsetshire* and *Cornwall*, carrier *Hermes* and destroyer *Vampire*' and that this indicated 'weak Japanese counter-surveillance, intelligence and reconnaissance'. Quite the contrary one would have thought, it was the Japanese reconnaissance that found and led to the destruction of *all* these vessels! It would have been more legitimate to have attributed that same conclusion to the failure of the Japanese carrier-born reconnaissance to find Somerville's main fleet, and for Japanese Intelligence to have failed to discover that this fleet was operating from Addu Atoll, something they never became aware of.

French Frigate Shoals were occupied and that all long-range probes from Wake Island toward Midway, were shot down should have indicated a high level of alertness on the part of the defenders.

There is more in this paper that rewards more detailed study, but essential as it is to give calm and reflective consideration to every scrap of evidence, one feels that there are some factors that just cannot be included in such a analysis such as the absolute self-confidence the IJN in general had in themselves and their ability. By May 1942 this was coupled with considerable contempt for the pretty poor showing and lack of ability exhibited by their opponents up to that time. 'Victory fever' certainly, and of course inexcusable then and in hindsight, it was still the 'X' factor or wild card that no scientific system can ever take fully into account. Nor was it unique to the Japanese: the French army had it in 1914, they called it *élan*, and it cost them hundreds of thousands of casualties in the Battle of the Frontiers in the first few weeks of that ghastly conflict; the Germans had it at the outset of the Battle of Britain in 1940, and also got a bloody nose; the British had it just before they went 'over the top' on the Somme in 1916 and lost 60,000 men in a single day; the Americans had it early on during the Vietnam tragedy, and the toll in young lives, and the self-confidence of the nation, was equally sobering.

James Bowen seemingly accepted the arguments of Professor John J. Stephan's book that losing Midway would have led to an assault on Hawaii between October 1942 and March 1943.[114] He even argued that Admiral King would have withdrawn the carrier *Saratoga* to the West Coast to join *Wasp* (and presumably, although he does not say so, *Long Island* and the 1st Battle Squadron) in the face of such a threat, though on what grounds he bases this assumption is hard to discern. If King would not abandon Midway, he was hardly like to leave Hawaii, its priceless naval and military facilities and its populace to its fate. Bowen argued, (presumably from a differing interpretation of the Japanese 'plan' to that of Stephan) that, while a Japanese invasion as such would not have taken place, a 'tight blockade' would have been enforced by Yamamoto. Just how the IJN was to have maintained such a tight blockade is not specified. Bowen pointed out that with '2,200 miles of unbroken ocean separating Hawaii from the American West Coast, providing support for the defence of Hawaii . . . would have been a logistical nightmare' for the Americans. One might assume that with 3,402 nautical miles of ocean, or eleven days' steaming time, separating mainland Tokyo from Hawaii, maintaining a tight five-month long blockade might also have been something of a logistical headache for the Japanese also![115] The development of this scenario envisages the American public turning against Franklin D. Roosevelt and insisting on the reversal of the 'Germany first' policy, the losing of the Battle of the Atlantic or at best the postponement of D-Day, resulting in Soviet armies replacing Nazi ones along the Channel Coast in 1945. It is rather a lot to conclude from Captain Kami's tentative theoretical study of January 1942, which itself considered such a prospect impossible for Japan to achieve.

On the other hand victory at Midway led, slowly but surely, to the strangling of Japan by naval blockade, mainly by submarine. Japan had gone to war because America threatened to cut off her oil supply. To have accepted such strangulation without fighting had been 'unthinkable' but the gamble had been taken and lost, and oil starvation followed anyway. One clear lesson *was* gained, for America no less than for Japan, as the famous parable of Moorer and Kurita demonstrated. Admiral Thomas Moorer[116], then a young naval officer in the devastated

114. James Bowen, an Australian military archivist of the Pacific War Historical Society, in his article 'Assessing the Place of Midway in World War II', http://www.users.bigpond.com/Pacificwar/Midway/assessing_Midway.html.

115. One of the reasons Kōchi Kido had warned the Emperor against the war, even before it began, was that, even if the Dutch East Indies oil fell easily into their hands, it would still need to be transported to the homeland and that it would be a simple task for the American submarine fleet and aircraft to cut those shipping routes. Prophetic words indeed, and how much easier would it have been for them to sever the long, long supply trail that would have to lead from Tokyo Bay or Soerabaya to the vicinity Diamond Head and back, should Hawaii be kept isolated for any length of time.

116. Admiral Thomas Hinman Moorer (1912–2004). b. 9 February 1912 at Mount Willing, Alabama. From 1927 raised at Eufaula. Graduated from Cloverdale High School, Montgomery. Served in USN from 1933 to 1974. Married Carrie Ellen Foy by whom he had four children. Graduated from US Naval Academy, Annapolis, 1933. 1936 completed naval aviation training at NAS Pensacola. Flew fighter aircraft from carriers *Langley* (CV-1), *Lexington* (CV2) and *Enterprise* (CV-6) before the war. 1941 serving as lieutenant with VP-22 at Pearl Harbor, December. 1942 Dutch East Indies (shot down off Australia, February, at Timor evacuation) and South-west Pacific campaigns. After the war Naval War College, and Operations Officer on carrier *Midway* (CVB-41) then on staff of Commander, CarDiv 4, Atlantic Fleet. September 1956 – September 1957 in command seaplane tender *Salisbury Sound* (AV-13) at Alameda. 1958 Promoted rear-admiral at age of 45. 1962 promoted to vice-admiral, i/c 7th Fleet. Promoted to admiral and major commands held include, 1964 C-in-C Pacific Fleet, and 1965 C-in-C Atlantic Fleet (first officer to command both fleets). 1967–70 Chief of Naval Operations (during the *Pueblo* and *Liberty* spy-ship incidents, he believed Israeli attack on USS *Liberty* was deliberate and covered up by President Lyndon B. Johnson). 1970–4 Chairman of Joint

Japan of 1946, approached the former head of the Combined Fleet, Takeo Kurita. He found him chopping potatoes in his garden dressed in ill-fitting clothes. As Moorer used to tell the story he asked Kurita through his interpreter what had gone wrong. 'we ran out of oil,' was Kurita's response. Moorer used to relate that tale, and the lesson it imparted. 'The lesson I learned was never lose a war'. And then Moorer would add, 'The way to lose a war is to run out of oil.'[117] The USA's policy since 1946 indicates that this particular lesson has undoubtedly been taken to heart.

Midway was undoubtedly a milestone battle, and a great achievement for the US Navy, but its effects were to be felt more in terms of morale (boosting American esteem and confidence and sowing doubt in the Japanese about their superiority) rather than such a pivotal moment as envisaged above. Like El Alamein for the British, Midway marked the moment when the retreating finally stopped[118].

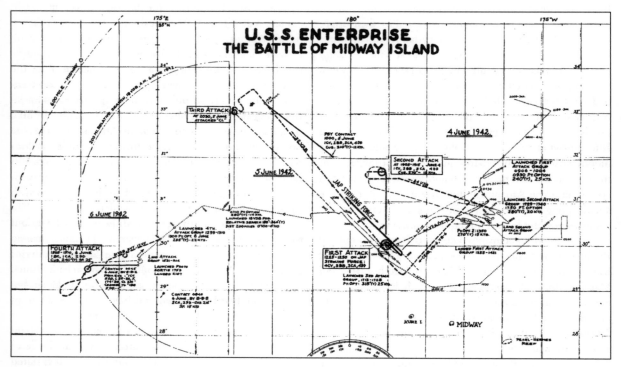

Map 3: The map of the battle as plotted by Spruance's flagship, the USS *Enterprise*. (NARA)

Chiefs of Staff. Defense Distinguished Service Medal twice, Silver Star, Distinguished Flying Cross, Purple Heart, Gray Eagle Award. 1974 retired on 2 July. Lived at Bethseda and worked for Texaco and CACI International. Wrongly accused by CNN and by *Time* magazine of using sarin gas in Laos in a story they ran with Peter Arnett, citing Moorer as their source, which he strenuously denied. Vindicated in court and by firing of two CNN producers. Died, following a stroke, on 5 February 2004 at Naval Medical Center, Bethesda. Just a few days short of his 92nd birthday. Interred at Arlington National Cemetery on 24 February 2004.

117. See *The Old Man and the Oil, a fascinating story about World War II: Good advice from Admiral Moorer*, from Len Kaine, Golden Rule Society, e-mail to the author from Norman Polmar dated 27 July 2006.

118. Interestingly, it is *this* facet of Midway's importance that has recently been resurrected. An older generation of Americans (and British for that matter), perplexed by a modern world in which the 'bad guys' always seem to be winning, and with a large section of the media that actively appears to support them rather than their victims, and moreover demonises any President (or Prime Minister) who dares to stand up them, is seeking a rock to cling to in a world turned upside down. Midway was one such certainty, (where we knew who the enemy was and beat him fair and square), as former Secretary of State Dr James Schlesinger discovered. His sixtieth anniversary commemoration, *'Midway to Victory'*, postulated the 'No Midway – No Normandy' theory and subsequently found a large audience ready and willing to embrace it.

Chapter Thirteen

The Chimera of 'Orient'

The fascination with the Battle of Midway continues. Many Americans claim that it still remains the 'underrated battle' of World War II, and they may very well be right.

To gauge the true impact of the victory at Midway on the outcome of the war it is essential to examine the position of the other powers involved in the world-wide struggle. With such a strange series of alliances any major outcome would be certain to have a ripple effect on them all, although, of course, some would be more affected than others.

To assess this impact we have to examine how things were perceived immediately before the battle was fought, and how the same perspectives were altered both materially and psychologically, after it. Each nation had its own set of goals and priorities, and these were hardly ever identical to those of its allies. We can also, in passing, examine in detail the recent phenomenon of the appearance, sixty years after these momentous events took place, of a whole new mythology, 'Operation Orient'.

British Fears

Long before the disasters of 1941–2 befell them, the British in the Far East, had known that, once totally committed against both Germany and Italy, and abandoned by France, their position *vis-à-vis* Japan was untenable. This was discussed and digested by the full War Cabinet at a meeting held on 8 August 1940. The final verdict of these worthies, '87 detailed paragraphs'[1], was far from upbeat. They concluded that if the Japanese moved against either the Vichy French in Indo-China or the wavering Thais there was no question of Great Britain being able to go to war to stop them. Moreover, should this happen then not only isolated Hong Kong, but Singapore, Malaya and the vast Dutch East Indian territories were indefensible also! With Nazi Germany just across the Channel and invasion expected at any time; with France not only prostrate but with Vichy openly collaborating with the former enemy, and with the Italian jackal taking the opportunity to assert himself in the Mediterranean, nothing could be spared for the Far East. Of course, it was an unpalatable fact that such a scenario would also, logically, encompass the overwhelming of Australia and New Zealand also, and, if Britain had nothing to spare for the rest of our Asian dependencies, then, equally, she had nothing to spare for them, even though their troops were fighting in the Egyptian desert far from home.

Rather predictably the embattled British civilian and war leaders preferred to keep this unpleasant knowledge to themselves, shielding it successfully from their trusting Commonwealth partners Australia and New Zealand, who continued to be kept in the dark. Any breath of such realism reaching Japan was also to be strenuously avoided, lest this knowledge of British impotence spur them into the very action that was feared. It was rather unfortunate then, that, in November 1940, the British, in what many of their ANZAC cousins still regard as 'the world's greatest intelligence disaster'[2] delivered this vital knowledge, plus a great deal more sensitive information, straight into the hands of

1. This section is mainly based on Ian Pfennigwerth, *A Man of Intelligence,* and Captain Eric Nave, OBE, RAN, and James Rusbridger, *Betrayal at Pearl Harbor*. See also the summary internet posting: James Rusbridger, 'Ultra: And the Sinking of the Automedon', nesa.org.uk.
2. *Military Intelligence Blunders and Coverups,* Constable & Robinson, London, 2004. Colonel John Hughes-Wilson is a retired NATO international political staff officer in Brussels, and a former Head of Policy Section and Senior British Intelligence Officer at Supreme Headquarters Allied Powers Europe (SHAPE), Mons, now a prominent author and broadcaster and Associate Fellow of the Royal United Services Institute. Books on the subject of intelligence and conspiracies include *The Puppet Masters: Spies, Traitors and the Real Forces Behind World Events*.

Japan's friend, the Germans. This was the unfortunate *Automedon* Affair.

Copies of the War Cabinet minutes for 8 August 1940, which committed to paper the full revelations on the total inadequacy of British defences in Malaya, and which had enjoyed highly restricted circulation for some weeks, were sent on this vessel to the British C-in-C, Far East, Air Marshal Sir Robert Brooke-Popham, at Singapore.[3] Why they could not have been given direct to him to take with him is unclear.[4] It has even been alleged that these important papers were sent thus on the direct orders of Air Chief Marshal Sir Cyril Newall[5], as a delaying ploy to avoid their unpalatable conclusions being discussed at the Singapore Defence Conference in October 1940.[6] If that is true it would have been doubly ironic, for Newall, who knew the contents of course, was himself sent out that same month to become Governor-General of New Zealand, one of the dominions kept strictly in the dark! Newall achieved a certain notoriety for his public gaffes during the war, and sending these documents by vulnerable steamship might have been seen by some to be rather in character!

Failing that, one would have thought that the C-in-C's status as a leading RAF officer would have triggered in someone's mind in London the thought that these vital documents might be more quickly (and securely) sent by the weekly Sunderland flying-boat service, but it was placed inside a canvas bag weighted with lead, and marked 'Safehand – British Master O/Ls'[7] and then delivered for transit, not to the safe-keeping of one of His Majesty's ships of war, but to a simple safe in the master's cabin aboard a slow (14 knots) and relatively defenceless mercantile vessel, the 7,528-ton Blue Funnel Line cargo liner *Automedon* (Captain R. B. McEwen) of 1922 vintage. She then independently (i.e. without any naval escort) sailed for Singapore.

It might be assumed by a general reader that, once beyond the reach of the German U-boats concentrated in the Western Approaches to Great Britain, the *Automedon* might be safe, but that was not the case, nor should it have been assumed to be the case in August 1940, for the exploits of both German warships like the pocket battleships *Admiral Graf Spee,* and *Admiral Scheer,* and the heavy cruiser *Admiral Hipper,* as well as the so-called armed merchant raiders (*Hilfskreuzer* or HK ships), were common knowledge. Even more relevant one raider, the very successful *Atlantis*[8], (Captain Bernhard Rogge[9]) had already dealt Britain a heavy security blow by capturing, on

---

3. Air Chief Marshal Sir Robert Brooke-Popham, GCVO, KCB, CMG, DSO (1878–1953). b. 18 September 1878 as Henry Robert Moore Brooke; the name Popham was added in 1904 by Royal Warrant in deference to an ancestor. Educated at Haileybury School and Royal Military College, Sandhurst. Commissioned May 1898 as second lieutenant Oxfordshire Light Infantry. 1899–1900 South African War against Boers. 1904 captain. 1910 Army Staff College, Camberley. Attached to Air Battalion during 1911 army manoeuvres applied to fly and gained RaeC Certificate No. 108 in July 1911. May 1912 major, became pilot in Air Battalion. April 1912, CO Aeroplane Company, Air Battalion. May 1912 seconded for duty with Royal Flying Corps (RFC). May 1912 CO No. 2 Squadron, then No. 3 Squadron, RFC. June 1913 temporary lieutenant-colonel, 20 November 1914 major, CO No. 3 Wing. May 1915 Chief Staff Officer, HQ RFC France. March 1916 colonel, as Deputy Adjutant & Quartermaster-General HQ RFC. Switched to RAF as temporary brigadier-general 1 April 1918, as Controller, Aircraft Production. After the war colonel, then group captain August 1919, then Air Commodore August 1919 and air vice-marshal January 1924. November 1928 Air Officer Commanding (AOC) Iraq. January 1931 air marshal, and Commandant, Imperial Defence College. 1933 AOC, Air Defence, Great Britain, opposed introduction of new fighter aircraft with enclosed cockpits and eight machine-guns. December 1933 ADC HM King George V. January 1935 Air Chief Marshal, Inspector-General RAF then AOC RAF Middle East. Retired at own request in 1937, married in March and appointed Governor and C-in-C Kenya. 1939 Head of RAF Training Mission, Canada, and 1940, Head of RAF Training South Africa. 18

    November 1940 appointed C-in-C, Far East Command, Singapore. 1944–6 President of NAAFI Council and Inspector-General ATC. Died 20 October 1953.
4. Brooke-Popham left the UK on 27 October.
5. Marshal of the Royal Air Force Cyril Newall, 1st Baron Newall, (1886–1963). b. India 15 February 1886. Educated Bedford School and Royal Military College, Sandhurst. Joined Royal Warwickshire Regiment, 1905, served on North-west Frontier of India. 1911 flying lessons in Bristol biplane. 1913 qualified as pilot at the Central Flying School. 1914 served on Western Front. 1916 wing commander under Trenchard. After the war 1926–31 Deputy Chief of the Air Staff. AOC Middle East 1932–5. Chief of the Air Staff (CAS) 1937. CAS retained ten fighter squadrons in England during fall of France June 1940. October 1940 Marshal of the Royal Air Force, replaced by Portal twenty days later and appointed Governor-General of New Zealand until 1946. Became Baron Newall of Clifton upon Dunsmoor. Died in 1963.
6. Alan Matthews, *SS 'Automedon': The Ship That Doomed A Colony.*
7. *Ibid.*
8. *Atlantis (Schiff* 16) was a 7,862 ton former Hansa Line, Bremen, vessel named *Goldenfels.* She was armed with six 5.9 inch guns, five AA weapons, 92 mines, six torpedo tubes and two Arado Ar196 aircraft. She had a top speed of 17.5 knots and eventually sank or captured twenty-two Allied merchant ships until she was sunk by the British heavy cruiser *Dorsetshire* on 22 November 1941.
9. *Konteradmiral* Bernhard Rogge (1899–1982). b. Schleswig, 4 November 1899. Joined the Imperial German Navy (*Kaiserliche Marine*) 1915 as ensign. World War I service

11 July 1940, the steamer *City of Baghdad*, thereby taking intact all the secret Merchant Navy cipher and call-signs currently in use.[10] That these documents were not destroyed was an incredible blunder, but it showed just how insecure such ships were. That the British were prepared to risk documents of even higher security to the same chance of capture, in the same area, may be considered to be criminal, but, again, it was done.

The *Automedon* very nearly got away with it, for she had reached an area about 250 miles off the north-western tip of Sumatra on 11 November, when the *Atlantis*, fully conversant with the details of her course and destination, courtesy of the already captured information, hove into view, dashing any hopes of reaching Singapore safely. Closing to within 4,600 yards of the British ship, where she had been mistakenly identified as a Dutch vessel, the *Atlantis* unmasked her battery of 5.9 inch guns at 0820 to fire a warning shot. At 2,000 yards, the *Atlantis* responded to the commencement of transmission of RRR (the raider-warning signal), by the British ship, and quickly smothered her target with well-aimed shots from her drilled gunners. The liner's bridge was hit almost immediately, and Captain McEwen, Second Mate Stewart, another duty officer and three crew members were all killed outright, with a further twelve badly injured. This did not prevent the *Automedon*'s radio officer getting off part of the standard pre-prepared 'Enemy Raider' report, which was picked up by at least two other merchant ships.[11]

There was no chance, of the slender green canvas bag and its sensitive contents being retrieved and thrown overboard into the Indian Ocean. It was found by the leader of the German boarding party, Lieutenant Ulrich Mohr[12], a fluent English-speaker. After the earlier coup aboard the *Baghdad*, Mohr was not the least daunted when, on opening the captain's safe, he discovered yet another Aladdin's cave full of treasure. He was able to get his hands on sixty sealed packages of top secret mail and then, with increasing elation, handed out a growing pile of Straits Settlements banknotes from the Bank of England printing presses, which finally totalled some 6,000,000 dollars. In the various packages the German discovered the British Admiralty weekly intelligence summaries, both Royal Navy and new Merchant Navy deciphering code tables 7, 8 and 9, which were not due to take effect until 1 January 1941. Spoilt for choice Mohr also found the bag containing the innermost thoughts of the British High Command on the Far East defence situation. Not of high priority to Berlin maybe, but the Germans thought that Tokyo might just possibly find them of interest!

Captain Rogge set course eastward toward Murag Island in the Japanese-mandated Mariana Islands to refuel and restock courtesy of the 'neutral' Japanese. Here the captured Allied ship's companies were sent over to a supply ship, the former Norwegian tanker *Ole Jacob*[13], and the captured documents went with her when she sailed for the Japanese port of Kobe, where she arrived on 4 December. Under very tight surveillance the British secrets were transferred ashore and taken at once to the German Embassy in Tokyo where, next day, a very intrigued Naval Attaché, Admiral Paul Wenneker[14], examined them and photographed those he felt were of particular value. Such obviously secret material was a hot item and they were

---

aboard several light cruisers North Sea. Between the wars commanded sail training vessel *Albert Leo Schlageter*. 1939 as *Fregattenkapitän* appointed in command of *Atlantis*. Awarded Knight's Cross with Oak Leaves. Promoted to vice-admiral by 1945, discharged service. 1957, June, re-entered *Bundesmarine* as *Konteradmiral* commanding Military Area Command 1 and also NATO Commander Land Forces, Schleswig-Holstein. 31 March 1962 retired. Co-authored with Wolfgang Frank (journalist) and R. O. B. Long (trans), *Under Ten Flags: the Story of the German Commerce Raider* Atlantis. Died 29 June 1982.

10. In 1940 the Royal Navy was still continuing to employ the cumbersome and time-consuming 'book cipher' system of four and five tabular columns, with subtraction tables laboriously coded and decoded by hand. The German SigInt team (*B-Dienst*) and had little difficulty in reading most British service and diplomatic signals traffic at this time.

11. The SS *Helenus* and the SS *Matara*. Captain P. W. Savery of the former vessel immediately forwarded this on to Colombo, but a sluggish response from that base caused a delay of one and a half hours before it was even acknowledged. British naval intelligence at Singapore is also alleged

to have learned of the interception of the secret documents aboard the *Automedon* from released Norwegian crew members from the *Ole Jacob* on 30 December 1940, and to have advised the Admiralty accordingly.

12. Mohr later wrote, in conjunction with British historian A. V. Sellwood, who acted as editor, *Atlantis: the Story of a German Surface Raider*. He listed his find as fifteen bags of secret mail, including 1 hundredweight of decoding tables, fleet orders, gunner instructions and naval intelligence reports. But it was in the chart room that he found 'a long narrow envelope in a green bag, equipped with brass eyelets to let in water to facilitate its sinking'. He subsequently claimed that there were details of the intended future strength of the RAF units (335 aircraft), naval strengths, assessment of the role of Australia and New Zealand plus copious notes on the fortifications of Singapore.

13. This 8,305-ton tanker laden with 10,000 tons of aviation fuel, was captured by *Atlantis* by a ruse and after being refuelled by the Japanese, eventually safely ran the British blockade to reach Bordeaux in occupied France.

14. Admiral Paul Wenneker (1890–1979). b. Kiel 27 February 1890 to a naval family. Joined navy as *seekadett* in 1909 with

---

entrusted to a trusted courier, and young naval officer named Paul Kamenz[15], for personal delivery to the naval HQ (*Oberkommando der Kriegsmarine* or OKM) in Berlin. Kamenz was hustled off hotfoot for the Reich via Vladivostok and the trans-Siberian railway.

Wenneker followed this up two days later by transmitting a summary of the British CofS's report direct to the OKM.[16] This telegram in four-part cipher, could not be intercepted by the British intelligence network because it went via the Soviet postal telegraph circuit, but it is quite possible that, because of this, Moscow was privy to its contents as soon as Berlin. When Hitler was informed of the coup he gave instructions that the Japanese Naval Attaché, Captain Yokoi, be shown a copy. In the tangled web being woven, Yokoi then cabled his summary of the summary back to Tokyo, and his message was intercepted by the United States listening stations. The cat should have been out of the bag, but, this signal was one of many that lay unread and was not deciphered by the Americans until 19 August 1945!

When the incredulous Vice-Admiral Kondo, Vice-Chairman of the IJN General Staff was given copies of the British report, he was loath to believe that such documents were anything but a 'set-up' by the Germans or a double-bluff by British secret service. When he was eventually persuaded that they were indeed the real thing, the knowledge of Britain's terrible weakness must have contributed to tipping the balance in favour of war the following month.[17] Indeed Kondo was alleged to have confirmed as much to Wenneker more than once.[18]

Who would not be grateful for such a detailed insight into the thoughts of a potential enemy? Indeed parts of it were subsequently repeated almost word-for-word by Japanese intelligence officers in subsequent reports as the move south was discussed.[19]

From the various sources mentioned, it seems obvious that Churchill and the Cabinet knew that their innermost thoughts on Far Eastern defence were in Japanese hands, but neither the Governor of Singapore, Sir Shenton Thomas[20], nor Brooke-Popham, the unfortunate C-in-C,

---

sea service aboard the armoured cruiser *Victoria Louise*. 1910 *Fahnrich zur See*. 1911–12 light cruiser *Mainz*. 1912 *leutnant zur see*. 1913 light cruiser *Königsberg* and 1913–14 *Mainz* again and when she was sunk by the British at the Battle of Heligoland Bight became POW. Released but interned in Holland 18 January – 10 December 1918. 1919 served with minesweepers clearing Baltic Sea. Promoted *oberleutnant zur see* May 1919 and *kapitänleutnant* 1920. Served aboard destroyer *S-18* and torpedo boat *T-109* then minesweeper *M-2* in 1919–20, then various minesweepers to 1922. Gunnery Officer cruiser *Nymphe* 1924–6, then Gunnery Officer armed merchant liners *Elsaff* and *Schleswig-Holstein* 1929–31. *Korvettenkaptän* 1928 and *fregattenkapaitän* 1933. 1933–7 Naval Attaché, Tokyo and built up excellent relationship with IJN. *Käpitan zur see* 1935 and *Konteradmiral* 1939. After brief period at home as captain of the pocket battleship *Deutschland* in Spanish Civil War and captain of pocket battleship *Lützow* in 1939 was reappointed March 1940 and remained until May 1945. *Vizeadmiral* 1941 and full admiral August 1944. Made available German U-boat technology to Japanese and tried to persuade them to switch from anti-fleet tactics to anti-supply route tactics, isolating Hawaii, but was unsuccessful. Interned May 1945 to November 1947. Released 5 November 1947. After the war lived quietly and died at Bergstedt, Hamburg, on 17 October 1979.

15. Kamenz had been the prize master of the *Ole Jacob* and had formerly been in command of a training vessel at Porsgrund in July 1938. An earlier capture, the Norwegian tanker *Teddy*, had her master transferred and shared a cabin with the *Automedo*'s mate, who informed him that he believed the raider had got legation mails and confidential books from his ship. He later informed the Naval Control Service Officer at San Francisco of this on his subsequent release and they, in turn duly notified the Director of Naval Intelligence in Ottawa, on 15 January 1941, so London must have known.

16. Cipher Tel Nr 209/40 gKdos to 212/40 gKdos to Navy High Command, dated 6 December 1940.

17. See S. Hatano and S. Asada, 'The Japanese Decision to Move South, 1939–41'.

18. Entry Wenneker War Diary, 1800, 12 December 1940. So grateful were the Japanese, that, when 'impregnable' Singapore later fell a year later Emperor Hirohito presented Captain Rogge with a ceremonial sword to mark his nation's gratitude.

19. Alan Matthews offers one example. Paragraph 33 of the CofS report read: 'Penetration of Indo-China: We should not under present circumstances go to war with Japan in the event of a Japanese attack on Indo-China'. Captain Yamaguchi Bunjoro, Chief 5th Intelligence Section and Captain Horiuchi Shigetada, Chief of 8th Section, in a report dated 21 January 1941: 'Even if Japan sends forces into Indo-China, Britain will not go to war'.

20. Sir Shenton Whitelegge Thomas (1879–1962). b. 10 October 1879 to the rector of Newton-in-the-Isle, Cambridgeshire. Educated at Syderston and then St John's School, Leatherhead Surrey. 1898 awarded scholarship to Queen's College, Cambridge. 1901 graduated with honours. 1901–08 taught at Aysgarth Preparatory School, Yorkshire. 1909 Joined Colonial Office, posted Kenya as Assistant to District Commissioner. April 1912 married Lucy Marguerite 'Daisy' Montgomery. One daughter Bridget, Nairobi, 1914. 1926 Colonial Secretary, Accra Gold Coast, then Acting Governor. 1929 Governor of Nyasaland. 1930 KCMG. 1932 Governor Gold Coast. 1934, appointed Governor and C-in-C Straits Settlements and High Commissioner of Federated Malay States. November disembarked Penang. February 1938 at official opening of the Singapore naval base. Returned to England on leave and appealed to the Joint Planning Sub-Committee of the War Cabinet for more troops for defence of Malaya and Singapore. This was approved by War Cabinet but over-

were told.[21] Nor, of course, were the Australian and New Zealand governments ever made aware of this embarrassing disaster.[22]

'Pride goeth before destruction, and a lofty spirit before a fall!' Never did the old adage seem more apt than in Japan's humiliation of Britain's Empire in the Far East during the first six months of 1942. Apart from the Soviet Union, Britain, because of her widespread possessions in the east, had the biggest stake east of the Urals, and so kept a close eye on proceedings. With the rapid overrunning of most of her lands in the opening months of the war, this indulgent watch turned to patent alarm. As late as January 1942, with Singapore still in British hands, the Foreign Office's tone was comparatively relaxed. Noting that Oshima had visited Hitler on 5 January and discussed 'political and military questions', they concluded: 'The course of the war during the next few months will to a great extent depend on whether Germany and Japan adopt a convergent strategy or whether each pursues its own political and military objectives without reference to the other'. With hindsight we now know that it was the latter policy that was taken, but in January 1942 that could not be foreseen let alone guaranteed.

The British assessed the possibilities in this way. 'If, in 1942, Germany again concentrates her main effort against Russia, while Japan fights the Anglo-Dutch-American forces in the East Indies, neither will be helping the other, except very indirectly'. This could have been Hitler or Ribbentrop talking. The Foreign Officer continued: 'A unified strategy would require either that Japan join the war against Russia or that Germany concentrate her striking power as far as possible against Britain and the USA.' They concluded:

The latter alternative is by far the more likely. Japan has a neutrality pact with Russia, and a Russo-Japanese war, in present circumstances, though very inconvenient for Russia, would probably be even more undesirable for Japan. Germany, on the other hand, is already at war with Britain and has deliberately declared war on the USA. Further, the intervention of the Japanese Navy especially if Japan gains control of the Malacca Straits, will have altered the general strategic position of the Axis *vis-à-vis* Britain and the USA more than the German invasion of Russia has affected the military position on the Manchukuo-Siberian borders.[23]

Surveying the future, the benefits to the Axis from an 'Orient' type strategy were as obvious then as they have been with sixty years of hindsight to 'alternative history' adherents. 'If Singapore is taken', the Foreign Office concluded, 'Japan will have an open gateway into the Indian Ocean through the Straits of Malacca and will be in a position to harry the shipping routes of the Indian Ocean (including those round the Cape to Egypt and the Middle East).

Any serious interception of shipping might seriously weaken the British position in Libya, Egypt and Syria, while at the same time determined Axis sea and air attacks on our Fleet in the Mediterranean might incur losses and make it difficult to counter the Japanese raids in the Indian Ocean. In this way it might be possible to create the necessary conditions for a serious Axis offensive in the Middle East, in

---

ruled by Churchill. 15 February 1942, on fall of Singapore interned by Japanese at Changi, then moved to POW Camp Karenko, and later Taihoku, Formosa: Moved to Hsian POW camp Manchuria until Japanese surrender. Flown to Calcutta via Chungking, returning to London September 1945. 1946 officially retired as governor. Died at his London home 5 January 1962, aged 82. The Shenton Way development complex in Singapore is named in his honour. Biography: B.Montgomery, *Shenton of Singapore: Governor and Prisoner of War*.

21. After the fall of Singapore, the Labour Peer Lord Addison had called Brooke-Popham a 'nincompoop' in the House of Lords debate and Thomas received similar vilification from left-wing politicians who, as Russell Grenfell sagely noted 'had worked the hardest against adequate defence preparations in peacetime. Perhaps an uneasy conscience on this latter point contributed to his Lordship's deplorable indulgence in personal abuse'.

22. After the war, the denial was continued by the Foreign Office, and, although the documents had been discovered in the Foreign Ministry archives in Berlin in 1945, this also was

not admitted. Three years after the war had ended Brooke-Popham was still being told his copy of the appraisal had been lost when 'the ship carrying the papers was sunk by a German submarine' (Squadron Leader G. Wiles, Air Ministry, Whitehall, to Brooke-Popham, dated 15 July 1948). They were still continuing to deny the affair fifty years later. No mention had been made in the belatedly published official history *British Intelligence in the Second World War*. Not until 1954 did the historian Captain Stephen Roskill make this brief reference to the *Automedon* disaster: 'The British ship *Automedon* was attacked and sunk, though not before she had sent a raider report and, in consequence, been savagely shelled. Again search of the captured ship yielded valuable intelligence to the enemy'. (*The War at Sea 1939–1945, Vol. I.*) And, he might have added, to a potential, enemy also! As usual, it was the more open Americans who finally blew the gaffe when the NSA declassified many Magic de-crypts in 1981, including Yokoi's summary.

23. Foreign Office Summary, *Enemy Activity*. Report No. 70 para. 3 (National Archives FO371/31831).

which Japanese naval power would be used to support a German drive either through Turkey or directly against Egypt. Though the Middle East falls outside the scope of Japan's 'Greater East Asia', and there might be a tendency in Japan not to take risks with Japanese warships outside the Western Pacific, Japan has now so vital an interest in a general Axis-Japanese victory in the war that such support would probably be forthcoming.[24]

With the rapid crumbling of the rest of her eastern empire, Burma having been written off, the spring of 1942 found the most prized possession, the British Raj of the Indian sub-continent, suddenly in the front line.

Just how big the risks Japan *was* prepared to take in the Indian Ocean was amply demonstrated a few weeks later of course; but it quickly transpired that the majority of the risks involved were taken by the British naval commander rather than the Japanese.

Churchill had for years scorned the Japanese navy, deeming it no match whatsoever for the Royal Navy or the USN. He persisted in sending tanks and Hurricane fighter aircraft to Stalin, who never asked for them and certainly never thanked him for them, while Malaya had to make do with what was left over, which was not much. Nor would the Premier ever believe what he was told by British intelligence about the potential of the IJN.[25] For example, in 1942 he was presented with a detailed assessment of the Japanese navy building programme.[26] He challenged it on every point. Yet he only had to ask his American ally. As long ago

24. *Ibid.*
25. The late Captain Stephen Roskill has recorded what he termed 'Churchill's pre-war blindness with regard to the Japanese threat'. For many examples of the continuing under-estimation of the Japanese navy, which included despatching the *Prince of Wales* and *Repulse* to Singapore against the advice of the Naval Staff instead of building up a balanced fleet, see Stephen Roskill, *Churchill and the Admirals*.
26. The Naval Intelligence Department's estimate of Japanese new construction which was admitted to be 'derived princi-pally from one particular source which is not regarded as

fully reliable', gave the following major warships under construction. In November 1941, Sir Robert Craigie telegraphed that in his opinion Japanese vessels under construction included four battleships and five heavy armoured cruisers of 15/20,000 tons. On 20 December 1938 it had been estimated by the Industrial Intelligence Committee that the maximum number of heavy ships the Japanese could build simultaneously was five battleships or large aircraft carriers, ten large and small cruisers, fifty destroyers and/or submarines. (ADM 2-5/13, National Archives, Kew, London, see Table 30 below). Churchill, who had cut the Royal Navy building programme of heavy

Table 30: NID Estimate of IJN's Building Programme 1942

Type/Est. Tonnage	No	Yard	Laid Down	Launched	Completed	Ships actually building
Battleships (40,000 tons)	1	Kure	1937	1939	1941	*Yamato* (62,315 tons)
	1	Sasebo [Nagasaki]	1937	1939`	1942	*Musashi* (62,315 tons)
	1	Yokosuka	1937	1941	1942	*Shinano* (62,315 tons) (completed as a carrier)
	1	Maizuru	1939	1942	1943	No. 797 (62,315 tons) (proposed only)
	1	Kure	1939	1943	1944	No. 111 (62,315 tons) (cancelled)
Heavy (Battle) Cruisers (20,000 tons)	1	Yokosuka	1938	1941	1942	No. 795 (32,000 tons) (proposed only)
	1	Kure	1938	1942	1943	No. 796 (32,000 tons) (proposed only
	1	Yokosuka	1939	1942	1944	–
Heavy Cruisers (14,000 tons)	1	Maizuru [Kure]	1937	1939	1940	*Ibuki* (12,500 tons) (to be completed as a carrier, cancelled)
	1	Nagasaki	1938	1940	1942	–
	1	Nagasaki	1938	1940	1942	–
	1	Maizuru	1939	1942	1944	–
Aircraft carriers (27,000 tons)	1	Nagasaki	1939	1941	1942	*Junyo* (24,140 tons)
	1	Kawasaki/Kobe	1939	1941	1942	*Hiyo* (24,140 tons)

as 1936 Admiral Osami Nagano[27], the Navy Minister, had boasted at a secret Diet meeting following Japan's withdrawal from all the detested naval treaties which the British and Americans were still clinging to:

> As a result of the coming no-treaty period we shall enjoy freedom of action in construction of warships in respect to category, quality and characteristics. With this freedom we may construct those ships particularly adapted for our national requirements, thereby gaining an advantage which obviates the necessity for numerical equality.[28]

This secret agenda was obtained by the American Naval Attaché, Captain Frederick F. Rogers, (who was also a fluent speaker and writer of Japanese, having been taught in Japan itself) who passed this interesting information on to Washington DC. He added that the Japanese were designing capital ships of 45,000–55,000 tons, way above the existing 35,000 ton treaty limit. The recipients might have scoffed, just as Churchill did six years later, but we now know that Rogers, if anything, vastly underestimated the lengths the Japanese were prepared to go to gain the ultimate advantage.

Despite his misplaced faith in the inferiority of the Japanese navy, even Churchill had to accept some plain facts, and, when in April, Nagumo's carrier force, the 1st *Kidō Butai*, sortied into the Indian Ocean and sank, in quick succession, the aircraft carrier *Hermes*, the heavy cruisers *Cornwall* and *Dorsetshire*, the destroyers *Vampire* and *Tenedos* and many lesser craft, with minimal loss to themselves, he had to face reality. In the aftermath of these further two naval disasters off Ceylon, Churchill had to swallow his pride and appeal directly to Roosevelt for help, not once but twice. He wrote on 15 April[29]:

> I must revert to the grave situation in the Indian Ocean mentioned in my No. 65.
>
> The consequence of this concentration of naval power might easily be:
>
> (a)   The loss of Ceylon
>
> (b)   Invasion of Eastern India with incalculable internal consequences to our whole war plan and including loss of Calcutta and of all contact with the Chinese through Burma.

But this is only the beginning. Until we are able to fight a fleet action there is no reason why the Japanese should not become the dominating factor in the Western Indian Ocean. This would result in the collapse of our whole position in the Middle East, not only because of the interruption to our convoys to the Middle East and India, but also because of the

---

cruisers when he was at the Treasury, and again cancelled four modern battleships on order for the Royal Navy in 1940, refused to believe it, asking, 'Is it credible that the Japanese have at present 9 capital ships and 2 large aircraft carriers all building simultaneously. If so, the future is indeed serious. On what evidence does this statement rest? We must on no account underrate the Japanese. Facts are however what is needed.'

27.   Admiral of the Fleet Osami Nagano (1880–1947). b. at Kochi, Kochi prefecture, on 15 June 1880 to a former *Samurai* family. Graduated Etajima Naval College, (2nd of 105) as midshipman on 13 December 1900. Joined protected cruiser *Hashidate*. 1901 served aboard battleship *Asahi*. 1902 sub-lieutenant aboard *Asama*. 1903 lieutenant (jg) at Yokosuka and student Gunnery Training Centre and aboard *Ariake-maru*. 1904 at Sasebo, then aboard the armed merchant cruiser *Hongkong-maru* with 1st Fleet. 1905 Lieutenant on staff of Ryojun Maintenance Yard and then aboard battleship *Shikishima* and Gunnery Training Centre again. 1906 Trainer at Naval Academy then to protected cruiser *Itsukushima*, as Chief Gunnery Officer until 1908. 1909, a course at Naval College, 8th. 1910 lieutenant-commander, Chief Gunnery Officer battleship *Katori*. 1911–12 Naval General Staff. 1913 to USA as language officer, studying at Harvard Law School. 1914 commander. 1915 XO of armoured cruiser *Nisshin*, then XO of armoured cruiser *Iwate*. 1916 Bureau of Personnel staff. 1919

appointed in command of light cruiser *Hirado*. 1920–3, Naval Attaché, USA, attended Washington Naval Conference. 1923 rear-admiral. 1924 Naval General Staff, commanding 3rd Squadron. 1925 commander 1st Expeditionary Fleet. 1926 General Staff. 1927 vice-admiral, commanding Training Fleet. 1928, Director, Naval Academy. 1930 Vice-Chief Naval Staff. 1931–2, Geneva Conference. 1933, C-in-C Yokosuka, Member Administration Committee. 1934 admiral, Navy Council. 1935 at London Naval Conference. 1936 Navy Minister. 1937 C-in-C Combined Fleet.1937–41 Navy Council, High Technical Committee, new warship design. 1941 Chief, Naval General Staff. 1943 Admiral of the Fleet. 1944, pressurized to resign by Tojo and Navy Minister Shigetaro Shimada, with the Emperor's tacit approval, resigned in February, after forty-four years continuous service and became a 'government advisor' for rest of the war.1946, March, arrested and brought before International Military Tribunal for Far East on class A war crimes charges. Held in Sugamo Prison, Tokyo, 1947, caught pneumonia in prison and died of a heart attack brought on by complications, aged 66 on 5 January.

28.   Fred F. Rogers papers, 1920–69, held at Naval War College, Rhode Island.

29.   Former Naval Person to President, Personal and Secret. No. 69, dated 15 April 1942 (T.570/2). (Contained in PREM 3/499/6 National Archives, Kew, London.)

interruptions to the oil supplies from Abadan, without which we cannot maintain our position either at sea or on land in the Indian Ocean area. Supplies to Russia via the Persian Gulf would also be cut. With so much of the weight of Japan thrown upon us we have more than we can bear.

He then went on to list some alternative, which would ease the strain, mainly detaching yet more American major warships to aid the British.[30]

Roosevelt, while sympathetic, could not offer any further detachments from the Pacific, nor did he seem to think the danger was acute as Churchill outlined. 'A Japanese land attack on Ceylon in my opinion won't be made for several weeks' time.'[31]

In the aftermath of the Nagumo raid and his demonstration of how to deploy air/sea power to influence worldwide events, the nations around the Indian Ocean reacted with a mixture of horror, alarm and concern according to their vulnerability. Although we know in hindsight that the Japanese naval excursions were not harbingers of a more general move west, it is hardly surprising that at the time this was not appreciated by those closest the threat. So how did these nations react?

Australian Alarm

As might be expected, real alarm was expressed in Australia after the Indian Ocean fiasco. For twenty years the

Australians has comforted themselves that, in the event of Japan breaking lose and attacking south, all would be well because the Main Fleet of the Royal Navy would sail to do battle and save them. That delusion was rapidly stripped away. Not one, but two Royal Navy fleets had been despatched; the first had been eliminated within a few days, the second had been given a sharp and humiliating lesson and dispersed, being reduced to no more than a nuisance-value 'fleet in being'. In its commanding officers words, 'Until I can get reinforced I shall have to lie low in one sense but be pretty active in another – keep the old tarts out of the picture and roar about with the others'.[32]

This 'strategy' was, of course, not known to the Australian premier, but what he and his government colleagues *did* know was that all the sure and steady shields, actual and promised, on which they had based the security of their homeland for two decades had vanished like smoke in less than five months. Quite apart from the naval disasters and the imperial fortresses falling with speed, almost it appeared, without a serious fight, the Nagumo carrier force had almost contemptuously, wiped out Port Darwin as a major base without breaking sweat. Nobody in Australia doubted where the Japanese were heading next, which was right down their throats![33]

At the time things appeared starkly serious. Prime Minister Curtin[34] telegraphed Churchill on 17 April:

I wish to let you know with what uneasiness we learnt of the sinking by air attack of the *Dorsetshire* and

---

30. Churchill asked for the new battleship *North Carolina* and the small carrier *Ranger* be sent to join Somerville's fleet in the Indian Ocean; alternatively *North Carolina* could join the US battleship *Washington* at Scapa Flow, releasing the British battleship *Duke of York*. The US carrier *Wasp,* badly needed in the Pacific, was already employed running British fighter reinforcements into Malta.

31. Telegram, For Hopkins for the Former Naval Person from the President. Message No. 133, dated 16 April 1942. (T.583/2).

32. Somerville to his wife, 7 April 1942. 'The old tarts' were the four 'R' class battleships, which had short fuel and water endurance and slow speed, which limited their value, together with their escorts, known as Force B; 'the others' were Force A, battleship *Warspite* and carriers *Indomitable* and *Formidable*, with their escorts. Within days, *Formidable* reported a stripped gearbox which reduced her speed to a mere 8 knots, which meant not much 'roaring about' from her. In the crucial matter of aircraft, these two British carriers embarked between them a total of six Wildcats (then known as Martlets in the Royal Navy) and eleven Sea Hurricanes (all single-seater fighters, but inferior to the Zero) and eight Fulmars, twin-seater fighters, totally outclassed at this period of the war. As for strike aircraft, these consisted of Swordfish

and Albacore biplanes, which again Somerville quite correctly described as 'useless against the Japs unless we can catch them at night'. Somerville Papers.

33. There is still bad feeling about this in Australia, although Australian troops were as ineffectual as any others in Malaya, and also earned a reputation for a serious lack of discipline in some accounts. 'Betrayal' is a word still bandied about, mainly by those who have little idea of the true facts. As one British Minister (Tom King) was forced to remind an Australian republican agitator, many decades later, 'the men of the *Prince of Wales* and *Repulse* were hardly running away when they went to their deaths'. But, of course, where raw emotions are concerned, facts hold little currency. Thomas Jeremy King (b.1933), Tory politician from 1970; Minister of the Environment then Employment Minister 1983–5; Secretary of State for Northern Ireland 1985–9; Defence Minister 1989–92, Life Peer Lord King of Bridgewater, 2001.

34. Australian Prime Minister, Rt Hon. John Joseph 'Ambrose' Curtin (1885–1945). Labour Party and Marxist (Victorian Socialist Party) activist in his youth; secretary of Timberworkers Union and anti-conscription activist. Became Labour Prime Minister in 1940. Due to war situation, reversed his earlier stance and introduced conscription

Cornwall, which is now followed by the sinking of the *Hermes*. These unfortunate happenings have been the subject of prolonged and anxious discussion by War Cabinet and Advisory War Council and they raise such vital questions that we feel constrained to ask you for full information as to the cause of them and for an appreciation of the United Kingdom, United States and Japanese position in regard to aircraft carriers, types of aircraft carried and views held as to relative efficiency of the aircraft and personnel. We would also ask for a statement of the United Kingdom's immediate and long range policy for combating the Japanese Naval forces.[35]

He added, 'I should be grateful to have information and advice on this vital matter as early as possible.'

Churchill's response included the statement that 'unknown fact is degree American action in Pacific will contain Japanese effort'. He also stated the obvious, telling Curtin: 'Next three months will be critical.'[36]

In his post-war memoirs Churchill converted these defeats into heroic actions which halted the Japanese with heavy losses, claiming, totally without foundation, that Nagumo's 'celebrated carrier force' had suffered such losses in the air that three of his ships had to be withdrawn to Japan to be refitted.[37] This was of course nonsense; the Japanese admitted the loss of five aircraft only during the whole operation, and even Michael Tomlinson, a former Station Intelligence Officer at Ratmalana, who gives the RAF's

figures maximum credence, claims only seventeen enemy aircraft destroyed.[38]

As a sop to Australian fears, Churchill proposed sending the four 'R' Class battleships (which he constantly disparaged when it suited his mood, as being obsolete ships, but whose modern replacements, the four powerful *Lion* Class, 40,000 tons, nine 16 inch guns, he had personally cancelled) to Australia.[39] The Naval Staff were eventually able to dissuade him from making yet another futile gesture.

The result of Midway brought 'a great easement'[40] to the British position in the Indian Ocean. Curtin and his Cabinet, however, from that point on, tended to place more trust in American action, which soon became apparent at both the Coral Sea battle and in the Solomon Islands, rather than vague British promises of some action of some kind, some time in the distant future. They also held the line in New Guinea mainly by their own efforts. The result of the Midway battle only reinforced this new-found reliance on the rising power of the United States rather than the increasingly irrelevant 'Mother Country'.

When, subsequent to Midway, Curtin visited Roosevelt in Washington, the Americans perhaps overcompensated for Churchill's lack of enthusiasm by telling the Australian Premier more than usual in order to keep him 'on side'. Captain Joseph J. Rochefort remembered[41]:

I recall having been sent for, two or three days after Midway, by my immediate superior[42], who was

against enormous opposition from his own party despite this was re-elected in 1943. Struck up surprising understanding with General Douglas MacArthur. Stress led to heart problems and he died in July 1945 just as the Pacific War was nearing its victorious conclusion. For further details see John Edward, *Curtin's Gift: Reinterpreting Australia's Greatest Prime Minister*.

35. Immediate – Most Secret. No 252. Prime Minister (Churchill) from Prime Minister (Curtin), 17 April 1942 10.30 p.m. (T.587/2) Churchill responded with a detailed report with a Narrative on the sinking of the British warships, a situation report on the aircraft carriers and aircraft of the three nations, including admission that the Japanese 'ability to strike at above our striking range gives them advantage'; that 'Japanese and Americans have air crews with many years training not yet diluted with war time entrants as are British' and that the reason British carriers embarked less than half the aircraft of Japanese and American equivalents was because 'they have armoured flight decks making them less vulnerable to bombing but reducing accommodation'.

36. Prime Minister to Mr Curtin. Most Secret. (T.636/2) dated 27 April 1942.

37. Churchill, *The Hinge of Fate*.

38. Michael Tomlinson, *The Most Dangerous Moment: The*

Japanese Assault on Ceylon 1942. However, Commander Eiziro Suzuki, who was also present, serving aboard the carrier *Soryū*, warned Tomlinson that this figure of seventeen was an 'exaggerated' one. When consulted by the publisher prior to printing, I independently gave exactly the same advice which was likewise ignored.

39. See exchanges contained in ADM 205/21(National Archives, Kew, London).

40. Stephen W. Roskill, *Churchill and the Admirals*.

41. The reminiscences (Oral History Tape in 1969) of Captain Joseph J. Rochefort, U S Navy (Rtd), for U S Naval Institute Annapolis, 1985, interview by Commander Kitchen.

42. Rear-Admiral David Worth Bagley (1883–1960). b. Raleigh, North Carolina, Annapolis. Graduated Naval Academy, 1940. Served in battleships, gunboats and with Great White Fleet in 1908. Commander destroyers during World War I, working out of Queenstown. Survived loss by U-boat attack of USS *Jacob Jones*. Between the wars served in destroyers, cruisers and as Assistant Naval Attaché at The Hague, and also had a stint in Naval Intelligence. As a rear-admiral he commanded BatDiv 2 from *Tennessee* (BB-43) and was at Pearl Harbor. He served in a variety of shore posts until the end of the war including Commander 14h Naval District twice. He retired in 1947 and died at the San Diego Naval Hospital on 24 May 1960.

Commander of 14th Naval District and I was told to sit down and listen.

I think it was the Prime Minister of Australia who was returning to Australia from Washington, and he told us how this whole thing had been done, the Intelligence at Midway. How this had been done by breaking the Japanese code. He had just come from Washington. In other words, somebody in Washington must have been talking, and this is almost impossible to stop. Somebody in Washington either in COMINCH's Office or at the White House, told him.

South African Determination

The lynchpin to holding the vital convoy route around southern Africa via the Cape of Good Hope, was of course the Union of South Africa. Her leader, the wise and thoughtful Prime Minister, Jan Christian Smuts[43], was one of the most respected leaders of the Commonwealth and had predicted the Japanese menace in discussions with his old friend Churchill, but his words had fallen on deaf ears then. Now he was listened to rather more carefully.

He signalled Churchill on 26 May 1942[44], expressing his fears.

I consider it essential for our ultimate victory that we should continue to hold the Middle East including Iran and Iraq and also India and Ceylon together with the Indian Ocean. Loss here would be such a set back as to affect our ultimate prospects of victory. The German attack on this land both from the West and the North this summer will be most formidable. The Japanese menace of the Indian Ocean and our lines of communication through it will be an added danger. We cannot safely rely on Russia to prevent an attack through Caucasus south-wards nor is India immune from attack or serious menace from Burma.

Smuts considered that 'neither by land nor at sea do we appear to have sufficient forces to guarantee this position should Russia be defeated or withdraws North from Caucasus'. He urged powerful reinforcements to the navy in the Indian Ocean, with 'the necessary American Naval Units. Together we should have a sufficiently powerful combination at sea in the Indian Ocean to prevent the Japanese threat and to bring the Japanese Fleet to action if opportunity offers'.[45]

Smuts thought it was a 'strategical mistake' that America was sending naval and land forces to Australia. He did not share Curtin's view of an imminent major Japanese attack there. On the contrary, he felt Australia 'lies off the real line of Japan's advance'. Major American forces for the Far East, Smuts felt, should be sent to the Indian Ocean to 'help check the Japanese advance to Ceylon, India and the Indian Ocean and to ensure the defeat of the Japanese Navy'. He urged that Allied strategy 'be based on the Indian Ocean rather than on both Indian and Pacific Oceans with division of forces involved'.

But, of course, the Americans had other priorities than the defence of the crumbling British Empire.[46] Also, in its result, Midway brought about the same result that Smuts's alternative strategy strove for, the defeat of the Japanese navy and, thereby, the ending of any further Japanese naval threat to the Indian Ocean.

Churchill's response also included much wishful thinking and underestimating of the Japanese threat. This was his invariable reaction and his wilful blindness does not seem to have been influenced by the events since December 1941. He confided to Smuts: 'My own belief is that Japanese will strike north and try to finish off Chiang-Kai-Shek, but the distances are very great.' He admitted, 'It will be difficult to find resources to meet really heavy

43. General Smuts, as he was generally known (1870–1950). Son of an Afrikaner farmer, educated at Cambridge and a lawyer in Cape Colony, had served as a Boer General during the war against British between 1899 and 1902 and organized the original commandos for irregular fighting. Prime Minister of the united South Africa for which he had striven, between 1919 and 1924, and again in 1939, Smuts was staunchly pro-Commonwealth. Among his many accomplishments were that he was the chief advocate of the League of Nations after World War I and of the United Nations after World War II. He lost the 1948 election and died two years later.

44. General Smuts to Prime Minister, No. 930. Most Secret and Personal Telegram. 26 May 1942, 3.20 p.m. (T.760/2).

45. Churchill replied the following day, promising Smuts that the battleships *Nelson, Rodney* and *Valiant* along with the carrier *Illustrious*, would join the Indian Ocean fleet at Colombo by the end of July. In fact, after Midway, not one of these warships joined Somerville, who himself was ordered to keep his fleet well clear of Colombo; moreover, *Indomitable* was withdrawn and sent to the Mediterranean.

46. Between 1936 and 1937 the essential harmony that was required between Great Britain and the United States if Japan was to be deterred had almost come to grief over Roosevelt's obsession with colonialism, when he accused Britain of, 'land-grabbing tendencies' for disputing ownership of a tiny island that America wanted for herself. See Ian Cowman, *Dominion or Decline, Anglo-American Naval Relations in the Pacific, 1937–1941*, Berg, Oxford, 1996.

German attack by the Caucasus and Caspian on the assumption that the Russian Front breaks to the southward'. But he added that there was 'no reason at present to assume such disaster. Anyway the year is advancing and the Germans have much to conquer and a long way to go before this occurs.'

The perceived Japanese threat included designs (imaginary as it turned out) on the large island of Madagascar. Axis submarines were despatched there to work against the Allied convoy routes, and occupation with the active assistance of the ruling Vichy French regime, which might prove as compliant as if had been in Indo-China, was on the cards. A pre-emptive move was made by the British (Operation Ironclad) and in a series of landings the whole island was quickly occupied and Vichy resistance was quickly overcome. Even so, this did not prevent some further casualties and yet another of the British battleships, *Ramillies*, was damaged by midget submarine attack , while several important merchant ships were sunk in the Mozambique Channel.

Indian Opportunism

Smuts also had wise words on India. He had met Colonel Louis A. Johnson, who had just returned from India as President Roosevelt's personal representative.[47] Johnson, Smuts warned Churchill, 'was pessimistic over the Indian situation. The Congress Party was not really intending any serious resistance to Japan while Gandhi appeared to him to favour Japan, under the impression (deluded as it turned out) that if the English were out of the way India could make an agreement with Japan.'[48]

In fact, the British were attempting to solve the complex issues involved and on 22 March 1942, Sir Stafford Cripps had arrived in New Delhi with a formula to present to nationalist leaders for the already promised post-war constitution. However, these leaders were in no mood to compromise on independence as they saw it and told Cripps to take the next plane home! Cripps, however, persevered, with Johnston's active input. It was a case of the blind leading the blind; neither man had been in India for much over a week and both were seeking fast fixes to problems that had bedevilled old India hands for decades! The failure of the British Government to agree to the appointment of an Indian defence minister became the official stumbling block on which the whole Cripps mission ultimately foundered. Johnson described the rejection by Congress of the offered solution as 'a masterpiece and will appeal to free men everywhere'.[49]

The failure of the Cripps mission led to a working committee of the Congress Party demanding an immediate end to British rule in India and the threat of a non-violent struggle under Mahatma Gandhi.[50] However the Criminal Investigation Department had ample proof that far from being 'non-violent,' firm plans were in place, in Hodson's words, to 'seize police stations and other key points, to sabotage railways and perform other acts of violence or acts inevitably leading to violence. They were more than enough to remove my doubts'. The Government, with the Japanese armies already on the border, could hardly stand by and allow this to take place, and, on 9 August the leaders of the Congress were arrested in Bombay and placed under detention. The resulting mayhem fully justified that action, for the 'Quit India' rioting (in effect an insurrection) was 'far worse and more dangerous than the public at home in Britain was allowed to know'. The strategic rail line between the north-west and Calcutta was severed for two weeks and there was open rebellion in the streets of Old Delhi and elsewhere.

Had the Japanese been able to move west, rather than merely to conduct raids into the Indian Ocean and Bay of Bengal, no matter how efficiently, or lightly bomb Calcutta, the results could have indeed been catastrophic to the Allied cause. However, as one Indian historian was forced to

---

47. The ever-perceptive Henry Vincent 'Harry' Hodson (1906–99), then Constitutional Adviser to the Viceroy, Lord Linlithgow, was a strong supporter of Dominion Status for India, but even he soon came to regard Johnson as, 'gravely ignorant of India, too easily impressed by Congress politicians, especially Nehru, who appealed to his predilections, and far too prone to see his role as that of negotiator and intermediary rather than observer and counsellor – in short, an indiscreet, ill-informed busybody'. See Harry Hodson, *Turning Point in India*, in his *Autobiography*. See also his *The Great Divide – Britain-India-Pakistan*. Hodson's judgement of Johnson was a pretty accurate summary of overall American opinion at this time also, especially that of the President, who never understood the complications of Muslim-Hindu-Sikh aspirations, hopes and fears within the

wider context of 'Independence', which Roosevelt's proposed 'Articles of Confederation' (based on the American model of 1783–9) were woefully inadequate to address let alone resolve. As Churchill sagely remarked at the time, the Americans had, ' strong opinions and little experience'.

48. *Turning Point in India,* Hodson.
49. For an Indian-American viewpoint see Dinyar Patel, *American Involvement in Cripps Mission.*
50. Mohandas ('Mahatma' – Great Soul) Gandhi (1869–1948). 'Father of India'. Barrister and leader of Indian nationalist movement. Adopted a non-violent protest and non-cooperation movement (*Satyagrha*) for the Indian National Congress. Post-independence, he tried to end Hindu-Muslim unrest by fasting. He was murdered by a Hindu fanatic, Nathuram Godse, in Delhi.

admit, the newly established 'Band of Brothers' relationship between Roosevelt and Nehru[51] was put on hold after Midway.

Unfortunately, the pressures of war prohibited India and the United States from further deepening their relations. With their soldiers 'island hopping' their way westward, America's attention increasingly shifted to battle in the Pacific Ocean. Languishing behind bars, Nehru and other Indian leaders were unable to continue their dialogue with Washington.[52]

But there were alternative Indian leaders, like Subhas Chandra Bose[53], who were eager to work with the Japanese and other members of the Axis, and they were free to continue organizing. Bose had escaped from jail in Calcutta in 1941 and fled via Afghanistan and Moscow to Berlin, where he helped organize the Nazi Anti-British Legion of 3,000 Indian POWs captured in the Middle East, who were to lead any German attack through the Caucasus to India. When this failed to materialize he took passage in the German submarine *U-180* to Madagascar, switched to a Japanese submarine *I-29*, which took him on to Sumatra and eventually reached Japan. Meanwhile Rash Behari Bose[54] had been similarly organizing the Indian National Army from disaffected POWs captured in Malaya and Singapore, under the leadership of Captain Mohan Singh[55], formerly of the 1/14th Punjab Regiment. They awaited the word to liberate eastern India, which again, never came.

Indian nationalists claim that, had Bose reached the Far East earlier and persuaded the Japanese to attack in the spring or early summer of 1942, India would have fallen. Some historians agree.

Rommel was in Egypt, the German invasion of Russia had gone smoothly, Nationalist China was on her knees, and India and Australia were expecting a Japanese invasion. Prospects for the Allies were dark in the Pacific and the Rising Sun was at its zenith from Japan to the Bay of Bengal . . . Britain was unable to dispute with the Japanese Navy, and there were not enough British and Indian troops in India to assure its defense. Even air protection was inadequate.[56]

Patel stated:

From the Himalayas to Cape Comorin there were virtually no anti-aircraft guns, air-raid floodlights [searchlights?], or radar sets. For Calcutta, in grave danger of attack by waves of Japanese bombers, the only defences that the Royal Air Force could muster were two barely workable fighter planes. British authorities in New Delhi hastily devised a scorched earth policy at least to slow down a Japanese advance. Surplus rice and grain was moved out of the northeast, and plans were drawn up to destroy Assam's Digboi oilfields and Calcutta's port. British

---

51. Jawaharlal Nehru (1889–1964). Lawyer turned politician and activist for Indian nationalism and socialism. Associate of Gandhi and President of Congress Party. Became first Prime Minister of India in 1947.
52. Dingar Patel *American Involvement in Cripps Mission*.
53. Subhas Chandra Bose (1897–1945). President of Indian National Congress twice, disagreed with Ghandi's 'non-violence' policy and resigned. Formed All India Forward Bloc. Much influenced by Fascist thinking, he once declared that democracy was not the way forward for an independent India. Was reported as being killed in air crash at Taihoku, Taiwan on 18 August 1945, while trying to reach Tokyo. Indian revisionist theories reject this and allege he sought sanctuary in Manchuria, which was under occupation by the last totalitarian regime, the Soviet Union, once more, the three Fascist states having been defeated, and that he died in captivity in Siberia in 1946/7. Indian historians have now elevated him to the status of a national hero in the fight for independence. For books relevant to this study, see Joyce C Lebra, *Japanese-Trained Armies in Southeast Asia: independence and volunteer forces in World War II*, the same author's *Jungle Alliance, Japan and the Indian National Army*, Peter Ward Fay, *The Forgotten Army: India's Armed Struggle for Independence* and, for an Indian viewpoint, Mihir Bose, *Lost Hero: a Biography of Subhas Bose*.

54. Rash Behari Bose (1885–1945). A former Bengali terrorist who became a naturalized Japanese citizen. Was involved in the Alipore bomb case in 1908 and jailed. Continued plotting after release, but it was one of his adherents, Awadh Bihari, who actually carried out the next attack, at Delhi in 1912, against the Governor-General and Viceroy Lord Charles Hardinge. Bose continued plotting but in 1915 fled the country and obtained refuge in Japan. During 1942 he helped organize the recruitment of volunteers from the captured Indian troops (helped by the fact that the Japanese shot many who failed to 'volunteer') as the Indian National Army (*Azad Hind Fauj*). He was also involved in the Japanese-organized Indian Independence League but the Japanese later threw him out. He died in Japan of natural causes in 1945.
55. Captain Mohan Singh (1909–89). Served as a regular with the Indian Army, and was in Malaya with 1/14th Punjab Regiment when he surrendered to the Japanese in mid-December 1941. Appointed as a 'General' to lead the INA, he fell out with his masters in 1942 and was arrested, but reinstated by Bose in 1943. Captured by the British in 1945 and then released. Later entered politics and served two terms in the *Rajya Sabha*, the Upper House of the Indian Parliament.
56. Lebra, *Jungle Alliance*.

authorities appeared resigned to defeat, yet made no attempts to engage the Indian independence movement, so at least to buoy the Indian spirit.[57]

This hardly equates with the facts; the Indian Army alone had 2½ million men under arms, of which the INA managed to subvert 45,000, mainly POWs under duress. Even so, Churchill constantly fretted about the reliability of this huge force should the Japanese arrive in force.[58] Even Allied intelligence had a gloomy prognosis in April 1942, and both the Joint Intelligence Committees (JIC) report of the 18th[59] and the Joint Planning Staff (JPS) report of the same date[60] concluded that Nagumo's highly successful foray, coupled with Japan's awareness of India's lack of defences could very well tempt them. Furthermore, they concluded that, in the face of any serious Japanese attack, Assam could not be held and that the whole subcontinent would fall. Richard J. Aldrich, in his definitive study, calls this period 'a background of near-panic'.[61]

However, the rosy picture of Japanese-Indian co-operation to bring the Raj crashing to its knees in 1942 as presented by Indian nationalist revisionists today has little credibility in fact. Distinguished Japanese historian Yōichi Hirama told me that the Japanese were never much more than luke-warm on the scheme and there were soon sharp differences of opinion.[62]

In the Autumn of 1941, Rash Behari Bose was invited by the Japanese General Staff to discuss how Indian independence could be achieved. The high proportion of Indian troops serving with the British in the Far East was of decisive importance, leading the Army General Staff on 18 September, to make the decision to send Major Iwaichi Fujiwara to Bangkok in order to set up a small unit, which later became known as the *Fujiwara Kikan*. Fujiwara would contact Pritan Singh, a Sikh revolutionary who had organized the Independence League of India in Thailand and was keen to co-operate with Japan.

The joint agreement was signed on 4 December 1941 and contained the following points: the Independence League of India would fight the British with a view to achieving independence fully and completely under the overall support of Japan. Japan was not to ask from India any kind of concession, either political, economic, territorial or military.

This policy was soon bound to clash over the further use of Indian prisoners-of-war. As the Indian nationalist visualized it, the prisoners-of-war were to be almost immediately transformed into freedom fighters and incorporated into an Indian National Army under Indian command: the Japanese military authorities, on the other hand, saw them merely in the role of useful auxiliary units only good for propaganda and sabotage purposes.[63]

After the Battle of Midway a very different atmosphere prevailed. By October 1942 (which it should be noted was

57. Dinyar Patel, *American Involvement in the Cripps Mission*.
58. Not without some foundation. As early as May 1940, the 19th Hyderabad Regiment, just arrived in Malaya from India, suffered constant and widespread unrest and came near to outright mutiny, so much so that the Argyll and Sutherland Highlanders had to be put on standby to quell such an outbreak. Once the Japanese attacked this unit soon disintegrated, Indian troops firing on Lieutenant-Colonel C. A. Hendricks, the CO of 1st Battalion. On 14 December they had to be disarmed and turned into a labour battalion. (Richard J. Aldrich, *Intelligence and the War against Japan: Britain, America and the Politics of Secret Service*).
59. Joint Intelligence Committee, Japanese Intentions, JIC (42) 141, dated 18 April 1942 (contained in CAB 79/20, National Archives, Kew, London).
60. Joint Planning Staff, *Indian Ocean- Strategy in Certain Eventualities*, JPS (42) 413, dated 18 April 1942 (contained in CAB 29/20, National Archives, Kew, London).
61. Richard J. Aldrich, *Intelligence and the War against Japan: Britain, America and the Politics of Secret Service*.
62. Rear Admiral Yōichi Hirama to the author, 17 December 2005.
63. Lieutenant-Colonel Iwaichi Fujiwara b. (1908). Graduated from the Nakano School of Military Intelligence, Tokyo. With his *aide*, Lieutenant Yamaguchi, established contact with Colonel Hiroshi Tamura, ostensibly the Japanese Military Attaché, but in reality the Japanese Head of Intelligence in Bangkok, who brought in Pritam Singh. They worked in conjunction with their equivalent intelligence ring under Colonel Keiji Suzuki in Burma and were believers in, and pushed hard on, the line of equal Pan-Asian partnership. Their success in instilling a high degree of this propaganda into the Indian Army was high, as was their recruitment of disaffected Malays for espionage purposes, as resulting events in Malaya and Singapore, soon illustrated. However, Colonel Hideo Iwakuro, Head of the Military Affairs Section of the Military Affairs Bureau, who had founded the Nakano establishment, later replaced Fujiwara, and he was far less sympathetic to the INA viewpoint. Iwakuru was a major intelligence player, with much political influence as well. He had visited the USA in March 1941, arousing much concern in American intelligence circles. Fort Shafter had radiogrammed the Adjutant General on 29 March that the Military Affairs Bureau was 'probably the most important office in the army. He is so influential that there is no one in army circles who does not know him. We do not know what mission this colonel is on but in view of the times the visit of so important an army personage is worth our attention'. (JTP 39WTJ dated 29 March, 1941, 8:32 AM. See *Proceedings of Clarke Investigation*. See also Richard J. Aldrich,

after Midway, but *before* El Alamein, Stalingrad or the North African landings), the British Chiefs of Staff Committee were able to submit a buoyant and upbeat report.[64] Now, they thought,

> . . . large scale attempt to invade either India or Australia appears unlikely. The collapse of Russia, or even a serious weakening which made necessary a reduction in strength of the Russian Far Eastern Army, would present such an opportunity to attack the Maritime Provinces, but, as long as Russian resistance in Europe remains strong, Japan would hesitate to embark on operations which would render her vulnerable to bombing, release a formidable submarine force to accentuate her naval and shipping difficulties, and impose a further strain on an air force already fully employed and declining in strength.

Chinese Impotence

There was, of course, another Ally on the spot, in close contact with the Japanese enemy, to be considered in the equation. Long used to being criticized by the Western power for their ineffectiveness in opposing Japanese encroachment on their homeland, the Chinese now began to revel in the Allies' own humiliating defeats and discomfiture. In contrast to the rapid ejection of the long-established colonial powers from the Philippines, Hong Kong, Malaya, Borneo, Singapore, the Dutch East Indies and Burma, China could now represent her long, if unsuccessful, struggle against Japanese aggression since 1937 as a heroic rearguard action of attrition. Despite the fact that General Chiang Kai-shek continued to feel that it was more important to give ground to the Japanese and so preserve his armies for future use against the Communist threat, the Americans held a trusting belief that, if only enough war supplies were sent the Chinese would eventually start to resist.

That did not prevent the Generalissimo scattering advice on how others should go about defeating the enemy. He paid a visit to India and, on his return, cabled Roosevelt that he was 'personally shocked by the Indian military and political situation'. He told the President, 'If the British

government does not fundamentally change their policy toward India, it would be like presenting India to the enemy and inviting them to quickly occupy India'. The President, ever suspicious of British colonial 'mismanagement', hardly needed such a spur to confirm his worst fears. Moreover he accepted the word of Chiang as the leader of a powerful military power.

The British did not share this view, nor were they ever to express much confidence in the Chinese army to stand up to the Japanese. Sir Horace Seymour, in Chungking, sent a confidential telegram to London on 13 April 1942, expressing the candid opinion of the men on the spot in this regard.[65] He commented dryly:

> As we see the matter here the Chinese feeling of superiority to the Allies has certain advantages from the point of view of morale but there is a danger of it developing to a point at which co-operation will become increasingly difficult. This tendency is encouraged by the optimistic attitude of the British and still more the American press, towards China's war effort.

Seymour pointed to some of the hard facts, which this new-found Chinese elation and overconfidence 'perhaps naturally' chose to ignore. They were:

> (a) On a front of some 4,000 miles inside China, at a time when Allied strategy urgently requires that Japan should be fully extended, neither regular nor irregular forces of China are on the offensive; (b) the fact that the Chinese armies are still in being is due fundamentally to the fact that they have had unlimited room to retreat; (c) the Chinese have always, even in their worst defeats, been greatly superior in numbers to their enemy; and (d) China's military apathy, which is in effect complete within her own territories, has allowed the Japanese to withdraw with impunity considerable forces for service elsewhere.

Seymour stated that it was not easy to suggest a remedy for the trend of Chinese opinion, but added, 'It would, no

---

Intelligence and the War against Japan. Fujiwara was interned in Pudu Prison, Kuala Lumpur at the end of the war, but, far from being 'hanged by the British Officer in charge' as Malayan sources have it, he went on to write several books, including the history of his unit, (see) Iwaichi Fujiwara, *F-Kikan: Japanese Army Intelligence Operations in Southeast Asia during World War II*.
64. Chiefs of Staff Committee, *American-British Strategy*, COS

(42) 345 (O) (Final), dated 30 October 1942. (contained in PREM 3/499/6, National Archives, Kew, London).
65. Seymour to Foreign Office, No. 500, dated 13 April 1942, 5.00 p.m. The telegram was considered hypersensitive and was marked 'This telegram is of particular secrecy and should be retained by the authorised recipient and not passed on'. (National Archives, Kew, London, CAB 21/1946).

doubt, respond to Allied military successes.' Whether Midway, a great naval victory in the middle of the Pacific Ocean, constituted such meaningful success to a land-warfare-orientated people, the majority of whom shared Stalin's ignorance and Adolf Hitler's abhorrence of the sea, seemed doubtful.

The Americans, of course, placed a very higher premium on the contribution of the Chinese army to the prosecution of the war. They were always more impressed by Chiang's promises, even if these rarely if ever translated into vigorous action. Roosevelt pretty much told Churchill that Chiang's needs took precedence over Britain's in the Far East. When Churchill requested heavy bombers be sent to India in April 1942. Roosevelt replied briefly: 'In my opinion it would be very unwise to curtail the planes now *en route* to General Stilwell. I have received from the Generalissimo a very despondent message and I feel that considerations of high policy call for aviation help to the Burma area immediately as the position of the Chinese must be sustained.'[66]

After Midway, the British Chiefs of Staff, while still not expecting much from China in the way of meaningful combat contributions, were of the opinion that Japan would now cease to expand eastward. Instead, they thought; 'Japan's aim will be to consolidate her position in the Pacific, which involves the final liquidation of the China Incident and the capture of the Maritime Provinces.'[67]

Even if that were so, the Allied strategy should continue to be 'Germany first'. 'By attacking Japan first we should give direct encouragement to China, but, provided we continue to give China some support, there is no reason to pre-suppose a Chinese collapse while we direct our main effort to the defeat of Germany'. They continued: 'Important though China is as an ally in the war against Japan, Russia is a far more important factor in the war against Germany. Moreover, when we have defeated Germany, Russia might subsequently become a very important factor in the defeat of Japan, whereas China could never

help us in the war against Germany'. There was one reason to keep China in the war. 'Chinese offensive power is small, but the potential value of her air bases and ports for our ultimate offensive against Japanese sea communications is very considerable. Her continuance in the war must be a major aim of Allied policy.'

Nonetheless the defence of the Middle East and India was considered by the British to be second in importance only to the defence of the United Kingdom herself.

> Until we reopen the Mediterranean, the Middle East and India depend for their maintenance on the adequate protection of our Indian Ocean communications and the security of the Abadan oil. A Japanese occupation of India would sever our communications with China, deprive us of the man-power and growing productive capacity of the Indian continent and seriously threaten the Middle East. It is vitally important to prevent the Germans and the Japanese joining hands.

The latter point is an acknowledgement that the Allies still considered this a threat, albeit a reduced one. Which leads us to the final question, did the Axis ever have a firm plan called Operation Orient to bring this much discussed link to fruition?

The Chimera of Operation Orient – Linking Hands?

On 22 October 1941, the Foreign Office[68] was reporting on a certain Captain Wiedemann.[69] He was recorded as being the Head of *Orientgruppe,* a German military espionage network, and specialized in sabotage and terrorism; he was liberally bankrolled by secret funds to further his work. Although officially appointed to Tientsin, this was merely a cover and he was sent out to direct the existing espionage-

66. Telegram, For Hopkins for the Former Naval Person from the President. Message No. 133.
67. Chiefs of Staff Committee, American-British Strategy.
68. Foreign Office Summary, Enemy Activity. Report No. 70 (National Archives FO371/31831).
69. *Hauptman* Fritz Wiedemann (1891–1970). Formerly Hitler's superior officer in Bavarian Regiment 16, met again in 1921 at a regimental reunion and was offered a position in SA [Sturmabteilung] by Hitler, but rejected it and became a dairy farmer. Through Hitler's former Top Sergeant, Max Amann, he got a position as aide to Rudolf Hess and joined the Nazi party. In 1935 became an aide to Hitler, becoming *Brigadeführer* NSKK [Nationalsozialistiches Kraftfahkorps] and by 1938 a Reichstag member. Used for foreign affairs, including the incorporation of Austria into the Reich and

with the British Lord Halifax in London, expressed admiration for America. Apparently had a falling out with Hitler in 1939; the latter accusing him of leaking sensitive information. Hitler is alleged to have said, 'You always said you wanted to be the Consul General in San Francisco; you've got your wish!' Had to leave America when Germany closed its consulates in June 1941, and finally ended up at Tientsin. He turned up in America again in October 1945 escorted from Tientsin by Lieutenant Guy Martin, and was sent to Washington DC to 'assist' the American authorities. *Time* magazine at that date had no hesitation in calling him a 'spy extraordinary for the Third Reich', but at Nuremberg he was dismissed without charge and returned to dairy farming. He kept his own counsel on whatever secrets he knew until his death in January 1970.

Gestapo organization in the Far East.[70] This latter assumption was reinforced by the fact that when he made an abortive attempt to sail direct for the Far East from San Francisco aboard the Japanese freighter *Yawata Maru* in July, there was no mention of any appointment to Tientsin. Under Widemann's control were two other major agents, Meisinger[71], based in Shanghai, and Hueber[72], in Bangkok. His arrival in the Far East was considered of major importance.

The main objective of *Orientgruppe* was to subvert Burma and India, and the organization was intended to act as the advance guard of a Far Eastern pincer movement designed to threaten the British Raj, with the other pincer being a German military advance into western Asia.[73] According to a Foreign Office informant 'who has sometimes proved reliable', Hitler attached 'great importance' to India.

The ambivalent attitude Hitler displayed towards his ally, was reciprocated by the Japanese themselves and further examples of this strange alliance abound.[74]

Japan's Ambitions

Japan was awash with fanatics in the 1930s, some of whom were associated with the Japanese secret service (*Kempei Tai*), while others obsessions owed allegiance to the army or navy factions[75] which were almost at war with each other over policy and resources: Other nationalist groups and cells formed and re-formed, often in bitter opposition to the governments of the day, but always with an expansionist agenda and the glorification of a 'great Japanese destiny' as their ultimate goal. These fanatics were not appeased by the war in the Pacific, even though it had proved successful beyond their wildest dreams; success huge as it was, only led to even wilder schemes of conquest in such minds. They would always support expansion, but the argument was mainly about the direction, north, toward Mongolia or south. The sudden opening of the doorway to India and beyond was alluring enough, but had appeared out of the blue. The door seemed wide open during a brief period in the spring of 1942, but Japan's forces were already at the ends of very long supply chains, had been fighting continually for six months and were just about at the natural end of their initial onslaught. Then there were the weather conditions in Assam and northern Burma to contend with; arrows drawn on maps in Tokyo in 1942, and on numerous amateur strategist web sites in 2007, look deceptively simple if one has not tried to fight in the middle of a monsoon! Nonetheless a dizzy array of shadowy figures and

70. Foreign Office Summary, Enemy Activity: Report No.66 para 1.
71. Colonel Josef Albert Meisinger (1889–1947), SS-*Standartenführer*, known as the 'Butcher of Warsaw' for his anti-Jewish activities. Tried to persuade the Japanese to exterminate the estimated 20,000 Jewish refugees that had found refuge in Shanghai from Europe. The Japanese refused to co-operate in any killings, but did place all Jews into the Hongkou district of the city as a 'designated area'. Meisinger served as liaison officer of the SD [Sicherheitsdienst] with the Japanese secret service in Tokyo and Yokohama. Arrested, tried and executed in Warsaw.
72. *Brigadeführer und Generalmajor der Polizei* in Munich before the war, Franz Josef Huber, former *Gestapochef* of Vienna, responsible for the death of many Hungarian Jews. He was of special interest after the war to the US secret service due to his vast store of knowledge and was preferentially treated during three and a half years in an American internment camp. At Nuremberg Huber received a light sentence, one year's probation and a 500 DM fine.
73. A useful source of information, which gives glimpses into German thinking at this period, is the von Rhoden collection 1911–47. *Generalmajor* Hans-Detleff Herhudt von Rhoden was head of the Historical Division (*8. Abteilung*), General Staff, Air Force High Command and was preparing an official history of the *Luftwaffe* during World War II for which he began to assemble documents, memoirs and official papers. After the war the USSTAF [United States Strategic Air Force] directed him to continue his work and complete a history assisted by other former *Luftwaffe* officers. These are on microfilm at the National Archives and Records Administration, Washington DC, Ref. T-971, with five reels nos. 65, 68–70 and 72 being available. Series 4407 contains a group on the 1941 situation in the Far East, including the war potential of Japan; propaganda pressure by the United States; the 'war of nerves' between Japan and the United States; and the enlargement of the US Military Mission to China. 4376/2810 dated 5 April 1941, *Kurze Auslandsnachrichten* N4. 55 contains Intelligence information regarding US efforts to supply war material to, among other places, British dependencies and British military interests in the Far East, as reported by the German military attaché in Washington DC. 4376/181 contains a report from the German Foreign Security Office of the OKW (Armed Forces High Command), concerning the visit of Japanese Foreign Minister Matsuoka to Germany on 10 April 1941, and a report from the Military Attaché in Tokyo concerning the possibilities of US involvement in a war between Germany and the USSR.
74. For further examples see Johanna Menzel Meskill, *Hitler and Japan: The Hollow Alliance*, Burkhart Mueller-Hillebrand, *German and Its Allies in World War II: A Record of Axis Collaboration Problems*, and Ernst L. Presseisen, *Germany and Japan: A Study in Totalitarian Diplomacy 1933-1941*.
75. The *Kaigun Kyookai* (Navy League) and the *Hoirusha Kai* (Military Servicemen's League) were respectable fronts for these two secret groups and were under active surveillance by the FBI.

groups would have given their wholehearted approval to any practical equivalent of an Operation Orient.

Extremist elements within the Japanese Kwantung Army, an IJA force based at Hsinking, on the Kwantung Peninsular Leased Territory, were involved with plans to establish a puppet state in eastern provinces of the USSR, in much the same way as they had turned Manchuria into Manchukuo in 1932. There they had installed the former Chinese Emperor Pu Yi as Emperor Kangde, in order to give superficial credence to the claim of 'independence'. But Manchukuo was a mere vassal state following the Tokyo line on everything, like joining the Anti-Comintern Pact on 16 January 1939. Following the Hakko Ichiu principle, (the slogan 'eight corners of the world' adopted by the expansionist groups) in the confusion following the Bolshevik uprising in 1917 Japanese troops joined the 'interventionist' force but went further in seeking to establish a so-called 'Republic of Littoral' with Vladivostok as its capital. The idea of an anti-Communist buffer state was also attractive to many of the former Allies, and even some local Russians, but eventually came to naught.

Nonetheless, in the late 1930s the idea was kept on the back burner to await a favourable opportunity. Even the royal family was involved; Prince Chichibu, with the full knowledge of Emperor Hirohito, travelled to Manchukuo with a hidden agenda to reconnoitre the possibility of further expansion north-westward. Already established as an expert on this region was the sinister figure of Motojiro Akashi. He belonged to a shadowy organization known as The Black Dragons.[76] His main role was to establish links with Muslim organizations, which he meshed into a web that eventually stretched across the Asiatic lands, and even into Europe, with particular emphasis on an affinity with Buddhist groups. This proved useful in the conquest of Malaya and Burma and would have been invaluable had the invasion of India been undertaken earlier than it was.

But the principal plotting remained the army in Manchukuo. Although, in principle, the Manchu Secret Service reported to the Kangde Emperor, as in everything else they were controlled by the Kwantung Army. Prominent among these was Jinzo Nomoto, an army intelligence officer with the Mongolian section in Manchukuo, who also visited Sinkiang and Tibet in 1939.[77]

Therefore between December 1941 and January 1942, with the Soviet Union seemingly on the verge of collapse, a similar idea again began to be touted in some Japanese circles, mainly among the hotheads of the Kwantung Army. They saw the establishment of such a 'bulwark state' as a logical move, as it would extend Japanese power and influence north-westward and seal off their already extensive mainland conquests from Communist infiltration. Using the same excuse as in 1918, that they would bring order out of the chaos of the Soviet collapse under the tracks of the German Panzers, this scheme had numerous other advantages to Japan. For a start it would have been a 'walk over', the bulk of the Soviet troops, certainly the finest, having been sacrificed far to the west defending Moscow. A victory would erase the bitter memories of the two vicious border clashes at Changkufeng in July and August 1938, and at Nomonhan between May and August 1939, when the Japanese had been worsted, especially in the air.[78]

Other benefits would include the elimination of the Soviet submarine base being built at Posyeta Bay close to the borders of Korea and Manchukuo. The plan would block any attempt by America to supply the Soviets and keep them fighting, and would eliminate any possibility of the USA establishing bomber bases around Vladivostok from which to attack Tokyo and other strategic sites in mainland Japan. The new territory would give the Japanese army yet another forward base from which to continue their encroachment westward, and they already had their eye on western Siberia and Outer Mongolia. These vast open spaces could be settled and colonized by the overspill of Japan's ever-booming population, and provide vast new mineral resources for her industry to exploit.

Those conspirators involved in drawing up these

---

76. Founded by Ryohei Uchida as long ago as the late nineteenth century as the innocuous sounding Amur River Society (*Kokuruy-kai*) this was an ultra-nationalist spying, intelligence gathering and subversion group, The Black Dragons had as their head Mitsuru Toyama, who worked for the Japanese secret service and included Kinoaki Matsuo, who was also an intelligence officer. Their former leader, who steered the group's intelligence-gathering activities, was none other than Koki Hirota, a foreign minister in an earlier government, who had the ear of the head of the army Hideki Tojo himself. The group established fifth column units ('wave-men') in China to undermine the Chinese Government, and in preparation for expansion had also set up similar groups in the Dutch East Indies, the Philippines and British India. From 1940 onward subsidiary spying groups known as the *Soshi* ('brave knights') were established in the USA, Canada, South America (especially Brazil with its large numbers of Japanese emigrants) and Morocco. They were monitored by US Navy Intelligence under Lieutenant-Commander K. D. Ringle, among others. See Violet Sweet Haven, *Gentlemen of Japan: A Study in Rapist Diplomacy*. See also Richard Storry, *Double Patriots: Study of Japanese Nationalism,* and Richard Deacon, *Kempei Tai: A History of the Japanese Secret Service*.

77. For his autobiography see Jinzo Nomoto, *Tibet Senko 1939*.

78. For details of the air fighting see Peter C. Smith, *Into the Assault*.

ambitious plans for Soviet Siberia had ready-made anti-Soviet allies in the forms of General Kislistin, one of the few remaining White Russian leaders, and Konstantin Vladimirovich Rodzaevsky, the leader of the Russian Fascist Party.[79] The Japanese could safely install such worthies as nominal rulers, knowing they would toe the line under the blanket of the Great East Asia Co-Prosperity Sphere concept, while, behind the scenes, the Japanese army would provide the physical guarantee of compliance. Reputedly the boundaries of this new 'Far East Republic'[80] would encompass the Amur *Oblast*, the Khabarovsk Krai, the Chita *Oblast* and the Primorsky Krai, and again the capital was to be Vladivostok or Khabarovsk, while the Japanese would annex North Sakhalin Oblast and exercise direct rule over it under the governance of Karafuto.

Despite the signing of the Soviet-Japanese non-aggression treaty, the plans for the execution of this programme called for an attack to be launched around July–August 1941, and would be triggered by the arrival of substantial *Wehrmacht* forces on the eastern bank of the Volga river. That did not occur, but the opportunity arose again the following summer. Known as the Kantouken Plan, or the *Othsu* ('B') Operation[81], the Kwantung Army was confident of success.

But all this plotting had its focus far away from the Persian Gulf and the symbolic linking of hands between the two nations claiming to be the master race.

The alliance between the Axis powers was a very different affair from that which developed between Great Britain and the United States. Although there were areas of policy on which the two English-speaking nations had huge disagreements, and although this grew more obvious as the balance shifted, with the experience of the British being steadily replaced by the dynamic industry-backed might of the United States, once a policy had been thrashed out it was more or less adhered to. It was rather different with the Axis. Italy was a lightweight and of little consequence in the overall scheme of things, other than providing Churchill with the temptation to postpone as long as possible the necessity of having to take on the main German armies in France, with the spectres of the Somme and Passchendaele World War I catastrophes still firm in the nations psyche.[82] On the American side her history led her to view the maintenance of the British Empire, from which she had fought to win her independence, with great disfavour, seeing expansion behind policies like opposing the Communist take-over of Greece, where none existed. But, generally, the two nations moved forward in remarkable harmony.

Relations between Germany and Japan were far more uncertain. Even before Japan attacked Pearl Harbor their intentions remained unknown to their German ally. Right from the start Hitler outlined what his interpretation of the Tripartite Pact meant to him, which he summarized in Directive No. 24 as 'to induce Japan as soon as possible *to take active measures in the Far East*', in order to tie down the British and divert American eyes to the Pacific. While hoping to keep the USA out of the war at this stage, Hitler made clear: 'The *seizure of Singapore* as the key British position in the Far East would mean a decisive success for the entire conduct of war of the Three Powers.'[83]

On 27 March Hitler urged Yosuke Matsuoka, the then Japanese Foreign Minister, that it was the time for Japan to strike; it was a moment 'unique in history'. A few days later he made a personal pledge to Matsuoka. 'If Japan got into a conflict with the United States, Germany on her part would take the necessary steps at once'. He repeated it so that there

---

79. Rodzaevsky, a bitter opponent of Bolshevism, had sought refuge in Kharbin in 1925 and worked his way up to leadership of the combined Fascist groups in exile in 1934. He organized a world-wide chain with similar White Russian refugees and built up party membership in Manchukuo to 12,000, adopting black shirts from Mussolini and the Swastika emblem from Hitler, while being secretly equipped with weapons by the Kwantung Army. His destiny was to lead the 'liberation' of Mother Russia from the Soviet grip. His party assisted the Russian-manned *Asano* Division, who were tasked for sabotage operations for the long-awaited invasion. He was tricked by Stalin into returning to Russia at the end of the war, promised good treatment and a job, but instead was arrested, given a summary trial and shot in Lubyanka jail. See John J. Stephan, *The Russian Fascist: Tragedy and Farce in Exile, 1925–1945*.

80. The Japanese proposal included name changes, with Amur becoming Hulun and the Primorsky region East Tartary. The renaming of many cities was also considered: Vladivostok would become Haishenwei, Nikolayevsk would become Miaoyie or Fuyiori, Chita-Ulan would become Transbaikal and Khabarovks to Bailim.

81. Stephan, *opcit*.

82. On just one day, 1 July 1916, the British had lost 20,000 men dead and 40,000 wounded in the Somme débâcle and the fighting continued for another three months with no worthwhile gain to show for it all; Passchendaele the year after, was much the same, with the cream of Britain's youth gassed, machine-gunned, blown apart by artillery, left hanging on the barbed wire of the German defences or drowned in a quagmire of mud. America, which did not enter the war until 1917 and was spared such appalling losses, and with a larger population, was distainful of the British reluctance to repeat this in 1942, before they were fully ready. They were to modify their tone somewhat after a much smaller butchers bill at Tarawa, Omaha beach and the Ardennes.

83. Emphasis in the original. Hitler, Top Secret, Basic Order No. 24, *Collaboration with Japan*, dated 5 March 1941. See H. R. Trevor-Roper (editor), *Hitler's War Directives 1939–1945*.

would be no doubt. 'Germany, as he had said, would promptly take part in case of a conflict between Japan and America.'[84] Both he and Foreign Minister Joachim von Ribbentrop kept urging Japan to seize Vladivostok and Singapore.

After such an unprecedented generous (and ultimately, fatal) offer, Hitler must have been rather peeved when, on 13 April, scant days later, Matsuoka stopping off at Moscow and the return journey to Tokyo, signed the Soviet-Japanese Neutrality Pact. This left the Japanese free to concentrate on the Pacific, but it also guaranteed that the Soviet Union would be left free to concentrate her forces on her western borders should the long-expected (and, unknown to the Japanese, already initiated) German attack materialize.

Hitler's long-term intentions, once the Soviet Union had been eliminated, were made clear on 11 June 1941. But, yet again, there was no mention of an Operation Orient. Instead the *Fuehrer* spoke only of the struggle against British positions in the Mediterranean and in West Asia, with 'converging attacks launched from Libya through Egypt, from Bulgaria through Turkey, and *in certain circumstances*[85] also from Transcaucasia through Iran.'[86] This was elaborated upon as a German operation from Bulgaria through Turkey, the aim being attacking the British position on the Suez Canal from the East also'. Not a mention of his Japanese ally. Again, the move against Iraq was to be a *major German*[87] initiative, exploiting the Arab Freedom Movement to be sure, but not involving Japan.

Of course, once Operation Barbarossa had commenced every effort was made to persuade the Japanese to renege on the neutrality treaty with Moscow and take advantage of the situation. Even the obtuse Matsuoka Yosuke, having had to admit to his superiors in Tokyo that, notwithstanding Ribbentrop's urgings, he had totally misread German intentions, now performed a remarkably *volte face* and asked that Japan immediately join in the attack on the Soviet Union. Such a 180-degree turn was so remarkable, even for a career diplomat, that one of his cabinet colleagues, unable to believe his ears, asked him to repeat that statement, which he duly did without a blush! The German ambassador General Eugen Ott, was also told by Berlin to do all he could to bring this about but despite his best efforts, the Japanese put on their inscrutable act, replying that such action would require 'profound reflec-

tion' and that although preparations were under way it would 'take more time for their completion'.[88]

But, to the Japanese, this was not the same as a link up in the Persian Gulf – quite the contrary, On 10 July Ribbentrop held out the picture of a different linking by the Axis partners. 'The natural objective still remains that we and Japan join hands on the Trans-Siberian railroad before winter starts'. But even this prospect, matching the existing secret Japanese *Othsu* Operation perfectly, failed to move Tokyo.

For a week after the German tanks rolled over the demarcation line and headed toward Moscow, the Japanese were in a ferment. Two liaison conferences were convened with representatives of the navy, the army and, the foreign ministries concerned and the Prime Minister all in attendance. They talked a great deal, but reached no conclusions. On 2 July an imperial conference took place, which finally came down on the maintenance, for the time being at least, of the *status quo*. Instead, the 'south first' men had their way, with the occupation of French Indo-China pencilled in as a preliminary and, secretly, the mobilization of a million reservists and fresh conscripts so that, whichever way they finally decided to jump, they would have the manpower to carry the plan through.

The British, commenting on the change of government in Japan that October, were wary. 'The German reaction to the new Government has so far been somewhat cautious,' they recorded. But they continued: 'At the same time there is no reason to believe that the change of Cabinet will interrupt the close cooperation between Japan and her Axis Allies'. They cited the growth of German secret organizations in Japan and occupied China and intensified liaison between the Japanese naval authorities and the Axis naval attachés as examples of this. On how this would affect the Soviet Union it was noted: 'One of the most notable factors in the new Government is the reappearance of the Manchurian totalitarian economists, Kishi and Hoshino, who are frank admirers of the German system, and the elimination of Baron Hiranuma's group, who were opposed to the introduction of non-Japanese totalitarian ideas, whether Communist or Nazi.'[89]

When the initial impetus of the German invasion of Russia had slowed down, thoughts in the Third Reich began to turn even more to a more active participation from their main ally. On 29 November 1941, at a meeting in which Ribbentrop enquired how the negotiations between

84. Paul Schmidt, *Statist auf diplomatischer Buehne 1923-45*.
85. My italics.
86. Hitler, Top Secret, Basic Order No. 32, *Preparations for the period after 'Barbarossa'*, dated 11 June1941. See H. R. Trevor-Roper (editor), *Hitler's War Directives 1939-1945*.
87. My italics.
88. William L. Shirer, *The Rise and Fall of the Third Reich: A History of Nazi Germany*, gives many examples of this urging, including Ribbentrop' s exhortations.
89. Foreign Office Summary, *Enemy Activity*. Report No. 70.

Japan and the United States were proceeding, and was told nothing whatsoever, advised the new Japanese ambassador in Berlin, General Hiroshi Oshima that Japan would lose the chance of a lifetime if they failed to move.

> It is essential that Japan effect the New Order in East Asia without losing this opportunity. There never has been and probably never will be a time when closer co-operation under the Tripartite Pact is so important. If Japan hesitates at this time and Germany goes ahead and establishes her European New Order, all the military might of Britain and the United States will be concentrated against Japan.[90]

He told the startled Oshima that, regardless of his earlier query, Berlin had a pretty shrewd idea of how the negotiations between Tokyo and Washington DC were heading.

> We have received advice to the effect that there is practically no hope of the Japanese-United States negotiations being concluded successfully, because of the fact that the United States is putting up a stiff front.
>
> If this is indeed the fact of the case, and if Japan reaches a decision to fight Britain and the United States, I am confident that that will not only be to the interest of Germany and Japan jointly, but would bring about favourable results for Japan herself.

Oshima could only repeat that he could 'make no definite statement, as I am not aware of any concrete intentions of Japan'.

Ribbentrop then indicated that the defeat of Britain would result in the division of her empire between Germany, the United States and Japan, although Germany was not much interested in the African colonies, which could be allocated to Italy. Germany was more interested in controlling European Russia. He also again threw in the *Fuehrer*'s earlier unilateral offer, which probably took Oshima's breath away. 'Should Japan become engaged in a war against the United States, Germany, of course, would join the war immediately. There is absolutely no possibility of Germany's entering into a separate peace with the United States under such circumstances. The *Fuehrer* is determined on that point.'

Actually, on this point, Hitler was to prove as good as his word. Although he was under no obligation to declare war on the United States, he readily did so on 11 December. If by so doing he hoped that Japan would similarly make a gesture of solidarity and tackle the rear of the Soviet Union, he was to be deeply disappointed. No such commitment was ever made. Hitler's one-sided gesture also got President Roosevelt off the hook with his many opponents in Washington and in the American press[91], for there had been no legitimate reason for the United States to declare war on Germany and Italy because of Pearl Harbor. However, that was the high point for the German-Japanese relations, and from then on each pursued their own agenda.

Carl Boyd had it exactly right when he wrote that 'the disharmony in the German-Japanese alliance derived from each power's refusal to subordinate selfish private goals to the common end'.

That is not to say that, following the unexpectedly tough Soviet resistance and the reverses of the winter of 1941/2, Germany did not make repeated efforts to get Japan to enter the lists against her. Hitler had wanted Japan to take Singapore, and by February 1942 she had done so, but now Hitler seemed almost to rue the victory he had urged for so long. When Ribbentrop drafted a communiqué celebrating this victory, Hitler tore it in half. It was, after all, an Oriental nation that had humiliated an Occidental one, and one for which Hitler, despite everything, still had the greatest respect. He told his puzzled minister, 'Who knows, in the future the Yellow Peril may well be the biggest one for us.'

Such an attitude hardly equates with the wholehearted co-operation assumed by post-war proponents of an 'Orient' type fusing of aims. It was still the question of taking the Soviet Union in the rear that occupied German thoughts

---

90. This statement was dutifully transmitted word for word by Oshima to his superiors in Tokyo, and, like everything else sent via that, route, duly read by the US Army Signals Intelligence Service (SIS) which, in 1940, had cracked the Japanese diplomatic codes enciphered by the Purple coding machine, (the resulting transcripts were known as Magic), so that within a few days, Hitler's inner-most confidences were in the hands of President Roosevelt, General George C. Marshall, and Chief of the Military Intelligence Service of the War Department General Staff, Brigadier-General Carter W. Clarke. This unique insight into the mind of the enemy was made even more valuable because Oshima himself was an expansionist, and continually urged Tokyo to join in the attack on Russia, that is of course, until the Stalingrad defeat opened his eyes to German military limitations. Of the 115,000 translated sheets thus acquired, which are held in Record Group 457 in the National Archives and Records Administration faculty in Washington D. C, some 2,000 of the most important and most revealing, were presented in book form by Carl Boyd, *Hitler's Japanese Confidant: General Oshima Hiroshi and MAGIC Intelligence,* 1941–1945.

91. Just how isolated President Roosevelt was during 1940–1 and how virulent the hatred of the press barons, who were almost all Isolationists and indeed, violently anti-British, is recorded in David Brinkley, *Washington Goes to War.*

in the spring of 1942. The war could only be won in the east as far as the Fuehrer was concerned. But the Japanese had their own ideas. Japan stalled, and kept on stalling. They never revealed to their closest ally the existence of the Kantouken Plan.

In July 1942, the German General Staff recorded that they knew nothing whatsoever of Japan's future intentions. In fact, in the aftermath of Midway, Japan had set her face even more resolutely against intervention in Russia, instructing the hawkish Ambassador Oshima to inform Ribbentrop, that:

> The Japanese Government recognises absolutely the danger which threatens from Russia and completely understands the desire of its German ally that Japan on her part will also enter the war against Russia. However, it is not possible for the Japanese Government, considering the present war situation, to enter into the war. It is rather of the conviction that it would be in the common interest not to start the war against Russia now. On the other hand, the Japanese Government would never disregard the Russian question.[92]

The disappointed German Foreign Minister could only respond with yet another warning about missing a moment of opportunity, stating that 'it would be more correct that all the powers, allied in the Three Power Pact, should combine their forces to defeat not just England and America, but also Russia, together. It is not good when one part must fight alone'.

We have seen how Hitler's concepts of racial superiority coloured his feelings toward his Japanese ally. He is reputed to have stated after the fall of Singapore that he would have 'gladly sent the British twenty divisions to help throw back the yellow men'.[93] For an example of how the Japanese themselves felt about their Axis partner of we can turn, incongruously, to the tranquillity of neutral Switzerland. On 13 July 1942, with Midway fought, Eric G. Cable of the British Consulate-General in Zurich, sent a letter to J. G. Lomax, at the British Legation in Berne. He revealed that 'an acquaintance' had dined with a member of the Yokohama Specie Bank, normally based in Berlin, but who was visiting Zurich as they were liquidating the Hong Kong

and Shanghai Banking Corporation and the Chartered Bank, spoils of the Japanese conquest of Hong Kong. A fluent German speaker, the Japanese banker spoke in English and volunteered a great deal of (possibly planted but seemingly genuine) information on German-Japanese relations.

'The Japanese hate the Germans and regret the necessity, as they put it, of fighting on their side against the Anglo-Saxon races. They fear the German competition much more than the Anglo-Saxon. Similarly, the Germans dislike the Japanese'. He also stated his view that Germany could not win, but he was entirely convinced that Japan would, 'because they control the Pacific absolutely'. That a knowledgeable and intelligent Japanese businessman could still believe that after the Midway catastrophe only shows just how much the true scale of Japan's defeat had been hidden from her people. He added that the Japanese 'have no intention of going beyond their present conquests, and if Germany wants to join up with the Japanese forces it is up to the Germans to do so'. The Japanese, he claimed 'have 900,000 men in the Southern Pacific and a million in China.' Finally, he averred, 'Japan will not attack Russia if the latter does not attack Japan, and he would not be surprised if one day the Japanese and Russians went together against Germany'.[94]

Such a view was surely extreme, and we know that many, like Oshima, who was once described as 'being more Nazi than the Nazis' had a very different view; nonetheless at least some of the expressed opinions expressed were widely held in Japan. Officially, of course, all was perfect harmony, and with the war going so well for the Axis, tension was low. All the same, repeated German requests for help against the Soviets continued to be politely ignored.

On 5 August 1942, the Japanese advised Major-General Alfred Jodl, German Chief of Operations when he pursued the same old German line, 'You must not demand too much of Japan'.[95] Ribbentrop would continue to repeat this request, with slight variations, and with increasing desperation, as the war on the Eastern Front deteriorated steadily, but always in vain. On 18 April 1943, he made it again, as Oshima diligently reported. 'The *Reichminister* for Foreign Affairs then stressed again that without any doubt this year presented the most favourable opportunity for Japan, if she felt strong enough and had sufficient anti-tank weapons at

92. Transcripts quoted as evidence for the Prosecution at the Trial of German Major War Criminals Sitting at Nuremberg, Germany, 7 January to 19 February 1946. Thirtieth Day, Wednesday 9 January 1946. Document 2911-PS

93. L. Rees, *The Nazis: A Warning from History*.

94. Eric G. Cable to J. G. Lomax dated 13 July 1942 (EGC/LVB.

A. 1431). Foreign Office Summary, *Enemy Activity*. Report No. 70 (National Archives FO371/31831).

95. OKW record of Joint German-Japanese staff talks, contained in *German Naval War Diary, and Annexes*, Part C, Vol. XV. Microfilmed in the PG- series and held by Bundesarchiv, Freiburg, Germany.

her disposal, to attack Russia, who certainly would never again be as weak as she is at the moment.'[96] By that date, of course, not just Midway but Stalingrad had been fought, and even the pro-Nazi Ambassador was having second thoughts.

Although the Americans had itemized the Japanese losses at Midway very accurately, and the Chinese had confirmed them, the Japanese themselves were not told very much at all, other than that the Aleutians had been occupied. The Japanese were equally coy when it came to informing their closest ally. Admiral Paul Wenneker, the German Naval Attaché in Tokyo for example, was later to complain to his post-war American interrogators that he did not receive the full story on how serious the losses to the IJN had been at Midway until 1943–4.[97] However, he knew enough to advise Berlin at the end of December 1942 that the losses at Midway, coupled with those in the subsequent Solomons campaign, were heavy. He made the point that these casualties were 'of grave consequence' to German hopes, rendering as they did any future Japanese naval involvement in the Indian Ocean highly unlikely – indeed, such operations were 'not even considered'.[98]

The recurring theme of many a study on this period of the war is that the Axis had the chance to finish the war in April 1942, and with a little more boldness could have done so, as the Allies were on the ropes. A typical example is H. P. Willmott, whose fine book contains a chapter entitled 'The Japanese Options, Spring 1942'.

As it was, news of the attack on Ceylon for a time threw the British war cabinet into utter dismay: it was believed that this indeed could be the beginning of the end. Wavell[99], writing of experiences that included service as Viceroy, referred to this raid as the supreme crisis of the war for India. The fact that the crisis passed and was not the beginning of the end can be attributed not to successful British resistance but to the enemy's choice not to press matters to a conclusion.[100]

But that presupposes that the Japanese actually had a plan ('Orient' perchance?), and the resources to follow up the Nagumo raid. The closest they got to such a plan was the so-called Kuroshima, or 'Western' strategy, devised by Kameto Kuroshima, but it was never put into practice[101]. It is frequently claimed that the Nagumo raid into the Indian Ocean was part of this scheme, but this was just not true. The plain and simple fact was that for the navy, the raid by the 1st *Kidō Butai* into the Indian Ocean was never meant to be more than just that, a sortie to keep the British quiet. They hoped to bring the remnants of the Royal Navy in the east to battle and destroy them but, failing that, they neutralized British naval power so effectively that it was to be two years before it could reassemble in sufficient force to even make light hit-and-run raids of its own. For the Japanese army, pushing up from Rangoon to the borders of India, triumphant but fully extended, the cutting of the war supply links from India to China was their goal, the cutting of the

---

96. *Ibid.* Document 2929-PS.

97. Admiral Wenneker, 'Report about My Stay in Japan', dated 20 March 1946, National Archives and Records Administration, Washington DC, RG 38/112, Headquarters 441st Counter intelligence Corps Detachment, Special Operations Section. Admiral Paul Wenneker (1890–1979) was twice German Naval Attaché, Tokyo (1933–7 and 1940–5).

98. *Ibid.*

99. Field Marshal Sir Archibald Percival Wavell, 1st Earl Wavell, (1883–1950). Fought in the Boer War with the Black Watch and in India. During World War I he was wounded at Ypres, and lost one eye. He served in Palestine and then took over Middle East Command, defeating a vastly superior Italian army with ease in 1940–1. He fell out of favour with Churchill after protesting when the latter had denuded his victorious command in North Africa and sent half his troops into the Greece and Crete disasters. He served as C-in-C India, then of the ABDA Command and became what is acknowledged as the best Viceroy and Governor-General of India. He knew the sub-continent and its people well and was sympathetic to their aspirations. He remained there until his replacement in 1947 by Lord Louis Mountbatten.

100. H. P. Willmott, *Empires in the Balance: Japanese and Allied Pacific Strategies to April 1942*, Orbis, London, 1982.

101. Of course there were *some* starry-eyed Japanese patriots who envisaged far wider horizons! In December 1941, the Japanese Ministry of War, Research Section in Tokyo produced the grandiose *Land Disposal Plan in the Greater East Asia Co-Prosperity Sphere* document. (*International Military Tribunal for the Far East*, Exhibit 1334, transcript pp 11969-11973). This dream of dreams had Japanese Governor-Generals running Alaska (as far south as Washington State), Australia, New Zealand, Ceylon, Central American (although excluding Mexico apparently) with compliant Monarchies being set up in Burma, Malaya and certain states of French Indo-China). For further details see Richard Storry, *The Double Patriots: A Study of Japanese Nationalism*, Greenwood Press, Westport, CT, 1957, Appendix II, pps 317-319. Perhaps the ultimate 'alternative history' was the first, the novel by Philip K Dick, *The Man the High Castle,* Victor Gollancz Ltd, London, 1975. It is a subtly-crafted and beautifully-written book which envisages an America where the Axis have triumphed, divided into three strips, an eastern, run by Japan, a western ruled by Nazi Germany and a neutral strip in the centre. It is science fiction at its best, and that is where the whole 'Orient' concept should be now laid to rest, as a work of science fiction.

Allied supply links to Russia via the Persian Gulf a remote dream impossible for them to realize in April 1942.

And yet TV programmes like *The Samurai and the Swastika* continue to advance the hypothesis that Operation Orient was hard fact. No sources are given, however; there is just speculation with odd bits of film almost incoherently strung together. Similarly web sites now abound promoting this thesis. We can just take one as an example of them all. 'Hitler appears to have conceived an alliance with the Japanese as a way of dividing the world in what he called Operation Orient. Prime Minister [*sic*] Ribbentrop became a major proponent of Operation Orient predictable as it was conceived by Hitler'. The site then totally contradicts itself and states that 'Operation Orient was largely a figment of Hitler's active imagination'.[102] So one can take one's pick. Finally there are the 'alternative history' adherents; to them any chance that 'Orient' might have existed is manna from heaven. Again, one example more than suffices to illustrate the inanities in them all. Peter G. Tsouras[103] gets straight off the mark in his chapter entitled 'Operation ORIENT: Joint Axis Strategy' in the book *The Hitler Options*.[104] He bases his theory squarely on the interception of the diplomatic traffic of Lieutenant-General Hiroshi Oshima . Tsouras claimed: 'Oshima's traffic to Tokyo harped on a German-Japanese plan, codenamed ORIENT, to link up somewhere in India. Its genesis was in Hitler's Draft Directive 32'. Later he talks of Oshima's 'chatter about ORIENT'. Tsouras even kindly provides us with a two-page map of how the plan was to be implemented.

Now, as we have already seen, Directive 32 made absolutely no mention whatsoever of a link-up between Germany and Japan; in fact Japan was not even mentioned, and there was certainly no reference to 'Orient'. Strangely enough also, the definitive work on Oshima's communications, which were being read by American intelligence, based entirely upon the Magic intercepts, also has no reference whatsoever to any Operation Orient.[105] The closest that Oshima appeared to come was to express in March the (forlorn as it turned out) 'hope that Japan can plan to co-operate in carrying out' such a scheme.

Yet the many exponents of the existence of 'Orient' continue to espouse it as an actual plan. Most serious historians do not share that view. David Irving, whose knowledge of the Third Reich is unrivalled, said of the 'Orient' plan, 'I have no idea what that is or was.'[106] On the Japanese side the very respected historian Rear Admiral Yōichi Hirama, co-author of the definitive study, *Reluctant Allies*[107], made no mention of an operation of that name. I asked him why not and he replied, 'I do not understand the meaning of Operation Orient.[108] I have never heard of such an operation'. He asked me what was thought to be the aim of such an operation, and when I told him what was alleged, he gave me his view of why no such operation was ever put in place.[109]

Pearl Harbor gave the German planners an entirely new chance: to try to co-ordinate military operations in Europe with those of Japan in the direction of the Indian Ocean. The Initiative rested with the German Naval Staff (SKL), which became the chief advocate of German-Japanese co-operation, since neither Hitler nor the OKW could disentangle themselves from the Russian labyrinth. As Japan wanted to play the role of a mediator for the conclusion of a separate peace between Germany and Russia, she did not therefore abandon their earlier plan of encouraging the Soviets towards the Persian Gulf and India.

Tokyo was aware of its weak bargaining position in the Indian question and went on inviting Berlin and Rome to co-sponsor a declaration of Indian independence in early April 1942.

Earlier, on 10 January, the Liaison Conference, which dealt with the Indian question for the first time

---

102. *War and social upheaval: World War II – Axis German and Japanese strategic cooperation.*
103. Lieutenant-Colonel Peter G. Tsouras, US Army Reserve. Analyst with US Army Intelligence and Threat Analysis Center, Washington D.C. and historian, (*Disaster at D-Day: The German Defeat of the Allies, June 1944; Gettysburg: An Alternate History* etc.) His imagined scenario throws in the invasion and occupation of Malta, Turkey and Palestine as well for good measure! His crushing naval battle of Dondra Head is another Tsushima for Japan, with lots of hyperbole, but such speculation had all been done before, many years earlier, see Lieutenant-Commander Tota Ishimaru, IJHN, *Japan must fight Britain*, Pasternoster Library, No. XI, London, 1936. Within twelve years, however, most of Ishikaru's seemingly far-fetched predictions had come to pass; the British and Japanese Empires were no more and the USA had the world supremacy she had long felt to be her right.
104. Kenneth Macksey (Ed and contrib.), *The Hitler Options: Alternative Decisions of World War II*, Greenhill Books, London, 1998.
105. Carl Boyd, *Hitler's Japanese Confidant.*
106. David Irving to the author, e-mail dated 15 September 2005.
107. Hans-Joachim Krug et al. *Reluctant Allies: German-Japanese Naval Relations in World War II.*
108. Rear-Admiral Yōichi Hirama to the author, e-mail dated 17 December 2005.
109. Rear-Admiral Yōichi Hirama, *India in Axis Strategy*, a summary prepared for the author, 17 December 2005.

since the outbreak of the Pacific war, merely amended the draft Proposal of 15 November 1941, which stated that co-operation between India and Britain should be boycotted, and 'anti-British movement schemes strengthened according to [the] development of [the] military campaign'. Fours days later, another Liaison Conference was held which dealt with the political and propaganda aspects of granting independence to Burma and India.

After the seizure of Singapore, [planning for] an amphibious operation in the Indian Ocean area started in the second half of February. These plans were finally discussed at the joint conference between the Army and Navy sections of the Imperial General Headquarters held in March. The question of invading India, as well as the necessity of co-operation with Germany and Italy, appeared again at the Liaison Conference on 7 March 1942, but as [the] Imperial Army was fancying German victory at [the] East Front, and still toying with the idea of one day invading the Soviet Far East; but [because] above all [they were] chronically short of reserves in trained troops, they refused to participate in the naval operations against Ceylon.

With the IJA's flat refusal to take part, no such grand scheme as envisaged by those who postulate a viable 'Orient' plan could ever take place. And even if the Japanese army had changed their minds and contributed an army large enough for the task, exactly how would they have been transported, supplied and maintained?

To make anything called Operation Orient a realistic option all Axis thrusts would have had to be not just overwhelming victories, but logistical miracles. In April 1942 the *Wehrmacht* was nowhere close to even reaching the western shores of the Caspian Sea (and nor would they ever be) let alone pushing on over the Bol'shoy Kavkaz and through Iraq, Iran and Afghanistan. The distance between the Japanese army spearheads at Myitkyina and Lashio (they were not yet over the Naga Hills into Assam) and Basrah at the head of Persian Gulf where it is stated the two Axis armies were supposed to meet, was at least 2,500 miles, and not of the easiest terrain either. The Germans would have had to defeat the Soviet army and then sprint another 1,000 miles to shake hands. It seems clear that Operation Orient is no more than a modern-day revisionist's or a web-site fantasist's pipe dream.

The three Axis nations might well discuss a military

agreement in January 1942, in order to ensure operational co-operation, but the only firm decision reached was to make Longitude 70 degrees east an arbitrary operational dividing line between them. As the distinguished German and Japanese co-authors of *Reluctant Allies* pointed out[110]:

> Beyond that, there was merely talk of 'contact' and 'cooperation'. Clues as to how this could be realized were utterly lacking. This document, which deals almost exclusively with maritime warfare, proves that the IJN's interest in merely loose cooperation had remained the same as Japan entered the war.

> But it was not just the Japanese navy that showed disinterest in close cooperation; the important German posts were also unenthusiastic.

Like the British and many others, the German naval staff could clearly see the possibilities. Leutnant Rost of the SKL[111] concluded from a long situational analysis that:

> The current weakened position of England in the Middle East gives us the great historical opportunity to achieve a position with a few divisions in a reasonable amount of time, that in cooperation with Japan will lead to the collapse of the entire British key positions at the three continent junction point and holds war-deciding consequences . . . The deployment of a few divisions will greatly compensate their lack on the Eastern Front through the strategic consequences achieved, not to mention the economic advantages that become clear with the acquisition of the oil in Iraq and the future connection to the raw materials in Asia. If Germany and Japan join hands at the Indian Ocean, the final victory should not be far off.[112]

Ah yes, *if*. But how to achieve that if the Japanese did not join in? On this point, Rost is silent.

The Position of the Soviet Union

With almost the entire weight of the main German armies at their throats and fighting for their very existence in a merciless war along a 2,000 mile front line, it would be expected that the Communist dictatorship of the USSR, in the malevolent form of Marshal Josef Stalin, would feel considerable relief at the outcome of the Midway clash. Any weakening of Japanese power would, many an outside observer might

---

110. Hans-Joachim Krug, et al. *Reluctant Allies*.
111. (*Seekriegsleitung* – German Naval Staff).

112. Hans-Joachim Krug et al. *Reluctant Allies*.

think, be a bonus for Russia in that it would force the Japanese to abandon any ideas of attacking them in the rear. Strangely, this was not the case. Stalin had already withdrawn seasoned troops from his Far Eastern provinces to fight before Moscow the previous winter, throwing in these fresh divisions to tip the scales just as German offensive ground to a halt in the mud and the snow. He had not seemed nervous about denuding the east of fighting men then, and this decision had justified itself, inflicting upon the Germans the first real defeat they had suffered in the war to that date. Although this proved but a temporary reprieve, the Soviets continued to use their distant empire as an almost unending supply of fresh cannon fodder to resist the new German offensives of 1942, equally without qualms.[113]

Was this just ignorance? After all Stalin was to be lectured by Winston Churchill in August that he knew more about sea-war than Stalin did. 'Meaning that I know nothing,' was Stalin's reply according to Churchill[114], but there might have been a question mark in that sentence had it been written instead of spoken. Even so, much later in the war Stalin had apparently freely confessed to President Roosevelt that he 'disliked ships and frankly confessed he knew nothing about them or the Navy and could never understand them'.[115] Certainly, unlike in 1904 when the Russian Baltic Fleet had sailed halfway around the world to its doom at the hands of Admiral HeihachiroTogo in the Tsushima Strait, Soviet warships did not venture very far from their shores during World War II, be it in the Black Sea, Baltic or Arctic when facing the German navy.

At this period, the Soviets principally used their warships as shore bombardment vessels to support their armies ashore in attack or defence, rather than seeking battle on the open sea. Often, too, the warships were laid up in ports for weeks or months inactive, because their crews were used to supplement the army units fighting at the fronts. A typical example of this policy was shown in the Far East when, following on the German invasion of June 1941, twelve so-called naval rifle brigades were formed that autumn and sent to the Moscow front line between November and December. This left the Soviet C-in-C of their Pacific Fleet, Vice-Admiral Ivan Stepanovitch Yumashev with little in the way of manpower for his few warships, even if he had been called upon to use them.[116]

The victory at Midway was certainly reported in the Soviet Union's strictly controlled press, usually with the by-lines 'According to Reuters' or 'According to the US Naval Command'. Official despatches from New York in June, followed the then current American line and claimed that the most recent information indicated that four Japanese aircraft carriers had been sunk in the Battle off Midway Island, along with 275 Japanese aircraft aboard the carriers and most of the crews as well. Little independent analysis by Soviet naval or political pundits resulted, although between July and August 1942, brief entries in the 'Chronicles of the War' section of the magazine *Morskoy Sbornik* appeared.

On 8 June, the magazine quoted the international news agency Reuters as saying that Admiral King had declared that in the northern part of the Pacific and to the west of Midway island, the battle was proceeding and that the Japanese ships were withdrawing. Again citing King, they declared that the losses of the American fleet were 'insignificant in comparison with the losses of their opponent'. In addition to the Japanese carriers sunk the Americans were claiming that they had damaged two heavy cruisers (true) and sunk a destroyer (false). They admitted a Japanese submarine had sunk a destroyer, but there was total silence on *Yorktown*'s torpedoing. On 10 June *Morskoy Sbonik* even-handedly quoted from a Tokyo communiqué that the IJN, operating in the eastern part of the Pacific on 4 and 5 June had made a surprise attack on Dutch Harbor and all the main bases in the Aleutian Islands group. Also, that a similar assault was made on Midway, and that two American aircraft carriers had been destroyed. The Japanese admitted losing one carrier themselves which had sunk, while another had been damaged, as well as one cruiser. The August chronicle printed the official New York bulletin of 29 June stating that, in the battle near Midway,

---

113. 'Massive troop traffic' continued from the Far East almost up to 1945, when, with the fall of Berlin, Soviet troops, tanks and vehicles began to move in the opposite direction!

114. Winston Churchill, *The Second World War*, Volume IV: *The Hinge of Fate*.

115. According to Admiral Sir James Somerville who had it from the President himself at a meeting on 20 November 1944, in Washington DC. See the Somerville Papers held in Churchill Archives Centre, Churchill College, Cambridge. Also mentioned in Michael Simpson, *The Somerville Papers*, Selections from the *Private and Official Correspondence of Admiral of the Fleet Sir James Somerville, G.C.B., G.B.E., D.S.O.*

116. Interestingly, Yumashev, who became a full admiral in 1943, did not suffer career-wise from this inactivity. Indeed in 1947 he was promoted to C-in-C of the entire Soviet Navy. He lasted four years in that post before Stalin got tired of him and dismissed him as a chronic alcoholic! During one of his sober moments he managed to compose an article on the Soviet-Japanese war of 1945 for a book on the subject, but made no other contribution to history. Ivan Stephanpvitch Yumashev (1895–1972). b. Tbilsi 9 October. C-in-C Soviet Naval Forces 1947–1952. Awarded six Orders of Lenin, three Orders of Red Banner D. Leningrad 2 Sept. 1972.

four Japanese carriers had been sunk and 275 aircraft destroyed and the crews of the ships had also been lost. This continued and on 30 June the names of the four carriers were announced as *Akagi, Kaga, Soryū* and *Hiryu*, with damage claimed on 'two or three battleships, with one suffering heavy damage' (all totally untrue) and two heavy cruisers, which were named as *Mogami* and *Mikuma,* sunk, with further damage inflicted on three more heavy and one light cruiser as well as three, or maybe four, destroyers sunk (all, save the sinking of one heavy cruiser and damage to another and two destroyers, pure fabrication!). For good measure bomb and torpedo hits were claimed on four transports of which one had 'undoubtedly' sunk!

It must be emphasized that, although the Soviet Union was not at war with Japan, she was obviously pleased at the American victory. Stalin was determined to have a reckoning with Japan, but at a time to suit himself; sheer survival against Germany was his only concern in 1942![117] Nonetheless, it should also be noted that in printing the hugely exaggerated false claims, the magazine was not just spouting the usual Soviet propaganda, but merely quoting from the misleading and totally false American claims. There was no need for the Soviets to exaggerate, the Americans were at that time proving quite capable of doing that for themselves.

The most significant Soviet analysis of Midway also appeared in that same journal later when they published an article by the distinguished naval historian and strategist, Rear Admiral V. A. Belli on the events leading up to Midway and the battle itself.[118]

Having failed in its approaches toward Australian and in the Battle in the Coral Sea, the Japanese fleet has undertaken, at the beginning of June, an operation in the central part of the Pacific Ocean. This operation was developed in two directions –

against Midway and against the Aleutian Islands. The purpose of the operation to capture Midway was, should the operation prove successful, the provision of a forward base to influence the effect of the Hawaiian Islands.

He observed that:

The Japanese command, obviously, expected its air attacks to suppress the American defences and weaken their fleet and, subsequently, to enable a landing on Midway Island, with the supporting guns of their battleships and cruisers. The sailing of the Japanese fleet was discovered owing to the depth of American submarine and air reconnaissance, which led to the sortie of the American fleet from Pearl Harbor to intercept.

He then quoted the various American communiqués, and repeated the air force's mythical B-17 hits on Japanese ships. He then wrote:

At dawn on 4 June, sixteen 'sea diving bombers' [SBDs] attacked the Japanese aircraft carrier *Soryū* and eleven aircraft of the same type attacked a Japanese battleship. *Soryū* received three hits and the battleship two hits by bombs. Preceding attacks by American aircraft had forced the Japanese squadron to change plans and by the morning of the 4th they began to depart in a north-west direction. While withdrawing the Japanese squadron had to undergo combined attacks by torpedo-bombers and diving bombers. As a result of direct hits by bombs and torpedoes the aircraft carriers *Kaga* and *Akagi* had sunk, and an American submarine found the burning aircraft carrier *Soryū* which it sank with three

117. Historian and former naval officer Alexander G. Bolnykh, reinforced this view recently. 'Once more I can say that there was no connection between the war in the Pacific and Soviet war planning. Indeed, in May 1942 it was the disastrous defeat of the Soviet attack at Kharkov-Barvenkov by the Germans that dominated all thinking. So, a carrier clash somewhere in the Pacific at the beginning of June, went totally unnoticed in Moscow!' Bolynykh to the author, 29 June 2006.

118. Rear-Admiral V. A. Belli, *Morskoy Sbornik*, July 1942. Vladimir Aleksandrovich Belli (1887–1981) b. St Petersburg. Soviet naval theorist and historian and candidate of naval sciences (1940), professor (1945). Served from 1903 and joined the Soviet Navy in 1918, specializing in mine warfare and radio-telegraphy. Served with the Baltic Fleet during the civil war 1917–22 commanded the destroyer *Captain Belli* (named after one of his direct ancestors) 1918–19; later became Naval Attaché in China 1922–4). Chief of Foreign Department of RKKF [Raboche-Krestyansky Krosny Flot – Workers and Peasants Red Fleet] then Assistant to Chief of Operative Management of Staff RKKF before joining the Naval Academy as a teacher. Arrested in 1930 and condemned in 1931, rehabilitated, released and restored to the Navy Staff in November 1932. Between 1937 and 1949 Chief of Strategy Faculty. Author of many scientific works on strategy and naval operations, international law of the sea etc. Many awards including St Vladimir, St Anna and St Stanislav under the Tsar, and Lenin and Red Banner under the Soviets. See also George E. Hudson, *Soviet Naval Doctrine under Lenin and Stalin*, in *Soviet Studies*, Vol. 28, No. 1, dated January 1976.

Table 31: Distribution of Allied War Materials supplied to Soviet Union 1941-45

Gateway	Tonnage of supplies	Sea-route length in miles	%
Vladivostok	8,2000,000	4,500	46.776
Persian Gulf	4,200,000	12,000	23.956
Murmansk	4,000,000	4,600	22.812
Black Sea	680,000	4,000	3.878
Arctic Ocean	452,000	4,500+	2.578
Total	**17,532,000**	-	**100**

torpedoes. The same day the planes lifted from the aircraft carrier *Yorktown* found the Japanese aircraft carrier *Hiryū* together with battleships and supported by cruisers and torpedo boats. As a result of attacks by carrier aircraft *Hiryū* received heavy damage and on the morning of 5 June had sank.

Early in the morning of 6 June the American planes found and attacked two groups of Japanese ships consisting of cruisers and destroyers. As a result of these attacks two cruisers, *Mogami* and *Mikuma*, and one destroyer, were sunk.

While it is clear that Belli had only the vaguest idea of what really occurred, it can be seen he based his article almost totally on American press releases. After describing the loss of the destroyer *Hammann* and the damage, but nothing else, of the *Yorktown* by Japanese carrier aircraft, Belli goes on to relate the Aleutian operations, again totally falsely claiming three Japanese destroyers were sunk and a fourth damaged. He summed things up:

It is difficult to judge whether carrier actions in the north were demonstrations only, as cover for the Midway operation, and were restricted by meteorological conditions, they concluded with the occupation of Attu. Or whether, on the contrary, the main purpose of the Japanese Command was to occupy the Aleutians with Midway as an incidental feature.

He was inclined to think that Midway was the main target, 'as for a mere demonstration against Midway the Japanese would hardly have committed to such an operation such great strength. It is possible also, that the plan stipulated a decision of two *parallel* tasks and they were both covered by the same covering force'.

Of one thing he was very clear. 'In the case of Midway Island, the Japanese have suffered defeat. However, occupation of Attu, if not repulsed by the Americans, gives the Japanese a useful base for action against Alaska and against the seaways of the northern Pacific Ocean'.

As the regular supply of vital war supplies (aircraft, munitions, transport) from America was a matter of vital self-interest to the Soviet's, this Japanese move north was far more relevant to them than the victory away to the southeast at Midway. It is interesting to examine just how the bulk of these war supplies actually reached the Soviet Union. The hard-fought Arctic convoys to the northern Russian ports of Murmansk and Archangel had been commenced by the British in the summer of 1941, and had been increasingly fed by American and British war materials carried on British, American and (a few) Russian merchant ships, and fought through by the Royal Navy in the face of heavy air and naval threats. The Allies suffered heavy losses carrying out this ghastly task, with the weather almost as much an enemy as the German battleships lurking in their Norwegian fjords or their torpedo- and dive-bombers on their Norwegian airfields. Naturally this battlefield attracted huge media and historical attention.

And yet it was not the Arctic convoy route that was the main gateway of Allied supply to the Soviet Union during World War II, as Table 31 clearly indicates.

Thus it can be seen that a Japanese move against the Soviet Union in the Far East would have cut off almost half of all Allied war material supplies to Stalin; it would also have prevented Russian reinforcements moving to the defence of Moscow. On the other hand, if proponents of a western move had existed, with the risky strategy of extending Japan's already over-stretched defensive perimeter to link up with the Germans in the Persian Gulf, it would, if successful, have only achieved half (23 per cent as against 46 per cent) that effect, cutting less than a quarter of such supplies.

Tactically, Belli observed clearly that: 'as in the Coral Sea battle, the outcome of the operation was decided by aircraft from aircraft carriers'. The battleships and cruisers only contributed by providing the carriers with cover and protection. He also observed:

The last prominent feature of naval operations in the central Pacific Ocean is endurance due to the huge distances involved. Such operations are only made possible by the modern engineering developments of the fleet, the high speed and long ranges of the ships and, chiefly, are due to the engineering and combat training of naval aircraft. Such operations will be characteristic of the big spaces of the Pacific Theatre.

In truth, whatever the outcome of the battle, Stalin knew he was safe from Japanese attack because of the wealth of information confirming that fact which reached him from his numerous spies, not least of whom was the infamous Richard Sorge. There were many Soviet spies in every land, but none quite as devastatingly effective as Sorge.[119] Born at Adjikent, Baku, Azerbaijan in 1895, the son of a German mining engineer and his Russian wife, he was raised in Germany when his family returned to the Berlin suburb of Lankwitz two years later. He enlisted in the German army on outbreak of war and fought on the Eastern Front for nine months until an artillery shell damaged both legs and put him in hospital. During his stay he was converted to Marxism[120], and committed himself to the Communist cause from then on. He was left with a permanent limp and had lost three fingers so, having no use for him as a fighting soldier, the Army sent him to Berlin University to study. But here he became even more radicalized, joining the German Communist Party (KPD). After study in Kiel and Hamburg he gained a PhD in political science, but his political extremism prevented him holding a job as a teacher.

Sorge became a journalist, a form of employment he was to find the perfect cover for his life of spying. By 1924 he was living and working in the Soviet Union and even married a young Russian ballerina, Christiane Gerta. His fanatical views soon saw him enlisted by the Comintern Intelligence Division, formed to spread the Bolshevik message worldwide. He visited England in 1929 and reported on the state of the far left there, but by the end of the year had been ordered back to Germany with instructions to infiltrate the growing Nazi party, which he did.

Sorge's Soviet secret service (OGPU) masters then despatched him to China and, based in the seething International melting pot of Shanghai, he duly learnt Chinese, studied agriculture and contacted other Soviet spies, German, Chinese and Japanese. All the time his ostensible object was writing for several German newspapers and magazine, including the Nazi *Geopolitik*. So well did he maintain his dual identity that he was ordered to set up a spy ring in Japan in 1933, reaching Yokohama in September of that year. Once established he carefully avoided all contact with the Soviet Embassy, reporting direct to the secret police in Moscow, with the code-name 'Ramsay'. He also kept well clear of the banned underground Japanese Communists, but still his network grew, with another German journalist/spy, Max Klausen, and Japanese converts, Ozaki Hotsumi and yet another journalist, Miyahi Yotoku who worked on the English-language *Japanese Advertiser*.

Sorge went out of his way to establish good working relationships with the German Ambassador in Tokyo, Herbert von Dirksen, and with the German military representative, Eugen Ott. Among the Japanese officials who became his (and therefore Stalin's) unsuspecting sources of information were various Foreign Office officials and the then Prime Minister, Fumimaro Konoye. He was outstanding in ferreting out secrets while in Tokyo, and tipped his Soviet master's off to the Anti-Comintern Pact of 1936, designed to counteract what he was working so hard for. The adherence of Japan to the Axis was also flagged up in advance. He even claimed to have forewarned the Pearl Harbor attack.[121] However, dedicated as he was, this brilliant work undermined his health and alcholism was hinted at. His greatest coup was to warn Stalin of the impending German attack in June 1941, Operation Barbarossa. But Sorge's warnings were ignored, just as Churchill's had been, and all his work was in vain. Even then, Sorge was not embittered by his master's incredible decision not to act, and he continued to send in a steady flow of reports of enormous significance. Incredibly he survived the attention of the Japanese secret service for more than nine years, but no matter how brilliant a spy he was, such immunity could not last. His patronage of the notorious Alt-Heidelberg restaurant in Tokyo brought unwelcome spotlight on his activities, secret messages fell into Japanese hands and, on 14 October 1941, the game was finally up when his close Japanese associate Ozaki was arrested. Ozaki did not keep his tongue still under expert interrogation and, inevitably,

---

119. Much has been written on Sorge, the most up-to-date source is Giovanni Volpi's on-line book in preparation, *Sorge Chronology*. But also see Robert Whymant, *Stalin's Spy: Richard Sorge and the Tokyo Espionage Ring*, and the fictional account by Hans Hellmut Kirst, *Letze Karte spielt dere Tod* (published in English as *The Last Card*, Pyramid Publications, New York, 1967).

120. Although it might have helped his conversion that an uncle had been a secretary to Karl Marx himself at one time.

121. It is alleged that when the Japanese Ambassador to Moscow, reported the outbreak of war with America directly to Stalin, the latter responded, 'I myself would not know how to beat the United States in a war'. The Ambassador maintained a discreet silence, but on the way back to the Embassy he confessed aloud to himself, 'And neither do I!' I am grateful to Giovanni Volpi for this titbit. (Volpi to the author, 6 May 2006.)

Sorge's arrest followed within four days. He joined Ozaki in the Sugamo Prison. But his information continued to exert influence in Moscow even after he had been taken, and Stalin had complete confidence that his rear was safe from the Japanese for a considerable period.[122]

Of principal concern to this book is the fact that Sorge was able to assure Stalin all through the crucial summer and autumn of 1941 that the Japanese had absolutely no intention to make war on the Soviet Union to aid their Axis partner. Even after he was caught and incarcerated his information continued to influence events. Just about the last item of intelligence he sent back to Moscow before the net closed on him revealed that Japan's intentions had changed. Now, he told them, Japan *would* one day attack the Soviet Union; the trigger for the assault would be the fall of any Soviet city on the Volga River[123], for such a move would sever Russian oil supplies from the south and American and British military equipment from the Persian Gulf via Iran. So, if Sorge was right, the battle of Stalingrad was to be far more crucial to continuing Soviet resistance, than the Midway effect. If, however Japan had linked up with Germany in the Persian Gulf, that supply route would have been sealed anyway, and at far less cost to the German army. However, just like Stalin, Hitler remained a land animal and did not understand sea power. 'On land I am a hero, on the sea I am a coward,' the *Fuehrer* once admitted in a rare moment of candour.

However secure Stalin felt against active Japanese intervention, and as little as the Soviet Union appeared to be affected by the American victory at Midway, it is interesting to note that just a month later, in July 1942, Vice-Admiral Stepanovitch organised a special expedition, bringing the Flotilla Leader *Baku* and the destroyers *Razumny* and *Raz'yarenny* from the Pacific north about to the Barents Sea via the Northern Seaway. These three ships left Vladivostok on 15 July 1942.[124]

British Relief

There is no doubt that it was the British who benefited the most from the victory at Midway. Australia was desperate and glad of the victory, even New Zealand felt threatened, but the most intense pressure was on Churchill. The battle was the first piece of good news the embattle Premier, who had yet to survive a motion of censure in Parliament following the fall of Tobruk on top of so many other disasters. The relief was palpable, and found full expression in his subsequent euphoria. His speech in July 1942 reflected the feeling of a burden being lifted from his shoulders. He was generous in his praise, and, as always, had to exaggerate, the politician in him always overcoming all else.

All this improvement in the position of Australia and New Zealand and of India has been clinched by the brilliant victories gained by the United States Navy and Air Force over the Japanese in the Coral Sea and at Midway Island. No fewer than five out of the twelve Japanese regular aircraft carriers have been sunk. When the Japanese came into the Bay of Bengal at the beginning of April with five carriers we were caused great anxiety, but five are now at the bottom of the sea and the Japanese, whose resources are rigidly limited, have now begun to count their capital units on their fingers and toes. These splendid American achievements have not received the attention they deserve in this island. Superb acts of devotion were performed by the American airmen. From some of their successful attacks on the Japanese aircraft carriers one returned in nine. In others the loss was more than half, but the work was done and the balance of naval power in the Pacific has been definitely altered in our favour.[125]

---

122. Typically, Stalin repaid this outstanding loyalty with contempt. Sorge might have survived, despite his devastating work, because three times the Japanese offered to exchange him with politically sensitive prisoners of their own. But, like Judas Iscariot, Josef Stalin and his Moscow NKVD disclaimed all knowledge of him, for the omnipotent dictator could not be seen to have made a mistake in not acting on the Barbarossa warning. Therefore both Sorge and Ozaki were executed by hanging on 7 November 1944. Not until 1964, with Stalin cold in his grave, did the Soviets finally acknowledge their debt to Sorge and make him a Hero of the Soviet Union. Even his Japanese prosecutor, Mitsusada Yoshikawa, had to express admiration for his work, stating, 'In my whole life, I have never met anyone as great as he was.'

123. This was, of course, the delayed version of the long-prepared and delayed Kantouken Plan, already discussed, which Sorge had finally got some details of.

124. Their voyage west may have merely been coincidence, however, for the planning of this operation most probably commenced as early as the late spring.

125. Draft and final speech with First Lord and Director of Naval Intelligence's amendments attached (NID 0638) dated 1 July 1942, contained in ADM 199/1935 (National Archives, Kew, London). The DNI quietly pointed out that it would have been more accurate, and make an even better case, to say 'No fewer than four of the eight Japanese regular aircraft carriers and one of the five vessels which had been converted to aircraft carriers have been sunk.'

In retrospect Churchill was equally generous, stating that Midway, 'this memorable American victory', was of cardinal importance, 'not only to the United States, but to the whole Allied cause. The moral effect was tremendous and instantaneous. At one stroke the dominant position of Japan in the Pacific was reversed.'[126]

These words contrast starkly with both the pessimistic predictions of doom coming from some quarters of America before the battle, and the revisionist writings downgrading the battle so prevalent on web sites nowadays. The former preached, 'Give up, its all hopeless, why go on', the latter, 'It was not so important; with America's industrial base we would have won eventually anyway'. Both are wrong. And stupidly wrong, because they do not take into account, as Churchill did, and as we surely still should, the effect on morale at the time – not just American morale, but the morale of the whole Allied cause, and also the effect on the enemy. Americans tend to be very parochial, and many, even today, seem incapable of seeing the wider picture. Churchill took the British view, used to seeing a larger canvas and he recognized Midway for what it was a decisive turning point. Let us look at these two negative viewpoints a little more closely.

Despair Turned to Hope

A rather different viewpoint from others recorded here was expressed by the American Marxist Joseph Hansen[127], writing in May 1942, just before the Battle of Midway. His attitude was pessimistic in the extreme, and it could be briefly expressed as 'A plague on all your houses!' Contemplating the advance of the Japanese across the Pacific Hansen wrote in black despair: 'Such enormous military forces will be required to dislodge Japan, such a titanic navy and air fleet, such colossal armies, such slaughter of troops, that American economy and the American people must be strained to the breaking point'. He poured scorn on the very concept of a fight-back as defiantly espoused by General Douglas MacArthur and others.

If we leave out the alternative of revolution and colonial uprising – a spectre which Wall Street fears above all else – this means taking and holding Java, Celebes,

Sumatra, Borneo and the lesser neighbouring islands, advancing into the blazing muzzles of the giant guns on Singapore (which is now being repaired and improved by the Japanese), advancing along the coast of China, retaking Hong Kong, Canton, Shanghai etc, recapturing the Philippines, and then landing on the Japanese islands themselves. If this project is ever carried out, the western waters of the Pacific will be dyed crimson with the blood of the opposing forces.

But of course hardly any of this tortuous course proved necessary; only the Philippines subsequently featured in the Allied advance, and that was a political invasion, not a necessary one. For Hansen, like Stalin and Hitler, did not understand sea power, which could cut off victorious Japan from its new-found oil riches simply by submarines sinking all the tankers that conveyed it; one did not have to occupy the lands the oil wells stood on to blockade Japan and starve her of fuel. Nor did any Allied army have to slog its way yard by gruelling yard across south-east Asia. They just sank the enemy ships and took the island bases by-passing everything else. If one controlled the sea, as Great Britain found in Napoleonic times, the enemy could bring a whole continent to heel and march to the very gates of Moscow, it would not matter one jot! What Hansen and his fellow travellers failed to see was that control of the sea negated his dismal prognosis. But it was the completely wrong-headed views of people like Hansen, if consistently repeated in the media of the day, that the Japanese ultimately put their faith in to make Americans war-weary. As the war continued it became their only hope, however misplaced. Fortunately, in those distant days, Hansen and his ilk were a minority; regrettably today's media, especially the BBC in Great Britain, but also some newspapers and, to a lesser extent some media outlets in the USA, have become even more tentative since those distant days, which in turn makes the general public much less resolute about confronting evil.

Certainly, the victory at Midway had a galvanizing effect; a real morale-booster after months of defeats. The Allied leaders were determined; the people were resolute but getting awfully tired of always losing. The Americans had suffered six months of reverses and withdrawals, the

---

126. Winston S. Churchill, *The Second World War*, Volume IV: *The Hinge of Fate*.

127. Joseph Hansen, (1910–79) b. in Richfield, Utah and worked as secretary and bodyguard to the exiled Leon Trotzky in Mexico from 1937 until his murder by Stalin's henchman Ramón Mercader in 1940. He then returned to the United States as editor of the Socialist Workers' Party magazine *The Militant* and then the United States Secretariat of the Fourth International's *World Outlook*. His jaundice eye found expression in a series of articles, '*On The War Fronts*', the issue quoted being that of May 1942.

British had undergone two and half years of almost continuous military disasters: Poland, Norway, Denmark, Belgium, France, Yugoslavia, Greece, Crete and most of North Africa, Hong Kong, Borneo, Malaya, Singapore and Burma, finally culminating in the Indian Ocean fiasco.

So I contend that Midway cannot be judged simply on the profit and loss basis of four aircraft carriers, one heavy cruiser and many aircraft against one aircraft carrier and one destroyer, although many still do. Nor can it be dismissed with the question 'Did it matter?', a rhetorical question as insulting to those who died there as it is silly. Of course it mattered. It gave a battered and shaken nation a beacon of hope. It gave desperate allies a signal that their powerful new ally was beginning to get her act together. It proved, for the first time, that the Japanese were not invincible – their expansion could be faced up to and halted. The road back might be a long one, but not as long as the Hansens of this world predicted. Heads up once more, the American people prepared to take the first step on that road, and soon the US Marines were wading ashore at a virtually unknown island in the Solomons Group, Guadalcanal.

The True Victors of Midway

If an 'Orient' type decision was an improbable dream for the Axis in April and May 1942, then it was totally impossible from June of that year. Once the Battle of Midway had been fought, the tide had turned for the Axis powers. As George Walsh stated[128]:

> The story of how a small force of US Navy carrier-based dive-bombers changed the course of the war for the United States and its Allies, is one of the most dramatic exploits ever achieved by a small group of men in any war. It was a victory where courage and sacrifice at the lowest levels of command overcame errors made at staff levels.
>
> Above all, it was the dive-bomber that delivered a visually thrilling, high-accuracy blow against the Japanese aircraft carriers that, in the space of five short minutes saved a battle that threatened disaster and changed the course of history.

With which we can agree. Honour to the SBD aircrews.

---

128. George J. Walsh, *Worldwide Impact of The Battle of Midway*, Summary submission to the author, 19 December 2005.

Appendix One

The Japanese Charting of Enemy Action and Damage Suffered by Their Carriers at Midway (ONI translation)

Table A: *Akagi*

TIME (TOKYO TIME/DATE)	ENEMY AIRCRAFT		# OF BOMBS OR TORPS.	# HITS	CHART OF HITS	TIME OF SCUTTLING SINKINGS	PLACE	REMARKS
	TYPE	#						
5 JUNE 0410	TORP.	4	3		1 TO STAR. 2 TO PORT (1 EXPLODED AUTOMATICALLY)			3 SHOT DOWN: 2 OF OUR MEN KILLED BY STRAFING
ABOUT 0415	ATTACK	1	1		500M STAR. ASTERN			
0726	DIVE B.	3	3	3	10 M. D # 1NEAR MISS 10M TO PORT #2 HIT ELEVATIOR AMIDSHIPS #3 HIT AFT EDGE OF PORT FLIGHT DECK (FATAL HIT- SEVERAL HOLES)	0200 6 JUNE SCUTTLED	30° 30' N 178° 40'W	

Table B: *Kaga*

TIME (TOKYO TIME/DATE)	ENEMY AIRCRAFT		# OF BOMBS OR TORPS.	# HITS	CHART OF HITS	TIME OF SCUTTLING SINKINGS	PLACE	REMARKS
	TYPE	#						
5 JUNE 0530	DIVE B.	3	3	0	20 M.			
0730	DIVE B.	9	9	4	INDUCED EXPLOSIONS IN GASOLINE (OR BOMB) STORAGE ROOM CAUSED SINKING	1625 5 JUNE SUNK	30⁰ 23' N 179⁰ 17'W	9 BOMBERS SHOT DOWN

Table C: *Soryū*

TIME (TOKYO TIME/DATE)	ENEMY AIRCRAFT		# OF BOMBS OR TORPS.	# HITS	CHART OF HITS	TIME OF SCUTTLING SINKINGS	PLACE	REMARKS
	TYPE	#						
5 JUNE 0535	B-17	3	ABOUT 11	0				
0630	TORP.	17	4	0	2 NEAR TORP. TO STAR. AND AHEAD			1 TORP. SHOT DOWN (WITH FIGHTERS)
0725	DIVE B.	12		3		5 JUNE 1620	30° 42 N 178° 37W	1 BOMB. SHOT DOWN

Table D: *Hiryū*

TIME (TOKYO TIME/DATE)	ENEMY AIRCRAFT TYPE	#	# OF BOMBS OR TORPS.	# HITS	CHART OF HITS	TIME OF SCUTTLING SINKINGS	PLACE	REMARKS
5 JUNE 0407	B-26	9	9	0				1 SHOT DOWN
0411	ATTACK	4	4	0				
0412	TORP	9	9	0				
0456	LEVEL BOMB	9	9	0	• ABOUT 100 M. • ABOUT 50 M.			
0508	BOMB.	4	4	0				3 SHOT DOWN
"	FIGHT.	4	M-GUN STRAFE		• 50 M. 150 M. 50 M. • 80 M. 4 KILLED SEVERAL WOUNDED			
0512	BOMB.	6	1	0	1 NEAR MISS; 1 'SELF-EXPLODED)			4 SHOT DOWN
0713	TORP.	16	16	0	TORP.TRACKS: 3 TO STAR. 1 TO PORT 2 AHEAD 1 TO STAR.			1 TORP. AND 2 BOMB. SHOT DOWN
0730	TORP.	5	5	0	TORP.TRACKS: 3 AHEAD 2 ASTERN			2 TORP. SHOT DOWN
1443	DIVE B.	13	13	4	TORPEDOED BY *MAKIGUMO*	6 JUNE 0210 SCUTTLED	31°27'N 179°23'E	2 BOMB. SHOT DOWN

Appendix Two

Midway and The Media

Before the Pacific War the press belittled the enemy and underrated Japan's potential and abilities. In the immediate aftermath of Midway it was seen at its worst. Before the true facts were known the Army Air Corps B17s were credited with the victory, when in truth they did not score so much as a single hit over the whole three-day battle. More seriously, in many respects, the whole Allied intelligence system, the very foundation of the American victory and of future victories to come, was almost totally destroyed by the selfish indiscretion of one reporter. Since the battle the whole media – press, film and television – have consistently and repeatedly turned the facts of the battle upside down.

Consider what actually happened at the time.

Stanley Johnson[1], an Australian journalist working for the notorious *Chicago Tribune*, filed a sensational story based directly on a CincPac bulletin transmitted to all Task Force commanders on 31 May. He had been aboard the carrier *Lexington* and, when she was sunk at the Coral Sea encounter, had been among the survivors sent home aboard the USS *Barnett* (AP-11) and USS *Elliot* (DD-146); a few others took passage aboard the heavy cruiser *Chester*. While aboard he managed to sneak a look at a copy of the Japanese Order of Battle, which the *Lexington*'s XO, Commander Morton T. Seligman, with whom he shared a cabin, had copied down as a list of Japanese warships present at Midway transcribed from CincPac's signal 311221Z May 42, on blue-lined paper. Trustingly, he left it unsecured. Johnson could not resist copying it and he then, with no apparent scruples, presented it to his boss, Pat Maloney. The latter used it to concoct a headline-grabbing story

which he deliberately avoided showing to the wartime censors. This yarn was thus run on 7 June 1942, not only in the *Tribune* but in the *New York Daily News* and the *Washington Times-Herald* as well as four Mid-western newspapers simultaneously. It not only blared out that the US Navy 'had word of Jap plan to strike' but also that it 'knew Dutch Harbor was a feint'. Although Johnson and his equally unscrupulous editor attributed their source to 'reliable sources in the Navy Department', that lie was soon exposed by an internal investigation. Millions of American and Allied lives were thus put at jeopardy, let alone the course of the war, by this 'scoop' which certainly sold a few more newspapers, but had no thought or care for the consequences.[2]

The press excused their behaviour by stating that the navy had failed to insist Johnson sign a security pledge before he went aboard the *Lexington* and there was no restriction on reporting the movements of enemy ships. On this legal technicality years of painstaking Intelligence work was casually thrown aside. Thomas Buell described King as being, 'in a white fury at his headquarters while his staff frantically tried to discover the source of the leak.'[3] Attempts to 'kill' the story by Secretary of the Navy Frank Knox failed, and the *faux pas* was compounded when respected radio broadcaster and journalist Walter Winchell joined in the feeding frenzy with a story on 5 July, which proclaimed to the world that the fate of civilization had twice been saved 'by intercepted messages.'[4] The editor of the *Tribune*, which was being investigated by the Judge Advocate General, had to testify before an investigative committee but Johnson refused to reveal his source for this top-secret leak.

---

1. Johnson had served in World War I and been decorated for bravery at Gallipoli and on the Western Front, so he certainly ought to have known better than to compromise the lives of servicemen.
2. One of which was the early retirement of Seligman, whom the

Secretary of the Navy and Ernie King had barred from any further promotion forever, and who left the Navy in 1944.
3. Thomas B. Buell, *Master of Seapower: Biography of Fleet Admiral Ernest J. King*.
4. Walter Winchell, *The New York Daily Mirror*, 7 July 1942.

At one point President Roosevelt even seriously considered changing the paper's owner, Robert R. McCormick, with treason but was talked out of it. BAD in Washington DC expressed dismay that all this publicity was now compounding the original gaffe and pleaded that the matter be dropped, adopting a 'least said, soonest mended' approach, but, in truth the damage had already been done. Prosecuted under the 1917 Espionage Act, the *Tribune* was exonerated by the grand jury on the technicality.[5] In Tokyo they read the verdict and no doubt shook their heads in amazement, but the result was that on 14 August 1942, they introduced the brand-new D book for the JN-25 code and, as Layton ruefully had to admit, 'the American cryptanalytic effort had to begin all over again'.[6]

During the Falklands War in the 1980s the Royal Navy thought the journalists that covered the war by travelling with the task force were, 'arrogant and intemperate'. The *Sunday Times* reported that there was an influenza outbreak in Port Stanley. That story, naturally, told the Argentine military that we were reading their codes, something that the media people had apparently not even considered! During the second Gulf War some British TV reports outdid even Saddam Hussain's own 'Comical' Ali in their bias against the Allies, so much so that British troops refused to watch what they termed bitterly the 'Baghdad Broadcasting Corporation'.

Hollywood, which even had a revered and respected member of their community present during the battle, John Ford himself no less, has got the Midway battle wrong time and time again, starting with the awful Don Ameche and Dana Andrews 1944 release *A Wing and a Prayer,* which set the trend by depicting the destruction of the four Japanese carriers as carried out entirely by Avenger torpedo-bombers, and this long after the true facts were known. It is full of fictional characters and incorrect ships and aircraft, but what it does have is the authentic 'feel' of the times; there is no moralistic preaching or liberal moral degrading of heroism, as in accounts from the 1960s onward.

The same scant regard for the truth followed with the 1952 *Crusade in the Pacific* and the long-running *Victory at Sea* television series, with, again, no mention of the pivotal

role of the SBD. And so it continued, ending with the factually farcical *Midway* feature film of 1976 starring such big-screen stars as Charlton Heston and Glenn Ford. Forget the pathetic politically correct and totally irrelevant love-story sub-plot between an American flyer and a Nisei girl. There are so many basic factual mistakes in this film, scores of them, that whole web sites have sprung up listing them and they grow almost daily. So we have films of SBDs diving and miraculously changing into German Bf.110 twin-engined fighters, swastika markings and all, on the way down, jet aircraft crashing on the decks (meeting one in the air, now that *would* have surprised the Zero pilots); and on and on it goes. Forgettable also, is actor Hal Holbrook's depiction of Joseph J. Rochefort, which turned out to be a grotesque misinterpretation of the man according to those who actually knew him.[7] But the greatest and most consistent error made by the film world has been the almost total silence on the role of the dive-bomber while 'Chuck' goes to his gallant death in an Avenger and takes out a Japanese carrier! The continued story line of the torpedo-bombers bringing about the destruction of the entire Japanese carrier fleet has been a feature of almost every film that has covered the battle; the Dauntless has been totally ignored by Hollywood, despite the fact that independent verifiable figures show that in 1942 alone, a staggering 83 per cent of all hits scored in carrier battles were credited exclusively to the SBD.[8] We in Britain are now wearily resigned to Hollywood bringing us films that rewrite history like *The Patriot, Braveheart, U-Boat 577* and other insults to our intelligence, but the real heroes of Midway, the SBD aircrew, surely deserved better at the hands of their own countrymen.[9]

TV-documentaries made by the likes of the Discovery and History Channels have even less excuse for what they turn out. After all, they have access to ample real footage lifted from Ford's original 1942 black and white film *Battle of Midway*, and the moving *Torpedo Squadron 8* from the same year, with which to work. They have also had fifty or sixty years of research to splice this and newsreel footage together, but their standards of accuracy are, if anything, worse than the epic-makers on the West Coast. Thus we see the British battleship *Barham* being torpedoed in the

5. See Richard Norton Smith, *The Colonel: The Life and Legend of Robert R. McCormick, 1880–1955.*
6. Edwin T. Layton, *And I Was There.*
7. See *Daily Mail,* 2 December 2006.
8. Admiral 'Mac' Showers stated that 'the moustachioed, cigar-smoking, loud-mouth, red-neck type portrayed by Hal Holbrook was totally out of character. Joe Rochefort was clean-shaven, occasionally smoked a pipe at his desk, was quiet-mannered and soft-spoken – a gentleman in all

respects'. The theory that circulated among veterans and others was that Holbrook had been playing the uncouth and loud-mouthed Mark Twain on the stage for so long that he seemed incapable of portraying any other character differently! See Ronald W. Russell, *No Right to Win.*
9. Lieutenant-Commander David L.Tidwell, *Attack Aviation in the Pacific Theater: Tactical Development, Employment and Effectiveness of Carrier-Based Attack Aviation by the US Navy in World War II.*

Mediterranean, or *Essex* Class carriers blazing away at *kamikazes* off Okinawa being depicted as American or Japanese warships in action at Midway, let alone SBDs being shown as Japanese Vals, and bent-wing Corsairs as F4Fs.[10]

There are many such documentaries out there, and no doubt they will be repeated *ad infinitum* without correction. The best of the bunch is the Thomas H. Horton film of 1999, *The Battle of Midway,* made for the Discovery Channel.[11] Contributions by many veterans lend this particular version some welcomed authenticity amid the usual incorrect footage, the old 'AF' ruse chestnut and an exaggerated emphasis on the influence of Nimitz. The most abysmal TV Midway of them all, which itself must be a kind of record, is the History Channel's *Command Decision* version of 2004, a total travesty of the facts. Like it or not, unless something more worthy is attempted, it will be through these hapless films that both present and future generations will recall the Battle of Midway long after books, which at least strive for accuracy, are pulped and forgotten.

Factual accounts *do* exist, notably George Walsh's amateur presentation for the New England Air Museum, *Dive Bombers, Smart Bombs and Suicide Aircraft.*[12] It is not perfect by any means, especially in historical background, but the gist of it is right. If one man can produce a passable documentary on the dive-bomber, alone and unaided, why cannot the TV companies with all their wealth and expertise? The answer is, they lack the will, while the likes of Walsh cannot get a hearing. What is desperately needed is a producer who will actually *listen* to a veteran like Walsh and combine correct footage with an accurate narration, and finally give the dive-bomber her just dues.

For the sake of history, may it be soon.

---

10. Attempts to get this issue raised have been continually rebuffed by the media. See George Walsh, *Searching for the Truth about the Battle of Midway.*

11. Typical, and only selected for inclusion here because it happened to be one of the most recently viewed, is the *National Geographic* documentary, *Midway,* one of their *Battlefront* series, directed by Richard Lysaek, with a voice-over by Jonathan Booth, which was screened between 1830 and 1900 on 22 November 2006 in the UK. It has some plus point including some retro-coloured film of PBYs, B17s, and Japanese aircrews. It is less than half an hour long but in that time the number of errors just a casual viewing reveals are legion and include many old favourites trotted out for the umpteenth time. Guest talking-heads included B5N2 pilot Taisuke Maruyama, which ought to have ensured some degree of accuracy but during his detailed account of his *torpedo*-dropping he is translated as saying he 'released the bomb'! There is the inevitable clip of the three SBDs diving on American ships, which appears in all such films; and the usual views of *kamikazes* diving into carriers off Okinawa and views of *Essex* class carriers (probably *Bunker Hill* or *Franklin*) ablaze purporting to be *Yorktown* which we have seen so many, many times before. The whole thing *appeared* to be half the 1999 documentary which originally featured the discovery of the *Yorktown* by Dr Robert Ballard, with the modern section removed.

12. George Walsh, an Octogenarian Productions film presentation.

Select Bibliography

Abbott, Jonathan, 'The Last Ride of Susie-Q', *Ghost Wings*, Issue 13.

Adolphus, Andrews, Jr, *Admirals with Wings: The Career of Joseph Mason Reeves*, Princeton University, Princeton, NJ, 1943.

Agawa, Hiroyuki and Bester John (trans), *The Reluctant Admiral: Yamamoto and the Imperial Navy*, Kodansha, Tokyo, 1979.

Aldrich, Richard J., *Intelligence and the War Against Japan: Britain, America and the Politics of Secret Service*, Cambridge University Press, Cambridge, 2000.

Allen, Thomas B., 'Return to the Battle of Midway', *National Geographic*, Vol. 195, No. 4.

Assistant Chief of Air Staff, Intelligence Headquarters, Army Air Force, *Mission Accomplished: Interrogations of Japanese Industrial, Military, and Civil Leaders of World War II*, UG Government Printing Office, Washington DC, 1946.

Ballard, Robert, *Return to Midway*, Madison Press Books, Toronto, Canada, 1999.

Bamford, James, *The Puzzle Palace*, Houghton Miffin, Boston, 1982.

Barde, Robert Elmer, *The Battle of Midway: A Study in Leadership*, transcript of dissertation, University of Maryland, College Park, MD, 1971.

Barde, Robert Elmer, 'Midway: Tarnished Victory', *Military Affairs* Vol. 47, No. 4, 1983.

Barker, Arthur J., *Midway: The Turning Point*, Macmillan, New York, NY, 1971.

Bates, Rear-Admiral Richard W. (ed), *The Battle of Midway: Including the Aleutian Phase June 3 to June 14, 1942. Strategical and Tactical Analysis*, US Naval War College, NAVPERS. 91067, Newport, RI, 1948.

Beach, Captain Edward L., *Salt and Steel: Reflections of a Submariner*, Naval Institute Press, Annapolis, MD, 1999.

Belli, Rear-Admiral Vladimir Aleksandrovich, *Morskoy Sbornik*, July 1942, *Chronicle,* The Rockford Institute, Rockford IL.

Bergamini, David, *Japan's Imperial Conspiracy*, William Morrow, New York, NY, 1971.

Bergerud, Eric M., *Fire in the Sky: The Air War in the South Pacific*, Westfield Press, Boulder, CO, 2001.

Best, Antony, *British Intelligence and the Japanese Challenge in Asia, 1914–1941*, Palgrave Macmillan, London, 2002.

Biard, Captain Forrest R., 'The Pacific War Through the Eyes of Forrest R Biard', *Cryptolog,* Vol. 10, Winter 1989.

Biard, Captain Forrest R., 'Breaking of Japanese Naval Codes: Pre-Pearl Harbor to Midway', article in *Cryptologia*, United States Military Academy, West Point, NY, via ProQuest Information & Learning, Vol. 30, 2006.

Bichento, Hugh, *Fields of Battle*: *Midway*, Cassell, London, 2001.

Bix, Herbert P., *Hirohito and the Making of Modern Japan*, Harper Collins Publishers, New York, NY, 2000.

Blair, Clay, Jr., *Silent Victory: The US Submarine War Against Japan*, Lippincott Williams & Wilkins, Hagerstown, MD, 1973.

Bose, Mihir, *Lost Hero: A Biography of Subhas Bose*, Quartet Books, London, 1982.

Boyd, Carl, *Hitler's Japanese Confidant: General Oshima Hiroshi and MAGIC Intelligence 1941–1945*, University Press of Kansas, Lawrence, KS, 1993.

Bradford, Richard, 'Learning the Enemy's Language: US Navy Officer Language Students in Japan, 1920–1941, *International Journal of Naval History*, April 2002.

Brief History of Seventh Air Force, 1940–5, Office of Information Services, Washington, DC. 1947.

Brinkley, David, *Washington Goes to War*, Alfred A. Knopf, New York, NY, 1988.

Brown, Captain Eric, CBE, DFC, AFC, RN, *Wings of the Navy: Flying Allied Carrier Aircraft of World War Two,* Airlife, Shrewsbury, 1980.

Brown, W. H., Memoirs, *Aerospace Historian, The Heritage of Flight,* Vol. 16, No. 2, 1969.

Browning, Miles, A., to Reeves, Admiral J. M., *A Short Discussion of Shipbased Aircraft Operations in the Fleet,* dated 1936, Robert P. Molten Papers, Operational Archives ranch, Naval Historical Center, Washington DC.

Budiansky, Stephan, *Battle of Wits: The Complete Story of Codebreaking in World War II,* Touchstone, New York, NY, 2002.

Buell, Thomas B., *Master of Sea Power: A Biography of Fleet Admiral Ernest* J. King, Little, Brown and Company, Boston, MA, 1980.

Buell, Thomas B., *The Quiet Warrior, A Biography of Admiral Raymond A. Spruance,* Naval Institute Press, Annapolis, MD, Revised Edition, 1987.

Burke, Arleigh, 'Admiral Marc Mitscher: A Naval Aviator', US Naval Institute *Proceedings* Vol. 101 (4), April 1975.

Burrell, Captain Robert S., USMC, 'Miracle at Midway', *Shipmate,* 2002.

Butcher, M. E., 'Admiral Frank Jack Fletcher, Pioneer Warrior or Gross Sinner?' *Naval War College Review,* Winter 1987.

Butler, Susan (ed), *My Dear Mr. Stalin: The Complete Correspondence Between Franklin D. Roosevelt and Joseph V. Stalin,* Yale University Press, New Haven and London, 2005.

Caidin, Martin, *The Ragged Rugged Warriors,* Ballantine, New York, NY, 1980.

Campbell, Mark A., *The Influence of Air Power Upon the Evolution of Battle Doctrine in the US Navy, 1922–1941,* Master's Thesis, History Department, University of Massachusetts, Boston, MA, 1992.

Cant, Gilbert, *America's Navy in World War II,* J. Day, New York, NY, 1943.

Cathcart-Jones, Owen, *Aviation Memoirs,* Hutchinson, London, 1934.

Chan, Victor, *American PT Boats in WWII,* Schiffer Publishing, New York, NY, 1997.

Chan, Victor, *Devil Boats: PT War Against Japan,* Random House, New York, NY, 1988.

Chihaya, Commander Masataka, IJN (Rtd), *IJN Yukikaze, Destroyer, 1939–1970,* Profile Publications, Windsor, 1972.

Chihaya, Masataka, *Teikoku Rengo Kantai* ('Imperial Combined Fleet'), Kodansha, Tokyo, 1969.

Chihaya, Masataka, *Nihon Kaign Senryaku Hassō* ('Strategic Concepts of the Japanese Navy'), Purjidento Sha, Tokyo, 1985.

Churchill, Winston S., *The Second World War,* Vol. IV: *The Hinge of Fate,* Cassell, London, 1951. Reprinted by Penguin Classics, London, 2005.

Cole, Wayne S., *Charles A. Lindbergh and the Battle Against American Intervention in World War II,* Harcourt Brace, New York, NY, 1974.

Coletta, Paolo E., *Patrick N. L. Bellinger and US Naval Aviation,* University Press of America, Lanham, MD, 1987.

Coletta, Paolo E. and Bernarr B., *Admiral William A. Moffett and United States Naval Aviation,* Edwin Mellon Press, Lampeter, Ceredigion, 1997.

Craigie, Sir Robert Leslie, *Behind the Japanese Mask,* Hutchinson, London, 1945.

Craven, Wesley Frank and Cate, James Lea (ed) *The Army Air Forces in World War II,* Vol. 1, *Plans and Early Operations (January 1939 to August 1942),* University of Chicago Press, Chicago, IL, 1948.

Cressman, Robert J., Ewing, Steve, Tillman, Barrett, Horan, Mark E., Reynolds, Clark, Cohen, Stan, '*A Glorious Page in Our History*': The Battle of Midway 4–6 June 1942, Pictorial Histories Publishing Co. Missoula, MT, 1990.

Cressman, Robert J., *That Gallant Ship: A History of USS Yorktown (CV-5),* Pictorial Histories Publishing Co., Missoula, MT, 1990.

Crowder, James L., Jr., *Osage General: Major General Clarence L. Tinker,* Oklahoma City Air Logistics Center, Tinker AFB, Midwest City, OK, 1987.

Davis, Burke, *The Billy Mitchell Affair,* Random House, New York, NY, 1967.

Deacon, Richard, *Kempei Tai: A History of the Japanese Secret Service,* Berkley, London, 1985.

Dull, Paul S., *A Battle History of the Imperial Japanese Navy (1941–1945),* US Naval Institute Press, Annapolis, MD, 1978.

Dulin, Robert O., Jr, Garzke Jr, William H., Haberlein Jr, Charles, Egan Robert, Mindell, Dr David and Jurens, William, *The Loss of the USS* Yorktown *(CV-5): A Marine Forensic Analysis,* Society of Naval Architects and Marine Engineers, Jersey City, NJ, 1999.

Dyer, Vice-Admiral George C., USN, Rtd., *The Amphibians Came to Conquer: the Story of Admiral Richmond Kelly Turner,* US Government Printing Office, Washington, DC, 1971.

Edward, John, *Curtin's Gift: Reinterpreting Australia's Greatest Prime Minister,* Allen & Unwin, London, 2005.

Edwards, C. P., Sc.Tech, '*Enemy Airborne Radio*

'Equipment', *Journal of the Institution of Electrical Engineers,* Issue 91, 1943.

Eggers, H. A., *Wake Survey of the Mark 13 Torpedo,* (ADA800161), David Taylor Model Basin, National Technical Information Service, Washington, DC, 1947.

Ellis, Major Earl H., USMC, *War Portfolio – US Marine Corps, Advanced Base Operations in Micronesia 1921,* FMFRP, USMC HQ, Quantico, VA, 1921.

Etisbree, W., *Japan's Role in Southeast Asian National Movements 1940–1945,* Cambridge University Press, Cambridge, 1953.

Evans, David C., and Peattie, Mark R., *Kaigun: Strategy, Tactics, and Technology in the Imperial Japanese Navy 1887–1941,* Naval Institute Press, Annapolis, MD, 1997.

Ewing, Steve, *Thach Weave: The Life of Jimmie Thach,* Naval Institute Press, Annapolis, MD, 2004.

Falke, Lieutenant-Commander Brian G., USN, *Battle of Midway: USS* Hornet *(CV-8) Air Group,* research report AU/ACSC/210/2000–04, to Air Command and Staff College, Air University, Maxwell Air Force Base, AL, dated April 2000.

Fay, Peter Ward, *The Forgotten Army: India's Armed Struggle for Independence,* Rupa, Calcutta, 1994.

Fenlon, Major B. T., USMC, *Remember Midway,* Executive Summary Thesis for Global Security Organisation, 1998.

Ferrier, H. H., 'Torpedo Squadron Eight, the Other Chapter', US Naval Institute *Proceedings,* Annapolis, MD, October, 1964.

Fisher, Commander Clayton, USN (Rtd), *Address to Victory at Midway Celebration,* North Island, CA, 2001, courtesy of Clayton Fisher, Coronado, CA.

Forbes, Bill, 'Pearl Harbor Story, World War II Encounters and Accomplishments by VP-23 December 7, 1941 through January 1943', in *Catalina Chronicles,* Vol. II, (undated).

Ford, Lieutenant-Commander Christopher A., USNR, with Rosenberg, Captain David A., USNR and Balano, Commander Randy C., USNR, *The Admiral's Advantage: U S Navy Operational Intelligence in World War II and the Cold War,* Naval Institute Press, Annapolis, MD, 2005.

Forrestel, Vice-Admiral E. P., *Admiral Raymond A. Spruance,* Government Printing Office, Washington, DC, 1966.

Fuchida, Mitsuo, and Okumiya, Masatake, *Midway: the Battle that Doomed Japan,* Naval Institute Press, Annapolis, MD, 1955.

Fujiwara, Iwaichi, *F-Kikan: Japanese Army Intelligence Operations in Southeast Asia During World War II,* Heinemann Asia, Hong Kong, 1983.

Gallagher, James P., and Nowarra, Heinz J. (contributors), *Navy Bombers (Ginga), Famous Airplanes of the World; Special Edition No.1,* Bunrindo Co. Ltd, Tokyo, 2004.

Gay, George, 'The Skipper – Torpedo 8', article in *Shipmate,* 1966.

Gay, George, *Sole Survivor: The Battle of Midway and Its Effect on His Life,* Naples Ad/Graphics Services, Naples, FL. 1979.

Gebhard, L. A., *Evolution of Naval Radio-Electronics and Contributions of the Naval Research Laboratory,* Naval Research Lanpratpru Report 8300, Washington, DC, 1979.

Genda, Minoru, 'Evolution of Aircraft Carrier Tactics of the Imperial Japanese Navy', *Stillwell,* Paul (ed) *Air Raid: Pearl Harbor!: Recollections of a Day of Infamy,* Naval Institute Press, Annapolis, MD, 1981.

Genda, Minoru, *Kaigun Kōkūtai Shimatsuki* ('A Record of the Particulars of the Japanese Naval Air Service'), 2 Vols, Bungei Shunjū, Tokyo, 1961-2.

Gladwin, Lee A., 'Diplomacy of Security: Behind the Negotiations of Article 18 of the Sino-American Cooperative Agreement', *Cryptologia,* January 2005.

Glines, Carroll V., *Attack on Yamamoto,* Crown, New York, NY, 1990.

Goren, Dina, 'Communication Intelligence and the Freedom of the Press'. The *Chicago Tribune's* Battle of Midway Dispatch and the Breaking of the Japanese Naval Code, *Journal of Contemporary History,* Vol. 16, No. 4, October 1981.

Gowan, R., Kameto Kuroshima: *The Man Behind Yamamoto,* ECU Press, London, 1973.

Grenfell, Captain Russell, RN, *Main Fleet to Singapore,* Faber & Faber, London, 1951.

Grenfell, Captain Russell, RN (as 'T124'), *Sea Power,* Faber & Faber, London, 1940.

Grenfell, Captain Russell, RN, *Unconditional Hatred: German War Guilt and the Future of Europe,* Devin-Adair, New York, NY, 1953.

Halsey, Fleet Admiral William F., USN, with Bryan, Lieutenant-Commander Joseph, USNR, *Admiral Halsey's Story,* McGraw-Hill, New York, NY, 1947.

Hirama, Yoichi, 'Japanese Naval Preparations for World War II', *Naval War College Review,* Vol. 44, No. 2, 1991.

Hashimoto, Mochitsura, with Colgrave, Commander E. H. M. (trans.), *Sunk: The Story of the Japanese Submarine Fleet,* Henry Holt, New York, NY, 1954.

Hata, Ikuhiko, *Nihon Riku Kai Gun Sougou Jiten,* Kokufan [Dictionary of the Japanese Navy] Tokyo, 1991.

Hata, Ikuhiko and Izawa, Yasuho, with Gorham, Don Cyril (trans), *Japanese Naval Aces and Fighter Units in World War II*, Naval Institute Press, Annapolis, MD, 1989.

Hata, Ikuhiko, 'Kaeri Zaru Tomonaga Raigekitai' ('The Tomonaga Torpedo Unit Departs'), *Kokufan,* Tokyo, 1976.

Hatano, S., and Asada, S., 'The Japanese Decision to Move South, 1939–41', Boyce, Robert, and Robertson, Esmonde M. (eds), *Paths to War: New Essays on the Origins of the Second World War*, Macmillan St Martins Press, Basingstoke, Hants, 1989.

Hattori, Takushior, *Dai-toa senso Zenshi (A Complete History of the Greater East Asia War),* Hara Shobo, Tokyo, 1953.

Hayashi, Saburo, *Kogun: The Japanese Army in the Pacific War*, Greenwood Press, Westport, RI, 1959.

Haven, Violet Sweet, *Gentlemen of Japan: A Study in Rapist Diplomacy*, Ziff-Davis, Chicago, IL, 1944.

Healy, Mark, *Midway 1942: Turning Point in the Pacific*, Praeger, Westport, CT and London, 2004.

Heinl, Lieutenant-Colonel Robert D., Jr, USMC, *Marines at Midway*, HQ US Marine Corps, Quantico, VA, 1948.

Heinemann, Edward H. and Smith, Glenn E., Jr, *Sugar Baker Dog: The Victor at Midway*, unpublished MSS, San Diego Aerospace Museum via Ray Wagner, San Diego, CA.

Herriges, Darrell L., *Operational Level Air Commanders: A Search for the Elements of Genius*, Thesis for School of Advanced Airpower Studies, Air University, Maxwell Air Force Base, AL, June 1994.

Heuer, Richard J, Jr, 'Strategic Deception and Counterdeception: A Cognitive Process Approach', *International Studies Quarterly,* Vol. 25, No. 2, 1981.

Hinsley, Francis A., *British Intelligence in the Second World War*, 3 Vols. Cambridge University Press, Cambridge, 1979–1983.

Hirama, Rear-Admiral Yōichi, *India in Axis Strategy*, summary prepared for the author, December 2005.

Hitsuji, Rear-Admiral Tsuneo, *Reflections of the Great Skies*, Anzen Zeppo, Tokyo, 1998.

Hodson, Harry, *Autobiography*, Routledge, London, 1999.

Hodson, Harry, *The Great Divide – Britain-India-Pakistan*, Oxford University Press, Oxford, 2001.

Holmes, Jasper W., Captain, *Undersea Victory* 2 Vols. Kensington Publishing Corps, MN.

Holmes, Jasper W., Captain, *Double-Edged Secrets: US Naval Intelligence Operations in the Pacific During World War II*, Naval Institute Pres, Annapolis, MD, 1939.

Horikoshi, Dr Jiro, *Eagles of Mitsubishi: The Story of the Zero Fighter*, Orbis, London, 1982.

Howorth, Captain Linwood S., USN (Rtd), *History of Communications-Electronics in the United States Navy*, BuOrd, Washington DC, 1963.

Hoyt, Edwin P., *Nimitz and His Admirals: How they Won the War in the Pacific*, Weybridge and Tally, New York, NY, 1979.

Hudson, George E., 'Soviet Naval Doctrine under Lenin and Stalin, in Soviet Studies', Vol 28, No 1, January 1976.

Hughes, Wayne P., *Fleet Tactics: Theory and Practice*, Naval Institute Press, Annapolis, MD, 1986.

Hughes, Rev. Paul A., M.Div., 'Hero of Pearl Harbor', article, believe his word.com.

Hughes-Wilson, Colonel John, *The Puppet Masters; Spies, Traitors and the Real Force Behind World Events*, Weidenfeld Military, London 2004.

Hurley, Alfred H., *Billy Mitchell: Crusader for Air Power*, Indiana University Press, Bloomington, ID, 1975.

Hunnicutt, Thomas G., *The Operational Failure of US Submarines at the Battle of Midway – and implications for Today*, Naval War College, Newport, RI, 2006.

Ikari, Yoshiro, *Kaigun Kugishō*, Particulars of Naval Aircraft, Kōjinsha, Tokyo, 1989.

Ike, Nobutake, (ed) *Japan's Decision for War: Records of the 1941 Policy Conferences*, Stanford University Press, Stanford, CN, 1967.

Irving, David, *Hitler's War*, Hodder & Stoughton, London, 1977.

Ishimaru, Lieutenant-Commander Tōta, IJN, *Japan Must Fight Britain*, Hurst & Blackett, London, 1936.

Isom, Dallas W., 'The Battle of Midway: Why the Japanese Lost', *Naval War College Review*, Naval War College, Newport, RI. 2000.

Isom, Dallas W., *They Would Have Found a Way*, article in *Naval War College Review*, 2001.

Japanese General Staff and War Ministry, *Summary Operational History of Japanese Naval Communications December 1941–August 1945,* Reprint by Aegeon Park Press, CA, 1995.

Kahn, David, *The Codebreakers: the Story of Secret Writing*, Macmillan, New York, 1967.

Karetka, Peter E., "Flags" at Midway: My Memories of Midway', article in *Naval History*, 2002.

Kenichi, Nakamuta, *Jihō Shikan No Kaisu* ('Recollections of an Intelligence Officer'), Daiya Mendosha, Tokyo, 1947.

Kernan, Alvin, *The Unknown Battle of Midway: The Destruction of the American Torpedo Squadrons,* Yale University Press, New Haven and London, 2005.

Kido, Marquis Kochi, *The Diary of Marquis Kido, 1931–45*, University Publications of America, Bethesda, MD, 1984

King, Admiral Ernest J., *First Report to the Secretary of the Navy; Covering our Peacetime Navy and our Wartime Navy and Including Combat Operations up to 1 March 1944*, CNO Archive, 23 April 1944.

Kizu, T., (ed), *History of Japanese Aircraft Carriers, Ships of the World No. 481*, Kaijinsha Co., Ltd, Tokyo, 1994.

Kizu, T., (ed), *History of Japanese Destroyers, Ships of the World No. 453*, Kaijinsha Co., Ltd, Tokyo, 1992.

Kleiss, Lieutenant (jg) N. J., *VS-6 Log of the War: Personal Diary*, Kleiss, San Antonio, TX, undated.

Knott, Richard, *Black Cat Raiders of World War II*, Nautical & Aviation Publishing Company, Annapolis, MD, 1981.

Krug, Hans-Joachim, Hirama, Yōichi, Sander-Nagashima, Sander-Nagashima, Berthold J. and Niestlé, Axel, *Reluctant Allies: German-Japanese Naval Relations in World War II*, Naval Institute Press, Annapolis, MD, 2001.

Kuznetsov, Admiral of the Fleet Nikolai Gerasimovich, with Krivoshchevkov, Vladimir (trans.), *Memoirs of Wartime Minister of the Navy of the Soviet Union*, Progress Publishers, Moscow, 1990.

Lacroix, Eric and Wells, Linton, *Japanese Cruisers of the Pacific War*, Naval Institute Press, Annapolis, MD, 1997.

Lamar, Commander Howell Arthur, USN, *I Saw Stars: Some Memories of Commander Hal Lamar, Fleet Admiral Nimitz's Flag Lieutenant 1941–1945*, Admiral Nimitz Foundation, Fredericksburg, TX, 1975.

Larabee, Eric, *Commander-in-Chief: Franklin D Roosevelt, His Lieutenants, and Their War*, Harper & Row, New York, 1987.

Layton, Admiral Sir Geoffrey, RN, *Layton Papers, Correspondence and Papers of Admiral Sir Geoffrey Layton Relating to the Naval War in the Far East 1940–1945*. Churchill Archives Centre, Churchill College, Cambridge.

Layton, Admiral Edwin T., with Pineau, Roger and Costello, John, *And I was There: Pearl Harbor and Midway – Breaking the Secrets*, William Morrow & Co, New York, NY, 1985.

Lebra, Joyce C. (ed.), *Japan's Great East Asia Co-Prosperity Sphere*, Oxford University Press, Oxford, 1953.

Lebra, Joyce C., *Japanese-trained armies in Southeast Asia: Independence and Volunteer Forces in World War II*, Columbia University Press, New York, NY, 1977.

Lebra, Joyce C., *Jungle Alliance: Japan and the Indian National Army*, Asia Pacific Press, Singapore, 1971.

LeCompte, Commander Malcolm A., USNR, 'Radar and the Air Battles of Midway', *Naval History*, Summer 1992.

Levy, James P., 'Race for the Decisive Weapon: British, American and Japanese Carrier Fleets, 1942–1943', *Naval War College Review*, 2005.

Locke, Rear-Admiral Walter M., 'Tomahawk Tactics: The Midway Connection', US Naval Institute *Proceedings*, Vol. 108, Issue 6, 1992.

Lord, Walter, *Incredible Victory*, Harper & Row, New York, NY, 1967.

Lundstrom, John B., *Black Shoe Carrier Admiral: Frank Jack Fletcher at Coral Sea, Midway and Guadalcanal*, Naval Institute Press, Annapolis, MD, 2006.

Lundstrom, John B., *The First Team: Pacific Naval Air Combat from Pearl Harbor to Midway*, Naval Institute Press, Annapolis, MD, 1984.

Lujan, Susan M., 'Agnes Meyer Driscoll', *Cryptologia*, Vol XV, Issue 1, January 1991.

McClusky, Rear-Admiral C. Wade, 'Historical Commentary, in *Midway Battle Manual*', Avalon Hill, Baltimore, MD, 1964.

MacPherson, B. Nelson, 'The Compromise of US Navy Cryptanalysis After the Battle of Midway', *Intelligence and National Security*, Vol. 2, Issue 2, April 1987.

Marder, Arthur J., *Old Friends, New Enemies: The Royal Navy and the Imperial Japanese Navy, Strategic Delusions 1936–1941*, Oxford University Press, Oxford, 1981.

Mars, Alastair, *British Submarines at War 1939–1945*, William Kimber, London, 1971.

Mason, Robert, 'Eyewitness', US Naval Institute *Proceedings*, Vol. 108, June 1982.

Matthews, Alan, 'SS *Automedon:* The Ship That Doomed a Colony', Forcez-Survivors.org.uk, 1999.

Maund, Rear-Admiral L. E. H., CBE, RN (Rtd), *Assault from the Sea*, Methuen, London, 1949.

Megumi, Ryunosuke Valentine, *Tekihei wo Kyuzyoseyo!* ('To Save Mine Enemy'). Soshisha, Tokyo, 2006.

Melhorn, Charles M., *Two Block Fox: The Rise of the Aircraft Carrier 1911–1929*, Naval Institute Press, Annapolis, MD, 1974.

Melinski, Hugh, *A Code-breaker's Tale*, The Larke Press, Guist, Dereham, Norfolk, 1998.

Meskill, Johanna Menzel, *Hitler and Japan: The Hollow Alliance*, Atherton Press, New York, NY, 1966.

Mikus, Andy, 'A Clear Day at Midway', USSYorktown.com/defendcv5.htm.

Milford, Frederick J., 'US Navy Torpedoes, part Two: The

great torpedo scandal, 1941–42', *The Submarine Review*, 1996.

Miller, Thomas G., Jr, *The Cactus Air Force*, Harper & Row, New York, NY, 1969.

Mingos, Howard, *American Heroes of the War in the Air*, Lanciar Publishers, New York, NY, 1943.

Ministry of Foreign Affairs of the USSR, *Correspondence: between the Chairman of the Council of Ministers of the USSR and the Presidents of the USA and the Prime Minister of Great Britain during the Great Patriotic War of 1941–1945, Vol 1, Correspondence with Winston S. Churchill and Clement R. Attlee (July 1941–November 1945)*, Foreign Languages Publishing House, Moscow, 1957.

Miyo, Captain, contributor, 'Captain Amagai', *Ano Umi Ano Sora* ('Memoir of the Heigakkou 51st Class Members'), Etajima, undated.

Mohr, Ulrich, with Sellwood, A V., *Atlantis: the Story of a German Surface Raider*, Hutchinson, London, 1957.

Montgomery, B., *Shenton of Singapore: Governor and Prisoner of War*, Secker & Warburg, London, 1984.

Moore, Jeffrey M., *Spies for Nimitz: Joint Military Intelligence in the Pacific War*, Naval Institute Press, Annapolis, MD, 2004.

Morison, Samuel Eliot, *History of United States Naval Operations in World War II*, 15 Vols, Little Brown Inc., Boston, MA. 1948–59.

Morison, Samuel Eliot, *The Two-Ocean War: A Short History of the United States Navy in the Second World War*, Galahad Books, New York, NY, 1997.

Mueller-Hillebrand, Burkhart, *Germany and its Allies in World War II: A Record of Axis Collaboration Problems*, University Publications of America, Bethesda, MD, 1980.

Nagagawa, Yasuzo, *Japanese Radar and Related Weapons*, Aegean Park Press, Walnut Creek, CA, 1998.

Nagumo, Chuichi, 'Action Report by the C-in-C of the First Air Fleet', *ONI Review*, May 1947.

Nave, Commander Theodore Eric, OBE, RN and Rushbridger, James, *Betrayal at Pearl Harbor: How Churchill Lured Roosevelt into World War II*, Summit Books, New York, 1991.

Nohara, Shigern, *Mitsubishi A6M Zero Fighter*, Aero Detail 7, Dainippon Kaiga Co. Ltd, Tokyo, 1993.

Nomoto, Jinzo, *Tibet Senko 1939* ('Tibet Underground 1939'), Yuyusha Publishing Co., Tokyo, 2001.

Okumiya, Masatake and Horikoshi, Jiro, with Caidin, Martin, *Zero! The Story of the Japanese Navy Air Force 1937–1945*, Cassell, London, 1957.

Okumiya, Masatake, *Nihon kaigun No Senryaku Hasso* ('The Japanese Navy's Conception of Naval Strategy'), Purejidentosha, Tokyo, 1982.

O'Neil, William D., *Military Transformation as a Competitive Systemic Process: The Case of Japan and the United States Between the World Wars*, Center for Naval Analysis Corporation, Alexandria, VA, 2003.

Parker, Frederick D., *A Priceless Advantage: US Naval Communications Intelligence and the Battles of Coral Sea, Midway and the Aleutians, Part Two: The Battle for Midway and the Aleutians*, United States Cryptologic History, Series IV, World War II, Vol. 5, NSA, Fort Meade, MD, 1993.

Parker, Frederick D., 'How OP-20-G got rid of Joe Rochefort', *Cryptologia*, 2000.

Parshall, Jonathan and Tully, Anthony, *Shattered Sword: the Untold Story of the Battle of Midway*, Potomac Books, Washington DC, 2005.

Parshall, Jonathan B., Dickson, David D., and Tully, Anthony P, 'Set and Drift: Doctrine Matters Why the Japanese Lost at Midway', *Naval War College Review, Summer 2001*, 2001.

Parsons, Lee M., 'Dive Bombers: The Pre-War Years', in *Naval Aviation* Confidential Bulletin, Washington DC, 1949.

Patel, Dinyar, 'American Involvement in Cripps Mission', *Span*, 2005.

Peattie, Mark R., *Sunburst: The Rise of Japanese Naval Air Power, 1909–1941*, Naval Institute Press, Annapolis. MD, 2001.

Pfennigwerth, Ian, *A Man of Intelligence: Life of Captain Eric Nave Australian Codebreaker Extraordinary*, Rosenberg Books, New York, NY, 1991.

Potter, Elmer B., *Nimitz*, US Naval Institute Press, Annapolis, MD, 1976.

Prados, John, *Combined Fleet Decoded: The Secret History of American Intelligence and the Japanese Navy in World War II*, Naval Institute Press, Annapolis, MD, 2001.

Prange, Gordon, *Miracle at Midway*, McGraw-Hill, New York, NY, 1983.

Prange, Gordon, et al, *At Dawn We Slept*, McGraw-Hill, New York, NY, 1981.

Prange, Gordon, Goldstein, Donald M., and Dillon, Katherine V., *God's Samurai: Fuchida – Lead Pilot at Pearl Harbor*, Brassey (UK) London, 1990.

Pratt, Fletcher, 'The Mysteries of Midway', *Harper's Magazine*, Issue 5, July 1943.

Pratt, Fletcher, 'The Knockout at Midway', *Harper's Magazine*, Issue 6, 1943.

Pratt, Fletcher, *Fleet Against Japan*, Harper and Brothers, New York, NY, August 1946.

Presseisen, Ernst L., *Germany and Japan: A Study in Totalitarian Diplomacy 1933–1941*, Martinus Nijhoff, The Hague, 1958.

Reese, Lee Fleming, MA, (ed.), unpublished book, *Looking Back Forty Years at the Battle of Midway 4–7 June 1942: as told by some of the men who fought for the United States of America against the Empire of Japan*, San Diego, CA, 1982.

Rees, L., *The Nazis: A Warning from History*, BBC Books, London, 1998.

Regan, Stephen D., *In Bitter Tempest, The Biography of Admiral Frank Jack Fletcher*, Iowa State University Press, Ames, Iowa, 1993.

Reynolds, Clark G., *Admiral John H. Towers: The Struggle for Naval Air Supremacy*, Naval Institute Press, Annapolis, MD, 1990.

Richardson, Vice-Admiral David C., 'The Uses of Intelligence', *Guest Presentations*, Harvard College, 1981.

Ring, Rear-Admiral Stanhope Cotton, USN, *Lost Letter*, *circa* 1946, courtesy of Susan Ring Keith, Coronado, CA.

Ringblom, Major Allan H., USMC, 'Dive-Bomber Pilot's Narrative, Battle of Midway', in *Marines in World War II*, historical monograph, *Marines at Midway*, USMC HQ, Quantico, VA, 1948.

Rochefort, Captain Joseph J., USN (Rtd), 'Finding the Kido Butai', US Naval Institute *Proceedings*, Vol. 118, No. 6, 1992.

Rochefort, Captain Joseph J., USN (Rtd), *The Reminiscences of Captain Joseph J. Rochefort, US Navy (Rtd)*, Oral History Series, Annapolis, MD, 1985.

Rogge, *Konteradmiral* Bernhard, Frank, Wolfgang, and Long, R. O. B., *Under Ten Flags: The Story of the German Commerce Raider Atlantis*, Weidenfeld & Nicolson, London, 1956.

Roscoe, Theodore, *On the Sea and in the Skies: A History of the US Navy's Airpower*, Hawthorne Books, New York, NY, 1970.

Roscoe, Theodore, *United States Submarine Operations in World War II*, Naval Institute Press, Annapolis, MD, 1949.

Roskill, Captain Stephen, W., *The War at Sea 1939–1945*, 3 Vols in 4 books, Her Majesty's Stationery Office, London, 1954–63.

Roskill, Captain Stephen W., *Naval Policy Between the Wars* 2 Vols, Collins, London, 1968 and 1976.

Roskill, Captain Stephen W., *The Strategy of Sea Power: Its Development and Applications*, Collins, London, 1961.

Roskill, Captain Stephen W., *Documents Relating to the Naval Air Service 1908–1918*, 2 Vols, Navy Records Society, London, 1970.

Roskill, Captain Stephen W., *Churchill and the Admirals*, Collins, London, 1977.

Rowland, Lieutenant-Commander Burford, USNR, *US Navy Bureau of Ordnance in World War II*, US Government Printing Office, Washington DC, 1947.

Roy, William G., 'I Filmed the Battle of Midway from USS Yorktown (CV-5)' in *Telling the Sailor's Story: US Navy Photographer's Mates Through the Decades*, USSYorktowncvs10@juno.com .

Rusbridger, James, *Ultra: And the Sinking of the Automedon*, nesa.org.uk.

Russell, Richard A., *Project Hula: Secret Soviet-American Cooperation in the War Against Japan*, Naval Historical Center, Washington DC, 1997.

Russell, Ronald W., 'Changing Course: The Hornet's *Air Group* at Midway', article in US Naval Institute *Proceedings*, Annapolis, MD, 2006.

Russell, Ronald W., *No Right to Win, A continuing dialogue with Veterans of the Battle of Midway*, University Inc., Lincoln, NE, 2006.

Rust, Kenneth C., 'Seventh Air Force Story . . . in World War II', in *Historical Aviation Album*, Temple City, CA, 1979.

Ryūnosukei, Kusaka, *Rengō Kantai* ('Combined Fleet'), Mainichi Newspaper Co., Tokyo, 1952.

Saburo, Sakai, *Samurai!*, Naval Institute Press, Annapolis, MD, 1992

Sanger, Grant, 'Freedom of the Press or Treason', US Naval Institute *Proceedings*, Vol. 103, September 1977.

Schlesinger, Dr James R., 'Midway to Victory', *Wall Street Journal*, New York, NY, 4 June 2002.

Schlesinger, Dr James R., 'Underappreciated Victory', US Naval Institute *Proceedings*, October 2003.

Schmidt, Paul, *Statist auf diplomatischer Buehne 1923–45* Koch Buchvig Bonn, 1949.

Schom, Alan, *The Eagle and the Rising Sun: The Japanese-American War 1941–1943*, W. W. Norton, New York, NY, 2004.

Schorreck, Henry F., *Battle of Midway: 4–7 June 1942: The Role of COMINT in the Battle of Midway*, Naval Historical Centre, Washington DC, SRH-230).

Senshi Sosho (War History Publications Series), Volume 43, *Midooei kaisen* ('The Midway Operations'), May–June 1942, Defense Headquarters History Office, Tokyo, 1971.

Sherman, Vice-Admiral Frederick C., USN. *Combat Command: The American Aircraft Carriers in the Pacific War*, E. P. Dutton, New York, NY, 1950.

Shibata, Masashi, *The Destroyer* Tanikaze *Returns from*

'*The Sea of Death*', unpublished manuscript (undated), via Commander Clayton Fisher, USN, Rtd., Coronado, CA.

Shirer, William L., *The Rise and Fall of the Third Reich: A History of Nazi Germany*, Secker & Warburg, London, 1962.

Shinsaku, Hirata, *Warera Moshi Tatakawaba* ('When we Fight!'), Shonen-Kurabo (Boy's Club), Dainihon yubea-kai, Tokyo, 1932.

Shōgen, Watashi, *No Showashi dai 4 kan* ('Evidence – My History of Showa, Vol 4'), Gakugei Shorin, Tokyo, 1969.

Short, Commander J. J., RN, *Was Japanese Defeat at Midway Inevitable?*, Student paper, MoD, London, 2005.

Showers, Rear-Admiral Donald M. 'Mac', USN, 'ULTRA-The Navy's COMINT Weapon in the Pacific', *Signals Intelligence and Information War*, Vol. 15, No. 1, Spring/Summer 1994.

Simpson, Michael, MA, MLitt, FR HistS, (ed.), *The Somerville Papers*, Scolar Press for Navy Records Society, London, 1995.

Slonim, Gilven M., 'A Flagship View of Command Decisions', US Naval Institute *Proceedings*, April 1958.

Somerville, Admiral Sir James, RN, *The Papers of Admiral Sir James Somerville*, (SMVL Series), Churchill Archives Centre, Churchill College, Cambridge.

Smith, Michael, *The Emperor's Codes: The Breaking of Japan's Secret Ciphers*, Arcade Publishers, New York, NY, 2001.

Smith, William Ward, *Midway, Turning Point of the Pacific War*, Crowell, New York, NY, 1966.

Smith, Peter C., *Into the Assault: Famous Dive Bomber Aces of the Second World War*, John Murray, London, 1985.

Smith, Peter C., *Ship Strike!: The History of Air-to-Sea Weapons Systems*, Airlife, Shrewsbury, 1998.

Smith, Peter C., *Douglas SBD Dauntless*, Crowood Press, Ramsbury, 1997.

Smith, Peter C., *Aichi D3A1/2 Val*, Crowood Press, Ramsbury, 1999.

Smith, Peter C., *Junkers Ju87 Stuka*, Crowood Press, Ramsbury, 1998.

Smith, Peter C. *Skua-The Royal Navy's Dive Bomber*, Pen and Sword, Barnsley, 2006.

Smith, Peter C. *Arctic Victory: The Story of PQ18*, Crécy, Manchester, 1994.

Smith, Peter C., *Vengeance!-The Vultee Vengeance Dive Bomber*, Airlife, Shrewsbury, 1986.

Smith, Peter C., *Straight Down! – the North American A-36 Dive Bomber in Action*, Crécy, Manchester, 2000.

Smith, Peter C., *Petlyakov Pe-2 Peshka*, Crowood Press, Ramsbury, 2003.

Smith, Peter C., *Action Imminent: Three Studies of the Naval War in the Mediterranean Theatre During 1940*, William Kimber, London, 1980.

Smith, Peter C., *Pedestal: the Convoy that saved Malta*, Goodall, Manchester, 2002.

Smith, Richard Norton, *The Colonel: The Life and Legend of Robert R. McCormick, 1880–1955*, Northwestern University Press, Chicago, IL, 2003.

Somes, Timothy E., 'Musing on Naval Maneuver Warfare', *Naval War College Review*, Vol. 51, Issue 3, 1958.

Spector, Ronald H., *Eagle Against the Sun: The American War with Japan*, Vantage Books, New York, NY, 1985.

Stark, Harold P., *Commanding the Fleet*, US Naval Institute Press, Annapolis, MD, 1953.

Stech, Frank J., and Elsässer, Christopher, *Midway Revisited: Detecting Deception by Analysis of Competing Hypothesis*, MITRE Corporation, McLean, VA, 2004.

Stefan, John J., *The Russian Fascist: Tragedy and Farce in Exile, 1925–1945*, Hamish Hamilton, London, 1978.

Stephan, Dr. J. J., *Hawaii under the Rising Sun*, University of Hawaii Press, Honolulu, Hawaii, 1984.

Stinnett, Robert B., *Day of Deceit*, Simon & Schuster, New York, 2001.

Storry, Richard, *Double Patriots: Study of Japanese Nationalism*, Greenwood Press, London, 1973.

Tagaya, Osamu, *Imperial Japanese Naval Aviator 1937–45*, Osprey Publishing, Wellingborough, 1988.

Tanabe, Commander Yahachi, IJN, 'I Sank the *Yorktown* at Midway', US Naval Institute Proceedings, 1963.

Taylor, A H, *Radio Reminiscences: A Half Century*, Naval Research Laboratory, Washington, DC, 1948.

Taylor, Theodore, *The Magnificent Mitscher*, Naval Institute Press, Annapolis, MD, 1991.

Thach, Admiral John S., *Reminiscences of Admiral John Smith Thach, U S Navy (Retired)*, US Naval Institute Press, Annapolis, MD, 1997.

Theobald, Rear-Admiral Robert A., *The Final Secret of Pearl Harbor*, Devin-Adair Co, New York, NY, 1954.

Thorne, Christopher, *Allies of a Kind: The United States, Great Britain and the War Against Japan 1941–43*, Oxford University Press, Oxford, 1978.

Tidwell, Lieutenant-Commander David L., USN, *USN Attack Aviation in the Pacific Theater: Tactical Development, Employment, and Effectiveness of Carrier-Based Attack Aviation by the US Navy in World War II*, Research Report, Air Command and Staff College: Air University, Maxwell Air Force Base, AL, 2002.

Tomlinson, Michael, *The Most Dangerous Moment: The*

Japanese Assault on Ceylon 1942, William Kimber, London, 1976.

Toyama, Saburo, 'Lessons From the Past', US Naval Institute *Proceedings,* September 1982.

Trevor-Roper, H. R. (ed.), *Hitler's War Directives 1939–1945,* Sidgwick & Jackson, London, 1964.

Trimble, William F., *Admiral William A. Moffett: Architect of Naval Aviation,* Smithsonian Institution Press, Washington DC, 1994.

Tuleja, Thaddeus V., *Climax at Midway,* W. W. Norton, New York, NY, 1960.

Turnbull, Archibald D., and Lord, Clifford L., *History of United States Naval Aviation,* Yale University Press, New Haven, CN, 1949.

Ugaki, Matome and Chihaya, Masataka (trans.), Goldstein, Donald M. and Dillon, Katherine V (eds), *Fading Victory: The Diary of Admiral Matome Ugaki, 1941–45,* University of Pittsburg Press, Pittsburg, PA, 1991.

United States Navy, U. S. Naval Technical Mission to Japan Report A-11, Government Printing Office, Washington, DC, 1946.

United States Navy, Bureau of Ships War Damage Report No. 25, *Loss of the USS* Yorktown at the Battle of Midway, June 1942, Government Printing Office, Washington, DC. November 1942.

United States Strategic Bombing Survey, Chairman's Office, *Japan's Struggle to End the War,* US Government Printing Office, Washington, DC, 1946.

Van Der Rhoer, Edward, *Deadly Magic,* Scribners, New York, 1978.

Walsh, George J., *Worldwide Impact of the Battle of Midway,* summary prepared for the author, Darien, CT, 2005.

Walsh, George J., *Searching for the Truth about the Battle of Midway,* unpublished research paper, 2004.

War Diaries, US Confidential, for Bombing Squadrons Three, Five (acting as Scouting Squadron Five), Six and Eight and Scouting Squadron Six and Eight for period 1–30 June 1942, CNO, Office of Naval Records and Library, held at NARA, College Park, MD, Xerox copies in Authors collection.

Weisheit, Major Bowen P., USMCR (Rtd), *The Last Flight of Ensign C. Markland Kelly, Junior, USNR: with a New, Corrected Charting of the Flight of VF-8 from USS* Hornet *During the Battle of Midway,* Self-published, Annapolis, MD, 1993.

Whymant, *Stalin's Spy: Richard Sorge and the Tokyo Espionage Ring,* St Martins Press, London, 1998.

Wildenberg, Thomas, *Destined for Glory: Dive Bombing, Midway, and the Evolution of Carrier Airpower,* Naval Institute Press, Annapolis, MD, 1998.

Wildenberg, Thomas, *All the Factors of Victory: Admiral Joseph Mason Reeves and the Origins of Carrier Airpower,* Potomac Books, Dulles, VA, 2003.

Willmott, H.P., *The Barrier and the Javelin: Japanese and Allied Pacific Strategies February to June 1942,* Naval Institute Press, Annapolis, MD, 1983. Published in UK as *Empires in the Balance,* Orbis, London, 1982.

Winter, Barbara, *The Intrigue Master: Commander Long and Naval Intelligence in Australia, 1913–1945,* Boolarong Press, Boolarong, 1995.

Woodrough, Fred C (trans.) for United States Office of Naval Intelligence, *The Japanese Story of the Battle of Midway,* Government Printing Office, Washington, DC, 1947.

Woods, David L., *Signalling and Communicating at Sea,* Vol. 2, Arno Press, New York, NY, 1980.

Worthington, Rear-Admiral Joseph M., USN (Rtd), 'A Destroyer at Midway', article in *Shipmate,* 2006.

Wrynn, Dennis V., 'Missing at Midway', article in *American History Illustrated,* Vol 27, July 1992.

Yokoi, Toshiyuki, *Nihon No Kimitsu Shitsu* ('Japan's Secret Chamber'), Rokumaisha, Tokyo, 1951.

Y'Blood, William, 'Point Luck: The Battle of Midway', article in *Air Power History,* Vol 39, Issue 2, 1992.

Zacharias, Rear-Admiral Ellis Mark, *Secret Missions,* G. P. Putnam & Sons, New York, 1946.

Zimmerman, Gene T., 'More Fiction Than Fact – The Sinking of the *Ostfriesland*', *Warship International,* Vol. XII, No. 2, 1975.

Glossary

(jg)	Junior grade
(P)	Permanent
(T)	Temporary
'R' Class	The four surviving battleships of the British *Royal Sovereign* Class, built in 1916–17 and unmodernized. Retained because 40,000 ton *Lion* Class replacements cancelled in 1940
1c	1st Class
2c	2nd Class
3c	3rd Class
A/S	Anti-submarine
A-26	Martin medium (torpedo-adapted) bomber (Marauder)
A6M2	Mitsubishi Type 0 Fighter (Zero or Zeke)
AA	anti-aircraft
ABDA	American-British-Dutch-Area Command
AC/S	Assistant Chief of Staff
ACDUTRA	Active Duty Training Naval Reserve
ACH	Analysis of Competing Hypotheses
ACIO	Air Combat Intelligence Officer
ACRM	Aviation Chief Radioman
ACTS	Air Corps Training School
AD	Aviation, Deck Merchant Marine (USNR designation)
ADF	Aerial direction finding
AE	Ammunition ship
AF	Air Force
AG	Air Group
AGC	Air Group Commander
AK	Attack cargo ship
AM	Aviation Metalsmith
AMM	Aviation Machinist's Mate

ANC	Aircraft Navigational Computer
AO	Naval Oiler
AOF	American Occupation Forces
AOIC	Assistant Officer in Charge
AOM	Aviation Ordnanceman
AP	Armour-piercing (bomb)
APA	Attack transport
APD	High-Speed transport (converted old destroyer)
ARM	Aviation Radioman
ATMC	Air Transport Movement Control
ATO	Air Tactical Officer
Av	Auxilliary vessel
A-V(N)	Aviation Officer (Navy)
A-V(R)	Aviator-Volunteer (Reserve)
Avgas	Aviation gasoline
B-17	Boeing heavy bomber (Flying Fortress)
B5N2	Type 97 T carrier attack (torpedo) bomber (Kate)
BAD	British Admiralty Delegation (in Washington DC)
BatDiv	Battleship Division
BB	Battleship
B-Dienst	*Beobachtung Dienst* ('Observation Service'), cryptological department of the German Navy
BOMRT	Battle of Midway Round Table
BT-1	Bomber Northrop.
BuAer	Bureau of Aeronautics
BuNav	Bureau of Navigation
buntai	group of two or three *shotai*.
buntaichō	Divisional leader (usually a lieutenant)
BuOrd	Bureau of Ordnance

BuPer	Bureau of Personnel	COS	Chief of Staff
C and R	Communications and Radio	CP (PA)	Communications Personnel (Photographers Assistant)
C&GSS	Commander and General Staff School		
CA	Communications Assistant	CP	Captain
CA	Heavy cruiser (8 inch guns)	CPO	Chief Petty Officer
CAP	Combat Air Patrol	CPO	Chief Petty Officer
CB	Battle Cruiser	CruDiv	Cruiser Division
CarDiv	Carrier Division	CTF	Carrier task force
CASU	Cooperative Administrative Support Unit	CV	Aircraft carrier
CEAG	Commander, *Enterprise* Air Group (McClusky)	CVE	Escort carrier
		CVL	Light carrier
CGO	Carrier Gunnery Officer	CW	Carrier waveband
CHAG	Commander, *Hornet* Air Group (Ring)	CWO	Chief Warrant Officer
chakkan shido‾to‾	carrier deck-landing lights	CXAM	RCA-built search radar
		CYAG	Commander, *Yorktown* Air Group (Pederson)
chutai	small or medium-size group of aircraft, usually of less than six machines (unofficial term)	D/F	Direction finding
		D3A1	Aichi carrier (dive-) bomber (Val)
CI	Communications Intelligence	DACD	Director, Airfields and Carrier Division
CIA	Central Intelligence Agency	*Dai-ich kōkūkanta*	First Air Fleet
CIC	Combat Information Center		
C-in-C	Commander-in-Chief	*Daitai*	Large air unit, usually three *chutai* or twenty-seven aircraft
CincPac	Commander-in-Chief, Pacific (Admiral Nimitz, Pearl Harbor)		
		DCNO	Deputy Chief of Naval Operations
CIS	Communications Intelligence Section	DCNS	Deputy Chief of Naval Staff
CIU	Central Intelligence Unit	DCS/O	Deputy Chief of Staff, Operations (USAF)
CL	Light Cruiser (6-inch guns)	DD	Destroyer
CLAA	Anti-aircraft cruiser	DesRon	Destroyer Squadron
CNO	Chief of Naval Operations	DFC	Distinguished Flying Cross
CO	Commanding Officer	DI	Decryption Intelligence
CoAir SoPac	Commander, Air, South Pacific	DIA	Defense Intelligence Agency
		DNAD	Director Naval Air Division
COM F/O Wing Pac	Commander, Flow Wing, Pacific	DNC	Division of Naval Communications
		DNI	Division of Naval Intelligence
COMB	Combined secure radio link	DOD	Director of Naval Ordnance
COMCAB-WEST	Commander, Marine Air Corps Bases, Western Area	DP	Dual purpose (guns for engaging both surface and air targets)
COMINCH CINCH	Commander-in-Chief Navy (Admiral King, Washington)	DTSD	Director of Training and Staff Duties
		Duty 'Q'	Intelligence Coordination Section
		ED	'Enemy Detected'
COMINT	Communications Intelligence	EM	Electrician's Mate
COMSowest-Pac For	Commander, South-West Pacific Force	EO	Engineering Officer
		F2F	Fighter Brewster (Buffalo)
COMSUB-PAC	Commander Submarine Pacific (Admiral English, Pearl Harbor)	F4-F	Fighter Grumman (Wildcat)
		FAA	Fleet Air Arm

Fantail	American for quarterdeck	MHz	Megahertz
FBI	Federal Bureau of Investigation	MO	Medical Officer
FDO	Fighter Direction Officer	MOAMA	Mobile Air – Materiel Area
FO	Flight Officer	Mob	Mobile
FRUPAC	Fleet Radio Unit, Pacific	MOCP	Measure of C2 Performance
FTU	Fighter Training Unit	MS	Motor ship
GP	General purpose (bombs)	MTBron	Motor Torpedo Boat Squadron
HE	High Explosive	NAGS	Naval Air Gunnery School
HF or H/F	High Frequency	NAP	Naval Aviation Pilot (enlisted flyer)
Hiko ̄cho ̄	Flight Operations Officer	NAS	Naval Air Station
Hinomaru	Nationality symbol painted on carrier flight deck (often a red circle with white border)	ND	Navy Department
		NID	Naval Intelligence Division
HK	*Hifskreuzer* German armed merchant raiders	*Nihon kaigun*	Imperial Japanese Navy
		NJROTC	Naval Junior Reserve Officer Training Cops
Hoirusha kai	Military Servicemen's League		
HQ	Headquarters	NKVD	*Narodnyi Komissariat Vnutrennykh Del* (Peoples Commissariat for Internal Affairs), Soviet Secret Police from 1917
IAS	Indicated air speed		
ICPOA	Intelligence Center, Pacific Ocean Area		
IFF	Identifier friend or foe	NMITC	Navy Marine Intelligence Training Center
IG	Inspector General	NRL	Naval Research Laboratory
IJA	Imperial Japanese Army	NSKK	National Sozialistiches Krafttfahkorps
IJN	Imperial Japanese Navy	NTS	Naval Training Station
INA	Indian National Army	NWC	Naval War College
Kaigun kyookai	Navy League	O/L	Ocean Liner
		OCNO	Office of the Chief of Naval Operations (OpNav)
Kanbaku properly kanjō kōgekiki	carrier (dive-) bomber		
		OGPU	*Ob'edinennoe Gosudartvennoe Politcheskoe Upravlene* (Joint State Political Administration), Soviet Secret Police from 1923
Kanko	Carrier-based attack or torpedo-bomber		
Kansen	torpedo		
Kempei tai	Japanese Secret Service.	OIC	Officer-in-Command
KHz	Kilohertz	OKM	*Oberkommando der Marine,* German Naval High Command
KIA	Killed in Action		
Kidō Butai	Mobile Force	ONI	Office of Naval Intelligence
Kōkū sentai	Carrier Division	Op	Operations
Ku koukuu	Aviation	OP-20-GI	Combat Intelligence
		OP-20-GY	Cryptanalysis
		OP-20-GZ	Translation
LF or L/F	Low Frequency	Opmm	Office Personnel Management
LSO	Landing Signals Officer	OPNAV	Office of Chief of Naval Operations
MACH	Warrant Machinist	OPVAN	Office of the Chief of Naval Operations
MAG	Marine Air Group	*Orientgruppe*	German Military Espionage Far East
MAW	Marine Air Wing	OTC	Officer in Tactical Command
MBAS	Master of Business Administration	PatRon	Patrol Squadron
MCAS	Marine Corps Air Station	PBY	Patrol Bomber Consolidated (Catalina)

PhoM	Photographer's Mate	SOC	Scouting/Observation Curtiss (Catapult-launched floatplane)
PIM	Position of Intended Movement	SS	Steamship (Mercantile Marine)
PO	Petty Officer	SS	Submarine
PO	Port Officer	SubDiv	Submarine Division
PT	Patrol torpedo vessel (motor torpedo boat)	SubFlot	Submarine Flotilla
R/G	Radioman/Gunner	SubRon	Submarine Squadron
RAF	Royal Air Force	TAIC	Technical Air Intelligence Center
RCA	Radio Corporation of America	TBD-1	Torpedo-bomber Douglas (Devastator)
RDF	Radio direction finding (Radar)	TBF/M	Torpedo-bomber Grumman (Avenger)
Regia Aeronautica	Royal (Italian) Air Force	TBS	Talk between ships
Renkō kantai	Combined Fleet, main battle fleet	TCO	Take-off Control Officer
RFP	Radio fingerprinting	TF	Task Force
RI	Radio intelligence	TG	Task Group
RIU	Radio intelligence unit *(embarked)*	TI	Traffic intelligence
RKKF	Raboche-Krest'yansky Krasny Flot (Workers and Peasants Red Fleet)	*Tokkogata*	'Special Type', usually applied to the new destroyer classes from *Fubuki* class onward, equipped with dual-purpose main armaments and Type 91 torpedoes
RM	Radioman	TSR	Torpedo-spotter-reconnaissance
RN	Royal Navy	TT	Torpedo tube(s)
ROV	Remotely operated vehicle	TV	Terminal velocity
Rtd	Retired	USAAC	United States Army Corps (to June 1942 then USAAF)
RU	Radio unit or remote unit	USAAF	United States Army Air Force
SA	Stürmabteilung	USCG	United States Coast Guard
SAP	Semi-Armour Piercing	USMC	United States Marine Corps
SAP	Semi-armour piercing (bomb)	USMCAS	United States Marine Corps Air Station
SAR	Search and rescue	USN	United States Navy
SB2C	Scout Bomber Curtiss (Helldiver)	USNA	United States Naval Academy
SB2U	Scout Bomber Vought (Vindicator)	USS	United States Ship
SBC	Scout Bomber Curtiss (obsolete biplane)	USSBS	United States Strategical Bombing Survey
SBD	Scout Bomber Douglas (Dauntless)	USSR	Union of Soviet Socialist Republics.
SC	General Electric-bomb search radar	USSTAF	United States Strategical Air Forces in Europe
SCAP	Supreme Command Allied Powers	VB	Dive Bomber Squadron
SD	Sicheriheitsdienst (Security Service)	VF	Fighter Squadron
Sea1c	Seaman 1st Class	VHF	Very high frequency
Seibiin	Flight Deck Officer	VMF	Marine Fighter Squadron
Seibiki	Control flag	VMSB	Marine Scout Bomber Squadron
Sentai	squadron of aircraft	VO	Observation Squadron
Shō-hickōchō	Deck Launching Officer	VP	Patrol Squadron
Shōtai	group of three aircraft	VS	Scouting Squadron
Shōtaicho	section leader	VSB	Scouting Bomber Squadron
SKL	*Seekriegleitung* German Naval Warfare Command	VT	Torpedo Bomber Squadron
SNLF	Special Naval Landing Force		

w/l	Waterline	WWMCCS	World-wide Military Command and Control System
WAVES	Women Accepted for Volunteer Emergency Service	XO	Executive Officer
WO	Warrant Officer	ZB	Zed Baker' or 'Hayrake,' homing beacon transmitting aerial
WP	War plans		

Index

Abe, Lieutenant-Commander Zenji 156
Abe, Lieutenant Heijiro 101
Adams, Captain John Paul 191
Adams, Lieutenant Samuel 203–204, 227
Adkins, Floyd 141
Admiral Graff Spee, German pocket battleship 300
Admiral Hipper, German heavy cruiser 300
Admiral Scheer, German pocket battleship 300
Ady, Lieutenant Howard Parmele, Jr 52
Akagi, IJN aircraft carrier 29, 34, 41, 83, 87–89, 93,
    101-1–2, 138–140, 151, 159–161, 164–167, 189,
    201–202, 206, 208, 209, 214, 324
Akashi, Motojiro 315
Akebono Maru, Japanese oiler 50
Aldrich, Richard J 311
Allen, Colonel Brooke E 218
Amagai, Captain Takahisa 146
Amari, Petty Officer 1c Yoji 102–103
Amaya, Commander Takahisa 159
Ameche, Don 335
Ammen, Ensign John N., Jr. 228
Anderson, US destroyer 176, 180, 198
Andrews, Dana 335
Arashio, IJN destroyer 92, 136, 185, 187, 216, 235–236,
    240
Archer, Henry 25
Ariga, Commander Kosaku Mikoto 185
Arima, Commander Takayasu 14, 18
Arizona, US battleship 21, 141, 201
Ark Royal, HM aircraft carrier 58–59, 61–62, 166, 198
Arnold, General Henry Harley 81
Arnold, Rear-Admirla Murr E 64, 76–77
Asashio, IJN destroyer 216, 235–236, 242
Ashford, Captain W H 270
Astoria, US heavy cruiser 148, 175–176, 178, 184, 188, 199,
    220
Atago, IJN heavy cruiser 238, 241
Atlantis, German armed mechant raider 300–301
Ault, Squadron Leader K 164
Automedon, SS 300–301

Ayao, Lieutenant Shirane 101

Bagley, Rear-Admiral David Worth 307 f/n
Baku, Soviet destroyer 327
Balch, US destroyer 188, 196, 198, 246
Ballard, Dr Robert 247
Bando, PO3c Masahi 189
Barde, Robert Elmer 108, 121–122, 133–134, 161, 209, 249
Barham, HM battleship 335
Barnes, Eric 25
Barnett, US transport 334
Barrett, Ensign James Clark 210
Bates, Commodore Richard W 69–70, 75, 121–122,
    269–276, 283, 293
Bates, Fred L 210
Belli, Rear-Admiral Vladimir Aleksandrovich 324–326
Bellinger, Rear-Admiral Patrick Nielson Lynch 47, 53–54,
    231
Benham, US destroyer 188, 196, 198, 246
Bennett, V M 176
Berwick, HM heavy cruiser 61
Best, Lieutenant-Commander Richard Halsey 51, 137140,
    202–203, 206–208, 249
Biard, Captain Forrest R 42–43
Bismarck, German battleship 151
Blair, Clay 90
Bloch, Rear-Admiral Claude C 28
Bolnykh, Alexander G 294–295
Bonaparte, Napoleon 284
Bond, Corporal Ronald 25
Bose, Rash Behari 310–311
Bose, Subhas Chandra 310
Bosquet, Marshal Pierre Francois Joseph 120
Bottomley, Lieutenant Harold Sydney, Jr 143, 254
Bowen, James 297
Boyd, Carl 318
Brassfield, Captain Arthur James 122, 176
Brockman, Rear-Admiral William Herman, Jr 90–92,
    200–201
Brooke-Popham, Air Marshal Sir Robert 300, 302

Brown, Colonel Julian P 222, 241
Brown, Second Lieutenant W H, RFC 168
Brown, Vice-Admiral Wilson, Jr. 8, 61–62, 272, 274
Browning, Captain Miles Rutherford 67–73, 77, 188,
    202–204, 211, 221–222, 235, 290, 292–293
Buckmaster, Captain Elliott 66, 75–77, 187, 192–193,
    197–198, 211, 247–248
Budiansky, Stephen 262
Buell, Commander Harold L 68
Buell, Thomas Bingham 67, 69, 203–204, 222, 294, 334
Buracker, Commander Willian Houck 202
Bush, President George, Jr 288
Butler, Ensign John C 148, 207

Cable, Eric G 319
Cachalaot, US submarine 91
California, US battleship 193
Campion, Lieutenat Kenneth O. 93
Carlson, Elliott 294
Carroll, Commodore 270
Carter, Ensign William D 232
Chase, Lieutenant (jg) William E 52
Cherpak, Evelyn M 270 f/n
Chester, US heavy cruiser 334
Chiang-Kai-Shek, Generalissimo 308, 312–313
Chichibu, Prince 315
Chihaya, Commander Masataka 282
Chikuma, IJN heavy cruiser 54, 97–98, 102, 126, 163, 175,
    210
Chochalousek, Walter George ARM1c 33, 241
Chokai, IJN heavy cruiser 33, 241
Churchill, Premier Winston Spencer 63, 304, 306–308, 311,
    313, 323, 326–328
City of Baghdad, SS 301
Clark, Captain Adolphus Dayton 166
Clarke, Commodore 166
Cleveland Class USN light cruisers 63
Cobb, Ensign P W 104
Collins, Captain James F, Jr 81–84
Colorado, US battleship 57
Cooper, Arthur 25
Coral Sea, Battle of 44–45, 62, 126–127, 129, 177, 252, 274,
    323–324
Cornwall, HM heavy cruiser 305–306
Courageous, HM aircraft carrier 168
Cressman, Robert J 74, 119, 239, 289
Cripps, Sir Stafford 309
Crommelin, Lieutenant (jg) Richard G 175
Cunningham, Admiral Sir Andrew Browne 286 f/n
Curtin, John Joseph, Prime Minister of Australia 306–307
Cuttlefish, US submarine 91

Davidson, Major-General Howard Calhoun 89, 229
Davies, Jack 25
Davis, Captain Arthur Cayley 53–54, 227

Davis, Lieutenant (jg) Douglas C 49
Davis, Lieutenant-Commander Ernest J 178, 180
Delaney, Lieutenant-Commander J F 194
DeRoin, Chief T J 48
Dickinson, Lieutenant Clarence Earle, Jr 143
Dobson, Benjamin R, ARM3c 185 f/n
Dolphin, US submarine 91
Doolittle, Lieutenant-Colonel James Harold 8, 28, 116, 275
Dorsetshire, HM heavy cruiser 305–306
Dow, Commodore Jennings B
Dow, Lieutenant-Commander Leonard J 175
Downey, Captain Charles 132–136
Driscoll, Ms Agnes Meyer 22
Duke, Lieutenant-Commander Claren E 200
Dyer, Captain Thomas H 24
Dyer, Lieutenant Thomas H

Eagle, H M aircraft carrier 61, 168
Earnest, Ensign Albert K 85
Edwards, C P 154
Egusa, Lieutenant-Commander Takashige 147, 166
Eiichiro, Lieutenant-Commander Jo 60–61
Eiji, Admiral Goto 17
Eller, Rear-Admiral Ernest McNeill 230
Elliott, US destroyer 334
Ellis, Lieutenant-Colonel Earl Hancock 212
Elsasser, Dr Christopher 296
Ely, Lieutenant Arthur V 97
Emerson, Lieutenant Alberto C 180
Emmons, Lieutenant-General Delos C 28
English, Rear-Admiral Robert Henry 90–91, 219
Enterprise, US aircraft carrier 41–42, 44, 56, 62, 64–65, 67,
    69–72, 74–75, 77, 97–98, 104, 112, 114–115, 117,
    131–132, 135, 136, 139–141, 144, 148, 175, 187–188,
    199, 202, 204, 206–208, 211, 220–222, 224, 226–227,
    232–233, 235, 238, 240, 243, 248, 253, 273, 279,
    280, 287, 291
Epps, Commander Richard C 52 f/n
Esders, Bill 148
Essex Class USN aircraft carriers 63, 336
Evasius, Alvin L 248 f/n
Ewing, Steve 289–290

Fabian, Lieutenant Rudolph J 26
Falke, Lieutenant-Commander Brian G 122–123
Fieberling, Lieutenant Langdon Kellogg 84, 101
Finnegan, Joseph 24
Fisher, Lieutenant (jg) Clayton Evan 59, 75, 111–116, 118,
    202, 206–207, 210–211, 223, 227, 235–236, 253–254,
    291
Fleming, Captain Richard Eugene 216–218, 240
Fletcher, Admiral Frank Jack 42, 45, 51–52, 54–55, 62,
    64–67, 69, 75–77, 116, 120, 128, 175, 177, 180, 184,
    188, 199, 202–203, 211, 219–220, 239, 243, 249, 254,
    274, 279, 285–286, 289, 292–193

Ford, Glenn 335
Ford, John 335
Formidable, HM aircraft carrier 162, 265, 286
Foster, Air Officer Hornet 74
Friez, Ensign Robert P 210
Fubuki Class IJN destroyers 223
Fuchida, Commander Mitsuo 101,139, 148, 283, 286, 292
Fujita, Commander Isamu 186
Fujita, Lieutenant Iyozo 99, 155–157, 289
Fujiwara, Lieutenant-Colonel Iwaichi 311
Fullenwider, Commander Ranson 42
Fulton, US submarine tender 90
Furious, HM aircraft carrier 61

Gaido, Bruno Peter, AMM1c 186
Gallaher, Lieutenant Wilmer Earl 136, 139, 141, 201–202, 204, 207–209, 221
Gandhi, Mohatma 309
Gay, Ensign George Henry 96–97, 116–119, 138, 249
Gee, Captain Roy P 119, 210
Genda, Commander Minoru 103, 166–167, 283, 289
Gerta, Christiane 326
Ginder, Lieutenant-Commander John B 180
Glidden, Lieutenant Elmer George 87–88
Glorious, HM aircraft-carrier 61, 149, 285
Gneisenau, German battle-cruiser 149, 285
Graves, Hubert 25
Gray, Lieutenant James S 72, 74, 97–98, 138, 203, 278–279, 288
Grayling, US submarine 242
Greene, Ensign Eugene Allen 137
Grenfell, Captain Russell 283–285, 287
Grouper, US submarine 200
Guerrierre, US frigate 57
Guillory, Ensign Troy Tilman 74
Gumz, Lieutenant Donald George 220
Gwin, US destroyer 246

Hadler, Jacques B 247
Hagikaze, IJN destroyer 201
Hale, Brigadier-General Willis Henry 228
Halsey, Admiral William Frederick, Jr 40, 4–45, 63, 65, 67–69, 184, 221–222, 257
Hammann, US destroyer 144, 176, 244–246, 324
Hansen, Joseph 328–329
Harada, Kaname 164
Hardeman, Ensign Gerald H 48
Harden, Bert LSO 135
Haruna, IJN battleship 33, 87, 93–94, 96, 98, 148, 186, 209–210, 223
Hashimoto, Toshio 190, 192, 194, 197
Hatsukaze, IJN destroyer 187
Healey, Dennis, MP 277
Heinemann, Ed 124–125
Henderson, Major Lofton R 86–87

Hermes, HM aircraft carrier 305, 308
Heston, Charlton 335
Hewitt, Admiral Henry Kent 272
Hibberd, Lieutenant (jg) Charles P 49 f/n
Hiei, IJN battleship 33
Hinoki, Major Yohei 153
Hirama, Rear-Admiral Yoichi 311, 321
Hirayama, Captain Shigeo 186
Hiranuma, Baron 317
Hirohito, Emperor 315
Hiryu, IJN aircraft carrier 29, 34, 84–85, 87–89, 96, 99, 101, 120, 138, 143–, 144, 147, 158–159, 165–166, 173–174, 176, 184, 188, 190, 196–197, 199, 202–211, 220, 223–224, 277, 290, 324–325
Hishin Maru, IJN aircraft transport 34
Hitler, Adolf, German Fuehrer 302–303, 313–314, 316–319, 321, 327–328
Hodson, Henry Vincent 309
Holbrook, Hal 336
Holmberg, Lieutenant (jg) Paul Algodte 143, 147
Holmes, Captain W J 24
Holtwick, Captain Jack Sebastian, Jr 261–262
Holtzworth, Commander Ernie 247
Hoover, President Herbert 57
Horii, PO1c Takayuki 189
Horikoshi, Dr. Jiro 154–155
Horikoshi, Jiro 290
Horne, Vice-Admiral F J 260
Hornet, US aircraft carrier 28, 41–42, 56–58, 62, 64–65, 69, 71–75, 77, 84, 98, 104–105, 108, 111–112, 114–118, 120–122, 136, 140–141, 168, 175, 187–188, 199, 204, 206–207,210–211, 220–221, 224, 226–228, 232–235, 237–238, 243, 248, 53, 257, 272, 279–280, 287, 291–292
Horton, Thomas H 336
Horwood, H 154
Hoshino, Banker 317
Howell, Earl E, ARM2c 186
Huckins, Lieutenant-Commander Thomas A 24
Hueber, Franz Josef 314
Hughes, US destroyer 176–178, 198, 220, 243–244, 246
Hunnicutt, Commander Thomas 219
Hussain, Saddam 335

I-29, IJN submarine 310
I-122, IJN submarine 18
I-123, IJN submarine 18
I-124, IJN submarine 18
I-168, IJN submarine 215, 243–247
I-171, IJN submarine 18
I-171, IJN submarine 18
I-175, IJN submarine 18
Ichikawa, Taemi 156, 166–167
Ikki, Lieutenant-Colonel Kiyonao 212
Illustrious, HM aircraft carrier 62–63, 162, 265, 286

Implacable, HM aircraft carrier 63
Independence, US light carrier 63
Indianapolis, US heavy cruiser 24
Indomitable, HM aircraft carrier 61–62, 265, 286
Irving, David 321
Isaman, Ensign Roy Maurice, Jr 146 f/n
Ise, IJN battleship 91
Ishizaka, Surgeon-Lieutenant Katsukichi 185
Isokaze, IJN destroyer 142
Isom, Dallas W 41, 291

Jacard, Ensign Richard 141
Jacobsen, Philip Hans 37
Jamieson, Lieutenant-Commander 25
Jarrett, Commander Harry B 179–180
Jeter, Commander T.P. 130
Jintsu, IJN light cruiser 91–92
Jodl, Major-General Alfred 319
Johnson, David F 143
Johnson, Corporal Meade T 88
Johnson, Lieutenant-Commander Robbin Ruffin 58, 115,
    119, 225, 228, 232–233, 235, 238–239, 280
Johnson, Colonel Louis A 309
Johnson, Stanley 334
Jordan, Lieutenant J M, MD 131
Junyo, IJN light carrier 7
Jupiter, collier 62

Kaga, IJN aircraft carrier 29, 34, 60, 96–98, 101–102,
    138–144, 146–147, 151, 156, 159, 165–166, 189,201,
    207, 209, 214, 273, 324
Kagero Class IJN destroyers 223
Kaku, Captain Tomeo 210
Kamenz, Paul 302
Kami, Captain IJN 297
Kamoi, IJN seaplane tender 18
Kkanechiko, Ensign Kojo 186
Karetka, Peter E 243, 248–249
Kashima, IJN training cruiser 17
Kato, Tateo 153
Katori, IJN light cruiser 13, 224
Katsumi, Commander Motoi 223–224, 226–227
Kawaguchi, Lieutenant-Commander Susumu 159, 197, 207,
    209
Kawasaki Type-2 (Emily) flying boat 11, 18, 34
Keith, Commander Bruce 25
Keith, Susan Ring 59
Kelly, Ensign C Markland, Jr 291
Kernan, Professor Alvin 60, 95, 100, 119, 291–292
Kido, Marquis Kochi 252
Kimes, Lieutenant-Colonel Ira L 86, 88, 214
Kimihawa Maru, IJN seaplane tender 282
Kimmel, Admiral Husband Edward 33
King, Admiral Ernest J 28, 36, 38–40, 44, 109, 184, 257,
    286, 297, 323, 334

Kleinsmith, Charles PO1c 187
Kirishima, IJN battleship 33, 210, 234
Kirk, Captain Alan Goodrich 37
Kishi, Nobusuke 317
Kislistin, General Pyotr Krasnov 316
Kitazawa, Commander Noritaka 156
Kitchen, Commander Etta-Belle 32–34, 64–66, 231
Kiyozumi Maru, Japanese troopship 150
Klausen, Max 326
Kleinsmith, Chief Charles
Kleiss, Lieutenant Norman Jack, Sr 130–132, 135–137,
    142–143, 197, 208, 226, 228, 234, 237, 249
Kniskern, Captain 247
Knox, Frank, US Navy Secretary 334
Kobayashi, Lieutenant Michio 143, 173–177, 182, 189–190
Komatsu, Vice-Admiral the Marquis Teruhisa 13–14, 17
Kondo, Admiral Nobutake 48, 250–251, 283, 302
Kongo, IJN battleship 33, 223
Konoye, Fumimaro 326
Kotaka, Sea1 C Kenji 189
Kroeger, Lieutenant (jg) Edwin John 137, 13–140, 206
Kuboki, Commander Hideo 235
Kumano, IJN heavy cruiser 211, 213, 241
Kurita, Rear-Admiral Takeo 190, 211–214, 297–298
Kuroshima, Captain Kameto 6, 9, 320
Kusaka, Rear-Admiral Ryunosuke 103, 289, 292
Kusumoto, Commander Ikuto 159
Kuznetsov, Admiral Nikolai Gerasimovich 295

Laing, Commander Michael Bryan 192
Lamar, Lieutenant-Commander Howell Arthur 28
Lane, Ensign C S 104
Langley, US aircraft carrier 57–58, 62, 68
Lanham, Lieutenanant H P 104
Lasswell, Major Alva B 24
Layton, Commander Edwin T 27–35, 41, 51, 230, 249, 251,
    260, 335
LeCompte, Commander Malcolm A 290
Leslie, Lieutenant-Commander Maxwell F 77, 104, 120,
    137–138, 146, 289
Lexington, US aircraft carrier 57, 62, 93, 168, 334
Linder, Captain Bruce 59
Lindsey, Lieutenant-Commander Eugene E 97–98, 100
Lomax, J G 319
Lion Class battleships 307
Long Island, US escort carrier 297
Lord, Walter 32, 83, 114, 242, 287, 290, 292
Lorenz, Lieutenant Jon D 179
Lough, Ensign John Cady 144
Lumpkin, Second Lieutenant George T 93
Lundstrom, John B 54, 68, 74, 120, 122, 157, 184, 188,
    197, 253, 264, 278, 288–289, 292–293
Lyle, Enisgn James Palmer O'Neil 47 f/n

MacArthur, General Douglas 19, 328

Maeda, Takeshi 103, 156, 166
Magda, Ensign John J 122
Maikaze, IJN destroyer 201
Makigumo, IJN destroyer 186, 210
Maloney, Pat 334
Manierre, Captain Ernest R 218–219
Masaji, Lieutenant Suganami 101
Masao, Lieutenantn Iizuka 101
Mason, Captain Charles P 117
Massey, Lieutenant-Commander Lance Edward 77, 98–99
Masuda, Commander Shogo 159, 161
Matsuoka, Yosuke 316–317
Maund, Captain Loben Edward Harold 198
Mayes, First Lieutenant Herbert C 83
Matsumoto, Sadao 176
McCarthy, Ensign John Reginald 143–144, 186
McClusky, Lieutenant-Commander Eade 72, 114, 118, 120,
    136, 138–140, 188, 202–204, 221–222, 272, 289–290
McCormick, Commander Lynde Dupuy 31
McCormick, Robert R 335
McCuskey, Lieutenant (jg) Elbert S 189–190
McInerny, Ensign John Edward, Jr 74, 122
McKellar, Lieutenant Clinton, Jr 215
McKewan, Captain R B 300–301
Meisinger, Colonel Josef Albert 314
Merrill, Ensign M A 104, 207
Michele, Ensign Vernon Larsen 142
Mikasuki, IJN destroyer 10
Mikuma, IJN heavy cruiser 133, 168, 211, 213–214,
    216–218, 221, 232, 235–, 236, 238, 240, 242–243,
    249, 324–325
Mikus, Andy 183, 191, 193
Miller, Thomas G, Jr 157
Minegishi, Warrant Officer Yoshijiro 189, 196
Minneapolis, US heavy cruiser 75
Mitchell, Lieutenant Samuel Gavid 74, 105, 115, 122, 280
Mitchell, Major-General Willliam 20, 228, 242
Mitscher, Rear-Admiral Marc Andrew 51, 56–57, 67, 72–75,
    104–105, 116–117, 119, 165, 167–168, 175, 199, 204,
    206, 220, 222, 233–234, 257, 272, 274, 280, 292
Miwa, Captain Yoshitake 8
Miyo, Commander Tatsukichi 7
Moffett, Rear-Admiral William A 57
Mogami, IJN heavy cruiser 168, 211, 213–214, 216–217,
    219, 221, 233–234, 236–238, 240–243, 249, 324–325
Mohr, Lieutenant Ulrich 301
Monaghan, US destroyer 245–246
Montgomery, General Bernard Law 19–20
Moore, Oral L Slim, ARM2c 107, 232
Moorer, Admiral Thomas Hinman 298
Mori, Lieutenant Shigeru 189
Morison, Professor Samuel Eliot 69, 271, 273, 286–287, 292
Morris, US destroyer 176, 179, 198
Muri, Lieutenant James P 83–84
Murphy, Lieutenant-Commander John Williams, Jr 219

Murray, Captain George D 70, 130, 135, 221
Murray, James Francis ACRM (PA) 208, 253
Musashi, IJN battleship 151, 167
Mutsu, IJN battleship 251

Nagano, Admiral Osami 305
Nagara, IJN light cruiser 85, 92, 175, 185, 187, 196
Nagato, IJN battleship 251
Nagumo, Vice-Admiral Chuichi 3, 9, 34, 38, 41, 45, 52,
    54–55, 64, 66, 68–71, 74–75, 81, 83, 86, 97–98,
    100–103, 121, 137, 140, 143, 156, 166–167, 175, 185,
    187, 190, 194, 196, 200, 211, 213,219–220, 223, 251,
    267, 275, 278, 281, 283–264, 287, 289, 290, 292,
    295, 305, 307, 311, 320.
Nagazawa, Captain Tasuku 138
Nakagama, Shizuo 176
Narwhal, US submarine 91
Nautilus, US submarine 91–92, 136, 185, 200–201, 247,
    273
Nave, Commander Theodore Eric 25
Nehru, Jawaharlal 310
Nevada, US battleship 193
New Orleans, US heavy cruiser 233
Newall, Air Chief Marshal Sir Cyril 300
Nicholson, Mac 247
Nickerson, Ensign Henry John 210
Nimitz, Admiral Chester William 19–20, 26–28, 31–32,
    35–36, 39, 42, 44–45, 51, 53–54, 56, 65–66, 90, 198,
    203, 211, 219, 221, 230–231, 247, 257–262, 265,
    267–269, 289, 336
Nishimori, Warrant Officer Susumu 189
Nobora, PO2c Todaka 174
Noland, CGM Robert 179
Nomoto, Jinzo 314
Normandie, French liner 49
Norris, Major Benjamin White 92–93, 214–215
Northampton, US heavy cruiser 44
Nowaki, IJN destroyer 155
Noyes, Rear-Admiral Leigh 37, 45
Numakaze, IJN destroyer 187

O'Flaherty, Ensign Frank Woodrow 144, 186
Ogawa, Commander Nobuki 101, 236
Ogawa, Lieutenant Shoichi 102
Ohara, Commander Hisashi 148
Okumiya, Masatake 290
Ole Jacob, Norwegian tanker 301
Oliver, Lieutenant Robert J 44, 69, 211, 294
Operation AL (Aleutians) 7, 17
Operation Barbarossa 317, 326
Operation FS (Fiji-Samoa) 6
Operation Ironclad 309
Operation MI (Midway = AF) 7, 17, 19, 296
Operation MO (Moresby) 6
Operation Othsu ('B') or *Kantouken Plan* 316–317, 319

Operation Pedestal 61
Oshima, Lieutenant-General Hiroshi 303, 318–319, 321
Osmus, Ensign Wesley Frank 185–187
Ott, General Eugen 317, 326
Ozaki, Hotsumi 326–327

Parker, Captain R C 270
Parker, Frederick D 20, 35, 38, 41
Parshall, Jonathan 41, 74, 148, 291–292, 294
Patel, Dinyar 309
Patriarca, Lieutenant Frank Anthony 104, 136
Peattie, Mark R 290
Pederson, Lieutenant-Commander Oscar 175
Pedeson, Commander Oscar 76
Penland, Lieutenant J R 144, 203, 236–237, 249
Pensacola, US heavy cruiser 188, 191
Pfeiffer, Ensign Carl D 144
Pichette, Norman 244
Pickett, Major-General George 75
Pineau, Lieutenant Roger 271
Pollard, Commander Joseph P 181, 194
Portland, US heavy cruiser 146, 175–176, 184
Potter, Elmer Belmont 27
Prange, Gordon 7, 292
President Polk, US Army transport 82
Prince of Wales, HM battleship 81, 151, 163
Princeton, US aircraft carrier 273
Propst, Ensign Gaylord D 49–50
PT-20, US motor torpedo boat 215
PT-21, US motor torpedo boat 215
PT-29, US motor torpedo boat 215
PT-30, US motor torpedo boat 215
Pu Yi, Emperor (as Emperor Kangde) 315
Pye, Vice-Admiral W S 274

Ramillies, HM battleship 309
Ramsay, Lieutenant-Commander Donald J 220
Ramsey, Captain Logan C 49
Ranger, US aircraft carrier 62, 68, 93, 109
Rausch, Ensign A L 104
Razumny, Soviet destroyer 327
Raz'yarenny, Soviet destroyer 327
Redman, Commander John Roland 39, 260–262
Redman, Rear-Admiral Joseph Reasor 38, 40, 260–262
Reeves, Rear-Admiral Jospeh Mason 63
Reid, Captain Jewell Harmon 47–48
Repulse, HM battle-cruiser 81, 163
Richards, Lieutenant William L 49
Richardson, Vice-Admiral David Charles 270–273
Ring, Commander Stanhope Cotton 57–60, 63, 68, 72–75,
    77, 108, 111–123, 136, 203–, 204, 206, 222, 224,
    226–227, 232, 234–235, 238, 278, 280–281, 290
Ring, Commodore James Andrew 57
Rio de Janeiro Maru, IJN submarine depot ship 13
Roberts, Lieutenant (jg) Wilbur Edison 144–145

Rochefort, Commander Joseph J 21–22, 24, 26, 28, 31,
    34–35, 42, 48, 231, 260–261, 262, 275, 3294,
    307–308, 335
Rodee, Lieutenant-Commander Walter Fred 58, 74–75, 115,
    118, 204, 224, 228, 232.238, 280, 291, 294
Rodenburg, Ensign Eldor E 104, 136
Rodzaevsky, Konstatntin Vladimirovich 316
Rogers, Captain Frederick Fremont 22, 305
Rogge, Konteradmiral Bernhard 299–300
Rommel, General Irwin 310
Roosevelt, President Franklin D 63, 248, 297, 306–307,
    309–310, 313, 318, 323, 335
Roskill, Captain Stephen Wentworth 285–287
Rost, Leutnant Wolfgang 322
Rothenberg, Ensign Allan 49
Roy, PhotoAsst2c William Glen 192, 248
Ruehlow, Captain Stanley Erdman 114
Russell, Ronald W 119, 287, 294
Russell, US destroyer 176, 198
Ryujo, IJN light carrier 7, 29, 167
Ryukaku, 29–30

Safford, Captain Laurence F 20–21, 23–24, 32, 37, 260
Sakai, Petty Officer Ichiro 85
Sakai, Saburo 153
Sakiyama, Captain Shakao 240
Salt Lake City, US heavy cruiser 19
Sanagi, Captain Sadamu 282
Saratoga, US aircraft carrier 53, 57–59, 62, 93, 109, 168,
    231, 297
Sasaki, Hitoshi, PO1c 196
Sato, PO1c S 186
Sauer, Captain Edward P 187 f/n
Scharnhorst, German battle-cruiser 149, 285
Schneider, Ensign Tony Frederick 104, 137
Schorreck, Henry F 34, 257
Schweikart, Larry 294
Second-K reconnaissance operation 11, 18, 34
Seligman, Commander Morton T 334
Seno, Commander Sadao 161
Seo, Tetsuo 176
Seymour, Sir Horace 312
Shafroth, Vice-Admiral John Franklin 274
Shelton, Ensign James Arnold 144
Sherman, Vice-Admiral Frederick Carl 61, 67
Shibata, Signalman Masashi 223
Shigematsu, Lieutenant Yasuhiro 101, 143–144, 174, 196
Shigeyoshi, Admiral Inouye 6
Shinsaku, Hirata 29
Shoho, IJN light carrier 10
Shokaku, IJN aircraft carrier 7, 10, 29, 296
Short, Commander J J
Short, Lieutenant Wallace C 55, 104, 120, 221, 234–235
Showers, Admiral Donald Mac 295–296
Shumway, Lieutenant DeWitt Wood 221, 224

Simard, Commander Cyril T 214
Singh, Captain Mohan 310
Singh, Pritan 311
Slonim, Captain Gilven M 43
Smight, Jack 287
Smith, Captain R S 270
Smith, Lieutenant L A 104
Smith, Lieutenant W A 89
Smith, Vice-Admiral William Ward 184, 274
Smuts, Prime Minister Jan Christian 308–309
Snowden, John Warren, ARM3c 142, 208
Somerville, Admiral Sir James 58–59, 63, 166, 267, 286
Sorge, Richard 326–327
Soryu, IJN aircraft carrier 29, 34, 88–89, 92, 96–97, 99, 101,
    138, 140, 146–, 148, 155, 158–159, 164–166, 185,
    201, 207, 209, 214, 223, 273, 324
Soucek, Commander Apollo 72–73, 222, 257
Soucek, Commander Zeus 72
Spruance, Rear-Admiral Raymond Ames 42, 44–45, 51, 55,
    64–72, 76–77, 90, 175, 184, 188, 199, 202–204, 206,
    211, 219–222, 224, 235, 243, 249, 251, 269, 271–274,
    278–279, 284, 287, 289, 293–294, 323
Stalin, Marshal Josef 304, 313, 322–324, 326–328
Stark, Admiral Harold Rainsford 37
Stebbins, Captain Edgar E 204, 216
Stech, Dr Frank J 296
Steele, Captain James M 102 f/n
Stephan, Professor John J 297
Steinman, William Burr, AMMIc 144
Stepanovitch, Vice-Admiral Ivan 327
Stewart, Second Mate Alec 301
Stillwell, General Joseph 313
Stillwell, Commander Paul 271–273
Stimson, Henry Lewis 82
Stone, Ensign Reid W 207
Strope, Jerry 247
Suekichi, Yoshimoto, Sea1c 174
Suzuki, Warrant Officer Shigero 189
Suzuya, IJN heavy cruiser 211, 213, 240–241
Sweeney, Lieutenant-Colonel Waltyer Campbell 89
Swope, Ivan L 118
Sylvester, Captain 274

Tama Maru No. 3 47
Tama Maru No. 5 47
Tambor, US submarine 213–214, 216, 219, 242
Tanabe, Lieutenant-Commander Yudachi 216, 243–246,
    253
Tangier, US naval transport 19
Tanikaze, IJN destroyer 203, 224, 226–227
Tankiowa, Lieutenant Kiyusumi 185
Talbot, Ensign Johnny A 74
Tappan, Ensign Benjamin 74, 115, 224, 226
Taylor, Theodore 74, 168, 280
Tenedos, HM destroyer 305

Thach, Lieutenant-Commander John Smith 64–67, 75–76
Theobald, Rear-Admiral Robert Alfred 274
Thomas, Sir Shenton Whitelegge 302
Thompson, Betty 60
Thompson, Lieutenant-Colonel Rufus B, Jr 59
Tinker, Brigadier-General Clarence Leonard 45, 231
Togo, Admiral Heihachiro 323
Tojo, Prime Minister Hibeka 6
Tomioka, Rear-Admiral Baron Sadatoshi 8
Tomlinson, Michael 307
Tomonaga, Lieutenant Joichi 101, 188–191, 196
Tone, IJN heavy cruiser 54, 96–97, 102, 126, 186, 196, 210,
    292
Tootle, Ensign Milton, Jr 191
Trendall, Professor Dale 25
Treweek, Major Athanasius 25
Trout, US submarine 242
True, Lieutenant-Commander Arnold Ellsworth 246
Tsuchiya, Takayashi 176
Tsouras, Peter G 321
Tsuda, Captain Hiroaki 240 f/n
Tucker, Lieutenant Alfred Bland 115
Tully, Anthony 41, 74, 148, 292, 294
Turner, Rear-Admiral Richmond Kelly 36, 38–40
Tyler, Captain Marshall Alvin 214, 216–217

U-81, German submarine 198
U-180, German submarine 310
Ud, Dr Shintaro 290 f/n
Ugaki, Rear-Admiral Matome 5, 7, 18

Valiant, HM battleship 61
Vampire, HMA destroyer 305
Vickrey, Bill 118, 139, 148, 208
Victorious, HM aircraft carrier 61
Vincennes, US heavy cruiser 188
Vireo, US tug 246
Virginia, US battleship 22
von Dirksen, Herburt 326
von Ribbentrop, Joachim 303, 317–319, 321

Wagner, Commander Frank D 63, 168
Waldron, Lieutenant-Commander John Charles 73–74,
    76–77, 94–97, 100–101, 112, 116, 118–120, 122,
    280–281, 292
Walsh, George 109, 133, 293, 329, 336
Ware, Lieutenant Charles Rollins 143–144, 186
Wasp, US aircraft carrier 63, 93, 297
Watanabe, Commander Yusumasa 185–187
Watanabe, Commander Yasuji 5
Wavell, Field Marshall Sir Archibald Percival 320
Weber, Ensign Frederick Thomas 134, 139–140, 206–208
Wiedemann, Hauptmann Fritz 313–314
Weise, George K 244
Weisheit, Major Bowen P 74–75, 121, 291

Wenger, Mike 164
Wenneker, Admiral Paul 301–302, 320
White, Ensign Harold H 210, 227
Whitten, Second Lieutenant Sumner H 215
Wildenberg, Thomas 74
Williams, Lieutenant-Commander Jack S 24
Willmott, H P 320
Wilson, Lieutenant A N Jr 195
Winchell, Walter 334
Wiseman, Lieutenant (jg) Obsorne Beeman 148, 207–208
Wright, Lieutenant Wesley A 24
Wright, US seaplane tender 57

Yagi, Dr Hidetsugu 290
Yamada, Lieutenant Shohei 101
Yamaguchi, Rear-Admiral Tamon 173–175, 185, 194,
    196–197, 210, 289,
Yamamoto, Admiral Isoroku 4–9, 13, 19, 28–29, 41, 44–45,
    50, 102–103, 167, 175, 189, 200, 204, 249–252, 278,
    281, 283–285, 288–289, 292, 296–297

Yamamoto, PO1c Akira 189
Yamamoto, PO2c Toru 189
Yamato, IJN battleship 3–4, 6, 9, 13,18, 41,151, 161, 167,
    223, 251
Yawata Maru, SS 314
Yokoi, Captain Tadao 302
Yorktown, US aircraft carrier 41–42, 55–56, 62–64–5, 67,
    71, 75–77, 98, 112, 114, 117, 120, 128, 136–137, 141,
    144, 175–178, 180, 182–183, 185, 187–194, 196–199,
    202–204, 207, 210–211,220, 243–249, 259, 264–265,
    276, 280, 290, 292, 323, 325
Yotoku, Miyahi 326
Young, Captain Grant C 293 f/n
Yubari Class IJN light cruisers 91
Yugumo, IJN destroyer 162, 186
Yumashev, Vice Admiral Ivan S 323
Yutaka, Petty Officer 3c Chiyoshima 174

Zacharias, Commander Ellis Mark 22
Zuikaku, IJN aircraft carrier 7, 29, 40, 285